ALSO BY JAMES BAMFORD

The Puzzle Palace
Body of Secrets
A Pretext for War
The Shadow Factory

SPYFAIL

—◆—

Foreign Spies, Moles, Saboteurs,
and the Collapse of America's
Counterintelligence

JAMES BAMFORD

12
TWELVE

NEW YORK BOSTON

Twelve
Hachette Book Group
1290 Avenue of the Americas, New York, NY 10104
twelvebooks.com
twitter.com/twelvebooks

First Edition: January 2023

Twelve is an imprint of Grand Central Publishing. The Twelve name and logo are trademarks of Hachette Book Group, Inc.

The publisher is not responsible for websites (or their content) that are not owned by the publisher.

The Hachette Speakers Bureau provides a wide range of authors for speaking events. To find out more, go to www.hachettespeakersbureau.com or email HachetteSpeakers@hbgusa.com.

Twelve books may be purchased in bulk for business, educational, or promotional use. For information, please contact your local bookseller or the Hachette Book Group Special Markets Department at special.markets@hbgusa.com.

Library of Congress Cataloging-in-Publication Data
Names: Bamford, James, author.
Title: Spyfail : foreign spies, moles, saboteurs, and the collapse of America's counter-intelligence / James Bamford.
Description: First Edition. | New York ; Boston : Twelve, [2023] | Includes index.
Identifiers: LCCN 2022037061 | ISBN 9781538741153 (Hardcover) | ISBN 9781538741177 (eBook) Subjects: LCSH: Espionage—United States. | Internal security—United States. | National security—United States. | Intelligence service—United States.
Classification: LCC JF1525.I6 B36 2023 | DDC 327.1273—dc23/eng/20220815
LC record available at https://lccn.loc.gov/2022037061

ISBNs: 978-1-5387-4115-3 (hardcover), 978-1-5387-4117-7 (ebook)

Printed in Canada

MRQ-T

10 9 8 7 6 5 4 3 2 1

To Mary Ann,
For the adventures past
And the adventures yet to come.
To Tom,
For your unfailing support,
and your enduring friendship.

CONTENTS

◆

INTRODUCTION

On the morning of August 8, 2022, a conga line of black SUVs, crowded with several dozen heavily armed FBI agents and escorted by local police cruisers, arrived at 1100 South Ocean Boulevard in Palm Springs, Florida. Ahead were a pair of closed white doors beneath an elaborate archway covered in glazed Spanish tiles, and in front was a small squad of armed Secret Service agents. For the first time in history, the home of a former United States president was about to be raided by federal law enforcement agents, as if on a drug bust or the arrest of a wanted fugitive. The unprecedented operation was being carried out by the Justice Department's counterintelligence section, responsible for catching spies. And the search warrant indicated that there was probable cause that the occupant was committing a crime under the Espionage Act by refusing to return classified documents.

The man behind the unprecedented raid was an obscure bureaucrat in a little known job in a nameless, nondescript building in downtown Washington, DC. He was Jay I. Bratt, the chief of the counterintelligence section of the Justice Department, who began his career prosecuting used car dealers for fraudulently changing odometers, and fruit drink companies for watering down orange juice containers. With an office behind the door to Room 10100 on the top floor of 600 E Street NW, a red-brick building plastered with torn handbills for the rapper YoungBoy and a march on Washington for voters' rights, Bratt was the country's top counterspy. And now instead of hucksters and secret agents, he was going after a former president of the United States.

Long before the raid at Mar-a-Lago, I began looking deeply into U.S. counterintelligence and security operations. And as detailed extensively in *SpyFail*, I discovered dangerous incompetence and vast politicization. Under both presidents Obama and Trump thieves were able to walk away with more than half a billion pages of documents classified higher than top secret, some dealing with U.S. war plans, many of which ended up in both Russia and China. And that was after the supposed crackdown following the million or so documents removed by whistleblower Edward Snowden, many of which were made public.

During the Obama administration, another thief was able to steal nearly all of the NSA's highly dangerous cyberweapons, the cyber equivalent of loose nukes, and put them up for auction. Eventually they ended up in the hands of Russia and North Korea, where in 2017 they were used to cause a worldwide cyberpandemic that shut down hospitals and medical facilities all over the world, including in the United States, thus turning our own weapons against us. And although the cyber thief left many clues, the counterintelligence agents have never come close to catching him. As a result, he continued to sell the weapons to whatever government or terrorist would pay for them. Instead, the FBI counterspies spent much of their time going after low-level whistleblowers like Thomas Drake, Chelsea Manning, John Kiriakou, Daniel Hale, Terry Albury, and Reality Winner, who was sentenced to nearly five years in prison for leaking a single document to the press.

Due to extensive politicization and incompetence, under both Obama and Trump, the country also became flooded with spies and covert operators. Many are Americans who have agreed to spy on and conduct operations against other Americans on behalf of a foreign government. And then there are the moles. During the entire 2016 election season, foreign moles went completely undetected and were able to penetrate the very highest levels of both the Trump and Clinton campaigns. In the same way, the FBI's own counterintelligence division—the people hunting for spies—was penetrated almost continuously for nearly forty years, until just recently, by both Russian and Chinese moles, resulting in dozens of deaths to cooperative agents in both countries.

Nor did the counterintelligence agents discover that in 2016 former CIA and FBI agents had gone to work for a foreign political organization planning a bloody Russian coup and assassination plot on a friendly ally. It was allegedly their job to exfiltrate the plotters. Around the same time, because of dangerous leaks at the highest levels of the CIA, the United States lost its most valuable spy in Russia, an agent-in-place in President Putin's Kremlin office—a spy who would have been invaluable during the war in Ukraine and as nuclear tensions escalate.

SpyFail is the first book to take a close look at this vast breakdown of America's counterespionage system. In my bestselling trilogy on the National Security Agency (NSA), I investigated how the agency targets countries around the world, and how intrusive the surveillance has become at home. Now in *SpyFail,* I investigate how foreign countries target Americans at home, and how ill equipped the United States is to stop them. These countries include adversaries such as North Korea, China, and Russia, and allies such as Israel and the United Arab Emirates.

And because of their highly secret nature, or the politics involved, many of these foreign spy operations within the United States have received little or no press coverage. Nor have the failures. They involve multiple countries, using multiple methods of espionage and covert activities, from spies to moles to saboteurs to cyber. But they all have one common denominator: They have succeeded where the U.S. counterspies and intelligence agencies have failed. I therefore take a very close look at the background, history, and personalities involved in each operation. Much of the information comes from restricted U.S. government documents, foreign government documents, and confidential sources.

The period I cover begins during the lead-up to the election season of 2016 and moves forward to the present day, 2022. And because Hollywood turns out to play a central role in a number of cases, its studios, films, and actors serve as the backdrop for much of the action. This allows me to combine the glitz and glamour of the movie world with the intrigue and mystery of the spy world. It is a combination that will attract a wide variety of readers, from fans of books about Hollywood to those of books about espionage and politics.

As with my previous books, *SpyFail* is fully documented and written in a storytelling, narrative style that delves deep into the espionage tradecraft involved and the people in the shadows. It is intended simply to explore the failures and the reasons behind them, not to lay out a detailed prescription for how to repair the system. I will leave that to others. And as always, I follow the facts where they lead regardless of special interest taboos, political ideology, or government censorship. To do otherwise would be to betray journalistic ethics.

Silence is the ultimate weapon of power.

Charles de Gaulle

The silence of the good people is more dangerous than the brutality of the bad people.

Martin Luther King Jr.

BOOK ONE

THE SABOTEURS

CHAPTER 1

◆

The Dinner

Retired general James Clapper peered out the window of the black Mercedes limousine and saw what appeared to be a brightly lit one-story bowling pin atop a modern rectangular chocolate brown building and wondered if they had come to the right place for dinner. As director of the Office of National Intelligence, he was America's top spymaster. Sitting next to him was North Korea's top spymaster, General Kim Yong Chol, head of the country's Reconnaissance General Bureau.

They were two old spies, and although they had never met before, for nearly half a century they had been battling each other on opposite sides of the most dangerous espionage war in history. Highly secret and little known to the public, it is a spy war that has cost the lives of scores of American intelligence agents and twice nearly led to all-out nuclear war. Rivals from the start, both spymasters began their espionage careers in the late 1960s, worked their way up to the general ranks, and eventually reached the pinnacle of their respective countries' intelligence services at about the same time, 2009 for General Kim and 2010 for General Clapper. And like General Kim, who reported directly to Chairman Kim Jong Un, North Korea's supreme leader, Clapper reported directly to U.S. president Barack Obama.

It was November 7, 2014, a chilly Friday evening below a waning gibbous moon as the car pulled to a stop in front of the Golden Lane Bowling Alley on Juche Tower Street in Pyongyang, North Korea. At seventy-three, General Clapper looked his age. Fleshy skin hung like handbags beneath his eyes, and wrinkles turned into trenches in the shadows. General Kim, a few years younger at sixty-eight, still had jet black hair, although it was receding like an outgoing wave. His cheeks were puffy and unwrinkled and expanded when he smiled, which was seldom on the car ride. Coming face-to-face for the first time, the two men shared an equal distrust of each other.

The trip had been spur-of-the-moment. Chairman Kim had decided to release two imprisoned Americans if the United States would send a letter from President Obama, along with a cabinet-level national security official to pick them up. Obama chose Clapper. But the offer of the prisoner release was simply Kim's excuse to explore the possibility of normalization of relations between the two countries. It was something that could only be discussed in secret with a senior cabinet-level official who had the ear of the president. Within hours, Clapper had packed his suitcase, assembled a small staff, and raced to Andrews Air Force Base.

————

By then the thirty-year-old supreme leader had been head of North Korea for nearly three years, and despite his youth and inexperience he was growing more and more confident. Twenty months earlier he had conducted his first, and the country's third, successful nuclear test, exploding underground a weapon with about half the destructive power of the atomic bomb dropped by the United States on Hiroshima. Above all else, he had inherited from his father, Kim Jong Il, who was in power for seventeen years, a critical understanding that only the development of nuclear weapons would allow the country to survive.

Kim Jong Un well knew that they were his nation's only insurance against becoming the next victim on America's long and bloody kill list of wars, assassinations, regime change, interventions, and drone attacks against small, Third World countries. Since the end of the Korean War, the United States has attempted to assassinate the leaders of Congo and Cuba; was extensively involved in the assassination and coup in the Dominican Republic, and according to the *Washington Post*, "the U.S. tried to change other countries' governments 72 times during the Cold War." In addition, it launched an offensive war in Vietnam that left over 1.3 million people dead; another in Iraq with 300,000 more killed; initiated other wars in Libya, Somalia, and Syria; provided weapons and direct support to Saudi Arabia and the United Arab Emirates in their punishing blockade and war in Yemen, a war that has led to hundreds of thousands of deaths from indiscriminate bombings and hunger; and engaged in extensive acts of torture at secret "black sites" around the world.

Within the intelligence community, Kim's decision to nuke up was seen as the only logical decision on his part. According to former North Korean CIA analyst Jung H. Pak, Kim has "made it clear that he will not give up North Korea's nuclear weapons, regardless of threats of military attacks or engagement, and that he sees the program as vital to regime security and his legitimacy as the leader of North Korea. The North Korean regime has often made reference to the fates of Iraq and Libya—the invasion and overthrow of their leaders—as key examples of what happens to states that give up their nuclear weapons." And had Ukraine kept its nuclear arsenal, rather than acceding to U.S. requests to disarm as part of the 1994 Budapest Memorandum on Security Assurances, it's unlikely that Russia would have invaded in 2022. And the United States stayed out of the war precisely because of Moscow's nukes.

Wendy Sherman, Obama's undersecretary of state for political affairs, was heavily involved with Clapper's mission. During the Clinton years she had served as the administration's North Korean policy coordinator. She expressed the same views as Jung Pak in a private talk to NSA employees in the agency's Friedman Auditorium. The North Koreans, she said, had followed the U.S. war in Iraq very closely and concluded "that a state without nuclear capability would always be vulnerable to attack." And former director of national intelligence Dan Coats put it very simply. The lesson is, he said, "If you had nukes, never give them up. If you don't have them, get them."

Even Clapper himself clearly understood Kim's position. Recalling the U.S. war against Libya, he said, "Gaddafi pleaded for the United States and then NATO to stop the attacks, citing his cooperation with weapons inspectors, his voluntary disarmament of his nuclear program, and his restraint from using chemical weapons in his current civil struggle." But it did no good. "No one in the West paid attention. However, I believe North Korea and Iran took careful note of what happens when you give up your nuclear program."

It was only politicians in Congress and the White House who, largely to look tough to their constituents and the public, refused to accept the inevitable and work out a sustainable and realistic solution to the issue. Nothing would change under Obama, who cynically adopted a killer-drone foreign policy that was, according to Pentagon documents, "plagued by deeply flawed intelligence, rushed and imprecise targeting and deaths of thousands of civilians, many of them children." As a result, prior to Clapper's departure for Pyongyang, Obama ordered him to have no discussions about anything unless Kim first agreed to give up his nuclear ambitions. It was a nonstarter from the start.

———

By the time Clapper's Air Force Boeing 737 landed on runway 01/19 at Pyongyang's Sunan Shuofang International Airport it was after sunset. Beneath spotlights and a large portrait of Kim Il Sung, the plane pulled to a stop on the tarmac where several officials were waiting. Nearby sat a Russian-made Air Koryo jet, the country's national airline, with North Korea's red-and-blue flag painted on its vertical stabilizer. Among the crew detailed to stay on board the 737 during the visit were several intelligence officers "with special skill sets," according to Clapper. They were likely manning specially designed eavesdropping equipment fitted into the plane.

There to greet the intelligence chief as he came down the boarding stairs was Kim Won Hong, the minister of state security. After brief formalities they took their seats in a dark Mercedes limousine and forty-five minutes later arrived at Paekhwawon, the state guesthouse, a villa and conference facility located on an artificial lake near the Taedong River. In front were well-manicured lawns and gardens, and behind lay thick woods. Paekhwawon's name is said to have come from a hundred kinds of flowers blooming around the facility. Clapper was given a spacious two-room suite with a French provincial–style bed. Later, his only comments about the guesthouse were that there was nothing on TV, all the books were uninteresting, the mattress was thin, and he didn't like the green carpet. He was simply an old man in a chain motel for the night, the espionage equivalent of Willy Loman.

About 8:45 p.m., another long black limousine arrived at the guesthouse. In the backseat with a translator was North Korean spymaster General Kim Yong Chol, Clapper's longtime rival, there to take him to dinner. The mood was as cool as a Pyongyang shaved-ice stall. As the Mercedes cruised the streets of the capital, occasional streetlights glistening like pearls in the black velvet night, Clapper said little and simply stared into the empty void. There would be no probing questions, no inquisitiveness, no search for nuggets of intelligence, not even polite conversation.

The car pulled to a stop in front of the bowling alley with its giant rooftop ten-pin and they entered a side door. An elevator took them up to a private dining room on the second floor where a table decorated with an assortment of colorful flowers had been set up for a thirteen-course dinner. Standing at the long plate-glass window before taking his seat, Clapper knew what lay in the darkness. Across the street was the shiny, mysterious Taedong River, a curving black ribbon. And a mile or so to the west, freshly painted and tied up to a pier, was a still fully commissioned U.S. Navy/NSA spy ship, the USS *Pueblo*. On orders of Kim's grandfather, Kim Il Sung, the ship had been captured in 1968, following a bloody Cold War naval battle, as it was eavesdropping off the coast. It remains the only U.S. Navy ship in foreign hands, and Clapper wanted it back.

Although they would never meet until now, it was that sea battle nearly half a century before that began the spymasters' careers as junior intelligence officers. Lieutenant Kim was an aide to Army major general Pak Chung Kuk. As North Korea's top negotiator at the UN's Military Armistice Commission, General Pak was the official negotiating with his American counterparts for the release of the *Pueblo*'s captured crew. Lieutenant Clapper, on the other hand, was an aide to Air Force major general Louis E. Coira, the commander of the U.S. Air Force Security Service (AFSS), the NSA's air spies. A key target of the flights was eavesdropping on the North Korean negotiators.

Now at the opposite ends of their careers, and as they were moving from course to course at dinner, they both were hiding one last secret. At that moment, Kim was covertly conducting the largest cyberattack in history against a U.S. corporation. And neither Clapper nor his army of spies had a clue. It was an intelligence blunder of enormous proportions. Should the dinner produce no hope for better relations, Kim would open the digital floodgates and release every embarrassing byte of information.

But Clapper also had a deep secret, one that could result in enormous retaliation if discovered. Several years earlier, under orders from Obama, he had launched a massive all-out cyberwar attack against North Korea. Similar to the devastating Stuxnet attack on Iran, it was designed to cause widespread physical damage and destruction to much of North Korea's nuclear infrastructure. But unlike in Iran, the attack ultimately failed, likely without anyone in North Korea, including General Kim, ever becoming witting of it.

Clapper more than anyone knew the dangers of serious retaliation should Chairman Kim Jong Un ever discover that act of war against his country. Harsh retaliation against the United States for perceived threats, regardless of the potential dangers, was not only in Kim's bloodstream, it was in his bloodline. A little more than a year after Kim's grandfather, Kim Il Sung, ordered the capture of the USS *Pueblo*, along with the imprisonment of its crew, he ordered the shootdown of an NSA EC-121 spy plane in international airspace, killing all thirty-one crew members on board. It was an act that nearly led to a nuclear war.

But for now, Clapper's act of war remained secret. Kim was instead retaliating against Sony Pictures for another reason, one very personal.

CHAPTER 2

◆

The Studio

Just beyond the glistening white Greek Revival colonnade that once served as the gateway to the legendary Metro-Goldwyn-Mayer studios is Sony's film empire. It is spread out over forty-four acres of soundstages, streetfronts, and back lots in Culver City, seven miles southwest of Hollywood and Vine. In its MGM heyday it was the lair of Leo the Lion and his famous roar. It was a fantasy world within a world of fantasy where, as children, Elizabeth Taylor, Mickey Rooney, and Judy Garland received acting lessons in "star school," now the Crawford Building. Where Clark Gable and Joan Crawford herself sat in dressing rooms and walked across soundstages. And where thick reels of film were shot, edited, and sent off to darkened theaters displaying in giant red letters on their marquees, and on colorful posters lining their walls, *Gone with the Wind*, *Ben-Hur*, and *Doctor Zhivago*.

In 1938, as the studio was filming *The Wizard of Oz* and Judy Garland was clicking her ruby slippers on the yellow brick road, a new executive office building was dedicated in the name of producer Irving Thalberg. With its lobby of butterflied walnut walls, terrazzo floor, and screen of Lalique crystal, it was considered one of the best examples of Moderne-style architecture in Southern California. And on the third floor was the office of studio chief Louis B. Mayer, a man who "defined MGM, just as MGM defined Hollywood, and Hollywood defined America," wrote biographer Scott Eyman.

By 2014, the painted plywood yellow brick road was long gone, but the trapdoor used for the Wicked Witch's ascent was still in place on Stage 27, the home to Munchkinland. And the foyer of the Thalberg Building still contained the twelve Best Picture Academy Awards won by MGM/Columbia between 1934 and 1987. But Mayer's office, with its balcony overlooking the Hollywood Hills, was now occupied by a new studio chief, fifty-six-year-old Amy Pascal.

Arriving every morning in a Land Rover from her $10 million home in the Mandeville Canyon area of Brentwood, Pascal had spent more than a decade at the top of Sony's Motion Picture Group. She also carried the additional title of co-chairperson of Sony Pictures Entertainment. Her light brown hair disheveled, her jaws in ceaseless motion chomping bubble gum, she would debate script changes with actors, or days of shooting with directors, while sitting, legs tucked beneath her, on her couch. At other times her fingers would be bouncing on her Sony Xperia Z2 sending out nearly incomprehensible emails as her assistant, who earned more than $250,000 a year, hovered nearby.

One floor above, where Mayer once had his private dining room, gym, and chiropractor, was the office of Michael Lynton, Pascal's boss as chairman and chief executive of Sony Pictures Entertainment. Under the arrangement, Lynton largely crunched the numbers dealing with the financial side of the business, leaving Pascal to focus on finding and producing the movies that were released under the Columbia Pictures, TriStar, and Screen Gems labels.

It was a difficult marriage at first. As president of Columbia Pictures since 1996, Pascal believed she had earned the right to the top job when it became open in 2003. When instead she was passed over and Sony's corporate boss, Howard Stringer, handed it to Lynton, an outsider who formerly ran AOL Europe, she was apoplectic. Sitting with Lynton in the studio commissary one day, Pascal told him bluntly, "I thought I should have your job. Howard thought you should have it. I said, 'I'm leaving.'" Nevertheless, the two worked out an amiable partnership and also became easygoing friends. They attended the same synagogue, and their children attended the same schools and even had sleepovers.

Slim and wiry with a bony, narrow face almost anvil-like in shape, and a shock of gray hair that hung like a rogue wave crashing on his broad forehead, Lynton came from inherited wealth; the giant Hunter Douglas wall covering company was the family business.

"Sony Pictures has made incredible progress in creating a more sustainable organization, across every part of the company," Lynton boasted. Yet instead of simply flying first class commercial, he constantly made use of Sony's fleet of private jets to get him wherever he wanted to go, including frequent cross-country meetings in New York at a cost of over $100,000. He even used them to fly his family on vacation to Martha's Vineyard. Then he would commute from the Vineyard to meetings in New York by private helicopter at a cost to the company of $10,000 round-trip, rather than simply taking a commercial flight for the one-hour journey.

And like much of the Hollywood upper echelon, Lynton had little use for the normal admissions process. Pay for play in colleges was apparently family policy. Lynton's sister, Carol "Lili" Lynton, a partner in the upscale chef

Daniel Boulud restaurant chain, was clearly an advocate. In February 2014, Michael wrote an email to Lili Lynton about their cousin David Sonnenberg, son of multibillionaire Ralph Sonnenberg. "[David] is obsessed with getting his eldest in Harvard next year. we should talk about that and what I should do." Lili appeared surprised even at the question. "If David wants to get his daughter in he should obviously start giving money," she said. "Did you tell him that? Maybe have him meet with Roger Cheever?" Roger P. Cheever was the associate vice president at Harvard in charge of "Principal Gifts."

"Giving money" was exactly what Lynton had in mind when his middle daughter, Maisie, wanted to attend Brown University in 2014. He therefore decided on a scheme involving a $1 million scholarship in the name of an old friend, Nathaniel Chapman, a CIA officer who graduated from Brown and died in 2008 of brain cancer. Unsurprisingly, the cash was highly appreciated. "This is great news! It is a wonderful thing that you will be doing," Brown's vice president, Ronald Margolin, wrote to Lynton.

As a result, unlike other prospective students who get the standard walk-around, Lynton and his daughter were invited for a private tour, where he would have a personal one-on-one meeting with Brown president Christina Paxson while his daughter attended a class. Secrecy in the form of anonymity, however, was key. "No one outside the board would see other than anonymous," Tom Rothman told him. As head of TriStar Productions, Rothman was a Lynton employee who conveniently served on the school's board of trustees. People seeing a million-dollar gift at the same time his daughter was applying for admission might somehow get the wrong impression.

Incredibly, Lynton even kept the scholarship secret from the Chapman family, in whose name the scholarship was given, despite the fact that Chapman's widow, Liza, had two daughters applying for admission to Brown that same year, and despite being godfather to Liza's youngest child. Chapman only discovered the scholarship by accident, from a secretary while touring the school with one of her daughters. It was a great surprise since it had been years since she had heard anything from Lynton, despite trying to contact him.

Finally, after locating an email address for Lynton, Chapman questioned him about the mysterious scholarship. Although he admitted providing the scholarship, Lynton nevertheless made no mention of helping her daughters get into Brown. "I have not been a good godfather (it is not really in the Jewish tradition and so I am on uncertain footing here)," he apologized.

Later Chapman asked for Lynton's help in putting a good word in with someone at Brown on her daughters' behalf. But the million dollars was to help *his* daughter get in, not Chapman's, so he simply blew her off. "I do not really know anyone at Brown" he said, despite having had personal meetings with officials from the president on down. "So I am not sure how I would go about it."

A year before Maisie went off to Brown, his older daughter, Eloise, entered Harvard. But since Lynton was an alumnus of both the college and the business school, on the Harvard Board of Overseers—which, among other things approves the appointment of the university's president—and a major donor, she likely had little trouble getting in. In 2012, the year before she was admitted, Lynton donated about $360,000 in rare photographs to Harvard's Fogg Museum. Then, the year she entered Harvard, in 2013, he donated an additional $550,000 in rare Ilse Bing and Leonard Freed photographs to Fogg.

By 2013, Pascal was in deep trouble. After more than a decade filling Mayer's old seat in the Thalberg Building, she was on the tail end of a six-year decline both in the quality of films she was greenlighting and the box-office numbers they were attracting. And that summer she went into free fall with *White House Down*, starring Channing Tatum. Produced by Sony's Columbia Pictures and Brad Fischer's Mythology Entertainment, the film was directed by Roland "Master of Disaster" Emmerich, who had already destroyed the White House twice before. (Full disclosure: Early on I was approached by the producers and director to be a technical consultant on the film but I declined.)

Almost immediately, *White House Down* produced a bomb worthy of an Emmerich special effect. The *Washington Post* called it "this summer's most cartoonishly bombastic exercise in sensory overload." To make matters worse, it followed on the heels of Sony's other summer blockbuster, *After Earth*, starring Will Smith and his son Jaden. Rotten Tomatoes gave it a mere 11 on its Tomatometer and the *Wall Street Journal* asked, "Is 'After Earth' the worst movie ever made?" In the end, *White House Down* lost the studio more than $50 million, and *After Earth* another $25 million. To make up for their disastrous disaster movies, Pascal and Lynton had a solution to save their studio: assassinate North Korean leader Kim Jong Un.

In their calculus, audiences would flock to theaters on opening day, Christmas 2014, to laugh uproariously as Kim's head gets blown up like a watermelon dropped from a skyscraper and hitting the pavement. And they had just the assassin to do the job: Seth Rogen, who would quadruple as killer, star, producer, and director. In the film, titled *The Interview*, Rogen and costar James Franco would portray journalists invited to North Korea to interview Kim, but who were secretly recruited by the CIA to assassinate him.

By the mid-2010s Rogen's frat-boy, stoner, scatological humor had become as stale as the air in his marijuana-saturated office on the Sony lot. Other Sony film executives, however, couldn't understand Pascal's attachment to Rogen and Franco, or the fact that she was planning to use them in still another puerile, dimwitted Christmas film the following year, 2015, with the title *The Night Before*. It was a decision that literally flummoxed a number of top company executives in confidential internal emails. "This was a SHOCKER...Are they serious? About making this film?" asked Executive Vice President Stephen Basil-Jones. "It could be one of the worse screenplays I have ever read...un-original, un-funny & no commercial playability...Not sure who the audience is for it."

Others signed off on a similar view of *The Interview*. "The unanimous point of view here is that this is another misfire," they advised, calling it "desperately unfunny and repetitive."

More than the film simply being in bad taste, company executives in South Korea warned it could also lead to trouble. "Above all," wrote an executive based in Seoul, Kim's exploding head along with the "strange North Korean accent is not acceptable to our audience. Also, there would be a big potential to produce the political issue about North Korea as well."

Based on a story idea by Rogen and his coproducer/codirector Evan Goldberg, the original screenplay was written by Dan Sterling. But Sterling's version involved a fictional dictator from a fictional country. "It never occurred to me that we would be able to use the real leader's name. I wrote the script—without any instructions from anybody—with a fake name," he said. "I wrote a name called Kim Il-Wan and that was the version that the studio green lit." Randall Park, the actor picked to play Kim, also understood that he would be playing a fictional character. "In the original version of the script that I got, it wasn't Kim Jong Un," he said. "But I was told right before my audition that it was going to be Kim Jong Un."

Later, at a meeting between Sony executives and Rogen and Goldberg, it was agreed that the script would be changed to feature the name of the real country and its real leader, Kim Jong Un. According to Sterling, it was something Rogen and Goldberg were insistent upon. "I think ultimately the studio said, 'Do what you've got to do.'" As a result, the title was then going to be *Kill Kim Jong Un*, until it was later changed.

This was a serious, unprecedented, and dangerous decision: satirizing a bloody CIA-ordered assassination of the leader of a potentially hostile country, followed by the violent overthrow of his government. A leader armed with both powerful nuclear weapons and cyberweapons and who had recently launched his country's third nuclear test. By naming names, Rogen and

Goldberg, along with Pascal and Lynton, had turned a mindless movie into a deep personal insult demanding a response.

The reason for the change was simply old-fashioned greed—principle had nothing to do with it. Real names would generate controversy, perhaps even a protest or worse by Kim himself. And controversy attracts paying customers. Rogen, who would make $8 million on the film, therefore insisted on the change. And Pascal and Lynton, who were projecting $100 million at the box office to help bail out their sinking studio, went along with it.

To make matters worse, Rogen started talking shit. Transformed into a foreign policy expert, he began championing regime change. At one point he declared, "Maybe the tapes of the movie will make their way to North Korea and cause a revolution." At another point he commented, "If it does start a war, hopefully people will say, 'You know what? It was worth it. It was a good movie!'" A high school dropout at sixteen, who claimed his research on North Korea consisted of "Wikipedia mostly," and who had posted a video of himself on Twitter asking his Alexa to fart, Rogen was in way over his head.

In November 2013, Rogen and Goldberg began shooting their film in Vancouver, Canada, transforming the city into a wintry Pyongyang, complete with a giant statue of Kim Jong Un in Robson Square. Back on the Sony lot in Culver City, Lynton and Pascal faced unhappy investors. CBS News headlined its article "Red Ink Runs at Sony Again, Cuts Profit Forecast." The result was a promise by Lynton and Pascal to slash $250 million, begin shifting away from film toward television, and start laying off hundreds of employees. "No cost is too sacred to cut," Lynton said.

In reality, as laid-off Sony workers picked up their last paychecks, both Lynton and Pascal went about life as always. Lynton, who made $13 million in 2013, kept his private jets and helicopters and bet a friend he wouldn't even have to give up his hefty yearly bonus. He was right; "Kaz" Hirai, the charismatic president and CEO of the Sony Corporation, let him keep it. "He gave me the bonus, the bet paid off," Lynton crowed to the friend. And Pascal, who made $12 million the same year, simply dismissed the whole exercise as nonsense. "Oh please, it's an investor conference," she privately wrote to an associate. "U know it's bs." "This is my fucking company," she declared. "I have outlasted everyone and always will."

But now the knives were sliding out from their sheathes and the *Hollywood Reporter* was going after Pascal. The magazine had learned that despite the massive losses the studio was accumulating, Pascal was still blissfully paying her personal assistant, who would help her pick out dresses and run errands, a whopping quarter million dollars a year in Sony salary. The article, headlined "New Life for Amy Pascal: From $250K+ Assistant to $250M in Cuts," was as bad as Pascal imagined. "So stupid," she said in an email to producer Scott Rudin, fifty-five, who had produced *The Social Network* for Pascal. "Entirely so," he replied.

For Pascal, the timing couldn't have been worse or more embarrassing. The next day she was joining many of her fellow film executives for a meeting with President Barack Obama at DreamWorks Animation's expansive campus in Glendale, outside Los Angeles. Obama was going to get a tour and give a brief talk. While awaiting Obama's arrival, she emailed a colleague back at the Sony lot. "I wish I was there so much Instead of at the DreamWorks animation building waiting for the rest of the Hollywood rat fuckers to try and look smart in front of Obama," she wrote. Then she and Scott Rudin began emailing back and forth with some racist humor at Obama's expense, attempting to name the president's "favorite movies," all of them with Black actors or themes. "Should I ask him if he liked DJANGO?" Pascal wrote, referring to the 2012 film about slavery. "12 years," Rudin replied, indicating *12 Years a Slave*. Seeming to enjoy the game, the two continued: "Ride-along. I bet he likes Kevin Hart," said Rudin. "Or the butler. Or think like a man?"

Given this cringe-inducing racial insensitivity displayed by one of Hollywood's top studio heads and one of its foremost producers, it is little wonder why *The Interview* was so repulsively racist and filled with Asian stereotypes. Noted national security author Tim Shorrock, "The film used every racist image and trope that Rogen could dream up, from the sing-songy caricatures of Asian speech that were a film staple in the 1940s and '50s, to the concept that Koreans are either robotic slaves (like Kim's security guards) or sex-starved submissives who crave American men."

"Now imagine this assassination farce was made not in Hollywood, but in North Korea or Moscow," wrote the *Washington Post*'s Justin Wm. Moyer, "and the leader assassinated in the film was a president of the United States. Or imagine the film was made by Iran, and the leader assassinated in the film was the prime minister of Israel. Not so funny, is it? The North Korean, Russian or Iranian version of 'The Interview' would be called racist. It would be called anti-Semitic."

Like tourists strolling through a minefield, as Lynton, Pascal, and Rogen continued pressing forward with *The Interview*, they had little idea how dangerous their path had become. On June 11, 2014, the world became aware of the film when Sony Pictures held a major press briefing, released a flashy trailer, and arranged numerous media interviews for Rogen. "Want to go kill Kim Jong Un?" Franco's character says. "Totally, I'd love to assassinate Kim Jong Un—it's a date," Rogen's character replies.

In Pyongyang, Kim Jong Un was not laughing. On the other side of the country from Lynton's and Pascal's lavish suites in the Thalberg Building was the drab North Korean Mission to the United Nations. Located on the thirteenth floor of a gray Manhattan office building above a Hallmark Card store, it sat behind a solid brown door with a peephole in the center. On a plaque on the wall was the country's formal name, the "Democratic People's Republic of Korea" (DPRK). Down the hall was the "Delegation of the Basque Country in the U.S." and a shared restroom.

On June 27, North Korean ambassador Ja Song Nam filed a formal complaint with the UN Security Council. "Those who defamed our supreme leadership and committed hostile acts against DPRK can never escape the stern punishment to be meted out according to the law, wherever they might be in the world," threatened the Foreign Ministry. "To allow the production and distribution of such a film on the assassination of an incumbent Head of a sovereign State should be regarded as the most undisguised sponsoring of terrorism as well as an act of war."

Hearing the news in his office on the Sony Pictures lot, a glass marijuana pipe on his desk beside an ashtray filled with the remnants of half a dozen joints, Rogen celebrated. "There was a lot of high-fiving," he later said. "It was exciting!" After all, it's not every day a gonzo stoner causes the United States to be threatened with thermonuclear war.

—◆—

CHAPTER 3

Pyongyang

General Kim Yong Chol walked quickly down the gold-trimmed red carpet for an important meeting with Kim Jong Un. The secretive office of the supreme leader was expansive, windowless, and had the airy appearance of a grad school library. Floor-to-ceiling bookshelves lined the mahogany walls end to end, colorful spines packed tightly cover to cover. The only openings were for two large flat-screen TVs, one on each side of the room. Above, three sparkling crystal chandeliers hung from a white carved ceiling. And below was a modern carpet in light shades of green that contained a calming, stylish pattern as if looking at stones beneath a clear pond.

There were no red buttons. Instead, Kim's long antique mahogany desk contained a dainty Victorian lamp with a silk fringe-lined bell-shaped shade; a large book-style calendar sat in the center; three white European-style phones were off to the right near his Android-powered HTC smartphone. A slim white Sonamu (Pine) brand cigarette rested in a crystal ashtray near a glass of iced coffee. Eschewing the standard executive-style swivel chair, he was seated in a powder blue high-back with four small cabriole legs.

Behind Kim were two red-and-yellow Workers' Party flags hanging limp in the still air, along with a large arched mirror above a mantel with a clock in a cherrywood case, and a colorful vase of fresh flowers. Running North Korea is Kim's family business, as two large paintings occupied most of the wall to his rear: on the right his father, Kim Jong Il, in his trademark tan flight suit, with teased hair and geometric glasses, was reading some documents; and on the left his grandfather Kim Il Sung, in a Western-style business suit, was sitting at his desk.

Dressed in a dark silk Mao suit, large buttons down the center, Kim Jong Un took his seat on a tufted leather maroon chair, the kind found in London clubs along Pall Mall. Horn-rimmed glasses rested on the bridge of his nose, and a black-dialed, American-made Movado Museum watch was strapped to his thick left wrist. General Kim sat down perpendicular to Kim at the end of an identical couch. The seating arrangement allowed the supreme leader to keep his eyes constantly on his spy chief, while the general had to continuously turn his head to the left to achieve eye contact with his boss.

For Kim Jong Un, his anger about *The Interview* was at a roiling boil, and he ordered General Kim to begin preparations for an immense cyberattack against Sony, one designed to greatly embarrass and humiliate—personally, professionally, and very publicly—those attempting to humiliate him. But while the preparations would go ahead for the attack, for now he was only authorizing a secret reconnaissance mission, exfiltrating and analyzing documents, nothing more, not releasing them or crashing the system. More important for Kim was simply getting Sony to fictionalize the leader and country, a reasonable request.

The key was finding a way to induce the Obama administration to pressure Sony to make the changes. But beyond giving up its nuclear program, there was only one thing the United States constantly wanted from North Korea: American prisoners. And at the time the country was holding three of them.

General Kim left the office through a pair of French doors and quickly returned to his Reconnaissance General Bureau headquarters. There he handed the assignment to one of his top cyber warriors, Park Jin Hyok. Shortly thereafter, Park opened several Facebook accounts under assumed identities, established a number of phony Twitter accounts, and on September 5 began spear-phishing Sony.

Changing his name to Andoson David, he sent a message to the Facebook account for *The Interview*. In the hopes of tempting someone at the company to click on an infected link, the message mentioned the name of one of the female actors, followed by "nude photos were leaked online. As you can see from attached file, somebody made screen saver with the photos." Below it was the link: "NudePhotoGallery.zip." But rather than nude images, it contained dangerous malware that would allow Park to digitally enter the person's computer and, through it, secretly begin hacking his way into Sony.

Ironically, at almost the same moment as Park launched his hack attack, the actor George Clooney sent Amy Pascal an email with the subject line "Knowing this email is being hacked." He had no way of knowing how correct he was. Clooney was hoping to get Pascal and Sony to finance a film he wanted to direct based on the book *Hack Attack* by journalist Nick Davies. Rather than North Korea, the book focused on the 2011 British phone-hacking scandal revolving around Rupert Murdoch's news empire.

And Clooney's reasons were decidedly political. "How much fun are we gonna have," he wrote to Pascal, "the stakes are higher than citizen kane...if we tell the truth in a compelling way...rupert won't get time/warner...cnn won't be fox...i'm so excited to do this film...and for those of you listening in...i'm the son of a news man...everything will be double sourced...so come on with your lawsuits...fuckers." In fact, Park soon *would* be listening in, and Clooney's email message would take its place with thousands of others from Sony in his Pyongyang database.

At thirty-two, Park Jin Hyok had been pounding keyboards since his earliest days. Slim, with thick jet black hair, a few wayward curls extending to the middle of his forehead, he enjoyed stylish clothes, occasionally dressing in a black mandarin-collared shirt beneath a brown wool sport coat. Following high school, he attended the Kim Chaek University of Technology in Pyongyang next to a large satellite dish on the banks of the Taedong River. With about ten thousand students and a heavy emphasis on computer technology and nuclear engineering, it was one of the country's leading sources of cyber warriors. In 2019 it ranked eighth out of over three thousand schools, ahead of Harvard and Stanford, in the International Collegiate Programming Contest, an annual event to find the top algorithmic programmers. Park studied English, Chinese, and a variety of computer languages, including Visual C++, a key skill for use in penetrating cyber networks. C++ is also required at NSA for those applying for exploitation cryptanalyst positions.

While in college, Park and a number of other high achievers joined Lab 110, a secret cyber warfare unit that was part of General Kim's Reconnaissance General Bureau, the country's equivalent of the CIA and NSA. Because at the time North Korea had little internet connectivity, Park and the others would be sent to China to take advantage of that country's high-speed internet while learning how to master it. Then, working full-time for the organization following graduation, Park was sent on one-year assignments to Dalian, China.

A city on Korea Bay north of the Yellow Sea and not far from North Korea, Dalian offered fast access to the internet. Based in the People's Square area near the municipal government buildings, Park and the others engaged in a combination of clandestine cyber warfare activities and also moneymaking commercial activities for the government while posing as employees of Chosun Expo Joint Venture. A North Korean front company, it served as a Korean-language online shopping site offering a variety of North Korean goods. Other cyber warriors worked out of assigned rooms at the Chilbosan Hotel in Shenyang, 243 miles northeast of Dalian. The sixteen-story four-star hotel, owned in partnership with China, was fully equipped with a gym, sauna, beauty parlor, and even a karaoke setup.

In 2011, Park was engaged and planning to be married that September; he was therefore looking for a way to return home to North Korea permanently. By then, with a new 3G network developed by Egyptian telecommunications firm Orascomcell, cell phones had proliferated, topping one million users. That number would leapfrog to nearly four million by 2015, according to South Korean intelligence. North Korea also developed growing internet connectivity through Star Joint Ventures, a Pyongyang-based company partly controlled by Thailand's Loxley Pacific.

In Pyongyang in 2012, a public internet café using North Korea's custombuilt operating system at last opened its doors. Its Red Star operating system mimicked Apple's OS X, unsurprising since Kim Jong Un was a fan of the iMac. Most local residents, however, can connect instead only to an internal intranet, called Kwangmyong. Likewise, most phones are unable to dial out of the country or receive international calls. However, foreigners with cell phones can purchase 3G SIM cards for about $200 and access a fast internet connection.

With internet connectivity finally adequate for cyber warfare, in 2013 Park moved back full-time to RGB headquarters in Pyongyang. A secretive complex of pearly white rectangular buildings, it is northwest of downtown in the Hyongjesan district. Nearby are three white satellite dishes. And in a heavily wooded hillside about a kilometer to the northwest there are another dozen large satellite dishes; these, however, are all painted green to camouflage them. Several buildings are close by.

For several months, since being assigned the operation in September, Park and his team had been spending hours conducting detailed reconnaissance on Lynton, Pascal, and Rogen as they developed ever more creative ways to explode Kim's head. The team searched the open web for business contacts on LinkedIn, read interviews they had given, plowed through their Twitter and Facebook accounts, checked out Sony's website, and put together an extensive dossier on each target. The personal and business data would give them clues for ways to develop realistic-looking spear-phishing emails, the hook that would enable the team to reel them in for capture. And occasionally, needing a break, they would check online for what was on TV that evening or what kind of pizza to order for lunch.

———

By 2014, Pyongyang, a wasteland of destruction following the Korean War, was no longer the drab, lifeless concrete metropolis in most people's imagination. Among Kim's first actions once his father died was to remove the oversize portraits of Karl Marx and Vladimir Lenin from the Foreign Trade Ministry building. While certainly a country with serious problems, under Kim Jong Un North Korea had been rapidly and quietly undergoing a metamorphosis, as many of the depressing Soviet brutalist designs fell victim to wrecking balls. "Visitors to North Korea over the years have returned with reports of new construction, streets crowded with imported cars and taxis, and new restaurants serving a dozen varieties of pizza and pasta accompanied by wine or beer," noted Jung Pak, the former CIA expert on North Korea. In early 2022, construction was nearing completion on a new street in Pyongyang featuring an eighty-story skyscraper and dozens of apartment buildings to house upwards of ten thousand families.

With his youth spent in the idyllic Swiss countryside, Kim has transformed much of Pyongyang from prison gray to a pallet of whimsical pastels. Streets are now filled with women in fashionable Western-style skirts window-shopping for stylish shoes. And couples now linger over demitasse cups of espresso or a chocolate frappé at the Vienna Cafe next to Kim Il Sung Square, a joint venture with Austrian roaster Helmut Sachers. Ornate, spotless subway platforms are lined with workers dressed for the office. Teenagers can be seen everywhere in distressed jeans lugging backpacks and sipping Cokes, with smartphone cords dangling from their ears and a pair of New Balance sneakers on their feet. And river cruises are offered aboard the 393-foot, 1,230-seat *Rainbow*, complete with a revolving restaurant on the third and fourth decks. Even in the countryside, water parks have begun to proliferate.

"Consumerism has been entrenched, embraced, and encouraged," the CIA's Pak said. "Since Kim came to power, more North Koreans enjoy smartphones, taxis, flat-screen televisions, and home appliances made in Japan and South Korea. A wide range of these and similar goods are available in hundreds of markets and state-run shops." She added, "Most North Koreans, not just the elites, now own or have access to advanced media devices, including computers, USB drives, and Chinese mobile phones."

In remote laboratories and test centers, Kim Jong Un was also quietly adding to his nuclear stockpile, his trump card should the United States decide it was time for regime change. Nevertheless, he also certainly realized that the only purpose of nuclear weapons was as a deterrent; the first time they are used for real it is the end of his country. Therefore, having grown up with computers and comfortable with technology, he saw cyber warfare as the great equalizer. It allowed him to compete with intelligence and cyber organizations like NSA both in terms of espionage and attack, while at the same time hiding his fingerprints because of the difficulty of attribution. The nuclear weapons, therefore, would give him his defense while the cyber-weapons would provide him with offense.

Beyond the hardware and software, what Kim needed was the human-ware like Park—mathematicians, computer scientists, and nuclear engineers in their twenties and early thirties. The solution was to greatly increase the focus on highly technical areas of study at Pyongyang's colleges and universities, and to build his own Silicon Valley. The centerpiece of Pyongyang's new high-tech zone is the glass-and-metal science and technology complex that, viewed from the sky, appears in the shape of the nucleus of an atom. And installed in the central hall of the main building is a three-story mock-up of the Unha (Galaxy) rocket that in 2012 launched a satellite into orbit. Since 1998, the country has launched five satellites, two of which have successfully been placed in orbit, including its last in 2016.

The extensive library contains a large selection of English-language books on thermodynamics, particle physics, and other technical topics. By 2020, students were writing research papers on the tracking and maneuvering of picosatellites, a key focus within the worldwide aerospace community. Two years later, in March 2022, Kim stared at a row of giant screens within the country's Satellite Control Center in Pyongyang. As he watched, a newly designed ICBM lifted off on a test flight from the Sohae Satellite Launching Ground in the country's northwest near the border with China. In the first such launch in five years, the Hwasong-15 rocket reached an altitude of over thirty-eight hundred miles in space and may eventually be used to place a reconnaissance satellite in orbit. It may also have the capability of reaching U.S. cities. Hours later, the U.S. Indo-Pacific Command ordered an Air Force RC-135S Cobra Ball reconnaissance jet into the air to spy on the intensified activity.

———

Sitting in front of his computer setup at RGB headquarters, Park and his team were physically in Pyongyang. But virtually they were inside Sony Pictures' studio lot, quietly emptying out its digital file cabinets and film vaults as if they were taking over the company—which in a sense they were. Command and control links had been established so that the voluminous data being transferred could not be traced directly back to Pyongyang. One of those was a server hidden at Thammasat University, a large public research institution near the Grand Palace in the heart of Bangkok, Thailand. Instructions from Pyongyang would flow through there to the Sony computers, and the stolen data would be returned the same way.

As the intercepted emails flowed in, Chairman Kim could clearly read in minute detail how on Christmas Day the world would watch his eyeballs liquefy and stream down his melting cheeks like runny egg whites. So in October another appeal was made, this time directly to Obama through the White House National Security Council. "The trailer of 'The Interview,'" it said, "has still impolite contents"; it threatened to take action if nothing was done.

CHAPTER 4

◆

Tokyo

At Sony's worldwide headquarters in Tokyo, just a short missile flight across the Sea of Japan from North Korea, there was immediate shock and pushback from Lynton's boss following the release of the *Interview* trailer. "Mr. Kaz Hirai, CEO, was very much concerned about this film," Noriaki Sano, the head of Sony Pictures Japan, notified others. At fifty-three, Kaz Hirai had been fascinated by technology since his days watching *Romper Room* on TV. He was perplexed why he couldn't simply reach through the screen and grab a cookie handed out to kids in the audience. Born in Tokyo and fluent in both English and Japanese, he was raised in Japan and the United States and had been with the company since graduating from college in 1984. Although Sony Pictures was part of his domain, he was far more comfortable wearing a pair of 3D glasses and experimenting with new digital games in the company's Tokyo demo room than wandering around a Hollywood soundstage.

Founded in 1946 amid the rubble of postwar Japan, the once-iconic company was widely known for groundbreaking products like the Walkman and the first CD player. But by 2012 Sony was rudderless, bloated, and falling behind rivals such as Apple and Samsung. Its huge losses were largely tied to the depressed consumer electronics business. That was when Kaz was tapped to lead the company back into profitability. His key focus was on dumping the company's personal computer business, cutting back on televisions, and pouring money into products like the PlayStation game console. He left movie premieres to Lynton and Pascal.

Kaz was also very physically removed from Hollywood's star-studded sidewalks and the carbon arcs of its Klieg lights. His office was on the twentieth floor of Sony's glassy headquarters in the embassy-cluttered Minato district of Tokyo. Much closer, across the Sea of Japan, was North Korea. He knew the hatred for Japan that remained there as a result of the brutal, horrific occupation of the country from 1910 to 1945. That was the year the

Japanese occupiers were finally booted out and Kim Jong Un's grandfather, Kim Il Sung, became ruler.

Rarely involving himself in the film side of the business, Kaz was greatly concerned that *The Interview* would trigger a hostile or violent reaction against Japan. Of special concern was the over-the-top death scene where Kim's head, hit by a tank shell, first melts like a gooey wax basketball as flames engulf his hair, then explodes as if he had sticks of dynamite up his nostrils and in his ears. Sitting in his thick-cushioned chair after viewing the trailer, Kaz picked up his phone and ordered Lynton to do something about the film—immediately.

The problem was that the studio had just released the trailer. Now Lynton was desperately trying to bury it. "Have to keep whole interview thing under wraps," he quickly notified Pascal. "Only on a need to know basis." Pascal then shot off an email to Sony Pictures vice chairman Jeff Black, telling him "we need sonys name off this asap everywhere." Like a pair of priests caught in a brothel, Lynton and Pascal scrambled to distance the company from the film, ordering the word "Sony" stripped from all billboards, magazine ads, and other promotional material. They even pulled back the trailer and told film editors to delete the logo from the end credit crawl and banned the film's release in Asia. Meanwhile, Sony Entertainment president Doug Belgrad, who reported to Pascal, spent more than half a million dollars having technicians digitally remove images of Kim Jong Un's father and grandfather from buttons, pins, and murals in more than five hundred shots.

Lynton, who hung out in Obama's elite social circles, next secretly began turning to the U.S. government for help. Soon after hearing from Kaz, he sent a message to Michael D. Rich, the CEO of the RAND Corporation. The quintessential Cold War military-intelligence think tank, RAND itself was once parodied by Hollywood as the warmongering "Bland Corporation" in *Dr. Strangelove*. And it played a critical role in the war in Vietnam, which led employee Daniel Ellsberg to quit, turn whistleblower, and release the secret RAND-produced Pentagon Papers that exposed the many lies underpinning the U.S. involvement.

Lynton had long been listed as a trustee of the organization, whose $100 million, five-story headquarters is in the beach community of Santa Monica, a brief drive from Lynton's Brentwood home. Happy to help, Rich put Lynton in touch with Bruce W. Bennett. Oddly, although RAND's expert on North Korea, he had never set foot in the country and was so untechnical he didn't even own a smartphone.

Bennett was, however, a certified card-carrying member of the U.S. military-intelligence complex and had long been eager for Kim to be overthrown. For that reason, he greatly enjoyed watching Kim's head liq-uefy and then detonate and hoped the film would spark his long-dreamed-of regime change. In fact, it was the theme of his recent book published by RAND: *Preparing for the Possibility of a North Korean Collapse*. It was there-fore not surprising that Bennett objected to toning down Kim's explosive death in the film, and he was very hopeful that the DVD version would leak into the North and "start some real thinking." Lynton replied, "Spoke to someone very senior in State (confidentially). He agreed with everything you have been saying. Everything."

Further involving the U.S. government secretly in the film's production, Bennett, as an advisor for the film, brought others from the Obama national security establishment on board for advice, including from the State Depart-ment. "We made relationships with certain people who work in the gov-ernment as consultants, who I'm convinced are in the CIA," Rogen would later claim. It was a bit like art imitating reality imitating art. The CIA was secretly encouraging filmmakers to make a film about the CIA encour-aging filmmakers to assassinate Kim Jong Un. The CIA's involvement was anything but unusual. The agency even has its own Entertainment Liaison Office. "I think probably Hollywood is full of CIA agents," actor Ben Affleck once said.

Other senior Obama officials shown the ghoulish ending also secretly gave Lynton the administration's thumbs-up rather than simply keeping their distance. This despite the dangers of risking an attack on the United States, or war, by placing an official U.S. seal of approval on a film depicting and advo-cating Kim's murder and the overthrow of his country by the CIA.

Although the U.S. government's role was intended to be secret, it quickly leaked, thus forcing the embarrassed State Department to lie and deny any involvement. But that backfired when one of the senior officials publicly admitted his role. "I'm the U.S. government official who told Sony there was no problem 'greenlighting' the movie *The Interview*," said Assistant Secretary of State for East Asia Daniel Russel. The result: Both official and unofficial members of the Obama administration secretly approved and encouraged the release of the film in its most violent form.

Over the next month, the degree to which the effects department would mangle Kim Jong Un's head became the subject of endless meetings, emails, and anguish. "We cannot be cute here," noted Lynton and echoing his boss, Kaz. "What we really want is no melting face and actually not seeing him die. A look of horror as the fire approaches is probably what we need." "We are gonna get rid of [his] face but we are gonna know he dies," replied Pascal in her usual clipped style. "Speaking of making Kaz comfortable," noted Doug

Belgrad, referring to an upcoming SONY New York meeting, "I have the shot that has embers in the hair, but more fireball to show in NYC."

By early August 2014, the launch of *The Interview* had been postponed from October to Christmas Day and what was left of Kim's head was pushed to a back burner as both Lynton and Pascal departed for vacation. As he did every year, Lynton took off for Martha's Vineyard with his family to join the Obamas and Clintons, and Pascal and her husband and son were going on an extensive trip to Asia.

Suddenly, on August 13, tremors rolled through the near-empty Thalberg Building. Someone had leaked details of the contentious meetings in which it was decided to pull back from the original concept of turning Kim's head into a burnt marshmallow. "Sony Altering Kim Jong Un Assassination Film 'The Interview' (Exclusive)," screamed the headline in the *Hollywood Reporter*. Below in bold print was the bizarre subheading "Military buttons disappear and face-melting could be cut as the Japan-owned studio preps the Seth Rogen comedy."

In a scramble to hide the truth—that the changes were ordered by Kaz, Sony's Japanese boss—the studio issued a series of bold lies. "A source close to Sony's decision-making says the move to alter the hardware was precipitated by 'clearance issues,'" the article said, "particularly because it involves a living person, Kim Jong Un."

At 7:43 a.m., Jean Guerin, Sony Pictures' senior vice president for media relations, emailed the article to Pascal, Rogen, and others. Rogen was in New York City near Union Square, just beginning to shoot his 2015 Christmas film *The Night Before*. In favor of greater head melting, not less, Rogen whined. "Well, this is pretty much the worst headline imaginable," he wrote to Pascal a few hours later. At the time she was still asleep in the Park Suite at the Park Hyatt Saigon Hotel where it was just after midnight. Partway through her vacation, she had checked into the ten-story French colonial–style hotel the day before, having just arrived in Vietnam's Ho Chi Minh City from Hanoi.

At Sony Studios, there was concern in the legal department because of the deception. "As I sit and process this a bit," wrote corporate attorney Aimee Wolfson, "and get past the sting, it occurs to me that we are not helped when someone 'close to our decision-making' implies that they are sharing attorney-client protected legal conclusions that are, in fact, incorrect public statements about a very volatile area of law."

Dawn was just breaking in Ho Chi Minh City when Pascal finally woke up. She quickly read the email from Guerin as well as the short and nasty message from Rogen. But she seemed in denial as she tapped out an email to

Rogen. "Just woke up. We didn't change any buttons," she wrote even though the studio just spent more than a half million dollars to do just that. She also approved of the lie. "And I like the idea that it was about clearances."

Rogen was confused. "I don't know what that means," he wrote back. "We did change hundreds of buttons." A few minutes later, in a string of emails, he wrote, "My conundrum is simple: I can't lie in every interview I do. I just can't. But I don't want to hurt the movie, and I know making it seem like there is a major turmoil between the filmmakers and the studio will do that. That's where I'm stuck...If your statement is not accurate to the truth it will not get me out of this situation. Because I'll just be asked if it's true or not... A statement saying that the studio didn't do this stuff will make things worse. I guarantee it."

Largely bypassed until now was Michael Lynton. At the time he and his wife, Jamie, were seated beneath a white vinyl tent top at an oceanside country club on Martha's Vineyard. The two were talking movies, money, and politics with Barack and Michelle Obama and Bill and Hillary Clinton. They were among 150 or so people who had gathered at the Farm Neck Golf Club in Oak Bluffs to celebrate the eightieth birthday of Ann Jordan, wife of former Clinton advisor Vernon Jordan. As guests in polo shirts and pressed chinos clinked bubbly flutes of champagne, waiters served plates of surf and turf and pasta and Secret Service agents whispered into their shirtsleeves.

Feeling the vibration, Lynton reached in his pocket and pulled out his cell phone. It was a message from Pascal briefly outlining the problem.

"Doug [Belgrad] and I agreed to a strategy," Lynton wrote back. "I am sitting between president Obama and Hillary Clinton. Otherwise I would get up and speak on the phone. If we need a change of strategy then I don't want anything done until we speak." Pascal said she understood. "I'm doing nothing now. Don't worry," she wrote. "That's fine. No worries." By then it was a little after 8 a.m. in Vietnam. "I will make a statement. I don't want to make this even bigger," she wrote. "We have to protect the movie and the filmmakers here. And looking like sony is kowtowing to pressure from Korea is the last thing they are gonna want...I'm happy to lie."

Rogen still didn't like this approach since it was his face that would be in front of the cameras doing the lying. "That does not fly with me," he said. Minutes later, Lynton got back in touch with Pascal and sympathized with her regarding Rogen. "Feels like he will drive you nuts for a while," he wrote. "God yes," she agreed. Soon after the story appeared, it quickly spread, including being picked up by *Time* magazine, adding to everyone's concern. "The THR [*Hollywood Reporter*] story has been widely picked up by numerous websites and bloggers and generally is being headlined that Sony is altering the film under pressure from N. Korea," Doug Belgrad warned. "Pretty bad spin for us."

On Thursday, August 14, Pascal flew to Bali, Indonesia, and late in the evening checked into the Four Seasons Resorts at Sayan. The next morning she once again emailed Rogen hoping to straighten out the mess. On the one hand Kaz and Lynton were against Kim even dying on camera, while Rogen was insisting that Kim's head melt like a wax pumpkin before exploding in a ball of flaming embers. "No one is asking you to lie about the process," she said. "How you want to handle it is entirely up to you. But the level of gruesomeness of shot in a movie is not an uncommon thing for a studio and a filmmaker to haggle over."

Rogen, however, wouldn't budge, claiming that eliminating Kim's melting head would somehow be an act of "censorship" infringing on his "creative vision." "The head melting shot described vividly in all these articles is universally received as awesome by the articles," he wrote. Speaking of the audience and critics, he said, "The second they DONT see a face melt, and they will hate it." But beyond the absurd "creative vision" argument and phony virtue signaling about standing up against "censorship" was the central issue: money. "Whether you want to accept this or not, this has become a real issue that we fully believe will impact the finances of the film," he wrote.

Frustrated, seated beneath palm fronds on the shores of Bali's Jimbaran Bay while tapping out emails about melting heads and dissolving faces, Pascal sighed to a friend, "Just arrived in Bali. Seth rogan is driving me nuts." And she pleaded with Doug Belgrad, "Can I be lost in the jungle?" Meanwhile, like Dr. Frankenstein, Belgrad was back at the studio hard at work on Kim's head. "Adding some melting while the heat ripples cross the screen in advance of the fireball would do the trick," he suggested as a compromise.

On August 17, Lynton and his family headed back to Los Angeles aboard one of Sony's fleet of private jets, a $44 million Dassault Falcon 900 (this despite accumulating an operating loss of $181 million during the last fiscal quarter). Later, after a meeting with Kaz in New York over the budget, he emailed Pascal. "Meeting pretty rough," he wrote. "We are just not making enough money... Too much overhead. Not enough hits."

By late September, the three-month debate over Kim's melting cranium was reaching its climax. It had become the pro-melt creatives championed by Rogen, versus the anti-melt suits led by Kaz. In the middle was Amy Pascal, vainly attempting to find some middle ground between the warring factions on Rosh Hashanah. "Shana Tova from temple," she wrote to Rogen. "I too have never ever in all the years I have worked at Sony (since 1988 before you were born) been in this situation ever," she pleaded. "No one has backed you more than I have and I am trying to do that now in a very peculiar situation."

Pascal was simply asking Rogen to make Kim's head "a little less gory" so she could keep her job. "I haven't the foggiest notion how to deal with Japanese politics as it relates to Korea," she told Rogen, exasperated. Then she tried to explain how unusual it was for Kaz to involve himself with a film "given that I have never gotten one note on anything from our parent company in the entire 25 years that I have worked from them. And this isn't some flunky it's the chairman of the entire sony corporation who I am dealing. With."

The back-and-forth began taking on the tone of two masters of torture in some medieval dungeon. "Burning face not as important as watermelon head explosion but everything that gets us out of this nightmare is good," said Pascal. "I hate doing this but maybe there are a few less fleshy parts that spurt out of the fire ball or maybe it's more chared [*sic*] than pink." "Shana tova," responded Rogen. "We took out three out of four of the face embers, reduced the hair burning by 50%...The head explosion can't be more obscured than it is because we honestly feel that if it's any more obscured you won't be able to tell its exploding...We will play with the color of the head chunks to try to make them less gross."

Hoping for the best, Pascal notified Kaz of the final version of Kim's head. "I think this is a substantial improvement from where we were," she said. "If we force them to go with the version where there is no head explosion it will be difficult but survivable...As you know, they have agreed to completely cut the head popping and reduce the violence generally in any international version of the movie. I'm sorry this hasn't already been resolved, but you know we will do what you need us to do." In the end, Kaz gave his approval with the caveat that whatever was done to Kim's head be removed entirely from any overseas release. Pascal emailed Rogen with the good news. "I need one night without dreaming about head explosions," she wrote. "But I am damn happy." Her joy, however, would be short-lived.

As Pascal sat in the synagogue discussing how many burning embers to leave in Kim's head, back at the studio an employee received an email from someone named Nathan Gonsalez with the address bluehotrain@hotmail.com. It had to do with a company involved in advertising and included an attachment that appeared to be a media file playable in Adobe's Flash player: "Video Clips (Adobe Flash).exe." Curious, the employee clicked on it to watch.

At that moment, Kim Jung Un took virtual control of Sony Pictures. Nathan Gonsalez was Park Jin Hyok.

CHAPTER 5

◆

Sony Down

Amy Pascal maneuvered her Land Rover down a secluded stone driveway nearly hidden by leafy, overgrown ferns and tall shafts of bamboo and turned onto a small Brentwood side street. Opposite were a dozen green and blue plastic trash barrels and a sign bearing the image of a camera warning that the exclusive neighborhood was under constant surveillance. It was early on a Friday morning, November 21, 2014, and she was on her way to the studio at the end of a trying few weeks.

"I don't care if Aaron is sleeping with the girl or not," she wrote in an email to other studio executives about Aaron Sorkin, the screenwriter and producer. "We paid him his insane fee on flashboys... He want's to get paid... He's broke." Sorkin, the man behind the hit TV series *West Wing*, was then producing the third season of HBO's *The Newsroom*. Sony had backed his hit films *The Social Network* and *Moneyball*, and now he was seeking the studio's financing for an adaptation of *Molly's Game*, a book about a woman who ran a star-packed underground poker ring in Los Angeles. Pascal instead wanted Sorkin to write the screenplay for the book *Flash Boys*, a financial story focused on Wall Street written by Michael Lewis. In the end, Sorkin jumped ship and went to another studio, leaving Pascal in the lurch and very bitter. "They are treating us like shit," she wrote.

She was also at war over another Sorkin-written screenplay, a biopic of Apple founder Steve Jobs. The film's producer, Scott Rudin, was demanding $33 million to do it with Danny Boyle as the director, but the problem was they couldn't find a top-tier star to take the role. Christian Bale turned it down, as did Leonardo DiCaprio, an action Pascal called "despicable." Instead, Rudin was offering it to Michael Fassbender, who had gained popularity for his roles in *The X-Men* series and also for his part in *12 Years a Slave*, the 2014 Best Picture winner.

But without a DiCaprio-level star, Pascal was only willing to go as high as $25 million, thereby setting off a very nasty battle with neither side willing to budge. Eventually, Rudin shopped it to Universal Studios instead. "Amy, it's closed. I'm sorry, I begged you to do it," he wrote. Pascal, having a long professional relationship with Rudin, was shocked. "Why are u punishing me?" Rudin didn't hold back. "You've destroyed your relationships with half the town over how you've behaved on this movie," he fumed, and added that she "behaved abominably" and "it will be a very, very long time before I forget what you did to this movie and what you've put all of us through." Regretting the loss, before leaving for the studio that Friday morning she wrote to Sony colleague Tom Rothman, "I feel like I just gave away a seminal movie like *Citizen Kane* for our time."

Once at the office, distracted by numerous problems, neither Pascal nor Lynton noticed an email that arrived that day from someone named Frank David with the subject line "Notice to Sony Pictures Entertainment Inc." It warned the studio that Sony Pictures had done "great damage," and they were seeking "monetary compensation" as a result. "Pay the damage, or Sony Pictures will be bombarded," it threatened. "You know us very well. We never wait long. You'd better behave wisely." It was signed by "God'sApstls." In reality, it was from Park Jin Hyok introducing himself as Pascal and Lynton walked out the door for the weekend.

The next day, as Pascal attended her regular 12:15 p.m. yoga class and then baked "cookie people" with Columbia Pictures executive Michael DeLuca and his young daughters, Park in Pyongyang went to work on Sony's computers. After having spent the past two months robbing them blind, stealing 100 terabytes of confidential internal communications and unreleased films, it was now time to let the show begin.

With long lists of captured passwords and stolen digital certificates, Park began installing a diabolical menu of super-destructive malware hardcoded with the names of ten thousand Sony computer workstations around the world. The nastiest weapon was Destover. A "wiper," it was similar to Iran's Shamoon that performed the cyber equivalent of a lobotomy on thirty thousand computers at the Saudi oil giant Aramco in 2012. It is designed to overwrite each computer's master boot record, the central repository containing key operating instructions. It then overwrites or deletes every file before deleting itself. By late Sunday night the operation was complete. Park and his team would masquerade as hacktivists although they would also leave no doubt about who they were or why they were there.

After a rainy and cloudy weekend in London the sun was bright on Monday morning, November 24, as Sony Pictures employees arrived for work on the tenth to thirteenth floors at the Brunel Building along the Grand Union Canal opposite Paddington station. As they switched on their computers, they were startled by a sudden high-pitched scream, followed by the sound of six rapid-fire gunshots—bang! bang! bang! bang! bang! bang!—coming from their speakers. At the same time a frightening image appeared on their screens of a menacing scarlet-colored skeleton with long skeletal fingers. "Hacked by #GOP," said the scrolling text message, standing for "Guardians of Peace." "We've already warned you, and this is just a beginning. We continue till our request be met. We've obtained all your internal data including your secrets and top secrets. If you don't obey us, we'll release data shown below to the world. Determine what will you do till November 24th, 11:00 PM." Listed at the bottom were links to a number of internal Sony Entertainment files.

Some thought it was a joke, until they had no way of logging on, their machines now turned into giant paperweights. Quickly, what became known as "the screen of death" spread next to company offices in South America and finally to Culver City where early arrivals at work first saw it at around 7 a.m. Lynton received the details from Sony's top financial officer, David Hendler, as he was driving to the studio from his Brentwood home.

With phones and email paralyzed, the news quickly leaked out. "Things have come to a standstill at Sony today, after the computers in New York and around the world were infiltrated by a hacker," Deadline's Mike Fleming reported at 10:50 a.m. Pacific. "As a precaution, computers in Los Angeles were shut down while the corporation deals with the breach. It has basically brought the whole global corporation to an electronic standstill." The normally loquacious public relations department could suddenly muster up only a few words: "We are investigating an IT matter." Several dusty boxes of ancient BlackBerrys were retrieved from the basement of the Thalberg Building and the devices passed out to some of the key executives.

Soon a team of FBI agents arrived from the Los Angeles cyber squad and a command center was established in the Gene Kelly Building, not far from the old soundstage where the dancer filmed *Singin' in the Rain* sixty-three years earlier. But by the next day, it was clear that the hackers had deftly penetrated Sony's nearly nonexistent cyber defenses when they posted online four movies, three of which had yet to be released, stolen from the studio's film vaults. They included Brad Pitt's World War II battle flick *Fury*, which had already opened but now quickly became the second most pirated movie ever, with more than 1.2 million downloads. Those not yet released included the upcoming musical remake of *Annie*; *Still Alice*, starring Julianne Moore; the biopic *Mr. Turner*; and *To Write Love on Her Arms*.

Two days later, a day before Thanksgiving, Park and his team increased the pressure in messages posted to Lynton, Pascal, and a few other top executives. "We Will PUNISH You Completely," it said. "We began to release data because Sony Pictures refused our demand. Sony Pictures will come to know what's the cost of your decision." Shortly thereafter, at 9:11 a.m. on Saturday, an email popped up in the inbox of Kevin Roose. The twenty-seven-year-old journalist had just left *New York* magazine and was now the news director for Fusion Media Group, a cable network targeting a multicultural, millennial audience.

"This morning, I received a link to a public Pastebin file containing the documents from an anonymous e-mailer," Roose wrote. "And the breadth and depth of the information I found is just *insane*." They included twenty-six large archives containing thousands of very private and confidential personnel files from the studio, including Social Security numbers for nearly four thousand employees as well as salaries. After some analysis, they showed enormously embarrassing gender and race gaps in pay. And over the following days hundreds of other news outlets around the world aired Sony's dirty linen, such as producer Scott Rudin's email to Pascal about actress Angelina Jolie. "I'm not destroying my career over a minimally talented spoiled brat," he wrote. Eventually the release would total an estimated thirty-eight million files. At one point someone stuck their head in Pascal's office and passed the news: "They have your e-mails."

While North Korea officially denied any involvement, they made scant effort to hide their fingerprints. Park and his team left little doubt who the "Guardians of Peace" were. Similarly, they made it very clear that the reason for the attack was Sony's decision to go ahead with *The Interview*, scheduled for release on Christmas Day. To make their point, they announced that they intended to send a special "Christmas gift" to movie theaters that dare show the film.

"We will clearly show it to you at the very time and places 'The Interview' be shown, including the premiere... Soon all the world will see what an awful movie Sony Pictures Entertainment has made. The world will be full of fear. Remember the 11th of September 2001. We recommend you to keep yourself distant from the places at that time. (If your house is nearby, you'd better leave.)" In another posting that day they called the film an act of "terrorism" and said showing it "can break regional peace and cause the War!"

Past the rainbow at Sony's Culver City lot there was little sympathy for Lynton, Pascal, and Rogen or their film, which was deliberately designed to provoke a reaction to increase box-office receipts. And now that they got their wish, they suddenly began playing victim, complaining that theaters were unwilling to screen the film out of safety concerns for their customers. On December 17 the studio announced that the only choice was to officially

scrap its elaborate Christmas Day release plans. "The lapse in judgment happened when they decided to call him by name," one studio executive told
Vanity Fair, referring to Kim Jong Un. "Their failure was to let Seth Rogen
and [Evan Goldberg] go ahead with this.... It's a movie! And not necessarily
a good one!"

The only person who came to their rescue was George Clooney, then
trying to get another film greenlighted by Pascal. A year earlier it was Pascal who was giving encouragement to Clooney during a troubling period.
She had greenlit *The Monuments Men*, a high-budget film for him to direct
and star in. It was about an Allied group from the Monuments, Fine Arts,
and Archives program charged with finding and saving a variety of artwork
before the Nazis could steal or destroy it during World War II.

But the reviews were savage. "It's not only the great works of European art that have gone missing in 'The Monuments Men'; the spark of
writer-director-star George Clooney's filmmaking is absent, too," said *Variety*. "Clooney has transformed a fascinating true-life tale into an exceedingly
dull and dreary caper pic cum art-appreciation seminar." Criticism greatly
affected Clooney.

As Clooney read the *Monuments Men* reviews, he was on Spain's Mediterranean coast finishing up another film in which he was staring, the futuristic
Tomorrowland for Disney Studios. And after a day of shooting in Valencia's
high-tech Ciudad de las Artes, he sought solace from Pascal. "So depressed,"
he wrote her in an email. "I need some protection from all the reviews. Let's
just make it a hit. I haven't slept in 30 hours. And it's 7 am." Later he added, "I
fear I've let you all down. Not my intention. I apologize. I've just lost touch...
Who knew? I won't do it again." Pascal responded, "We will protect you. By
making money. That's the best revenge." *Tomorrowland*, however, would also
bomb badly both critically and financially.

Now, in early December, Clooney was meeting with Pascal and Lynton for
lunch in the studio's Commissary Dining Room, located in the Harry Cohn
Building, still named after the former head of Columbia Pictures despite his
well-deserved reputation as the Harvey Weinstein of his day. "Cohn expected
sex in exchange for a chance at stardom. And as one of the most influential figures in Tinseltown, he usually got it," noted journalist Erin Blakemore.
"He was one of the men responsible for instituting the system of Hollywood's
'casting couch,' which demanded women trade sexual favors with powerful
executives for a chance at a movie role." During the studio's major renova-
tion, Lynton decided to keep the name on the building and move the company's television employees into it.

To help Pascal through the *Interview* mess, Clooney created a simple petition of support calling on industry executives to "stand together" in order to present a unified front behind Sony. But, as Clooney would sadly tell the pair, he couldn't get a single signature. "Nobody stood up. Nobody took that stand," he said later. While admitting that "this was a dumb comedy that was about to come out," he added, "We cannot be told we can't see something by Kim Jong Un, of all fucking people."

Perhaps most surprising to Lynton was the criticism of his old friend and summer neighbor, President Barack Obama. On Friday, December 19, Obama took to the stage in the White House briefing room and began his year-end press conference before a packed crowd of note-taking journalists. The first question was about the Sony attack. "I think they made a mistake," he said about canceling the film. "I wish they had spoken to me first." Lynton at that moment was watching the event live while sitting in the green room of CNN headquarters in New York.

From the beginning, it was clear the Obama administration had a quiet but vested interest in using the film as propaganda to undermine the North Korean government. After all, RAND's Bruce Bennett, who had long advocated regime change, had argued against toning down Kim's melting head and expressed his hope that "once the DVD leaks to the North (which it almost certainly will)" it would cause "some real thinking" by the public in the North. At the same time, the State Department's top East Asian diplomat officially and secretly greenlit the film rather than play no role in the matter, as should have been the case. And then there's Rogen's comment about making "relationships" with CIA consultants.

Following the briefing, Lynton, in his standard mortician's black suit, black tie, and white shirt, took a seat opposite CNN's Fareed Zakaria for the taping, which was to air the following Sunday. "The president, the press and the public are mistaken," he argued, saying it was the theaters that refused to show it. "We do not own movie theaters," Lynton said. "We cannot determine whether or not a movie will be played in movie theaters."

Although Obama later characterized the attack as "cyber vandalism," rather than an act of cyber terrorism, during the widely watched briefing he nevertheless promised that the United States would retaliate. It was a very unusual move to make such an action public. "We will respond proportionally, and we will respond in a place and time and manner that we choose," he said.

The next day, Saturday, North Korea's National Defense Commission, chaired by Kim Jong Un, angrily responded. Rather than Sony, Kim clearly put the blame on the White House and the U.S. government for the film, which he saw as advocating his bloody, head-melting assassination and the violent overthrow of his government. Obama, the statement said, was "the chief culprit who forced the Sony Pictures Entertainment to 'indiscriminately distribute' the movie" and warned, "If the U.S. persists ... [it] will face inescapable deadly blows."

————

That Sunday, as Rogen in shorts and hoodie strolled barefoot beneath overcast clouds along a beach in Malibu, cyber warriors at the U.S. Cyber Command headquarters at Fort Meade, Maryland, began focusing on North Korea. A sprawling complex of newly constructed buildings next to NSA headquarters, the organization was run by NSA director Mike Rogers, a Navy admiral, under his dual authority as commander of Cyber Command.

At 12:30 p.m. on Monday, Washington time—1:30 a.m. Tuesday in Pyongyang—the operation was launched. Known as a distributed denial of service (DDOS) attack, it quickly overwhelmed the country's minimal bandwidth, estimated at about 2.5 gigabits per second (Gbps), with about 6 Gbps. This immediately clogged and crashed the system, like shoving a mountain of trash down a narrow gutter pipe, thus preventing legitimate traffic from getting through. But given the time, mostly in the middle of the night, and the short duration, less than ten hours, combined with the country's reduced dependency on the internet, it likely caused minimal disruption. The entire country has only 1,024 IP addresses, less than many universities in the United States. Later, Texas Republican congressman Michael McCaul, chairman of the House Homeland Security Committee, confirmed that the attack was payback for the Sony hack.

On Christmas Day, Lynton was able to get a small number of independent art-house theaters to screen the film, and he also managed to have it released on Google Play and Microsoft's Xbox Video at $5.99. But for a film with an original projected profit of $100 million, it produced instead only barrels of red ink, especially when the enormous legal costs were factored in. Immeasurable were the losses in personal reputations and bad publicity.

In the war between Chairman Lynton, Chairman Pascal, and Chairman Kim, only Kim would survive virtually unscathed, in power and with the last laugh. Where Sony sought to ridicule Kim, it was Lynton and Pascal who were ultimately humiliated and scorned, their most secret and embarrassing communications exposed to the world like a clothesline of dirty skivvies. Their stoned and dimwitted CIA agents, Rogen and Goldberg, were no match for Kim's real and highly trained cyber warriors, Park and his team.

However, RAND's Bruce Bennett's wish that the movie would leak to North Korea did come true. Lee Min Bok, a South Korean activist, said that from the back of his truck he carried out numerous cross-border launches of helium balloons with bundles of *The Interview* DVDs tied to the bottom. "I launched thousands of copies," he said, "near the western part of the border." At one point, North Korean border guards attempted to shoot down some of the balloons, leading to an exchange of heavy machine-gun fire between the two sides. But in the end, rather than regime change in Pyongyang, there was regime change in Culver City, with Pascal quickly ousted. "All I did was get fired," she said. And Lynton left Sony, Hollywood, and the film business altogether two years later to run Snap, an app company.

Kim's war, however, was far from over. Just as the digital dust was settling from his battle with Hollywood, he discovered Clapper's deepest secret—that shortly after Obama took office, the president and Clapper had launched a massive and highly secret cyberattack against his country. Designed to destroy thousands of physical objects—centrifuges used for uranium enrichment—it was an illegal act of war, even according to the Pentagon's own definition. But it failed, and now it was payback time.

However, rather than a cyberattack limited to crashing computers networked together within a company, like Sony, Park at General Kim's RGB headquarters sought to develop a far more powerful weapon. What he wanted was a super-virus, a weapon that would spread robotically to millions of unlinked computers throughout cities, countries, and even continents. Combined with a ransomware program, designed to lock the contents of a computer until a ransom was paid, such a super-virus could help the country's depressed economy resulting from the crippling U.S. sanctions—sanctions Obama refused to even discuss despite Kim's overture to Clapper and his prisoner release.

Finally, after several years of searching and trial and error, Park found the perfect solution, a weaponized super-virus developed by Obama and Clapper's own ultrasecret National Security Agency. And then stole it.

BOOK TWO

THE
EXTORTIONISTS

CHAPTER 6

◆

The Man in the Mirror

In a windowless, cavelike conference room behind a cipher-locked door, Mike Rogers and his most senior staff were attempting to comprehend the incomprehensible on a Friday in May 2017. A Navy four-star admiral, director of the National Security Agency, commander of U.S. Cyber Command, and chief of the Central Security Service, he was like the plenipotentiary of a small country. On the other side of the door was a hidden city, home to the most intrusive and powerful surveillance organization the world had ever known. Never before in history had a single person controlled so much secret power to pry into so many private lives, or launch attacks through cyberspace with the capability of sabotaging vast networks, silencing millions. But something had gone terribly wrong.

Three years earlier North Korea had been able to perpetrate the worst cyberattack in history against an American company, Sony, to the complete surprise of Obama, Clapper, the FBI's counterspies, the NSA, and the rest of the U.S. intelligence community. Now, almost unbelievably, the NSA had suffered the worst loss of powerful and potentially deadly cyberweapons in history—three-quarters of their entire arsenal had been stolen. And many of those weapons were now in the hands of North Korea. Among them was a diabolical super-virus designed by NSA that was now ripping across the world, shutting down hospitals, wiping out critical medical histories, and crashing computers used in operating rooms and ICU wards. And now it was headed for the United States.

How could such a disaster have happened? Rogers and his top agency officials were asking each other behind the closed door. How could Kim Jong Un have pulled off such a feat? In their desperate scramble for answers, they would eventually turn their attention to a longtime contract employee, and a shadowy cyber thief.

Hal Martin had a secret. In fact, he had half a billion of them. In his tan, unlocked garden shed, they were stacked floor to ceiling like old newspapers, and covered shelves alongside hedge trimmers and spray bottles of weed remover. In his home office, not far from an arsenal of assault weapons and other guns, they overflowed from his file cabinets, blanketed his desk, and filled dozens of computers, optical discs, thumb drives, and external hard drives stashed on, under, and behind bookshelves. Others resided invisibly in digital clouds, downloadable at the touch of a key. Codeword documents, classified higher than top secret, were scattered like fast-food wrappers in his aging teal-colored Chevy Caprice, near the loaded revolver under his front seat.

Many of the drives contained some of the agency's most dangerous cyberweapons. Others held documents at the "eyes only" level. One, an operational plan against an enemy of the United States and classified "Top Secret/Sensitive Compartmented Information," bore an additional warning at the top: "THIS CONOP CONTAINS INFORMATION CONCERNING EXTREMELY SENSITIVE U.S. PLANNING AND OPERATIONS THAT WILL BE DISCUSSED AND DISSEMINATED ONLY ON AN ABSOLUTE NEED TO KNOW BASIS. EXTREME OPSEC PRECAUTIONS MUST BE TAKEN."

For over two decades, without a hint of suspicion and passing his regular polygraph exams, Martin had been walking out of NSA headquarters and other spy agencies with somewhere on the order of 50 terabytes—about half a billion pages—of the country's most valuable secrets and dangerous cyber-weapons. It was the largest loss of classified information in American history.

Obese, with a serious binge-drinking problem, financial troubles, and severe psychological issues, Martin was a poster child for security risks. Nevertheless, he spent decades working and rising as a contractor in the intelligence community's innermost sanctums. "I have 20 years in the IC," he wrote to me in a letter, "starting with the NRO," the National Reconnaissance Office, responsible for managing the country's spy satellite program. "Then DIA headquarters, where I watched 9/11 out the window at Bolling Air Force Base." After a stint at NSA in 2007, he said, he transferred to the CIA to work on a Red Team, testing cybersecurity.

Eventually he returned to NSA, working as a contractor for Booz Allen, the same company that formerly employed whistleblower Edward Snowden, who also walked out of NSA with upwards of 1.7 million pages of highly classified documents, according to the agency. The company, which earned $3.6 billion from its intelligence and defense work in 2016, is into hacking and hackers in a big way. "Are you a hacker?" a Booz ad asks. "Show us your hacking skills!" Once hired, the hackers are assigned to the company's "Dark Labs" that employ "an elite team of security researchers, penetration testers, reverse engineers, network analysts, and data scientists," it says, who "apply the same tools, techniques, and mindset as today's most advanced hackers."

At NSA, Martin was assigned to the highly sensitive Office of Tailored Access Operations (TAO), the elite unit charged with planting malware and hacking foreign systems. He was, in essence, the NSA's version of North Korea's Park Jin Hyok at RGB headquarters. Within TAO, Martin worked in S3241, the Telecommunications Network Technologies unit, which was responsible for developing unique cyberweapons to penetrate vast telecom networks enabling the agency to hack into millions of computers. "I spent a little over two and a half years there, till early 2015," Martin said.

While in TAO, Martin said he had access to a wide variety of eavesdropping technologies, including XKeyscore. According to NSA whistleblower Edward Snowden, with XKeyscore, "You could read anyone's email in the world. Anybody you've got an email address for, any website you can watch traffic to and from it, any computer that an individual sits at you can watch it, any laptop that you're tracking you can follow it as it moves from place to place throughout the world." Other programs Martin said he worked with included TURBINE, a massive cyberweapons program that allows the agency to covertly and automatically insert malware into millions of worldwide computers, steal data, or launch cyberattacks. According to a top secret NSA document, the system is designed to allow the current network to scale up to "millions of implants." On his "HAL999" Google Profile, Martin called himself a "TAOist at heart."

From TAO he transferred to S31, the NSA's even more secretive codebreaking unit, Cryptologic Exploitation Services, which focuses on breaking difficult encryption systems. Among the sections in S31 is the BULLRUN Project Office, which specializes in developing backdoors into encryption systems, including internet services like Google's Gmail. Sometimes the operations are carried out covertly and at other times with the secret assistance of the encryption company. For a cyber thief, TAO and S31 are the NSA's crown jewels; one develops cyberweapons to break into networks, and the other develops computer algorithms to unscramble what's in them.

Ever curious, in the fall of 2015 Martin transferred to the Pentagon's top cyber office, which works closely with U.S. Cyber Command, also run by Admiral Rogers at the time. "I wanted to do CNA—Attack—after seeing all there was in CNE," Martin told me. CNE, Computer Network Exploitation, is the eavesdropping side of NSA, while CNA, Computer Network Attack, is the weaponization of cyber, sabotaging vast networks or critical infrastructure. There, he said, he became "heavily involved" in "offensive software."

———

An American flag hung prominently from the front of the modest Cape Cod–style home on Harvard Road in Glen Burnie, Maryland, a short twenty-minute drive to NSA. At sixty years old, the red bricks and pale blue siding were showing their age, offering no hint that within them was a mountain of freshly stolen secrets. Nor were the friendly couple who lived there, as they rested on lawn chairs handing out candy to children on Halloween, or gener-ously offering to look after a neighbor's sick rabbit.

At fifty-one, Hal Martin was eager to take part in the conflicts of the future, the ones that will be fought in cyberspace with keyboards instead of on battlefields with tanks. He was a fan of Major Motoko Kusanagi, the cyborg hacker with a neuro-cyberbrain in the popular Japanese manga series *Ghost in the Shell*. And he saw himself as "a special breed of warrior" in the new "great game." "It's really a calling," he wrote in the *Cyber Defense Review*, "due to the sacrifices required to be top flight in this new, electronic, version of the great game."

After graduating with a degree in economics from the University of Wis-consin in 1989, Martin became a surface warfare officer in the U.S. Navy, serving aboard the fast combat support ship USS *Seattle* when it was sent to the Middle East to take part in the 1991 Persian Gulf War. A few weeks before, he married his first wife, Marina, an accountant with a degree in psy-chology, after they had dated for about a year. They would have an amicable divorce in 1995 and he would later marry Elizabeth, a Maryland police offi-cer. Around the same time, he began work in the intelligence community and also started amassing his labyrinth of secrets.

By 2015, Martin had remarried again; his new wife, Deborah Shaw, helped lead a ministry at nearby Abundant Life Church, which focuses on helping people with addictions. He had earned a master's degree in infor-mation systems from George Mason University and had completed course-work for his Ph.D. in the same field at the University of Maryland's Baltimore County branch. There his papers had such titles as "Virtual Interfaces for Exploration of Heterogeneous & Cloud Computing Architectures." But as he patrolled cyberspace for the NSA, he also continued to exfiltrate secrets and cyberweapons from its vaults and air-gapped computers.

In a sense, Martin, an avid reader, was less an individual than a cast of characters. It was as if every time he looked into the mirror, he would see the face of someone else, usually someone from a classic book or Hollywood film. "Who is that 'man in the mirror'?" he once asked in a letter. At one point he was Antonius Block, "searching for knowledge, and playing chess for the rightest of reasons," he wrote. Block, a medieval knight in Ingmar Bergman's classic film *The Seventh Seal*, was forced to play a game of chess with the personification of death. In the end, Block was determined to outwit death, as Martin outwitted the intelligence community for two decades.

At another point he viewed himself as "Major Pugachev, fighting to be free," a reference to Yemelyan Pugachev, a disaffected former officer in the Imperial Russian Army who led, heroically, a Cossack revolt to end serfdom. Among the most intriguing comparisons was to view himself as possibly the "new Number Six, episode 17," a cryptic reference to the final episode of the classic British TV series from the 1970s, *The Prisoner*, starring Patrick McGoohan. In it, McGoohan plays a spy, Number Six, who is trapped in an Orwellian village where he is constantly eavesdropped on and monitored Big Brother–style, but who finally breaks free. At still another time he pictured himself as Harry Palmer, the dull, unglamorous, rule-breaking British spy played by Michael Caine in the 1965 film *The Ipcress File*.

Then on August 13, 2016, Martin suddenly and inexplicitly sent several curious and unauthorized Twitter direct messages to Moscow. For a person who outwardly appeared so normal, it was a very odd act, among many others—especially since the day before, a suspected Russian hacker calling himself "Guccifer 2.0" had dumped a trove of stolen Democratic Party data on the internet.

Whatever his avatar and fantasy role in the great game might be, Hal Martin was not the only one collecting NSA's secrets and cyberweapons. So was Moscow.

———

Astonishingly, at the same time that Martin was walking out the door with gigabytes of secrets in his pockets, so was another TAO worker, this despite the claims by Admiral Rogers that he had tightened security following the massive leak by Edward Snowden.

Martin's counterpart was sixty-seven-year-old Nghia Hoang Pho, a naturalized U.S. citizen originally from Vietnam who had been employed full-time as a developer at NSA since 1995. Ironically, he was assisting in the development of replacement cyberweapons for the ones stolen by Snowden. And by 2015 he had been stealing TAO's secrets for half a decade and keeping them in his Ellicott City, Maryland, home.

Just as NSA director Rogers had no idea that many of his agency's highly destructive cyberweapons were piled in unguarded homes in Maryland, he also had no idea that a large cache of them were also sitting in heavily guarded vaults in Moscow. The tip-off came from Israel's equivalent of NSA, Unit 8200. Headquartered north of Tel Aviv, it sits near Glilot Junction, a busy intersection where the east–west Trans-Samaria Highway bisects the north–south Coastal Highway. Behind high fences, the organization occupies a labyrinth of dull, yellowed, and nearly windowless concrete buildings near a stand of withering eucalyptus trees. Not far away is a cluster of sun-drenched saucer-shaped satellite antennas along with a dozen or more radomes, some perched atop tall steel towers like giant teed-up golf balls. For years, the NSA and Unit 8200 had secretly collaborated with each other.

In 2014, I traveled to Moscow on behalf of *Wired* magazine for an extensive interview with Edward Snowden. Over three days of hanging out together, he detailed a great many of the agency's highly secret operations directed against Americans. Among the most shocking revelations was that NSA was routinely passing along the private communications of Americans—emails as well as phone calls—to Unit 8200. The intercepts, Snowden stressed, included those of countless Arab and Palestinian Americans whose relatives in Israel and the occupied Palestinian territories could become targets based on the communications. "I think that's amazing," he told me. "It's one of the biggest abuses we've seen." Later, striking and protesting members of Unit 8200 would courageously reveal that Israel used such information for "political persecution" against innocent Palestinians.

That same year, Unit 8200 was also busy targeting Russian communications, and using a highly sophisticated cyberweapon known as Duqu 2.0, it managed to secretly penetrate the computer network at Kaspersky Lab. Products of the Moscow-based antivirus software manufacturer were used by upwards of four hundred million people around the world, including many U.S. government agencies. Like all virus protection companies, in order to eliminate viruses in a computer it was necessary for Kaspersky to scan it for signatures of suspected malware. Once that's done, the suspect software is removed and a sample is sent back to Kaspersky for analysis to aid in future scans, especially if the malware is new.

By then the Russian FSB had already penetrated Kaspersky, most likely covertly. They were looking to secretly piggyback. As the company scanned the millions of computers belonging to its worldwide customers, the FSB's own computers would also be secretly scanning them. But rather than searching for malware, the FSB computers were instead programmed to search for useful intelligence, like code words, passwords, cover words, and other telltale signs of secret U.S. communication.

Because the NSA never installed Kaspersky software on any of its computers, there was no way the Russian spies would be able to steal any of its cyberweapons or other secrets. The problem, however, was that Pho had installed Kaspersky virus protection on his home computer, so when he loaded his stolen data from the agency's TAO organization in his machine, not only Kaspersky but also the FSB spies were able to detect it, and then steal it.

As a result, in the several months before Kaspersky discovered and removed the Israeli spyware from their system, Unit 8200 was able to detect the presence of both the Russians and the signatures of NSA cyberweapons in the data collected from Kaspersky. And in 2015 they passed on a warning to their unwitting counterparts at Fort Meade. As a result, in an effort to track down the leak the agency launched an investigation, code-named Red Magic, which would lead to Pho.

But it would come far too late. By then the Russian spies would have already copied much of the NSA data that Pho had placed on his computer over the five years he was actively stealing TAO secrets.

To make matters worse, a review by Kaspersky determined that because Pho had also installed on his home computer a pirated version of Microsoft Office, the machine was crawling with malware, including a "backdoor." That would have given both Russian intelligence and criminal hackers easy access to the highly secret NSA and TAO documents and any cyberweapons installed on Pho's computer.

Kaspersky also presented another problem for NSA. For years the company had been collecting malware found on customer computers and attempting to discover where it came from and what it was designed to do. Over time it acquired a number of very sophisticated samples of malware and concluded that, because of its complexity, in all likelihood it came from a secret unit at NSA. But rather than publicly identify the agency by name and its secret unit, TAO, Kaspersky simply invented a name for it: "the Equation Group." It was, they said, "one of the most sophisticated cyber-attack groups in the world." Kaspersky added, "they are the most advanced threat actor we have seen."

To NSA's horror, in addition to unmasking TAO in a public report—albeit under a pseudonym—Kaspersky went even further. It also described in enormous detail the technical makeup of the cyberweapons used by the unit. And it released the names of the dozens of countries in which the weapons were found. Some of them were designed to give the NSA total and persistent control of targeted computers for years, programming them to vacuum up data and monitor activities while remaining hidden beneath complex layers of encryption. While stopping short of unmasking the "Equation Group" as an arm of the NSA, the report left little doubt in most people's minds.

To NSA and its British partner, GCHQ, Kaspersky has long been viewed with suspicion and hostility since it's the job of the spy agencies to act like burglars and use weapons to break in and steal data. And it's Kaspersky's job, like a cop, to discover the break-ins, identify the cyberweapons used, and then remove them to protect the customer. Such concerns are explicit in a top secret GCHQ document. "Personal security products, such as the Russian anti-virus software Kaspersky, continue to pose a challenge to GCHQ's CNE [computer network exploitation] capability," it said. But Kaspersky worked for its customers, not NSA or GCHQ, a fact that seemed to miff the government spies. And it was the leadership at NSA, not Kaspersky, that was responsible for the sloppy and inept security that led to the agency's enormous loss of secrets.

But Kaspersky was only one of a long list of antivirus companies NSA and GCHQ covertly targeted in a sort of cyber search-and-destroy mission, thereby turning their millions of customers seeking protection from destructive hackers into the agency's unwitting victims. According to a top secret NSA document, twenty-three other antivirus companies around the world are also listed as agency targets. Conspicuously absent, however, are the American antivirus corporations McAfee and Symantec and the British antivirus firm Sophos.

All of which made it very suspicious when the agency discovered that a highly cleared contractor, Hal Martin, was secretly attempting to contact Kaspersky headquarters in Moscow.

———

By August 2016, all eyes were on the presidential election and the disruption caused by the hack into the Democratic National Committee. As a result, across the Potomac River at the Pentagon no one was watching Hal Martin as he continued stealing more and more secrets to add to the hundreds of millions he already had stashed away. And now he could add to his collection highly classified details of cyberwar attack plans directed at Russia. He had been assigned by Booz Allen as a technical advisor and investigator on offensive cyber issues to the key Pentagon office working with U.S. Cyber Command. It was the top of the cyber food chain at a time of great tension, with the dangerous potential of morphing from a dormant cold war to an active code war.

As a result of the Russian interference, Admiral Rogers, the NSA director, was spending more and more time wearing his other hat, that of commander of U.S. Cyber Command, which was also under his direct authority. Whether he would be part of the new administration, whoever might win, Trump or Clinton, or fired by Obama as some were suggesting, was an issue he confronted daily during the election season of 2016. His predecessor, Keith Alexander, had held the job for nearly nine years, longer than any other American spy chief in history, while accumulating more power each and every year. But Rogers, who replaced him on April 2, 2014, wasn't sure he would survive three years.

Rogers had a stocky build and the constant appearance of a man who had gone weeks without sleep. Below a shock of hair the color of strong coffee, his eyes were sunken in a well of darkened skin, as if he had received twin black eyes, the loser in a barroom fight. At fifty-six, he was around the same age as his fellow cyber czars in China and Russia: Zheng Jungie, head of China's National Security Division; and Sergey Gizunov, deputy chief of Moscow's military intelligence agency, the GRU. But where both were well-qualified technologists, Zheng with a master's degree in electrical engineering and Gizunov with a Ph.D. in math, Rogers was a technophobe. There is an odd irony that the man picked to run an organization that employs seven hundred Ph.D.s and the most mathematicians of any organization in the world dropped calculus to avoid a failing grade. "I was terrible at math," he admitted.

Born in the Chicago area, Rogers grew up in Winnetka, Illinois, where his father was employed in an A&P grocery store, eventually rising from stocker to vice president of the company. In 1977, Rogers graduated from New Trier East High School, where, according to a school alumni publication, "he managed to avoid significant notice or accomplishment." "My grades were not very good and I failed spectacularly at trying to get into the Naval Academy," Rogers would later say. "Then I thought I would try to get an ROTC scholarship. I failed miserably at trying to get a ROTC scholarship...I failed everywhere else I tried to get in."

Nevertheless, after a college recruiter volunteered to put him up during orientation, he enrolled at Auburn University in Alabama, where he graduated in 1981 with a degree in business. Eventually obtaining a commission, Rogers spent most of his career working his way up in the Navy's cryptologic branch, eventually taking charge of the 10th Fleet, also known as the Fleet Cyber Command, and its fifteen thousand sailors and civilians. "I'm not a computer engineer. I'm not a computer scientist. I'm not a mathematician," he said. "But I'm comfortable."

Instead, Rogers was in way below the waterline. He had been picked because he was wearing the right color uniform at the right time. It was the Navy's turn to run the agency, Air Force and Army generals having previously served as director, and he was at the top of the Navy's cyber food chain.

To counter the Russian hacking operation, Rogers was proposing a series of covert cyber counterstrikes against Russia. They included exposing President Vladimir Putin's well-hidden financial links to the country's oligarchs and disabling restrictions on Russia's internet to give dissidents an opportunity to protest against him. But Rogers was also being pressured to develop far more aggressive responses. And the Obama White House wanted to send a clear message that it was fully prepared to escalate, a point made clear by

Vice President Joe Biden during an appearance on *Meet the Press*. "We're sending a message" to Putin, he said, implying a cyberattack, and "it will be at the time of our choosing, and under the circumstances that will have the greatest impact."

As both sides began arming their cyberweapons, the danger of a tit-for-tat cyberwar escalating into a real war continued to grow. Such a prospect has long worried Richard Clarke, the former White House cyber czar under President George W. Bush. "It's highly likely that any war that begins as a cyberwar," he told me, "would ultimately end up being a conventional war, where the United States was engaged with bombers and missiles."

————

Now working under Rogers at Cyber Command, Hal Martin found himself in the middle of the action. The question was, which side was he on? On Friday, August 12, 2016, Guccifer 2.0, a Russian GRU employee pretending to be a truth-seeking freelance journalist, made public a pile of hacked internal Democratic Party documents. The next day, back at his house in Glen Burnie, Martin used an anonymous Twitter account to tap out two odd messages from "HAL999999999" to several researchers at Kaspersky headquarters in Moscow. He was apparently looking to set up a conversation with the company's CEO, Eugene (Yevgeny) Kaspersky. For a member of the intelligence community, such a secret exchange would be a strict security breach. "So…figure out how we talk. With Yevgeny present," he wrote. Then, moments later, as if making a limited-time offer, he sent another Twitter message: "Shelf life, three weeks."

At the same time Martin was contacting Kaspersky, outside in his car he had a printed email chain containing top secret information. On the back of the document he had handwritten a description of the agency's highly classified computer infrastructure and detailed descriptions of classified technical operations along with basic security concepts, as if they were intended for someone outside the intelligence community.

Then, just thirty minutes after Martin's cryptic and suspicious private Twitter message to Kaspersky, another Twitter message appeared online, but this one was open for anyone to see. It was from a very mysterious group that called themselves the Shadow Brokers. And in it they announced that not only were they in possession of vast amounts of NSA's cyberweapons, but they were putting them up for sale to the highest bidder as part of an online auction.

Immediately, suspicions would turn to Martin. After all, many of the cyberweapons being auctioned off were identical to the ones to which he had access.

CHAPTER 7

◆

Shadowland

"How much you pay for enemies cyberweapons?" read the Twitter message from the Shadow Brokers announcing the auction for NSA's most valuable, and dangerous, lines of code. "We hack Equation Group [i.e., NSA's TAO]. We find many many Equation Group cyberweapons...We give you some Equation Group files free, you see. This is good proof no? You enjoy!!!...We auction best files to highest bidder."

The message was written in what would become the sender's faux and often changing foreign accent in order to hide his speech pattern.

Included were links to sites where the Shadow Brokers had uploaded free sample files to serve as proof that the stolen NSA cyberweapons were authentic, samples with bizarre code names, such as EXTRABACON, EPIC-BANANA, NOPEN, and FALSEMORSE. And within minutes of opening the sample files at NSA there was panic—it was no joke, they were the genuine article, actual working cyberweapons developed by NSA's TAO. Most shocking to those in the field were "zero-day exploits," the most valuable weapons in the agency's vast armory.

The key to penetrating a computer system or network is finding a vulnerability, a weak spot, like a hole in a bank vault that only you know about and, as a result, only you can exploit to steal bundles of cash. Zero-day exploits are vulnerabilities in computer programs like Windows that the company, Microsoft, has no knowledge of—that is, has known about for zero days. This gives the NSA the opportunity to secretly exploit that vulnerability on every computer using that program, which may be millions worldwide with Windows.

Through that hole in the program, the agency can secretly plant malware to spy on its targets or sabotage an entire network, the cyber equivalent of a high explosive. And it can continue doing it until the company discovers the vulnerability—the hole—and patches it, which may be months, years, or never. The Shadow Brokers' free sample package provided a number of zero-day exploits.

"There are a lot of people in Ft. Meade shitting bricks," declared Nicholas Weaver, a computer scientist at the University of California, Berkeley, in a Twitter message. "Without a doubt, they're the keys to the kingdom," said one former TAO employee. "The stuff you're talking about would undermine the security of a lot of major government and corporate networks both here and abroad." Another former member of TAO, Jake Williams, also confirmed the authenticity of the cyberweapons soon after analyzing the sample data. "This is real," he said. "This isn't a hoax. This is real stuff."

On Monday, August 15, two days after the Shadow Brokers posted the notice of their cyberweapons auction, and the first full workday, the NSA's entire website suddenly crashed for nearly twenty-four hours. The agency was silent as to the cause, but it may have been the Shadow Brokers telling the agency that they were not kidding and were fully armed and capable of carrying out surprise attacks at a time and place of their choosing.

Transpiring simultaneously as the Shadow Brokers' auction was Hal Martin's attempts to contact the head of Kaspersky. But the researcher at the company to whom he sent the "Shelf life, three weeks" message never received it; he was on vacation. It was not until the following Tuesday, August 16, three days after it was sent, that he finally had a chance to read it. By then the researcher had seen the news about the Shadow Brokers' auction and became suspicious about the odd post and its mysterious sender, "HAL999999999." His Twitter profile picture contained a silhouette illustration of a man in a chair taken from the TV series *Mad Men*. And alongside him was the image of a CD-ROM bearing "TAO2," which the researcher was aware referred to the NSA's highly secret Tailored Access Operations unit. Hoping to connect with the sender, he sent him a request for his email address and PGP encryption key. Instead, apparently fearful of revealing his identity, Martin quickly blocked the researcher's account.

Two days later, on August 18, Martin sent three more private tweets to Kaspersky in Moscow, but now to a different researcher. "Still considering it...," the first said. Puzzled, the researcher asked, "What are you considering?" Martin again turned cryptic, projecting his life through plots on a movie screen. "Understanding of what we are all fighting for...and that goes beyond you and me," he wrote. "Same dilemma as last 10 min of latest Bourne." The film, *Jason Bourne*, had opened on screens across the country two weeks earlier.

Tech-heavy and topical, the movie's plot focused on Matt Damon as renegade CIA agent Jason Bourne. In the film, he is caught up in a world of surveillance, cyber, lies, and fighting against a corrupt intelligence bureaucracy. With all his years at NSA, CIA, and the rest of the spy world, it was a world Martin could certainly identify with. Now, based on his comment, it appeared to be a world in which both Martin and Bourne were wondering what it was all for. In the end of the film, there is deception masquerading as patriotism, with the head of cyber operations waving the flag to get Bourne to come back to the CIA. "Things are changing at the agency," she lies. She had already made alternative plans if Bourne decided not to return. "He'll have to be put down," she tells the director of national intelligence.

Four minutes after sending the message, Martin thought of another film the researcher should watch to understand the man at the other end of the cryptic tweet. "Actually, this is probably more accurate," he wrote, and included a YouTube clip of the final scenes from the film *Inception*. Released in 2010, the film stars Leonardo DiCaprio as a professional thief who infiltrates the subconscious of his targets in order to steal information. In the end, the audience is left with questions about the gray line between free will and the secret manipulation of people's minds, the same gray line the NSA was constantly crossing.

Curious as to whether there was a connection between the mysterious Twitter messages from "HAL999999999" and the post by the Shadow Brokers that quickly followed after it, the researcher held off replying and instead, along with a few colleagues, decided to check out the sender. After all, it was a quiet time at Kaspersky Lab. In mid-August the headquarters was nearly abandoned as most employees were on their annual vacation, including the boss, Eugene Kaspersky, who was traveling in the mountainous Altai region of Siberia.

A pair of boxy modern glass buildings, Kaspersky Lab was located in Moscow's Olympia Park on the banks of the Khimky reservoir, next to a beach and a small yacht club in the northwestern part of the city. In the lobby stood Salvador Dalí's *Éléphant de Triomphe*, a bronze sculpture of an emerald green elephant with spindly mosquito-like legs and a gold angel above its back, trumpeting success and prosperity. Nearby, computer virus hunters would hang out at the lobby's central hearth, a fireplace in winter and a fountain in summer, or have a meal and a beer in the company's BarKas restaurant.

Given their backgrounds, the researchers had little trouble pinpointing the identity of the sender. The username, Hal999999999, also turned up in a personal ad looking for female sex partners at a bondage and sadomasochism website. Accompanying it was a picture of Martin, along with his age, height, and location in Annapolis, Maryland. The username also turned up a LinkedIn profile of a Hal Martin employed as a researcher in cyber issues in Annapolis Junction, Maryland. As many in the cyber world would be aware,

Annapolis Junction is directly across the highway from NSA headquarters and serves as the agency's office park for contractors such as Booz Allen. The profile also indicated that Martin's work involved assignments throughout the defense, cyber, and intelligence communities.

For years the NSA and FBI had constantly accused Kaspersky of being little more than a handmaiden to Russia's FSB, despite strong denials by Kaspersky and clear evidence that the FSB had the ability to penetrate the company covertly without their help, just as the Israelis had done.* Nevertheless, rather than sit on the information about Martin, as the Russian government would have no doubt preferred, or leaked it to the press, which would have been good for Kaspersky's business, on August 22 the company instead quietly turned Martin over to the NSA.

Despite the tens of billions of tax dollars spent on NSA, its biggest secret seemed to be its near-total incompetence. After the agency missed 9/11 and got the war in Iraq wrong, it was the Dutch who alerted the NSA that Russia had penetrated the DNC, and it was the Israelis who tipped them off that Pho was stealing secrets. Likewise, they had no idea that Edward Snowden had taken a million or so documents until he flew to Hong Kong and told the press. Then it was the Shadow Brokers who informed them that the group had just nearly cleaned out their cyberweapons armory. And now it was the Russians who were warning them about Martin. By then he had already stolen half a billion pages of documents from between the agency's electronic ears.

Suspecting that Martin was possibly connected with the Shadow Brokers, NSA officials quickly alerted the FBI, and five days later, on August 27, a search warrant was approved by Magistrate Judge Stephanie A. Gallagher of the U.S. District Court in Baltimore. As justification for probable cause, an affidavit listed the tweet Martin had sent to Kaspersky saying, "Shelf life, three weeks," which was interpreted as being an offer for information that would only be useful or valuable for a short time. It also noted that at NSA, Martin had access to some of the same information offered by the Shadow Brokers.

Early that afternoon, nine members of a SWAT team gathered for a briefing at the Baltimore field office. Located just outside the city in Windsor Mill, it was a modern four-story, 236,000-square-foot redbrick building protected by a vehicle-resistant perimeter barrier. Dressed in camouflage, and wearing helmets and bulletproof vests, the SWAT members were armed with M4

---

*In March 2022, following Russia's invasion of Ukraine, the U.S. Federal Communications Commission added Kaspersky Lab to its list of entities that pose an "unacceptable risk to US national security."

rifles slung across their chests and Glock handguns strapped to their waists. After being handed pictures of Martin, they piled into their SWAT vans for the seventeen-mile drive to Glen Burnie.

It was a little after 2 p.m. when the SWAT team approached Harvard Road. Over the radio, the team leader suddenly received an urgent message from the surveillance crew secretly watching the house. Martin was in his driveway, he was told, just leaving his vehicle and heading for the front door. We "expedited our plan," said Ryan Davis, one of the SWAT members. "Because dealing with an individual outside of a residence is a lot safer for us as opposed to when he could be inside and have access to weapons." And although they didn't know it, Martin had ten guns, some fully loaded and many not registered, in his house and car.

Moments later they arrived, as three Maryland State Police cruisers blocked the road to traffic. Quickly jumping from the van, they raced toward Martin, their assault weapons pointing at his back, as he was heading for the house with a portfolio of top secret documents. Davis was carrying a long steel battering ram to bash down the door if necessary. He shouted for Martin, in shorts and a T-shirt, to show his hands, walk away from the door, and get down on the ground.

Abandoning the battering ram, Davis grabbed Martin's right wrist, pushed him facedown on the grass, and snapped handcuffs on him, two cuffs linked together because of Martin's size. Almost simultaneously a loud explosion and bright burst of light took place at the front door, shaking the ground and leaving a cloud of gray smoke. It was an FBI flash-bang device used as a diversionary tool to distract dogs and others in the house, allowing the SWAT team to charge in. The surprise raid followed by the flash-bang caused Martin to defecate in his pants.

Davis brought Martin into the house and put him, still cuffed, on a couch in the living room. It was a chaotic scene, with about twenty FBI agents and technicians searching, barking on cell phones, entering and leaving, and holding hushed mini-conferences. Other agents began lugging in boxes of hard drives and documents from the garden shed.

In the midst of the confusion, Laura Pino, the counterintelligence division task force case agent, entered the house wearing a blazer and button-down shirt and took a seat on the couch next to Martin. With her were two men in khakis and untucked shirts hiding their weapons, Paul M. Scarzello and Jeremy L. Bucalo. As Martin's handcuffs were removed, Scarzello sat down on the other side of Martin and Bucalo pulled up a chair opposite them. On a small coffee table in the middle, Scarzello placed a binder containing a hidden recorder; another was secreted in a key fob.

Scarzello, forty, was familiar with eavesdropping, having spent the past decade and a half employed by NSA. Attached to the dreaded Q5, the internal spies of the Office of Security, he had had a number of assignments ranging from the director's protective detail, to Q7, the Office of Counterintelligence, to the Security Operations Command Center. Then in 2013, following the Snowden leaks, he was detailed to the FBI task force involved with rooting out leakers and spies.

Across from Scarzello was Bucalo, thirty-five, a twelve-year veteran of the FBI who specialized in cyber crimes and was eager to take a look at Martin's hoard of hard drives, CD-ROMs, laptops, and other electronic media. Fit and muscular, Bucalo was a winner in the World's Toughest Mudder competition where teams compete in a ten-mile race over a rugged, obstacle-laden trail. "You need my help," Bucalo told Martin. "I need your help. We can help you fix the mistake... This is your chance to work with us."

Thin and dark-haired, Pino, fifty, a former accountant, joined the bureau in 1997 and spent most of her career in the counterintelligence division of the Baltimore field office. A few years earlier she was the lead agent on a number of disastrous investigations involving NSA. One of her targets was Thomas A. Drake, a former senior agency official. Eventually charged with multiple counts of espionage for leaking documents to the *Baltimore Sun*, he faced decades in prison. Pino had pursued him relentlessly for four years, nearly ruining his life.

But in the end, Pino and the prosecutors were forced to drop all ten counts against Drake when the defense, federal public defenders James Wyda and Deborah Boardman, proved that the documents he was accused of leaking were in fact not secret. In court, Judge Richard Bennett strongly chastised Pino and the prosecution for their handling of the case, calling it "unconscionable." It was one of the very few times the government had been forced to abandon an espionage case. (Full disclosure: I was a consultant for the defense on the case.)

Pino also went after others at NSA, including former senior NSA officials William Binney, J. Kirk Wiebe, and Ed Loomis, and also Diane Roark, a top staffer on the House Intelligence Committee. With no evidence, she suspected they were behind the leaks to the *New York Times* that exposed the NSA's involvement in the massive and illegal warrantless eavesdropping program code-named Stellar Wind. As a result, as with Drake, heavily armed FBI SWAT teams raided the homes of Binney, Wiebe, and Roark. But the cases turned out to be a bust, with no charges ever brought.

As Pino, Scarzello, and Bucalo interrogated Martin, other agents placed a hidden tracker on his car. And in his home office they drained his laptop onto a Computer Online Forensic Evidence Extractor, a small flash drive containing commands to decrypt passwords, extract information, and perform other tasks. It was a device Martin was very familiar with, having read about it in an online article and dropped a note to the writer. In his message, from "HAL999," he made a curious comment, seeming to imply that Microsoft secretly built into its systems backdoors to aid law enforcement.

"Would one not then infer that there are either prestored keys or some sort of built in back door into all MS OSes [Microsoft operating systems] that the vendor 'provides' as a 'service,' to support LEOs [law enforcement organizations]?" he asked. He then seemed to answer his own question. "More validation for MS being the OS of choice for security and trusted applications." Obviously happy as a hacker to have a backdoor into Microsoft systems, Martin added, "Goody goody."

With top secret documents piled high in his office, Martin quickly admitted that he had unauthorized documents at home. But he briefly denied he had any stolen digital files, until Pino told him they had found classified documents on the electronic media. For four hours the interrogation continued, as the agents pumped questions at Martin while the secret recorders captured every word.

But in the end, it was amateur hour; neither Pino nor anyone else bothered to read Martin his Miranda rights, the most basic rule in law enforcement, one even a cop on his first day in uniform knows. Judge Bennett therefore threw out the entire interview. "The Defendant's interrogation lasted approximately four hours," said Bennett in his ruling. "The agents never gave the Defendant Miranda warnings...Miranda warnings were required."

In fact, the entire drama involving the SWAT team was unnecessary. Pino, Scarzello, and Bucalo could have easily approached Martin quietly at work on Monday, where he would have had no access to guns, and simply read him his rights and interviewed him discreetly in a secure government office. At the same time, another team could have executed the search warrant on Martin's house with far less notice, and in that way eliminated the *Zero Dark Thirty*-like atmosphere, accompanied by the very loud flash-bang, that brought neighbors out to watch on a quiet Saturday afternoon. But as with the raids on the homes of Drake, Binney, Wiebe, and Roark, Pino and the SWAT teams seemed to enjoy the drama simply for the sake of drama.

In the hope that Martin might lead Pino to the Shadow Brokers, the arrest was kept secret, even though due to the SWAT raid it was the talk of the neighborhood and far beyond. By nightfall, Martin was behind bars, and on Monday, August 29, Bucalo obtained a sealed criminal complaint and arrest warrant against him. That same day Martin made a secret initial appearance in a sealed courtroom. Search warrants were also executed for Martin's accounts at Google, Yahoo, Samsung, and Verizon Wireless.

Following his arrest, Martin was represented by federal public defenders James Wyda and Deborah Boardman, the same defense team that had successfully battled Pino in the Thomas Drake case. As a result, Piro and her task force would no longer have free access to Martin as they did for four hours in his living room. And with their secretly recorded and illegally conducted interrogation thrown out as evidence, they would have to start again from scratch, now going through Wyda and Boardman. Nevertheless, Martin did agree to cooperate within limits.

It appears that the prosecution wanted to keep the arrest under wraps for six months while they questioned Martin in secret about any connection with the Shadow Brokers or others, and also possibly used him in a sting operation. The judge therefore agreed to extend the date for a formal indictment and court appearance until the following March. But the secret would be short-lived. As might have been expected from the circus-style arrest, news of it had leaked and the *New York Times* had the story. A neighbor, Murray Bennett, eighty-four, told the paper, "I thought the third world war had started." Another article, also published on October 5, noted, "The Justice Department unsealed the complaint after The New York Times notified the government it intended to publish a story about Mr. Martin." That was two major mistakes in rapid succession by the FBI's counterspies.

Despite a twenty-count indictment, Pino and company were likely realizing they once again had the wrong man. For a few weeks it appeared as though there might be a connection between Martin and the Shadow Brokers since the group's posts stopped at the same time the arrest took place. But in September, a new message from the Shadow Brokers was released, and with it any hope that Martin was the lone mastermind behind the posts evaporated. At the time the message surfaced, Martin was dressed in a gray-striped jumpsuit and sitting in a cell in Maryland's Harford County Detention Center as inmate #134683.

And an analysis of his electronic media showed he likely had nothing to do with the Shadow Brokers. There was no evidence that he had ever sent or received any communication with anyone associated with them. Instead, it appeared to be mental illness, not bitcoin enrichment, that drove his actions. The evidence points to a combination of compulsions, including hoarding, an obsession he shared with his mother, along with the thrill of the steal, like shoplifters who habitually pocket unnecessary items simply for the adrenaline rush.

It was the worst news the NSA could receive. It meant that in addition to the more than half a billion pages of secrets stolen by Snowden, Pho, and Martin, someone else, someone unknown, had nearly emptied the agency's arsenal of what would later be estimated as 75 percent of its dangerous and potentially deadly cyberweapons. And now they were being offered up to the highest bidder. Yet neither the NSA nor the FBI had a clue as to who was behind the theft, how they got the cyberweapons, or where on the planet they were located.

By then the Shadow Brokers were also becoming frustrated. A little after noon on August 15, Mike Damm, a cyber security tester for Walmart, announced on Twitter that he was the highest bidder. But eventually the "auction" brought in only 1.6 bitcoins, or less than $1,000. That disappointing result inspired the Shadow Brokers' "Message 2," this one accompanied by a cartoonish image of North Korean leader Kim Jong Un and the words "Why Are People So Fucking Stupid!!!" It was likewise written with a sort of mock Asian-slang accent: "We say roser not get money back, we know not idear." ("We said the losers in the auction will not get their money back; we know that's not ideal.").

It was an angry post, with much of the anger directed at the hacker community. The Shadow Brokers were astonished and furious that no one was taking them seriously. Translated from mock Asian:

> We dump files. You say real. We say no shit! Where does this leave us? We just kicked the biggest bully on the planet in the dick, took their shit, offered to sell it in public, and you value it at $1,000? Fucking pussy ass cowards. We feel sorry for you. It must be hard living with such tiny balls. It's good proof why cyber defenders always lose. Too pussified to take risks. Is this what the hacker culture has become? Quiet little pussies brought to heel by decent paychecks at big business and big government? Sad!

With no other suspect, most of the media simply went into their standard default mode and pointed the finger at Russia, even though logically it made little sense. It would be as if Russian intelligence spent millions planning the theft of the blueprints for the most powerful and secret U.S. Navy submarine, and after successfully pulling off the operation, auctioned off the plans on the internet. Nevertheless, the *New York Times* quoted James A. Lewis of the Center for Strategic and International Studies, who commented, "This is probably some Russian mind game, down to the bogus accent," based on absolutely no evidence.

So, who are/is the Shadow Broker(s)? The name is apparently derived from the role-playing video game series *Mass Effect 2: Lair of the Shadow Broker*. In it, the Shadow Broker is a ruthless information dealer, always selling his data to the highest bidder. "It is pointless to challenge me," the Shadow

Broker says at one point. "I know your every secret, while you fumble in the dark." It was an apt expression if directed at the bumbling NSA. And like NSA, the Shadow Broker has information on virtually everyone in the galaxy. As the group mentioned in their posts, their use of faux accents was simply to disguise their normal speech pattern. "If theshadowbrokers be using own voices, theshadowbrokers be writing peoples from prison or dead," they noted. "TheShadowBrokers is practicing obfuscation as part of operational security (OPSEC). Is being a spy thing." It was a wise move since in a *Mass Effect* sequel the Shadow Broker became the victim of data breaches about himself.

A close reading of many of his posts, stripped of the faux accents, gradually brings them into much crisper focus, like an old negative that's been digitally enhanced. Rather than multiple actors, the Shadow Brokers is likely a sole individual, a Shadow Broker rather than Shadow Brokers. And he is also probably a male, given that the majority of military and civilians working for TAO are male, as are the vast majority of spies. At one point he refers to then vice president Joe Biden as "DirtyGrandpa," possibly indicating he is in his late twenties. Also like many people in TAO, he likely had prior military service because he once indicated he had taken an oath "to protect and defend the constitution of the United States against all enemies foreign and domestic." And in the military the Shadow Broker was almost certainly assigned to a cryptologic unit and after leaving got a civilian job at NSA, which assigned him to TAO, the origin of the stolen materials.

Within TAO, the Shadow Broker apparently came to know—or know about—former TAO employee Jake Williams, who had confirmed the authenticity of the cyberweapons. Williams had never previously made his affiliation with the organization publicly known, yet the Shadow Broker outed him after becoming angry over comments Williams directed at him in a blog. "Shadow Brokers is not in the habit of outing [TAO] members but had to make exception for big mouth," he wrote. He even posted technical details of some of the projects Williams had worked on. "[The Shadow Brokers] had operational insight that even most of my fellow operators at TAO did not have," said Williams, who spent five years in TAO. "Whoever wrote this either was a well-placed insider or had stolen a lot of operational data."

In TAO, the Shadow Broker was likely employed as a cyber intelligence subject matter expert, a title the agency bestows on advanced hackers. By contrast, notes the Shadow Broker derisively, Edward Snowden was "a contractor tech support guy posing as a infosec expert." At one point, when Vice President Biden threatened to unleash a CIA-sponsored cyberwar with Russia, the Shadow Broker displayed some interagency rivalry by criticizing him for picking the agency over the NSA. "Why not threating with NSA or Cyber-Command?" he said. "CIA is cyber B-Team, yes?"

In May 2013, Snowden fled to Hong Kong with his pocketful of flash drives containing hundreds of thousands or more pages of top secret NSA documents exposing the agency's widespread domestic and international eavesdropping activities. Around the same time, someone assigned to NSA's TAO, possibly the Shadow Broker, also began stealing NSA's documents as well as its cyberweapons. Because much of the material was likely air-gapped on networks physically separated from the internet, stealing the data would require physical internal access. A few months later, in the summer or fall of 2013, that person also likely quit, taking with him his stolen materials, probably on flash drives. He may have been concerned about new post-Snowden security measures or taking a new polygraph.

After leaving NSA, the Shadow Broker became heavily involved in the hacker community, as indicated by his support of it and his anger at the community's lack of respect for his "kicking the biggest bully on the planet in the dick and stealing their data." He also indicated that he continued to work for the government after leaving NSA. He noted that his job was writing "TRADOC [training doctrines], Position Pieces, White Papers, Wiki pages, etc."

Then in 2016, he came up with the cyberweapons auction idea. "Auction is sounding crazy but is being real," he wrote, this time in a sort of pidgin English. But he was a man with a plan. "How do you sell secrets and make money fast, with the least amount of effort and while still maintaining anonymity: an auction," he wrote (faux accent translated).

In many respects, the Shadow Broker is the un-Snowden. Where Snowden was left of center, later decrying Trump and his right-wing agenda, the Shadow Broker was far right and a strong Trump supporter who supposedly voted for him even though the Shadow Broker opposed the Republican Party. Instead, he appears to have been stanchly in favor of the right-wing Tea Party movement. He was also an avid listener to far-right radio, especially Michael Savage, whose vile and often bigoted screeds were so extreme they once got him banned from entering the United Kingdom for "fostering hatred which might lead to inter-community violence." Banned along with Savage was the former Ku Klux Klan grand wizard who set up the racist website Stormfront. "Dr. Savage is correct, liberalism is a disease!" said the Shadow Broker, who argued in favor of using tax dollars to buy a one-way plane ticket to Africa for anyone who wants one.

On a number of points, the Shadow Broker contrasted himself with Snowden, including the issue of fight or flight. He said that between the U.S.

and Russian governments, he was surprised Snowden was still alive. Unlike Snowden, living in exile in Russia, he—the Shadow Broker—was planning to remain in the United States. "Fuck running from these bastards?" he said. "TheShadowBrokers is not running. America is our fucking country and we staying and fighting for it!"

Above all, the Shadow Broker's key target was Hillary Clinton, who was nominated as the Democratic candidate for president a little more than two weeks before he sent his first message. "Wealthy elites," he called her and her close political allies. They were people, he complained, who break the law but unlike ordinary people never go to jail. Instead, he noted, they call their top friends at the FBI and Justice Department and make deals, alluding to the lack of prosecution for Clinton's use of a private, unsecured email server in her home. Through such server passed unprotected and easily targeted top secret emails, among them a discussion of North Korea's nuclear-weapons program, according to an analysis by the intelligence community's inspector general.

Despite their political differences, Snowden and the Shadow Broker also had a number of things in common, especially a great distrust of the tremendous Orwellian power of the NSA, and also the "Military, Industrial, Intelligence, Complex." "Fuck the MIIC," the Shadow Broker said at one point. He also strongly opposed the secrecy state. "No more secrets. Secrets Equal Control," he wrote. "Secrets between government and governed, governed is getting fucked...No more classifying bullshit. No more black budgets and black ops."

Although the Shadow Broker's original intent for stealing the cyber-weapons was to make money, actually releasing them to the public was not necessarily part of the plan. "TheShadowBrokers is not being irresponsible criminals," he said. Instead, while he would put the weapons up for auction, allowing people to bid up the price to get them, in the end he was convinced that the NSA itself—"responsible parties" in his words—would buy them at the inflated price to find out what he had and keep them from the public.

But the NSA had other ideas. They took the point of view that if they gave in and purchased the stolen materials back from the Shadow Broker, other employees would quickly also begin holding the agency's secrets for ransom. Thus there was no deal, and as a result, the Shadow Broker would eventually turn angry and desperate. Given what he held, that was a truly dangerous condition.

"When you are ready to make the bleeding stop, payus, so we can move onto the next game," he wrote. "The game where you try to catch us cashing out! Swag us out!"

CHAPTER 8

◆

Apocalypse

By New Year's Day 2017, the Shadow Broker's bitcoin wallet was nearly bare. Despite his angry and threatening posts, he had only raised just over 2 bitcoins (about $1,400) from a total of sixty-nine bids. Changing tactics, on January 8 he made a new offering. Dispensing with the auction, he decided to open up his "firewall tool kit" and sell the weapons inside individually, like entrées on an à la carte menu, each with individual prices. Among them was FuzzBunch, a suite of powerful Windows zero-day exploits, including one code-named EternalBlue.

The Shadow Broker knew that EternalBlue, originally developed for use against countries such as Russia and China, was top-of-the-line when it came to zero-day exploits. The internet equivalent of a super-virus, it implants itself within a system like a microbe and then releases a cyberweapon called DoublePulsar that acts like a secret back door. Through it runs the malware to spy, destroy, or hold the system for ransom. Then EternalBlue begins to spread like a plague, bypassing firewalls, passwords, and antivirus programs as it infects all other systems with the same vulnerability. A similar NSA super-virus discovered by China in 2013 was later found to have affected hundreds of targets in forty-five countries for over a decade. The countries included such allies as Switzerland, Israel, and Belgium. The Chinese analysts code-named the cyberweapon "Telescreen" after the all-seeing and hearing surveillance device in George Orwell's novel *Nineteen Eighty-Four*.

Knowing its capabilities, the Shadow Broker priced EternalBlue alone at 650 bitcoins, about half a million dollars. It was likely a very difficult decision. He knew that once he opened up the tool kit and revealed the names of the weapons inside, such as EternalBlue, NSA would have what they needed in an attempt to neutralize them before they became active. But by then he was desperate. He had to let buyers know he had actual powerful weapons, that it wasn't just a scam. Nevertheless, he still had no takers, and four days later, on January 12, he decided to call it quits.

"So long, farewell peoples," he wrote. "TheShadowBrokers is going dark, making exit. Continuing is being much risk and bullshit, not many bitcoins. TheShadowBrokers is deleting accounts and moving on so don't be trying communications. Despite theories, it always being about bitcoins for The-ShadowBrokers... You are being disappointed? Nobody is being more disappointed than TheShadowBrokers." He added, however, that should someone deposit 10,000 bitcoins (about $8.2 million at the time) in his digital wallet, he would return and reward the person with the password for some of his best weapons.

As might have been expected, once the agency discovered what weapons he had, from the names on the à la carte menu, they quickly and secretly contacted Microsoft to alert them to the vulnerabilities. The company could then begin working on patches to plug them. The news of the breach came as a severe shock to officials at the Microsoft Security Response Center. The NSA had known about the vulnerabilities for five years without offering the company a warning of any kind—five years in which any number of hackers, criminals, and state-sponsored cyber warriors may have discovered the same holes and used them to attack Windows computers throughout the country and around the world. According to Microsoft, six billion records were stolen by hackers in 2017.

From an array of flat-screen monitors displaying the unseen rivers of digits around the world, the center was the company's war room for fighting security breaches. About fifteen miles east of Seattle, it was located on the company's sprawling Redmond, Washington, campus, an insular fortress-like city within a city made up of eighty-three buildings and over forty thousand employees stretched across 502 acres. Alerted by NSA, the response team began an emergency effort to quickly develop patches for EternalBlue and the other zero-day exploits in a frantic race to beat the Shadow Broker before he changed his mind and sold or released them.

At 10 a.m. Pacific time on the second Tuesday of every month, the center issues an updated list of security fixes. But on February 14, 2017, Valentine's Day, the software engineers were still working desperately in secret on the zero-day patches. They therefore made the unprecedented decision to cancel that month's "Patch Tuesday" alerts less than two hours before their scheduled release, raising suspicion within the tech world.

A month later, on March 14, Microsoft released the patches. But the question remained whether it was five years too late, and whether and when the Shadow Broker would once again offer the weapons up for sale despite his claims that he was giving up. As both NSA and Microsoft knew, the patches were only a partial solution since millions of people, businesses, and institutions simply ignore updates, delay installing them, or never learn of them. They would continue to be just as vulnerable as before, and potential targets if the cyberweapons were released.

Learning of the patches, the Shadow Broker was likely furious considering the risk he had taken, the time he had spent, and the efforts he had gone to for no ransom. He was also extremely angry that his man Trump, someone whose views he had promoted in his posts during the campaign, now appeared to be backtracking on a number of key policies since becoming president. As someone long opposed to U.S. involvement in foreign wars, he was particularly upset over Trump's decision to become more heavily engaged in the conflict in Syria. And on April 8, he let Trump know in a long, fifteen-hundred-word post. "Dear President Trump," he wrote. "Respectfully, what the fuck are you doing? TheShadowBrokers voted for you. TheShadowBrokers supports you. The ShadowBrokers is losing faith in you. Mr. Trump helping theshadowbrokers, helping you. Is appearing you are abandoning 'your base,' 'the movement,' and the peoples who getting you elected."

Before signing off, the Shadow Broker attempted to justify his actions as acts of patriotism. "Some American's consider or maybe considering TheShadowBrokers traitors," he wrote. "We disagreeing. We view this as keeping our oath to protect and defend against enemies foreign and domestic." But the Shadow Broker's solution was destructive rather than constructive. In the end, like many of those who took part in the January 6, 2021, attack on the U.S. Capitol, what the Shadow Broker wanted was to overthrow the government. "TheShadowBrokers wishes we could be doing more, but revolutions/ civil wars taking money, time, and people," he wrote. "TheShadowBrokers has is having little of each as our auction was an apparent failure." In fact, it is highly likely the Shadow Broker was among those who stormed the Capitol.

He then included another free giveaway of cyberweapons. "Be considering this our form of protest," he said. The next day he taunted the FBI and NSA for their seemingly hapless efforts to find him. "TheShadowBrokers has being operating in country for many months now and USG is still not having fucking clue."

By now the Shadow Broker was burning with anger. The auction was a flop, and no one even wanted the weapons once he revealed their names, thereby decreasing their future value. And there was one final humiliation: Despite the risks he had taken in exfiltrating most of the NSA's cyberweapons, the media was completely ignoring him. Not that he had any love for the media. In his memo to Trump he asked, "Why haven't you served search warrant to NYT, Washington Post, Goldman Sacks, Jeff Bezos, and all other Globalist for investigation and prosecution of treason, sedition, and un-American activities during a time of war?"

Snowden, on the other hand, generated months of flattering headlines for his theft; the suspected Russian hacker Guccifer 2.0 received enormous press with the release of leaked Democratic Party documents; and Julian Assange achieved tremendous notoriety with his WikiLeaks disclosures. But besides some tech sites and a few one-day stories, virtually no one was paying any long-term attention to the Shadow Broker, especially on television. "Where is being 'free press'? Is ABC, NBC, CBS, FOX negligent in duties of informing Amerikanskis?" he asked. He even agreed to clean up his act to please the media. "TheShadowBrokers is making special effort not to using foul language, bigotry, or making any funny. Be seeing if NBC, ABC, CBS, FOX is making stories about now? Maybe political hacks is being more important?"

Finally on Good Friday, April 14, six days after his Twitter message to President Trump and at the start of the long Easter weekend, it was time for the endgame. "Last week theshadowbrokers be trying to help peoples," he wrote, referring to a number of suggestions to help President Trump regain the support of lost followers like himself. Then he offered some suggestions. "Maybe you be making YouTube video is in order, to be explaining to your voters, your supporters, you didn't fuck them all over," he wrote to Trump. Unsurprisingly, he never heard back. "This week theshadowbrokers be thinking fuck peoples."

With that, the Shadow Broker opened the cyber equivalent of Pandora's box by releasing the password for the zero-day exploits and other weapons he had on his à la carte menu, including EternalBlue and DoublePulsar. "Password = Reeeeeeeeeeeeeee." He certainly knew the potential for a worldwide cyberpandemic such a release would cause since millions had probably not yet installed the patch, nor ever would. "Is being too bad nobody deciding to be paying theshadowbrokers for just to shutup and going away," he wrote. "Maybe if all surviving WWIII theshadowbrokers be seeing you next week. Who knows what we having next time?"

"This isn't a data dump, this is a damn Microsoft apocalypse," tweeted Matthew Hickey, a.k.a. @hackerfantastic. He added that the release would provide "God Mode" to hackers in terms of access. "This is really bad, in about an hour or so any attacker can download simple toolkit to hack into Microsoft based computers around the globe." Worse, he said, the exploits could be repurposed to launch a worm or virus with the ability to spread itself, the catalyst for a cyberpandemic.

Ignored by the press and feeling snubbed by President Trump, the Shadow Broker did have one enormous fan. On the other side of the world, Kim Jong Un had had been closely following the Shadow Broker and his auction. And he also had a very large score to settle.

◆

CHAPTER 9

Yongbyon

In May 2015, about six months after his dinner with Clapper, Kim discovered the spy chief's deep secret. He learned that in 2010 President Obama had authorized Clapper to launch a massive and highly secret cyberwar attack against North Korea. The target was a long rectangular building at the country's Nuclear Scientific Research Center in Yongbyon, about a ninety-minute drive north of Pyongyang on the Myohyang–Pyongyang Expressway. Buried among the rugged, low-lying Myohyang Mountains, the complex of 390 buildings makes up a secret city that occupies fifteen square miles and is pockmarked with security checkpoints. It is home to ten nuclear research institutes as well as three reactors. Running through the sprawling campus is the Kuryong River, the source of the enormous amounts of water needed for cooling. Within the long rectangular building was a new uranium enrichment facility fueled by nearby uranium mines and containing about two thousand spinning centrifuges.

The attack on the Centrifuge Enrichment Facility was carried out with a cyberweapon known as Stuxnet, fueled by four zero-day exploits. Developed by the NSA, CIA, and Israel, it was the world's first cyberweapon designed to destroy physical objects, specifically sophisticated nuclear centrifuges built by Siemens. About the same time as the attack on Yongbyon, the weapon was also used against Iran's nuclear enrichment facility at Natanz. But where it successfully destroyed thousands of centrifuges within Natanz, the operation was a complete bust when it came to North Korea's Yongbyon facility, likely due to far greater security controls.

Nevertheless, when Kim belatedly learned of the failed attack, shortly after his battle with Sony, he viewed it as a clear act of war, thus giving him the legal right to retaliate in kind. After all, the Obama administration believed it was fully within its legal rights to launch a retaliatory attack against Pyongyang following what he labeled only an act of "cyber vandalism" on Sony. Now it was up to North Korea to pick a "time of their choosing." And in a supreme touch of irony, Kim was hoping to use America's own powerful cyberweapon against itself.

But rather than a tit-for-tat retaliation, Kim was instead interested in cash for his poor country to make up for America's UN-imposed sanctions, which act as a near-total trade blockade, strangling the country's economy. To that end, in a windowless room filled with the soft blue glow of computer screens, Park Jin Hyok and his team were hard at work in Reconnaissance General Bureau headquarters. They were developing software for a massive ransomware attack, one where computers by the hundreds of thousands would be encrypted and locked forever if their owners failed to pay in bitcoin what he was asking.

A year before, according to the FBI and NSA, Park managed to pull off the most successful cyber bank heist in history. Using the U.S. Federal Reserve Bank of New York as a go-between, he and his team were able to execute an enormously complex scheme that allowed them to steal $81 million from a bank in Dhaka, the capital of Bangladesh. And by April 2017, Park had largely developed the lines of code needed for their ransomware attack. What Park still lacked, however, was an adequate method of infection, a means of spreading the malware from computer to computer to maximize the attack.

What Park needed was a zero-day exploit to help proliferate the ransomware to millions of computers. But they were rare and very expensive, and unfortunately the Shadow Broker with his menu of zero-days for sale had just called it quits. The only other alternative was sending out spear-phishing emails in an attempt to trick someone to click on a link so he could steal their passwords and other credentials. It was obviously something that Park was very good at, having just tricked a bank out of nearly $100 million with the technique.

Then, on April 15, when the Shadow Broker released the password for EternalBlue and the other cyberweapons with their zero-days, everything changed. Immediately, Park and others on his team began analyzing the weapon's complex digital wiring to find a way to understand what they had. It was as if a loose nuke had just fallen into their hands and they were looking for the on-switch and how to make it work. It was a time-consuming and complicated task. But three days later, Park noticed that someone else was not only analyzing the inner workings of the NSA cyberweapon, but actually posting his research on his website, https://zerosum0x0.blogspot.com. The researcher worked for RiskSense, a private cybersecurity company in north Albuquerque, New Mexico.

As the company reverse engineered the complex cyberweapon, and posted details online, Park kept a close watch. Finally, on May 9, RiskSense, in an effort to aid other researchers, posted on github.com the entire source code for EternalBlue—in essence its internal wiring diagram. That was the final clue Park needed. Now he had it all—his own NSA-built, multimillion-dollar weapons-grade zero-day exploit. Three days later he attached the backdoor cyberweapon DoublePulsar, also released by the Shadow Broker. Although he hoped to target the United States, this ad hoc creation was the cyber equiv-alent of an unguided missile. Finally, Park inserted his ransomware program and hit the send key. In so doing, he launched into cyberspace what would quickly become the world's first cyberpandemic, eventually given the appro-priate name: Wannacry.

CHAPTER 10

◆

Cyberpandemic

Anthony Brett, fifty, sat in a wheelchair, his head covered in a dark wool knit cap that seemed large for his thin face, cheekbones narrowing to a chin gray with whiskers. It was springtime, May, 12, 2017, a Friday morning in London, and Brett had on a winter coat over a gray sweater and black T-shirt in the chilly, damp air. He was being wheeled into St. Bartholomew's Hospital in the central part of the city for a serious operation. A stent was to be put in his liver to treat his cancer.

But in a place where there should be focus, careful attention, and order there was confusion, bewilderment, uncertainty. In one of the country's largest medical institutions, which served millions of patients every year with a staff of fifteen thousand, the doctors and nurses were hustling, charts and thermometers in hand, as if a fire alarm had just gone off. Behind a pair of narrow amber-colored glasses, Brett looked concerned as he was told the operation was off, something had gone wrong.

Already in the operating room, his chest shaved and going through final preparations, was Patrick Ward, forty-seven, a sales director for an ice cream company. He had been waiting nearly a year for the open-heart surgery, but a doctor rapidly walked in, leaned over him, and said the operation would have to be postponed. Nearby in another operating room, a surgeon was in the middle of a heart operation when the computer screen first flickered and then turned black. MRI scanners and devices for testing blood and tissue samples went dead. And across town at the Royal London Hospital, Richard Harvey, fifty, also wheelchair-bound due to a motorcycle accident, a pale blue blanket covering his legs wrapped in a hospital gown, was suddenly told his hip procedure would have to be canceled, leaving him to wheel himself home.

On that cool morning in May, Ray Neal waited patiently in line in the lobby of the Royal London Hospital, located in the Whitechapel district of the city's East End. A week before, Neal had been urgently booked into the hospital after tests indicated a severe heart ailment. It was an immediate concern because just two years earlier he had had a triple heart bypass operation. Now, after traveling an hour from his home in Wanstead, he was hoping to have the problem corrected. But suddenly there seemed to be confusion, and people heading in were told to turn around. Then, just before being admitted, he was told he would have to come back some other time; a problem had come up at the hospital. "I am fuming," he said. "When it's your heart—it's your life isn't it? It's really worrying. I want to know what's wrong with me. I just want peace of mind."

Nearby, dressed in a hospital gown, fifty-two-year-old Martin Hardy was in agony. Seated in a wheelchair, he was about to be admitted to the operating room for surgery on a broken kneecap when his surgeon told him the operation would have to be called off. The computer system had just crashed, the surgeon said. "I was in my hospital robe literally about to go in," Hardy said, wincing, as he made his way out the door with a pair of silver crutches strapped to his arms.

The same thing was happening throughout London at Mile End Hospital, Newham Hospital, Whipps Cross Hospital, and many more. It was the same story to the northeast of the city in Essex. Grant Gowers, a fifty-year-old grandfather from Clacton-on-Sea, was scheduled for a prostate cancer biopsy at Colchester General Hospital. But he was told instead that it would have to be postponed for several weeks, a very worrying development. "They said nothing was going ahead unless it was life or death," he said. "But to me, cancer is life and death—and I won't know whether or not I have cancer until the biopsy results come back."

Across the country and even in Scotland hospitals were on the brink of shutting down, ambulances were being diverted, medical histories were no longer available, nor access to X-rays and blood tests. Internal phone lines and email were inaccessible. Someone had taken over the computer system for much of the National Health Service (NHS) throughout the UK and was threatening to sabotage it unless a ransom was paid. At the entrance of Royal London Hospital, a sign was quickly put in place that read: "The emergency department has no IT facilities, there are significant delays occurring." Inside, every computer screen now contained only a message in red demanding payment of various sums in bitcoin, or every record would be permanently and irretrievably destroyed—patient histories, appointment schedules, diagnoses, everything.

"Many of your documents, photos, videos, databases and other files are no longer accessible because they have been encrypted," it read. "Maybe you are busy looking for a way to recover your files, but do not waste your time. Nobody can recover your files without our decryption service. You only have three days to submit the payment. After that the price will be doubled. Also, if you don't pay in seven days, you won't be able to recover your files forever."

As the NHS became catatonic, Prime Minister Theresa May held an emergency "Cobra" meeting and announced that the havoc engulfing the hospitals and other victims had reached unprecedented levels and was part of a much wider assault. At 4 p.m. the NHS declared the attack a major incident, and at 6:45 p.m. it launched its Emergency, Preparedness, Resilience and Response plans. Others began looking for both solutions and culprits. "The attack against the NHS demonstrates that cyber-attacks can quite literally have life and death consequences," said Mike Viscuso, chief technology officer of the security firm Carbon Black.

The techno-plague spread at lightning speed. As hospitals across the UK closed, nearly twenty thousand appointments had to be canceled, including many for patients who had an urgent referral for potential cancer. Jumping the English Channel, it continued to spread. In Spain it was about 9:24 a.m., just as the workday started, when the attacks began. "One major hospital group is having a rough time right now. Everything has gone to hell," a hospital worker told the newspaper *El País*. At the giant telecom Telefónica, audio warnings were played over speakers directing workers to quickly shut off all computers.

In Germany, passengers waiting for trains watched as the electronic displays flickered and quit; in France, carmaker Renault was forced to stop production at many locations. At Europol, Europe's international police agency, director Bob Wainwright said the attack was "unprecedented in its scale. At Europol we are running around 200 global operations against cyber crime each year. But we've never seen anything like this." He added, "The global reach is unprecedented."

It was the start of a worldwide cyberpandemic, crashing more than three hundred thousand computers in at least 150 countries, with health care systems a key victim. Like a row of tumbling dominos, networks were going black not only throughout London and the UK but across Europe and moving rapidly beyond. Russia quickly became the hardest-hit country as banks, railways, and mobile phone networks went down. "Humanity is dealing here with cyberterrorism," said Frants Klintsevich, the deputy chairman of the Russian Senate's defense committee. "It's an alarming signal, and not just a signal but a direct threat to the normal functioning of society, and important life-support systems...The attacks hit hospitals, railroad transport and police. Over these days, the world got a serious warning."

And in China, over thirty thousand institutions, universities, immigration checkpoints, and other locations were suddenly returned to the pre-computer era. Around the same time, Japan's Computer Emergency Response Team said two thousand computers at six hundred locations were down, and hospitals as far away as Indonesia were affected as the pandemic moved west toward the United States. "The spread is immense," exclaimed Adam Kujawa, the director of malware intelligence at Malwarebytes, the first cybersecurity company to discover the attack. "I've never seen anything before like this. This is nuts."

Yet at NSA headquarters, as hundreds of thousands of computers crashed around it, taking down thousands of hospitals and other critical institutions in 150 countries, accumulating tens of billions of dollars in damage and lost business, there would be only silence. The agency was to blame for the worst cyberattack in history, having managed to lose three-quarters of its cyberweapons to the Shadow Broker, from where they eventually ended up in North Korean hands. Nevertheless, the agency would offer no clues to help stop it, no apology, not even an acknowledgment. Instead, Admiral Rogers and other top officials simply gathered around a table in a windowless cavelike secure conference room, unable to come up with answers or solutions.

In London, as the cyberpandemic seemed unstoppable, a twenty-two-year-old hacker named Marcus Hutchins came to the rescue, almost by accident. A security researcher at Los Angeles–based Kryptos Logic, he was on vacation, taking some time off, and only discovered the attack after returning home from lunch, hours after it began. Nevertheless, sitting in his bedroom, he began reverse engineering the code and soon discovered that instantly after the ransomware installs itself on a computer, it pings an odd, unregistered web address. Curious, Hutchins registered the address to see what would happen. This was a very good idea.

If the address the virus pings remains unregistered it will continue with the encrypted lockdown. But if the address is registered when it is pinged, the system is designed to shut itself off, like a kill switch. Therefore, by registering that address Hutchins instantly ended the worldwide cyberpandemic, which appeared to be headed for the United States at the time. Apparently never realizing that someone would figure out the kill switch, Park's ransomware operation had by then netted only $130,634.77 in bitcoin from 327 payments. At least for a short while, there would be a reprieve.

But EternalBlue and the other zero-days were still out in the wild, and ready to be put to use again by Park or anyone else. And within a few days a new variant-like version was detected, this one missing the kill switch. "It's very important everyone understands that all they need to do is change some code and start again," warned Hutchins. Pandora's box was still wide open. To make matters exponentially worse, the Shadow Broker seemed to be rejuvenated by the cyberpandemic. Rather than give up, he decided to start selling NSA cyberweapons by subscription, calling it a sort of wine-of-the-month club.

CHAPTER 11

◆

Eternal Blowback

In what may be the ultimate irony, within weeks of the Shadow Broker's release of the NSA cyberweapons, President Putin, like Chairman Kim, ordered his spies to add them to his own cyber armory. Eventually these weapons would be used to attack America's close ally—and Russia's great adversary—Ukraine. Since February 2014, Russia had been locked in a crushing territorial war with its southern neighbor, much of it waged in the shadows and in cyberspace. The conflict had been touched off by Russia's seizure of Crimea.

Far less visible, however, was the long-running economic war between the two countries, especially the fight over fuel to power Ukraine's Russian-built nuclear power plants, critical utilities that supply half of the country's energy needs. For years, Russia had supplied nearly all fuel for Ukraine's nuclear reactors, a profitable deal for Moscow. But now because of the crisis, Ukrainian energy officials were becoming increasingly worried. Because much the country was completely dependent on nuclear power for electricity, Russia at any time, for any reason, could slow down or cut off the fuel supply and thus plunge millions of people into darkness. As a result, and to Russia's great anger, Ukraine began negotiations with an American company, Westinghouse Electric, the world's largest nuclear fuel producer, to supplement and potentially replace the supply chain of Russian fuel rods.

To spy on the negotiations, the Kremlin turned to Unit 26165, the Signals Intelligence Collection Department of Russia's military intelligence agency, the GRU. The elite hackers were based at Moscow's Khamovnichesky Barracks, a rambling, multiblock-long structure not far from the former home of Leo Tolstoy, an elegant wooden house with a green roof and shutters behind an orange fence. Constructed in 1807, a few years before Napoleon invaded the city, the high walls of the barracks hid a modern cyber command center made up of two rectangular buildings seven stories tall. On their roofs were more than a dozen parabolic satellite dishes oriented toward a diverse range of azimuths.

The team was led by thirty-year-old Ivan S. Yermakov, a veteran hacker with a boyish face and a fringe of choppy brown hair, as if cut by a shredder. He had been born in the closed territory of Chelyabinsk, not far from the Ukraine border. And for two years, unknown to the FBI and U.S. intelligence, he and his fellow cyber warriors had been digitally entering and leaving, like apparitions, Westinghouse Electric's massive nuclear engineering headquarters near Pittsburgh. Once inside, they began penetrating deep into the company's digital bloodstream, eavesdropping on communications and stealing documents between Westinghouse and Ukraine to give the Kremlin insights that could lead to potential sabotage.

Now with the NSA's prize cyberweapons in its arsenal, the Kremlin's capability for destructive attacks had increased exponentially. The goal would be to secretly crash and destroy much of Ukraine's financial infrastructure. This time the assignment went to the GRU's Main Center for Special Technologies (CST). Also known as Unit 74455, the center specializes in information operations and occupies space in a modern blue-glass twenty-story high-rise office building. Owned by the Ministry of Defense and known within the GRU as "The Tower," it is located on a restricted section of road at 22 Kirova Street in the northwestern Moscow suburb of Khimki.

In charge of the operation was Aleksey Potemkin, one of the CST's key cyber warriors. Sitting in The Tower, with its view overlooking the eighteen-thousand-seat Khimki Arena, home of the Dynamo Moscow football team, he began plotting the assault. Over the years, the CST had launched a variety of cyberattacks on Ukraine's government offices, businesses, and political sectors in order to discourage or prevent opposition groups from organizing against Moscow. But as with North Korea, zero-day exploits were out of the question because of their rarity and enormous expense.

EternalBlue, therefore, was a game changer. As was another NSA zero-day released by the Shadow Broker, EternalRomance. Now the Kremlin was no longer limited to simply targeting a dozen computers networked together in a Kiev political party, or the machines connecting branches of a bank. Suddenly in their sights was anyone using unpatched Microsoft Windows, which included much of the country. Therefore the decision to infect the servers in Kiev that supplied updates to users of M.E.Doc, a piece of accounting software similar to Quicken or TurboTax. It was the perfect common denominator since about 90 percent of the companies in Ukraine used it for filing tax statements, and it was installed on an estimated one million computers in the country.

At 12:14 p.m. Moscow time, on June 27, 2017, the eve of Ukraine's Constitution Day and a little more than a month after North Korea launched its cyberpandemic, the Russian hackers initiated their attack. First, like putting up a detour, they altered the route of internet traffic carrying the routine M.E.Doc accounting update to a secret server in France. There the malware, including EternalBlue and EternalRomance, was added to the update before it was sent on its way to the computers of the thousands of unsuspecting victims. Expecting to see spreadsheets, they instead saw a ransom demand to unlock their files. But the ransomware was simply a cover to make the operation look like it was part of the North Korean attack and hide Moscow's involvement. In reality, there was no way to ever decrypt the data. The goal was sabotage, not ransom; the files were permanently locked, as if sealed in cement.

Unfortunately, NSA's zero-day exploits were never designed to respect lines on a map in their lightning-speed hunt for vulnerable computers. As a result, the agency's EternalBlue was once again spreading pandemic-like around the world, this time together with its twin, EternalRomance. And rather than simply demanding money, they were sabotaging every susceptible computer they came across. In Ukraine, they crashed the radiation monitoring system for the Chernobyl Nuclear Power Plant, in addition to banks, ATMs, ministries, metro systems, train depots, electricity companies, and the international airport.

Merging with the cyberpandemic launched by North Korea, the super-virus jumped border after border, quickly spreading to sixty-four countries as it turned computers into bricks and paperweights. "A New Ransom-ware Outbreak Similar to WCry Is Shutting Down Computers Worldwide," said a headline in *Ars Technica*. Now, like a cyber boomerang, Eternal-Blue was returning home to the United States, creating chaos in hospitals and the medical industry. At 7:23 a.m., a little more than two hours after EternalBlue and the rest of the malware was launched by Moscow against computers in Ukraine, it arrived at the Heritage Valley Health System in Sewickley, Pennsylvania.

Just a few hundred miles from NSA, where EternalBlue and Eternal-Romance had been brought to digital life, thousands of computers and hundreds of servers at Heritage Valley began crashing and dying. Patient medical histories were lost, lab records were destroyed, workstations went black, and thousands of appointments disappeared. In cardiology, nuclear medicine, radiology, and surgery, doctors, surgeons, and nurses were returned to the pre-computer era. "The incident is widespread," said an announcement, "and is affecting the entire health system including satellite and community locations."

In New Jersey, the giant pharmaceutical company Merck sent out a tweet: "We confirm our company's computer network was compromised today as part of a global hack. Other organizations have also been affected." In company offices around the world, thirty thousand computers and seventy-five hundred servers had instantly become junk. Medical supply lines were also massively disrupted. Maersk, the world's largest shipping line, responsible for transporting millions of tons of medical supplies to the United States and around the world, was computer dead, its ships suddenly in limbo.

Now with the cyberpandemic finally reaching U.S. shores, some in Congress began at last to wake up to the danger and look for answers. "It appears these two global ransomware attacks likely occurred because the NSA's hacking tools were released to the public by an organization called the Shadow Brokers," Democratic congressman Ted Lieu wrote to NSA director Rogers. "My first and urgent request is that if the NSA knows how to stop this global malware attack, or has information that can help stop the attack, then NSA should immediately disclose it. If the NSA has a kill switch for this new malware attack, the NSA should deploy it now."

Admiral Rogers had neither ideas nor a kill switch. There would just be more meetings behind cyber-locked doors, producing more meetings behind cyber-locked doors. And in the end the NSA and Cyber Command managed no meaningful actions during the entire cyberpandemic, a worldwide terrorist event for which Rogers and the people hidden behind those doors were fully responsible. The secret organizations knew only how to launch cyberpandemics, not how to stop them. At the same time, despite the enormous number of clues, leads, and messages left by the Shadow Broker, the FBI has never even come close to making an arrest or even identified a suspect or person of interest. It was a massive failure across the board, yet there would be no public congressional hearings, no unclassified inspector general reports, and no consequences.

———

By 2021, EternalBlue variants were still very active and remained the most commonly detected strain of malware on the planet, according to security firm Trend Micro. "Many of the versions we see spreading in the wild today are modified versions of the original," said Rik Ferguson, the company's vice president of security research. "And they do not have—or else they bypass—the kill switch, which contributes to the spread."

It turned out to be a banner year for Park and his seven thousand-plus fellow hackers at the RGB. "They've been very successful," said Erin Plante, a senior director of investigations at Chainalysis, a company that helps governments and financial institutions battle cyber crime related to cryptocurrency. The company's report for 2021 said North Korea stole nearly $400 million in cryptocurrencies that year, making it, according to South Korea's *Chosun Ilbo* newspaper, the "world's third biggest hacking powerhouse" after the United States and Russia.

But in the summer of 2022, rather than Sony Studios it was the Pentagon that was exploring ways to turn Kim Jung Un's head into a flash of burning embers. As part of the first war games between the United States and South Korea in five years, the plans included a "decapitation" exercise involving exploding not just Kim's cranium but his entire command structure. And no one could be happier than RAND's Bruce Bennett. The "task could be done by a drone or reconnaissance aircraft," he told the Daily Beast's Donald Kirk, but Seoul also has decided "to create a brigade of special forces to help perform this function."

In the end, however, it could turn out as bad for the United States and South Korea as *The Interview* did for Sony. "I personally think that the preemptive strike option against North Korea is a bad idea," said Steve Tharpe, an official with the U.S. Command in Seoul. "It would immediately lead to a full-scale war—a resumption of full-scale warfare—Korean War: Part II."

———

Less than three years after the cyberpandemic shut down hospitals in the United States and around the world, a viral pandemic, COVID-19, sent millions to those same hospitals, overtaxing them along with other vital systems. Like powerful trains heading for each other on the same track, the pair of pandemics came close to colliding, one sending millions around the world into overcrowded hospitals and the other shutting down many of those very same hospitals as well as other critical medical services around the planet. Had the collision occurred, both taking place at the same time, it would have added countless more deaths to the millions who got sick.

One virus was created by nature deep in the belly of a bat, its genetic code transforming and mutating before escaping into the wild. The other virus, however, was created by hackers deep in the bowels of the U.S. National Security Agency, its computer code transforming and mutating after escaping into the wild. Thereafter, both developed variants that allowed them to continue to spread. But while the bats had no control over their deadly end product, the NSA hackers did. And the cyberweapon that brought down much of the world's health care systems was just one of hundreds of cyberweapons the NSA carelessly allowed to escape its control and fall into the hands of criminals, adversaries, and terrorists.

One way to avoid cyber blowback is to switch to human spies and intelligence. But at times this spy game can be even more dangerous, especially when the goal is to steal nuclear secrets.

And one of those spies has lived and worked for decades in the heart of Hollywood, the same place where the first domino fell that led to the cyberpandemic.

BOOK THREE

THE SPIES

CHAPTER 12

The Propagandist

Sony Pictures boss Michael Lynton looked like he was going to be late for dinner and sent an email to warn his host. A long stretch of the Pacific Coast Highway had been blocked off and only one lane was open. Studio co-chair Amy Pascal was also rushing to the dinner, and likely hoping not to bump into Scott Rudin, the producer behind such shows as *The Social Network* and Broadway's *To Kill a Mockingbird*. The two had recently had a heated argument over a remake of *Cleopatra* staring Angelina Jolie. "Watch how you talk to me!" Rudin barked at Pascal in an email. "Do not fucking threaten me!!" she shot back. Both Lynton and Pascal were also on edge because of arguments over their Kim Jong Un assassination film, which had just had a terrible test screening.

The dinner was at the Malibu home of Arnon Milchan, one of Hollywood's top producers. It was going to be a celebration; just three days earlier he had won the Best Picture Oscar for his *12 Years a Slave*. He was on a very big roll. A year later he would win Hollywood's top prize again for *Birdman*, followed the next year by a Best Picture Oscar nomination for *The Revenant*, which would go on and win a Best Actor Oscar for Leonardo DiCaprio and a Best Director Oscar for Alejandro González Iñárritu. For more than three decades Milchan had been behind some of the city's most awarded and well-known hits, among them *JFK*, *Pretty Woman*, *L.A. Confidential*, *Once Upon a Time in America*, *Mr. & Mrs. Smith*, *The Big Short*, *Gone Girl*, and more than a hundred others. And with a net worth of $3.6 billion, Milchan was number 240 on *Forbes* magazine's list of the World's Billionaires. In addition, he also had another half billion dollars hidden away in a Virgin Islands tax dodge, according to the leaked Pandora Papers, putting his true worth at over $4 billion.

Located on Carbon Beach, labeled by *Forbes* "the world's most expensive sandbox," Milchan's 9,655-square-foot home was once owned by legendary director John Frankenheimer, whose films included such classics as *The Manchurian Candidate*. In addition to a ninety-foot pool outside, its cream-colored walls were lined with original Picassos, Pissarros, and Basquiats, part of a $600 million art collection. It was just one of seven homes Milchan owned around the world.

The reason for the traffic backup was the Secret Service partially blocking the road near Milchan's house for his guest of honor: Benjamin Netanyahu. Bibi had just flown in from Washington, where he had delivered a harsh attack on the Boycott, Divestment, and Sanctions (BDS) movement at the annual AIPAC conference. "Those who wear the BDS label should be treated exactly as we treat any anti-Semite or bigot. They should be exposed and condemned. The boycotters should be boycotted," he said with rising anger. "That movement will fail." However, given that he devoted a considerable amount of his speech to attacking the group, it was instead likely succeeding.

As Pascal and Lynton arrived, Milchan greeted them at the front door, along with Secret Service agents there to protect Netanyahu. A citizen of Israel and Monaco, where he enjoys tax-free citizenship, Milchan had a Kojak-style shaved scalp and wore a small pair of wire-rimmed glasses that lent him a bookish, academic look. And despite having once been a star center forward for Israel's national soccer team, beneath his dark gray suit was a paunch that pushed tight against the buttons of a stiff white shirt. Among the sixty or so other guests already there or arriving was Barbra Streisand in a floppy black beret, Leonardo DiCaprio wearing a tan Stetson newsboy cap and matching scarf, Keanu Reeves and Kate Hudson dressed like twins with matching low-cut black V-necks beneath gray suit jackets, and a coatless James Caan in a powder blue shirt and silver tie.

Despite the high profiles of the invitees, according to the Israeli newspaper *Yedioth Ahronoth* the guest list was kept a secret out of fear that some of the stars would cancel their participation if their names were leaked. At the time, Israel was carrying out its latest ruthless war against the Palestinians trapped in Gaza. "This is not the best time to be seen with the Israeli prime minister, especially in Hollywood," said the paper. Another guest, humorist and political commentator Bill Maher, was stunned by the number of Secret Service agents at the dinner. "I couldn't believe the amount of security," he said. "There had to be 300 cops there. Such overkill. I mean, I understand he's the Israeli prime minister, but that's what we do in this country: We overdo everything."

Avoiding the lens side of cameras had long been a Milchan trademark. "Posing for pictures is anathema," noted the *Los Angeles Times* about Milchan. Writer Ann Louise Bardach agreed. "He remains the town's most secretive mogul," she said. "In a town where disclosure and revelation are as banal as cereal, Arnon Milchan has kept his secrets to himself."

Following the dinner, once all the guests had cleared out, Milchan was planning to discuss some of his darkest secrets with Netanyahu. Secrets that concerned his years of covert work as Israel's top nuclear spy in the United States. In the process he had used well-known actors, such as Richard Dreyfuss, as unwitting fronts to recruit Americans as spies, getting them to betray their country. Now one of them was secretly talking to FBI counterintelligence agents, and Milchan was very worried. If arrested he could face life in prison for espionage. He needed Netanyahu to quietly intervene at a very high level with the Obama administration. The prime minister would eventually agree, but there would be a very big price for his help. A price that might put them both in prison in Israel.

Very concerned about his future, Milchan likely thought back to the past and how it all began, and how he hoped that past would always remain a very dark secret. Including the fact that the man who had just won the Best Picture Oscar for *12 Years a Slave* had begun his secret life as a top arms dealer for South Africa's White supremacist government. For years, Milchan supplied arms, including nuclear materials, to the apartheid regime. Arms used to brutally kill and torture the country's Black population as they fought back. And nuclear materials to help the apartheid regime secretly develop atomic bombs so they could stay in power. At the same time, Milchan served as a top propagandist for the South African government, helping them hide their racist policies from the rest of the world, and promoting pro-apartheid propaganda internationally in news outlets, and also in plays and films. It was, after all, how he became a Hollywood producer.

———

In the summer of 1975, Arnon Milchan sat down to dinner at a restaurant overlooking the Mediterranean Sea in Cannes on the French Riviera. On the other side of the stiff white tablecloth and silver setting was Eschel Rhoodie, thirty-eight, the tall, suave, smartly tailored chief propaganda minister for the apartheid government of South Africa. He had a critical problem: A recent survey had confirmed the worst. Due to the country's brutal treatment of Blacks and its harsh segregation policies, South Africa had become "the most unpopular nation barring one—Idi Amin's Uganda," said the report. As a result, Israeli officials had secretly offered to help. And Milchan, an Israeli covert operative with worldwide connections, was looking forward to it. "Sure, it sounds like fun," he told Rhoodie. The idea was to launch a covert propaganda war to hide the apartheid regime's cruel and reprehensible actions against its majority Black population. It was a war in which, Rhoodie would say, "morality flies out the window."

The dinner was the result of a high-level meeting between Rhoodie, South African prime minister John Vorster, and several others on February 6,

1974. As they sat in stinkwood chairs around Vorster's desk in the prime minister's Cape Town office, Rhoodie was given authorization to embark on "a full-scale psychological war" against the media around the world. "In this unconventional propaganda offensive," Rhoodie had argued, "no rules would apply, no regulations would stand in our way. Only objectives would count, and the end would indeed justify the means—any means." Vorster approved, but also offered a warning: "You should keep your paperwork to an absolute minimum and anything not necessary should be destroyed. In fact, where you can do without documentation, you should do so."

Rhoodie and his secret Joint Secretariat for Political and Psychological Warfare were soon given a near-bottomless budget. With it, they began working closely with General Hendrik van der Bergh, the head of the brutal Bureau of State Security (BOSS). Nicknamed "Lang Hendrik" ("Tall Hendrik") because of his six-foot-five-inch height, van der Bergh had a well-earned reputation for the violent enforcement of the country's apartheid policies against Blacks. He once told a government commission, "I have enough men to commit murder if I tell them to kill. I don't care who the prey is. These are the type of men I have." And the British *Independent* referred to him as "probably the most feared man in South Africa."

Milchan became involved as a result of a highly secret June 1975 visit to Israel by Rhoodie, his deputy Les de Villiers, Interior Minister Connie Mulder, and BOSS chief General van den Bergh. Welcoming them were Israeli prime minister Yitzhak Rabin, Defense Minister Shimon Peres, and top Mossad agent David Kimche, who specialized in African affairs. At the meeting, Peres introduced the propaganda minister to Milchan and pledged his cooperation. It could not have gone better for both governments. In a letter to Rhoodie following the meeting, Peres praised South Africa's leading role in initiating "a vitally important co-operation between the two countries." And BOSS chief van den Bergh said he "enjoyed every minute there. I told the prime minister when I got back that as long as Israel exists, we have a hope." But writer Breyten Breytenbach, a White South African who had long opposed apartheid, and served years in prison as a result, saw the pact very differently. Israel had become, he said "White South Africa's political and military partner in 'the alliance of pariah states.'"

Over the following years, Rhoodie, with Milchan's help, would conduct nearly two hundred secret propaganda operations targeting the United States, Europe, and other locations. At the same time Milchan would also become the top arms dealer for the White supremacist government, supplying weapons to ensure that there would be no Black uprisings, rebellions, or outside interference in its racist policies.

Milchan first stepped through the looking glass nearly a decade earlier, in the mid-1960s. At the time, his favorite hangout was Mandy's Discotheque, a club on Ben Yehuda Street in Tel Aviv, a mile of bright lights and noisy and arty nightlife. The star attraction was the club's namesake, Mandy Rice-Davies, a former model and call girl who had gained fame and notoriety several years earlier for her involvement in the Profumo affair. A political sex scandal, it nearly took down the British government, and led to the resignation of Minister of War John Profumo. Later she moved to Israel, converted to Judaism, and married businessman and former El Al steward Rafi Shauli. Together they opened the club and several others.

A close friend of Shauli and Mandy, Milchan began using the club as a makeshift office. Then in his twenties, he had recently taken over the family's chemical and fertilizer business. Soon he met and became close personal friends with another regular customer, Shimon Peres. At forty-two, with his styled hair, penchant for well-cut suits, and reputation, according to former prime minister Yitzhak Rabin, as "an indefatigable schemer," he was Israel's deputy minister of defense. Among his schemes was overseeing the development of the country's secret nuclear and biological weapons programs, and then compulsively lying to the United States about their existence. Sensing that same deceitful trait in Milchan, he began offering him work as a defense contractor and then recruited him into the world of nuclear espionage. "Arnon is a special man. It was I who recruited him," Peres would later admit. "Arnon was involved in numerous defense-related procurement activities and intelligence operations."

The centerpiece of Israel's nuclear weapons program was a secret reactor largely built by France in the late 1950s and completed around 1964. It was located eight miles outside of Dimona, a dusty, isolated town deep in the rocky and blistering Negev Desert. In 1867, following a visit, Mark Twain described the Negev as "a desolation that not even imagination can grace with the pomp of life and action." Charged with turning the reactor into a black hole, ensuring that many secrets went in but none ever came out, was Benjamin Blumberg.

Tall, with dark wavy hair and thick ebony brows, Blumberg was quiet and reserved. He had been picked by Peres to organize and run the country's most secret intelligence agency, the Bureau of Scientific Relations. Known by its Hebrew acronym, LAKAM, it was responsible for acquiring both nuclear intelligence and nuclear weapons material for Dimona, and at the same time ensuring the facility's airtight security. Blumberg had similar responsibilities for the biological weapons plant at Ness Ziona. Known as the Israeli Institute for Biological Research, it is a fortress-like structure that rises from the dunes south of Rishon LeZion, southeast of Tel Aviv. And reporting to Blumberg were Israel's science attachés, specially trained to collect nuclear and biological intelligence, at key embassies in the United States and other countries.

After a recommendation by Peres, Blumberg checked out Milchan in the Zionist Organization of America (ZOA) House on Ibn Gabirol Street in Tel Aviv. His secret office was a few miles south, on the third floor of a dingy, nondescript four-story office building at 21 Carlebach Street, in a busy neighborhood of noisy buses, shoppers, and crowded falafel shops. Blumberg's goal was not to be noticed. But the meeting went well and Milchan even moved his company's office from a wholesale agricultural market area, with its battered vegetable carts, into an identical building next door at 29 Carlebach Street. It was a wise decision and allowed for easy and secure conferences with Blumberg over cups of strong tea. What made Milchan particularly appealing was his established company. Taken together, Milchan controlled over thirty companies in seventeen countries, many of which would serve as fronts for LAKAM's various covert operations.

———

Given a South African passport, Milchan's job was to secretly assist Rhoodie and the White supremacist government in developing a nuclear weapons capability, running arms into the country, and hiding from the world the desperate, horrific conditions of the country's Black population. Rhoodie saw little difference in Israel's racist treatment of its Palestinians and his own country's racist treatment of its Blacks, except in the biased coverage by the Western media. "Eschel Rhoodie expressed his envy of Israeli public relations successes in the West, and compared the merits of apartheid and Zionism, which he found basically similar," noted Benjamin Beit-Hallahmi, a psychology professor at Haifa University, who studied the relationship between the two countries. "Despite its openly discriminatory policies, Israel is described in the Western media as a 'Western democracy,' while South Africa is almost universally condemned."

Eventually, the relationship became close. Rhoodie even sold Milchan his condominium in Plettenberg Bay, an exclusive all-White South African beach resort. With $100 million to spend, the plan was to target key opinion shapers in Western media circles, including mainstream journalists, television personalities, entertainers, and politicians. And the method was to use Milchan's dozens of front companies to secretly purchase controlling interests in news organizations, magazines, newspapers, publishing houses, and film studios around the globe. Then, to hide any connection to the apartheid regime, Milchan's Israeli fronts were again used to launder the payments.

Once secretly in control of the media companies, the cabal would use disinformation and fake news to whitewash South Africa's policies of racial segregation by putting a positive spin on them. After all, according to Prime Minister Vorster, "The Whites of South Africa understand the mentality of the Black man." And Israel, through Milchan, intended to help the racist government as much as it could, according to Rafi Eitan, a top Mossad official who would take over LAKAM from Blumberg. "The idea was that we, together with the director of the South African Ministry of Information, Eschel Rhoodie, would take over the world media and that way we would help both him and ourselves, and show the world the 'beautiful face' of South Africa," he said. "They recognized me as someone who could help them with public relations, through connections on television, in newspapers, in articles. Even with financial support," Milchan said. "And I do it happily."

Relations between Israel and South Africa quickly blossomed to the point where Israel, in April 1976, literally rolled out a red carpet to the plane for visiting Prime Minister Vorster. Waiting to greet him at the other end of the carpet was Prime Minister Yitzhak Rabin and a crowd of dignitaries. The four-day visit had been arranged the month before during a secret trip to South Africa by Shimon Peres.

It was a very odd collaboration. Nicknamed "Jackboot John," during World War II Vorster was an admirer of Adolf Hitler and a member of the pro-Nazi Ox Wagon Guard (Ossewabrandwag) movement, rising to "Chief General." As a result, Britain imprisoned him for twenty months as a Nazi sympathizer. "To this day," noted *Time* magazine in June 1976, "Vorster maintains that what he did during the war 'was right.'" Nevertheless, Rabin even honored him at the Yad Vashem Holocaust memorial, where the Hitler admirer laid a wreath on a mass grave for Nazi concentration camp victims.

A few months later, the South African government's yearbook described the two countries as having one thing in common above all else: "They are both situated in a predominantly hostile world inhabited by dark peoples." Therefore, both countries also had a mutual interest in keeping their oppressed "dark peoples," Palestinians in Israel and Blacks in South Africa, under brutal military control. As a result, in addition to his roles as key money launderer and propagandist for the racist government, Milchan also became the principal arms dealer between Israel and South Africa, its biggest weapons customer.

It was a time when Pretoria was focused on purchasing from Israel powerful counterinsurgency weapons to prevent Black insurrection or revolt. "We created the South African arms industry," said Alon Liel, a former Israeli ambassador to Pretoria. "After 1976, there was a love affair between the security establishments of the two countries and their armies... The link was very intimate." Among the weapons were 106mm recoilless rifles and four hundred M-113A1 armored personnel carriers for use against protesters in the Black townships. The arms deals included many American-made weapons supplied to Israel and then covertly and illegally transshipped to Pretoria. Thus, through Israel and Milchan, Americans were unwittingly supplying the arms the apartheid government was using to violently oppress its Black population.

In addition, Israel was offering for sale such locally made weapons as Uzi submachine guns and the Galil, a light assault rifle that converts into a submachine gun, sniper rifle, automatic rifle, light machine gun, or grenade launcher capable of firing antitank or antipersonnel ammunition. Israel was also sending advisors to train South African military forces in anti-guerrilla warfare. And South Africa wasn't the only White supremacist government Israel was helping stay in power. It was also assisting Rhodesia maintain its White rule by illegally supplying U.S.-made Bell helicopters with the use of false end-user certificates.

But as Milchan and Rhoodie lobbed tennis balls and sunned themselves on Plettenberg Bay's all-White beach, the racial tensions throughout the country were seething. The repression and daily humiliations for the country's eighteen million Blacks were reaching a breaking point. Finally, on June 16, 1976, two months after Vorster's visit to Israel, the world learned of another new place in the divided country: Soweto. It was just one of the many dilapidated slums for Blacks outside Johannesburg. But over three harrowing days and nights it captured the world's attention as it became the scene of enraged rioting and lopsided battles between stone-throwing Blacks and heavily armed White police. At least eight hundred people were killed and more than a thousand were injured, dwarfing the death toll at an earlier massacre, that of Sharpeville. The violence quickly spread to at least seven other nearby segregated Black townships.

Soon in Israel, like mirror images, there would be desperate uprisings by stone-throwing Palestinians during the Intifada, and violent responses by heavily armed Israeli forces. Ronnie Kasrils, a White Jewish South African, rose up in the ranks of the anti-apartheid African National Congress (ANC), eventually becoming the intelligence chief. In 2004, he visited the Palestinian territories and was shocked by what he saw. "This is much worse than apartheid," he said. "The Israeli measures, the brutality, make apartheid look like a picnic. We never had jets attacking our townships. We never had sieges that lasted month after month. We never had tanks destroying houses. We had armored vehicles and police using small arms to shoot people but not on this scale."

And just as apartheid South Africa fought back against the world with lies, propaganda, and psychological warfare, so would Israel. "At the UN we kept saying: 'We are against apartheid, as Jewish people who suffered from the Holocaust this is intolerable.' But our security establishment kept cooperating," said Liel, the former Israeli ambassador. Therefore, both Blacks and Palestinians would constantly be labeled "terrorists" whenever they attempted to end their brutal occupation, even though international law recognizes the right to resist such actions. "The repressed are demonized as terrorists to justify ever-greater violations of their rights," noted Ronnie Kasrils. "We have the absurdity that the victims are blamed for the violence meted out against them."

With the Soweto riots bringing worldwide attention on the desperate conditions in South Africa, there was a scramble for cover. Rhoodie issued instructions "on the advice of both Prime Minister Vorster and General van den Bergh" that they destroy all "unnecessary documentation." Nevertheless, the propaganda operations would continue, now with an increased focus on film and entertainment. In 1976, with Milchan's help, there were 1,160 screenings worldwide of documentaries putting a positive spin on the country's apartheid policies, and Rhoodie hoped to extend that to both movies and television programs.

For Milchan, it would offer good cover as South Africa's key arms dealer. And his role grew exponentially following the Soweto massacre as a result of a UN-imposed mandatory arms embargo on South Africa, as well as the declaration of the International Anti-Apartheid Year. That opened the floodgates for Milchan, giving him a near monopoly on the South African arms trade and making him the regime's largest weapons procurer.

Through Milchan's dozens of phony front companies, some of the same ones used for the disinformation campaign, weapons would be secretly and illegally sent to South Africa. Some would be sent from the United States to Israel and then be illegally transshipped to Pretoria. Others would come from third countries with the use of phony end-user certificates. And as many millions of dollars' worth of weapons flowed into South Africa, millions of dollars' worth of commissions flowed into Milchan's bank account.

At the time, both Israel and South Africa were also secretly becoming nuclear weapons partners. Pretoria coveted Israel's nuclear capabilities, and Israel needed South Africa's natural uranium, known as yellowcake, to keep Dimona running. It was an area Milchan knew a great deal about. The topic of nuclear weapons had first come up on June 4, 1975, during a meeting between Peres and his counterpart, South African defense minister (and later president) P. W. Botha. The venue was the palatial Baur au Lac Hotel in

Zurich, in the shadow of the Swiss Alps. And the focus was Israeli nuclear warheads.

According to minutes from the meeting, what Botha was interested in were Jerichos, short-range Israeli missiles capable of launching nuclear warheads. But there was a catch: They had to come with "the correct payload." Peres said, "The correct payload was available in three sizes." Another memo makes it clear that Botha was referring to "nuclear-armed Jerichos." In the end, largely due to financial issues, the deal was apparently never completed.

Nevertheless, Prime Minister Vorster eventually agreed to sell Israel fifty metric tons of yellowcake. But there was a catch. Pretoria was also secretly developing nuclear weapons and they wanted something specific in return: 30 grams of tritium. A radioactive form of hydrogen, tritium is used for "boosting," or enhancing, the explosive power of nuclear weapons. According to secret South African court records, that quantity of tritium was sufficient for use in twelve atomic bombs. The deal was agreed to, and in 1977 the tritium, under the code name "Tea Leaves," was delivered to the apartheid state by Blumberg in a series of shipments over eighteen months packed in tiny capsules containing 2.5 grams in each. Among those serving as escorts for the tritium on the special C-130 Hercules flights were Blumberg, Milchan, and Rhoodie.

In return, another fifty-ton shipment of yellowcake, code-named "Mutton," was sent to Israel. But now Blumberg was after more. Back in the mid-1960s, South Africa had entered into an agreement to transfer ten tons of yellowcake to Israel, followed by regular shipments. Pretoria, however, had placed severe restrictions on its use. They included regular inspections by South Africa of the sealed barrels to prevent its being converted into weapons grade. By the mid-1970s, the stockpile had grown to five hundred metric tons, and Blumberg wanted it all. But that required ending the inspections and getting all restrictions lifted.

Working through General van den Bergh, Blumberg got his wish. In the late 1970s, Botha lifted all restrictions and threw out the safeguards, thereby making the grand total of yellowcake received from South Africa an enormous six hundred metric tons. For Israel, it was a highly secret windfall, enough fuel to allow Dimona to continue operating for another decade. But it was obtained at an unspeakable cost to the Black population of South Africa, apparently with no remorse. Nevertheless, there was certainly a lingering fear that the next Soweto, or the one after that, would bring an end to the White supremacist government.

––––––––––

With the deal for the yellowcake in place in the late 1970s, the next need for Israel was for two other critical ingredients. One was highly enriched weapons-grade uranium for the nuclear cores of the bombs, and the other was rare, highly specialized nuclear triggers to make them detonate. Both of these required covert operations to steal them from the United States, Israel's ally. Luckily, for years Blumberg had an American working as a spy smuggling out bomb-grade uranium and other critical items from a nuclear plant he ran in Apollo, Pennsylvania. Known as the Nuclear Materials and Equipment Corporation, or NUMEC, it was little more than a nuclear pigsty. But the sloppy conditions served as excellent cover for smuggling highly enriched uranium to Israel.

Milchan's job, therefore, would be to recruit another American spy to secretly smuggle out the critical nuclear triggers, as well as other key supplies and intelligence. But first he would need to develop a cover, one that allowed him to spend a great deal of time in Southern California, the heart of America's defense industry. He would become a wealthy movie producer. At the same time, working with Rhoodie, he could secretly extend their pro-apartheid propaganda program to America's film and entertainment industry. What they would call "Operation Hollywood."

CHAPTER 13

◆

The Producer

Arnon Milchan stepped off his private jet at California's Burbank Airport flush with tens of millions of dollars he had made from arming the racist South African government, arms used to suppress the raging Black population and prevent future uprisings like Soweto. Now in the summer of 1978 he was on his way to Warner Bros. Studios to recruit an American as a spy for LAKAM, and at the same time build his cover as a wealthy Hollywood producer.

As part of Operation Hollywood, according to a high-ranking South African official, Milchan recommended that the apartheid regime begin penetrating the U.S. entertainment industry with techniques similar to those used with the media. The idea was to expand from secretly investing in newspapers and magazines to also begin clandestinely funding movie, television, and Broadway deals. Such a move would greatly expand their covert propaganda operation, allowing them to put a favorable spin on the government's brutal segregation policies, or alternatively, cast a harsh light on the Black freedom movement.

Soon Milchan turned up as a producer for a Broadway musical about joyful native Blacks living happily under apartheid, the theme that Rhoodie and the government were trying to project. *Ipi Tombi*, produced along with fellow Israelis Avrham Dashe and Chaim Topol, started previews at Harkness Theater near New York's Lincoln Center on December 28, 1976, and instantly attracted angry protests and pickets. Among the groups was the Emergency Committee to Protest the South African Production of *Ipi Tombi*, which included an executive from WNET, the local PBS station; the editor in chief of *Essence* magazine; and the president of the Black Theater Alliance. The grievances focused on "the exploitation of blacks by South Africans" and "America's cooperation and support of the present South African government."

According to an article in the *New York Times* at the time, "The protesters contended the musical, conceived and produced by whites, offered an unrealistic picture of blacks in South Africa and could be considered pro-apartheid propaganda." There was a similar reaction when the play opened in Los Angeles. Protesters picketed the theater shouting, "Shut down *Ipi Tombi*," calling it "racist garbage" and "a coverup of South African apartheid." In New York the production was such a disaster that it ended up sinking the entire theater. A few months after it opened, the wrecking balls started knocking down the walls. "The closing of 'Ipi Tombe' may have been the final blow that led to the decision to sell," said the *Times*. "The marquee told the story. It read, 'Happiness Is an African Musical Called Ipi Tombe.' Over that message, a sign announced the liquidation sale."

Around that same time, Milchan happened to meet film producer Elliott Kastner in a Tel Aviv restaurant. Born into a Jewish family in New York in 1930, Kastner started out in the industry as a talent agent and later set up shop as a movie producer. He had just arrived in Israel following a disastrous western, *The Missouri Breaks*, starring Marlon Brando and Jack Nicholson. Not only did the film flop at the box office, but it was panned by critics and Nicholson ended up suing Kastner for cheating him out of money. Nevertheless, Kastner hit it off with Milchan so well that he invited him to tag along on a trip to Austria to meet actress Elizabeth Taylor, who was going to star in his next film, *A Little Night Music*. It would end up another financial and critical dud, but Kastner's very wealthy new friend had now become his partner. "Suddenly we are doing business together producing movies," Milchan would later say.

Flush with South African cash from Rhoodie for his secret Operation Hollywood propaganda plan, Milchan had agreed to pump money into a British movie, *Black Joy*. The film had its origins as a play, *Dark Days, Light Nights*, written and directed by Jamal Ali. It was intended as a political "call to arms" to oppose the rampant oppression that Blacks go through in a White-dominated society, especially in the ghetto, and to highlight the struggles they must endure. During its performance at the Black Theatre of Brixton, a largely Black section of London, Ali was approached by director Anthony Simmons, who suggested turning the play into a film and asked if Ali would write the screenplay. Excited by the prospect of attracting a wider audience to his political message, Ali agreed and soon thereafter was introduced to Kastner, who would produce it along with Milchan, the moneyman.

On the first day of filming, Kastner jetted in from California, but by then Ali already regretted his decision. To his horror, without any consultation the script had been radically changed and stripped of its powerful political message. "I don't like how the script is turning out," he told a friend. "It ain't *my* play anymore." He later complained, "The play was quite lost and they wanted to make a kind of blaxploitation film." Simmons, he said, "made the movie into what I did not want the movie made into...the radicalness had gone and had become a joyous situation. Whereas I was thinking it was much more brutal than that." At one point Ali became so frustrated by what he was seeing that he suddenly shouted, "Cut!" But Simmons simply ordered him off the set and continued with the filming.

As with *Ipi Tombe*, the message Rhoodie and Milchan wanted the film to convey was for Blacks to give up dangerous political ideas and instead simply be happy with their lot in life. Simmons, who was also Jewish, would later say, "I don't want to get involved in a story of the Blacks and the issue of slavery and all of the rest of it. The object is that I wanted to make [a] comedy film... I wasn't going to do *Black Joy* as a Black film about how terrible it was to be Black." He added, "I would [imagine]...the whole thing as a...Jewish story." The result was to deliberately mute the outrage and oppression of Black voices for the sake of the box office, and clandestinely for the benefit of the racist South African government.

————

Rhoodie was apparently pleased with the final result. Kastner entered the film in the 1977 Cannes Film Festival, and although it came away with no awards, Rhoodie was there to celebrate. During the May event, Rhoodie, Milchan, and two other members of their propaganda clique, financiers David Abramson and Stuart Pegg, shared a table at the ceremony. Joining them at the table and toasting to their success was another new Milchan friend, forty-three-year-old American filmmaker Roman Polanski.

Just two months earlier Polanski had been arrested at the Beverly Wilshire Hotel in Los Angeles for drugging, raping, and performing sodomy on a thirteen-year-old girl, crimes that didn't seem to trouble Milchan. Later, facing the prospect of prison, Polanski fled to France and became a fugitive from the American legal system. Nevertheless, a few years later Milchan produced Polanski's French staging of *Amadeus*, with Polanski directing and starring as Mozart. "He's fun," Polanski said about his decades-long friendship with Milchan. "Dinners, parties, nightclubs."

Israeli spymaster Blumberg cannot forget the evening he spent with Polanski at Milchan's luxurious villa near Paris. Milchan suggested that they all go out for a night on the town at a cabaret. Polanski immediately agreed. Blumberg, the LAKAM chief, was hesitant. "I went with them but after half an hour I wanted to leave. Naked girls were dancing on stage, it's not my taste. I asked Milchan to take me back to the hotel, but we could not move because Polanski was so enthusiastic he refused to go. So I had to spend half the night there watching that. It was horrible."

On the heels of *Black Joy*, Milchan suggested another joint project with Kastner. He wanted him to produce a fictionalized film about himself, Milchan, as a heroic arms dealer, full of derring-do. A new book had just been released on the trade, *The Arms Bazaar*, by longtime British author and journalist Anthony Sampson, and Kastner wasted little time contacting him about turning it into a movie. "Kastner had the style of an amiable gorilla," recalled Sampson. "He conveyed his enthusiasm for the book in the weird, electrical language of the movie trade: he liked the vibes, he wanted to pick up the activity, he didn't want any static: 'The word of mouth is big.'" After Sampson agreed to write the screenplay, Kastner said he wanted him to meet "the real backer of the film." He was "an Israeli called Arnon Milchan...who enjoyed courting danger and flew around the world with a briefcase containing $75,000 in different currencies."

But around the same time, an internal investigation by authorities in Pretoria began looking into Rhoodie's years of wild spending and misappropriation of funds. And then Milchan's name started to appear. As a result, with millions in the bank thanks to his weapons and propaganda deals with the apartheid regime, Milchan decided to distance himself from Rhoodie and go it alone as a producer. In a messy separation, he dumped Kastner, accusing him of overcharging him. Kastner angrily responded, "He wanted to be as famous as me in restaurants and hotels, and to fuck every girl that I fucked."

Despite his enormous wealth, fights over every last dime would become a constant Milchan trademark. "He's as cheap as they come," said filmmaker Oliver Stone, who worked with Milchan on such films as *JFK* and *Natural Born Killers*. "He's sick about money, obsessed with losing it. I learned a very hard lesson, and it cost me a lot of my personal money. I don't want to get into a pissing contest, but Arnon can be very nasty." As if to make the point, Italian spaghetti western director Sergio Leone, who directed Milchan's film *Once Upon a Time in America*, presented Milchan with a gift. It was a life-sized sculpture of a man sitting at a table in front of a plate piled with money. The name of the artwork is *The Last Supper of a Greedy Man*.

In 1976, now in sole charge of the *Arms Bazaar* project, Milchan called Sampson and said he wanted to meet him urgently. He then chartered a jet, flew to London, and showed up at Sampson's home in sports clothes and tennis shoes, and carrying a black briefcase with a row of six combination locks. Getting down to business, Milchan told Sampson that he had been in the arms trade himself and had dealings with South Africa. "As he talked about the plot," Sampson said, "I began to suspect that he wanted the story to be about himself."

Later Sampson was flown to Paris, picked up by Jose, Milchan's chauffeur, and taken in a Range Rover to meet with Milchan, who by then owned an eighteenth-century chateau, Montfort l'Amaury, on a fifty-acre estate an hour's drive outside Paris. A hunting lodge that had formerly been used by French kings, it sat on the edge of a pond and was close to the comparatively humble abode of future French president Jacques Chirac. Milchan had purchased it a few years before, while just in his early thirties. When Blumberg was in Paris he would often stay there. "I never saw such luxury, elegance, size," he later said.

The chateau was a convenient place to unload some of his growing mountain of blood-soaked cash—millions earned at a high cost to South Africa's oppressed Blacks who found themselves at the receiving end of his tons of imported weapons. Lives that apparently didn't matter to Milchan. Now he was planning to launder more of it through Hollywood film studios as he turned himself into a producer. It was a nice cover as he resumed his espionage activities for Blumberg and Israel's LAKAM, and began targeting Americans for nuclear secrets and technology.

But rather than the chateau, the chauffeur drove Sampson to Elysée-Matignon, a restaurant and club with faux gold bullion walls that Milchan used as an informal office. Sampson joined Milchan for lunch and they discussed a draft of Sampson's screenplay. Next, they went to Milchan's apartment in the city, a stately building on Rue Singer in the 16th arrondissement, one of the most expensive sections of Paris, between the Arc de Triomphe and the Bois de Boulogne. As Milchan's blonde Swedish girlfriend played pinball, the two discussed the script in his study, a dimly lit room with dark tiles made of rugged tree bark that reminded Sampson of the lair of some nocturnal forest creature. "The atmosphere was placeless and creepy," he said, "with strange young men waiting around and phones ringing with messages from foreign airports."

Shortly after Sampson returned to London, Milchan called again. "I've got Sydney Pollack and Sidney Lumet interested," he said, referring to two of Hollywood's most prolific producers and directors. Later he called back saying he had talked to Lumet, Pollack, and Robert Redford, who were filled with ideas and asked Sampson to fly to Hollywood and discuss the film with Pollack. Arriving in July 1978, Sampson was put up at the fashionable Sunset Marquis Hotel in West Hollywood, an enclave for the 1970s rock-and-roll crowd, from David Bowie to Bruce Springsteen.

The next day he was driven to Warner Bros. Studios in Burbank and was escorted to Room 1206, Pollack's small and largely nondescript office on the sprawling lot. By then Pollack was an established director of such films as *They Shoot Horses, Don't They?*, with Jane Fonda, and *The Way We Were*, which starred Robert Redford and Barbra Streisand. At the time, Pollack was heavily involved with both Fonda and Redford in a new film, *The Electric Horseman*. It centered on Redford as a former rodeo champ who reluctantly goes to work as a spokesperson for a cereal company. As a prop he is given Rising Star, a $12 million champion Thoroughbred racehorse outfitted in an elaborate electric light costume. Redford soon realizes that Rising Star has been badly maltreated and identifies with its plight. He then steals the horse and makes his way cross-country to release it in a remote canyon to join a herd of wild horses. Fonda is cast as a television reporter who finds him, tags along, and the two become lovers.

Sampson got the impression that Pollack was interested in the idea, but oddly he seemed even more interested in exactly who Milchan was, along with his motivation. Pollack found it puzzling that he traveled on a South African passport and gambled extravagantly at Caesars Palace, where he was said to have lost $200,000 in a single night. "What did he *really* want?" was the impression Sampson got from Pollack, implying that making movies was not Milchan's real goal. Nevertheless, the concept of a film about an arms dealer was appealing and Pollack brought in a screenwriter, Bob Garland, for Sampson to collaborate with in London. At the meeting, Garland pitched Robert Redford to play the lead.

Although Sampson had no way of knowing, what Milchan *really* wanted was to turn Pollack into a spy for LAKAM, and then become his control agent, his handler. And, Milchan hinted, it was something he eventually accomplished. Pollack "was my partner," he would later admit, in "all kinds of things." When asked if Pollack knew of and participated in all of Milchan's activities, Milchan said, "He had to decide what he was willing to do and what he was not willing to do. On a lot of things he said no. On a lot of other things he said yes."

Just what assistance he provided Milchan is still unknown, since Milchan revealed Pollack's role only after the director's death. Burbank, however, was in the center of the defense and aerospace industry. And Warner Bros.' neighbor was Lockheed's highly secret Skunk Works, where the U-2 and SR-71 spy planes were designed. At the time of Sampson's visit, the Skunk Works had just received a new highly secret contract to build the F-117 stealth fighter. While there's no indication that Pollack had access to the plant, the question remains just what help he might have provided, or who else he might have recruited for Milchan, such as someone high up at the plant. Ironically, just a few years earlier Pollack had directed *Three Days of the Condor*, a cat-and-mouse spy thriller. Based on the novel *Six Days of the Condor* by author James Grady, it starred Robert Redford as a covert CIA agent fighting back against a corrupt agency.

Soon after Sampson returned to London, Milchan called to ask how the meeting went. But almost before Sampson could answer, Milchan said he wanted a new script written, one that would attract Robert De Niro. By then De Niro was well established, with a Best Supporting Actor Oscar for his role in *The Godfather II* playing the young Vito Corleone, and a nomination for Best Actor for his portrayal of the violent, mentally disturbed Travis Bickle in *Taxi Driver*. The next month Sampson returned to Paris for another meeting with Milchan and a further discussion about a possible film to snare De Niro, who Milchan saw as key to his entrée into Hollywood. Sampson, however, was starting to become suspicious. "I remained baffled by his real motivation and loyalties," he said.

In the end, nothing came of Sampson's screenplay because Milchan had a better idea. He knew that De Niro, like much of Hollywood, was very pro-Israel. So rather than dump another unread screenplay on De Niro's doorstep, he would make "the Godfather" an offer he couldn't refuse. He would fly him to Israel to meet with Defense Minister Ezer Weizmann, soon to become president, and General Moshe Dayan, the high-profile war hero and minister of foreign affairs. The pretext was for Milchan to produce a film about Dayan with De Niro playing the general. Whether or not a film would ever develop, it would give the gregarious Milchan a unique chance to spend quality time and bond with De Niro, who was the same age as him.

The invitation would also offer Milchan a perfect opportunity to show off his connections and enormous wealth, which was key for a producer. Shortly after arriving, a beaming De Niro sat at a dinner table next to a smiling Dayan, clad in a suit and tie along with his trademark black eye patch covering his left eye. Likely nearby was Milchan's boss, LAKAM chief Benjamin Blumberg, sizing up Milchan's next possible recruit. Later Dayan introduced De Niro to his family. And afterward, a tanned, fast-talking Milchan gave him a tour of the city while pitching him on his willingness to invest heavily in his films. It was important, he told De Niro, "for the producer to be real partners with the stars and the director, for the producer to put his neck on the line financially and for them to do it artistically."

The move quickly put Milchan on the inside track with De Niro and his wide circle of friends in Hollywood just as he was reaching his apex with a Best Actor Oscar win for *Raging Bull*. And soon, rather than Milchan pitching De Niro, it was De Niro pitching Milchan on screenplays in which he wanted to star, while Milchan paid the bills. The first was *The King of Comedy*, a dark dramedy about fans obsessed with celebrities to such a degree that they stalk them like prey, and occasionally resort to violence.

De Niro had originally purchased the screenplay from *Newsweek* film critic Paul D. Zimmermann years earlier but had trouble interesting anyone in it. Until Milchan came along and agreed to finance the $19 million project, and thereby finally turn himself into a major Hollywood producer. At the same time, Milchan now had an outlet for his millions in dirty apartheid cash. In the film, which was directed by Martin Scorsese, De Niro was to play the stalker, a wannabe Seinfeld-like stand-up comedian, with Jerry Lewis his target as a Johnny Carson–style late-night talk show host.

During the filming of *The King of Comedy*, Milchan's name began appearing in newspapers tying him directly to South Africa's arms and propaganda scandal. The revelations greatly angered Anthony Sampson, who was close to Nelson Mandela, then still in a South African prison, and he was happy to have parted ways with Milchan over the *Arms Bazaar* project. "The revelations about Rhoodie are an important warning of how far a determined and embattled nation can 'throw morality out of the window,'" he wrote in an opinion piece, quoting Rhoodie's own words. And he wanted an explanation from Milchan. "When I rang to ask him how he had become involved in such a shady operation," Sampson said, "he protested his innocence, a little too much."

Unlike Sampson, the idea that Milchan made his millions weaponizing the White supremacist government at the expense of South Africa's oppressed Blacks, and helped run the regime's worldwide propaganda operation, didn't seem to bother De Niro. Nor did the fact that that same blood-soaked money was financing his film and paying his salary. Unconcerned, he remained close to Milchan and went on to do two more films with him in rapid succession, *Once Upon a Time in America* and *Brazil*.

———

As Milchan built his cover while at the same time recruiting American spies, work at Dimona had greatly speeded up. Around the same time, a number of Dimona scientists suddenly became very interested in the capabilities of U.S. spy satellites to detect secret nuclear explosions. Among them was Avraham Hermoni, LAKAM's chief of station in Washington and one of the key developers of the Israeli bomb. That sudden interest struck Dr. Alan Berman, the director of research at the U.S. Naval Research Laboratory in Washington, as very odd. "My close Israeli friend Dr. Dror Sadeh, who had worked at Dimona," said Berman, "seemed to have more than a casual knowledge of the issues related to nuclear weapon design. Somehow, whenever I met him, or the Israeli science advisor at the Israeli Embassy in DC, Avraham Hermoni, the conversation always nudged to how American satellites could locate a nuclear detonation."

Hermoni had reason to be curious. Two years earlier, in 1977, the Russian spy satellite Cosmos 932 returned to Earth with detailed photographs of a South African military installation deep in the Kalahari Desert. It took little time for analysts to conclude that the facility was designed for nuclear testing. And in an unusual move, the Russians passed the intelligence on to the United States, hoping that the Carter administration would be able to prevent a test from taking place—something that was in the interest of both countries. In response, U.S. spy satellites verified the Russian intelligence and pressure was immediately placed on South Africa to cancel any tests, presently and in the future, which they did. Now, in 1979, the lesson for Hermoni was to find out as much as possible about U.S. spy satellites, and then, unlike South Africa, find a way to successfully hide a nuclear test from them.

CHAPTER 14

——◆——

The Bang

Sixty-five thousand miles above Earth, in the frigid blackness of deep space, a U.S. spy satellite was dying of old age. VELA 6911, shaped like a giant twenty-six-sided Christmas tree ornament hanging weightlessly in the empty void, had been launched on May 23, 1969, with an expected lifetime of seven years. A decade later, in late September 1979, it was still alive, but just barely. Its heartlike power source was growing weaker and it was losing control of its functions.

The VELA satellites were designed to act as America's sentinels in space, watching eagle-like for any signs of nuclear detonations far below on any part of the planet—explosions that would constitute violations of the 1963 Partial Test Ban Treaty, signed by most countries in the world, which outlawed nuclear explosions in all environments except underground. It was especially watchful for rogue tests by nuclear pariah states like Israel, one of the very few countries that had refused to sign both the 1970 Nuclear Non-Proliferation Treaty and the 1975 Biological Weapons Convention, in spite of the fact that it had a hidden arsenal of nuclear weapons and a secret biological weapons program.

But after a decade in orbit watching over about a third of the Earth, VELA 6911's electromagnetic pulse sensors, used to discover sudden bursts of electrons indicating a nuclear blast, were no longer working. Nor was the sensor that was designed to pinpoint where in its field of vision a blast might have taken place. Nevertheless, it still had two working and unblinking mirror-like "eyes" known as bhangmeters, designed not to "see" a burst but to record its light intensity. And in the early morning blackness of September 22, 1979, at 00:52:43 UTC, the twin bhangmeters recorded what appeared to be a very bright flash, followed quickly by a second. They were the classic indicators of a powerful nuclear explosion. Somewhere down below, in a broad, isolated expanse of ocean stretching from the South Atlantic southward to the coast of Antarctica, eastward past the tip of Africa, and onward to the edge of the

Indian Ocean, someone had set off a nuclear bomb. Someone who was hoping not to get caught.

At 10:15 p.m. on Florida's Atlantic coast, an hour and twenty-three minutes after the blast, technicians in a secret office began a routine download of VELA 6911's nuclear event detection payload memory. As they watched a fresh sheet of graph paper roll out of a gray computer, long thin styluses like a spider's legs began swinging back and forth. In black ink, the styluses drew two hump-shaped images from each bhangmeter, representing light flashes. The first camel-like hump was caused by the initial fireball. And the second occurred a millisecond later when the bright sunlike orb was overtaken by, and hidden behind, the rapidly expanding shock wave.

The technicians worked at a secret headquarters with a bland and meaningless cover name: the Air Force Technical Applications Center. It was housed in a tan four-story brick building on Patrick Air Force Base, a few miles south of Cape Kennedy. Stretched across the front, as if ready for war, were life-size mock-ups of powerful missiles and rockets. And beyond a tall fence was the busy A1A Highway and the crashing waves of the Atlantic Ocean. The job of AFTAC was, and is, to clandestinely monitor the world for any indications of nuclear detonations, NUDETs, overt or covert.

The little-known organization was born in secret two decades earlier, in 1959, in preparation for the eventual enactment of the Partial Test Ban Treaty. Signed in Moscow in August 1963 by the United States, the Soviet Union, the United Kingdom, and eventually 123 other countries, including Israel, the treaty banned nuclear weapons testing in the atmosphere, under the sea, and in outer space. The only exception was for tests conducted underground. The idea was to prevent a proliferation nightmare, a race where every country expended billions to build and test ever more powerful nuclear bombs to destroy their neighbors, and eventually engulf the world in a deadly radioactive cloud.

Outside AFTAC's radiochemistry laboratory, rotating red lights in the hallway ceilings warn that uncleared persons are in the area. Inside the entrance, the logo embedded in the floor succinctly sums up the organization's mission. Surrounding an image of a lithium atom are the words "In God We Trust, All Others We Monitor." It was scientists in white lab coats and blue rubber gloves in the lab who analyzed, atom by atom, environmental samples secretly collected near Dimona by John Hadden, the CIA's chief of station in Tel Aviv. Using mass spectrometry and other techniques, they determined that the samples contained trace amounts of highly enriched uranium produced by a U.S. government plant in Portsmouth, Ohio. And Portsmouth's only customer was the NUMEC plant in Apollo, Pennsylvania, which meant it had to have been stolen by Israel.

Over the years, AFTAC's secret Atomic Energy Detection System would encircle the world with thirty-six hundred sensors that listen, sense, sniff, and watch 24/7 for indications of a nuclear blast. "We've got them in space. We've got them at sea. We've got them in the air. We've got them on land on all seven continents, to include Antarctica," said AFTAC commander Colonel Chad Hartman. And in Antarctica, a sensor is buried beneath the South Pole.

At 11 p.m., forty-five minutes after discovering and confirming what AFTAC determined was a "low-yield atmospheric nuclear detonation," the organization initiated a NUDET "pre-alert." Then, four and a half hours later, following a more thorough analysis, AFTAC declared "Alert 747" at 3:30 a.m. on September 22. They then began searching through data from other sensors for additional details, as well as attempting to pinpoint roughly where in millions of possible square miles the nuclear event had taken place. Whoever set off the clandestine explosion was either very lucky or very well informed about VELA 6911's inoperable sensors. Nevertheless, clues began arriving from other dark recesses around the world.

Twelve hundred miles to the south in Puerto Rico, the giant thousand-foot Arecibo radio telescope picked up an unusual disturbance. An odd and powerful electromagnetic ripple on the lower surface of the ionosphere had occurred about the same time as the event detected by VELA 6911. Known as a traveling ionospheric disturbance, it originated from the southeast, the area in which the blast occurred, heading toward the northeast. "The initial examination," wrote John Deutch, the undersecretary of the Department of Energy, "may confirm the signal from the VELA system." And a memorandum from the National Security Council noted that "the signal from this disturbance is similar to some recorded during U.S. and Soviet atmospheric tests in the early 1960s." And it "represents the best lead yet in the search for corroborative data."

Another clue came from the sea. Among AFTAC's monitoring locations was Ascension Island, a bleak and rugged volcanic speck in the middle of the South Atlantic Ocean. One of the most isolated places on earth, it lies near the equator halfway between Africa and South America. It is also one of the most secret places on the planet. Over the years, both the United Kingdom and the United States have turned its eighty-eight square miles into an Orwellian surveillance world. There's a massive British GCHQ eavesdropping base that targets communications satellites far above, as well as communications to the west in South America and to the east in Africa. Then there are giant American golf-ball-like radomes hiding radar for tracking the final splashdown of ICBM missiles test fired from Florida. And under the waves are networks of eavesdropping systems that stretch out octopus-like from the island in order to listen for foreign ships and submarines thousands of miles away, and the splashdown offshore of the ICBM nosecones. Both governments also have military bases on the island, along with aircraft on Wideawake Airfield.

The long-standing joke is that the island has more antennas than people, which apparently is the way both governments want to keep it. The local authorities of the British possession have been accused of uprooting the few long-term residents and maintaining the island exclusively for highly cleared government employees and contractors. And when their contracts or assignments are up, they must leave. "There is no indigenous population, or 'islanders,'" one official said dismissively. "On Ascension, everyone is an expat, present by virtue of an employment contract."

Both the secrecy and isolation are critical for AFTAC and Navy intelligence in taking advantage of a discovery made years earlier: Deep in the ocean, at just the right depth, sounds thousands of miles away can be heard. Known as the SOFAR (Sound Fixing and Ranging) channel, it is a horizontal layer of water that acts as a sort of waveguide for sound. A key factor is water temperature. At the surface where the sea is the warmest, sound travels rapidly, but also dissipates rapidly. But thousands of feet down, in a layer that remains constantly cold and under high pressure, sound becomes trapped and travels more slowly, but for great distances, at about five thousand feet a second. It's a bit like finding a clear frequency among a great deal of static on a shortwave radio.

To tap into the SOFAR channel around the world, Navy intelligence established a highly secret program known as the Sound Surveillance System, or SOSUS. On Ascension, as part of the system, the Navy set up two arrays of undersea microphones, known as hydrophones, one seventy-four miles south of the island and the other seventeen miles north. Each array consists of three widely separated hydrophones that are suspended at depths of between fifteen hundred and three thousand feet by cables anchored to the seafloor. Undersea cables then connect them to a small white analysis building on Northwest Bay, a small sandy beach on Ascension.

The sensors are also used by another program, the Air Force Missile Impact Location System (MILS), which pinpoints the exact splashdown location of nosecones from ICBMs test fired from Florida. Both systems are extremely sensitive and accurate. In 2006, 109 miles off the coast of New York, a power supply for underwater oceanographic equipment suffered a small accidental explosion. Five thousand miles away on Ascension Island, the SOSUS hydrophones picked up the sound, and technicians were able to calculate nearly exactly when and where the explosion took place.

About 110 minutes after the mysterious nuclear blast, Ascension Island's SOSUS and MILS hydrophones suddenly detected a powerful signal, a "large impulsive release of energy" within "the deep South Atlantic sound channel"—that is, SOFAR. It was also picked up about 20 minutes later by another SOSUS station, this one at Argentia, Newfoundland, in Canada. Technicians were quickly able to triangulate the direction of the signal as emanating from the south-southeast. And given that hydroacoustic signals travel through the SOFAR channel at about five thousand feet per second, they could also calculate when the energy burst occurred. It took place at 00:52:00 UTC, almost identical to the time of the VELA 6911 detection, 00:53:43 UTC, which was 8:53 p.m. on the U.S. East Coast. The speed of the signal also allowed the technicians to determine that the event occurred about sixty-two hundred miles away. And given the south-southeast direction, that would have put it in a remote and isolated stretch of the South Atlantic near Antarctica. Far from any human inhabitation, or shipping and air routes, it was as close as one could come to a geographical void, terra incognita.

South of that void was Japan's Syowa Station on the eastern coast of Antarctica. A small, ice-covered base in Queen Maud Land, where the temperature has dropped to as low as minus 50 degrees Fahrenheit, its facilities included a satellite building as well as ionospheric and radiosonde stations. Among those wintering over was geophysicist Takeshi Morikawa from the Earthquake Research Institute of the University of Tokyo. At 00:52:10, almost the exact time that VELA 6911 detected the nuclear blast, a bright, colorful aurora lit up the sky above the station. A study by the Los Alamos Scientific Laboratory noted that "the Syowa auroral patch might have been caused by…a few-kiloton SNB [surface nuclear burst], detonated possibly at Prince Edward Island [no connection to the Canadian island of the same name] +/- 2,200 km [1,367 miles] north of Syowa." The blast generated an electromagnetic pulse in the ionosphere about a hundred kilometers northeast of Syowa.

———

In Washington at the time of the nuclear blast, President Jimmy Carter and First Lady Rosalynn Carter were sitting in a pair of plush red velvet armchairs in the bordello-like red-on-red White House movie theater. It was a place he spent more time at than any other president, watching 408 films during his single term, including *The Cat from Outer Space*. And that night he and the first lady were viewing the old 1960 Spencer Tracy flick *Inherit the Wind*, about the famous 1925 Scopes "monkey" trial. At 10:30 p.m., half an hour before AFTAC issued its pre-alert, they were in bed with the lights out.

At six the next morning, a pleasant Saturday with temperatures in the mid-70s, Carter received his usual wake-up call from the White House signal board operator and fifty-three minutes later walked into the Oval Office. At 9:17 he met for about ten minutes with Zbigniew Brzezinski, his national security advisor. But it wasn't until midafternoon that AFTAC developed enough corroborating detail about VELA 6911's discovery to send out a Flash message to the White House. At 2:50 p.m. the Situation Room duty officer notified Brzezinski "that according to a JAEIC [the CIA's Joint Atomic Energy Intelligence Center] statement a possible South African nuclear explosion had occurred." Brzezinski said he would notify the president and several other principals "and set-up a meeting of the matter ASAP." Four minutes later he called Carter, but the first lady answered, and he left a message. They finally connected at 4:56 p.m.

Twenty minutes earlier, the emergency "Mini-Special Coordination Committee Meeting" had begun in the White House Situation Room. Among those attending was Gerald Funk, the senior Africa specialist on the National Security Council. He had been called by Brzezinski, he said, and told to "get my *toucus* to work, that we had a bit of a problem." Others included the chairman of the Joint Atomic Energy Intelligence Committee.

The meeting was led by the National Security Council's Henry Owen, who summed up the evidence. There was "strong positive evidence" and "no negative evidence" indicating a nuclear blast. The assumption, said Funk, was "that there had been in fact a legitimate sighting…that satellite had never failed to react positively and had never given a false signal." Nevertheless, there was also deep concern that the United States may have been responsible. "Defense is to verify all U.S. strategic force locations so that we can be certain that no U.S. weapons accidentally exploded in the region," said Owens. "Defense will also check Soviet force locations for the same purpose."

At Patrick Air Force Base, two specially equipped WC-135B aircraft, code-named Constant Phoenix, were quickly scrambled to hunt for particulate nuclear debris and residue in the South Atlantic and over Antarctica. Known as "sniffers," they were modified Boeing 707s and belonged to AFTAC's Technical Operations Squadron. The on-board atmospheric collection systems and filters allow the crew to detect radioactive "clouds" in real time. Later joined by three other WC-135Bs, they would eventually conduct a total of twenty-five sorties totaling more than 230 hours of flying time within that remote void. In requesting from the government of the French island of Mauritius permission to operate out of their airfield, officials were simply told the planes were conducting weather missions.

That night, Carter and his family traveled by motorcade to Spring Hill, Brzezinski's secluded estate nearby in McLean, Virginia, for dinner, returning at 10:33 p.m. Shortly thereafter, as he did several times a day, Carter made a note in his private diary. "There was indication of a nuclear explosion in the region of South Africa," he wrote, "either South Africa, Israel using a ship at sea, or nothing."

The next day, the committee reconvened at 11 a.m. in the crowded Situation Room. For Brzezinski, it was his home away from home, his having once even judged a pumpkin-carving contest there. A briefing board had been sent over from CIA headquarters displaying the broad area where the blast took place. "Limited satellite detection information suggests that a nuclear explosion (1–3KT [kilotons]) probably occurred early Saturday morning in the South Atlantic, southern Indian Ocean, southern Africa, or Antarctica," said the notes. A decision was made to keep news of the clandestine nuclear detonation as secret as possible, only informing the top members of the House and Senate Intelligence Committees.

Eventually, as more and more evidence arrived, the spy agencies became unanimous in their view. "The Intelligence Community has high confidence, after intense technical scrutiny of satellite data, that a low yield atmospheric nuclear explosion occurred in the early morning hours of September 22," said a Secret/Sensitive Department of State document. It was prepared for a high-level White House meeting on October 23. The CIA agreed in a separate secret report, and "assessed the probability of a nuclear test as 90% plus."

Around the same time, doubts began to grow about the technical ability of South Africa to build and test a completed nuclear weapon. "[South Africa] had enough fissile material (95% enriched) to test in 1979," said Professor Anna-Mart van Wyk, a South African nuclear historian. "And had enough material to have assembled a bomb by the end of 1979, though may not have had enough for [both] a test and a bomb." Attention, as a result, turned to Israel. Dimona had long since ceased to be a secret, and the question wasn't whether Israel could construct a nuclear weapon, but how many it had already built. Both the State Department and CIA addressed the issue of Israel in their reports. "We must consider the possibility that Israel could have detonated a device in this remote geographical area," said State.

And addressing the issue of "A Secret Test by Israel," the CIA outlined a number of reasons why the state might have wanted to carry out a hidden nuclear test. Among them was "developing the fission trigger [an atom bomb] for a thermonuclear weapon [an H-bomb]... A low-yield nuclear test conducted clandestinely at sea could have enabled them to make basic measurements of the device's performance." It also considered as a possibility a joint Israel–South Africa nuclear test. "Clandestine arrangements between South Africa and Israel for joint testing operations might have been negotiable," it said, with South Africa providing Israel with logistical assistance.

Finally, the report noted, "Indeed, of all the countries which might have been responsible for the 22 September event, Israel would probably have been the only one for which a clandestine approach would have been virtually its only option."

The problem for Israel was the Glenn Amendment to the Arms Export Control Act passed by Congress in 1977. Aimed particularly at the nuclear pariah states, it mandated an end to arms assistance, and an automatic application of extensive U.S. sanctions, if the president determined that any state (other than the nuclear states authorized by the Nuclear Non-Proliferation Treaty) detonated a nuclear explosive after 1977. For Israel, it would mean an instant end to their annual $3.8 billion aid package, along with other harsh sanctions, such as travel restrictions. And that would not be good for Carter, since he was hoping to win reelection the following year and needed support from the Jewish community. He therefore had a political interest in ensuring that Israel's secrets remained secret, regardless of the detrimental effect on the United States and the world, by turning a blind eye to its nuclear lawlessness. Lawlessness that included turning Americans into spies and stealing U.S. nuclear materials, traitorous acts that could be punishable by death.

The concern over a potential Jewish backlash greatly troubled the president's top aide, Hamilton Jordan, according to Carter biographer Kai Bird. "Hamilton Jordan was specifically apprehensive about the 'Jewish lobby,'" noted Bird. In a candid and confidential 1977 memo to Carter, Jordan outlined the risks of offending the lobby. "We are aware of its strength and influence," he wrote, "but don't understand the basis for that strength nor the way that it is used politically." Money and power were key, he noted, pointing out that Jews made up less than 3 percent of the U.S. population but comprised 60 percent of the large donors to the Democratic Party.

Jordan then outlined the role of Israel in American politics. "When people talk about the 'Jewish lobby' as relates to Israel, they are referring to the American Israel Public Affairs Committee (AIPAC)." And AIPAC, said Jordan, had "one continuing priority—the welfare of the state of Israel as perceived by the American Jewish community." Among those in agreement was Carter aide David Rubenstein. "Ever since 1948," he said, "the Jewish American community thought it was their job to support Israel ninety-nine percent. You don't criticize the Israeli government." Outing it as a nuclear thief, or finally admitting its nuclear pariah status with its stash of illegal atomic bombs, something known by virtually everyone, verged on political suicide.

Beyond politics, American's national security was very much at risk. The Camp David peace accords between Israel and Egypt had concluded the previous March. But before the meetings, Egypt, Syria, and Iraq had made it clear to Carter that confirmation of a nuclear test by Israel would force them to also seek an Arab nuclear capability, if not war. A war that would certainly draw in and involve the United States.

Unlike plutonium, the secret of this clandestine nuclear test had a very short half-life, lasting barely a month. On the evening of October 25, ABC News correspondent John Scali let the atomic cat out of the bag on the network's nightly news program. And immediately, the Carter White House chose obfuscation and concealment over candor and honesty. The next day at a press conference, Secretary of State Cyrus Vance declared that "it is not clear that there has been a nuclear detonation," despite the unanimous opinion of the entire intelligence community that one had taken place. It was the political equivalent of "move along, there's nothing to see here," and a substantially different response than if Russia, or any other country, were suspected. It was also the opening lie in what would eventually become an elaborate cover-up.

Following the disclosure on ABC, the Carter White House began a series of briefings for members of Congress, attempting to downplay and raise questions about the evidence of the nuclear event. Among those attending some of the briefings was Leonard Weiss, the top aide to Ohio Democratic senator John Glenn, America's first person in space. Weiss had an extensive scientific background, having served for a number of years as a professor of mathematics and electrical engineering at Brown University and the University of Maryland. He therefore also acted as Glenn's chief advisor on the Senate Subcommittee on Energy and Nuclear Proliferation.

What astonished Weiss was the aggressiveness with which the Carter administration officials were attempting to shut down legitimate questions and inquiry into the VELA 6911 detection. At one point, Louis Nosenzo, a deputy assistant secretary of state, actually threatened him. "My questioning," said Weiss, "caused Louis Nosenzo, who was present at the briefing…to take me aside during a temporary recess of the briefing, and caution me that if I persisted in suggesting that a nuclear test had taken place, my reputation would suffer." He added, "I was surprised that a Carter State Department official would issue a veiled threat because of my view of the 'flash' expressed in a non-public setting. But all it did was to make the administration look desperate to me in its desire to promote a benign explanation for the Vela event."

What officials believed privately, however, was a different matter. At another point, during a party while Weiss and Glenn were chatting, they were approached by Gerald Smith, the U.S. representative for nonproliferation matters. According to Weiss, Glenn happened to mention that he thought that the Indian government had been " 'bad guys' on nonproliferation issues."

"At this," Weiss said, "Smith bristled and said, 'You think the Indians are bad guys? You want to talk about bad guys, talk about the Israelis!'" According to Weiss, "I think Smith may have been telling Glenn that he believed those analysts in the intelligence community who thought Israel was the most likely perpetrator."

Much to the chagrin of the White House, secret study after secret study confirmed that a clandestine nuclear detonation had taken place, including one convened by the CIA. Unwilling to accept the evidence and opinions of his own government agencies as they were coming in, all of which pointed unanimously to a nuclear detonation, with Israel as the likely culprit, Carter instead opted for a cover-up. The idea was to bury details of the blast, along with the identity of the likely perpetrator, under layers of Restricted Data secrecy, then establish his own panel, run by his own White House science advisor, and reporting only to Carter. The end goal was delay, confusion, and obfuscation until no one cared anymore. Carter's science advisor, Frank Press, picked nine scientists with a wide variety of backgrounds, histories, and disciplines. Then he chose an old friend, Jack Ruina, as chairman. A professor of electrical engineering and computer science at MIT, Ruina had once headed the Pentagon's Advanced Research Projects Agency.

The group began their work on November 1, and just a week later, after their first meeting, they had already come up with "preliminary results." Much to Carter's liking, they quickly rejected the nuclear detonation explanation and instead suggested the bhangmeters were triggered by a meteoroid, a theory rejected by previous studies. From then on, the panel seemed irritated that they had to listen to witness after witness from the intelligence and nuclear weapons communities present their evidence that a nuclear explosion had in fact taken place. The Arecibo scientists who detected the anomaly in the ionosphere referred to their meeting with the panel as "mass confusion" and "an exercise in distraction."

Among the members of the White House panel was Richard Garwin, who a few days after the VELA 6911 alert was convinced, by two-to-one odds, that the evidence indicated a nuclear detonation. But mysteriously, as more and more evidence began pouring in pointing to Israel as the perpetrator, he changed his mind. It would later come out that Garwin believed that Israel, and only Israel, is justified in maintaining a secret, illegal cache of nuclear weapons. "Israel certainly has more than 100, maybe 200 [nuclear weapons], and is the state among them all that needs nuclear weapons most," he said in 2008, "because they could easily be overrun by the populous neighboring states in a matter of hours without nuclear weapons." In fact, nuclear weapons aside, "Israel remains the most powerful and well-equipped military force in the region, supported by its strategic ally, the United States," according to the Institute for International and Strategic Studies. And according to a 2019 headline in the *Jerusalem Post*, "Israel ranks as the 8th most powerful country" in the world. As *Haaretz*'s Nir Gontarz noted, "It's an open secret that with regard to military power and military superiority, Israel is no longer the tiny David facing the giant Goliath. For several decades now, the roles have been reversed." Which raises the question, Why has U.S. defense funding remained at the same extraordinarily high levels?

By January 1980 the White House panel was ready to wrap up its work and issue its report rejecting the nuclear explosion explanation in favor of the meteoroid. But suddenly there was angry pushback from the spy agencies. Even CIA director Stansfield Turner never "bought" the panel report and had always believed that the Israelis were behind the nuclear detonation. The rebellion greatly worried the Carter White House, enough to make them re-review the evidence, if just to mollify the spy agencies. "They have sufficient doubts about the [White House] panel report to make it very dangerous to proceed without another look," said a secret internal White House memorandum.

As a result, it was decided to appease the intelligence community by extending the review. Otherwise, said the secret memo, "there will be continued internal dissent and an appearance that policy people (including the White House) did a whitewash for political reasons." Another secret memorandum referred to the intelligence officials derogatorily as "dissenters," as if they were refusing to proclaim a Kremlin-dictated explanation. A memorandum from White House staffer Jerry Oplinger confirmed the view of the intelligence community that the second review was simply for show. He wrote that the "main objective [of the new review] is to hear the dissenters out so that we can more safely ignore them."

In the end, Carter got what he wanted, although in private even he didn't believe the meteoroid explanation. Instead, in secret, he preferred the unanimous views of the intelligence community scientists. On February 27, 1980, as the panel was nearing completion of its report, Carter again made an entry in his private diary. "We have a growing belief among our scientists that the Israelis did indeed conduct a nuclear test explosion in the ocean near the southern end of South Africa." He would later note that during his time in the White House, he never intended his diary to ever become public. It was a decision he made much later after leaving office, a time when he no longer had to protect Israel in order to win votes and receive millions in donations.

In May, after a total of just three meetings, the panel completed its report. As it had concluded in its very first meeting, rather than having detected a nuclear explosion, VELA 6911 was instead the victim of a micrometeor impact. The White House quickly released the report to the press in the middle of Carter's presidential campaign. "For political reasons," Brzezinski responded years later when asked why Carter did what he did. The problem of confronting Israel, and thereby outraging AIPAC and the numerous other pro-Israel special interest groups, was eliminated. But it came at a high cost to the nation in terms of honor, credibility, and safety.

By 1979, at the time of the test, Dimona would likely have produced at least dozens, if not scores, of atomic bombs, which rely on fission, the splitting of an atom.

The next step would be to develop far more powerful thermonuclear hydrogen bombs, which use fusion, and are a thousand times more powerful than the early atomic bombs. Rather than destroying a few square miles of a city with a bomb measured in kilotons, thermonuclear weapons are designed to take out hundreds of square miles with megatons of destructive power. And critical would be supplying them all with professionally made triggers to make them explode, triggers identical to the ones developed for "Fat Man," the bulbous plutonium-fueled atom bomb dropped by the United States on the Japanese city of Nagasaki, killing upward of eighty thousand people.

The nuclear equivalent of blasting caps, the triggers, known as "krytrons," consist of cold-cathode gas-filled tubes and appear somewhat similar to small halogen lightbulbs, but with four long, thin electrodes at the bottom.

Despite their diminutive appearance, however, these triggers are highly complex instruments capable of emitting simultaneous high-powered electrical pulses in a fraction of a millionth of a second. The long, spidery electrodes are attached to detonators connected to the bomb's spherical shell, which is made up of thirty-two geometric-shaped high-velocity explosive charges arranged in a sort of soccer-ball pattern. Once the krytrons trigger the detonators, the simultaneous explosions create a massive shock wave that races inward to the weapon's plutonium core. Suddenly compressed to a supercritical state, the core implodes violently as it is heated to billions of degrees Celsius. That is followed by an enormous fireball, a mini-sun, as a shock wave simultaneously radiates outward. Then comes the familiar mushroom cloud and the widespread release of radiation. But it all starts with a krytron.

The men behind the development of the krytron were Dr. Harold Edgerton, Kenneth J. Germeshausen, and Herbert E. Grier. After the war they formed a company, EG&G Corporation, based in Massachusetts. Joining them was Bernard J. O'Keefe, who installed the krytrons on "Fat Man" before it was dropped on Nagasaki. In addition to selling a variety of advanced electrical equipment, EG&G was the only company in the world that offered the highly restricted krytrons. EG&G, therefore, had now become Blumberg and Milchan's top target.

What they needed was a secret American agent to operate a clandestine U.S.-based front company like NUMEC, which covertly supplied Israel with weapons-grade uranium. A company that could legally order the krytrons, and then illegally ship them to Israel. That was where Richard Kelly Smyth came in.

CHAPTER 15

The Triggerman

Arnon Milchan had finally bought his way into the big time as a Hollywood producer. Seated on a chair on the seventh floor of a midtown Manhattan office building, the headquarters of Murjani, the maker of Gloria Vanderbilt jeans, he was watching his $19 million in action. Leased by the production company, the reception area had been repainted a deep blue and silver white to turn it into a set for *The King of Comedy*. Off to the side, director Martin Scorsese, in T-shirt and jeans, took sips from a Styrofoam cup of iced tea. Robert De Niro, in a pair of slightly baggy poplin trousers, Japanese zori slippers, and a blue chambray shirt, rested on a folding chair. Suddenly, beneath a straw Stetson, assistant director Scott Maitland yelled, "Quiet." Scorsese shouted, "Action." And De Niro, a thin pencil mustache beneath his nose, rose and stepped into character as Rupert Pupkin, a deranged amateur stand-up comedian hungry for fame.

As Milchan was pouring millions into *The King of Comedy* to become a Hollywood producer, he was also dumping hundreds of thousands of dollars into a New York theater to become a Broadway producer. There his play was *It's So Nice to Be Civilized*, a musical that opened at the lavishly decorated, Moorish-inspired Martin Beck Theatre in the heart of the theater district. Unfortunately, the production closed for good just eight performances later. "The show," a *New York Times* reviewer wrote, "never appears to know what it is, or where it is going."

Much the same could have been said about Milchan. In the end, *The King of Comedy* would likewise bomb badly at the box office, earning back a mere $1.2 million from Milchan's $19 million investment.

But Milchan the operative had other things on his mind, namely the FBI. All while the FBI was chasing their tails.

The small blue-collar community of Parks Township sits along the banks of Pennsylvania's winding Kiskiminetas River, a gentle, dark blue ribbon that occasionally gives way to foamy whitewater rapids deep in the state's coal country. Known to the locals simply as the Kiski, its twenty-seven miles are bordered by old mill towns and thick, dense woods where white-tailed deer and osprey are a frequent sight. In the village of 2,744 people and fourteen square miles, the major event is the annual Kidspalooza festival sponsored by the local fire department, Kochka Towing Company, Big Dogs Performance, and other local businesses.

Residents were therefore shocked when suddenly one day in September 2011 a number of U.S. Homeland Security vehicles arrived, lights flashing, and men clad in uniforms and armed with high-caliber military assault rifles jumped out. They took up a perimeter around an empty field as workers began erecting a tall chain-link fence topped with barbed wire. Signs were attached warning "Danger: Radioactive Materials." What was once a place to walk and play ball was now a very dangerous no-man's-land.

Buried just below the surface, the Kiski valley townsfolk would eventually learn, was a witches' brew of potentially deadly nuclear-weapons-related chemicals, enough to make dirty bombs, which was the reason for the 24/7 armed presence. The chemicals included americium-241, radium-228, uranium-235, and various types of plutonium. That may also have explained, residents feared, their high rates of suffering and dying from various cancers, including those of the lung, thyroid, prostate, and brain—sicknesses resulting from decades of radiation soaking into their soil, air, water, and clothes.

Decades earlier, a building on that site had produced deadly plutonium, and another five miles down the road in the small town of Apollo, manufactured bomb-grade uranium. They belonged to the Nuclear Materials and Equipment Corporation, or NUMEC, which secretly provided Israel with regular supplies of highly enriched uranium. It also served as Israel's nuclear dump. Shallow trenches in the field became the graveyard for the radioactive waste, products with half-lives of twenty-four thousand years. An inspection by the Nuclear Regulatory Commission would conclude that NUMEC was "devoid of adequate physical safeguards to insure proper handling of the nuclear material." And "even the trees and bushes surrounding NUMEC would be covered by a white residue indicating obvious losses of [radioactive] material," said another report. Still another inspection, by Oak Ridge National Laboratory, simply labeled NUMEC "a dirty operation."

Stretching along several blocks of Apollo's main street, the facility was an odd and dangerous place to locate a nuclear plant. Just outside the door was Warren Avenue, and across the street was a residential neighborhood of handsome Victorian houses with broad porches dotted with tan wicker chairs. Years later, many of those residents would become tragic victims of NUMEC.

With Dimona in the early stages of development, it would take years to produce the critical cores of the Israeli nuclear bombs, which at first were made of highly enriched uranium and later of plutonium. A much quicker way would be to steal the nuclear materials from the United States, and Benjamin Blumberg therefore took aim at NUMEC. As the country's first privately owned plutonium development and fabrication plant, it had far less security and oversight than government operations, making it an ideal target, especially since it was run by people with secret ties to Israel. After decades of enormous secrecy, only recently have a number of key CIA and FBI documents been released shedding light on the covert Israeli operation. Thousands of additional documents remain locked in vaults and buried under multiple security classifications.

NUMEC's president was Zalman Shapiro, who also served for a time as president of the local Pittsburgh chapter of the Zionist Organization of America. Thick-chested, with brown hair, a high forehead, and dark horn-rimmed glasses, he was born in 1920 and grew up the son of a Russian-born rabbi in an Orthodox Jewish home in New Jersey. Avoiding military service during World War II, in 1948 he earned a Ph.D. in chemistry from Johns Hopkins University. With very close ties to the Israeli nuclear scientists involved in the secret nuclear program at Dimona, by the mid-1970s he had become the chief suspect in the unexplained loss of five hundred pounds of highly enriched uranium from the plant.

"The relationship of the company's president," said Thomas Bullock, a supervisor in the plutonium plant, "with the Israelis opened speculation as to how they obtained a large quantity of HEU [Highly Enriched Uranium] for their atomic bomb program. Hundreds of pounds of HEU missing from the Apollo plant were written off as normal production losses, or material unaccounted for." Among other things, according to Bullock, "At NUMEC we processed hundreds of kilograms of plutonium."

What was strange, however, given the secrecy and sensitivity of the plant, were the comings and goings of numerous Israelis. "There was," said Bullock, "a contingent of Israelis as part of a technology exchange between Israel and the United States." Soon after NUMEC opened its doors, Shapiro entered into an agreement to provide technical assistance to the Israeli Atomic Energy Commission, the cover for the country's secret nuclear program.

Bullock spent thirty-five years as an engineer involved in nuclear weapons production and previously worked at the U.S. government's Hanford,

Washington, facility, which produced the plutonium "pits" for hydrogen bombs. He described NUMEC's appalling safety and security conditions, which at times were both reckless and highly dangerous. "The first attempt at oxidizing metal plutonium was a near disaster," he said. "We first tried to oxidize a whole 2.5 kg [5.5-pound] button in a copper-bottomed frying pan from a hardware store in Leechburg...and ignited it with a barbecue starter." The plutonium then began to burn and melted out the bottom of the frying pan and nearly burned a hole in the surrounding containment box. "We ended up with a glob of plutonium/steel/copper," said Bullock.

At other times, the containment units, known as gloveboxes, exploded, dispersing plutonium and injuring and heavily contaminating employees. Still another employee accidentally had his hand cut off inside a plutonium glovebox. "NUMEC gave the [Pittsburgh Presbyterian-University] hospital a lot of hands-on experience in treating plutonium-contaminated patients," said Bullock. Outlets for the radioactive nuclear residue to escape included "the numerous exhaust stacks, the river, and waste drums shipped off site, or buried in a field behind the plutonium plant." Inside, he said, "Fumes from the chemical conversion process permeated the open bay." Security was also a joke, with not even a fence around the plutonium plant.

As for the CIA, the evidence was clear. At the time, the agency's chief of station in Tel Aviv was John Lloyd Hadden, newly arrived from Germany. A well-built man of average height, he had a twice-broken nose and black shiny hair, slicked back with Vitalis. His cover was a midlevel diplomat, a second secretary, and his office was behind a cipher-locked door on the top floor at the embassy. Following a supposed "picnic" with his family near Dimona, Hadden covertly collected samples of nuclear residue from around the plant.

A chemical analysis of the material then directly linked the uranium being used at the nuclear plant with that from NUMEC, a conclusion that caused CIA director Richard Helms to notify the Justice Department. "Given the aforementioned circumstances," he wrote, "I urge that the Federal Bureau of Investigation be called upon to initiate a discreet intelligence investigation of an all-source nature of Dr. Shapiro in order to establish the nature and extent of his relationship with the Government of Israel."

Soon, every morning a local FBI agent began tailing Shapiro's dark blue Buick Electra from his brick home in Pittsburgh to his plant in Apollo, and then back every night. "He is known to generally travel at a very high rate of speed," noted the agent, who was forced to press hard on the accelerator to keep up. Other agents tapped his phone. Adding to the suspicion were mysterious visits to the plant by high-ranking Israeli intelligence agents, including

Raphael (Rafi) Eitan, who would take over LAKAM. "Source advised that [Shapiro] is closely associated with high-ranking officials of the Israeli Government and recently he observed photographs of [Shapiro] shaking hands with Ben Gurion and Moshe Dayan in Israel," said one report.

Shapiro and some of his supporters tried to claim that the nuclear materials simply vanished into thin air, but the scientists at the CIA weren't buying it. "The clear consensus of CIA was indeed that the most likely case was that indeed NUMEC material had been diverted and had been used by the Israelis in fabricating weapons," said Carl E. Duckett, the CIA's deputy director for science and technology at the time. "I certainly believe that to be the case...I believe that all of my senior analysts who worked on the problem agreed with me fully." Glenn R. Cella, the political-military affairs officer on the Israel desk at the State Department during the early 1970s, saw the espionage close up. "They have this vast network of sympathizers who are willing to do pretty much anything that the Israelis ask," he said. "We're talking about leading edge developments, technological developments and that sort of thing, real breakthroughs. I think it's true that they don't have to conduct espionage the way any other country would do it."

The problem with making an arrest, however, was not a lack of evidence, but special interest politics. According to John Davitt, the longtime head of the Justice Department's internal security section until his retirement in 1980, Israeli intelligence services were "more active than anyone but the KGB." Another senior FBI counterintelligence official, Raymond Wannal, said that he knew of at least a dozen incidents in which American officials transferred classified information to the Israelis but the Justice Department declined to prosecute.

And a secret CIA document on Israel's "Foreign Intelligence and Security Services" noted that two of Israel's first three intelligence priorities involved the United States. The report went on to extensively detail the methods of operation for Israeli intelligence organizations, noting how, in the United States, they target almost exclusively Jewish citizens for recruitment as spies. "The Israeli intelligence representatives usually operate discreetly within Jewish communities...The Israelis select their agents almost exclusively from persons of Jewish origin...The recruitment of Gentiles is comparatively rare."

Soon after taking office in 1976, President Jimmy Carter learned the secret details behind the NUMEC investigation, and he ordered one of his National Security Council staffers, Jessica Mathews, to investigate. Immediately she ran into a series of roadblocks, with both the FBI and CIA refusing to release documents to her until, she said, I "had a handwritten note literally from [the] president." It was only then that she was able to finally see the complete picture.

"So I carried this note around, my hall pass, and this time they did talk, and the first thing that was most clear was that neither agency had spoken to the other, and they were principally concerned about keeping what they knew from the other. I mean, it was extraordinary. But I came back with some pretty clear conclusions from it. My conclusion was that the material did come from the Apollo Plant in Pennsylvania and that we had pretty good evidence." Nevertheless, as with Israel's secret nuclear test, Carter would prefer political cover-up to political courage. "Who shut off the investigations?" a frustrated John Hadden would ask.

In the end, NUMEC left a grim legacy. "Both the Apollo uranium and Parks Township plutonium plants were decontaminated and dismantled," said Bullock, the former plutonium supervisor. "But the notoriety about its operations and lasting radiation caused health concerns [to] continue." The local newspaper, the *Valley News Dispatch*, conducted a yearlong investigation involving reviewing thousands of documents and interviews with scores of people whose lives were affected by the now defunct company. "As reported in the paper, lawsuits, and in claims to the federal government," said Bullock, "several hundred Kiski valley workers employed at NUMEC died or have illnesses attributed to nuclear fuel processing."

Many others in the surrounding communities met similar fates. Among the victims is Patty Ameno, a Navy veteran and former Defense Department investigator who grew up right across the street from the Apollo facility and suffered from several bouts of cancer. For more than three decades Ameno battled the company's owners and successfully helped organize litigation, including lawsuits that have resulted in over $80 million in payments to her and scores of neighbors who have demonstrated illnesses from the radioactive contamination.

Not content, Ameno also relentlessly badgered federal bureaucrats until Congress finally enacted a law requiring a cleanup of NUMEC's deadly mess—one in which Israel secretly played a major role and derived great benefit from the theft of nuclear materials. But it will be the American taxpayers who will be stuck with the final bill for the cleanup, estimated at half a billion dollars. No cost can be put on the lives lost or the pain suffered. Sadly, about 40 percent of the claimants had died by the time the lawsuits were settled.

There is, noted CNN's Wolf Blitzer, "a widely held attitude among Israeli officials that Israel can get away with the most outrageous things. There is a notion among many Israelis that their American counterparts are not too bright, that they can be 'handled' thanks partially to the pro-Israel lobby's

clout in Congress." Blitzer should know, having previously served as the editor of AIPAC's propaganda arm, *Near East Report*, the newsletter mailed to
the group's membership every week. And two veterans of the AEC and the
NRC, Victor Gilinsky, a physicist, and Roger J. Mattson, who led the NRC
task force investigation of NUMEC, decried the government's historical
blind-eye approach to Israel: "Perhaps the most worrisome aspect of the
NUMEC affair is that the government itself did not seem to want to find out
what happened because it feared the answer."

Now Arnon Milchan was hoping that the same powerful political pressure groups and special interests that kept the FBI at arm's length from his
fellow LAKAM spy at NUMEC would do the same for him in Hollywood.

From Milchan's hangout at Hollywood's Chateau Marmont, it was a forty-
five-minute drive to his front company in the oceanside community of Huntington Beach. Named Milco International, it acted as Israel's hidden supplier
of technical equipment for its nuclear program and was run by an American
agent Milchan had recruited years earlier, Richard Kelly Smyth.

The two first met in 1970, when Smyth arrived in Tel Aviv as the new
Middle East regional manager for Autonetics, a major American aerospace
manufacturer before it merged into North American Rockwell and later
Rockwell International. Landing at Ben Gurion International Airport, Smyth
got into the crowded passport line, exhausted after his long flight from Los
Angeles to Frankfurt and then to Tel Aviv. In his early forties, he had a bushy
brown mustache graying on the sides, and a receding hairline also beginning
to turn the color of stone.

A talented engineer, Smyth had attended Caltech on several scholarships,
graduating with a degree in physics. For spending money, he ran the dorm
laundry and acted as a part-time chauffeur for an elderly woman, studying
as she popped in to visit friends. Eventually he received a Ph.D. in electrical engineering and mathematics from the University of Southern California while working for Autonetics. There he became an expert in designing
guidance control systems for aircraft and missiles and was named the chief
engineer of avionics for the F-111 fighter. Now his job was drumming up
new business in the volatile Middle East, which meant seeking contracts with
the oil-rich Arab countries. However, inducing them to go with Autonetics meant decreasing business with Israel, which provided relatively little
income. Passing on that message to his Israeli customer, the Ministry of
Defense, was one of the reasons for the trip.

Blumberg and Milchan, however, had other ideas. During a meeting
before Smyth's arrival, they discussed ways to turn him into Milchan's spy.

Pay close attention to his weaknesses and vulnerabilities and use them to Israel's advantage, Blumberg told Milchan. And chief among those would be money. Although Smyth was a well-paid executive, he was also in financial difficulty. It was a fact that would have been easily discovered by Israel's intelligence agents at its Los Angeles consulate, a hotbed of espionage.

Several years earlier Smith had quit Autonetics and used the family's savings to purchase his father-in-law's failing business, a wholesale refrigeration company. Thinking he could revive it, Smyth traveled around the world looking for customers, but found few. The company, said his wife, Emilie, "continued to lose money in spite of all Richard's efforts." For a family man with five children; an expensive waterfront home at 16532 Cotuit Circle in Huntington Harbour, an exclusive island near Los Angeles; and a thirty-six-foot masthead sloop named *Pleiades* docked at the Cabrillo Beach Yacht Club where he once served as commodore, times became tough. "We put our house up for sale to get money to pay for the bills piling up," said Emilie, who went to work as a first- and second-grade teacher to help pay the bills. Eventually, Smyth's father-in-law took the company back, but for no money, leaving the engineer to lick his financial wounds as he rejoined Autonetics.

For Blumberg and Milchan, Smyth was to become their front man in California in order to get them the supplies they needed for their missiles and atomic bombs, especially the nuclear triggers. First, however, they needed him to make a lot of money for Israel, and for Milchan, in a series of contracts already largely arranged in Iran. What was missing, however, was a major American weapons contractor as a partner since Israeli companies were too small. At the time, Iran was controlled by Shah Mohammad Reza Pahlavi, who was friendly to both the United States and Israel. And the shah was looking to spend half a billion dollars on a secret plan to build a series of both land-based and airborne surveillance platforms, code-named Ibex, to watch and eavesdrop on the activities across his borders. The shah was in the market for a major American defense contractor to carry it out, and Israel wanted a piece of the action. That would be Richard Kelly Smyth's role, although he did not yet know it.

Milchan, whose cover was acting as Israel's business agent for Autonetics, spotted Smyth in the line at the airport and gave him a warm bear-hug greeting. He then immediately whisked him past the crowd directly to the passport control station, and minutes later to his red Chevrolet convertible illegally parked at the curb, greatly impressing the visitor, which was the idea. From the airport, Milchan drove Smyth to the Tel Aviv Hilton, the brutalist concrete leviathan that dominated the city's coast, for a night's rest.

The next day, Milchan told Smyth that he was well aware of the situation, that Autonetics needed to switch its focus from Israel to the rest of the Middle East. But, he said, they had a new plan that would make Autonetics very happy. Informed of Iran's half-billion-dollar project IBEX, Smyth was told that Israel would be willing to use its considerable influence to make sure that Autonetics/Rockwell landed the deal. In return, the company would need to assure Israel that its state-owned company, Israel Aircraft Industries (later Israel Aerospace Industries), would get 20 percent, $100 million, as a subcontractor for supplying the antenna systems.

Smyth's original trip to Tel Aviv was to inform the Israelis that their business was too small for their company. Now he had to worry whether the potential new business was instead too big. But those were the kind of worries he knew his bosses would like. That night, Milchan picked him up at the Hilton and took him to dinner at one of the two best restaurants in town, the Alhambra in Jaffa. Its long nouvelle French and North African menu offered such specialties as warm goose liver slices, mushrooms, and pine nuts on a bed of sorrel in a vinaigrette dressing. Sitting at a nearby table with several guests was another friend of Milchan, Defense Minister Moshe Dayan. And in an action that was likely prearranged, Milchan introduced him to Smyth, just as he had with Robert De Niro. The meeting gave Milchan another chance to impress Smyth, and to allow Dayan an opportunity to briefly size up LAKAM's potential American recruit.

Eventually the deal was made, and while Israel made at least $100 million off the shah, Milchan also increased his wealth considerably with side contracts. Then came Act II, the pitch.

 · Milchan attempted to convince Smyth to leave Rockwell and, with Milchan's money and behind-the-scenes help, establish his own company in the center of the defense and aerospace industry in California. By then, Smyth had come to admire the young Milchan, who was making millions on deals, driving expensive cars, eating in the best restaurants, and seeming to know everyone of importance. He had tried to make it on his own earlier, but that was selling refrigerators from a dying company. Now Milchan had promised that he would become rich from all the orders he would fill as Israel's military and defense needs continued to grow.

Smyth agreed and in January 1973 named the company Milco International, which stood for "Milchan's company," since in reality it was little more than his covert Israeli front. At first Smyth operated the company part-time from his bedroom while also working for Rockwell, but a year later he quit and set up a storefront office in Huntington Beach. Under the deal, Milchan would supply about 80 percent of its business and receive 60 percent of the profits from those deals, with 40 percent going to Smyth. Milchan would also pay Smyth's expenses.

Soon, through Smyth's U.S. back door, Israel began obtaining questionable technology that might cause suspicion if purchased directly from the Pentagon or from other companies, including critical products for Israel's ballistic missile program. Among them were barrels of butyl, a compound used to bind explosive powders into solid rocket fuel. The material was destined for the Jericho, a solid-fuel tactical missile capable of launching a nuclear warhead. As part of a concealment effort, Smyth used code names for many of the items sent to Milchan, such as "mirror" for a laser, "Carl" for a radar system, and "refrigerator" for oscilloscopes.

And most important now that the bombs were being built, Milchan needed to find a way to steal American-made nuclear triggers to make them detonate. Convinced that his Milco International channel was running without any hitches, in 1975 Milchan decided it was time for Project Pinto, his code name for the operation to smuggle hundreds of the forbidden krytrons to Israel. Smyth was therefore asked to place an order for four hundred of the "pintos" with EG&G. He was then instructed to ship them to Milchan's Tel Aviv business, Heli Trading Company, a front for LAKAM. The "end user" was listed as Rehovot Instruments Ltd., and to mask their true purpose, Smyth indicated that they would be used as "remotely located intrusion detectors."

By now the CIA was well aware of Smyth's trips to Israel. Although the agency was not allowed any law enforcement authority in the United States, as with the FBI, as part of their standard domestic contacts program a CIA officer would routinely connect with Smyth to see if he had any information of intelligence value. Smyth therefore told the CIA officer, Ron Romano, that "Arnon Milchan [had] requested that a certain number of krytrons be shipped to Israel." The officer, aware of the restrictions, warned Smyth that he needed to obtain a munitions control license from the State Department. Smyth complied and, as might have been expected, such a large order set off alarms at the U.S. Nuclear Regulatory Commission. After a call from an official, Marvin Peterson, who recommended that the Israeli government certify that the "end use" would be nonnuclear, Smyth reduced the request to twenty krytrons. The request went through a special interagency Middle East Task Force that had been set up to monitor U.S. arms transfers and the Pentagon representative simply rubber-stamped an approval.

But then, unfortunately for Milchan, it came across the desk of Glenn R. Cella, the State Department's member of the team. A veteran foreign service officer with tours of duty in Morocco, Egypt, and Algeria, he handled political-military affairs on the State Department's Israel desk. Over the years, he had become appalled at the institutional "look the other way" attitude when it came to Israel and its illegal development of a nuclear bomb. He quickly caught the mistake and prohibited the shipment.

In addition to stopping the shipment of the krytrons, Cella was holding up a long list of other potentially restricted items Israel was hoping to quietly slip past the committee. Unsurprisingly, Cella's actions greatly angered Israel's Washington ambassador, and future prime minister, Yitzhak Rabin. Playing Israel's political card, he began calling friendly members of Congress, virtually all of whom received large donations from pro-Israel organizations and political action committees, to complain. They, in turn, put pressure on senior State Department officials.

Preventing the illegal shipment of restricted weapons-related items to Israel was an endless struggle, according to Cella, who was one of the few with the courage to speak out about it. "They have total contempt for our spineless system, in my judgment. Yes, there were a few cases where they didn't do things that we didn't want them to do, but in general they got their way and got their way rather easily." It was politics, not national security, that mattered, he said. "They could count on the automatic support of 76 senators, automatic."

On top of that, said Cella, was the constant slandering of people who actually tried to do their duty and hold Israel to account, especially regarding their development of nuclear weapons. "I thought we ought to face up to the fact that they had [the atomic bomb], but nobody was allowed to talk about it," he said. "Anything that was seen as even remotely critical to Israel is branded as anti-Semitic. And something that perplexes me very much is the way the anti-Semitic label is used to intimidate people, or to apply a gag on what should be honest and open debate." It was a frustration he shared with a friend, John Hadden, who was engaged in the same battles across the Potomac at CIA headquarters.

The agency's former Tel Aviv chief of station, Hadden had been confronted with the problem while attempting to warn of Israel's theft of bomb-grade uranium from NUMEC. Now he was the CIA's senior Middle East analyst and still up against Israel's iron grip on U.S. policies. Early one evening he and Cella took a walk across Washington's Memorial Bridge, which ran over the Potomac between the Lincoln Memorial and Arlington National Cemetery. Under the dim streetlights, Cella turned serious and asked the CIA official a question. "Do you think there's any chance that the Israelis would assassinate me?" he said. Hadden shook his head. "No," he replied. "They're pretty confident they're going to get what they want in the end anyway so why run any risk whatsoever in, you know, poisoning Glenn Cella's Sanka?"

As a result of Cella, rather than receiving his nuclear triggers, Milchan instead received several surprise visitors at his office door in Tel Aviv. They were officials from the U.S. embassy who told Milchan he would have to cancel his order for krytrons. No doubt shocked by this American cold call, Milchan later that day contacted Smyth and complied. Not being informed about the visit, Smyth simply assumed Milchan had changed his mind. "Richard was unhappy because he had counted on the money he would make for shipping the krytrons to Arnon to put in his little business," said Emilie, Smyth's wife.

Nevertheless, over the years Milchan would continue sending Smyth coded messages requesting other military-related items as his business grew. In the meantime, both Blumberg and Milchan knew that people in government jobs are constantly in motion, changing positions along with promotions, transfers, and new opportunities. Therefore, it was just a matter of time before the bureaucrat who halted the trigger shipment would be gone, and likely replaced by another bureaucrat, and then Israel gets what it wants, one way or another, American laws and national security notwithstanding.

CHAPTER 16

◆

The Pitch

Milchan's first attempt at smuggling the krytrons failed because of a single diligent bureaucrat, State Department official Glenn R. Cella. Now, four years later, in 1979, Milchan pushed Smyth hard to try again, telling him Blumberg needed over a thousand of the triggers.

This time Smyth would avoid the problematic bureaucrat by illegally bypassing the required munitions control license and State Department approval process. Rather than krytrons, he would fraudulently list them instead as "pentodes." Although they were small glass electrical tubes like krytrons, pentodes were simple voltage amplifiers and had no weapons-related functions. Therefore, they required only an approval from the Commerce Department rather than a munitions license from State.

Becoming a smuggler of nuclear triggers was a very risky move for a family man like Smyth. His five children, some of whom also worked at his small company, along with his wife, could easily be implicated.

The krytron order was eventually handled by Smyth's son, who either didn't know about Milchan's warning or forgot. As a result, on October 1, 1979, less than ten days after the secret Israeli nuclear test, Ernest Smyth sent a telex to Milchan's Tel Aviv office quoting a price of $46,200 for a total of twelve hundred krytrons. "Hope to receive delivery schedule this week," wrote Smyth. "Will forward it to you upon its arrival." Smyth suddenly realized the error, Milchan's insistence on small orders, and twenty-three minutes later sent a telex to Milchan's assistant in Tel Aviv, Dvora Ben-Itzhak, asking for a time and phone number where he could quickly reach Milchan. Eventually Milchan wrote back, "As pointed out during your visit, no further inquiries for price quote of larger quantities should have been made." He added, "This is of utmost importance." It was eventually agreed that for security, each order would contain just fifty krytrons.

Finally, on January 7, 1980, a truck from Overseas Airfreight arrived at Milco International, a bland office in an industrial strip at 15628 Graham

Street in Huntington Beach, California, to pick up the one-pound package. Hours later it was on Lufthansa Airways Flight 604 to Israel with a stopover in Frankfurt. The destination was Heli Trading Company, Ltd., Milchan's LAKAM front company, at 29 Carlebach Street in Tel Aviv. It would be the first shipment of the planned twelve hundred krytrons. Yet with highly restricted nuclear triggers leaving the country for a rogue foreign nuclear state, the question is, where was the FBI or the CIA? Especially since Smyth had earlier attempted to acquire them without the proper license.

As the shipments began arriving without interference, Milchan's assistant, Ben-Itzhak, would simply take them next door to Blumberg's secret LAKAM headquarters. In the meantime, Milchan turned his attention to finding and recruiting Americans who were expert in the secret workings of thermonuclear weapons and ballistic missiles. For that, Smyth would also be crucial, and they would frequently get together for dinner to discuss strategies. The idea was to identify the experts and then invite them to become members of Milco International's board of directors. That, in turn, would give Smyth an opportunity to introduce the experts to Milchan. And Milchan would then seduce them with dinners and parties packed with his growing stable of high-profile stars like De Niro and magazine-cover models. "Anyone who lives in California is a star-fucker," Milchan said of his plan. "They hear 'star,' they come running."

At the top of the list of potential recruits was Dr. Arthur T. Biehl, likely chosen by Blumberg. Few people knew as much about the design of thermonuclear weapons, or the United States' current hyper-secret nuclear war plan. He was there at the very beginning. In the early 1950s, Biehl worked alongside Edward Teller, known as "the father of the hydrogen bomb," at what is now Lawrence Livermore National Laboratory. Also working with the two was Harold Brown, who was now President Jimmy Carter's secretary of defense. At the top, it was a very small, close-knit group.

In addition, Biehl was one of the few people in the country with the very highest security clearances due to his position on the Joint Strategic Target Planning Staff's Scientific Advisory Group. Known as the "targeteers," the 350 members of the JSTPS are the people who decide who will live and who will die in World War III. Their nuclear war plan, known as the Single Integrated Operational Plan, or SIOP, contains the hyper-secret National Strategic Target List. It details which H-bombs will target and destroy which cities from an ever-changing list of approximately four thousand "desired ground zeros" (DGZs) in Strangelovian SIOP-talk. They are the documents assembled in a binder known as the "Blue Book" that is always just a few feet from the president in the thick black briefcase nicknamed "the football."

Smyth and Biehl crossed paths a number of times over the years. Both had top secret clearances and belonged to the Air Force Scientific Advisory Board. And both also were experienced yachtsmen who competed in a number of Transpac races from Los Angeles to Honolulu, Biehl in his thirty-seven-foot sloop named *Quasar*, and Smyth in his thirty-six-foot masthead sloop, *Pleiades*. Nevertheless, it was rather unusual for Smyth to invite Biehl to join his small board of directors. But Biehl believed that Milco International's primary business was developing aerospace software for U.S. military and space programs, and in 1980 he agreed to join. For Israel, turning Biehl into a clandestine agent could give them enormous insight into America's most secret H-bomb program, as well as its current nuclear war plan.

Shortly thereafter, another person was roped in as a board member, Dr. Ivan Getting, who was a founding member of the Air Force Scientific Advisory Board. It was where he, Smyth, and Biehl first came together. Getting later became the chief scientist for the Air Force. At the time he joined Milco's board, he had no way of knowing it was a clandestine Israel front company. Shortly before, Getting retired as president of the Aerospace Corporation, a company he founded in 1960. There are few organizations more secret. Its principal function is providing technical support to the super-secret National Reconnaissance Office, which runs the country's spy satellite program, as well as other highly classified space and missile projects. Like both Smyth and Biehl, Getting was an avid sailor aboard *Sirena*, his fifty-foot wooden sloop.

Still another person Smyth recruited for his board was Robert Mainhardt, who had been in charge of the materials laboratory for the atomic bomb program in Los Alamos, and afterward worked at the Atomic Energy Commission's intelligence division. He later became a partner with Arthur Biehl in MB Associates. Among the dozens of classified projects they developed was the Gyrojet pistol. For use in clandestine operations, it fired miniature rockets called microjets.

Focusing first on Biehl, Milchan's idea for turning the H-bomb designer into a spy was to invite him and Smyth to several dinner parties at the home of Richard Dreyfuss, who throughout the 1970s was one of Hollywood's most successful actors. Among his most popular films were *Jaws*, *Close Encounters of the Third Kind*, and *The Goodbye Girl*, for which he won a Best Actor Oscar at the age of twenty-nine. In *Close Encounters*, Dreyfuss played an electrical lineman in Muncie, Indiana, who has a close encounter with a UFO and thereafter becomes obsessed by it. Later, U.S. government scientists attempt to communicate with the alien spacecraft using mathematics in the form of light, colors, and musical tones. So Milchan convinced Biehl to come to the dinner parties by telling him that Dreyfuss needed some help on another project involving music in which Biehl's mathematical skills were needed. The story made little sense, but Biehl nevertheless agreed. And Dreyfuss had no knowledge that Milchan was using him as a shill to recruit an Israeli spy, and thereby subjecting him to possible arrest as a co-conspirator.

Disproving Milchan's theory that "anyone who lives in California is a star-fucker," and "they hear 'star,' they come running," Biehl decided instead to run the other way. He began to suspect that Milco International was what it was: an Israeli front company. Rather than software for the U.S. space program, Smyth was purchasing items such as "green salt," a product that can be processed by centrifuges into weapons-grade uranium. Then Biehl began peppering Smyth with questions about proper compliance with export regulations, and why so many shipments were going to Israel, and what's the deal with this Israeli Milchan?

Fearful of losing Biehl or, worse, having him talk to the FBI, Milchan and Blumberg changed tactics. Biehl was invited to another dinner with Milchan and Smyth. But this time it was at the nail-polish-pink Beverly Hills Hotel, where Milchan had moved from Chateau Marmont. They met in the Polo Lounge, a haven for celebrities with its deep forest green banquettes, pink tablecloths, and plug-in phones. It was an appropriate venue, having been used by another of Milchan's spies, Sydney Pollack, to film scenes with Barbara Streisand and Robert Redford in *The Way We Were*.

In a darkened corner beneath the candy-striped ceiling, Biehl took his seat and shook hands with a graying, middle-aged Israeli introduced only as "Benny." "He's maybe the third most powerful man in Israel," Smyth gushed, as Benjamin Blumberg, Milchan's spymaster, began sizing up ways to recruit the H-bomb designer. What followed was Blumberg's standard flag-waving, pro-Israel sales pitch, but Biehl wasn't buying.

Ivan Getting had also become very suspicious, especially after he was asked to help Israel obtain missile-range instrumentation radars by escorting a pair of Israelis to several major defense contractors, including RCA and Raytheon.

Instead, both resigned from Milco International's board of directors. Robert Mainhardt stayed on the board for a while, but he also resigned after Smyth began pressuring him for details on an advanced nuclear reactor. "That's it for me," he said later. "I know espionage laws. I grew up in Los Alamos [as head of the materials laboratory] when we were putting together the first atomic bomb. Klaus Fuchs was my dorm-mate and David Greenglass was one of my best friends," he said, referring to two of the Soviet spies who helped steal atomic bomb secrets. "So, I know espionage."

Blumberg's failure to recruit Biehl and the others would be his swan song.

Shortly afterward, incoming defense minister Ariel Sharon unceremoniously tossed him out in the cold. "I never even saw Sharon," said Blumberg. "I was driving north to Tel Aviv and on the way I heard on the radio that Sharon plans to replace three senior officials. I had a bad feeling. I stopped by and I called from the pay phone to someone who told me that Sharon had fired me. So that's when I knew I was fired after 40 years of defense work." As he told the Hebrew newspaper *Ma'ariv* years later, he was left with just a small pension. "When I left, the LAKAM offered me to become an arms dealer. I had many contacts all over the world, and I imagine I would've made a lot of money. I refused. I never liked this kind of pursuit of the money," he said.

Blumberg would eventually become bitter about those like Milchan, a man who made millions off his espionage and arms deals while Blumberg labored as an innominate. "For years I worked for the country," Blumberg said. "While other people took care of themselves, built beautiful houses and saved money, I traveled the world and worried about the country. Today all those former colleagues live well, and I'm in debt." While Milchan would become a multibillionaire with homes, villas, and chateaus around the world, Blumberg ended up in a tiny, cramped apartment in Tel Aviv unable to even afford needed surgery. He was turned down for a loan to pay for a private doctor. "They won't increase my pension, even though I need the money to survive," Blumberg said. "I am hurt by the fact that I did so much for the country, and this is how I am treated." The minute Blumberg was fired, Milchan simply turned on his heels and left him to wither in the cold. "When I left the LAKAM he severed our relationship," said the former nuclear spymaster.

Replacing Blumberg was Rafi Eitan, a favorite of Sharon. Born in 1926 in a kibbutz, at eighteen he joined the Palmach, the pre-state underground Jewish militia, and eventually rose to deputy chief of operations for Mossad. He also worked with LAKAM on the NUMEC highly enriched uranium smuggling operation, even visiting the plant. "Sharon took advantage of a baseless complaint lodged against Blumberg by a person with business interests in order to remove Blumberg from his post and appoint me in his place," Eitan would later admit.

It would be a star-crossed assignment: Less than two years after Eitan took over LAKAM, things suddenly began to unravel.

BOOK FOUR

THE SMUGGLERS

CHAPTER 17

◆

Escape

By 8 a.m. on New Year's Day 1983, hundreds of thousands of spectators had already lined the streets of Pasadena for the annual Tournament of Roses Parade. As the Salvation Army Band played "Everything's Coming Up Roses," dozens of colorful floral floats decorated with eighteen million fresh flowers began their slow, two-mile-an-hour crawl down Orange Grove Boulevard. On the Rose Bowl's bright green field, the UCLA Bruins would soon face off against the Michigan Wolverines.

Forty-five miles south in Huntington Beach, Richard and Emilie Smyth had little interest in parades or football games. For them it was a quiet Saturday and a good time to catch up on work. But soon after entering the office, they saw only empty spaces on the desks where their computers used to be. Shocked, they quickly called the police. "Richard thought the robbery was espionage," said Emilie. "U.S. industrial security rules required Richard, as president of Milco International, Inc., to write a report for the FBI with a copy to the CIA." She added, "He included a phone call from Arnon Milchan the week before the robbery."

The previous week, Smyth had been notified by the State Department that an export license he had requested for an encrypted radio Milchan ordered was denied. Israel had tried to import the radio previously from another U.S. source, but the State Department had turned them down. Thus their attempt to try again, this time through their front company. The radio had probably been ordered so Israel could reverse engineer it, break the encryption, and then eavesdrop on the system.

Smyth in turn passed the bad news on to Milchan by telex. He did not take it well. "Arnon phoned Richard and angrily stated we should ship the radio without a license," said Emilie. "Of course, Richard said he couldn't do that. Arnon suggested we carry the radio to the Los Angeles Israeli Consulate, and they would forward the radio to Israel by diplomatic pouch. Again, Richard said he couldn't do that." Now furious, Milchan insisted that the company immediately send back the money it had been paid for the radio project. Smyth, however, said he was currently short of cash and would repay him shortly. "Arnon added he would order some more krytrons, and Milco could repay him from that money," said Emilie.

Soon thereafter, Milchan placed his order. "[Sixty] additional units (bigger model) were needed," he said. By then Smyth had already transferred 810 krytrons to Israel in fifteen separate shipments. "Then Arnon repeated three times, with great emphasis, 'Send the krytrons the same way as before,'" said Emilie. Meaning with only a commerce license instead of the required State Department munitions control license, which both Milchan and Smith knew was a serious crime. Now worried about the FBI because of the burglary, Smyth refused just as he had with the encrypted radio.

Smyth's sudden change of heart greatly alarmed Milchan. Something was up, possibly involving the FBI. As a result, he immediately shut down all communications with Smyth, fearing that both he himself and LAKAM could be implicated. As far as Milchan was concerned, Smyth was "burned," and the front company was history. From then on, whenever Smyth attempted to contact Milchan, at no matter what number, he could never reach him. Smyth was suddenly the spy left out in the cold.

Instead, Milchan turned his attention to *The King of Comedy*, which was to premiere in New York the next month.

Although the burglary turned out to be a simple theft by a part-time employee, Smyth was beginning to feel as though he was being squeezed in a vise. Within a few days both the CIA's Ron Romano and an agent from the FBI would pay a visit for an interview. He was greatly worried that they would begin discovering his hundreds of illegal krytron shipments to Israel, a fact easily discernible with a review of his incoming and outgoing shipping records. He therefore decided to lie by downplaying his actions, saying he had simply "bent the law" by sending shipments of "vacuum tubes" to Israel.

But Smyth only seemed to dig himself in deeper, setting off alarm bells at both the FBI and the Customs Service. On April 13, agents from both organizations visited Smyth at Milco to learn more about how he had "bent the law." This time he went a bit further, calling the krytrons "pentodes," which was still a lie since pentodes are similar in appearance but far different in function. Finally, after another visit by the FBI two days later, he at last admitted sending krytrons to Milchan at Heli Trading Company in Israel. Back at the office, both agents checked with the Office of Munitions Control and learned that a munitions license was required because krytrons, they were told, were used as "triggers for atomic weapons."

On May 13, Smyth and Emilie took off for a NATO meeting in Europe, and while changing planes in New York, Richard made a call to their son Ernest at Milco to see if everything was running smoothly. It wasn't. "On the phone, Ernest was clearly upset," recalled Emilie. "Seven U.S. Customs agents had pushed into the office with a search warrant... They took all the original records from the files about the krytron shipments." Then the agents demanded access to the safe and took a document Richard had written describing the shipments. "And why did they want it?" asked Emilie. "Later we figured out it was to read the part about Arnon ordering more krytrons." By the time he landed in Europe, Richard Kelly Smyth realized he had been hung out to dry by his onetime partner, Arnon Milchan.

———

As Smyth twisted slowly in the wind, nearly broke and possibly facing an indictment or arrest, Milchan at that very moment was also in Europe, but he was in a much better mood. He was with Robert De Niro, Jerry Lewis, and Martin Scorsese at the Cannes Film Festival to celebrate the showing of *The King of Comedy* at the new Palais des Festivals convention center.

By now the Festival international du film had become an annual event for Milchan. A year earlier while staying at the Carlton Hotel he had spotted Sergio Leone, the director of spaghetti westerns such as *The Good, The Bad, and the Ugly* and *Once Upon a Time in the West*. Milchan introduced himself in French, told him he was a big fan, and asked about any new projects.

"There is this movie that I have been working on for ten years now, and no one wants it," Leone said. "It's a big American saga; do you want to hear about it?" Milchan smiled. "Of course!" The two quickly pulled up chairs at an awning-covered table on the hotel's terrace, a broad plaza looking out at the palm trees and La Croisette, the promenade that links the beach and the city. And for the next four hours, as the sun sank below the dark blue Mediterranean, Leone outlined frame by frame his concept for the gangster film *Once Upon a Time in America*. Milchan was impressed. "I committed to finance the movie on the spot," he said. Eventually, it would cost $28 million and, like *The King of Comedy*, it too would flop at the box office and be scorned by critics.

Now in May 1983, Leone's film was in production with Robert De Niro as the star, and Milchan was back on the Carlton Hotel's terrace. As Elton John was filming a music video for his recording of "I'm Still Standing," Milchan, off to the side, was once again pushing another new film he had agreed to produce. This time it was director Terry Gilliam's Orwellian black comedy *Brazil*. Milchan and Gilliam had first met in March 1982 at Elysée-Matignon, Milchan's Paris hangout. And as with Leone's film, Milchan agreed to produce it after a single meeting.

The dinner had been arranged by Robert De Niro's agent, Harry Upland. And for the third time in a row, De Niro would star in another Milchan production, this one costing between $10 and $15 million. Gilliam, a former member of the Monty Python comedy troupe, had originally been warned about Milchan. "People that I talked to said, 'Stay away from this guy, he's an arms dealer making movies. He's too slippery, he can't be pinned down.'" By then Milchan's name had begun turning up in news accounts pointing to his involvement with arms deals and propaganda operations on behalf of apartheid South Africa. "In Hollywood they don't like working with an arms dealer, ideologically," Milchan acknowledged, "with someone who lives off selling machine-guns and killing."

As a result, much of Hollywood, including many of the stars and directors on the receiving end of Milchan's millions, were well aware of his weaponizing the White supremacist government. Yet hypocritically, while constantly proclaiming their support for racial justice, human rights, and other liberal causes in public, they had no problem financing films with his bags of apartheid-tainted cash. "I figured if everybody in Hollywood is badmouthing him, if everyone's against him, he must be OK," said Gilliam. De Niro heard that Milchan was not only an arms dealer on behalf of the racist South African government, but had even admitted to his involvement in smuggling of U.S. nuclear triggers on behalf of Israel, a very serious criminal offense. But De Niro just shrugged. None of it seemed to bother him as long as Milchan continued to put up the money.

But it wasn't just Hollywood; people in Washington were also quietly badmouthing Milchan. By now it was clear that both he and Israel were heavily involved with Smyth in the krytron smuggling operation. As a result, the matter quickly moved from FBI headquarters up Pennsylvania Avenue to the White House of President Ronald Reagan and over to the State Department. What began as a simple theft had quietly metastasized into a full-blown international incident requiring discreet, back-channel negotiations with officials at Israel's embassy. That meant dealing with the newly appointed deputy chief of mission, Benjamin Netanyahu. Potential public relations nightmares like this were the precise reason he was hired the previous year.

Soon, Netanyahu's portfolio increased substantially. As a result of Israel's disastrous invasion of Lebanon and the subsequent massacres at two refugee camps, Sabra and Shatila, General Ariel Sharon had been booted out as minister of defense. Replacing him was Moshe Arens, Israel's ambassador to Washington. That left Netanyahu in charge of everything as acting ambassador, including figuring a way out of the Milchan mess. Although Meir Rosen, the Foreign Ministry's legal counsel, was eventually chosen to replace Arens, there was little question that it was Netanyahu who was really running the show.

"Officially [Rosen] was Israel's ambassador to Washington, but Netanyahu continued to function in that capacity de facto," noted Netanyahu biographer Ben Caspit. "Rosen was older, heavier, an old-fashioned diplomat, conservative and restrained. In comparison, Bibi was a firebrand. Energetic and self-confident, he paid no attention to Rosen and acted on his own counsel. He stole political meetings from under Rosen's nose, took advantage of his absences to make appearances on *Nightline*, and did everything in his power to dwarf and undermine the older man."

Netanyahu was the shadow ambassador in more ways than one. He also oversaw all espionage operations in the United States, including those run by LAKAM, as well as its agents posing as science attachés, in his Washington embassy and the consulates in New York and Los Angeles.

Over the next two years, there was a quiet battle between CIA, FBI, Customs, and the Los Angeles U.S. Attorney's office on one side, all of whom wanted Milchan to face justice for the krytron smuggling operation. On the other side was Israel, which was greatly concerned with Milchan's past unraveling in a U.S. court of law. After all, he was a man with a head full of embarrassing secrets, from arms dealing, propaganda operations, and nuclear deals with racist South Africa to acting as a spy, smuggler, and bagman for LAKAM. After a year and a half of behind-the-scenes moves, the first shot was fired by the U.S. Attorney's office in Los Angeles.

The long, business-size envelope stood out among the Christmas cards that arrived at the Smyth residence on December 24, 1984. "I was stunned and dismayed," said Smyth. "It was an order to appear during the week between Christmas and New Year's Day at the Federal prosecutor's office in Central Los Angeles to answer questions about exporting krytrons." Smyth reached for the phone to call his lawyer. "I told him the Federal attorney had ordered me to come to a meeting to discuss 'high crimes and misdemeanors,' a phrase that scared me to death."

The meeting eventually took place in early January 1985. It did not go well. The assistant U.S. attorney, William Fahey, looked at Smyth as the fall guy and wanted him to reveal what he knew about Milchan and Israel. But Smyth, exercising misguided loyalty, refused to give him anything useful. "Richard did not think Fahey had a 'right to know' about what Israel did with the things they ordered from Milco; that was confidential to the Israeli government," said Emilie. Also, because ignorance of the law was his defense, pointing the finger at Milchan for knowingly violating the law regarding krytrons was also pointing the finger back at himself as a co-conspirator. The same with Milchan's attempts to recruit his board members and others as spies.

As a result, a secret grand jury was empaneled focusing on both Milchan and Smyth. Hoping to question Milchan one way or another, Fahey ordered a Rome-based Customs investigator to fly to Tel Aviv and knock on the door of his front company, Heli Trading Company. But without any legal authority or help from the Israeli government, he was quickly and unceremoniously turned away. Israel had a great deal to lose if Milchan was convicted of smuggling the nuclear triggers, including cancellation of Israel's annual $3.8 billion military aid package. Under legislation introduced by Congressman Stephen J. Solarz, a New York Democrat, such aid would be barred from any country violating U.S. export laws for the production of nuclear explosive devices. Had Fahey known about Milchan's confession to Robert De Niro, the actor could have also been hauled before the grand jury, and possibly been a key witness for the prosecution.

News of the grand jury investigation was leaked to a reporter for *Newsweek*, and he called Milchan in Paris to get his reaction, thereby tipping him off. "The first time I heard the word 'krytron' was last Thursday," Milchan lied to a reporter. "I have never heard this name before." The reporter responded, "What do you mean? There is a grand jury in the United States investigating you about this." According to Milchan, "I told him that I had just arrived [in Paris] from Los Angeles and had been staying at the Beverly Hills Hotel, so how could I be under investigation there? I told him that maybe one of the 30 companies that I own around the world was buying or selling these things, but I have not been involved in these businesses for 12 years." It was another lie. Upon hanging up the phone, Milchan quickly headed to the airport and took off for the safety of Israel, leaving Smyth shivering in the cold.

Milchan's next stop was to see his old friend, the man who first recruited him for LAKAM, Shimon Peres, now the prime minister. "I'm asking for your help," Milchan pleaded. "Call [President Ronald] Reagan or whoever and fix this... All I'm asking is that something be done to make this go away." Peres agreed, and Milchan would later donate large sums of money to a center named after Peres.

Soon after, a deal was quietly finalized between Netanyahu and the U.S. government. The 460 remaining krytrons "still in stock" would be returned to the United States, with no penalty for 350 already illegally smuggled to Israel and now attached to nuclear bombs. Israel would falsely claim that the unreturned krytrons were used only for "conventional research and development" rather than nuclear weapons. These were just lies piled upon lies, but President Reagan, like President Carter before him, would do what was politically expected and accept them, thereby preventing a cutoff of billions in foreign aid for Israel—and likewise a cutoff in millions in political donations for Reagan. Milchan would thereby get off without a scratch, Netanyahu would be promoted to Israel's ambassador to the United Nations, and Smyth would be the patsy and take the fall for everything and everyone.

Finally, in May 1985 the grand jury investigation ended, and Smyth was quietly notified by his attorney that he was about to be indicted. Bitter and unbelieving it would really happen, he was finally realizing how much his claims of innocence lacked credibility, and that he should have given up Milchan when he had the chance. "The U.S. government was prosecuting me and planning to send me to prison for sending krytrons to Israel," Smyth would later say. "What was the U.S. government going to do to Arnon Milchan who ordered the forbidden krytrons...who was now a billionaire movie producer. Nothing!"

As if choreographed, the same day the indictment was publicly announced, May 16, Israel came out with a prepared statement, all of it false. "Israel was not aware of any ban on purchasing those devices," said a spokesman from the Ministry of Defense. "It purchased the krytrons without knowledge of any restrictions."

To make matters worse for Smyth, on the day he was due in court to hear the indictment, he and his family had tickets to leave on a long-planned trip overseas, including attending a NATO meeting in Netherlands. To pay for their tickets, he had cashed in all his frequent-flier miles. After pleading with the prosecutor, Smyth was allowed to postpone the date of the court appearance, but not the date of the indictment. He was given permission to travel provided he post a $1 million bond, requiring $100,000 cash down payment, to ensure his return. Smyth quickly remortgaged his house, paid the bond, and they took off on a TWA jet.

But after a stopover in Paris, as the flight attendant was passing out fresh newspapers high above the French countryside, Smyth's eyes widened. The headline of an article in the *International Herald Tribune* announced that he had been indicted for smuggling nuclear triggers to Israel. "I was shocked," Smyth recalled, as he looked around at others reading the same article. Then came the line that truly scared him: "Smyth could expect 105 years in prison and a one-and-a-half-million-dollar fine for this crime." He suddenly realized he was potentially facing the rest of his life in prison, and then some. And had he talked, Milchan would have faced the same charges, if not more.

From Paris, the next stop was Tel Aviv. Smyth was going to hunt down Milchan, and possibly seek asylum.

———

Once assured he was in the clear and not named in the indictment, Milchan simply washed his hands of Smyth. His agent was now facing life in prison and over a million dollars in fines for running Milchan's smuggling operation. Yet even though Milchan knew the indictment was coming, he never offered Smyth to help pay for his defense. Nor could he even answer the phone. Instead, he continued pumping millions of those billions into star-laden, money-losing Hollywood movies.

As the Los Angeles U.S. Attorney's office announced Smyth's indictment, across town at almost that same moment Milchan's latest movie arrived at Universal Studios. Packed into seventy-eight heavy cartons, the reels of *Brazil* had been sent from PooPooPictures in London, the company owned by the movie's director, Terry Gilliam. It had been a long and torturous journey. Four months earlier, on January 23, 1985, Milchan and Gilliam met at Universal's 325-seat Alfred Hitchcock Theater to screen the film for the studio executives. Among them was Sidney Sheinberg, the president of MCA, the parent company of Universal. Afterward, Gilliam came away with a bad feeling. From Sheinberg's body language, he told Milchan, he suspected his reaction was, "I don't know what the fuck this thing is." Nevertheless, back at the Beverly Hills Hotel and hoping for the best, Gilliam and Milchan celebrated by popping champagne corks.

The next day Milchan and Gilliam met with Sheinberg in his office on the fifteenth floor of the Black Tower, the studio's stylish, ebony-glass headquarters on the Universal lot. Gilliam's feelings the previous day were confirmed. An unhappy Sheinberg insisted that Gilliam make a number of changes, including coming up with a different ending, something Gilliam considered unacceptable. "The ending is not negotiable," insisted Gilliam. Sheinberg, however, was equally insistent. "The movie is not going to be released in this form," he said firmly. "There are going to be some changes." Gilliam was now furious. "Before that happens, I'll burn the negative *and* the Black Tower," he barked, his face turning crimson. Off to the side, Milchan could see his movie, and his millions, going up in those same flames.

Gilliam eventually agreed to edit the film, but Sheinberg had one more demand: that Gilliam ship to Universal cartons of the film shot but not used in the movie so *his* editors could create their own version. Then they would test the two before a live in-studio audience. And in May, as the U.S. Attorney's office announced Smyth's indictment, those cartons began arriving. Shortly thereafter, when Gilliam finally sent his newly edited version back to Universal, Sheinberg was shocked to see that all he had done was shorten it by eleven minutes but left everything else, including the ending, unchanged. Furious, over the phone he told Gilliam that he had put a stop on release of the film. With that, Gilliam exploded. "Take the fucking thing and do anything you want with it," he screamed. "Just take my name off and put your name on. 'Sid Sheinberg's *Brazil*.' It has a nice ring to it."

As Smyth landed in Tel Aviv following his indictment, Milchan was also back in Israel speed dialing between Gilliam and Sheinberg in an attempt to find a solution to save *Brazil*. Unlike his movie, however, Milchan had no interest in saving his clandestine agent. As a result, every time Smyth called Heli Trading, Ltd., Milchan's assistant, Dvora Ben-Itzhak, told him that her boss was unavailable. Eventually she agreed to meet with Smyth herself. By now he was very familiar with Ben-Itzhak, having traveled to Israel between fifteen and twenty times since first meeting Milchan.

Over coffee, Ben-Itzhak began pumping Smyth for any information he had passed on to the prosecutor regarding Milchan. Smyth said he had told them nothing, then pleaded for some financial help or asylum. After all, he had been Milchan's faithful agent for more than a decade and despite the indictment kept his silence. In a subtle threat, he implied that that could change depending on whether a deal might eventually be struck with the U.S. attorney. What Smyth didn't know was that a deal had already been struck, far above the U.S. attorney's head, and he was not part of it.

"Dvora set up some meetings with government officials and reported things looked hopeful," said Emilie. Then everything changed. Ben-Itzhak told Richard, "The Israeli government had discussions with U.S. officials regarding the krytrons Israel had purchased," and as a result "the Israeli government would not be able to provide any assistance to him." Smyth was shocked. The fix was in. There would be no money, no lawyers, no asylum. He was standing alone in a wilderness of mirrors.

The rest of the day, Smyth tried to track down Milchan. Years earlier, Milchan had given him a home address on El Al Street in Herzliya, an affluent city just north of Tel Aviv. But when he got to the location it was just a rundown abandoned building, obviously a phony address. In fact, Milchan did have an ocean-view penthouse in Marina Towers in Herzliya Pituah, the toniest part of the city, but it wasn't anywhere near El Al Street. Frightened and abandoned, Smyth suffered through the rest of the trip for the sake of his family.

"We returned to Los Angeles," said Smyth. "We reported to the L.A. court where I turned in my passport, was taken to the jail segment of the courthouse and was fingerprinted. How mortifying." He and his wife then drove back to their home, now up for sale to pay his legal expenses. Later, a secret FBI counterintelligence report on Smyth's trip to Israel would be titled "Termination Phase." Milchan, who had masterminded the nuclear trigger smuggling operation, returned about the same time aboard his private jet to work out a negotiated settlement to save his movie. As he passed quickly through passport control, the customs agent smiled, said welcome back, and Milchan was driven to his suite at the Beverly Hills Hotel.

As August rapidly approached, Richard Smyth was becoming increasingly desperate and could see no way out. Emilie was also going through a very rough period. After an argument with Richard at the office, she said, "I drove home and drank a lot of vodka—not to get drunk but specifically to commit suicide." After passing out she was discovered by her daughter, who called 911, and an ambulance brought her to a hospital emergency ward, where she was revived. Then, a few days before the trial was to begin, Richard received a candid assessment from his attorney regarding the outcome of the trial. On the phone was his lawyer's assistant. "Your lawyer informed me that you will go to prison," he said starkly. Minutes after hanging up, Richard and Emilie made a decision they had been contemplating for days. They would flee the country.

Within minutes, the two were stuffing clothes into a pair of carry-on suitcases. Next, they withdrew $15,000 from the bank that had been their emergency fund. And because the FBI had confiscated his passport, Richard grabbed the one that belonged to his middle son, hoping he would be able to bluff his way into a country. Then, as he dyed his stone gray hair jet black, Emilie made reservations on a nonstop Lufthansa flight to Frankfurt. Where they would go after that they would decide when they got there. Finally, they raced to the Los Angeles airport and abandoned their cream-colored Oldsmobile in the parking lot with its keys in the ignition. As far as their children knew, the two were simply going to Catalina Island, just off the California coast, to relax for a few days before the start of the trial. "We didn't want them to be accused of helping us get away," said Richard.

For the amateur fugitive and his now criminal accomplice, it was learning by doing. Once in the Lufthansa terminal they decided to sit apart in case the FBI was looking for a couple. But when Emilie returned from a trip to the restroom, someone had taken her seat, so she found another. However, because she didn't tell Richard, he thought she had become frightened and returned home. For the next forty minutes, the two frantically searched the terminal for each other, finally connecting only when they both lined up for boarding. Once on the jet, their hearts were still pounding like jackhammers. "All that we were carrying after our 34 years of marriage were the two under-the-seat luggage pieces," said Richard. "We both scanned all around the cabin. How we expected to recognize a threat, I can't imagine."

The nine-hour flight gave them a chance to relax a bit, but then came the first great challenge for Richard: passing through German immigration control with his son's passport. On the flight they had worked out a scheme. When the inspector questioned Richard, he would act embarrassed and say that in his rush to leave the house he had accidently grabbed his son's passport. Once at the immigration window, Richard slid the passport across, and after a moment, as expected, the official exclaimed in a growl, "This isn't you!" The two were then taken to a back room, but after Richard offered his explanation, he was released with a warning to go straight to the U.S. embassy and resolve the problem.

Having vaulted over their first hurtle, they rented a car at Frankfurt airport and drove to Zurich, Switzerland, the city they decided would act as their hideout. The country's largest city, it was a good place to disappear, especially since Richard knew some German and Zurich was in the German-speaking part of Switzerland. After spending the first night in a hotel in the center of the city, they located a branch of the Union Bank of Switzerland and opened a numbered account to deposit the $15,000 in cash they had brought with them. Richard thought it was an ironic choice since it was the same bank to which he would regularly send Milchan's 60 percent profit from the krytron purchases.

Next, they bought a copy of *Neue Zürcher Zeitung*, the popular German-language Swiss newspaper, and began looking for an apartment to begin, in their midfifties, their new lives. They spotted a small, unfurnished flat in the northern part of town for $400 a month and quickly snapped it up. Like first-years in a college dorm, at a discount store they bought an inflatable mattress, a feather comforter, kitchen and bathroom supplies. And after dropping the rental car off at Zurich's airport, they began exploring their new neighborhood. Conveniently, a tram line ran out front, and behind them was Uetliberg, a scenic tree-covered low-rise mountain very popular with local hikers and climbers. "We liked our little apartment," said Emilie, "but we were still paranoid that agents or Interpol police would find us." Richard added, "We thought they were searching for us everywhere. We were frightened and kept looking for anyone following us."

They were right. Six thousand miles away, in a shocked courtroom, the defendant was a no-show for a key hearing, and a week later the trial opened without him. "Frankly, we are in a limbo situation," Assistant U.S. Attorney William Fahey told the court. He said an arrest warrant had been issued and the FBI, Customs Service, Interpol, and other agencies were searching for Smyth and are pursuing "a couple of leads." He added that he hoped to have the fugitive in custody in a "short time." Meanwhile, Smyth's $100,000 bond was forfeited.

Also in the courtroom, and more terrified than shocked, were the couple's relatives, who were never informed of the plan to escape. "This is a nightmare, except in a nightmare, you wake up," said Pauline Smyth, Richard's mother. Emilie's mother, Gene Manns, was also perplexed. "We are scared to death," she said. Speculation was wild. The *Los Angeles Times* reported, "Sources close to the case have various theories about what happened to the Smyths, ranging from a suicide pact to kidnaping by either Arabs or Israelis concerned about Smyth's possible knowledge of Mideast nuclear capabilities."

As the two settled into their new Zurich hideaway that August, they nervously avoided eye contact with locals and peered through their door's peephole at every sound. To ease their family's concern, they sent a brief message indirectly to Emilie's mother, who was living in Laguna Hills, California. The quick phone call to an acquaintance simply said, "Tell my mother I'm safe." Soon after arriving, Richard secretly appealed for financial help to LAKAM chief Rafi Eitan through Dvora Ben-Itzhak. He also reached out to Milchan. But every time he checked, there were no new deposits in his numbered account at the Union Bank of Switzerland. They were on their own.

In fact, Milchan was just to the south, a few hundred miles away at the Venice International Film Festival.

———

By the time Arnon Milchan arrived on the Venetian island of Lido, a twenty-minute vaporetto ride across the lagoon from Piazza San Marco, throngs of paparazzi were crowding the entrance to the theaters in the Palazzo del Cinema on the Lungomare Marconi. Universal's Sidney Sheinberg had finally relented and allowed Milchan and Gilliam to release *Brazil*, starring Robert De Niro, with its ending intact. But it was the disaster Sheinberg had feared, making back only $9.9 million at the box office from its $15 million price tag.

The movie did Milchan no favors for his reputation as a movie producer. "No one has asserted that Mr. Milchan has any known talent in this business," said Sheinberg. "He has a string of total failures. I think the greatest help he can be to the future of the movie business is to continue his activities in other businesses," apparently referring to selling weapons to apartheid South Africa. Gilliam was equally caustic. "Arnon has to screw everyone—partners, friends—literally, figuratively, in every sense of the word," he said. "It's pathological. He can't stop himself. At some point, he needs to invent an enemy."

Gilliam's cowriter, Charles McKeown, also got to know Milchan during the filming and didn't like what he saw. "You just never know whether he was telling the truth or not," he said. "The kind of deals he was in, the level of finance and the way he operated, seemed to me like a world upside down. I felt we were dealing with a sort of dangerous, shady quality. He boasts enormous wealth and clearly wants to be seen as the most generous individual." But, added McKeown, "when it came to getting £10,000 out of him for some work he actually owed me, forget it. My agent spent months phoning him all over the world and getting no reply. He seemed to be quite pathological in his desire not to part with money."

On Lido Island, Milchan made his way to the theater showing his latest film, *Legend*. Directed by Ridley Scott and starring Tom Cruise, it centered on the Lord of Darkness who seeks to cast the world in eternal night. It also had a familiar ending: red ink and odorous reviews. It earned less than $15 million on a $25 million budget, and garnered a dismal 48 on Rotten Tomatoes.

Another film that Milchan would later produce was the romantic spy thriller *Mr. & Mrs. Smith*, starring Brad Pitt and Angelina Jolie, and paying the pair millions for their performances.

Feeling betrayed, the other Mr. and Mrs. Smyth remained in Zurich, peering out their peephole at every sound, constantly checking for a secret deposit, and getting shorter and shorter in cash as the days grew darker and colder. Three months later, in November, the world was about to change dramatically for all of them.

CHAPTER 18

◆

Deceit

In November 1985, LAKAM chief Rafi Eitan suddenly had a much bigger problem than the hunt for Richard and Emilie Smyth. Jonathan Pollard, an analyst for U.S. Naval Intelligence and another of his U.S. spies, was about to be arrested. Over the past year, Pollard had secretly delivered truckloads of highly classified files from various sensitive U.S. agencies to Eitan. The number of secret documents was so voluminous they could fill a six-by-ten-foot room, with the stacks rising six feet high. At the time it was the most secrets that had ever been stolen from the U.S. government.

But now Pollard's days were numbered. He was under surveillance by the FBI and knew his arrest was imminent.

At thirty, Pollard smoked two packs of Marlboros a day, was overweight, and had wavy brown hair that receded from his broad forehead. Below his dark brows were a pair of wide owlish glasses, a thick dark mustache, and a dimpled chin. Growing up in Indiana, he loved spy novels, especially Graham Greene's *The Quiet American*, and was brought up in a Jewish family obsessed with Israel. "Israel was with me every waking moment since I can remember," he said. "The first flag I remember was the Israeli flag. It was the first flag I could identify."

A few months earlier, Pollard had secretly flown to Tel Aviv for a meeting with Eitan. It was at the same time that Richard Kelly Smyth was desperately and unsuccessfully seeking money or help as his trial was about to start. Pollard was extremely concerned because despite Eitan's continuous promises, he had never bothered to provide him with an escape plan if he, like Smyth, came under suspicion. As a result, their meeting became very heated.

Arriving in Israel, Pollard found Eitan lying prostrate in a bed in the ophthalmic ward of Beilinson Hospital, a few miles east of Tel Aviv, recovering from eye surgery. For security, the room was guarded and all visitors and unnecessary people had been cleared from the entire floor. Standing at the end of his spymaster's bed, Pollard was engaged in an increasingly vocal shouting match with him. Eitan was demanding that Pollard fulfill a ten-year spying contract, and Pollard was demanding a detailed escape plan should he end up like Smyth. Greatly annoyed by the question, Eitan told Pollard not to worry, that "no drastic action would be taken against you—it hasn't happened in the past." When in fact it had just happened to Smyth. "Any action that was initiated could be contained by Israel," Eitan assured Pollard, implying top-level pressure on the White House and Justice Department officials as with Milchan. But Milchan was a wealthy and powerful Israeli, unlike Pollard and Smyth.

"Rafi just kept blowing me off," Pollard said. At one point the argument became so heated that the guard outside the door had to look in to make sure everything was all right. Rather than find a solution to Pollard's problem, Eitan wanted Pollard to find a solution to his: to locate another safe house for additional Israeli spies in the Washington area. "Here I was, complaining about my lack of security, and Eitan wanted me to operate a 'safehouse' for Israeli agents," said Pollard. "This certainly wasn't what I had in mind." The comment clearly indicates that Pollard was not the isolated spy Israel would later claim, but one of many.

Now in late November and back in Washington, Pollard's nightmare had come true. He was being constantly tailed by the FBI and he knew the game was almost up. Desperate and, like Smyth, with no escape plan, he had one final option. He and his wife, Anne Henderson, would flee to the Israeli embassy and ask for asylum. Since the embassy was considered Israel's sovereign territory, the FBI would be forbidden from entering. Once inside the gate Pollard and Henderson would announce that they were Jews and ask for citizenship and asylum under the so-called law of return. The law creates a reality where a Jew anywhere in the world, even if they and their ancestors have never set foot in Israel, can show up in the country and automatically be granted citizenship.

Early on the morning of Thursday, November 21, Pollard and Anne loaded a suitcase in their car along with their wedding album and cat, Dusty. Then they headed to the Washington Hospital Center near Howard University for a previously scheduled appointment for Anne, a short twelve-minute drive away. Knowing they would be followed by the FBI, Pollard had previously alerted the bureau of the appointment. And if they spotted them loading the suitcase, they may have assumed it was in the event Anne might be required to remain overnight.

As they departed the hospital an hour or so later, at least half a dozen unmarked FBI cars were waiting. Seeing Pollard's green Mustang exit the parking garage, Special Agent Mike Rolince pulled out ahead of them and

Agent Max Fratodei got behind as they and the others jockeyed in and out of position to hide their presence. At the time, they knew Pollard was a spy, but they didn't know for what country. The agents assumed the couple would simply return to their apartment since there had been no notification of any additional travel. But instead, Pollard began driving aimlessly, possibly attempting to ditch the parade of surveillance vehicles.

A short time later, he was driving along busy Wisconsin Avenue in northwest Washington. "As we drove up Wisconsin Avenue, Anne and I could see at least six FBI cars," said Pollard. From Wisconsin, he turned right into a series of residential neighborhoods, eventually coming to the intersection of Van Ness Street and International Drive. By now Pollard's pursuers suspected the couple were preparing to seek asylum, but where? Within a dozen or so blocks were the embassies of China, Singapore, Morocco, Ethiopia, Jordan, Bahrain, Bangladesh, Ghana, Israel, Pakistan, Malaysia, Nigeria, Egypt, and others.

Suddenly, at about 10:20 a.m. Pollard made a right onto International Drive and then another sharp right, following a car through a gate that had just opened, which then closed behind him. Seeing the blue-and-white flag with the Star of David atop the sand-colored building, the FBI agents finally realized where Pollard's massive cache of documents had gone. One of the agents quickly notified FBI headquarters, "Pollard just turned into the Israeli embassy!" Later, Special Agent Eugene Noltkamper said, "A diplomatic vehicle was going into the compound, through the gate, and the Mustang followed it through." Surveillance cars began arriving from all directions as agents got out and began peering through the gate and fence with bulky black binoculars.

As the steel gate clanked shut behind him, with the growing crowd of angry FBI agents on the opposite side, Pollard pulled up to an underground garage and stepped out. "I'm a Jew!" he shouted as loudly as he could. "I need help. The FBI is after me." Almost instantly, a security guard with a cocked pistol confronted him. "This isn't good," Pollard thought to himself, seeing that he might suddenly be caught in a crossfire between Israeli guards and FBI agents. Then a group of five or six embassy people came out and gathered with the guards a short distance away.

Meanwhile, inside the embassy, frantic calls were made to Tel Aviv, where it was about 8:30 p.m. Rafi Eitan was at home when he got the message and quickly reached for his secure "red phone." "I immediately said, 'Throw him out,'" Eitan later recalled, adding that he had no regrets. "If we hadn't removed him," he said, "officials in the United States—including the Jewish lobby—would have been compelled to remove him from there by use of force...

Granting asylum to Pollard in the embassy, even for a few minutes, would have immediately caused an extremely serious diplomatic conflict between the countries, [and] not have prevented his arrest."

One of the security guards left the group and approached Pollard, telling him forcefully that under orders from Israel, he was to leave immediately. Pollard couldn't believe what he was hearing, and Anne suddenly began crying hysterically. "This is where the knife really went deep into the back," she would later say. Pollard said that there were twenty FBI agents waiting for him outside. "Do you know what they'll do to me?" he asked in a near shout. Now the guard was even more firm. "Those are the orders from Jerusalem. Leave!" he said. Pollard was incredulous. "I said, 'I know what's going to happen and I'm not prepared for this. Just shoot me. You'll say that you thought I was a terrorist, and it was a car bomb. Just do it now, quickly. Don't think about it.'" But no one took him up on his suggestion.

Instead, Pollard got back in the driver's seat next to his hysterical wife, turned the car around, and slowly slid through the gate like a turtle emerging from his protective shell. Moments later his arm was grabbed, he was ordered to turn off the engine, and a pair of shiny silver handcuffs were slapped on his wrists. It was the ultimate betrayal. "Any country that could do this to a loyal agent was capable of anything," he said later. "I grew up on this myth that you never leave a soldier behind, which is bullshit. We do. It's not just me." He added, "I simply couldn't believe that Jews were capable of abandoning their own since that was something only the *goyim* [a Jewish slur for non-Jews] did." With regard to Eitan, his spymaster, Pollard would never forgive him. "He abandoned me, he lied about me, he buried me, and he did everything he humanly could to make sure I never came home," he said. "The quality of tradecraft exhibited by Rafi in this affair was less than poor, it was criminally irresponsible."

Anne was arrested the next day and both she and Pollard were placed in isolation cells in separate wings of the District of Columbia jail. Seeing no alternative, Pollard confessed and spent the next few weeks undergoing daily interrogations, filling top secret page after top secret page with details of his short but spectacular career as an Israeli mole. "Ron, you know the government shouldn't give high clearances to Jewish people," he told Naval Investigative Service investigator Ron Olive. "Jews like me," he said, "who can't afford to travel to Israel or give money. When asked to help, we're willing to do anything for the love of our country."

———

Thousands of miles away, news of the Pollards' highly publicized capture outside the Israeli embassy in Washington sent shivers down the spines of another couple: Richard and Emilie Smyth. Eight days later, on Friday November 29, 1985, they piled what little they had left of their lives into an Avis rental car. And shortly before 7 a.m., they watched Zurich disappear for good in their rearview mirror as they headed down an icy highway to once again escape into the loneliness of another new and distant country. "We headed south to Málaga," said Richard, "worried we would have trouble crossing the many borders between Switzerland and Spain."

A freezing northerly wind was just beginning to blow, and there were patches of snow on the ground. Every time they came to a border, Emilie, with a valid passport, would be at the wheel. Making good time on the super-highways, they spent the first night in the French city of Lyon, and the second in Barcelona after reaching the Spanish border by dark. Finally, on the third night they pulled into Málaga. Exhausted, they checked into a seedy $7-a-night flophouse on Calle Redding and Richard registered under his new alias, "Jon Schiller."

Richard and his wife, now Emilie "Schiller," had searched a map for a new hideaway. They settled on the Andalusian city of Málaga on Spain's Costa del Sol, far from the snow and bitter cold of Zurich. The area had long been a haven for international fugitives hiding in plain sight. In 2020, 116 fugitives were arrested along the coast, likely a small percentage of the actual number.

Luckily, Richard spoke fairly good Spanish and they were able to find an out-of-the-way auto company. For $1,000 a year they leased a small white Fiat Panda registered in the name of the company, so there was no need for their names to be exposed. After dropping off the Avis car, they bought a copy of the local *Diario Sur* newspaper and looked for an apartment. Málaga was a good choice; in two days they found a fully furnished four-bedroom apartment, C/2, at 6 Calle Marcos de Obregón. It was a small side street just a half block from Playa La Caleta, a sandy beach on the Mediterranean. The six-story tan brick building had wide balconies covered with green awnings and was just $400 a month, the same as they were paying for the drab and much smaller place in Zurich. When the landlady asked them how long they planned to stay, Richard quickly answered, "Forever." "We were still fearful of being tracked down," he later said, but "we planned to live the rest of our lives in Spain."

As the years went by, the Smyths became more and more integrated into Málaga's society. They joined a group of English speakers and became active participants in the American Club of Southern Spain, to which Richard was elected vice president. They savored tapas, enjoyed the cheap prices on the *menu del día*, and downed generous glasses of tinto de verano on breezy Malagueña summer nights. They shopped in the market stalls on Calle Larios, attended classical music recitals, celebrated *Semana Santa* every spring, and took long walks in Teatinos, Málaga's university district. And eventually they ventured out, traveling around Europe while staying at campsites.

For money, Emilie's parents gave them $50,000, which was delivered personally by their middle son, and they worked hard to stretch it out. Richard also began having success trading options. Using the email address jonsch@ vnet.co.es, they continued their relationship with Milchan's assistant, Dvora Ben-Itzhak. But Milchan himself, Smyth's former handler, offered no assistance whatsoever, in the same way that Pollard was left in the cold by his Israeli handlers. Milchan even forbade Ben-Itzhak from visiting them.

Like the Smyths, Milchan also followed closely the news of the arrest and sentencing of fellow LAKAM agent Jonathan Pollard. After all, both Milchan and Pollard had worked for Rafi Eitan, and both had risked arrest for espionage, among other crimes. But where Pollard was an American with little money and no escape plan, Milchan was an Israeli billionaire with private jets and homes in Israel and Paris, as well as a near-permanent suite at the Beverly Hills Hotel. Nevertheless, the question was, how long could his luck last?

For over two decades Milchan had been one of the stars in LAKAM's small pantheon of spies, first for Benjamin Blumberg and then Eitan. Now, as a result of the scandal following the Pollard arrest, Eitan had been fired and LAKAM had been dismantled, its functions transferred to Mossad. Suddenly Milchan was on his own in the United States, and without the protection of diplomatic immunity. Except for Prime Minister Shimon Peres, who first recruited him for LAKAM, and a few close friends like Robert De Niro, no one knew of his secret life. But all it would take was one mistake. If he were arrested for espionage and smuggling nuclear triggers, his life would be reduced to a nine-by-six-foot cell and watching reruns of his films in an orange jumpsuit.

Now focusing full-time on becoming a successful Hollywood producer, he could not hide out in Israel. He needed to spend a considerable part of his time in the United States working on his films. And he also needed to travel extensively internationally, both for foreign films and the various film festivals. Should a grand jury issue a secret indictment, however, he, like Smyth, would be subject to arrest anywhere in the world under an Interpol "Red Notice." And he would never know about it until the silver handcuffs were snapped on his wrists.

In early September 1987, as the Smyths were acclimating themselves to their new hideout in Málaga, Milchan was next door in France. Attending the Deauville American Film Festival, he was clinking long-stemmed glasses of bubbly Dom Perignon with members of Hollywood's royalty at Chez Miocque and other chic hangouts in the town. Among the forty films to be screened was his latest, *Man on Fire*, about a rogue former CIA agent. As with Milchan's previous films, however, *Man on Fire* flamed out at the box office and received scorching reviews.

But by 1989, Milchan's fortunes began turning around with *The War of the Roses*, starring Michael Douglas and Kathleen Turner. It was a brutal black comedy about a couple, the Roses, who go from marital bliss to mortal combat. This time for Milchan, the silver ball on the roulette table landed on black rather than red, as the film earned a nice profit by grossing $87 million in the United States and $160 million worldwide.

Milchan had turned the corner, and his next film would be even bigger. Titled *3,000*, it was a dark and gritty script about a wealthy businessman who hires a down-on-her-luck prostitute in Hollywood to become his escort for a week of business and social functions. The fee was $3,000. They eventually develop a close relationship over the course of the seven days. But in the end, they sadly go their separate ways: the businessman off to New York and another deal, and the prostitute forlornly off to Disneyland with a female friend. Milchan got Disney to sign on as the studio, and he recruited Julia Roberts for the female lead, with Richard Gere playing the businessman.

Finally, when *3,000* was nearly done and in rough cut, Ehud Olmert, the mayor of Jerusalem, paid Milchan a visit. Invited to the studio, he listened as Milchan and Disney executives Michael Eisner and Jeffrey Katzenberg were trying to decide on a key song for their film. As they were listening to Roy Orbison's "Pretty Woman," Olmert said, "This should be the title of the movie." Milchan cocked his head and looked at him. "What the hell do you know?" he said. "How can you call a movie 'Pretty Woman'? I mean, I've never seen something more heavy-handed than that title." Not giving up, Olmert again suggested *Pretty Woman* as the film's title. Milchan shot back, "What do you know about movie titles?"

In the end, the Israeli mayor became responsible for replacing the title *3,000* with *Pretty Woman*. The film quickly became a smash hit, and the $14 million investment paid off by grossing $178,406,268 in the United States and another $285 million in other countries.

Olmert's visit was anything but unusual for Milchan, who had now become Mossad's man in Hollywood. Whenever Mossad director Meir Dagan needed help in Hollywood on a clandestine operation, needed assistance with the film industry, he would secretly call Milchan. Therefore, when Dagan was attempting to cultivate a relationship with a top Russian oligarch with close ties to President Vladimir Putin, he turned to Milchan. Dagan knew the oligarch's young daughter was a budding musician interested in an international music career, so he asked Milchan to help expedite it in Hollywood.

Milchan quickly flew back to Tel Aviv and invited Dagan, the oligarch, and his daughter to his palatial seaside home. Located behind two electric gates on Mitzpe Yam Street in Beit Yanai north of Tel Aviv, it is built on a bluff above Arsuf Beach and offers stunning views of the Mediterranean. It was created by joining together three adjacent houses, and to keep it all very private, he spent another $3.5 million to buy a lot for an access road to the house. The meeting went well and Milchan put the woman in touch with a Hollywood recording studio. The favors would continue.

Milchan would also meet frequently in Hollywood with Yossi Cohen, Dagan's successor as head of Mossad. At one point, Cohen secretly discussed with Milchan, an expert in pro-Israel propaganda, the possibility of quietly producing a favorable movie about the Mossad. Over the years, Milchan would become a member of Cohen's inner circle, meeting him dozens of times in both Israel and the United States. "We did a few operations together," Milchan would later say. Despite secretly carrying out numerous espionage activities on behalf of Israel and its intelligence services over decades on U.S. soil, from LAKAM to Mossad, Milchan has never been arrested or even questioned by FBI counterintelligence agents. Nor has he registered, as required, as an agent of a foreign government, a serious criminal violation.

Instead, protected by his wealth, fame, and high-level political connections, he simply continued making films. Films that throughout the 1990s included *JFK*, *Natural Born Killers*, *Heat*, *The Client*, *L.A. Confidential*, *City of Angels*, *Fight Club*, and dozens more.

Then in 2000 he came across another script he liked, *Freddy Got Fingered*. It would be considered one of the worst films of all time, earning five Golden Raspberry Awards.

It also had an ironic title. Just a few months after it was released, on April 20, 2001, Richard Kelly Smyth also got fingered.

———

By 2001, after sixteen years on the run, Richard and Emilie Smyth were settled in their Málaga hideout, but continually strapped for money on which to live. Despite Richard's repeated pleading for financial assistance from Milchan, now a billionaire and then some, his former handler offered him not a single euro. Like Pollard, he was stiffed and left in the cold. As a result, the Smyths decided to take a chance, a big chance, by applying for U.S. Social Security payments in their real names. It worked, and for several years they received about $2,000 a month that helped sustain them. The money would be sent automatically to an account Richard had opened in a nearby branch of Banco Bilbo.

Then in June 2001, the branch manager mentioned a new requirement. Richard needed to have a standard nonresident form filled out and stamped at the local police office in order to receive the proper permit for his account. "But I've been able to use this account for over six years. Why do I need this permit now?" he complained. The manager was in no mood to argue. "Get the police permit or this account will be frozen," he snarled.

Richard chalked it up to growing bureaucracy, since he had registered to vote in the local elections without having to fill out such a form. On the drive home they stopped at the police station, submitted the form, and were told to return on Monday, July 9, to pick up the permit. A few days later, on the Monday, they returned to the station and were told to take a seat. Finally, an officer appeared. Tall with blond hair and blue eyes, he wore a dark blue police uniform and directed them to stand by a fax machine on the other side of the room. Then, slowly pulling a piece of paper from its output tray, the officer handed it to Richard.

Instead of the expected permit, he was suddenly staring at a twenty-year-old photo of himself. "I saw the word 'INTERPOL' at the top of the page and a knot tightened in the pit of my stomach," he said. "The officer asked me, 'Is this you?' I managed to choke out the words, 'Yes, it appears to be me, but it's an old picture.'" The officer then turned to Emilie and said she could leave as he grabbed Richard's wrists and placed them in handcuffs. Richard looked at Emilie in disbelief. "She turned white, her eyes wide open in shock," he recalled. "Emilie didn't realize it, but this was the last time she would see me as a free man for many years."

Richard was marched to the police station's jail and placed into a stark, windowless cell. For a bed, there was simply a raised cement area with a thin cushion and a soiled blanket. There also were no toilet facilities in the cell, which meant requesting permission to use the facility down the hall, simply a hole in the floor. At night, because of a medical condition, he would have to urinate several times, but there was no guard on duty. "The only solution was to wet on the floor," said Smyth. "I had to wet on the floor twelve times during the thirty hours I was confined to that cell . . . I had never felt so wretched and discouraged in my whole life."

Later, at a brief hearing, Smyth raised no objection to his extradition back to the United States, hoping the conditions there would at least be more humane. But it turned out to be a very slow process. From the courtroom, Smyth was transferred to a prison in Alhaurín de la Torre, a small town about twenty minutes west of Málaga. Unhandcuffed, he was placed in Cell 62 on the prison's third floor in Module One, the high-security section of the prison. Conditions were only slightly better; he had an occasionally malfunctioning toilet in his cell and a variety of ever-changing cellmates as the weeks dragged on. By late August he had been held for a month and a half with still no clear idea when he would be sent back. His anger at Milchan growing ever stronger, on August 22, 2001, he wrote out a long letter to him. "To: Arnon Milchan, Big Time Movie Producer," he began.

I really wish you could learn what it's like to be in prison. I can tell you, it's not very pleasurable. The worst part is that I'm separated from my wife, Emilie, on our 50th Wedding Anniversary, which is 30 August 2001...You are the reason I'm in prison because I sent to your company, Heli Trading in Tel Aviv, some electronic tubes called Krytrons. Remember? I thought you might...So the U.S. government thought I should go to prison for 105 years. I read in the newspaper that you sold $450 million worth of movies to Channel Plus, the TV Channel for "coded" [subscription] movies. I hope you put most of that money in your Union Bank of Zurich secret bank account like the 60% profit on each of the things, including Krytrons, that I shipped to Heli Trading.

I also saw the movie, "Pretty Woman" that you produced. Congratulations! It was an excellent movie. What's it like to have so much money? I've often wondered what it would be like to have the $1.5 billion you are reputed to have...

Smyth sent the letter to his wife to forward to Milchan, but, fearing his power and potential reaction, she decided not to mail it. Milchan, however, likely knew Smyth's feelings toward him even without the letter.

Finally, after over four months in the Spanish prison, on Saturday, November 16, Smyth was driven by two hulking U.S. marshals to Madrid and escorted onto a Delta Airlines flight to Los Angeles via Atlanta. Landing at 8:45 p.m., Smyth was once again back in California after sixteen years in hiding. From LAX he was taken in handcuffs to the city's federal Metropolitan Detention Center, a sleek stucco-and-glass ten-story high-rise that had the appearance of an insurance company home office. Inside, however, instead of smiling receptionists there were gruff prison guards handing Smyth his uniform, maroon pants with elastic waists and tan T-shirts. Placed in a cell high above the ground, from his window he overlooked the freeway and on the few clear smog-free days he could see the mountains near Mount Wilson, where he had proposed to his wife more than fifty-one years before.

With the original thirty-count indictment still in place, in addition to the escape charges, he was once again facing a maximum sentence of years in the three digits. Now seventy-two years old, he had little recourse but to plead guilty, confess to everything, and hope for the best. By then both the FBI and the U.S. Attorney's office were far more interested in Milchan than Smyth. As a result, in exchange for his plea, they agreed to drop twenty-eight of the counts, and in December Smyth pled guilty to violation of the U.S. Arms Export Control Act and also making a false statement about one shipment of krytrons.

On January 2, 2002, the FBI opened a formal Full Field Counterintelligence Investigation on Milchan on suspicion of espionage. Smyth had agreed to cooperate, but he knew the agents and the prosecutors were out of their league when it came to putting a wealthy Israeli spy in prison. "Frankly, I think the U.S. Attorneys are wasting their time," he wrote his wife, "but I'll tell them everything I know, which isn't much." He later wrote, "The Government had to get someone instead of the billionaire Israeli movie producer who had ordered the Krytrons. They couldn't get him, he's too rich and powerful. So they got me."

The interview with the prosecutors took place on February 21, 2002, at the U.S. district courthouse, just two blocks away. Sitting in a large glass-walled conference room, Smyth spent two hours detailing, for the first time, his long history with Milchan—a history that included dozens of illegal shipments of krytrons to his spymaster, along with the profitable markups. On April 16 and 17, Smyth was taken back to the courthouse conference room for another interview, this time by FBI counterintelligence agents.

Two weeks later, Smyth once again was taken to the courthouse, but this time it was for sentencing. Because of his cooperation, guilty plea, and frail health at age seventy-two, he was fairly convinced that he would receive about a ten-month sentence. That would mean release, since he would have by then served ten months, including his time in the Spanish prison. In fact, that was the recommendation of the probation department.

But when he had failed to show up for his original trial sixteen years earlier, the judge who was left without a defendant was Pamela A. Rymer. Since then, she had been elevated to a seat on the U.S. Court of Appeals. Still angry over Smyth's no-show, Rymer made the unusual decision to briefly return to the lower court in order to impose his sentence, and she had no intention of letting him walk. Instead, she sentenced Smyth to forty months in prison and tacked on a fine of $20,000. Smyth was stunned. "I sat at the table in the courtroom, unable to move or think," he later said. "I felt like screaming, but no words would form." In early June, he was transferred to the Federal Correctional Institution in Lompoc, California.

By then there was certainly more than enough evidence for the FBI to indict Smyth's spymaster, Milchan, as a co-conspirator. In addition to Smyth's testimony, the bureau had detailed receipts and other documents from the original search showing the transfers. Numerous other potential witnesses included Smyth's family members who also worked at Milco and dealt personally with Milchan, as well as members of Milco's board of directors who quit because of Milchan and the covert dealings with Israel. Then there were his close associates, such as De Niro, to whom Milchan acknowledged his connection to the krytrons and who could be forced to testify in a criminal trial.

But in the United States, there has long been a different set of laws for the super-rich and the politically powerful like Milchan, especially since he was a well-connected Israeli, making him off-limits without the highest-level approval. After all, an arrest and prosecution could lead to the loss of hefty donations from wealthy, pro-Israel voting blocs, and blowback from muscular lobbies like AIPAC. There was little surprise, therefore, that somewhere in the political stratosphere above the FBI's Los Angeles division, reaching potentially as high as the George W. Bush White House, Milchan's dossier was quietly slipped back into a locked file drawer. It's the small-fry agents like Pollard and Smyth who take the fall, not their spymasters and handlers with their political backers. Nevertheless, diligent FBI counterintelligence agents, ignoring Milchan's fame, money, and backers, continued to probe and gather evidence with the hope of one day prosecuting him the same way his agent, Smyth, was prosecuted for carrying out his orders.

On June 12, 2005, Milchan's romantic spy comedy, *Mr. & Mrs. Smith*, opened to a very successful weekend, with box-office earnings of $50,342,878. By then, the other Mr. & Mrs. Smyth were at last back together. Richard had been released on probation after being incarcerated for three and a half years. The two were living in a small mobile home in Lompoc, not far from the tall prison walls, barely making ends meet on their $2,000-a-month Social Security checks. And Smyth still had the $20,000 fine hanging over his head like an anvil.

Then in December, as Smyth's probation was finally about to end, he was once again contacted by the same FBI agents who had interviewed him nearly four years earlier. As before, they wanted more details on Milchan. This time the meeting took place at the FBI's Los Angeles division, located in the Wilshire Federal Building, seventeen stories of windows and stark white concrete in the middle of a former golf course. For three hours, in a sea of gray desks and boxy cubicles, the agents again questioned Smyth about Milchan's role in the krytron smuggling operation, and other potentially criminal activities.

"I could sense a great relief on the part of the two FBI agents when I made it clear that I would be their ally should they prosecute the man who had been the cause of my imprisonment," recalled Smyth. But as before, there was a mysterious political intervention, and the investigation went nowhere; Milchan was not even allowed to be questioned.

CHAPTER 19

◆

The Fix

In the fall of 2009, the cast and crew of Arnon Milchan's new production, *Knight and Day*, were about to begin shooting in Richard Smyth's former hideout, Andalusia in Spain. But the film had nothing to do with Smyth. Instead, it starred Tom Cruise as a disgraced spy trying to clear his name. Milchan, however, was a bit more generous with Cruise than he had been with his former agent, paying the actor $11 million (down from his usual $20 million because he liked the part). Another in a long line of cartoonish Cruise spy flicks, it nevertheless pulled in a worldwide gross of $262 million from an investment of $117 million.

By then, the only thing more sizable than Milchan's bank account, which hovered at around $4 billion, give or take a few hundred million, was his ever-expanding ego. With his own version of modesty, he once described himself as "young, slim, good-looking, amiable and clever." He was also a man with a spy inside trying to break free, to boast to the world that he, Arnon Milchan, was what Tom Cruise only pretended to be, a dashing, daring, heroic spy out to save the planet. Or at least Israel. He would drop hints every so often. But then when asked directly, he would affect a sly adolescent grin, a wink of sorts, before offering a deliberately ungenuine denial.

By late November 2013, that spy could no longer be restrained. Milchan needed to let it out, but just to the right crowd, the people who would put him in a pantheon of heroes, rather than a prison of criminals. He therefore accepted a rare invitation for an interview at his Malibu home, and aboard his private jet, to be aired on the Israeli television show *Uvda*. Broadcast in Hebrew from Tel Aviv, the segment was titled "Operation Hollywood," just like Milchan and Eschel Rhoodie's plan to spread pro-apartheid propaganda in the film industry.

The program was hosted by Ilana Dayan, a relative of Moshe Dayan, who said she was surprised that Milchan would admit to being a spy, thus exposing himself to criminal liability in the United States, and to his role as an arms dealer and top propagandist for the White supremacist government of South Africa. "In retrospect, it was in there, it was in him, it was waiting to burst out. It is very evident. Two minutes before landing, all of a sudden it comes out. 'I did it, I did it for Israel,'" she said.

For the program, Dayan also interviewed De Niro at the actor's upstate New York estate in Gardiner. And to her surprise, as the two old friends sat side by side on a tree-covered patio, De Niro revealed how Milchan years ago had confessed to him. "Milchan was in the midst of the biggest drama of his life, when one of the shipments of nuclear triggers for Israel went wrong," she said. It was early 1983, just when the FBI began investigating his partner, Richard Kelly Smyth, and Milchan left him to take the blame and dangle in the wind. But Milchan had other things on his mind. "This was the time in which he was filming *Once Upon a Time in America*," Dayan said. "He was dying for De Niro to take the leading role."

He "told me that he was an Israeli and he of course would do these things for his country," De Niro said. "There was something with the little things that trigger a nuclear thing." At that point, Milchan offered De Niro a little technical help. "A krytron," he said, as De Niro continued. "I remember at some point I had asked Arnon something about that. Being friends, I was curious. Not in an accusatory way, I just wanted to know. And he said, 'Yeah, I did it. I'm Israeli, that's my country.' And he gave me that answer and I accepted it."

Milchan simply smiled and did not contradict De Niro. In fact, he was very proud of his espionage against the United States, and how much fun it was. "Wow!" he gushed. "The action! That was exciting." He managed, however, to leave out the parts about the lives he ruined, the agents he turned his back on, the American security he undermined, or the numerous serious laws he had broken in the country that made him a multibillionaire, the country that had been his home for decades. Dayan believed that Milchan assumed he was too powerful to be touched by law enforcement. "It has to do with the fact that nobody can really harm him today—he's wealthy enough, he's successful enough, he's powerful enough, who cares?"

Milchan also revealed that he had recruited Hollywood director Sydney Pollack as "a real partner" to assist him in his covert acquisitions of arms and sensitive military equipment for Israel. The director of such films as *Tootsie* and *Out of Africa* died in 2008. When Dayan asked if Pollack knew about the details of the clandestine activities, Milchan said he did. "Pollack knew, but I didn't want to scare him because he's American," Milchan acknowledged. "He could have said 'no.' He said 'no' many times, but he also said 'yes' many times." Milchan, however, would not reveal the names of any living agents he recruited. Over the years there were likely others in Hollywood with divided loyalty, people like Pollack who also bought into his "do it for Israel" pitch. Others were still alive and working in movies.

With regard to Milchan's espionage activities in the United States on behalf of Israel, Dayan asked media mogul Rupert Murdoch if they had tarnished Milchan's reputation in Hollywood. In response, the owner of the *Wall Street Journal* and Fox News, and former chairman of 21st Century Fox, pointed to the sensitive issue of divided loyalties within the overwhelmingly Jewish film community. "Hollywood is a very Jewish industry. Very pro-Israel," he said. "Many would honor him for it. Others," he added with a tinge of regret, "might be a bit frightened by it, but that's all right." Dayan also interviewed Tom Rothman, another ex-chairman of Fox, about Milchan's spying against the country on behalf of another. "Didn't it ever raise an eyebrow in this town in terms of dual loyalty?" she asked. Rothman said it didn't. "He says, you know what? In this town there's one loyalty, one religion, one god: make hits, bring profits, that's the only thing that matters in Hollywood."

Milchan also admitted his role as a top financier and propagandist for apartheid South Africa, something that seemed to shock Dayan. It was a time, she said, when Israel entered into one of the "darkest alliances it ever made...The apartheid regime was at its worst...He's speaking on it on camera. I was amazed because for many years people have spoken about it, have heard about it, it was kind of rumored, but I didn't really imagine him coming on camera and confessing."

Despite the fact that the program was in Hebrew and not intended for audiences outside Israel, somewhere in the bowels of the U.S. State Department someone caught wind of it and courageously decided to take some action. Almost immediately, Milchan's usual ten-year U.S. visa was canceled. It was a minor move, but one that would take on a butterfly effect that would help cause the downfall of the Israeli government in Tel Aviv and the end of Benjamin Netanyahu's long career.

An Israeli citizen living permanently in the United States, Milchan was outraged that some low-level faceless bureaucrat, like a character in his film *Brazil*, could abruptly cancel his visa. All for simply committing espionage against the United States, recruiting others to do the same, and smuggling out hundreds of nuclear triggers. Crimes for which the maximum penalty would be several lifetimes in prison, if not death. He was therefore also worried that other faceless bureaucrats, this time within the FBI, might likewise decide to finally take action, so he quickly began searching for cover.

For thirty years, Hadas Klein, forty-eight, had been Milchan's closest personal assistant in Israel. Trim, with blonde hair cut in a boyish, carré style, she was also the person who knew where all of Milchan's proverbial bodies were buried. Now her top job was to help Milchan find a way to get his ten-year visa restored. "Then began a series of emotional calls by Arnon to any-one who he thought could help," she later said. "'You have to help me,' he would tell them."

First, he turned to the U.S. embassy. "He asked me to reach out to Dan Shapiro, U.S. ambassador to Israel, but he didn't answer," she said. "So he asked me to reach Netanyahu." After numerous calls to the prime minister's aide, Ari Harow, Netanyahu finally called her back in the middle of the night and told her it would be no problem. "Why is Arnon so worried?" he asked. "As long as he's rich and healthy, what does he have to worry about? It'll be taken care of."

Netanyahu then met with Shapiro in Jerusalem over coffee and urged the diplomat to help Milchan. Shapiro then reported back to the State Department in Washington about the strange meeting, saying Netanyahu was "very agitated" over the matter. In December, Klein said, "I got a call from Dan Shapiro or his assistant telling me the visa was approved." The bad news, however, was that the approval was only for one year, the most the local embassy could grant. Once again Milchan began to panic. Now he needed Netanyahu to go right to the top in the State Department, to Secretary of State John Kerry. And in March 2014, Netanyahu was planning to fly to the United States to speak at the AIPAC annual conference in Washington and Milchan saw an opportunity. He would invite the prime minister to his home in Malibu for a party, giving him an opportunity to plead his case in person for help with the visa.

March was a busy time for Milchan. Principal photography was under way at the Sunset Gower Studios in Hollywood on his newest film, appropri-ately titled *Rules Don't Apply*. A romantic dramedy loosely based on the life of Howard Hughes, the American business magnate, investor, and film director, it was written, produced, and directed by Warren Beatty, who was also part of the ensemble cast. Hughes was played by Beatty, the actor's first time on the big screen in a decade and a half. Others in the cast included Beatty's wife, Annette Bening, Matthew Broderick, and Lily Collins. Beatty first happened to see Howard Hughes in a hotel lobby in the early 1970s, and since then he had been working on a screenplay based on his life.

On March 6, 2014, a week after the shooting began, Milchan threw a very large and very glitzy Hollywood party at his expansive beachfront Mal-ibu house. Just three days earlier he had won the Best Picture Oscar for *12 Years a Slave*. It was an ironic award for the man who had secretly been a top propagandist and arms runner for the White supremacist leaders of apart-heid South Africa. Invited by Milchan as the guest of honor was Benjamin

Netanyahu, who would be accompanied by his wife, Sara, and son Yair. For Milchan, that meant a bit of redecoration. "If the Netanyahu couple arrives [for a visit]," said his aide, "Arnon says, 'Quick, quick, quick, take off all the pictures of Shimon Peres and hang pictures of him [Netanyahu] instead.'"

The number of celebrities juggling canapés in one hand and flutes of champagne in the other was extraordinary even by Hollywood standards. "Am I at the Oscars?" quipped Netanyahu, who had agreed to give a short talk. The glitterati on the confirmed list included Sony Pictures top executives Michael Lynton and Amy Pascal, director James Cameron, humorist and political commentator Bill Maher, and actors Robert De Niro, Warren Beatty, Barbra Streisand, Leonardo DiCaprio, Keanu Reeves, Kate Hudson, James Caan, Clint Eastwood, Anthony Hopkins, Ben Affleck, Billy Crystal, Annette Bening, Jeremy Renner, and many others.

Cohosting the party was Australian casino magnet James Packer, a close friend of both Milchan and Warren Beatty. Heir to a multibillion-dollar fortune, with a desire to expand into the film industry, he was coproducing *Rules Don't Apply* along with Milchan. Packer's late father, Kerry, had previously been a partner in Milchan's New Regency film company. At forty-seven, Packer was tall and lanky like a basketball player, with short-cropped black hair. Once planning to marry singer Mariah Carey, he had given her a $10 million engagement ring. Their relationship ended, however, in a messy breakup. Unhelpful was his habit of guzzling bottles of vodka and tequila, sometimes downing half the contents in less than a minute.

Introduced by Milchan, Packer quickly became a close friend and an enormous fan of Netanyahu, who seemed to enjoy the company of billionaires. Eventually, at Netanyahu's encouragement, Packer even purchased a beachfront villa next to the prime minister, at 71 Hadar Street in Caesarea, for about $2 million. Netanyahu soon had his own key. While Packer was away, which was most of the time, Bibi would use the estate as a luxurious annex to his own villa, taking advantage of the private gym, the heated swimming pool, the huge Jacuzzi, the outdoor fireplace, and the 103-inch television. And sitting on the driveway was Packer's blue Audi Q7 and an all-terrain vehicle, useful for navigating the nearby sand dunes. There was "a kind of convenience in moving from house to house, from yard to yard, from pool to pool, from food island to food island," said Milchan. At other times, Packer would moor his 287-foot yacht, the *Arctic P*, near the Caesarea marina.

The party was also a key opportunity for Milchan to have a quiet and confidential conversation with his old friend Bibi. The two had first crossed paths more three decades before, when Netanyahu was Israel's acting ambassador in Washington during the Reagan administration. As the krytron scandal exploded, Netanyahu had come up with the plan that saved Milchan from arrest and prosecution, while leaving Smyth to take the fall. They grew closer in 1999, following Netanyahu's ouster after his first term in office. It was a depressing period. "I was a political cadaver at that time," Netanyahu later said. "I had no future. I was a goner."

But Milchan's flashy, Hollywood-style exuberance was like a tonic for the dejected Netanyahu. Later, after he once again became prime minister, their relationship continued to develop. And knowing Milchan's covert activities in the United States from the beginning, he also began sharing some of his government's highest secrets with him. "Bibi personally tells me everything," Milchan once told Yuval Diskin, the head of Shin Bet, the country's internal security service.

During their private discussion in Malibu, Milchan once again brought up the cancellation of his visa and asked if Netanyahu could help. The prime minister made a few suggestions, such as appointing Milchan as honorary consul in Los Angeles, or even nominating him for the role of president of Israel. Both would give Milchan a diplomatic passport, eliminating the need for a visa. But they were long-term ideas, and his status could quickly change depending on politics in Israel.

What Milchan needed was a ten-year visa as soon as possible. But that was something only Secretary of State John Kerry could grant, so he felt it was critical that Netanyahu arrange a face-to-face between Milchan and Kerry as soon as possible. Given his billions, his Hollywood status, his power, and his connections with Netanyahu, Milchan believed he could convince the secretary of state to overlook the FBI reports about his years of espionage and nuclear materials smuggling in the United States and restore his ten-year visa. And Netanyahu was the only one who could set up such a meeting. But he knew that favors from Netanyhau didn't come cheap, and that there would be a high price to pay. A high price in the form of very expensive "gifts" for Netanyahu. "Gifts" that were not gifts but bribes according to Milchan, who would complain that they were always demanded and not voluntarily given. Bribes that could go on for years as repayment. But as he would later tell Klein, "there's no choice," and Netanyahu agreed to connect Milchan and Kerry.

Keeping his end of the bargain, Netanyahu telephoned Kerry at least three times attempting to resolve the matter with Milchan. At one point, Netanyahu's special envoy, Isaac Molho, called a State Department official and said, "The prime minister wants to speak with Secretary Kerry urgently." A few hours later, Kerry and Netanyahu connected. But because of the request for urgency, Kerry assumed that Netanyahu wanted to talk to him about

the Israeli-Palestinian peace process, then on the top of the Obama administration's agenda. Instead, the "urgent" phone call had only to do with the
upgrading of Milchan's visa. At the time, Kerry couldn't be bothered with the
issue, but Netanyahu turned more aggressive, almost demanding his personal intervention.

"One day I got a phone call from abroad, it was John Kerry calling me
himself," Hadas Klein, under oath, would tell an Israeli court in July 2022.
Milchan was in Malibu sleeping at the time, but soon Klein connected the
two by phone. They would eventually meet in New York, she said. But there
was a strange catch. What Milchan wanted was not a green card or "work"
visa, but a ten-year "tourist" visa, as if he was going to spend the decade
visiting national parks in a camper. Instead, California was where he lived,
worked, made his billions, and where his company, New Regency Productions, was based. Yet as Kline told the judge, "He doesn't pay any taxes in the
United States." Implying a sort of tax-evasion scheme with the "tourist" visa,
she added, "He counts the days in each country he goes to in the framework
of his businesses."

Believing his wealth and power made him immune from arrest in the
United States, Milchan also apparently assumed, unlike everyone else, he was
also absolved from paying taxes. However, under the IRS "Substantial Presence Test," a person is a U.S. resident–and thus required to pay taxes–if he
or she was physically present in the country "on at least 31 days during the
current year, and 183 days during the 3-year period that includes the current
year and the 2 years immediately before that."

Also revealed in July 2022, Milchan even found a way to avoid paying
taxes in his homeland of Israel. "According to an accumulation of evidence
in recent years, plus declarations given in court," reported *Haaretz*, Milchan "apparently also paid no taxes at all, anywhere, from 2008 to 2018."
To accomplish such an enormous feat, he and his attorneys engineered the
so-called "Milchan Law," which grants full and complete exemption from all
payments and reporting of taxes for new immigrants and returning Israelis
for ten years upon arrival. According to the paper, "The law created a global
tax haven for Jewish and Israeli millionaires." Applied to Milchan, "each year
he would have saved capital gains tax to the tune of about $50 million–which
over the 10 years of the exemption comes to about half a billion dollars."
That's of course in addition to what he saved by allegedly not paying U.S.
taxes.

According to the *Times of Israel*, the "Milchan Law" flies in the face of
"international anti–money laundering standards, and for years the then-
finance minister [now temporary prime minister], Yair Lapid, had tried to

get rid of it. But each year the efforts to cancel it [were] scuttled, putting Israel in danger of being placed on international sanctions lists," said the paper. Lapid saw his opportunity to finally end the exemption when it was due to expire in 2018, but Milchan strongly lobbied Netanyahu to renew it for another decade. As a result, that action became part of a secret Israeli bribery investigation. "The central favor they believe Netanyahu provided both Milchan and Packer, in exchange for gifts," said the *Times of Israel*, "was an attempt to alter a little-known tax exemption law."

Never satisfied, Milchan also hid hundreds of millions of dollars offshore in a number of tax dodges according to the secret Pandora Papers, a leak of 12 million files from more than a dozen offshore companies around the world. The papers revealed that Milchan stashed nearly half a billion dollars in seven secret accounts in the Virgin Islands. In his Century Mark Company, Milchan had antiques and artworks valued at almost $453 million, much of it decorating the walls of his home in Malibu. His Fairway Isle Limited company owned his prestigious $7.6 million Manhattan apartment, purchased from Rupert Murdoch's family. Millions of dollars more were in the form of real estate in Malibu.

In the end, Kerry granted Milchan his wish and approved his visa, apparently proving him right about wealth and power. It was an absurd move by the Obama administration, rewarding an admitted high-level foreign spymaster rather than having him arrested like Smyth, his American agent, or anyone else who commits espionage and smuggles U.S. nuclear materials to a foreign country.

Around the same time Kerry approved Milchan's visa, frustrated senior U.S. intelligence officials were testifying about Israeli espionage in secret sessions before the House Judiciary and Foreign Affairs Committees. "U.S. intelligence officials trooped up to Capitol Hill to tell U.S. lawmakers considering visa waivers for Israelis that Jerusalem's spying here had 'crossed red lines,'" said *Newsweek*'s Jeff Stein. The extent of the spying was "quite shocking," one staffer who was there told Stein, adding that he found the testimony "very sobering...alarming...even terrifying." Others called it "unrivaled" and "unseemly," and noted that "it has been extensive for years." And a former staffer who attended a similar classified briefing exclaimed, "No other country close to the United States continues to cross the line on espionage like the Israelis do."

Unsurprisingly, an anonymous official from the Israeli government was quoted in the Israeli media as saying that Stein's *Newsweek* report "had the whiff of anti-Semitism in it." It was the standard slander used to intimidate journalists and media organizations with the intention of frightening them away from critical reporting on Israel. "There is a small community of ex-CIA, FBI and military people who have worked this account who are absolutely cheering on the [*Newsweek*] story," responded a former U.S. intelligence official. "Not one of them is anti-Semitic. In fact, it has nothing to do with anti-Semitism. It has only to do with why [Israel] gets kid-glove treatment when, if it was Japan doing it or India doing it at this level, it would be outrageous."

It's a view that is virtually unanimous among those in the intelligence agencies, and those who cover them. "Former counterintelligence officials describe Israeli intelligence operations in the United States as quite extensive, ranking just below those of China and Russia," said Scott Shane, who covered intelligence for the *New York Times* for many years. His counterpart at the *Wall Street Journal*, Adam Entous, agreed. "U.S. officials said Israel has long topped the list of countries that aggressively spy on the U.S., along with China, Russia and France," he said. Paul Pillar, the CIA's former national intelligence officer for the Near East, also confirmed that Israel posed a serious threat. "Israel should be assumed to continue to have an aggressive intelligence collection operation against the United States," he said. And according to a top secret document leaked by NSA whistleblower Edward Snowden, "A NIE [National Intelligence Estimate] ranked [Israel] as the third most aggressive intelligence service against the U.S."

For FBI counterintelligence, it means agents are constantly required to close their eyes when it comes to criminal activity by Israel. According to I. C. Smith, a former top FBI counterintelligence officer, "Dealing with the Israelis was, for those assigned that area, extremely frustrating. The Israelis were supremely confident that they had the clout, especially on the Hill, to basically get [away] with just about anything." Another former top intelligence official said, "You catch them red-handed, and they shrug and say, 'Okay now, anything else?'" Milchan was a prime example.

———

Thus, few things are more guaranteed to make a senior FBI official break out in a cold sweat, and then clam up, than being asked about Israel. During a long interview over lunch with Frank Figliuzzi Jr., the bureau's former assistant director for counterintelligence, I asked, "Why haven't you looked into Israel?" Suddenly his eyes widened, and he immediately reverted to sign language. He put one finger to his lips and waved another over my tape recorder in what seemed an attempt to make it disappear. Understanding the strange pantomime, I turned off the recorder.

Smith's reaction reflected the secret influence exerted by pro-Israel lobbies on both parties. According to an investigation by *The Guardian*, pro-Israel donors spent over $22 million on lobbying and contributions in 2018. The report was based on an analysis of data from the nonprofit, non-partisan Center for Responsive Politics, which uses election records to track campaign finance spending. "I haven't observed many other countries that have a comparable level of activity, at least in domestic lobbying data," said Dan Auble, a senior researcher at the center. Money translates into political power and influence, which in turn translate into "Get Out of Jail Free" cards for Israeli spies like Milchan. The result is serious damage to U.S. national security, and fat bank accounts for corrupt politicians.

————

The meeting with Kerry was a success, and Milchan now had a ten-year tourist visa stamped in his passport. Netanyahu had carried out his part of the secret quid pro quo. It was now Milchan's turn, something he was not happy about. "Our prime minister and his wife are hedonistic, and they have no limits," he would later angrily tell Israeli investigators. "I find it disgusting, it comes from a place of hedonism." According to an unprecedented Israeli criminal indictment, in return for his intervention with Kerry, Netanyahu allegedly began secretly demanding hundreds of thousands of dollars' worth of gifts from Milchan, both for himself as well as his wife, Sara.

Despite his billions of dollars in the bank, and millions more secretly stashed away in offshore accounts, Milchan was well known for his hatred of parting with money, no matter how small or inconsequential the amount. His assistant, Hadas Klein, told prosecutors how he insisted on approving expenditures as little as 20 shekels, $5.70. "Milchan never gave anybody anything without a reason," his former business partner Yossi Maiman testified. And Sheldon Adelson mockingly said of Milchan, "He has deep pockets and short arms. He can't reach into his pockets with his short arms." At one point Milchan asked Klein to call Adelson and ask him where he might pay less for cigars. Faced with growing demands from Netanyahu for more and more expensive bribes, Milchan turned to his old friend, partner, and fellow multi-billionaire James Packer for help with the expenses. Among them was keeping Sara Netanyahu fully supplied with an ocean of champagne.

In the iconic *Breakfast at Tiffany's*, the glamorous Holly Golightly, played by Audrey Hepburn, loved her champagne so much she would often crack open a bottle before breakfast. Like Holly, Sara Netanyahu, a short and hefty woman with dark blonde hair, was also an ardent fan of the French fizz. As part of the conspiracy, therefore, she allegedly turned Milchan into her private vintner, constantly demanding cases and cases of the very best bubbles, Dom Pérignon Rosé, at more than $400 a bottle.

Whenever her stock was running low, Sara would call Hadas Klein and request more "pinks," the code name for the champagne. "Sara would ask for boxes of six or 12 bottles of champagne," Klein testified. Milchan's chauffeur, Jonathan, would then drive his boss's Jaguar to the Hinnawi Wine Store in Herzliya, hide the heavy wooden crates in large black bags, and drive them to the prime minister's official residence in Jerusalem. "We received crates of champagne from Milchan's driver and we brought it up to the top floor, where the kitchen was," recalled Meni Naftali, the chief caretaker. More crates of champagne were stored in the gym at Packer's beachfront home next to Netanyahu, giving the prime minister easy access.

Secrecy was critical. "Sara was afraid of being recorded. She asked to speak only by landline or meet face to face," Klein testified. At another point, when Packer was away his housekeeper at the beach house called Klein, who also acted as Packer's aide, and said Sara wanted to come by and pick up some bottles of champagne. Klein told her to put them in a black bag, seal it up so no one can see, and leave it by the door. "She's scared to death," Klein told the housekeeper. And failure to do as told was never tolerated by Sara. "She shouted at me many times regarding gifts," said Klein, who once complained to Bibi, "I don't work for your wife."

Sara also had expensive tastes in clothing and jewelry and soon allegedly began demanding that Milchan also provide those items as part of the secret arrangement. According to the prosecutors, they included a bracelet made of 18-karat yellow and white gold with 121 diamonds valued at over $45,000, delivered by Packer. It had been purchased at her favorite shop, the glitzy Caprice near Milchan's office in the Ramat Gan section of Tel Aviv, home to one of the world's major diamond exchanges. "When you step out into the world," says the store on its website, "the wearer is immediately recognized as a person with a style that matches no one else." Other jewelry was purchased and delivered on Milchan's behalf by Klein. Worried about the growing numbers of expensive gifts, she asked Milchan about them. "He said there's no choice," Klein told prosecutors, clearly indicating that he considered them demands for bribes.

And then there were the "gifts" for Netanyahu. In the same way Milchan was to keep Sara well stocked in expensive champagne and jewelry, he was to keep Netanyahu's humidors well supplied with the world's most extremely expensive Cuban cigars, among them smooth, tightly hand-rolled Cohiba Siglo V cigars. A box of twenty-five goes for around $1,200. Others on the list included equally pricy Trinidad and Montecristo brand Cuban cigars. "He would phone and say, 'Hey, are there any leaves?'" Milchan would later tell investigators, indicating the code word for cigars.

Like Sara, Bibi was also very demanding. When he requested a box of his favorite Cohiba 56 cigars from Milchan, Hadas Klein could only find a box of Cohiba 54 at Cabinet, the cigar store. Netanyahu then angrily complained to Milchan. Eventually, he would secretly pass to the prime minister about $85,000 worth of "leaves." And because Netanyahu liked to dip his cigars in a glass of Cointreau, bottles of the orange-flavored French liqueur also became part of the "gifts."

Soon, said Klein, Sara began getting nervous. "Arnon told me a few times that Sara had said to him, 'Do you trust Hadas to never talk?' and that he had replied, 'Listen, Hadas has been with my banks for 30 years, my life is in her hands, you have nothing to worry about,'" Klein told the prosecutors. Sara listened to Milchan, Klein said. "But she was scared." Packer was also growing increasing fearful of a potential criminal probe. "We would buy iPads every two days because of his fears," according to Klein. Then, "he was sure there were all sorts of things [on them] and he would throw them in the pool."

––––––––

With a fresh ten-year visa now in his passport, personally approved by Secretary of State Kerry, and under the protection of Netanyahu thanks to the regular supply of expensive "gifts," Milchan likely assumed he no longer had to worry about the FBI showing up unannounced and hauling him in for questioning. What he never expected was that the proverbial knock on his door would come instead from Israeli investigators. Unlike their American counterparts, the Israeli police were undeterred when it came to power, privilege, and money. Eventually they caught wind of the secret deal between Milchan and Netanyahu, and without being told why, Milchan was asked to come to the headquarters of the department's National Fraud Unit while on a visit to Israel. At the time he had just released *Rules Don't Apply*, Warren Beatty's romantic dramedy (adding to his troubles, it became an enormous box-office disaster, bringing in only $3.9 million against its budget of $25 million).

Nevertheless, on a rainy day in early December in 2016, Milchan showed up at the Israeli police office for the mysterious appointment and was placed in a stark white interrogation room. Two officers soon entered and began questioning him about the "gifts" to both Netanyahu and his wife, Sara. Reluctantly, given that they had already collected a great deal of evidence, Milchan confessed. He told the investigators that the "gifts" were the price of admission to Netanyahu and his circle of power. "Gifts that I don't bring voluntarily, but am asked to bring," he told police, making clear that they were involuntarily given rather than friendly gifts. Milchan said the "gifts" made him "feel sick." They included the expensive jewelry requested by Sara and approved by Netanyahu. Hadas Klein would later confirm that the bribes were demanded, not simple presents. "I want to emphasize," she told investigators, "nothing was volunteered." Following police searches of Milchan's office and elsewhere, investigators turned up evidence indicating "gifts" totaling nearly a quarter of a million dollars.

Unknown to Milchan, in another interrogation room just down the hall was Sara Netanyahu, also being grilled, but involving an entirely separate fraud case. She had no knowledge that Milchan was also there, or that she was a subject in a major bribery investigation. Therefore, she was being questioned "under caution," meaning subject to possible arrest, rather than as just a witness. It was a stormy interview that would last nearly twelve hours. Ironically, the bribes from Milchan continued even during the investigation of her. Shortly after Netanyahu left the police station, Hadas Klein received a familiar signal from the prime minister's official residence in Jerusalem demanding more "pinks."

Milchan couldn't believe what was happening. "Arnon was shocked," said Klein. "The sky fell on him and he said: 'how will I go around the world with the word bribe [attached to my name]?'" Much later, he would receive an even greater shock when he learned that the person who threw both him and Netanyahu under the bus, from the very beginning, was his trusted aide, Hadas Klein. Sara Netanyahu's suspicions had proved correct. Klein would tell Milchan she had an appointment at the dentist or the doctor's office, and instead pay a visit to the prosecutor. Once there, she would reveal the code names they used, the gifts hidden in bags, the rages Sara would fly into when her requests were turned down, and the fact that Bibi Netanyahu was fully aware that he was unlawfully receiving the "gifts"—committing very serious crimes. Later, according to Klein, Sara would attempt to pressure her not to cooperate with law enforcement, pressure Klein rejected.

Enter the chief superintendent.

CHAPTER 20

◆

The Trial

In charge of the investigation was a determined chief superintendent, Shlomo "Momi" Meshulam. A cross between TV's Columbo and the fictional French *commissaire* Maigret, he slowly and methodically began building his cases against both Milchan and the prime minister, as well as exploring the involvement of Milchan's film partner, billionaire casino tycoon James Packer. Although those interviewed were cautioned not to discuss the case with anyone, rumors of the investigation soon began to circulate. Around the same time, Packer showed up offshore on his megayacht, and Chief Superintendent Meshulam began making preparations to bring him in for questioning. But before he could act, Packer received an urgent call from Prime Minister Netanyahu, who demanded forcefully that Packer and his *Arctic P* "beat it out of here." Packer obeyed, never to return.

Nevertheless, Meshulam was able to have investigators interview Packer in Australia. Distance was no barrier. While in Israel and ordered to undergo another interrogation, Milchan quickly flew to London, where, unlike in Israel, British law allows lawyers to be present during an interrogation. Meshulam quickly followed, and then pursued him to his home in Malibu for more questioning. Formally advised that he was now a principal suspect in a serious criminal investigation, Milchan reportedly was "boiling" mad and "feels betrayed," according to one of the investigators. "This man destroyed my life," Milchan charged, referring to Netanyahu. "Suddenly, you see he's lying to you. He says it's all legal, that he checked with the attorney general and friends are allowed to give gifts, except for homes. And suddenly I'm in the papers, and my children have bodyguards. I'm deathly afraid." Finally, Milchan pleaded, "Don't throw me under the bus because of him."

During the secret interrogations, Milchan called the idea that his "gifts" were simply normal offers of friendship laughable. Asked whether Sara Netanyahu ever gave him gifts, Milchan responded, "Do you want me to fall on the ground laughing? The answer is no." Then he was asked, What about Bibi? "Do you know him as a person who gives presents?" Milchan laughed.

As the interrogations ended, Milchan seemed to realize the irony of his situation. While the country he harmed turned a blind eye to his activities due to his wealth and power, the one he claimed to have helped ignored his elite status and was looking to put him in prison. "I'm sad—sad that they don't remember all I did for this country," he said. "I wake up in the morning sad; I go to sleep at night sad. I feel wounded." But in the end, as always, it was all about Milchan. "Maybe they'll see the damage they've done to me."

Adding to his troubles, a group of investors who had pumped millions into his Warren Beatty film were now suing him for $50 million in a fraud complaint. It alleged that the film bombed because he failed to market it adequately. "Among other results of Milchan's utter failures to keep his false promises concerning marketing," said the suit, "the Picture was so poorly and ineffectively marketed that it had a disastrous public 'unaided awareness' score of 1% at the time of its release." Around the same time, Milchan launched his own $18 million suit against Beatty, claiming the actor failed to repay the promotional and advertising costs of the disastrous film.

On Monday, January 2, 2017, Chief Superintendent Momi Meshulam turned his attention to Netanyahu, without letting on that he had spoken with Milchan. It was sunny and in the 60s when his car pulled up to the high gray steel gate. Beyond was Agion House, the prime minister's official residence. Located in the upscale Talbiyeh section of Jerusalem at 9 Smolenskin Street, it is a boxy 1930s Bauhaus affair coated in pale tan limestone and surrounded by a high wall. Outside, the area is festooned with cameras and triple barricades, and a huge black curtain at a nearby intersection blocks the view of the entrance.

Accompanied by two investigators, Meshulam was escorted to a study where Netanyahu soon entered and took his seat at a polished rosewood desk. Behind him was a map of the Middle East, to his right a bookcase with family photos and a flat-screen television, and next to him two phones, one black and one white and red. Nearby was a gray paper shredder. Netanyahu was not allowed to have a lawyer next to him and the chief superintendent was uninterested in small talk. Instead, the questions were tough and direct, and it was clear that the prime minister was unprepared and very rattled by Meshulam.

Soon, to Netanyahu's astonishment, he slowly began realizing that Milchan had already been secretly interviewed, and that he had thrown him under the proverbial bus. Cornered, Netanyahu exploded, pounding the desk between them with his fist. Bang! Like a hammer. "I don't believe you're asking me about this," he growled at Meshulam. "But go on, it's your right." Without skipping a beat, the chief superintendent shot back, "It's our obligation, by the way," and continued with his questions:

Q: *Did you see the quantities of champagne bottles?*
A: From time to time I saw a bottle here, a bottle there... What do you think, that I count bottles?... Maybe I count different things that are related to our existence here? Such as how many missiles are aimed at us, things like that?... In Milchan's home, champagne was drunk in lakes, in cascades, in rivers.

Netanyahu would often give one answer, only to be contradicted when Meshulam quoted Milchan:

Q: *Did your wife receive a piece of jewelry from Milchan?*
A: No. I don't know that she received [one].

Q: *You don't?*
A: Maybe she did, maybe not.

Q: *You don't know?*
A: I don't know, maybe.

Q: *Last September your wife received a piece of jewelry worth almost 11,000 shekels [approximately $3,000 at the time].*
A: I don't have the foggiest idea.

Q: *You don't have the foggiest?*
A: I don't have the foggiest... Nothing.

Q: *I say that you knew about the item of jewelry your wife received from Milchan.*
A: About the last piece of jewelry? A total lie.

At another point, Netanyahu denied making a tape recording of a conversation, only to have Meshulam produce it.

Q: *You told us you didn't make recordings. That is a lie.*
A: My dear Momi, it is not a lie, just a memory problem.

Q: *If it's not a lie, sir, I don't know—and forgive me for saying this—I don't know what a lie is.*

Q: *Do you believe what you're saying?*
A: Every word.

Q: *It's even embarrassing...*
A: The truth embarrasses you.

Q: *Embarrassing, embarrassing...*
A: Don't talk to me like that...I'm asking you.

There would be at least three more interrogations of Netanyahu that month. They would lead, according to close associates, to haunting fears by both Bibi and Sara of once again staring at the moldy walls inside the police interrogation rooms in Petah Tikva—the same facility where Palestinians are regularly detained and often tortured. Soon after Netanyahu's first-term defeat in 1999, around the time he became close to Milchan, both Bibi and Sara were suspected of accepting $50,000 in bribes. Although the police recommended that they both be indicted, the attorney general eventually declined. "The Netanyahus thus escaped a criminal trial by the skin of their teeth," said *Haaretz* columnist Yossi Verter.

For Milchan, one of his many problems was eliminated in September 2017 when his former agent, Richard Kelly Smyth, suddenly died of a stroke. At the time, Smyth and his wife were still living meagerly in a mobile home in Lompoc, California, not far from the prison where he had been held. Nevertheless, other members of the Smyth family who worked at Milco and dealt with Milchan and the krytrons, as well as former board members, could still testify against him. And then there was Robert De Niro, to whom he had confessed. In addition, all the documents showing the transfers, as well as the phone call records, were still in FBI custody, as was Smyth's statement to the FBI confirming Milchan's role.

Milchan's luck was running out. Five months later, on February 13, 2018, Chief Superintendent Meshulam recommended that he be indicted on bribery charges for showering Netanyahu and his wife with $215,000 worth of lavish "gifts" in exchange for interceding on his behalf with John Kerry and the Obama administration for his visa. He also recommended charging him with bribing Netanyahu to renew the "Milchan Law" tax exemption to save him tens of millions of dollars. However, the scheme was eventually rejected by then minister of finance Yair Lapid, now Israel's interim prime minister.

"It was not my job to help Milchan or any other tycoon, but rather to look after the country's coffers," said Lapid. "Despite all the pressure, I refused to pass the law."

———

But after yearlong negotiations, on February 28, 2019, the prosecutors agreed to set aside the charges provided Milchan appear in court and give testimony as a key witness against Netanyahu. Some of Milchan's friends worried that Netanyahu might retaliate somehow, given his power as prime minister. But Milchan had much more dirt on his old friend. "He won't attack me," he told them, sounding like a character in one of his more subpar films, "because he knows I have more bullets in the chamber."

The prosecutors had also requested the testimony of former secretary of state John Kerry and former U.S. ambassador Dan Shapiro. But, standing behind his corrupt ally in Bibi, President Donald Trump denied the request. By then, after years of investigation, the police had discovered even more evidence of graft, bribes, and corruption by Netanyahu. And as before, to save his own skin, Milchan agreed to become a principal witness—or, as in countless Hollywood Mafia flicks, principal "rat."

Finally, six years after the butterfly fluttered its wings in Malibu during the *Uvda* interview, a hurricane engulfed Tel Aviv. On November 21, 2019, Attorney General Avichai Mendelblit formally charged Prime Minister Benjamin Netanyahu with multiple crimes involving corruption, including bribery, fraud, and breach of trust. "You took the favors," said the indictment, "in full awareness that you were taking a bribe." It was an almost unheard-of action against a sitting head of state. Milchan was featured prominently in the indictment, which focused on his hundreds of thousands of dollars in "gifts" to Netanyahu for his visa intervention.

Among the actions mentioned as a reward for the bribes was Netanyahu agreeing to show up at Milchan's glitzy, star-packed *12 Years a Slave* Best Picture Oscar party. "As part of the relationship between you and Milchan, you acceded to his request by making a speech in his home in the United States in 2014," it said. Bibi also let Milchan join his official party when Netanyahu addressed the U.S. Congress in 2015. Tzipi Livni, Israel's former foreign minister, accused Netanyahu of "living at the expense of others," adding that he no longer had "the moral right" to serve as prime minister. And former Labor leader Shelly Yachimovich said that the prime minister's acceptance of gifts from his "sugar daddy" Milchan was "corruption exemplified."

It was a supremely anxious time for Milchan. In his homeland of Israel he was under criminal investigation for bribery, and in his adopted homeland of the United States he was under criminal investigation for espionage and nuclear smuggling. Nevertheless, he had just begun filming his latest movie, *Deep Water*, an erotic thriller starring Ben Affleck and Ana de Armas and directed by Adrian Lyne. The title of Lyne's earlier film *Indecent Proposal* seemed to fit Milchan's predicament.

On February 8, 2021, a Monday, the trial of Benjamin Netanyahu opened in Jerusalem District Court on Saladin Street in East Jerusalem. Outside, grim-faced police officers, Border Police, Shin Bet agents, and members of the court security service had ringed the building in case of violence. Only a month before, thousands of insurrectionists had stormed the U.S. Capitol to overturn the U.S. election. The street was divided with Bibi-bashers on one side shouting, "He's a thief" and "He's an undertaker," while across the invisible divide, a lone Bibist was draped in a "Bibi vaccinated me" T-shirt. Beyond were roadblocks, police vans, explosives detection dogs, and a low-hovering helicopter. "It was a war zone," noted Moran Sharir in *Haaretz*. "It looked as though half the security and policing forces of the State of Israel were concentrated in the streets around the courthouse."

Inside was an unusual sight. Benjamin Netanyahu, the prime minister of Israel, was sitting in a seat at the defendant's table, twitching, as one commentator noted, like "a drugged cockroach in a bottle," as he waited to be called. For a dozen years, Netanyahu had instead been a man for whom others waited and waited, hoping to be called.

After about twenty minutes, the panel of three black-robed judges appeared and everyone clambered slowly to their feet as hoarse chants of "Bibi go home! Bibi go home!" could be heard through an open window. When addressed by the judges, he was shorn of his grand title and became simply "Mr. Netanyahu."

In the meantime, on March 23, 2021, Israeli voters could at least decide whether to evict Netanyahu and Sara from the prime minister's residence with another election, the fourth in two years. Sensing the mood throughout the country, Bibi had long had fears of voters heading to the polls at the same time that he was under indictment for bribery and other felonies, and those fears were justified. Although his Likud Party won the most seats, Netanyahu needed to form a coalition government by May 4 in order to remain prime minister. It proved to be a difficult task and instead, like his pal Donald Trump, he wanted a redo—still another election, giving him a second bite at the apple.

But that required getting the support of one of his chief rivals, former defense minister Naftali Bennett, another denizen of the extreme far right. Desperate, Netanyahu turned into Vito Corleone. "When he realized that I didn't intend to let him drag Israel into a fifth election, he really threatened me," said Bennett. "'Listen,' he said to me, 'if I understand correctly what you're going to do, you should know that I am going to employ my entire machine, the army against you.'" Netanyahu then "demonstrated with his arm," Bennett said, an aircraft coming in for an attack. "I will send the drones at you, and we'll see," Netanyahu snarled.

Despite the threats, Bennett refused. And in the end, it was he and former finance minister Yair Lapid who formed a coalition government without Netanyahu. On June 13, 2021, Bennett was sworn in as the new prime minister. Asked about his predecessor's corruption case, he said, "I would not like to see Netanyahu in jail, in a prisoner's uniform. That is not an image that would bring honor to him or the country's citizens."

Stunned by the defeat, Netanyahu seemed for a time as if he would need to be physically removed from the official mansion, his home for a dozen years. The delay in leaving gave him time to order a massive shredding operation in the "aquarium," a sterile area where the prime minister and his most senior aides sit. "Before I left, I took documents out of the safe, gave them to my deputy and told her to shred them immediately," said Tzachi Braverman, Netanyahu's cabinet secretary. "She shredded them, and with that, it was over." In the meantime, others volunteered to help evacuate Netanyahu from the residence. "We decided to come with our truck, and we are ready to help him anytime," said one of the demonstrators who had crowded nearby Paris Square for months, chanting for the defeat of the "Crime Minister."

Finally, late on Sunday July 11, the Netanyahus departed the mansion in a modest Skoda, heading toward their oceanside villa in Caesarea. Left behind was their former car, a shiny armor-plated Audi. Moments after they disappeared down the road, protesters took to Facebook. "The defendant and his family fled as the last of the thieves in the night," one wrote. For many activists, however, it was joy mixed with anxiety. While happy to see the Netanyahus vanish into the darkness, come the next morning they were not welcoming his replacement, Naftali Bennett, a pro-settlement right-wing ultra-nationalist. "There will never be a peace plan with the Palestinians," he has said. "I will do everything in my power to make sure they never get a state."

Among the protesters was Guy Hirschfeld. "Until Sunday I'll fight for the establishment of a new government," he said. "And beginning Monday morning I'll fight that government." He added, "In the end, the main problem is the occupation." Nor did Bennett's election help Israel's image with its diaspora in the United States. In January 2022, leaders of the two largest streams of U.S. Judaism signed letters sharply critical of Bennett, describing his actions as "unacceptable" and expressing "outrage" and a sense of "betrayal."

After originally entering a plea of not guilty, by early 2022, with so much evidence against him, Netanyahu was instead looking to settle with a plea deal. It was an outcome even endorsed by the right-wing *Jerusalem Post*. "The time has come for the country to move on from Netanyahu-gate," said an editorial. The question was whether the plea would contain a clause that his crimes involved "moral turpitude," thus ruling out any future in Israeli politics for seven years. For Netanyahu, with visions of one day returning to the prime minister's residence, the clause was a deal-breaker and he therefore rejected the plea agreement.

Nor would the deal have ruled out jail time. "A bribery conviction, should there be one, would send him at the age of 76 or 77 to Wing 10 at Maasiyahu Prison, the maximum security facility near Ramle, for several years," noted an analysis by Yossi Verter in *Haaretz*. "There he will find the tabulation of remaining days scratched into the wall by his predecessor Ehud Olmert." In March 2015, former prime minister Olmert was convicted of fraud, breach of trust, and tax evasion and sentenced to eight months in prison. "It's about time Israel had a prime minister who didn't need investigating," said Netanyahu's former defense minister, Moshe Ya'alon. Corruption in Israel, he added, "causes me more sleepless nights than the Iranian bomb."

But by the summer of 2022, with the trial still going on, the public was left to wonder whether Netanyahu would eventually end up in Olmert's dingy cell or back in the lavish prime minister's residence, which had been unoccupied since his departure. Prime Minister Naftali Bennett, in contrast, chose to live in his home on Chipman Street in the Tel Aviv suburb of Ra'anana. But despite an enormous $14 million in security upgrades, he had to endure constant "deafening" pro-Netanyahu demonstrators. Known as "Bibists," they used powerful megaphones, sirens, and drums to let Bennett know their displeasure at his replacing their dear leader. "They were insufferable," said a neighbor. "They said terrible things about Bennett's children."

In June, Bennett was out following the collapse of his coalition government, and Netanyahu was looking to take his place with a repugnant, anti-Palestinian race-baiting campaign. He said he would "never agree to allow" any Arab politicians to join his coalition. "One benefit of a victory," noted the London *Times*, "is that Netanyahu could engineer a law change that would end a corruption trial in which he is accused of three counts of fraud and one of bribery."

This time Netanyahu would be facing off against Yair Lapid, Bennett's former foreign minister and now, with end of Bennett's government, the caretaker prime minister until the November 1, 2022, election. Like his predecessors, Lapid promoted Jewish supremacy over Palestinians' rights and planned no changes in the occupation. Human rights groups were the enemy; he accused Breaking the Silence of "smearing Israel abroad" for telling the truth about apartheid.

As his temporary official residence, he even chose to move into Villa Hanna Salameh at 2 Balfour Street, a home that Palestinians fled during the war in 1948. Like all property owned by Palestinians, many fleeing as a result of massive ethnic cleansing operations they call the Nakba, or "catastrophe," it was stolen by the government with no compensation to the owners and no right of return. Known as the Absentee Property Law, a *Haaretz* editorial called it "incomparably broad and draconian," and said it must be repealed. At least two former prime ministers had declined to move into similar confiscated homes.

Years before, as he waited to be called to take the witness stand, Milchan had flown back to Hollywood in his private jet. What had been a dangerous and complicated situation became even more so with Lapid now prime minister, since the two had a long history. And Lapid had worries of his own. He had also been grilled by the police about his possible involvement with Milchan and Netanyahu regarding bribes and fraud. "I remember [Milchan] and me sitting with George Clooney on the balcony," he told the investigators. "His closeness to Bibi came from his need to be close to power for publicity. I told him: 'He'll just use you and you'll become like his servant . . .' 'I remember I talked about it once with [Avigdor] Lieberman . . . I said: 'Well, you can't rely on Arnon, he has become like Bibi's servant.'"

Sometime after the election, Lapid was also scheduled to testify at the trial, a time when he might be the newly elected prime minister testifying against former prime minister Netanyahu. Or it might be newly elected Prime Minister Netanyahu testifying against former prime minister Lapid. And Lapid making accusations against Milchan, or vice versa. He first became acquainted with Milchan in 1994 when working as an Israeli television journalist. "I interviewed the Dalai Lama, Arnold Schwarzenegger, and Bill Gates," Lapid told investigators. "I was traveling with a film crew abroad, and that's how we became friends." A year later, Milchan offered Lapid a job managing his television company in Los Angeles. He agreed but left after just six months.

In 2013, Netanyahu appointed Lapid finance minister, despite the fact that he had never even finished high school, never managed a large bureaucracy, and never served in government. Eventually fired by Netanyahu, *Haaretz* would report, "Lapid's 22 months as finance minister were a disaster." But Milchan was delighted by the appointment of his former employee and he even sent him a huge bouquet, which Lapid quickly returned.

By the summer of 2022, worried about arrest or other charges, Milchan hadn't set foot in Israel for five long years, even staying away from his mother's funeral. Then, as the time for his testimony approached, he began seeking ways to continue avoiding a return to Israel, including claiming ill health, an excuse the prosecutors weren't buying. Every witness must testify, he was told, implying there were no exceptions for multibillionaire Hollywood producers or Israeli spies. And since he promised to testify in exchange for not being indicted, his failure to show up could lead to his extradition and sharing an adjoining cell with Netanyahu. "It's difficult to guess how he will behave when the moment of truth arrives," noted one Israeli commentator.

For decades, Milchan had gone to great lengths to hide his racist, traitorous, money-grubbing, Scrooge-like past by giving few serious interviews unless he was convinced they would be puff pieces. Now his government had turned on him, and finally, so had the public and the press. "All those who are clucking their tongues at the Netanyahus' disgusting behavior are holding their noses to the stench of the Milchans and their aides, a stench that is possibly even worse," wrote Gideon Levy in *Haaretz*. "One of the things he sought to get through this bribery was particularly stingy: He wanted to avoid paying taxes in the United States, where he lives, and also in Israel, where he was born, despite making a loud display of his patriotic emotions for Israel, as far-off Diaspora Jews are wont to do."

While waiting, he turned his attention to his latest flick. The $80 million screwball comedy opened in October 2022 to "withering reviews and bad buzz," according to *Variety*, along with a 28 percent "rotten" ranking on Rotten Tomatoes. The Daily Beast called it an "all-around disaster." Among the stars was his old pal Robert De Niro, who by then was deep in his own troubles and reduced to making commercials for Warburtons bagels and Kia automobiles. Then there were the films where he would demand an exorbitant amount for little more than a walk-on part to boost a B movie's overseas sales, like the low-budget 2022 *Savage Salvation*—low-budget except for De Niro's fee of $11 million, transportation in a Gulfstream IV, and $100,000 for a family vacation, via a Gulfstream, all for eight days' work. "Fees for De Niro," said the *Los Angeles Times*, "ate up half the film's budget." Which meant minimal pay for the rest of the hardworking, full-time cast and crew.

Like Milchan, De Niro also seemed to believe that multimillionaires and multibillionaires should be immune from paying taxes. According to his divorce lawyer, Caroline Krauss, the actor was millions of dollars behind on his taxes. On top of that were millions more owed to his estranged wife, Grace Hightower. He was also being sued for $12 million by a former employee, Graham Chase Robinson, who accused him of "gratuitous unwanted physical contact," being "verbally abusive," and making "sexually-charged comments to her." Among the evidence was a voicemail recording De Niro once left her when she didn't pick up the phone: "You fucking don't answer my calls. How dare you? You're about to be fired. You're fucking history," he screamed. "This is bullshit. How dare you fucking disrespect me? You gotta be fucking kidding me, you spoiled brat! Fuck you!" De Niro denied all the charges.

But for Milchan, remaining in the United States also has its dangers. Since there is no statute of limitations for espionage, he may someday face arrest. In that case, Netanyahu may be subpoenaed as a witness against him, along with John Kerry. And if Milchan testifies against the former prime minister, the former prime minister may look forward to testifying against Milchan. And then there are the questions surrounding his alleged failure to pay any taxes, despite making billions, for a decade or more.

Given the mountain of evidence against Milchan, it is now up to President Joseph Biden to decide whether political courage should finally win out over political expediency, and likewise justice for millions of Americans over millions in cash from politically powerful special interests. But the odds are unlikely. According to the nonprofit campaign data site OpenSecrets, Biden was the top recipient of pro-Israeli donations over the years, totaling over $4,228,000.

———

By the time Milchan arrived back in Malibu from Israel, it was nearly sixty years since he first joined LAKAM and began his career secretly assisting Israel build its covert stockpile of nuclear weapons at Dimona. It was a complex process that over the decades has created enormous amounts of highly lethal nuclear waste, much of it with a half-life measured in tens of thousands of years. By comparison, when the San Onofre Nuclear Generating Station in Southern California was closed down in 2013, it had accumulated sixteen hundred tons of nuclear waste in the form of spent fuel rods over its forty-five-year life span. Dimona, by contrast, was built ten years earlier and is still in operation. And its volatile waste has been sitting in aging containers, buried or aboveground, dangerously close to the nuclear plant. Considering the nuclear disasters at Chernobyl in 1986 and Fukushima in 2011, such conditions represent a great risk.

Around the same time that both Milchan and Netanyahu were coming under investigation, nuclear scientists at Dimona were realizing they had a very serious problem. With the deadly waste possibly leaking into the soil, there was the potential for widespread contamination as well as the risk of explosion from escaping gases. The problem was exacerbated by secrecy due to Israel being the only country in the world to conceal the existence of its nuclear weapons program. Along with North Korea it is also one of four rogue countries not a member of the Non-Proliferation Treaty.

As a result, Israel has continuously rejected any international safeguards, inspections, or accountability, a position that is coming increasingly under attack as unsustainable. What "the Israeli government is doing at this secret nuclear weapons plant is something for the Israeli government to come clean about," argued Daryl G. Kimball, executive director of the Washington-based Arms Control Association. In contrast, Iran is a full signatory to the treaty and allows UN inspections.

By the 2000s, fears of a nuclear disaster began growing, and in 2004 the Israeli military even began passing out iodine pills in Dimona in the event of a radioactive leak. Though the reactor was initially slated for closure around 2023, Israel decided instead to extend its life span to 2040, at which time it will be over eighty years old. This was a potentially dangerous decision, with the city of Beersheba and its population of 209,000 to the north and the resort city and port of Eilat to the south. Soon, as concern over a home-grown nuclear catastrophe at Dimona began outweighing the potential of a nuclear attack from Iran, scientists and engineers at the facility began looking into ways to rebury the corroding waste. And in early January 2021, just a few months before the election, cameras on China's SuperView-1 commercial satellite captured an image of the first new sizable project at Dimona in decades.

What Princeton University's International Panel on Fissile Materials called a "significant new construction" consisted of a large hole several stories deep, about 165 yards long, 65 yards wide, and a few feet from the aging heavy-water reactor. Then just over a mile from the plant were boxes stacked in two rectangular-shaped holes with concrete bases. While there were a number of possible explanations for the excavation, high among them was digging up the old, worn containers of nuclear waste for reburial in more secure containers.

And just as the United States had long conspired with Israel to cover up the country's illegal nuclear stockpile, hiding its existence from both the American public and the world, they would now help Netanyahu bury much of the deadly evidence.

According to U.S. Department of Energy documents, the first steps in Washington's quiet assistance to Netanyahu began when a joint project was formed that included scientists from Dimona with those from the U.S. Sandia National Laboratories in Albuquerque, New Mexico. For a number of years, Sandia had been experimenting with the idea of burying highly radioactive nuclear waste deep in boreholes drilled three miles down into crystalline rock. But due to objections first in North Dakota and then South Dakota, they had largely given up—until Israel came along. Following a number of conferences and visits both in the United States and Israel, the two organizations began looking for locations in the Yamin Plain near Dimona to begin drilling the boreholes.

But where Sandia's original U.S. plans involved burying the plutonium and other waste miles underground beneath groundwater for complete safety, Dimona was only interested in going down several hundred yards. "With limited geological options for disposal, intermediate-depth borehole disposal is being considered in the arid Yamin Plain region of the northeastern Negev desert at depths of several hundred meters below ground surface," said a Sandia report in March 2020. By 2022 a number of potential borehole sites had been mapped and the project was continuing, although no waste had yet been buried and there was no guarantee of success. Thus the danger would remain.

———

Despite the billions in yearly aid and the extensive U.S. assistance to Netanyahu with Dimona, there was no letup in Israel's extensive spying and covert operations against Americans. By 2015, Israel was facing a new enemy, one against which its armory of nuclear weapons was useless. Where once the greatest threat to the state's survival was incoming missiles, foreign invasion, and vast armies of soldiers, it was now incoming boycotts, foreign isolation, and vast armies of activists. The new enemy was delegitimization, the loss not of Israel's territory but of its moral authority—to be judged like apartheid South Africa in the eyes of the world, an odious, racist, pariah state boycotted, sanctioned, and scorned.

In 2013 Israel's highly respected *Haaretz* newspaper carried the distressing headline "Israel Among World's Least Popular Nations." It noted that the "only states less popular are North Korea, Pakistan and Iran." The article reflected the results of the annual BBC World Service Country Ratings Poll, made up of the views of nearly twenty-five thousand people in twenty-four countries around the world. It was clear that through its actions, Israel was rapidly delegitimizing itself in the eyes of much of the world.

But rather than deciding to finally bring his country in line with international laws, norms, and basic human rights obligations, Prime Minister Benjamin Netanyahu chose instead to go on the offensive. The United States was the one country Netanyahu dared not lose, the one country that filled his coffers with billions of American taxpayer dollars every year, and the one country that stood between Israel and scores of harsh UN resolutions and sanctions. But it was also the country where the Boycott, Divestment, and

Sanctions (BDS) movement was increasingly gaining in popularity, an unsustainable situation. He would therefore declare war on the movement, and on other human rights groups involved in the nonviolent struggle to force Israel to end its military occupation of Palestine.

And because a new and different enemy required a new and different spy organization, Netanyahu assigned the mission to the highly secret Ministry of Strategic Affairs, run by Gilad Erdan. He quickly began plotting his covert operations in the United States.

BOOK FIVE

THE
INFILTRATORS

CHAPTER 21

◆

Adelson's Army

Sheldon Adelson's Venetian Resort sits at the heart of the Las Vegas strip like a neon nirvana. Along with its adjacent Palazzo, it contains seventy-one hundred all-suite rooms and forty restaurants, making it the second biggest hotel in the world, after only Adelson's Venetian Hotel in Macau, the largest occupied building on earth. Beneath the trompe-l'oeil sky ceiling, opera-singing gondoliers transport tourists in motorized gondolas over two man-made canals of chlorine blue water. Elsewhere, visitors marvel at Disneyesque replicas of the Rialto Bridge, the Doge's Palace façade, and the Campanile di San Marco tower. To empty their wallets and bank accounts, the casino covers 120,000 square feet of space with over 1,247 slot machines, 139 games, and a high-limit salon for baccarat and other tables.

For the big winners, shops along the canal sell items such as a baccarat decanter of Rémy Martin Cognac Louis XIII Legacy for $24,499.99, or a Greubel Forsey Grande Sonnerie watch for $1.2 million. And for the super-rich, the hotel offers the four-day "Want the World" package for $450,000. It includes transport to Las Vegas in a private jet, pickup in a Maybach, a key to the sixty-five-hundred-square-foot presidential suite, a private butler, and monogrammed red silk pajamas.

On the weekend of June 5–6, 2015, several hundred well-dressed and well-heeled visitors entered the Venetian's frescoed lobby with its gilded sphere held up by four golden female statues. They then bypassed the baritone gondoliers, the faux St. Mark's Square, and the acres of vices as they quietly made their way to a side conference room in the hotel's complex. Gathering behind closed doors was an army of middle-aged millionaires and billionaires on a mission. "All proceedings," participants were told, "shall remain strictly confidential." The invitation warned that that they must agree "not to discuss the events of the conference with media before, during and after" the meeting. What happens in Vegas, stays in Vegas.

Adelson, long the mogul-in-chief of Sin City and at the time the eighth richest human on the planet, with $40 billion, was used to holding court in his gaudy palace, especially during a presidential election year. In a traditional spectacle some referred to as "the Sheldon Adelson suck-up fest," political hopefuls seeking his cash unashamedly took turns prostrating themselves in front of him, or jogging alongside the scooter he used to navigate around his empire, a dark blue three-wheeled Afikim Caddy complete with headlight and cane holder.

In 2012 he spent over $150 million, more money than anyone else in American history, according to ProPublica, to elect Mitt Romney and other Republican candidates. And in April, in preparation for the 2016 election, he hosted a three-day gathering of the Republican Jewish Coalition, on whose board he sits. As expected, the candidates came bearing gifts, inevitably with Israel rather than the United States in mind. "It's not complicated for Republican politicians to come to the RJC and say, 'We should stand with Israel,'" exclaimed Texas senator Ted Cruz. "Unless you're a blithering idiot, that's what you say when you come here."

Republican Party bundler Fred Zeidman, a friend of Adelson who attended the 2014 RJC conference, agreed. "His priority is Israel," he said. "I assure you that the first question is 'tell me where you are on the safety and security of the state of Israel.'" Adelson's single-minded obsession with Israel long ago morphed into dangerous fanaticism. "I had this crazy Jewish billionaire, yelling at me," President George W. Bush told an Israeli official after Adelson discovered that Bush was considering a restart of the Israeli-Palestinian peace process. Adelson was opposed to any and all concessions to the Palestinians.

But the June conclave would be very different from the RJC gatherings, and it would take place behind tightly closed doors. Consisting of about two hundred people from fifty of the most far-right pro-Israel organizations in the country, many of them super-rich who had arrived on private jets, they would make up what would become Adelson's Army, a task force of Gulfstream warriors. The objective was the launch of a secret psychological and propaganda war targeting Americans on behalf of Israel.

On the stage joining forces were the opposing generals, megabillionaire Adelson, the largest donor to Donald Trump and the Republican Party; and multibillionaire Haim Saban, the largest donor to Hillary Clinton and the Democrats. Both Saban and Adelson's wife held dual Israeli/American citizenship. Adelson, however, seemed to regret only having U.S. citizenship. In a talk in Israel a few years earlier he had disparaged the American military and implied he felt a greater loyalty to Israel than the United States. "The uniform that I wore in the military, unfortunately, was not an Israeli uniform. It was an American uniform," he complained. He added that both his wife and one of his daughters served in the Israel Defense Forces (IDF), and four of his five children were born in Israel. And he hoped that one of his sons would become "a sniper for the IDF." "He's a gun freak," Adelson boasted.

Leading the charge from Israel would be the commander in chief, Benjamin Netanyahu. "Greetings from Jerusalem," he told the crowd in a letter read from the podium by Adelson. Dressed in a chestnut brown suit with a maroon tie and matching handkerchief, an Israeli flag to his left, Adelson issued Netanyahu's call to arms. "Delegitimization of Israel must be fought, and you are on the front lines," he said, adding that "the Israeli government is committed to launching assertive and innovative programs and to joining you and many others around the world to combat the lies and slander that are leveled against us." Then, engaging in rabid fearmongering, Saban warned of "an anti-Semitic tsunami that's coming at us." It was a lie, as Adelson himself would admit in Israel. There is "little to no sign in American society" of significant anti-Semitism, he said.

Netanyahu was asking Adelson's task force to launch, on Israel's behalf and with its secret financial and intelligence support, a nationwide covert operation targeting Americans. It was a dangerous proposition with the potential of turning those taking part into foreign agents of the State of Israel, a serious crime. Before the night was over, the group had raised upward of $50 million for Netanyahu's propaganda war inside the United States; tens of millions more would covertly come from the Israeli government through a variety of hidden fronts and shell organizations. At the same time the summit was taking place, Netanyahu was meeting with his top national security and intelligence officials. He told them they would receive at least $30 million from the government for the secret offensive, and with the help of Adelson's group and others possibly as much as $900 million.

The target of Netanyahu's secret war in the United States was not a team of Iranian terrorists with plans to blow up the Israeli embassy, or a plot to assassinate Israeli diplomats. Instead, it was the Boycott, Divestment, and Sanctions (BDS) movement, a dedicated and growing assortment of college students and human rights supporters scattered across the country armed with Twitter followings as bullhorns. Their goal: to rally the world to boycott, divest from, and sanction Israel until it ends its brutal, racist, and illegal occupation of the Palestinian territories.

And the best way to counter this movement was with lots of money to buy political power in America. Haim Saban, the cosponsor of the secret conclave, along with his Israeli/American wife, would donate $6.4 million to Hillary Clinton's campaign, more than any other Hollywood donor. And less than a month after the secret Las Vegas meeting, Clinton wrote a "Dear Haim" letter to Saban expressing her "alarm" over the BDS movement. It was an organization she had never before paid any attention to. "I am seeking your thoughts and recommendations on how leaders and communities across America can work together to counter BDS," she wrote. "From Congress and state legislatures to boardrooms and classrooms...I will be speaking out on this issue in the weeks ahead."

Netanyahu's problem, however, was that the more Israel's atrocities came to light, the more the BDS movement gained strength around the United States and the world, both on campuses and throughout Western society. In 2003, Rachel Corrie, a twenty-three-year-old American college student and Palestinian human rights activist, was killed when she was run over by an Israeli military armored bulldozer during a protest. At the time, wearing an orange fluorescent jacket with reflective stripes, she was bravely attempting to protect a Palestinian home in the Rafah refugee camp from demolition. "The driver cannot have failed to see her," said eyewitness Richard Purssell. "The driver didn't slow down; he just ran over her. Then he reversed the bulldozer back over her again." She was far from alone, noted London's *Observer*. "On the night of Corrie's death, nine Palestinians were killed in the Gaza Strip, among them a four-year-old girl and a man aged 90."

The BDS movement began a few years after Rachel Corrie's horrific death and modeled itself after the successful worldwide nonviolent anti-apartheid campaign against South Africa. Leading the group as cofounder was Omar Barghouti, a Palestinian and a 1993 graduate of Columbia University with a master's degree in electrical engineering. He later moved to Israel to pursue a Ph.D. from Tel Aviv University. In 2017 he received the Gandhi Peace Award.

Among the movement's supporters was the late South African archbishop Desmond Tutu, who along with Nelson Mandela had long battled the White apartheid government in Pretoria. During an emotional address and press conference in Boston in 2007, Tutu called Israel "worse" than South African apartheid in some respects, including the illegal use of "collective punishment" of Palestinians. He also criticized the government for its brutality and its "gross violation of human rights." Mandela was likewise outraged by Israel's apartheid as well as its key role in supporting South African apartheid and undermining the global boycott against it. "We know too well that our freedom is incomplete without the freedom of the Palestinians," he said during an address in Pretoria at the International Day of Solidarity with the Palestinian People in 1997.

And in July 2022, South Africa's foreign minister, Naledi Pandor, said Israel should be classified as an apartheid state and that the UN should establish a committee to investigate whether it satisfies the charge. "The Palestinian narrative evokes experiences of South Africa's own history of racial segregation and oppression," she added.

By 2015, thanks to a variety of dedicated human rights organizations, within

Israel as well as internationally, the evidence was becoming impossible to hide or cover up. Between 2006 and 2012, violent settlers' attacks on Palestinians nearly quadrupled, with 324 incidents reported in 2014, averaging more than six attacks a week. They often came from outposts manned by religious settlers with kippahs on their heads and automatic weapons over their shoulders. Little would change over the years. In January 2021, settlers from the Mitzpeh Yair outpost attacked a seventy-eight-year-old Palestinian farmer with clubs. Then a gang of about ten returned with pistols, rifles, clubs, axes, and iron chains and went after his family. "Violence by settlers (and sometimes by other Israeli civilians) toward Palestinians has long since become part of daily life under occupation in the West Bank," concluded a report by B'Tselem, the Israeli human rights organization. And then there are the near-daily home destructions. Protected by heavily armed Israeli troops, powerful tractors claw at the walls and roofs of Palestinian homes as workers toss children's cribs, toys, and family beds into makeshift trash piles.

Over the years, Israel has continued to ethnically cleanse Palestine of Palestinians, land on which they have lived for centuries. Today, about six million Israelis live on 85 percent of the area that was Palestine during the time of the British mandate. As a result, behind four hundred-plus miles of concrete walls over two stories high, Palestinians are squeezed into the remaining 15 percent, with their cities and towns trapped between Israel's ever-expanding settlements and a network of segregated roads, armed security barriers, and military fortifications. B'Tselem has accused the government of creating conditions that bear "clear similarities to the racist apartheid regime that existed in South Africa." John Dugard, a South African lawyer and UN human rights monitor, also sees little difference between the two. "Apartheid was about keeping the best parts of the country for the Whites and sending the Blacks to the least habitable, least desirable parts of the country," he said. "And one sees that all the time here [in the occupied territories]." Israel also now allows its draft-age youth to volunteer to protect settlers in the occupied territory rather than serve in the army.

According to Amnesty International, 2015 was a cruel year for occupied Palestinian families, but then again it was not much different from any other year, before or since. The previous summer, during Israel's bloody war on those living in Gaza, Israeli forces killed over five hundred children, according to a United Nations report. Children seemed to be a key target,* among

---

* According to a 2019 report by the Commission for Detainees and Ex-Detainees' Affairs of the Palestine Liberation Organization, Israeli occupation authorities had arrested more than fifty-three thousand Palestinian children since 1967. That includes more than nine thousand Palestinian girls and boys detained between 2015 and March 2019. See "Israel Has Arrested 50,000 Palestinian Children Since 1967," Middle East Monitor, April 29, 2019, www.middle eastmonitor.com/20190429-israel-has-arrested-50000-palestinian-children-since-1967/.

them four boys playing soccer on a beach, blown apart by an Israeli shell. In stark, dry, emotionless statistics, Amnesty International offered an equally grim review of 2015:

> The authorities detained thousands of Palestinians from the OPT [Occupied Palestinian Territories]; most were held in prisons inside Israel, in violation of international law. Hundreds were held without charge or trial under renewable administrative detention orders, based on information withheld from them and their lawyers; some engaged in prolonged hunger strikes in protest... The Israeli authorities launched a new clampdown on protests by Palestinians in the OPT amid the escalation in violence from October, arresting more than 2,500 Palestinians, including hundreds of children, and significantly increasing their use of administrative detention.
>
> Israeli military and police forces, as well as Israel Security Agency (ISA) personnel, tortured and otherwise ill-treated Palestinian detainees, including children, particularly during arrest and interrogation. Reports of torture increased amid the mass arrests of Palestinians that began in October. Methods included beating with batons, slapping, throttling, prolonged shackling, stress positions, sleep deprivation and threats. Jewish suspects detained in connection with attacks on Palestinians also alleged torture. Impunity for torture was rife. The authorities had received almost 1,000 complaints of torture at the hands of ISA since 2001 but had yet to open any criminal investigations.
>
> Israeli soldiers and police killed at least 124 Palestinians from the OPT in the West Bank, including East Jerusalem, 22 in the Gaza Strip, and 10 inside Israel during the year. Many of those killed, including children, appeared to be victims of unlawful killings.
>
> Israeli forces, including undercover units, used excessive and lethal force against protesters in both the West Bank and the Gaza Strip, killing dozens, including 43 in the last quarter of the year, and injuring thousands with rubber-coated metal bullets and live ammunition. While many protesters threw rocks or other projectiles, they generally posed no threat to the lives of well-protected Israeli soldiers when they were shot. In September, Israel's security cabinet authorized police to use live ammunition in East Jerusalem. On 9 and 10 October, Israeli forces used live ammunition and rubber-coated metal bullets against Palestinian protesters in border areas of the Gaza Strip, killing nine, including a child, and injuring scores.

Conditions would only grow worse. On July 22, 2019, nine hundred Israeli soldiers and border police arrived in the Palestinian neighborhood of Wadi al-Hummus to demolish thirteen apartment blocks. Following the destruction, the former residents, poor, destitute, and psychologically traumatized, would sit on the broken slabs of cement and watch as the same tractors returned. This time, however, the dust would be caused by the construction of modern homes in a new illegal Jewish settlement surrounded by a chain-link fence, barbed wire, and armed guards.

Among the victims was fifty-two-year-old Abdul-Ghani Awawdeh. "They startled us with no prior notification," he said. "We slept on the ground covered with a plastic bag." By then, according to a scorecard maintained by the Israeli Committee Against House Demolitions (ICAHD), the total number of Palestinian structures deliberately destroyed by Israel had reached nearly fifty thousand. Israel's aim, according to ICAHD, is "to Judaize Palestine, to transform an Arab country into a Jewish one."

In May 2022, fear ran through the Najjar family when a neighbor called with the message "The bulldozer is coming." By then, the house demolitions had eclipsed a thousand since the day Biden took office, according to the UN Office for the Coordination of Humanitarian Affairs. Among them was the home of a ninety-five-year-old physically disabled woman. Her family had built it on the ruins of the house in which she had lived for the last fifteen years to make it wheelchair-accessible.

"Gangs of settlers carry out raids in the dead of night, attacking in Ku Klux Klan style," said Michael Sfard, an Israeli attorney and expert in humanitarian law who represents Israeli and Palestinian human rights organizations. "The evidence of how the Israeli government abets settler criminality is extensive and unequivocal."

Even members of the government could no longer keep silent. "We, members of the Jewish people, which has suffered pogroms throughout history, come and perpetrate a pogrom on others. These aren't people. They're subhuman," Deputy Economy Minister Yair Golan told Israeli television viewers in January 2022. "This extremist, nationalist wild behavior will bring disaster upon us." But rather than take action against the settlers, the Israeli government instead condemned Golan, calling his comments "shocking" and "bordering on blood libel."

Netanyahu's greatest fear was that as a result of the growing strength of the BDS movement, the public would finally begin seeing Israel in the same light that many people in the rest of the world, and even in Israel, saw it: as a brutal apartheid state.

———

Unlike many in their parents' generation, the students who supported the Boycott, Divestment, and Sanctions movement rejected Israel's claims of being a democratic country while at the same time denying not only the vote but even basic human rights to millions of people under military occupation. Nor did they accept the pious assertions that God had given Israel exclusively to the Jews. These were claims blindly accepted by generations of older Americans captivated by the *idea* of Israel rather than its *reality*. It was a faux Israel propagated by well-financed pro-Israel pressure groups, powerful lobbies, and politicians pandering for payoffs.

The BDS student activists seemed to even have a layer of Kryptonite as phony charges of anti-Semitism, the tired, go-to weapon used to instantly silence the press and critics of Israel, simply bounced right off them. But most of all they had the courage to fight against an unjust regime in Israel, as an earlier generation of American students fought against an unjust war in Vietnam.

Originally dismissed as inconsequential by Netanyahu and other Israelis, by 2015 the boycott movement had become one of the country's biggest political threats. On the same weekend that Adelson's secret task force was forming in Las Vegas, an Associated Press news article noted, "In boardrooms and campuses, on social media and in celebrity circles, momentum seems to be growing for a global pressure campaign on Israel. The atmosphere recalls the boycotts that helped demolish apartheid South Africa a quarter century ago ... Increasingly prominent is the so-called 'BDS' (boycott-disinvestment-sanctions) movement, run by Palestinians and leftist activists from around the world."

To Israel's shock, the week before the launch of Adelson's task force, FIFA, the world's main soccer body, considered the country's expulsion at the request of the Palestinians, but at the last minute the Palestinians withdrew it. Shortly afterward, Orange, the giant French telecoms company, notified the Israeli government that it wanted to terminate its relationship with the Israeli company that licensed its brand. And around the same time, the National Union of Students in the UK voted to support boycotting Israel.

Then the European Union ruled that goods produced by Israelis in the illegally occupied territories be labeled "made in settlements." Norway, although not a member like Sweden and Finland, followed suit. It was a deep embarrassment, reminiscent of actions against apartheid South Africa, and would make it easier for countries to boycott Israeli goods. The action coincided with a critical Human Rights Watch report that noted how Israeli businesses had exploited the occupation for profit, calling it unlawful and abusive.

Over the years, the movement quickly would spread. The 5.6-million strong British Trade Union Congress voted unanimously in favor of a motion to "encourage affiliates, employers and pension funds to disinvest from and boycott" Israel. The organization charged, "For too long the international community has stood idly by as the Israeli state has been allowed to carry out its crimes and this cannot be tolerated or accepted any longer. Decisive action is now urgently needed in relation to Israel's illegal actions against the Palestinians." And later the British Labor Party Conference voted in favor of a motion to identify Israel as a state practicing the crime of apartheid. The motion committed the party to implement sanctions, including ceasing UK-Israel arms trade and trade with illegal Israeli settlements.

At Cambridge University, in a demonstration that recalled the anti-apartheid campaigns in South Africa, students demonstrated against visiting Israeli ambassador Tzipi Hotovely. Protestors chanted, "Silence is complicity, acceptance is complicity, platforming is complicity." And in an open letter, the students wrote, "Hotovely is a proud supporter of Israeli settler colonialism."

In the United States, the BDS movement was gaining significant ground with both religious and educational organizations. The New England Conference of the United Methodist Church condemned Israel's apartheid system by an 88 to 12 percent vote. According to the resolution, "Israel has blatantly codified a racist governing principle in the Nation State Basic Law of 2018, which grants self-determination *exclusively* to the Jewish citizens of Israel; Jewish supremacy was thereby made a binding constitutional principle and all state institutions *must* now promote Jewish supremacy." Therefore, "the Conference calls on the U.S. government to condition U.S. funding to Israel upon Israel's willingness to dismantle its apartheid system and implement all the rights due to Palestinians under international law." (emphasis in original)

Adding to the pressure, the U.S. Presbyterian Church during its 2022 General Assembly also voted overwhelmingly to recognize that "Israel's laws, policies and practices regarding the Palestinian people fulfill the international legal definition of apartheid." They determined that Palestinians have been systematically oppressed through inhuman acts for the objective of racial domination and called on the United States to take action against Israel. "Christians spoke out in the 1950s against segregation in the United States and later against apartheid in South Africa," said the resolution. "They must again raise their voices and condemn Israel's discrimination against Palestinians and give a name to the crime against humanity that this discrimination represents, the crime of apartheid," it said.

Around the same time, the Episcopal Church in the U.S. at its Baltimore convention passed resolutions that "condemn the continued occupation, segregation and oppression of the Palestinian people" and called on President Biden and Congress to "oppose legislation that punishes supporting nonviolent boycotts and divestments on behalf of Palestinian human rights." Then the governing body of the World Council of Churches charged that Israel's "discrimination against Palestinians is overt and systemic, and the ongoing half-century-long occupation continues to contradict the equal human dignity and human rights of Palestinians living under this system of control, while the response of the international community continues to reflect egregious double standards."

And in a surprising move, the North Carolina Democratic Party adopted a resolution calling for Israel to end its "commission of the crimes of apartheid and persecution." Titled "A Resolution in Support of Human Rights in Israel/Palestine," it said the United States should end its arms sales to Israel and impose "targeted sanctions, including travel bans and asset freezes, on those individuals and entities that continue to commit" human right crimes. It also alleged that Israel had engaged in massive ethnic cleansing with the forcible transfers of tens of thousands of Palestinians, and the seizure of 65 to 85 percent of Palestinian land within Israel in service of Jewish settlements.

In the state of Washington, the Seattle Education Association passed a resolution expressing solidarity with Palestine and endorsing the BDS movement. "As a Jewish Educator, I am proud to be a member of SEA," said Emma Klein. "Educators and institutions from around the world have come forward, as part of a vibrant and growing international movement in opposition to Israeli colonization and apartheid. We call on others to join us." Shortly before, the United Educators of San Francisco, a union representing sixty-two hundred public school teachers and aides in the city, also passed a resolution endorsing BDS. "Over 1,500 Palestinians from neighborhoods in Jerusalem are facing the threat of forced displacement and home demolitions by Israeli authorities," said the resolution. "This pattern and practice of dispossession and expansion of settlements has been found to be illegal under international law."

For Netanyahu and many Israelis the greatest humiliation came when actress Natalie Portman, who is Jewish and was born in Israel, refused to accept one of Israel's highest honors, the Genesis Prize, known as the "Jewish Nobel." Her decision, noted *Haaretz*, is "a very big deal" that "has touched a very raw nerve." Presented during a high-profile ceremony, it comes with a $1 million prize that recipients are free to direct toward causes of their choice. "The mistreatment of those suffering from today's atrocities is simply not in line with my Jewish values," Portman said. "Because I care about Israel, I must stand up against violence, corruption, inequality and abuse of power." Regarding Netanyahu, she has said, "I find his racist comments horrific."

———

In the days leading up to Adelson's task force summit, Netanyahu called his BDS war cabinet together to plan the Israeli government's long-term strategy.

Placed in charge was Gilad Erdan, a close Netanyahu confidant with a broad and shadowy array of powers. He was in charge of the Ministry of Strategic Affairs, an organization so secret that even its location was long hidden. It was largely responsible for developing clandestine agents, relationships, and financial resources in foreign countries, predominantly the United States, to counter the boycott movement. According to *Haaretz*, Erdan and his top officials "see themselves as the heads of a commando unit." At the same time, Erdan also ran Israel's Ministry of Public Security, which oversees the Ministry of Internal Security, making him Israel's top political spook, top cop, and top internal spy.

At forty-five, with dark, neatly trimmed hair and a strong build, Erdan had the looks of a local TV anchor. A former chairman of the Knesset Subcommittee on the War on Traffic Accidents, and the Subcommittee for Sports, he was nevertheless a dedicated war hawk from his earliest days. He even opposed the Oslo peace accords while studying law at Bar-Ilan University. Afterward, he became a political advisor to far-right politician Ariel Sharon before Sharon joined the Knesset as a member of the Likud Party. In 2003, Erdan also won a seat in the Knesset and eventually made a name for himself opposing any effort by the Obama administration to end Israel's occupation of the Palestinians. "Israel does not take orders from Obama," he said, while at the same time not objecting to taking billions from American taxpayers.

With his wife and four children, Erdan lived in the upscale Tel Aviv suburb of Kiryat Ono. It is just a few miles away from the Petah Tikva Police Station, which Erdan oversaw as minister of public safety. Inside the station, which is located at 57 Stampfer Street in Petah Tikva, is housed a feared and notorious interrogation center for Palestinians. With a decades-long reputation for brutality and torture, it is where Palestinians from the occupied territories are regularly and illegally taken.

In 2010, the European Union financed an investigation of the interrogation center by B'Tselem, the Israeli human rights organization, and the HaMoked Center for the Defence of the Individual. Titled "Kept in the Dark: Treatment of Palestinian Detainees in the Petah Tikva Interrogation Facility of the Israel Security Agency," the report read like something out of Stalinist Russia. Always arrested in the middle of the night, the Palestinians were thrown into tiny gray cement cells, then taken to interrogation rooms where they were strapped to a chair for hours while being threatened, subjected to physical violence, deprived of sleep, and forced into painful positions.

An earlier report by Human Rights Watch described similar conditions suffered at Petah Tikva by journalist Rashid Hilal, who was hooded and chained to a "kindergarten chair." "When he tried to remove the hood by rubbing his head against the wall, he said, guards came and punched him in the head and upper body." Titled "Torture and Ill-Treatment: Israel's Interrogation of Palestinians from the Occupied Territories," the 335-page report examined conditions throughout Israel.

As the 2010 EU report noted, "This doctrine appeared in the CIA interrogation manuals of the 1960s and 1980s, used as guides to interrogators operating in Latin American dictatorships...According to the manuals, these methods result in the mental regression of the detainee, who becomes putty in the interrogator's hands." After sixty-eight pages of testimony and documentation, the report on Petah Tikva's chamber of horrors offered a grim conclusion. "The measures depicted in the report constitute cruel, inhuman, and degrading treatment, and in some cases constitute torture. All are prohibited, absolutely and without exception. International law unequivocally stipulates that no state of emergency may be invoked to justify such acts."

As with the settler attacks, little has changed over the years. In May 2022, according to *Haaretz*, two Palestinians reported that they had been tortured for over a month by Shin Bet in order to extract a confession of rock throwing. "Investigators left me tied to a chair with my hands cuffed behind me and legs cuffed in front," said twenty-year-old Yazan al-Rajbi. "I stayed that way for two days, without going to the bathroom, without drinking and without eating." A month later, the Public Committee Against Torture in Israel referred its own country to the International Criminal Court after concluding that Israel is "not interested and unable to stop the use of torture against Palestinians."

This was far from being a concern of Erdan; his covert job was to ensure that reports like those of the EU and Human Rights Watch get buried beneath millions of dollars of pro-Israeli propaganda and never see the light of day. That was where Adelson's task force came in with its moguls, millions, and manpower.

————

If Adelson was the field marshal of Netanyahu's secret propaganda war, California multimillionaire Adam Milstein was his commanding general, rallying the troops and organizing their battles. A close associate of Adelson and a key organizer of the task force summit, Milstein spoke on camera to a reporter with Israel National News following the conclave at the Venetian Hotel. Despite the prohibition on speaking to the American press, Adelson wanted to make sure Israelis knew he was fighting for them.

"We just had a historical conference in Las Vegas," said Milstein. Then, speaking about those Americans taking part in the nonviolent boycott, he began comparing them to Nazis out to commit genocide in Israel. "We know what happened during the Nazis in Germany. Our Jews were boycotted and then later on exterminated." Then he added, "This boycott movement is not about borders, it's not about peace, it's not about policies, it's about eradicating the Jews living in Israel." It was an indication of the over-the-top fanatical nature of Adelson's secret task force. The boycotters are the equivalent of the Nazi Gestapo, therefore any actions against them are justified.

"We should emphasize this summit was basically led by Israeli Americans living in America," Milstein said. "We have always told everybody around that we are a strategic asset for the State of Israel, but it's now becoming clearer and clearer that we indeed are the ambassadors for the State of Israel here in the United States. We care and we are willing to go on the offense, which not too many Jews are willing to do."

There was a reason why the Adelson task force formally demanded pledges of secrecy before, during, and after the meeting. Once they closed the door at the Venetian, they opened the door to potential criminal prosecution as agents of a foreign power, a very serious offense punishable by up to a decade in prison.

According to the law, 18 USC § 951, "Whoever, other than a diplomatic or consular officer or attaché, acts in the United States as an agent of a foreign government without prior notification to the Attorney General...shall be fined under this title or imprisoned not more than ten years, or both... For purposes of this section, the term 'agent of a foreign government' means an individual who agrees to operate within the United States subject to the direction or control of a foreign government or official."

Milstein was a dangerous man to follow. Few besides Adelson were aware of his criminal background as part of an international organized crime ring run by a crooked New York grand rabbi. Headquartered in a Brooklyn yeshiva, a Jewish children's school, it used Orthodox Jewish organizations and yeshivas as phony charity fronts. The fraud involved millions of dollars, went on for decades, stretched from Jerusalem to Los Angeles, and was made up of more than one hundred members of the Jewish communities in New York and California.

Wealthy Jews who were members of the ring, like Milstein, would donate large sums of money to the phony Jewish charities, enabling them to deduct the full amount from their taxes. By claiming the deductions, they could save tens or hundreds of thousands of dollars that would otherwise go to the U.S. Treasury. Later, after being laundered through an Israeli bank, the full amount of the "donation" would be returned to the members of the ring minus a 10 percent cut for the grand rabbi and his co-conspirators. By the time Milstein joined, it was so entrenched that even following an extensive investigation there was no idea how long it had been going on undetected. "I believe this goes on beyond living memory," said one of the prosecutors.

As the FBI began their raids, Tuvia Milsztein, Adam Milstein's real name, was arrested along with his Israeli-born business partner, David Hager, a "bundler" for the crime ring. A key problem for prosecutors, however, was the issue of *mesira*, the Jewish version of the Mafia's practice of *omertà*, silence. One key witness came forward, but others may have been afraid of retribution within the close-knit Orthodox community. Despite the seriousness of the crime, many were instead angry at the witness for "ratting out" fellow Jews. "People are very shell-shocked about the whole thing on many levels," Rabbi Daniel Korobkin, a West Coast representative of the Orthodox Union, told the Jewish *Forward*. Sounding like a Mafia kingpin he added, "Number one, that our neighbors and friends are implicated, and number two, that an act of mesira on this level was perpetrated by one of our own."

Milstein's bond was set at $100,000 and he faced ten years in prison, but he worked out a felony guilty plea for a reduced sentence with the help of an expensive Beverly Hills attorney. He tried to lessen the charges by claiming he was a "philanthropist" because he donated money to a number of far-right pro-Israel causes. But the prosecutor wasn't buying it. "There is an obvious concern that much of his philanthropy appears to have been merely a device to defraud the government," said Assistant U.S. Attorney Daniel J. O'Brien. "This was simply a case about greed," scoffed Leslie P. DeMarco, the IRS special agent in charge of the investigation.

In September 2009, soon after his release from confinement, Milstein made a very odd request to the Justice Department. The ex-con wanted permission to fly to Israel where, among other things, he would "meet with Israel's Prime Minister." It was part of an exclusive AIPAC trip for the very highest rollers, the President's Cabinet, whose members donate $25,000 or more a year. The permission was granted. One of the topics Milstein and Netanyahu likely talked about was the Israeli-American Council (IAC), an organization Milstein had cofounded at the same time he was committing tax fraud.

Backed by Adelson's millions, the IAC brought together thousands of expat and dual-citizen Israelis who became soldiers in Adelson's Army, supporting Netanyahu in his war in the United States. In the process, Milstein and the others would weaponize the phony charge of "anti-Semitism" and constantly use it as a bludgeon against those advocating for Palestinian human rights. Instead, there are likely few things more anti-Semitic than the use of Judaism and Jewish schools as fronts to commit fraud, theft, tax evasion, and other crimes. The real anti-Semites were the grand rabbi's nationwide ring of wealthy, greedy Jewish tax thieves, including Milstein.

CHAPTER 22

The Blue Network

Sheldon Adelson's powder blue limousine, a stretch Maybach with dark-tinted windows, pulled through a black wrought iron gate and turned left onto Trophy Hills Drive. Behind him was an identical limo containing agents from his Executive Protection Team. And behind them was Adelson's 44,870-square-foot mansion. Nearly the size of the White House with its East and West Wings, and so big it was stocked with Segway transporters to get around, it was once on the market for $85 million.

It was October 2015, four months after Adelson's secret task force meeting, and he was on his way to his private hangars at McCarran International Airport in Las Vegas for a flight to Washington, DC. The hangars contained Adelson's Air Force, a presidential-level fleet of private jets, including two special-performance custom-fitted Boeing 747SPs designed for extremely long nonstop flights, such as his trips from Tel Aviv to Hawaii. In addition to the jumbo jets, through his company, Las Vegas Sands Corp., he also owned an Airbus A340-500, a Boeing 767-300ER, six Boeing 737s, six Gulfstream Vs, and three Gulfstream IVs, for a total of nineteen aircraft. All were painted in the colors of Israel's flag, white with powder blue stripes.

On the long flight, as the 747SP with its multiple bedrooms, marble bathrooms, and circular lounges, cruised high above the Grand Canyon and Nebraska's cornfields, conversations likely focused on a troubling federal criminal bribery investigation then taking place. Its venue was Macau. A once-depressed Portuguese enclave along the Chinese coast near Hong Kong, in 1999 it reverted back to China as a special administrative region. It has since become the world's gambling capital, and also home to an entire Las Vegas–style strip of Adelson's hotels and casinos, which soon became the largest revenue stream for his company.

In addition to gambling, crime had also become a growth industry in Macau, especially bribery, corruption, and money laundering. According to a report by the U.S. Congressional Executive Commission on China, $202 billion in "ill-gotten funds" channel their way through the enclave each year. That obviously raises questions regarding the origins, and cleanliness, of the money Adelson passes out to his prize slate of pro-Israel Republicans every election. "Much of Mr. Adelson's casino profits that go to him come from his casino in Macau," noted the late Arizona Republican senator John McCain. "Maybe in a roundabout way, foreign money is coming into an American political campaign."

Landing at Dulles International Airport's private terminal, Adelson's motorcade quickly made its way to the Washington Hilton, an iconic hotel with a gleaming white curvilinear façade. A few blocks down Connecticut Avenue were the outdoor chess tables of Dupont Circle, and beyond was the White House. In the marble lobby, waiting to check in, was a crowd dotted with yarmulkes, and voices murmuring in Hebrew and Yiddish. Many wore Israeli flag pins and patches. They were there to attend the annual conference of Adelson's Israeli-American Council. An organization designed to bring together the growing community of nearly two hundred thousand Israelis and ex-Israelis in the United States, the IAC had become another division in Adelson's Army. They, like the members of his task force, were willing participants in Netanyahu's secret war targeting Americans involved in the boycott movement.

To give the group guidance and support, Netanyahu sent over members of his war cabinet. They included Gilad Erdan; Major General Amos Yadlin, the former chief of Israel's military intelligence; and Israeli justice minister Ayelet Shaked. He told the crowd of about thirteen hundred that Israel must seize the initiative and "move from defense to offense" against American members and followers of BDS. At the time, the Americans they were planning to attack, and others like them, were involuntarily subsidizing Israel with nearly $4 billion a year in direct foreign assistance.

Beginning to rival the long-dominant and far better-known AIPAC in power, the IAC was even further to the extreme right in its pro-Israel/anti-Palestinian views. "Attila the Hun was too liberal for me," Adelson once half-joked during a talk in Israel, a place "I've been coming a million times a year at least," he said. The organization was largely supported with Adelson's money, including more than $10 million in donations from 2015 to 2016.

Haim Saban soon dropped out as the organization grew more extreme. At the IAC annual conference the year before, in 2014, Saban and Adelson had an onstage debate over the "two-state solution," whereby Israel would end its illegal military occupation, thereby enabling the Palestinians to establish their own sovereign nation. But Adelson would have none of it; Israel would continue its vicious occupation regardless of its status as an international outcast. Responding to a question about how to deal with "the problem of six million Palestinians," he answered, "I don't think the Bible says anything about democracy…[God] didn't talk about Israel remaining a democratic state, and if Israel isn't going to be a democratic state—so what?" He added, "Democracy is overrated."

Adelson was not alone in his disdain for the democratic process. Members of the Knesset also rejected democracy. "The State of Israel was created for the Jewish people, and its democracy is supposed to serve the Jewish people," noted Deputy Speaker Moshe Feiglin. And in 2022 lawmaker Miri Regev announced, "There are enough democratic countries. Another democratic country is not what is needed. What we need here is the only Jewish state in the world, which must be protected." Another Knesset member threatened a "Nakba," a mass expulsion, if Palestinian students at Israeli universities fly the Palestinian flag. "If you don't calm down we'll teach you a lesson that won't be forgotten," warned Israel Katz, a former minister of intelligence under Netanyahu.

Around the same time that Saban dropped out, Adelson put in his $10 million and effectively took over the IAC. A few months later, on March 1, 2015, Adam Milstein met with a reporter for the *Jewish Journal* and announced that the IAC had formed a Washington, DC, office. Seated in the twelfth-floor M Club of the Marriott Hotel in the capital, Milstein explained that it would be "an advocacy arm for Israeli-American interests on Capitol Hill." He added, "We feel that we have the natural knowledge to be the ambassadors for Israel." It was a clear acknowledgment by Milstein that he and his group intended to act as foreign agents—"ambassadors"—on behalf of the Israeli government while engaging in lobbying activities with members of Congress.

From the beginning, according to Milstein, it was the Israeli government that secretly originated the idea of the IAC and has long been behind it. The concept came about in 2006 when Ehud Danoch, Israel's consul general in Los Angeles, outlined the idea on a napkin and presented it to several local expat Israelis. "He challenged them to establish an umbrella organization that would unite and empower the local Israeli community to support the State of Israel and get involved in pro-Israel advocacy," said Milstein. That led Milstein and a few others to form the Israeli Leadership Council, which later changed its name to the Israeli-American Council (IAC).

At the IAC conference in Washington, Adelson related to the members a conversation with Netanyahu in which the prime minister expected loyalty to Israel from Israeli-U.S. citizens. "Would you be willing to recognize Israeli-Americans as Israelis to all intents and purposes?" Adelson asked. To which Netanyahu replied, "Of course, because otherwise we'd have to send emissaries to do the jobs that they can do." It was a response that raised many troubling questions dealing with dual loyalty and the expectation that Israelis living in the United States, including naturalized American citizens, would have a duty to act as agents of Israel. It was an issue that troubled Israeli journalist Chemi Shalev, the U.S. editor of *Haaretz*, who attended the conference. "Which raises the question: emissaries representing who, exactly, and to what purpose?" he wrote. The answers would be secret.

As the members of the IAC checked out the next morning, Netanyahu's war began. Key Jewish donors in the United States were secretly approached with a proposal by Psy Group, an Israeli psychological warfare firm with close connections to Mossad. Code-named "Project Butterfly," the proposal outlined a clandestine operation that would seek to damage specific Americans and U.S. organizations associated with the boycott movement. It would develop ways to disrupt their activities, lead them to be falsely investigated by the authorities, and run a hidden media influence campaign against them.

Champion Tower in the Tel Aviv neighborhood of Bnei Brak was an odd place for a clandestine organization, one hidden from Israelis as much as the rest of the world. Built on a former car lot, Champion Motors, the ground floor of the forty-story glass and cement structure served as showrooms for Audi, Volkswagen, Seat, and Skoda automobiles. On the twenty-ninth floor was the secret headquarters of the Ministry of Strategic Affairs. And standing at his wide plate-glass window, not far from his 24/7 ops center, Minister Gilad Erdan had a clear view of two distinct worlds.

To the west were the skyscrapers of modern, cosmopolitan, and largely secular downtown Tel Aviv, and beyond was the crescent of beaches along the Mediterranean Sea. Below, in contrast, was the most densely populated neighborhood in Israel, a center of Haredi Judaism, the world of the ultra-Orthodox. Permitted a large degree of autonomy, it is a world of rabbi-politicians and misogynistic gender segregation, including even sex-segregated department stores and laws forbidding women from driving or even possessing a driver's license. Until it was finally declared illegal in 2011, female bus passengers were required to sit in the back and enter and exit through the rear door, if they were allowed on the bus at all.

However, it wasn't the anti-Palestinian racism and blatant sexism in his own society that concerned Erdan, it was secretly attacking and subverting American society that had become his mandate.

According to Erdan's deputy, director-general Sima Vaknin-Gil, a reserve brigadier general, Israel was waging its covert war so that the "narrative in the world won't be that Israel equals apartheid." The ministry needed to quickly silence the growing boycott movement and its messengers, by any means necessary, before what happened in apartheid South Africa happened to Israel. In Washington, addressing a private meeting of Adelson and Milstein's Israeli-American Council, General Vaknin-Gil issued a stark warning. "In order to win," she said, "we must use tricks and craftiness." They would include threats, intimidation, harassment, covert influence operations, troll farms, fearmongering, blacklists, and espionage. The key was turning thousands of Americans into clandestine Israeli agents to spy on and carry out the operations against their fellow citizens. Secrecy, emphasized Vaknin-Gil, was therefore critical. "We are a different government working on a foreign soil, and we have to be very, very cautious," she said. What she didn't know was that there was a spy in her midst, recording her on a hidden video camera.

Among those present for the private talk was Antoine "Tony" Kleinfeld, a fast-rising star within what Vaknin-Gil termed the "Blue Network." The color of Israel's flag, as well as that of Adelson's Air Force, the network was a spiderweb of scores of well-funded organizations in the United States and around the world that work with and carry out actions on behalf of Israel. And as Gilad Erdan noted, it was a network that wanted to keep their relationship with his intelligence organization very covert. "One of the principles for success is keeping our methods of action secret," he said. "Since most of the ministry's actions are not of the ministry, but through bodies around the world who do not want to expose their connection with the state, we must protect the information whose exposure could harm the battle."

Slim, Jewish, extremely pro-Israel, an Oxford grad fluent in six languages including Yiddish and Hebrew, Kleinfeld was a perfect fit for the Blue Network. With a crisp North London accent and a smart wardrobe, he was also very sociable. He would throw lavish parties for members of the network in his tony Dupont Circle apartment, its walls covered with vibrant pro-Israel posters and its bookcases stacked with thoughtful writings about Israel and Judaism. And then there was his enthusiasm, his constant appearances at private fund-raisers and exclusive conferences, chatting it up with powerful members of the network, like Adam Milstein, and officials from the Israeli embassy.

In reality, Kleinfeld was a British filmmaker engaged in an undercover investigation for Al Jazeera television focusing on Washington's role in the network. And as Vaknin-Gil spoke, Kleinfeld's hidden camera was rolling.

Kleinfeld had arrived in town from London in the summer of 2016. At the time a similar undercover investigation was taking place there. Over drinks at the Aubaine, a shabby-chic French restaurant directly opposite the Israeli embassy in Kensington, West London, the undercover reporter turned on his hidden camera. What he caught was Shai Masot, an Israeli diplomat with a military and intelligence background, plotting to "take down" members of Parliament considered hostile to Israel, among them Deputy Foreign Minister Sir Alan Duncan, a vocal advocate for Palestinian human rights. Masot also told senior Labour MP Joan Ryan that he had obtained "more than £1 million" to pay for Labour MPs to visit Israel, visits that were simply luxury propaganda junkets.

Soon after the documentary aired on UK television, however, Israel quickly recalled Masot. "The diplomat in question seems no longer to be a functionary of the embassy in London," said Prime Minister Boris Johnson, unable to repress his obvious satisfaction. "So, whatever he may have been doing here his cover may well be said to have been truly blown." And Duncan, a Conservative member of Parliament for nearly three decades, accused Israel of "disgusting interference in our public life."

As might have been expected, a number of Jewish and pro-Israel groups launched bitter protests over the film, including hurling knee-jerk accusations of anti-Semitism. But following a lengthy investigation, Britain's top broadcast regulator, Ofcom, found no validity to the charges. "I think anti-Semitism as a smear is not what it used to be," said one disappointed Jewish supporter of Israel. Nor did the British authorities find any other issues, and they fully cleared the program. In its lengthy verdict it concluded that the film was "a serious investigative documentary" produced in the public interest. "Surreptitious filming," Ofcom confirmed, "was necessary to the credibility and authenticity of the program because without it, the program makers would have had to rely on second-hand accounts." And as Boris Johnson's comments indicated, he was happy the program put an end to at least one instance of Israeli treachery on British soil.

With the success of the British production, including a positive endorsement from the prime minister, the producers were hoping for a similar reaction in the United States to their American version, especially with their very convincing undercover agent, Tony Kleinfeld. But nowhere in the world is the pro-Israel lobby as powerful as in the United States. Thus, prior to the release of the completed film, horrified U.S. Jewish and pro-Israel groups initiated a massive pushback effort to spike the entire program, as they did in London. And once again they lobbed tired, overused accusations of anti-Semitism at the mostly British and American producers. But unlike in the UK, the American version greatly implicated the Trump administration and members of Congress in allowing and encouraging Netanyahu's blatant espionage and covert actions within the country, actions that also implicated a number of the same Jewish special interest groups protesting the loudest.

As a result, the groups received powerful backing from both Congress and the administration in their efforts to kill the film and bury its harsh and embarrassing truths. In the end, the Qatari ministers, facing problems with their neighbors in the Gulf and fearful of ending up on the wrong side of the powerful and vengeful Trump White House, buckled and folded, killing the program as it was set to air on al Jazeera.

Nevertheless, the completed film was eventually leaked on YouTube, and the revelations were startling. Among other things, they captured the director-general of the Ministry of Strategic Affairs, Vaknin-Gil, in Washington quietly laying out to members of Adelson's IAC the details of Israel's war plans against the United States, plans that included setting up a covert intelligence unit to spy on Americans involved in the boycott movement and take action against them. According to Vaknin-Gil:

> Ambiguity is part of our guidelines, that's why I'm not going to say anything too much about each one of the legs. The first one is intel, intelligence, or data, or information. What we've done is mapped and analyzed the whole [boycott] phenomena globally. Not just the United States, not just campuses, but campuses and intersectionality, labor unions and churches. We started to establish a project called Israel Cyber Shield. This is actually a civil intelligence unit that collects, analyzes and acts upon the activists in the BDS movement, of its people, organizations, or events. And we give it everything we collect. We are using the most sophisticated data system, intelligence system in the Israeli market.

Israel Cyber Shield, therefore, was a clandestine Israeli intelligence organization designed to spy not just on American students, but also on Christian churchgoers and labor unionists. And it was the recipient of Israel's massive intelligence resources. Once their targets were identified, according to Vaknin-Gil, the ministry then "acts upon" them using covert operations. Key was hiding all Israeli government links to the operation and its targeting of Americans. The ministry therefore created a phony, innocent-appearing front organization, "Concert." Supposedly a nonprofit "charity," it was anything but.

Instead, it was funded by $36 million from the ministry, and an equal amount or more was expected to be supplied by donors within the "Blue Network" of covert collaborators. In that way, U.S. donors could pretend their cash was going to a "charity," rather than an Israeli intelligence organization targeting fellow Americans.

From the beginning, Concert had very close ties to the Adelson/Milstein Israeli-American Council. In 2015, Sagi Balasha left his position as CEO of the IAC to become the first CEO of Concert. Milstein in turn took over as head of the IAC. Another founder of Concert was Ehud Danoch, Israel's former consul general in Los Angeles and the man who helped launch the IAC along with Milstein. Other Concert directors included retired brigadier general Yossi Kuperwasser, a former director-general of the Ministry of Strategic Affairs as well as a former top military intelligence official; former IDF military intelligence chief Amos Yadlin; ex–senior IDF intelligence officer Miri Eisin; and former national security advisor Yaakov Amidror. It was hardly the board of a benevolent charity dedicated to aiding the elderly or other noteworthy causes.

A key reason for attempting to hide the ministry's activities behind the phony charity was concern that cooperative Americans from the Blue Network could be arrested as illegal agents of Israel. Before the decision to create this front, the ministry attempted to pass millions of dollars to the network to pay for support and cooperation in carrying out its operations. One involved flying members of the network to Israel to be trained as "influencers," then back to the United States to spread propaganda and perform other secret tasks on behalf of the Israeli government.

But fearing charges, some of the organizations within the network turned the ministry down, including the Jewish Federations of North America as well as the Jewish Council on Public Affairs. They knew that without formal registration, such actions would be violations of both the Foreign Agents Registration Act (FARA) and the law against agents of a foreign power, known as Section 951, serious crimes. The turndowns left Erdan and his top officials "anxious and frustrated," according to one of the American Jewish officials approached. Erdan and his ministry were "anxious to figure out a way to spend the money." The result was the creation of the phony "charity," Concert. Nevertheless, the front was far from opaque.

Within Israel, the link between Concert and the ministry was little more than a badly kept secret. And among those warning of its dangers was human rights attorney Shachar Ben-Meir. In a petition to Israel's Supreme Court, he argued that Concert was used for "surveillance and espionage" as well as propaganda, and that those activities were carried out by proxies, like the Blue

Network. "In the case before us," he wrote, "the ministry [of Strategic Affairs] not only is 'aided' by private organizations in carrying out its activities, but also transfers much of its power—draconian powers to surveil, spy on, and spread propaganda—to private organizations that are not directly accountable to the government." In other words, turning American Jewish and pro-Israel organizations into clandestine conduits for the ministry.

One of those secret conduits is the Washington-based Israel on Campus Coalition (ICC), a key player in the Blue Network. Because much of the boycott activity takes place on college campuses around the United States, targeting and spying on student activists has become a high priority for Israel. This is often done secretly by fellow students belonging to Jewish and pro-Israel on-campus organizations. Once gathered, that intelligence on their fellow Americans is fed to the ICC, which acts as a sort of command center for on-campus spying. "The ICC pools resources from all of the campus organizations. So that they're tapped in on all angles," Lila Greenberg, the senior national field organizer for AIPAC, told undercover reporter Tony Kleinfeld.

"We built up this massive national political campaign to crush them," boasted Jacob Baime, referring to Americans on campuses across the country who support Palestinian human rights and the boycott. The ICC's executive director was meeting with Kleinfeld at the organization's Washington headquarters. On the hidden camera he described ICC as basically a clandestine Israeli military command. "It's modeled on General Stanley McCrystal's counterinsurgency strategy in Iraq. We've copied a lot from that strategy that has been working very well for us, actually. And one of the pieces is this Operations and Intelligence Brief."

That intelligence brief, containing secret details about targeted American students, is then passed on to the Ministry of Strategic Affairs, according to Baime's director of operations, Ian Hersh. "In terms of information sharing, we did add the Ministry of Strategic Affairs to our Operations and Intelligence Brief," he said. Baime told Kleinfeld that he also "coordinates with" and "communicates with" the ministry. Kleinfeld asked if he might be able to join in on the conversations occasionally, but Baime said no. "It's a pretty sensitive conversation."

They were striking revelations, indicating that Israel is illegally operating a secret nationwide campus spying operation within the United States, and Baime and his staff may potentially be acting as covert foreign agents for Israel. Beyond spying, the ICC engages in covert operations against the innocent American students, with its "massive national political campaign to crush them."

According to Baime, the ICC's war-room-like command center with its wall of flat-screen monitors uses the most advanced intelligence technology on the market. At the time it included Radian6, which monitored online conversation in real time from more than 150 million social media sources, including Facebook, Twitter, YouTube, blogs, and other online communities. A dashboard provided geolocation data and other details. "We're phasing that out over the next year and we're bringing on more sophisticated technology that is developed in Israel," Baime said. "The research operation is very high-tech. When I got here a few years ago the budget was $3,000. Today it's like a million and a half, or more. Probably it's two million at this point. I don't even know, it's huge. It's a massive budget."

Unsurprisingly, the ICC is heavily funded by Milstein, who also sits as a director on its board.

Money, therefore, seems to be no object. The group even paid over $1 million to a high-powered Washington political consulting firm, FP1, to set up a network of anonymous websites and social media accounts to attack students who supported Palestinian rights. Hidden behind its opaque digital wall, the ICC is free to name and shame, leveling spurious and outrageous charges of anti-Semitism and terrorism, and even likening students protesting Israel's occupation to members of the Ku Klux Klan. Intimidation is the goal, all without fear of being held to account, or showing their direct links to the Israeli government. Secrecy is therefore paramount. "We have a lot of communications capabilities, and what's most interesting about it, I think," said Baime on the hidden camera, "is that 90 percent of the people who pay attention to this space very closely have no idea what we're actually doing, which I like. We do it securely and anonymously and that's the key."

Israel also secretly hires Americans as spies to work out of its Washington embassy and its consulates around the United States to covertly surveil and monitor fellow Americans. Thoroughly vetted to ensure loyalty to Israel, many of those hired have spent years heavily involved in pro-Israeli activities from the time they were in college and before. Among them was Julia Reifkind, who led a pro-Israel group at the University of California at Davis before moving on to become an activist with AIPAC. In October 2017 she was hired by Israel and assigned to its embassy in Washington.

Reifkind had good preparation for her assignment. Thinking that Kleinfeld was a fellow pro-Israel activist, over dinner at Washington's Mari Vanna restaurant she revealed that while at AIPAC she spent much of her time deceiving college students about her covert connection to the organization. "Obviously I'm an AIPAC-trained activist," she said. "When you're lobbying on behalf of AIPAC, you don't say AIPAC, you say, 'I'm a pro-Israel student from UC Davis.' And when you're meeting with students on campus I would never say, 'I am the AIPAC Campus Rep.' I'd say, 'My name is Julia and I'm a pro-Israel student.'"

At the embassy, Reifkind focused on developing intelligence on fellow Americans, including students on college campuses. "So nobody really knows what we're doing," she said. "But mainly it's been a lot of research like monitoring BDS...It's mainly gathering intel, reporting back to Israel. That's a lot of what I do. To report back to the Ministry of Foreign Affairs, the Ministry of Strategic Affairs, and make sure they have the right information." Among the ways she spies on boycotters and Palestinian human rights supporters is with fake Facebook accounts. "I have my fake Facebook that I follow all the SJP [Students for Justice in Palestine] accounts. I have some fake names. My name is Jay Bernard or something."

Once Reifkind collects the intelligence on her targets, she passes it on to her boss at the embassy, who translates it into Hebrew. Then it is sent to Erdan's Ministry of Strategic Affairs and other offices over a very secure encrypted system called Cables. It's "really secure," she said. "I don't have access to it because I'm an American...I've seen it, it looks really bizarre... And then they'll send something back and he'll translate it and tell me what I need to do." What Reifkind didn't know was that the FBI had the embassy wired. Like a comic strip from *Mad* magazine, it was the spies spying on the spies.

CHAPTER 23

◆

The Eavesdroppers

Just north of Washington, DC's Beltway, in the small bedroom community of Calverton, Maryland, a bland, unmarked six-story office building sits between a Kingdom Fellowship AME Church and a Wendy's fast-food restaurant. Located in the Calverton Office Park at 11700 Beltsville Drive, the hundred-thousand-square foot structure could be just another regional insurance headquarters, or a place to visit the eye doctor or tax accountant. Instead, inside is a highly secret SCIF, a sensitive compartmented information facility, where the FBI's Hebrew-speaking spies eavesdrop on Israeli diplomats while sharing space with agents posing as young children to catch online pedophiles.

For years, the FBI's team of Hebrew-speaking eavesdroppers occupied space in the Language Services Unit, a large L-shaped room off-limits to most agents on the fourth floor of the bureau's field office in downtown Washington. Behind cipher-locked doors, between two hundred and three hundred linguists targeting a variety of languages sat in long rows of waist-high cubicles, earphone cords dangling from their ears, as they transcribed conversations, many from nearby embassies. Other eavesdropping and analysis are done by the bureau's secretive Data Intercept Technology Unit at the FBI's complex of buildings on the Marine Corps base in Quantico, Virginia. But as the FBI's eavesdropping and data intercept operations exploded in the early to mid-2000s, many linguists, including members of the Hebrew team, were moved to the nondescript office building in Calverton.

It's clear that the FBI's counterintelligence organization is fully cognizant of virtually everything Israel is doing in the United States, including the employment of Americans as spies at its embassy, its clandestine campus activities, and its secret dealings with American members of Congress, but chooses to do nothing about it. According to Itamar Rabinovich, Israel's former ambassador to the United States, the NSA even broke the embassy's encryption system, a fact later discovered by Israel's Shin Bet counterintelligence organization.

"Every 'juicy' telegram was in danger of being leaked," he said. "We sent very few of them. Sometimes I came to Israel to deliver reports orally. The Americans were certainly tapping the regular phone lines, and it became clear that in later years they were also listening to the secure line." Rabinovich, who served in Washington from 1993 to 1996, said the leak happened years after his appointment ended, and then continued undiscovered for many years. The result, he said, was that everyone at the embassy is constantly warned about the possibility of conversations leaking, even on the heavily encrypted lines, such as Cables.

Located at 3514 International Drive NW in Washington, the Israeli embassy is the country's epicenter of spying in the United States. A few years ago, FBI Counterintelligence determined that Israel was most likely behind the placement of cell phone surveillance devices that were discovered close to the White House and other sensitive locations within Washington. Known as international mobile subscriber identity-catchers, or IMSI-catchers, they are traditional tools of trade for spies because they mimic standard cell phone towers and thus fool cell phones into revealing data, including the contents of calls and email.

"It was pretty clear that the Israelis were responsible," a former senior intelligence official told *Politico*. "The devices were likely intended to spy on President Donald Trump, as well as his top aides and closest associates." Other U.S. officials, including several who served in top intelligence and national security posts, told *Politico*, "Based on a detailed forensic analysis, the FBI and other agencies working on the case felt confident that Israeli agents had placed the devices." Nevertheless, as is always the case when it comes to Israeli spying in the United States, no action was ever taken by FBI Counterintelligence. "The Trump administration took no action to punish or even privately scold the Israeli government," a U.S. official told *Politico*. "I'm not aware of any accountability at all."

Among the Hebrew-speaking spies, commuting to Calverton every day from his home in nearby Silver Spring was Shamai Kedem Leibowitz. Hired in January 2009, Leibowitz, a thirty-nine-year-old attorney and Orthodox Jew, had dual American/Israeli citizenship and was a former tank gunner in the Israeli army. But despite his ties to Israel and his service in the Israeli military, he had long been opposed to the state's oppression of Palestinians and in favor of the boycott. "As a young soldier serving in the Israeli army, I was ordered to commit war crimes in the Palestine Occupied Territories," he wrote in the journal *Against the Current* in 2005. "My platoon meted out collective punishment on whole Palestinian communities, shot live ammunition at unarmed civilians, killed women and children, enforced prolonged curfews, creating humanitarian disasters, arrested and detained Palestinians without charge, demolished their homes, and arbitrarily destroyed crops and property." He therefore argued for Americans to "support divestment from Israel."

Assigned to eavesdrop on the Israeli embassy, Leibowitz was growing increasingly angry and fearful as a result of the numerous conversations he was monitoring and the emails he was reading, as well as the daily reports from the NSA and the voluminous archives at his disposal. What concerned him most was the embassy's secret and illegal efforts to influence Congress, especially the constant push to support an Israeli nuclear strike against Iran, as well as the hidden collaboration with American pro-Israel lobbies and pressure groups, what the Ministry of Strategic Affairs called the Blue Network.

It was a situation Tom Hayden, a former California assemblyman and ex-husband of actress Jane Fonda, was very familiar with. A former president of the Students for a Democratic Society (SDS), and a prominent anti–Vietnam War activist, in the 1980s he decided to run for the state assembly. Familiar with political battles, having been a member of the infamous "Chicago Seven," he expected to face opposition. But what he didn't expect was to be confronted by the Mafia-like Israeli lobby. "Twenty-five years ago I stared into the eyes of Michael Berman, chief operative for his congressman-brother, Howard Berman," Hayden revealed decades later. " 'I represent the Israeli defense forces,' Michael said. I thought he was joking. He wasn't. Michael seemed to imagine himself the gatekeeper protecting Los Angeles' Westside for Israel's political interests, and those of the famous Berman-[Congressman Henry] Waxman machine. Since Jews represented one-third of the Democratic district's primary voters, Berman held a balance of power." It was also home to many of the actors, directors, and producers who make up the film industry.

Howard Berman eventually became chairman of the powerful House Foreign Affairs Committee. He said, "Even before I was a Democrat, I was a Zionist," and that Israel "is why I went on the Foreign Affairs Committee." According to Hayden, the brothers Berman were actually in favor of a then young Jewish prosecutor named Adam Schiff, now chairman of the equally powerful House Intelligence Committee. "But they calculated that Schiff couldn't win without name recognition, so they were considering 'renting' me the Assembly seat, Berman said. But there was one condition: that I always be a 'good friend of Israel.' " Schiff apparently passed the lobby's test and has certainly become a certified "good friend of Israel."

In 2016, for example, Schiff sided with AIPAC and Benjamin Netanyahu and urged President Barack Obama to veto UN Security Council Resolution 2334, which condemned Israeli settlements as "a flagrant violation of international law." "I would urge the Administration to make every effort to oppose its being brought forward and make it clear that it will veto the measure if necessary," he said. Like Berman, Schiff was protecting Israel on AIPAC's behalf while ensuring its continued illegal occupation and abuse of the Palestinians. He later led the congressional investigation into Russiagate, hunting for conspiracies between the Kremlin and the Trump campaign, but never found any. His having won AIPAC's seal of approval certainly ensures that there will be no similar penetrating investigations of Israel, at least on his watch. And it also might help explain why the FBI Counterintelligence Division constantly looks the other way when it comes to Israeli espionage and covert operations in the United States.

"I can offer my real-life experience to the present discussion about the existence and power of an 'Israel lobby,'" said Hayden, who served eighteen years in the California state assembly and senate. "I had to be certified 'kosher,' not once but over and over again. The certifiers were the elites, beginning with rabbis and heads of the multiple mainstream Jewish organizations, especially each city's Jewish Federation. An important vetting role was held as well by the American-Israel Public Affairs Committee (AIPAC), a group closely associated with official parties in Israel. When necessary, Israeli ambassadors, counsels general, and other officials would intervene with statements declaring someone a 'friend of Israel.' In my case, a key to the 'friendship issue' was the Los Angeles–based counsel general Benjamin Navon."

Because an open endorsement by Navon would be a violation of laws that prohibit foreign interference in an American election, it was agreed that the endorsement would instead be "communicated indirectly," said Hayden. "We would be seen and photographed together in public. Benny [Navon] would make positive public statements that could be quoted in campaign mailings. As a result, I was being declared 'kosher' by the ultimate source, the region's representative of the state of Israel."

But then came Israel's bloody siege of Beirut. "Benny Navon wanted Jane and me to be supportive," said Hayden. "I decided we should go to the Middle East." It was, he said, "the mistake of my political career...I found myself defending Israel's 'right' to self-defense on its border, only to realize privately how foolish I was becoming." He also witnessed many other abuses. "I remember watching Israeli soldiers blow up Palestinian houses and carry out collective punishment because, they told me matter-of-factly, punishment is the only language that Arabs understand."

These were the kinds of illegal activities that Shamai Leibowitz and the other Hebrew eavesdroppers, sitting in the FBI's SCIF hidden in the Maryland office building, were regularly recording. But to Leibowitz's increasing anger, nothing was ever done about them by either the FBI or the Justice Department. It was a situation that even frustrated a former head of the FBI's counterintelligence division. When I asked him why no one would talk to me about Israel's massive espionage in the United States, he simply shook his head. "You don't think Israel's a sensitive topic?" he asked, astonished, requesting that his name not be used. "So, Israel has been looked at and is being looked at and that's all I can tell you," he said. "But nobody's doing anything."

"Why not?" I asked.

"You can imagine," is all he would say. I then said that I was planning to write about the topic. "I hope you do. I hope you do," he said. Then, sighing and looking frustrated, he added, "I've been there done that. I know it. I've brought cases to the Department of Justice on Israel." Cases that were never opened.

Among the cases that caused such frustration at the bureau was that of former congresswoman Jane Harman, whom FBI eavesdroppers had recorded speaking a number of times with a suspected Israeli agent—an agent who was the target of a secret FISA warrant, signed by FBI director Robert Mueller. The warrants are used when the target is a foreign intelligence agent. At the time, in 2006, Harman was the top Democrat on the House Intelligence Committee and she was lobbying hard for Nancy Pelosi, soon to become Speaker, to name her head of the committee. The problem was, Pelosi was planning to appoint someone else to the position.

Thus a quid pro quo from the secret Israeli agent: If she would use her powerful position on the Intelligence Committee to intervene with the Justice Department on behalf of two AIPAC lobbyists charged with espionage, he would see to it that she got the top slot on the committee. Specifically, he promised that Haim Saban would threaten to withhold campaign contributions to Nancy Pelosi, a recipient of more than half a million dollars in pro-Israel cash, if she did not select Ms. Harman for the intelligence post. It was an act of political extortion by a clandestine Israel agent to put a very pro-Israel member of Congress as head of the U.S. House Intelligence Committee, and in return to obtain reduced charges for two people awaiting trial for espionage on behalf of Israel.

But rather than immediately slam the phone down, call the FBI, and report the potential crime, as was her obligation, Harman instead agreed to the proposal. She even suggested that she might have more influence by going directly to someone at the White House. Then, before hanging up, she told the Israeli agent, "This conversation doesn't exist." The problem was it did exist, and it was sitting in an FBI computer. Harman certainly knew how much power Haim Saban had. A billionaire and dual Israeli/American, Saban was one of the most powerful members of the Democratic Party and often its top contributor. He was also a major contributor to AIPAC, and he made no secret of his single-minded goal: "I'm a one-issue guy, and my issue is Israel." Thus, when Saban talks, Pelosi listens.

Details of the phone calls and the conversation quickly raised a number of serious alarms within both the bureau and the Justice Department. In the intelligence and public corruption units, attorneys who read the transcripts decided Harman had committed a "completed crime," meaning that there was evidence that she attempted to complete the act. The transcripts also raised great alarms at CIA. The director, Porter Goss, was himself a previous chairman of the House Intelligence Committee, and he "deemed the matter particularly urgent because of Harman's rank and the panel's top Democrat."

Harman boasted to a Jewish news service that "I'm proud of my friend-ships with members of AIPAC, I have conversations with them," but she never realized she had been recorded. Ultimately, she said, she never approached either the Justice Department or the White House on behalf of the AIPAC officials charged with espionage. But despite the belief by Justice Department prosecutors that Harman had nevertheless committed a crime, the attorney general at the time, Alberto Gonzales, quickly killed any further investigation into the matter, for strictly political reasons. In the end, Harman was never appointed chair of the Intelligence Committee, never approved for another term on the panel, and less than two years after the scandal broke she unex-pectedly resigned her seat in Congress after sixteen years in office.

Details from the transcript of Harman's calls with the secret Israeli agent finally leaked on April 20, 2009, first to Jeff Stein of *Congressional Quarterly* along with his *SpyTalk* blog, and then to the *New York Times*. It was likely the result of frustrated officials at either the FBI or Justice. Then, at almost the same time, Shamai Leibowitz's fears and disgust over inaction by the White House and Justice Department also reached their apex. Eavesdrop-ping on the Israeli embassy, he knew that illegal activities were regularly tak-ing place between Israeli agents, members of Congress, and others. But as with Jane Harman, it was all being brushed under the rug due to political considerations.

Therefore, within days of the Harman leak he also decided to leak about two hundred pages of transcripts containing secret intercepted Israeli con-versations to Richard Silverstein, a fellow Jew who shared his views on Israel's human rights violations. Hiding Leibowitz's identity, Silverstein published some of the details in his blog, *Tikun Olam: Make the World a Better Place*. "Thanks to a confidential source," he wrote on April 28, 2009, "I'll be lifting the veil, in this post, on Israeli intelligence gathering regarding members of Congress from the Midwest."

In this and other blog posts, Silverstein focused on questionable and potentially illegal activities engaged in by Israeli agents in their widespread influence operations. "I've been informed by a confidential source that in September 2008, before one of the presidential debates," he wrote, "an Israeli operative attempted unsuccessfully to meet with a debate panelist in order to plant a question about war against Iran: would the candidates take military action against that country or accept a nuclear armed Iran?" Silverstein added, "I wonder what an Israeli voter might think if he or she discovered that U.S. intelligence operatives were planting questions during Israeli election debates."

By midsummer 2009, the FBI was closing in on Leibowitz, and in August he quit the bureau. At the same time, a panicked Silverstein quickly deleted the blog posts that referenced the leaked material (I obtained them from another source) and burned the hundreds of secret intercept transcripts in his backyard. Nevertheless, by December the FBI had linked Leibowitz to the Silverstein disclosures and the former bureau linguist was arrested and charged with espionage. Soon after, he pled guilty and was sentenced to twenty months in prison. At his sentencing, Leibowitz, a lawyer, explained that his decision to leak the secret documents was because he "saw things which I considered were violation of the law." But as part of his sentence, he was forbidden from mentioning anything he learned while with the FBI.

With FBI counterintelligence agents focused solely on arresting those leaking details of Israel's illegal influence operations targeting Congress, rather than those perpetrating the crimes, the spying and subversion would grow exponentially. Six years later it was discovered that Israel was spying on U.S. secret negotiations with Iran over a nuclear agreement, one designed to protect Americans.

Much worse, however, was the discovery that Israel was using results of that espionage in a clandestine congressional influence operation aimed at killing the agreement. In so doing, Israel, for its own benefit, was deliberately putting Americans at risk of becoming involved in a nuclear war. It was a situation Leibowitz had earlier warned of. "It is one thing for the U.S. and Israel to spy on each other. It is another thing for Israel to steal U.S. secrets and play them back to U.S. legislators to undermine U.S. diplomacy," said one senior U.S. official who had been briefed on the case.

With FBI counterintelligence agents forbidden from taking action against Israeli agents, the clandestine influence operations in Congress would continue unimpeded. And their American spies at the embassy, the consulates, the ICC, and elsewhere would have no fear of arrest. It was therefore time to launch General Sima Vaknin-Gil's "tricks and craftiness," the covert operations.

———

At Adelson and Milstein's IAC conference in Washington in the fall of 2015, Minister of Strategic Affairs Erdan and other officials made it clear that now was the time to go on the offensive against the boycott movement. And as if on cue, a small group of wealthy Jewish donors was quietly approached by officials from Psy Group, the secretive Israeli psychological warfare company.

In a crowded and eclectic Tel Aviv neighborhood of weathered Bauhaus apartment buildings and tired art deco dry goods shops, Psy Group was well hidden. Its offices were located three floors above a busy Tiv Ta'am grocery store at 47 Nahalat Binyamin Street. Staffed by former Israeli spies and with links to the Israeli government, the secretive company was known as a "private Mossad." Uniquely, it specialized in psychological warfare, a field that focused on changing people's perceptions, and thus their actions, often unwittingly, through the manipulation of social media, the use of fake online identities, and phony news sites. In other words, bots.

With the motto "shape reality," Psy Group billed itself as specializing "in innovative influence and intelligence activities tailored to a client's unique needs." It was founded in 2014 by Royi Burstien, a lieutenant colonel (res.) in Israeli military intelligence and a veteran of an elite Israeli military unit that specialized in psychological operations. "These guys came out of the [Israeli] military intelligence army unit," said George Birnbaum, a U.S. political consultant familiar with the company. "And it's like coming out with a triple Ph.D. from MIT. The amount of knowledge these guys have in terms of cybersecurity, cyber-intelligence." The company's owner was Joel Zamel, the Australian-born son of a wealthy mining engineer and businessman. He later moved to Israel, where he earned a master's degree and joined the country's burgeoning army of private electronic spies-for-hire.

A major Israeli export, Psy Group's intrusive surveillance techniques and technologies were sold and contracted out to countries, including despots, with little regard to how they would be used on the victims. Since 2010, Zamel had also been running a shadowy "crowdsourced" rent-a-spy firm called Wikistrat at the same Tel Aviv address as Psy Group but also with an office in Washington. It largely sold its intelligence services to foreign governments, especially the UAE and the United States. In 2016, Psy Group formed a strategic partnership with Cambridge Analytica LLC. A digital media firm, it was employed by the Trump campaign and secretly and improperly harvested the data of up to eighty-seven million Facebook users.

What Psy Group was after from the Jewish donors was millions of dollars to help finance Project Butterfly, a covert operation within the "theater of action," as the company referred to the United States. According to its secret internal operations plan, Project Butterfly was aimed at "executing intelligence and influence efforts" against Americans by creating an "infrastructure for narrative warfare—alternative messaging and negative platforms." In other words, by creating fake news outlets, phony Facebook personas and posts, and other forms of information warfare, Psy Group's specialty was to deceive the American public. Psy Group was seeking $2.5 million from the Jewish donors for the operation's first year of a three-year plan and promised it would conduct its activities in utmost secrecy. All links to the donors would be hidden and, according to Burstien, none of the actions would be traceable to Jews or Israelis.

The importance of the operation and its closeness to Netanyahu can be seen in Project Butterfly's top officials. Among them was Netanyahu's former deputy director of Mossad and director-general of the Ministry of Intelligence and Strategic Affairs, Ram Ben-Barak, who was the project's strategic advisor. Comparing the effort against the American boycotters to "a war," he said, "you don't kill them but you do have to deal with them in other ways." Another project advisor was retired major general Yaakov Amidror, Netanyahu's former national security advisor.

According to the Jewish magazine *Forward*, Psy Group approached the donors through Misha Galperin, a Russia-born former psychotherapist with a shock of curly white hair and a scruffy white beard. Galperin had recently stepped down from his New York–based, $750,000-a-year position as CEO of international development for the Jewish Agency for Israel. An organization with close ties to the Israeli government, it raises hundreds of millions of dollars from donors in the United States to aid and encourage Jews to return to Israel. After leaving the Jewish Agency, Galperin started his own firm, ZANDAFI, that specialized in advising philanthropic groups, foundations, and not-for-profit organizations. They were precisely the target audience of potential donors Psy Group was after.

Galperin had been in communication with the Ministry of Strategic Affairs over the past several years. But due to the secrecy of the operation, what assistance, if any, he eventually provided to Psy Group is unknown since he declined to discuss his role. Nevertheless, Psy Group was soon successful in raising $1.2 million from Jewish donors in New York and elsewhere and quickly launched its secret operational plan. The document read as if drafted by Mossad preparing for a war against a violent enemy. "The Butterfly initiative uses PSY's proprietary intelligence-gathering and influence techniques to destabilize and disrupt anti-Israel movements from within," it said. The organization's on-the-ground clandestine agents:

- Conducted 2 tours of main theater of action [the U.S.]—executing intelligence and influence efforts, collaborating with partners.
- Executed 5 rapid-response operations nationwide.
- Obtained unique and sensitive intelligence relevant to Israeli national security.
- Damaged effectiveness of anti-Israel movement.

Among the activities carried out was creating fake news outlets and other disinformation platforms in an Orwellian effort to brand the nonviolent boycotters and their supporters as "terrorists." "Narrative Warfare/Influence: Reinforced and increased awareness of main message that anti-Israeli activity equates with terrorism," said the document. The operation "achieved high-impact results against targeted individuals" while making sure its own activities are "not connected to Israel."

The "targeted venues" included "2-3 high-value campuses that serve as local hubs/hotspots for anti-Israel activity...Expanded focus on 6-7 additional campuses" as well as "individual targets," including "movement leaders, thought leaders, influencers, major supporters, etc." The actions included efforts to destroy the reputations of students and faculty, subjecting people to unwarranted investigations, and charges of "persecution," that is, endless phony accusations of "anti-Semitism":

- Damage to target's standing/reputation (bad reviews, fall in support, etc.)
- Cancellation or disruption of events
- Online and offline echoing of "persecution" by targets
- Inquiries/Investigations commenced
- Lawsuits filed/threats to sue
- Media coverage and masked PR (i.e., not attributable to us)

One of those targeted was Hatem Bazian, fifty, a lecturer at the University of California at Berkeley and a leader in the boycott movement. One morning, as he was about to drive his daughter to school, he discovered a flyer on the windshield of his and other cars parked along the street of his quiet North Berkeley neighborhood. To his horror, they contained his picture along with the caption in large bold letters "HE SUPPORTS TERROR."

In addition to flyers, Psy Group's agents in the United States also put together a dossier on Bazian, as well as other targets, that included false and misleading data as well as the phony and ever-present charges of "anti-Semitism." These flyers were distributed to a number of legitimate organizations in an effort to destroy the reputations of their targets. "Bazian," noted a secret Psy Group document, "got our full attention in the last few weeks." The document noted, "a HUMINT [on-the-ground human intelligence] operation is conducted on each of the individuals."

As Psy Group's agents conducted their espionage and covert operations with no pushback, or even investigation by the FBI, Erdan and other Israeli groups expanded their operations. The key was to get wealthy Americans to secretly pay for the spying, slander, and destruction of their fellow Americans on behalf of Israel—while also saving money on their taxes.

CHAPTER 24

◆

The Thugs

Under ashen clouds on a mild Wednesday in May 2020, a cavalcade of noisy, unwashed cars and utility vehicles traveled slowly down Pacific Avenue in San Francisco's Pacific Heights, the most expensive neighborhood in the city. "Housing is a Human Right," read the sign on a red SUV. "#House the Homeless," said another. And taped to the side of a tan Toyota was a handwritten poster declaring in red ink, "I'd Be Safier If Jackie Wasn't A Landlord." As the convoy approached a boxy modern slate gray mansion trimmed with redwood, the drivers began leaning on their horns, honking and shouting. "We know you live here," roared a man from an open car window. "We don't need corporate landlords pushing people onto the street." From another vehicle someone yelled, "Stop disrupting our neighborhoods, and we won't disrupt yours."

The target of the protest was the $13 million home of billionaire Jaclyn Safier, the fifty-five-year-old CEO of Prometheus Real Estate Group, the largest private owner of apartments in the San Francisco Bay Area. Safier controlled over thirteen thousand apartments in the city and the Northwest. With a net worth of $1.3 billion, she was also a key Republican donor, contributing over a quarter million dollars to the party's coffers in 2016 as Donald Trump was running for president. After Trump won, he appointed her to a prestigious post, the board of directors of Presidio Trust, in charge of managing the Presidio of San Francisco.

The protest was organized by the nonprofit Housing Is A Human Right, the housing advocacy division of the AIDS Healthcare Foundation. It was directed at Safier due to her leading role in blocking rent control measures in California. "The level of greed on display by corporate landlords like Safier comes as no surprise," said the group's director, René Christian Moya.

"After all, Safier and Prometheus shelled more than 2 million dollars to defeat Proposition 10 in 2018, which would have expanded rent control." The group noted the extra hardships faced by many renters during the

COVID-19 pandemic: "Safier wants to maintain the status quo, a California where seniors sleep in their cars, hard-working citizens are priced out of their communities, and there are very limited tenant protections. For her, it's good business."

Prometheus was founded by Safier's father, publicity-shy billionaire Sanford Diller. Also a major Trump backer, he came under investigation for a possible bribery attempt involving a presidential pardon for a friend in prison. Hoping to free psychologist Hugh Baras, who had been convicted of tax evasion, Diller donated $6 million to a pro-Trump political committee and suggested there was much more where that came from, that he had the potential to rival fellow billionaire Sheldon Adelson in the size of his donations. In the end the deal fell through and the pardon never materialized. It was only after Diller's death in 2018 that an investigation uncovered details of the potential attempt to purchase a pardon from Trump.

A pro-Israel extremist, Diller supported a long list of right-wing Islamophobic organizations. They included the American Freedom Law Center, which even the Jewish Anti-Defamation League said has a "record of anti-Muslim, anti-immigrant and anti-black bigotry," and Stop Islamization of America, which "has sought to rouse public fears about a vast Islamic conspiracy to destroy American values," according to the ADL. He also became the largest financial backer of the Tea Party Patriots, one of the organizations involved in the January 6, 2021, insurrection at the Capitol.

Another major cause was aiding Israel in its war against the American boycott movement. Because much of the funding for Israel's secret war against the movement was to come from Americans themselves, Jewish millionaires and billionaires like Adelson, Milstein, Diller, and others were critical to support organizations like Psy Group, Israel on Campus Coalition, and the Israeli-American Council. Diller's focus was funding a clandestine Israeli psychological terror organization known as Canary Mission. As support for Palestinian rights increased on college campuses around the country, Canary Mission was secretly established in Israel to intimidate and frighten American students away from the boycott movement.

For years the Diller family had used their billions to combat and quash support for Palestinian human rights. In 2004, Sanford's wife, Helen, offered to donate $5 million to the University of California at Berkeley's Center for Middle East Studies to underwrite a series of visiting Israeli scholars. "You know what's going on over there," she said to a reporter for the San Francisco Jewish newspaper *J.*, referring to the Berkeley campus. "With the protesting and this and that, we need to get a real strong Jewish studies program in there...Hopefully, it will be enlightening to have a visiting professor and it'll calm down over there more." Instead, as the first Diller visiting professor the university chose Oren Yiftachel, a professor at Ben-Gurion University in Beersheba and a harsh critic of Israel. In an article, he wrote, "The actual existence of an Israeli state (and hence citizenship) can be viewed as an illusion," adding, "Israel has created a colonial setting, held through violent control."

Based in Israel with a hidden operational center in the United States, Canary Mission was established to frighten American college students away from voting for divestment by placing their names, pictures, and personal details on an online blacklist. It was designed to be viewed by future employers and accused the students of being in favor of terrorism and other false charges, while the hatemongers themselves cowered behind a digital wall of anonymity. And to reinforce the fear of being placed on the blacklist, muscular men in yellow canary costumes showed up on the eve of a vote and engaged in a frightening demonstration.

Compiled largely by pro-Israel campus spies, the blacklists targeted students who, through their overt actions or their comments on social media, demonstrated opposition to Israel's illegal occupation or showed support for the boycott movement. The lists were professionally done, complete with derogatory "dossiers" of their targets; the idea was to cause havoc in the student's life, including difficulty obtaining employment upon graduation. Despite the psychological damage done to thousands of students throughout the country, there has been so little reported on the secretive organization that Project Censored named Canary Mission one of the Top Ten Underreported Stories of 2021. "Even at the peak of the 'cancel culture' panic," the Project said, "perhaps the most canceled people anywhere in America—pro-Palestinian activists and sympathizers—got virtually no attention."

In a video put out by the group, the human rights activists are referred to as "anti-Semitic and anti-American radicals" and likened to Nazis as the video tracks slowly across a picture of the Holocaust, including images of Jews with yellow stars on their clothes. "Soon they will be part of your team," it warns companies. It then adds, "It is your duty to ensure that today's radicals are not tomorrow's employees." The program targets professors as well as students who fight against apartheid and the oppression of Palestinians. Among them was Corey Robin, a political science professor at Brooklyn College and the CUNY Graduate Center. It's "classic McCarthyism," he said, "because what you're really saying is, we're going to exile you from all aspects of society."

Canary Mission's blacklist quickly grew to more than two thousand names, including faces and screenshots, some with "charges" running for thousands of words, much of them cobbled together from Facebook and other social media. Over five hundred professors also found themselves targets, including David Biale, a Jewish studies professor at the University of California at Davis and the author of over ten books on Jewish history. "It's essentially a spying operation they run on college campuses," he said. "The problem is, there's pretty persuasive evidence that Israel is using this website to block people from entering the state of Israel. The Ministry of Strategic Affairs, they evidently have very close ties to Canary Mission."

Included are Jews who belong to pro-Palestinian human rights groups like Jewish Voice for Peace, an American organization with seventy chapters and fifteen thousand dues-paying members. Among them was Sophie Hurwitz, a student at Wellesley College who was from a Jewish community in St. Louis. Hurwitz's "crime" was attending a rally protesting Birthright Israel and its major funder, billionaire Sheldon Adelson, as well as speaking out about it. The program offers free trips to Israel for all American Jews ages eighteen to thirty-two. In explaining why she refused the expenses-paid trip, Hurwitz called them one-sided propaganda tools used to justify the occupation and abuse of Palestinians. "It was scary," she wrote to the *St. Louis Jewish Light*. "I'm a college sophomore, I didn't expect to start my second year living away from home by feeling stalked by an international, shadowy organization. Seeing your face, and details about your life, on a website that you know means to slander you is a surreal, disconcerting experience…It's a deliberate attempt to shut down dialogue on Palestinian issues."

Ari Kaplan, a Jewish student at NYU, also faced Canary Mission's wrath. After he made a comment at a Jewish dinner critical of the Trump administration's decision to move the U.S. embassy to Jerusalem, Canary Mission charged that he was "demonizing Israel at a Jewish event." Such a comment could severely affect potential employment, especially by a Jewish or pro-Israel employer, which was the idea. Some students have even reported receiving death threats online following tweets about them by Canary Mission. "My first quarter at UCLA, someone said they were going to come to UCLA and kill me. And I had to move out of my dorm," one student, a member of Students for Justice in Palestine, told *The Intercept*.

Not content with online slander and blacklisting, Canary Mission agents soon began physical intimidation. At George Washington University, on the eve of a vote on a divestment resolution involving Israeli violations of Palestinian rights, two powerful men in yellow canary outfits suddenly turned up outside the building in which the vote was to take place. They then engaged in a strange and frightening dance. Their purpose was to dramatically reinforce earlier Canary Mission messages sent to students advising them to vote against the resolution and attacking the student activists. "THERE ARE NO

SECRETS. WE WILL KNOW YOUR VOTE AND WILL ACT ACCORD-INGLY," said one threatening Canary Mission message. Abby Brook, a Jewish student at the school who was active in pro-Palestinian groups on campus, found the event "pretty unbelievably terrifying," she said. "These two fully grown, muscular men in these bird costumes, strutting." On the walk home that night she said she was careful to watch her back.

In-your-face intimidation of students is the hallmark of Canary Mission, an organization that remains very active. "When a BDS vote comes to a U.S. college campus today, a pro-Israel cavalry arrives, whether or not they're called," said Josh Nathan-Kazis, a reporter for the Jewish magazine *Forward*, who has written extensively on the topic. "The total amount of American Jewish and Israeli government funds flooding the anti-BDS effort is easily in the tens of millions of dollars each year." He also noted that only a small fraction of Canary Mission's targets are Jewish. Instead, most are Muslim, including many Palestinians. "For those students," Nathan-Kazis said, "the risks can be far greater."

One of those was Natalie Abulhawa, a 2019 graduate of Temple University in Philadelphia. Her mother, Susan Abulhawa, is a writer whose books have sold over a million copies and been translated into thirty-two languages. Her 2020 novel *Against the Loveless World* was headlined in the *New York Times*: "A Beautiful, Urgent Novel of the Palestinian Struggle." In November 2021, Natalie was summarily fired from her job as an athletic trainer for the Agnes Irwin School in Bryn Mawr when some parents brought an old Canary Mission profile to the attention of administrators. The profile charged that she had been a chapter member of Temple's Students for Justice in Palestine club and cited comments critical of Israel going back nearly a decade. "Employment discrimination against Palestinian Americans and Muslim Americans is a real problem," said Abulhawa. "Agnes Irwin School did not think twice before bulldozing my life, without even a pretense of due process. It only took a known hate site to profile me for them to derail my career," a profile, she said, that was "based only on my support for an indigenous people's struggle against colonialism."

For Israel's Ministry of Strategic Affairs, Canary Mission acts as a key intelligence asset, as does the Israel on Campus Coalition. The list of Americans identified by the group's campus spies is used to prevent those individuals from entering Israel, including both Jews and Palestinians attempting to visit family. Among them was American student Lara Alqasem, twenty-two, who was planning to study in a master's program at the Hebrew University in Jerusalem. Although she had a valid visa, she was dragged in for interrogation shortly after landing at Tel Aviv's airport.

During the process, the Ministry of Strategic Affairs sent over a document marked sensitive. It contained a printout from Canary Mission that listed her crime: She had served as a local chapter president of Students for Justice in Palestine at the University of Florida. Even worse, her chapter had called for a boycott of some Israeli hummus. Afterward she was placed in detention pending deportation procedures. According to an investigation by *Forward* and *Haaretz*, the documents "show clearly that the [Canary Mission] site is indeed the No. 1 source of information for the decision to bar entry to Alqasem." There were many others before and after Alqasem who fell victim of Israel's campus spies.

The Diller family and other Americans who were financially supporting Canary Mission were potentially committing a serious crime, acting as agents of a foreign power. They were financing a clandestine foreign organization, with ties to an Israeli intelligence agency, that was engaged in secretly spying on thousands of Americans, and in many cases threatening, intimidating, and terrorizing them for the benefit of Israel. Also, because the victims were targeted specifically due to their religion, ethnicity, or political beliefs, these acts could be considered hate crimes. The Diller family and others therefore had great reason to keep their $100,000 donation to Canary Mission secret. "We have a steadfast policy as a family and business to not release our net worth and keep all financial information private," said daughter Jackie Safier, president of the Diller Foundation board and CEO of Prometheus Real Estate.

However, a slipup on a tax form revealed a paper trail. For donations to a variety of causes, the Diller family maintains the Helen Diller Family Foundation. But in order to get a tax break, they turn it over to a much larger trust, the Jewish Community Federation of San Francisco, which then directs the funds. In return, the federation receives a percentage of each donation. As a result, in 2016 the Diller Foundation donated $100,000 through the Jewish Community Federation to an obscure Israeli nonprofit called Megamot Shalom. Untraceable, off the grid, unheard of, Megamot Shalom was actually the front for Canary Mission.

Confident that their dark donations would never be revealed, other donors around the country poured cash into Megamot Shalom via similar Jewish charities, among them the Jewish Community Foundation of Los Angeles. There a contributor, whose name was legally hidden behind foundation rules, donated another quarter of a million dollars to Canary Mission's front. The foundation manages assets of more than $1.3 billion and, like San Francisco's Jewish Federation, has distributed millions of it to right-wing pro-occupation groups. Yet at the same time, it turns down donations to human rights groups *opposed* to the occupation, as foundation board member Lisa Greer discovered. When she attempted to donate $5,000 to IfNotNow, a group against the occupation, it was rejected. "I'd never heard of this happening before," she said. "I was beyond shocked. I really did start shaking."

Not content to secretly fund Canary Mission to carry out its spying and intimidation on American college campuses, many of the wealthy donors also wanted generous federal tax breaks for their donations. The problem was that tax breaks are not allowed for donations to foreign charities, just those in the United States, and since Megamot Shalom was in Israel that would rule out the deduction. To solve the problem, years ago a family living in Israel's illegal settlements came to the United States and set up shop in New York City as a nonprofit "charity," calling itself the Central Fund of Israel. Therefore, the Diller family, through San Francisco's Jewish Federation, actually "donated" their money to the Central Fund in New York, and in return received a substantial tax rebate. And then the Central Fund simply transferred the money to Megamot Shalom's bank account in Israel. Under the scheme, billionaires and wealthy Jewish foundations get richer while American taxpayers subsidize the blacklisting and terrorizing of their own children in college.

Among the many other organizations taking advantage of the loophole was the New York–based Jewish Communal Fund, with assets of more than $1.5 billion. In both 2016 and 2017 the fund made grants of $1 million to the Central Fund. From there the money may have been sent to Megamot Shalom or any of the three hundred or so other "charities" in Israel and the occupied territories it supports. In 2014, the Central Fund's revenues were $25 million, and $23 million of those were transferred to Israel. "For years the federations managed to keep the specifics of their support for the settlement enterprise out of the public eye," said Uri Blau, a reporter for *Haaretz* who conducted a long investigation of Jewish charities and foundations.

Nearly invisible, the Central Fund for Israel was hidden in the back room of a fabric company in Manhattan's garment district. Across from a Chick-fil-A, Marcus Brothers Textiles was located on the third floor of "The Vogue," an apartment building at 980 Sixth Avenue. It has since moved into a back room of J.Mark Interiors on Central Avenue in Cedarhurst, Long Island. The family business is run by Jay Marcus, a gray-haired sixty-year-old settler with a kippah on his head and a second home in Efrat, an illegal settlement in the occupied West Bank.

From the textile company, the Diller family's $100,000 was wired to the Israeli bank account of Canary Mission's front organization, Megamot Shalom. Unsurprisingly, the actual physical address for Megamot Shalom was simply a run-down abandoned building in Beit Shemesh, a city west of

Jerusalem. Near a few broken chairs and a scattering of pigeon droppings, or perhaps those of a canary, was a heavily scuffed powder blue door from which hung a rusty padlock.

Hidden deep in the shadows, the man behind both Megamot Shalom and Canary Mission was a smiling, pleasant-looking middle-aged rabbi with receding dark brown hair beneath a black felt fedora, Jonathan Jack Ian Bash. Although he has denied involvement, Bash signed the financial reports for Megamot Shalom, and two people separately confirmed to the *Forward* that he was in charge of Canary Mission. Megamot Shalom is what is known in Israel as a "public benefit corporation," and documents seem to clearly describe its work: to "ensure the national image and strength of the state of Israel via the use of information disseminated by technological means."

Within hours of Bash being identified, the website was shut down and much of Bash's background was carefully scrubbed from the internet. Nevertheless, enough clues were left behind to put together some insight into the rabbi's history. A British citizen born in May 1973, Bash grew up in a middle-class section of Ilford, a busy retail area just east of London, and spent time working with his parents at a local London shop, Body Clock Health Care Limited. In 2011 he told a group called Israel Shabbat Experience that he had a law degree from Brunel University in London, and a master's degree in information technology from Aston University in Birmingham. In his twenties he moved to Israel, and in June 2004 he married Kim Silverstone, a woman from South Africa who had worked for a Jewish organization in New York before also moving to Jerusalem.

Soon after arriving, Bash became a follower of Rabbi Noah Weinberg. A white-bearded ultra-Orthodox Jew who was born and grew up on New York's Lower East Side, Weinberg founded Aish HaTorah (Fire of Torah). An aggressive right-wing organization with an annual budget of about $40 million and three dozen full-time branches on five continents, it has a history of propagandizing Islamophobia in the United States. And according to Charity Navigator, it has a "failing score." Over the years, the connections between Bash and Aish HaTorah became a dark maze of intertwining links and relationships.

Today Bash and his wife, a real estate broker, along with their five children, live within the pale sand-colored limestone walls of the Jewish Quarter in Jerusalem's Old City, a cloistered enclave of snaking, dimly lit passageways, curved arches, barred windows, and crowded yeshivas. Nearby, on HaTamid Street, is the World Center of Aish HaTorah, a modern facility with a sleek wood-paneled interior and a Chihuly-created blown-glass sculpture in the middle of its atrium. From the roof, students attending Aish's yeshiva can view the Western Wall, supremely holy to Jews. And from the classrooms they have a view of the lead-domed Al-Aqsa Mosque, supremely holy to Muslims. Sitting at their desks, they are taught "a politicized form of Judaism," according one former student.

While Bash has long run Canary Mission's operations, the man with the money pulling the strings appears to be Adam Milstein, the convicted felon in charge of Sheldon Adelson's Israeli-American Council. In 2016, during his undercover investigation, Tony Kleinfeld discussed Milstein with his then "boss," Eric Gallagher, fund-raising director for the Israel Project, a Washington-based pro-Israel media organization. At the time, Gallagher believed that Kleinfeld was a like-minded pro-Israel advocate. Asked about Canary Mission on Kleinfeld's hidden camera, Gallagher said, "It's him, it's him," to which Kleinfeld asked, "Adam Milstein?" Gallagher replied, "Yeah, I don't know who he hired to oversee it. Adam Milstein's the guy who funds it."

Kleinfeld then asked, "So Adam Milstein funds the Israel Project and he's funding the Canary Mission website?" Gallagher answered, "Yeah, which is interesting because it makes us [the Israel Project] seem as though we're part of it. But we're not." Gallagher also said that he himself was involved during the early stages of Canary Mission. "Actually, I was involved in the effort to start it, the name-and-shame. He called a group of us to ask us what we thought. I told him actually I thought it was a bad idea. But he did it anyway."

At another point on the hidden camera, Milstein himself told Kleinfeld how best to handle critics of Israel. "First of all, investigate who they are. What's their agenda?" he said. "We need to expose what they really are. And we need to expose the fact that they are anti everything we believe in. And we need to put them on the run. Right now they can do whatever they like." Kleinfeld then asked, "How do we put them on the run, though?" To which Milstein, who has praised the blacklist, answered, "We're doing it by exposing who they are, what they are, the fact that they are racist, the fact that they are bigots, they're anti-democracy." It is a perfect description of the activities of Canary Mission.

In addition, Milstein's obsession with the nonviolent student-led boycott movement borders on the psychotic. A 2019 opinion piece he wrote for the right-wing evangelical Christian Broadcasting Network was titled "The Nazi-Like Boycott of Jews Is a Global Menace: Why BDS Is All About Eradicating the State of Israel." In it he called BDS a "terrorist-led movement," and used the word "terror" or "terrorist" ten more times in the short piece. Another item in his newsletter was captioned "The BDS Movement: Proudly following in Hitler's Footsteps." At the top was a picture of Nazi storm troopers in jackboots on one side and a photo of peaceful protesters carrying a white "Boycott Israel" sign on the other. And his "Milstein Family Foundation Newsletter" leads off with a picture of jackbooted Nazis and the phrase, the BDS movement "alarmingly resembles the Nazi movement in WWII-era Europe." Next to it is another picture of Nazis. Canary Mission's YouTube video also attempted to compare the boycott movement with the Nazi movement.

In a carefully worded statement, Milstein claimed, "Neither Adam Milstein nor the Milstein Family Foundation are funders of Canary Mission." But Canary Mission is simply the name of the website; the funds actually go to its front organization, Megamot Shalom, which Milstein never mentioned. He also has a history of lying, including under oath on federal tax forms, and spent years in a combination of prison and on probation for his membership in the fraud ring.

In fact, Milstein has personally backed Bash in his many endeavors for more than a decade. In 2010 Bash became a founding member of a media watchdog organization called Honest Reporting, and Milstein became one of its principal financial backers. Bash also created an online Jewish university, OpenDor Media, then churned out pro-Israel propaganda, which was financially backed by Milstein. And while Bash was heavily involved with Aish HaTorah in Jerusalem, Milstein also began financially supporting the organization, as well as studying under Aish HaTorah's Dov Heller in Los Angeles.

So wherever Bash went, Milstein's money seemed to follow. Similarly, soon after Bash created Megamot Shalom it received more than a quarter million dollars from the mysterious donor to the Jewish Community Foundation of Los Angeles, Milstein's hometown. Soon the organization grew considerably, including adding a secret operational center in the United States employing Americans as professional character assassins.

Eventually, Gilad Erdan and his Ministry of Strategic Affairs, along with Sheldon Adelson and Adam Milstein, moved on to their next project. From hundreds, they would now turn thousands of Americans into secret Israeli bots.

CHAPTER 25

◆

The Trolls

Wearing a powder blue tie and a banner across his chest announcing in blue letters, "Honorary Grand Marshal," New York governor Andrew Cuomo marched up Fifth Avenue's freshly blue-painted pavement. Behind him, stretching for blocks, were eleven marching bands decked out in blue ribbons and blue bunting. June 4, 2017, was Celebrate Israel Day in Manhattan, and the guest of honor, smiling broadly as he marched alongside the governor, was Gilad Erdan, Israel's minister of strategic affairs.

Erdan was being honored by the same country he was spying on and attacking in a covert war. It was quite a coup. Under his direction, wealthy Americans were secretly financing other Americans to spy on, intimidate, and terrorize their fellow citizens on behalf of Israel.

As governor, Cuomo spent much of his time pandering to his nearly two million Jewish voters. A year earlier he had signed an executive order that blacklisted institutions and companies that engage in or promote the boycott. "If you boycott against Israel," he declared, surrounded by Jewish officials and leaders, "New York will boycott you." That prompted Ido Aharoni, Israel's New York consul general, to declare that Israel "has had no truer friend" than Cuomo.

But voters in New York, as in the rest of the country, were increasingly rejecting the ever-present Jewish lobbyists and politicians constantly demanding absolute loyalty to Israel and its corrupt, apartheid policies. "Shame on Governor Cuomo for using an anti-democratic executive order to push through a McCarthyite attack on a movement for justice," scolded Rebecca Vilkomerson from across the East River in Brooklyn. The executive director of Jewish Voice for Peace, she was a key target of Erdan's spies and Canary Mission thugs. "This executive order shows how out of touch the political leadership is with the growing numbers of Americans who support the use of nonviolent tactics to achieve freedom and equality for Palestinians."

Following the parade, as champagne sparkled in tall, tapered flutes during a cocktail party atop the Dream Hotel, Erdan repaid New Yorkers for the honor by secretly unleashing his latest weapon. It was a cyber army made up of thousands of Americans.

Like Vilkomerson, fellow Brooklyn resident and Cuomo constituent Linda Sarsour was at the top of Erdan's hit list. A leader in the boycott movement, three days earlier she had given a powerful commencement speech at City University of New York.

A slight five foot two, with a placid smile and a velvet complexion, Sarsour often dresses in stylish, multicolored hijabs. Born in Brooklyn to Palestinian parents, she had long been a leader in both the boycott movement and Black Lives Matter, which endorsed the BDS boycott in 2016. "Israel is an apartheid state with over 50 laws on the books that sanction discrimination against the Palestinian people," said a formal Black Lives Matter announcement. "Palestinian homes and land are routinely bulldozed to make way for illegal Israeli settlements. Israeli soldiers also regularly arrest and detain Palestinians as young as 4 years old without due process. Every day, Palestinians are forced to walk through military checkpoints along the US-funded apartheid wall."

But despite her years as an activist, Sarsour had maintained a relatively low profile. That, however, changed a few months before the parade, on January 21, when she gained notice as one of the primary organizers of the Women's March following President Donald Trump's inauguration. The largest single-day protest in U.S. history, the Women's March drew over 470,000 demonstrators in Washington and upward of five million across the United States. Worldwide, it was estimated that over seven million took part. Suddenly, the boycott movement had another high-profile leader, one who was giving interviews to top-line newspapers, magazines, and television shows. And then came her commencement speech at City University of New York. It was time for Erdan to take action.

Thumbtacked to a tan corkboard in Sarsour's apartment was a crooked pale orange sign near a haphazard assortment of photos, notes, letters, and announcements. "Spying on Muslims produced ZERO leads!!" it said. "Stop unwarranted surveillance!" The notice was directed at the FBI and New York police. But it might also have been a warning to a clandestine Israeli organization known as Israel Cyber Shield (ICS), had Sarsour known such an intelligence organization even existed. It was in fact a secret unit within Erdan's Ministry of Strategic Affairs, and Sarsour had acquired a bull's-eye on her back. By then, Erdan had earned a well-deserved reputation for trashing human rights with what some were calling his "Thought Police." "With frightening speed," noted an editorial in *Haaretz*, "Minister for Public Security and

Strategic Affairs Gilad Erdan is becoming the Israeli heir to notorious U.S. Senator Joseph McCarthy."

Virtually unheard of, the ICS was briefly mentioned by Erdan's deputy, General Vaknin-Gin, during a private discussion with the Adelson/Milstein Israeli-American Council. Captured on Tony Kleinfeld's hidden camera, Vaknin-Gin said, "We started to establish a project called Israel Cyber Shield. This is actually a civil intelligence unit that collects, analyzes, and acts upon the activists in the BDS movement, of its people, organizations, or events. And we give it everything we collect. We are using the most sophisticated data system, intelligence system in the Israeli market."

Over the years, with virtually no oversight, Israel has become one of the world's most prolific exporters of covert surveillance technology. And as Sophia Goodfriend reported in *Foreign Policy*, much of that spyware is tested out on unsuspecting Palestinians before it is sent abroad to spy on others, like the BDS supporters. "Innovation in AI-powered surveillance continues to outpace regulatory frameworks," she wrote. "Reining the private industry in is a small but necessary step to clamp down on the abuse of new technologies—in Palestine and beyond."

Just one of Israel's many sophisticated spying tools targeting Americans, the ICS is a system designed to monitor and collect vast amounts of information on its victims in the United States, possibly by illegally hacking American computers. In charge was Eran Vasker, a lawyer from Netanya, a beach resort a few miles north of Tel Aviv. He previously worked for Israeli police in the anti–money laundering unit and later joined a firm specializing in investigative auditing. His specialties included computer forensics and counterintelligence. And among the employees of ICS were former members of Unit 8200, Israel's equivalent of the U.S. National Security Agency.

One of them was Rebecca (a pseudonym), who spent nearly four years in the intelligence organization, rising to team leader before leaving in the spring of 2016. After a few years working in the private sector as a business intelligence analyst, she was hired by ICS in November 2017 as a project manager. Among her assignments was recruiting. At one point, without revealing the name of her organization, she posted a notice in an online Israeli jobs forum. What she was looking for, she said, was an experienced "webint analyst" for a web intelligence position in Tel Aviv. In terms of qualifications, the organization was looking for applicants with "Cyber intelligence experience" and "experience working for official Israeli security organizations," such as Unit 8200. "Perfect English—[a] Must," the post said, and added that the job "involved a deep sense of satisfaction knowing that they are contributing to the future of the State of Israel." In the summer of 2020 she left to work as a webint analyst at another cyber intelligence firm, ActiveFence, north of Tel Aviv. Others at the company worked as influence operations analysts.

According to an investigation by Uri Blau of *Haaretz*, among the information the ICS was able to collect on Sarsour was a file protected by a password that contained details about her parents. Another was over ten pages long and all marked "Confidential." And still another contained legal documents related to a court case in which she was involved. It was the kind of information only obtainable by illegal and sophisticated hacking, indicating a very serious criminal act by both Americans and Israelis. The documents were then analyzed and organized by the ICS, which produced an executive summary highlighting Sarsour's vulnerabilities for future attacks.

Once the ICS spies collect the intelligence on its targets like Sarsour, it is turned over for action to the Blue Network thugs, such as Canary Mission and Psy Group.

Still another avenue of exploit is the secret cyber army Erdan launched the day of his being honored by Governor Cuomo. Following a series of secret meetings over a number of months, the Ministry of Strategic Affairs budgeted $570,000 to create a computer and smartphone application that would turn thousands of Americans into a robotic army of Israeli trolls.

While Canary Mission focused mostly on students, Netanyahu's trolls would attack everyone else. Assigned "missions" from troll headquarters near Tel Aviv, they would hide their links to Israel and launch online attacks against their U.S. targets, including critics of Israel, boycott supporters, and human rights activists. "Call it a human 'botnet,'" said *Forward*'s Josh Nathan-Kazis. "It has thousands of mostly U.S.-based volunteers who can be directed from Israel into a social media swarm."

Named "Act.il," the app soon had over twenty thousand online potential trolls, mostly American and Jewish, and a budget of $1.1 million. While developed and controlled by the Ministry of Strategic Affairs, as part of the Blue Network arrangement it was largely financed by Sheldon Adelson and Adam Milstein through their nonprofits. Headquarters for the operation is a large room on the campus of the Interdisciplinary Center at Herzliya, near Tel Aviv. A private university, it was heavily endowed by Adelson and has extensive ties to Israel's military and intelligence services.

Known as the Hasbara War Room, *hasbara* being the Hebrew term for propaganda, an early version of the operation began in 2014 when it was used to fight worldwide condemnation following the country's bloody war on Gaza. Greatly expanded with the infusion of half a million dollars by the Ministry of Strategic Affairs, Act.il used the same propaganda war room. Inside, tables were cluttered with laptops, plastic water bottles, and backpacks; a maroon "Stanford University" blanket hung from one. A long Israeli flag was draped vertically from ceiling to floor, flat-screen monitors covered one cream-colored wall, and on another was a map of the world in Israeli blue on a black background.

Still in charge was Yarden Ben-Yosef, who first created the Hasbara War Room. Paunchy, with his head shaved smooth and shiny as a cue ball, he calls himself "a world expert in cognitive influence operations." While running Act.il he also serves as a reserve major in what he called "an elite intelligence unit," possibly Unit 8200. Like Psy Group and Israel Cyber Shield, most of the Act.il staff is made up of current and former Israeli intelligence officers. "We work with the Ministry of Foreign Affairs and the Ministry of Strategic Affairs, consult with them and manage joint projects," Ben-Yosef said. "The same with the intelligence agencies," he added. "We talk with each other. We work together." Staffers like Daniel Gavriel work simultaneously for both the Israeli security services and Act.il.

From the beginning, therefore, the idea was for the war room to become a secret arm of the Ministry of Strategic Affairs. "In the months before the app's launch, we ran a pilot [program] among a group of some 800 students, most of them Americans," Ben-Yosef said. "We're working with the IDF and the Shin Bet, who are giving us information on such inciting content." And in June 2017, Minister of Strategic Affairs Erdan Gilad personally visited the war room to observe his secret trolls in action. Some of the messages were sent by the notoriously Islamophobic Morton Klein, head of the Zionist Organization of America. Among his tweets was "[Congresswoman] Omar and [Congresswoman] Tlaib you're both frightening insensitive terrorist supporting, Jew hating, America hating Israelophobes. You're a curse on America. You're worse than White supremacists." Also pleased with the launch were Adelson and Milstein, as well as Shoham Nicolet, one of the founders of the IAC and its CEO at the time. "Nicolet," said Ben-Yosef, "was visibly excited as he spoke to the team at the new operations room via Skype. 'Imagine 20 more rooms like this, not just in the United States but all over the world,' he enthused."

From the war room, often made up of dozens of Americans sitting in front of their laptops, Ben-Yosef issues "missions" to his thousands of online troll-commandos in the United States. "This is a new kind of war," he said. The missions involve groups of trolls collectively attacking their American victims like digital wolf packs. As ammunition, they often use scripts or data prepared by the ministry based on intelligence collected by Israel Cyber Shield, the ICC, Canary Mission, American campus spies, and other agents attached to the Israeli embassy and consulates. The targets are subjected to constant doxing, harassment, and slanderous charges, such as publicly comparing them to Nazis. As before, there is likely a considerable use of fraudulent digital manipulation. "Spearheaded by the Ministry of Strategic Affairs, the campaign enlists Israel's supporters as foot soldiers," noted *Haaretz.*

The targets are any Americans Ben-Yosef, the ministry, or the intelligence services choose, including students, academics, writers, public speakers, Christian church members, union members, or anyone in need of silencing or canceling. Thus, once the ICS turned Sarsour's stolen files and list of vulnerabilities over to Act.il, the trolls went to work. Among other actions, they used the confidential details and whatever slanderous information they could find to prepare a letter that was sent to the heads of colleges and universities where she had spoken. It was part of a secret joint Act.il/ICS effort to silence Sarsour, and other critics of Israel, by quietly encouraging schools to cancel future speakers and not recommend past speakers.

Numerous clandestine operations were carried out by Americans targeting other Americans on behalf of a hostile foreign intelligence agency, ICS, and a government propaganda organization, Act.il. It should have been clear to those who signed up that they were accepting "missions" from a foreign government, and that by hiding their links to it when carrying out those "missions" they were acting as clandestine agents of that government. They have a due diligence obligation to check out the organization assigning them "missions" to covertly attack other Americans. Certainly they would face criminal charges if they were clandestinely carrying out "missions" on behalf of a Russian government propaganda or spy organization.

By 2018, the operation was completing 1,580 missions a week, according to the organization's internal-only annual report. It noted, "Every 5.4 minutes a mission is accomplished on the app." The top trolls and cyberbullies, some of whom complete five or six missions a day, "receive points that can be redeemed for cool prizes," as well as a letter of congratulations from a government minister, such as Gilad Erdan. The trolls therefore receive both compensation and awards for their clandestine work on behalf of Israel. Still another goal for the trolls is to manipulate Google's algorithm so that when someone Googles "BDS," the first three responses are "BDS undermines peace," "BDS promotes hate," and "BDS lies." According to the internal annual report, the trolls are as young as thirteen years old.

Beyond its war room in Israel, Act.il operates troll farms across the United States, targeting Americans on behalf of Israel with impunity. According to Ben-Yosef, "[We have] five situation rooms across the USA—Boston, New Jersey, New York, Philadelphia and [Orange County] California—to be ready for action." The U.S. situation rooms "mimic those used by the Israel

Defense Forces," said the *Times of Israel*. By 2018, two additional troll farms were launched, one in Florida and another in Los Angeles, Adam Milstein's hometown. There the troll farm was jointly funded by the Adelson/Milstein Israeli-American Council and the Jewish Community Foundation of Los Angeles. That was the same organization that distributed the mysterious quarter-million-dollar donation to Canary Mission's cover, Megamot Shalom.

In Boston, the troll farm was cosponsored by IAC and the Combined Jewish Philanthropies of Greater Boston. During a meeting there, the trolls requested that the war room in Israel develop a mission to target a local Boston church that was showing a documentary they felt was critical of Israel. As a result, across the country the ministry's trolls disguised their links to Israel and attacked the Christian churchgoers, accusing them of anti-Semitism. The charges were completely absurd, but they were designed to cause havoc and "cancel" the documentary. According to the internal report, by 2018 the Boston troll farm had conducted 120 online missions.

Israel frequently uses Act.il to support its other covert operations in the United States, such as Canary Mission. Despite the thugs in their yellow canary costumes physically threatening students at George Washington University, attempting to scare them away from voting in favor of divesting from Israel, the vote nevertheless succeeded. In retaliation, Israel sent out a new mission to their American trolls to "out" the offending voters and punish them. They were instructed to push a new Facebook page that exposed the names and pictures of those they suspected of having dared vote in favor of divestment, information likely acquired by the campus spies. It also slandered them as "anti-Semites," to ensure that the students would be harassed and turned down by future employers.

Another Blue Network organization that uses Americans to harass, intimidate, and silence other Americans, including Sarsour, is Video Activism, which, like Canary Mission, is run by Jonathan Bash. Set up around 2015, it supplements the troll farms with a video component. The organization trains American Jewish college students to become propagandists on behalf of Israel. During seven-week visits to Israel, they receive instruction from Bash in ways to create, edit, and produce pro-Israeli propaganda videos targeting Americans.

"Video Activism is the only organization that specifically trains young Jewish leaders to spread pro-Israel content on YouTube," according to its pitch to American Jewish donors. Over the years it has trained "in excess of 500 students" who have "produced a total of 300 videos that have received several hundred thousand views." Based at Aish HaTorah headquarters in Jerusalem's Old City, near Bash's home, the program is run by Hasbara Fellowships. Not surprisingly, Adam Milstein was once again heavily involved.

In addition to being a major funder of Hasbara Fellowships, he also sat on its board of directors, thereby overseeing Bash's video propaganda school.

Like many of the other Blue Network operations, Video Activism is simply an organ of the Ministry of Strategic Affairs, which also funds Hasbara Fellowships, thereby making Bash's propagandists, like Israel's Act.il trolls and their Canary Mission thugs, clandestine agents of the Israeli government targeted against Americans. In 2016, for example, the ministry funded Hasbara with an $882,000 grant, giving the ministry the right to determine what videos to produce.

As a result, when eleven American students arrived in Jerusalem in the summer of 2017 to take part in Bash's program, one student, Emily Biffinger from Colorado State University, was assigned to do a hatchet job on the ministry's key target, Linda Sarsour. The upshot was "Is Linda Sarsour Really a Feminist?," a five-minute video trashing the former Women's March leader, largely with hyped and dubious clips from Fox News. Made to order for Erdan and his Ministry of Strategic Affairs, it received thousands of views when uploaded to YouTube. With the operation a success, the ministry's funding for the anti-American propaganda program soon increased to more than $1 million. The money was passed to Hasbara through its cover organization, Concert. "We are the elite," Bash proudly assured Biffinger. By April 2022, the video had 4,092 views.

Little had changed by then. Following an organized campaign of pro-Israel groups, Sarsour was suddenly canceled from an event celebrating Middle Eastern and North African (MENA) Heritage Month by the giant auto insurance company GEICO. The ADL's Jonathan Greenblatt had charged that Sarsour was someone with a history of "slandering and delegitimizing Israel," and warned that "GEICO must act fast and reverse course." Which they immediately did, since the warning came from a member of the powerful pro-Israeli lobby. The sudden cancellation "shocked me—and broke my heart," said Sarsour. "GEICO publicly justified their decision by smearing my work advocating for marginalized communities as 'hatred' across their social media accounts." Supporters were outraged. "This is disgraceful @GEICO and defamatory. Islamophobia in 15 minutes," tweeted Yousef Munayyer.

With propaganda their specialty, Erdan's ministry was even paying tens of thousands of dollars a year to Israeli news organizations to secretly print positive propaganda masquerading as "news" about the ministry's own activities, including over $30,000 to the *Jerusalem Post* alone. In an attempt to show what a great job Erdan and his ministry were doing on the boycott movement, the ministry paid the *Post* to print a special supplement in which his staff were thrown softball questions by the paper's top journalists. "BDS and its true intentions have been exposed and as a result began suffering a series of blows," General Vaknin-Gil crowed in the article titled "Winning the Battle Against BDS." Texas senator Ted Cruz was even interviewed and described as a "brave warrior" for Israel. Thus the Israeli public was paying thousands in taxes to read fake news about how great its government was doing.

It was therefore time for a major promotion for the man who achieved those enormous accomplishments, at least as outlined in his own propaganda. And in May 2020, Netanyahu named Erdan ambassador to both the United States and the United Nations. An extremely powerful appointment, it would allow him to oversee all espionage, covert activities, and influence operations in both the United States and the UN, thereby permitting him to continue and expand on his past successes. Three months later, on August 10, Erdan and his family boarded a blue-and-white El Al jet for a night flight to New York.

––––––

In the end, however, it was all for naught. Addressing the members of the Israeli-American Council, General Sima Vaknin-Gil said in 2015 that the key purpose of Netanyahu's espionage and covert propaganda war in the United States was so that the "narrative in the world won't be that Israel equals apartheid." But by January 2021, even Israel's largest human rights organization, the Jewish-led B'Tselem, would finally acknowledge the obvious. In a major report the group declared to the world that Israel does in fact equal apartheid. Its title left no ambiguities: "A Regime of Jewish Supremacy from the Jordan River to the Mediterranean Sea: This Is Apartheid." Unlike Erdan's fake news, B'Tselem's report was real news.

The report concluded that the "bar for defining the Israeli regime as an apartheid regime has been met after considering the accumulation of policies and laws that Israel devised to entrench its control over Palestinians." Just as Israel's longtime close ally, apartheid South Africa, had a White supremacist government, Israel, according to B'Tselem, has a Jewish supremacist government. "Israel cannot be considered a democracy, for it works to advance and perpetuate the supremacy of one group of people, Jews, over another, Palestinians." And supremacy, by definition, is racism. As Yossi Sarid, a former Israeli cabinet minister and thirty-two-year veteran of the Knesset, put it, "What acts like apartheid, is run like apartheid and harasses like apartheid, is not a duck—it is apartheid."

B'Tselem's report was a courageous act in a country where many human rights groups are labeled terrorist organizations, and their workers are often intimidated and harassed by both the public and the government. In 2021,

Defense Minister Benny Gantz pinned the terrorist label on six human rights organizations in the West Bank, thereby outlawing them. And in the hope of cutting outside funding for the groups, "evidence" was presented to a number of European countries. It was, said *Haaretz*, an "extreme measure—one befitting a military dictatorship, not a democracy." But in June 2022, after eight months of analyzing the material given them by Israel, the European countries said the evidence simply wasn't there. It was instead another on a long list of Israeli lies. "It's simple, we were given evidence, and we did not find it to be compelling enough," said one diplomat.

Nevertheless, such accusations have had an enormously harmful effect on the courageous individuals within the organizations. Yuli Novak, an Israeli who headed the anti-occupation group Breaking the Silence, was accused of treason by cabinet ministers and received threats on her life. "People here were told that they have an enemy, and the enemy is within, and it's Breaking the Silence or B'Tselem," she said. "It was standard fare for people to call and say, 'We're coming to kill you.' People wished us different forms of death."

Employees of Human Rights Watch, including Lama Fakih, have also had their phones hacked by Israel's secretive spyware company, NSO. An American citizen and the organization's crisis and conflict director, Fakih oversaw investigations in both Israel and occupied Palestine. An analysis discovered five separate hacks by NSO on two of her iPhones. "It's heart-rending," she said. "My job is to talk to and about vulnerable people all day...There was no way I could protect against this."

The U.S.-based Human Rights Watch was an obvious target of Israeli intelligence since the organization was working on its own lengthy report, titled "A Threshold Crossed: Israeli Authorities and the Crimes of Apartheid and Persecution." Released three months after that of B'Tselem, it also condemned Israel as an apartheid state. The group accused Israel of "committing the crimes against humanity of apartheid and persecution," and added, "We reached this determination based on our documentation of an overarching government policy to maintain the domination by Jewish Israelis over Palestinians coupled with grave abuses committed against Palestinians living in the occupied territory, including East Jerusalem."

In 2018, Israel went so far as to enact racism and apartheid into the law with its "Nation-State Law." The legislation, said the Human Rights Watch report, "affirms the supremacy of the 'Jewish' over the 'democratic' character of the state." Therefore, Israel cannot claim to be a democracy since the "exercise of the right to national self-determination in the state of Israel is unique to the Jewish people...The Nation-State Law contains no language about equality."

Despite the spies, thugs, and trolls, the reports by the human rights organizations were clear evidence that Israeli intelligence had lost its covert war in America's classrooms, boardrooms, and living rooms, and even in its synagogues. In January 2022, Foreign Minister Yair Lapid issued a stark warning to the Israeli public. "We think that in the coming year, there will be debate that is unprecedented in its venom and in its radioactivity around the words 'Israel as an apartheid state,'" he said. "In 2022, it will be a tangible threat." Lapid didn't have long to wait.

CHAPTER 26

◆

The Reckoning

Within a month of Yair Lapid's warning, in February 2022, the esteemed human rights organization Amnesty International made it unanimous. Joining with its sister human rights groups, Israel's B'Tselem and America's Human Rights Watch, the British group issued a meticulously researched 280-page report titled "Israel's Apartheid Against Palestinians: A Cruel System of Domination and a Crime Against Humanity." In a statement, Amnesty International's secretary-general summed up the charges: "Our report reveals the true extent of Israel's apartheid regime. Whether they live in Gaza, East Jerusalem and the rest of the West Bank, or Israel itself, Palestinians are treated as an inferior racial group and systematically deprived of their rights. We found that Israel's cruel policies of segregation, dispossession and exclusion across all territories under its control clearly amount to apartheid. The international community has an obligation to act."

The report also pointed the finger directly at the United States for its years of supplying Israel "with arms, equipment and other tools to perpetrate crimes under international law and by providing diplomatic cover, including at the UN Security Council, to shield it from accountability." This included cover for such crimes as the "massive seizures of Palestinian land and property, unlawful killings, forcible transfer, drastic movement restrictions, and the denial of nationality and citizenship to Palestinians," according to the report.

In a panic, Israel's $1.1 million secret troll army across the United States was immediately called to action over its Act.il app. From its command center near Tel Aviv, the trolls were instructed to discredit the report by using the hashtag #AmnestyLies. One of many "missions" listed a CNN report on Twitter that outlined Amnesty's findings. "COMMENT on this tweet and let the readers of CNN and the world know that #AmnestyLIES," Act.il ordered its militant U.S.-based disinformation commandos. "Complete the mission and collect your points!"

The reports from the three highly respected human rights groups were an enormous setback for Netanyahu and Erdan and their covert propaganda war in the United States. And confirmation came in the form of a 2021 survey by the Jewish Electoral Institute. It found that fully one out of four American Jews agreed that Israel is an apartheid state, a third agreed that the Jewish state's treatment of Palestinians is similar to racism in the United States, and 22 percent even believed that Israel was committing genocide. Nearly 60 percent also supported restrictions on U.S. military assistance to Israel, to avoid funding settlements. The survey also showed that younger Jews are even more alienated by Israel, with 38 percent of those under forty believing that it is an apartheid state, and 33 percent saying Israel was committing genocide. "The results were shocking to many," said Arno Rosenfeld, a staff writer for the Jewish magazine *Forward*. "The findings," he said, "raised eyebrows at a time when activists and politicians are accused of antisemitism for voicing similar criticism."

But an even more disturbing Pew poll was released in 2022. It clearly showed that Democrats and the young were rapidly turning against Israel and in favor of Palestine. Whereas Democrats and Democratic-leaning independents held a 64 percent positive view of Palestinians, only 60 percent held the same view of Israelis. And while 61 percent of U.S. adults under thirty viewed Palestinians warmly, only 56 percent viewed Israelis the same way. By then, even a number of synagogues were denouncing Israel.

In Illinois, Tzedek Chicago officially declared itself "anti-Zionist." "We are anti-Zionist, openly acknowledging that the creation of an ethnic Jewish nation-state in historic Palestine resulted in an injustice against the Palestinian people—an injustice that continues to this day." The action was unanimously endorsed by the congregation's board and 73 percent of households voted in favor of the motion. Rabbi Brant Rosen, the synagogue's founder, defined an anti-Zionist as someone who "opposes the very concept of an exclusively Jewish nation-state in historic Palestine." According to *Forward*, the synagogue was one of at least half a dozen congregations to take similar positions. Jewish Voice for Peace called Tzedek Chicago's decision "a HUGE step toward Judaism beyond Zionism in the U.S."

It was a trend that Eric Alterman, the author and distinguished professor of English and journalism at Brooklyn College, long saw coming. "The American Jewish rabbinate is turning pro-Palestinian. The rabbinical students are turning pro-Palestinian," he told students at Tel Aviv University in May 2022. "American Jewish youth are walking away from Judaism. So, they are either turning away from Israel by and large or they're walking away from Judaism entirely. Because Judaism has no answers for them, because the answer they get is, 'Pro-Israel, watch out for antisemitism.' There is no content . . . secular American Judaism is dying on the vine, because it's been replaced by nothing but pro-Israelism, and pro-Israelism doesn't work anymore."

Nor did Alterman see any hope for the future. "Because the powers that be are so entrenched. And the Republican Party is so dedicated to its position on Israel, and Democrats are so afraid of taking on this monster that will come down on them if they step over the line, that there's no value in it." The result is the rise of the boycott movement. "The BDS movement," he said, "is now I would say mainstream thought in most universities. It's not really challenged very much."

Some of those views were likely shaped by Israel's latest bloody war on Gaza, in March 2021, which killed over 240 Palestinians and wounded more than 1,900 others. More than half of the dead were civilians. And an investigation by *The Intercept* showed that much of the destruction, including that of hospitals and schools, was carried out with U.S.-supplied weapons, despite laws prohibiting such use. "The vast majority of ammunition used by Israel is manufactured or subsidized by the U.S.," said Raed Jarrar, advocacy director at Democracy for the Arab World Now. "It's fair to say that every Israeli munition is subsidized by the U.S. one way or another, by U.S. tax dollars."

As the various human rights reports were released, international organizations began taking action. Shortly after the March 2021 attack, the International Criminal Court in The Hague opened a major criminal case against Israel focused on its alleged war crimes in Gaza and other violence directed at the Palestinians, among them the killing of entire families. One of those was the family of Zainab Shukri Al-Qolaq, twenty-one, whose residential apartment building on Al-Wehda Street, west of Gaza City, was bombed by Israeli warplanes. The building was completely destroyed; forty-two civilians were killed, including sixteen women and ten children. Fifty others were injured. Zainab remained under the rubble for twelve hours before being rescued. Twenty-two members of her family perished in that attack, including her mother and three siblings.

"I remember that my mom in my right hand and my sister in my left hand, but both of them passed away. And I hear them that—when they are dying. I can't do anything," she said soon after being rescued. "My mom, she's the most kind person you will meet ever. My sister—my only sister, Hanna— she's the source of happiness for everyone. She's still young. She's a student at school. She has friends. She has hopes. She has dreams. I know all of her dreams, but all of them just go." Surrounded by debris, all Zainab was left with were questions. "We are civilians. So we don't have—just why? Why they are just bombing us? What they want?"

"I am satisfied that war crimes have been or are being committed in the West Bank, including East Jerusalem, and the Gaza Strip," prosecutor Fatou Bensouda wrote. The court served notice on Netanyahu that it also intended to investigate Israel's endless occupation "despite the clear and enduring calls that Israel cease activities in the Palestinian Territories [that have been] deemed contrary to international law." And in May 2021, in an action the *Times of Israel* called "unprecedented," the United Nations established a special permanent "Commission of Inquiry"—the most serious tool at the council's disposal—"to investigate violations of international humanitarian law and all alleged violations and abuses of international human rights law . . . in the Occupied Palestinian Territory, including East Jerusalem, and in Israel." The focus would include issues related to racism and apartheid, such as "systematic discrimination and repression based on national, ethnic, racial or religious identity."

The commission was approved overwhelmingly by 125 countries and opposed by only eight outliers: Israel, the United States, Hungary, and the Pacific nations of the Marshall Islands, Micronesia, Nauru, Palau, and Papua New Guinea. The action placed Israel in very bad company. In 2013, a similar commission of inquiry was established to investigate the human rights abuses in North Korea. Among the witnesses before the new commission was Michael Lynk, the special rapporteur on human rights in the occupied Palestinian territory. "I conclude that the Israeli settlements do amount to a war crime," Lynk wrote in his report. "I submit to you that this finding compels the international community . . . to make it clear to Israel that its illegal occupation, and its defiance of international law and international opinion, can and will no longer be cost-free."

And in Geneva in March 2022, Zainab Shukri Al-Qolaq called on the commission to explain what progress had been made in its war crimes investigation and to hold Israel to account. "I know my loss is too great to be compensated," she said. "But my mother, my sister, my brother, and my family will rest in peace only when the perpetrators are held accountable. I want to know the progress has been achieved by the commission of inquiry that you formed after the Israeli attack. Was it able to identify those responsible for wiping [out] my family? Will real actions be taken to prevent similar tragedies? I am now 22, and I have lost 22 people. Will I lose more when my next birthday comes before the international community takes tangible steps to bring me justice?"

Israel announced it would not cooperate with either the International Criminal Court or the UN Special Permanent Commission of Inquiry. And to make the point, Israeli ambassador Gilad Erdan brought a stone into the

Security Council chamber so members could visualize the violence that Israelis confront from stone-throwing Palestinians. But Palestinian ambassador Riyad Mansour would have none of it. "I am so sorry," he said, "but the doors of this chamber could not fit Israeli F16s, tanks, warships, military jeeps, drones, bombs and missiles." Then, fearing what might be revealed in the ICC's investigation, acting prime minister Yair Lapid took a page out of Stalinist Russia. In August 2022 he ordered the Israeli military to storm the offices of the Palestinian human rights organizations assisting the court. After using explosives to blow open the doors, the soldiers raided the offices, went after the files, then sealed the entrances with large iron plates. Attached were orders shutting down the organizations. Lapid was convinced that thanks to Israel's powerful political lobbies and wealthy supporters, the United States would always have Israel's back regardless of how many horrendous war crimes or despicable human rights violations it racked up. The humiliating vote in the UN proved it.

———

As the Israeli government suppressed the truth, journalists had become the enemy. In May 2021, after filming a clash in the occupied West Bank between Palestinian protesters and the Israeli army, Hazem Nasser, a reporter for a Palestinian television network, was arrested and placed in detention. For more than a month he was interrogated by Shin Bet, Israel's internal security service. "All the questions were about my journalism," he said. Between January 2020 and March 2022, Israel imprisoned at least twenty-six Palestinian journalists for doing their jobs.

And one year later the dangers for journalists in Israel and the occupied territories would only increase. In May 2022, the killing of Palestinian American journalist Shireen Abu Akleh by Israeli forces in the West Bank instantly sparked global outrage. At the time, she was reporting for Al Jazeera on a military raid targeting Palestinians in the occupied city of Jenin. During the assault, she was shot in the head by an Israeli soldier while wearing a blue flak jacket and a helmet marked with the word "Press" as she attempted to escape the army's gunfire.

Like Hazem Nasser, Abu Akleh was an experienced journalist who had reported for years on the Israeli occupation of the West Bank and was greatly admired by Palestinians. Thousands took to the streets of Jerusalem during her funeral even as Israeli police officers beat and kicked mourners carrying her coffin, nearly causing it to tumble to the ground. Israel denied that its military was involved in the shooting, saying it was "most likely" the Palestinians themselves. But an investigation by the Palestinian Authority said there was no question that the armor-piercing bullet was fired by an Israeli soldier and that she was deliberately targeted.

An investigation by CNN agreed. "They were shooting directly at the journalists," said the report. "Videos obtained by CNN, corroborated by testimony from eight eyewitnesses, an audio forensic analyst and an explosive weapons expert, suggest that Abu Akleh was shot dead in a targeted attack by Israeli forces."

The *Washington Post* also conducted its own investigation. According to the paper, it "examined more than five dozen videos, social media posts and photos of the event, conducted two physical inspections of the area and commissioned two independent acoustic analyses of the gunshots. That review suggests an Israeli soldier in the convoy likely shot and killed Abu Akleh."

The *Post* also rejected the Israeli contention that the reporter was instead likely killed by a Palestinian. "Israel's military has not released any evidence showing the presence of a gunman. The available video and audio evidence disputes IDF claims there was an exchange of fire in the minutes before Abu Akleh was killed and supports the accounts of multiple eyewitnesses interviewed by The Post, who said there was no firefight at the time... The IDF did not respond to a question about what, if anything, Israeli footage of the incident—from drones or body cameras—may show." Similar investigations by the *New York Times*, the Associated Press, and the investigative group Bellingcat came to the same conclusions. As did the UN High Commissioner for Human Rights.

The deliberate murder by the Israeli military of an American journalist doing her job triggered an enormous response. The United Nations and the international community called for an independent probe, and fifty-seven members of Congress signed a letter calling for the FBI to investigate Shireen's death. But as usual, the Biden administration chose instead to do the very minimal. On July 4 they issued a press release concluding "gunfire from IDF positions was likely responsible for the death of Shireen Abu Akleh." Yet there was no FBI investigation and no call for an Israeli investigation to determine who pulled the trigger and why, critical answers when a foreign army kills an American citizen. Especially one that receives more American tax dollars than any other country.

As one of the largest recipients of pro-Israel PAC money, Joe Biden had long ago learned to turn a blind eye to Israel's blatant racism, its extreme brutality, and its domestic espionage to keep the millions in donations flowing. While vice president in 2011, he gave an address to a group of fund-raisers and supporters of Yeshiva Beth Yehuda, a Jewish day school in Detroit. "I've raised more money from AIPAC than some of you have," he said to great applause. He added, "I was speaking to the Zionist Organization of Baltimore. And I said, I am a Zionist, for I learned you do not have to be a Jew to be a Zionist."

Later at an AIPAC conference he boasted of his support for the settler movement. "As recently as last year, the only country on the United Nations Human Rights Council to vote against—I think it's 36 countries, don't hold me to the exact number—but the only country on the Human Rights Council of the United Nations to vote against the establishment of a fact-finding mission on settlements was the United States of America." He added, "I did more fundraisers for AIPAC in the '70s and early '80s than—just about as many as anybody."

Thus, with a self-declared Zionist in the White House, grateful for pro-Israel PAC money, and in favor of the brutal and illegal settler movement, Prime Minister Bennett felt free to launch Israel's biggest eviction of Palestinians in decades just ahead of Biden's planned visit to Israel in July 2022. A visit in which U.S. ambassador to Israel Thomas Nides described Biden to the Israeli press as a "Zionist...who loves Israel." And in August 2022, Israel approved construction of 1,400 new illegal settlement units in occupied East Jerusalem.

As *Haaretz* columnist Gideon Levy observed, "No one is ever held responsible...Soldiers serving in the occupied territories know very well that nearly anything they do is treated as permissible: shooting, killing, abusing, humiliating. They will never be punished, not by Israel nor by anyone else. Every day there are more killings, politically motivated arrests without trial, collective punishment, home demolitions, land confiscation, torture and humiliation, settlement expansion, and exploitation of natural resources."

Around the same time as the murder of Shireen Abu Akleh, United Nations special rapporteur Michael Lynk issued a devastating eighteen-page report on Israel's institutionalized racism and human rights abuses, officially charging the Jewish state with "committing the crime of apartheid."

"The political system of entrenched rule in the occupied Palestinian territory," Lynk wrote, "which endows one racial-national-ethnic group with substantial rights, benefits and privileges while intentionally subjecting another group to live behind walls, checkpoints and under a permanent military rule '*sans droits, sans égalité, sans dignité et sans liberté*' [without laws, without equality, without dignity, and without liberty] satisfies the prevailing evidentiary standard for the existence of apartheid."

He added that in many areas, Israel's version of apartheid went well beyond that of even South Africa. It included "segregated highways, high walls and extensive checkpoints, a barricaded population, missile strikes and tank shelling of a civilian population, and the abandonment of the Palestinians' social welfare to the international community." And then there were the acts of cold-blooded murder, "arbitrary and extra-judicial killings," as well as "arbitrary detention" and "collective punishment."

Lynk also brought up the racist and oppressive nature of the country's settlement policies. "Over the past five decades, Israel has created 300

Jewish-only civilian settlements, all of them illegal, with 700,000 Israeli Jewish settlers now living in East Jerusalem and the West Bank in the midst of, but apart from, three million Palestinians," he wrote. "In Gaza, Israel has barricaded the two million Palestinians into what former British Prime Minister David Cameron called 'an open-air prison,' a method of population control unique in the modern world." To fight back, the Israeli government began stepping up its efforts to cancel anyone daring to speak the truth. "In recent months Israel has intensified its efforts to censor and discredit anyone who uses the word apartheid. This strategy is failing in the face of the growing consensus among experts that Israel is committing apartheid," said a report by Amnesty International.

Despite the threats, for many the level of disgust had become intolerable. "I am a Jew. I am an Israeli citizen. I am a veteran of a combat unit in the Israeli army," said Rafael Silver in March 2022. He left Israel and emigrated to Canada, he said, "because I felt that I could no longer be a part of a system that practices apartheid against the Palestinian people. I do not use the word apartheid lightly but instead reluctantly. I choose to use this word to describe the reality the Palestinian people have been enduring for generations because I have seen it in action with my own eyes. I have enforced it during my military service in the West Bank and in the Gaza Strip and supported it as an Israeli taxpayer." He added, "A system that applies separate laws and practices to one group of people yet denies it to another based solely upon ethnicity is apartheid by definition. It was the case in South Africa in the past and it is the case in Israel today."

———

For others, joining the boycott was the only way to protest. Ben & Jerry's, the popular worldwide ice cream company, announced they were shutting down all their shops in the illegal settlements in the West Bank and East Jerusalem. "We're a values-led company with a long history of advocating for human rights, and economic and social justice," they said. "We believe it is inconsistent with our values for our product to be present within an internationally recognized illegal occupation."

Although they no longer had operational control of the company, Ben & Jerry's founders, Bennett Cohen and Jerry Greenfield, both Jewish, declared that they "unequivocally support" the boycott decision. "It is a rejection of Israeli policy, which perpetuates an illegal occupation that is a barrier to peace and violates the basic human rights of the Palestinian people who live under the occupation," they wrote in a *New York Times* op-ed. Cohen later added, "I'm against some of [Israel's] actions. One of these is oppressing a whole group of people in the occupied territories." They also rejected the attempts to intimidate critics with endless accusations of "anti-Semitism." "We fundamentally reject the notion that it is antisemitic to question the policies of the State of Israel," they wrote.

The decision by Ben & Jerry's was a crushing blow to Netanyahu's and Erdan's covert war in the United States, and their efforts to muzzle critics through intimidation and disinformation. Attempting to fight back, newly elected president Isaac Herzog went so far as to liken the decision to stop selling cartons of Caramel Chew Chew to an act of "terrorism." "The boycott of Israel is a new sort of terrorism," he said. "We must oppose this boycott and terrorism in any form." Then Prime Minister Naftali Bennett, who replaced Netanyahu in the election, placed a threatening, thuglike phone call to Alan Jope, the CEO of Unilever, Ben & Jerry's parent company. There would be "severe consequences" by the Israeli government, he warned. Finally, Ambassador Gilad Erdan even called the decision to end the sale of ice cream cones "the dehumanization of the Jewish people." And Jacob Baime, who runs the Israel on Campus Coalition, wrote in the *Jerusalem Post* about "Unilever's war on the Jewish state," and that the "capture of Unilever by antisemitic radicals" should not be allowed to stand.

The next move in Israel's ice cream war was to activate its allied forces in the United States. "Following Erdan's call, most of the U.S. Jewish establishment and pro-Israel organizations," noted *Haaretz*, "applied pressure to Unilever and U.S. governors alike, while progressive Jewish organizations called on states to avoid legal action." Over the years, pro-Israel lobbyists had donated millions of dollars to state politicians to get them to pass anti-boycott laws favorable to Israel. Now it was time for Erdan and Israeli foreign minister Yair Lapid to call them to action.

As if taking over as U.S. attorney general, Lapid ordered law enforcement organizations throughout the country to take punitive action against the South Burlington, Vermont, ice cream maker. "Over 30 states in the United States have passed anti-BDS legislation in recent years," he tweeted. "I plan on asking each of them to enforce these laws against Ben & Jerry's. They will not treat the State of Israel like this without a response." Saluting smartly and quickly springing into action was conservative Oklahoma senator James Lankford. He urged his state's government to "immediately block the sale" of Ben & Jerry's ice cream to Oklahomans.

About the same time, a group of congressmen and senators began pushing for the U.S. Securities and Exchange Commission to launch an investigation into Unilever over the action by Ben & Jerry's.

Others, however, pushed back. When the Illinois state investment board voted to divest from Unilever because of the actions of Ben & Jerry's, a group of Illinois rabbis protested. "We find the IIPB's [Illinois Investment Policy Board] punitive actions against companies exercising their free speech rights to engage in boycott to be patently unjust," they wrote.

In the summer of 2022, after months of pressure by U.S. pro-Israel groups and politicians, Unilever simply dumped the company in Israel, selling it to a local owner. Unilever would receive no profits from it, the name would no longer be allowed in English, only in Hebrew or Arabic, but once again the illegal settlements would get their ice cream. "The anti-Semites will not defeat us. Not even with ice cream," barked newly appointed caretaker Prime Minister Yair Lapid.

Apparently among Lapid's "anti-Semites" are Ben and Jerry themselves. "We do not agree with it," said an angry Ben & Jerry's tweet. "We continue to believe it is inconsistent with Ben & Jerry's values for our ice cream to be sold in the Occupied Palestinian Territory." And on July 5, 2022, Ben & Jerry's took action, suing Unilever in an effort to block the sale, thus launching a new front in the ice cream war. A battle that has placed a spotlight on the issue of brutal racism and Jewish supremacy similar to the way early boycotts brought world attention to the violent racism and White supremacy in apartheid South Africa.

Because it was such a high-profile company, and one founded by highly respected Jews, the action would lend enormous legitimacy to the worldwide boycott movement, encouraging other companies and organizations to do the same. "Ben & Jerry's Could Be the First in a Wave of BDS Victories," said a headline in *Haaretz*. Soon, others in the academic, business, and cultural worlds joined in. In 2022, General Mills, the country's third-largest consumer food products company, said it would divest from Israel and no longer make Pillsbury products in the occupied territories. The move was cheered on by five members of the Pillsbury family who earlier wrote an op-ed in the *Minneapolis Star Tribune* titled "Why We Must Boycott Pillsbury." "We cannot support the products bearing our name when its parent company is benefiting from Israel's war crimes," they wrote.

Beyond the United States, boycott and divestment actions were also taking place around the world. KLP, the enormous Norwegian pension fund, which manages more than $100 billion in investments, pulled out, divesting from sixteen Israeli companies, among them Israel's largest telecommunications firms and banks. And New Zealand's $33 billion national pension fund announced that it had excluded five Israeli banks from its portfolio because of their role in financing Israeli settlements in the occupied West Bank.

There were also major advances within the academic community. In May 2022, in a severe blow to Israel, the editorial board of the *Harvard Crimson* issued a very strong endorsement of the BDS movement. "As a board, we are proud to finally lend our support to both Palestinian liberation and BDS—and we call on everyone to do the same," it said. "We do not take this decision lightly," they noted. "The weight of this moment—of Israel's human rights and international law violations and of Palestine's cry for freedom—demands this step." The editors went on to praise the college's Palestine Solidarity Committee "that has forced our campus—and our editorial board—to once again wrestle with what both Human Rights Watch and Amnesty International have called Israel's 'crimes against humanity' in the region."

They also acknowledged the constant intimidation faced by anyone critical of Israel. "Israel remains America's favorite first amendment blindspot," it said. "Dare question Israel's policies or endorse Palestinian freedom and you will be shunned from the newsroom, past accomplishments or legitimate arguments be damned. For college students like ourselves, speaking bluntly about events in the region can prompt online harassment or even land you on a blacklist." A blacklist such as Canary Mission. "Even on this campus, many of our brave peers advocating for Palestinian liberation can be found on watchlists tacitly and shamefully linking them to terrorism...Even for journalists, openly condemning the state's policies poses an objective professional risk."

The board went on to criticize the Israeli lobby–led efforts to criminalize boycotting Israel. "Companies that choose to boycott the Jewish state, or otherwise support the pro-Palestine Boycott, Divest, and Sanction movement face legal repercussions in at least 26 states." Finally, they compared the BDS movement with similar movements that brought an end to apartheid in South Africa. "The tactics embodied by BDS have a historical track record; they helped win the liberation of Black South Africans from Apartheid, and have the potential to do the same for Palestinians today."

Within a few days, there were very worried voices within the Jewish community. "I must admit I saw this coming," noted Dany Bahar in the Jewish Forward. "But it is still terrifying, because it is yet another sign that public opinion among young elites is turning against Israel."

Around the same time, the faculty at City University of New York Law School unanimously backed a Student Government resolution that "proudly and unapologetically" embraced the Boycott, Divestment, and Sanctions movement. The resolution criticized the university's complicity "in the ongoing apartheid, genocide, and war crimes perpetrated by the state of Israel against the Palestinian people through its investments in and contracts with companies profiting off of Israeli war crimes."

And at Georgetown University in Washington, DC, a coalition of graduate and undergraduate students successfully prevented $30,000 in student funding from being used for a propaganda trip to Israel sponsored by a group called itrek, formerly "Israel & Co." According to the students' "Victory Statement," they "fully cut the trip's institutional links to Georgetown University... in line with BDS principles of academic boycott." The students charged that "itrek (or International Trek) is an organization that is explicitly pro-Israel and has previously received money from the Israeli government." Its purpose, they charged, was "to whitewash the Occupation of Palestine" by organizing a "trip to an Apartheid state that enforces military rule on millions of Palestinians and occupies their land... Over the span of just a week, the opposition to the trip and its financing became too grand to ignore... We hope that what happened here at Georgetown University can serve as a model for students at other universities."

The movement has also been spreading rapidly on college campuses around the world. In August 2022, the student union of Australia's highest-ranked college, the University of Melbourne, overwhelmingly passed a pro-BDS motion. The organization, with about 35,000 members, accused the "apartheid colonial state" of the "ethnic cleansing of more than 350+ Palestinian villages and towns" and "forcefully displacing over 750,000 Palestinian from their homes."

Among the writers taking part in the boycott was critically acclaimed Irish novelist Sally Rooney. In a widely publicized statement, she praised the BDS movement and announced her "solidarity with the Palestinian people in their struggle for freedom, justice and equality." Going further, she refused a request from an Israeli publishing firm to produce a Hebrew translation of her new novel, *Beautiful World, Where Are You*. The recent report by Human Rights Watch, she wrote, "confirmed what Palestinian human rights groups have long been saying: Israel's system of racial domination and segregation against Palestinians meets the definition of apartheid under international law." Rooney added, "I am responding to the call from Palestinian civil society, including all major Palestinian trade unions and writers' unions."

Comparing Israel's "grievous human rights abuses" to those of apartheid South Africa, Rooney said she was open to such a translation, but only from a company "that is compliant with the BDS movement's institutional boycott guidelines." Earlier she signed a "Letter Against Apartheid" that called on artists "to exercise their agency within their institutions and localities to support the Palestinian struggle for decolonization to the best of their ability. Israeli apartheid is sustained by international complicity, it is our collective responsibility to redress this harm." Rooney's homeland has long had similar views about Israel. In 2021, Ireland passed a motion condemning the "de facto annexation" of Palestinian land. And three years earlier, resolutions were passed by Dublin's city council endorsing a boycott of Israel and calling for the Israeli ambassador to be expelled.

Following Rooney's action, scores of other writers came out supporting her stand. Pulitzer Prize–winning novelist Michael Chabon, who is Jewish, wrote that he "supports the Palestinian people in their struggle for equality, justice and human rights." He added, "I say *yasher koach* (Hebrew for 'Good job' or 'More power to you') to Rooney." And seventy notable writers and publishers signed a letter of support, vowing to "continue to respond to the Palestinian call for effective solidarity, just as millions supported the campaign against apartheid South Africa."

Infuriated, Netanyahu and Erdan once again activated their hidden troll army in the United States, Act.il, in an attempt to take down Rooney. From Tel Aviv, Israel's American cyber soldiers were given the command to attack: "This is hateful behavior at its finest, and we must put an end to it! LIKE this Facebook comment saying that her decision reflects her antisemitic behavior!" For years, such efforts to deliberately muzzle critics of Israel have been successful, according to the American Civil Liberties Union. "Those who seek to protest, boycott, or otherwise criticize the Israeli government are being silenced," warned ACLU attorneys. It was a trend that "manifests on college campuses, in state contracts, and even in bills to change federal criminal law" and "suppress[es] the speech of people on only one side of the Israel-Palestine debate."

As with Act.il, much of that silencing was the result of deliberate and blatant efforts by the Israeli government to interfere in U.S. domestic affairs. Over the years, Netanyahu and Erdan had transformed thousands of Americans into clandestine Israeli spies and covert operatives; still other Americans would become the regime's secret propagandists, selling its lies to their fellow citizens. American collaborators were even used to illegally finance much of the espionage and covert operations. All while U.S. politicians, the mainstream press, and the FBI deliberately looked the other way, as they have always done with Arnon Milchan.

Soon the pro-Israel lobby decided it needed to buy a great deal more influence with Congress. Therefore, in December 2021, AIPAC announced that it was launching a new political action committee, a "super PAC." Deliberately hiding the word "Israel," it was called the "United Democracy Project." "The AIPAC PAC is now the largest bipartisan, pro-Israel political action committee (PAC) in the country," the lobby announced. "And it is quickly emerging as a leading force in American politics." The beneficiaries would be both Democrats and Republicans, the sole criteria being blind, unquestioning support for Israel.

Soon after, billionaire Hillary Clinton supporter Haim Saban donated $1 million and AIPAC itself put in another $8.5 million. In just the first three months of 2022, the super PAC took in nearly $16 million, which is in addition to millions from at least a dozen other pro-Israel pressure groups. AIPAC's slate of endorsements included 109 of the 147 Republicans who refused to affirm President Joe Biden's election on January 6, 2021, among them Congressman Scott Perry of Pennsylvania who, noted *Forward*, "invoked the Nazis in a tirade against the Democratic Party."

Others, according to *Forward*, had had enough of AIPAC and its endless bags of cash on behalf of Israel, including former New York City mayor Bill de Blasio. In June 2022 he said he no longer supported AIPAC, wouldn't accept its endorsement even if it was offered, and called the organization "unacceptable." He was particularly angry at the lobby using its PAC money to help defeat progressive House candidate Nina Turner, who lost a primary election in Cleveland. Turner had dared express solidarity with a Jewish group that accused Israel of "apartheid." Truth being an unforgivable offense to the bloated lobby.

With the FBI officially neutered when it comes to Israel, unsurprisingly in January 2022 Prime Minister Naftali Bennett increased funding for Concert, the cover organization for the covert war in the United States against the boycotters, students, writers, and protesters. The new effort would now receive a total of $62 million. And as before, half of the war chest would come from the Israeli government and half from "donations"—in other words, the Blue Network made up of pro-Israel American citizens and organizations. By subsidizing Israel's clandestine operations in the United States, they would be acting illegally as agents of a foreign government.

"At the end of the day, what you see is a financial transfer from a public utility company, rather than an official government transfer. That is the idea," said the previous minister of strategic affairs about the scheme—which ran into problems, according to *Haaretz*, "likely caused by reluctant donors hesitant to identify themselves with covert propaganda operations" and thus hesitant to go to prison. As a result, although the Netanyahu government put in nearly $50 million for the secret war, they were only able to raise $7 million from U.S. private donors. Bennett's idea was to push much harder on the wealthy Americans in the Blue Network. Wasting little time, the operation was launched at the end of January 2022. And as in the past, the FBI was sure to look the other way.

At the same time Gilad Erdan's Ministry of Strategic Affairs was launching psychological warfare operations in the United States, and building up his army of spies and covert funders, his boss had much higher ambitions. Using his own secret agent, Netanyahu was determined to put Donald Trump, his favorite candidate, in the White House.

BOOK SIX

THE MOLES

CHAPTER 27

◆

The Asset

"Roger, hello from Jerusalem," said the message from the secret Israeli agent. Dated August 12, 2016, it was addressed to Trump associate Roger Stone. "Any progress? He is going to be defeated unless we intervene. We have critical intell. The key is in your hands! Back in the US next week." Later he promised, "October Surprise coming!"

The Israeli connection was by far the most secret (and perhaps overlooked) aspect of the Russiagate investigation. No details of it were ever revealed in the heavily redacted Mueller Report. "References to some sort of Israeli involvement in Trump's 2016 campaign cropped up during Robert Mueller's official investigation of the so-called Russia collusion affair," noted *Haaretz*, "but were thoroughly redacted." Nor was there any mention of an Israeli plot in the similarly redacted Senate Intelligence Committee Report, or in any of the indictments or trials. Nor did it ever leak into the press. What it involved, however, was an elaborate operation directed by Prime Minister Netanyahu to use secret intelligence, presumably concerning Hillary Clinton, to clandestinely intervene at the highest levels in the presidential election on behalf of Donald Trump.

While the American media and political system fixated on Putin and his armies of cyber warriors, trolls, and bots, what was largely missed in 2016 was that Israel had developed a great deal of experience in secretly manipulating elections around the world.

—————

On the sixth floor of a glass-and-cement high-rise just south of Tel Aviv, behind a door marked only with a mysterious "Unit 17" in Hebrew, political operatives plot newer and more creative ways to use fraud to win elections across much of the planet. The sixteen-story Azrieli Business Center in Holon is home to Archimedes Group, a private intelligence company that boasts, like Psy Group, that it can "change reality according to our client's wishes." Those clients stretch from Africa to Latin America to Southeast Asia.

In Nigeria in 2018, the company's campaign of lies and misinformation helped reelect former military coup leader Muhammadu Buhari as president. Scores of phony Facebook pages were set up pretending to be news organizations, flooding Nigerians with fake news and disinformation promoting Buhari and denigrating his opponent, Atiku Abubaker. Others, pretending to be run by local Nigerians, spread false rumors about Abubaker that raced through the country like wildfire. One trolling campaign aimed at Abubaker used the theme "Make Nigeria Worse Again." In fact, they were all created, managed, and controlled in Israel.

Hired by other would-be presidents and politicians around the world in at least thirteen countries, Archimedes soon had three million people following their phony Facebook and Instagram accounts. They even created phony "fact-checking" accounts to lie about their fake news stories, claiming they were based on solid facts. According to the analysis think tank DFR Lab, "The tactics employed by Archimedes Group, a private company, closely resemble the types of information warfare tactics often used by governments, and the Kremlin in particular."

The man behind the "Unit 17" door is Elinadav Heymann, a bald, thick-necked former senior intelligence agent for the Israeli air force. Prior to Archimedes, Heymann was the Brussels-based director of the NGO European Friends of Israel (EFI). A powerful lobby organization, it pushed Israeli-related causes, including anti-boycott legislation, to European members of Parliament. Journalist David Cronin has called the EFI "the closest thing this side of the Atlantic to the American Israel Public Affairs Committee (AIPAC)."

In 2016, Heymann started Archimedes Group and quickly began using his lobbying skills to sell his company's reality-changing electioneering to much of the world. But in May 2019 Facebook caught on to the various scams and removed 265 Facebook and Instagram accounts. "Archimedes Group," it said, "has repeatedly violated our misrepresentation and other policies, including by engaging in coordinated inauthentic behavior. This organization and all its subsidiaries are now banned from Facebook, and it has been issued a cease and desist letter." Archimedes and Psy Group are hardly alone. An Israeli government official told the *Times of Israel* that 265 accounts "is a drop in the bucket, and that there are probably tens of thousands of bogus accounts operated by numerous companies in Israel."

According to the Israeli official, outsourcing fake news and voter manipulation is a growth industry in Israel because many young Israelis who serve in intelligence units in the army are trained in the use of "avatars," or fake identities, on social media. "IDF intelligence likes to use avatars," he said. "They use them against Israel's greatest enemies and they're extremely effective. The problem is that you have all these young people who served in the 8200 intelligence unit and who know how to create fake profiles, and when they leave the army some of them say 'I want to make money' and they sell their skills to whoever will pay them." There appears to be no effort by the Israeli government to halt or even curb the activity, likely because the groups also provided Netanyahu and Minister of Strategic Affairs Gilad Erdan with intelligence, access, and the ability to secretly manipulate elections to Israel's benefit.

An example was Minnesota Democrat Ilhan Omar, who had a long record of fighting for Palestinian human rights. In an effort to silence her, Israel's cyber war room issued a mission to its loyal battalions of secret American trolls to try and oust her from Congress, especially since "her district is very Jewish." Apparently, Israel's Ministry of Strategic Affairs preferred a Jewish member of Congress in her district. "Her anti-semitic acts don't have a place in the congress especially given the fact that her district is very Jewish. SHARE this post to notify people about her anti-semitic comments."

Another mission asked the troll army to promote a letter from "ACT! For America," demanding her ouster from the House Foreign Affairs Committee. "ACT!" was a notorious Islamophobic organization labeled a hate group by the Southern Poverty Law Center. Neither Israeli operation was apparently discovered by the FBI, or if it was, no action was taken. And because the trolls are instructed to hide their connection to Israel, no one on Omar's staff apparently realized they were being targeted by the Israeli government. Still another mission directed the trolls to contact their U.S. senators to support a federal anti-boycott law.

These were clear and deliberate covert acts by a foreign power to interfere in U.S. domestic politics. In 2018 the Justice Department's special counsel announced a sweeping indictment of the Internet Research Agency, a group of Russian internet trolls. Thirteen individuals and three companies were charged with taking part in a long-running conspiracy to criminally interfere with the 2016 U.S. presidential election. It also charged that the suspects engaged in extensive online conversations with Americans who became unwitting tools of the Russian efforts. The indictment, however, did not accuse the Russian government of involvement in the scheme. Yet when it came to Act.il, the FBI and Justice simply closed their eyes and never brought any charges.

In the spring of 2016, no issue was more important to Benjamin Netanyahu than Donald Trump winning the White House. The candidate was key to everything he was after, from ending the Iran nuclear agreement, to moving the capital from Tel Aviv to Jerusalem, to continuing the occupation of Palestine. But November was months away, and there was no guarantee Trump would win. In the meantime, he was under mounting pressure from President Obama, hoping for another Nobel Peace Prize before leaving office, to finally resolve the issues surrounding Palestine. And leading the charge on behalf of Obama was Secretary of State John Kerry, who was equally determined to find a solution after many years of trying.

Adding to Netanyahu's problems, Kerry was not alone. There was also the Middle East Quartet, representatives from the United Nations, the European Union, the United States, and Russia who were also seeking a solution to issues surrounding the occupation. And they were about to release a long-awaited report that was expected to be highly critical of Israel.

For years, the man Netanyahu relied on to do battle with both Kerry and the Quartet was his top personal aide, Isaac Molho, a secretive and shadowy private attorney who was trusted with the prime minister's most sensitive missions. It was Molho who helped arrange the secret meeting between Kerry and Milchan regarding Milchan's visa. "There has probably never been a person in the history of this country in such a desirable position as Isaac Molho," noted *Haaretz*. "He enjoys almost complete silence from the media…On Prime Minister Benjamin Netanyahu's instructions, Molho undertakes sensitive missions to countries with which Israel has no diplomatic ties. The Mossad supplies him with logistical backing, security and transport."

Some of Molho's assignments are too sensitive even for the Mossad, a fact that has at times frustrated those at the spy agency. "The Mossad gritted its teeth over the past eight years while watching the diplomatic missions carried out by Isaac Molho, without any requirement to take a polygraph test and as a private citizen with business and other affairs that are not subject to civil service regulations," said *Haaretz*. In addition to national loyalty there is even family loyalty, since Molho is related to Netanyahu, having married his cousin.

In the spring of 2016, with so much on the line, Netanyahu made a drastic decision. He would dispatch a discreet, highly trusted aide, armed with critical intelligence, to covertly "intervene" in the U.S. election to put his man Trump in the White House. Shadowy hints of the plot only became visible with the little-noticed release in 2020 of a heavily redacted 2018 FBI search warrant and its accompanying affidavit. Part of the Mueller investigation, the warrant was directed at secretly securing the Google accounts for a mysterious Israeli agent.

Although the secret agent's name was redacted from the search warrant, as outlined in the accompanying affidavit his profile was strikingly similar to that of Isaac Molho. Like Molho, the agent was highly trusted and very close to Netanyahu. He was also a "discreet man for sensitive missions," as *Haaretz* described Molho. Most importantly, the agent would eventually be summoned from the U.S. at a moment's notice to be by Netanyahu's side during critical negotiations with Secretary of State John Kerry regarding the Quartet and the Palestinians. It was a critical role played exclusively for many years by Molho. In addition, the agent had enough clout and authority to direct the actions of two other very high-ranking Israeli officials involved in the clandestine operation. An operation designed to secretly steal the election from the American voters.

The numerous potential criminal charges laid out in the FBI documents spoke to the seriousness of the Israeli plot. They included violation of the foreign contribution ban, which prohibits foreigners from contributing money or something of value to federal, state, or local elections. Others included aiding and abetting, conspiracy, unauthorized access to a protected computer, wire fraud, and attempted conspiracy to commit wire fraud. And based on the emails and text messages contained in the documents, the conspiracy began in the late spring of 2016, a time when it appeared that Trump had a good chance of winning the Republican nomination.

The key for the Israeli agent was finding a back door, an asset, a covert channel to Trump, and Roger Stone fit the bill. With his sculpted platinum-dyed hair, round Cutler and Gross sunglasses, and bespoke suits from Wiggy & Cheats, he had long been a key Trump aide.

And although Stone had formally left the campaign, he and Trump spoke frequently and confidentially. For the calls, Trump would often use the phone of his security director, Keith Schiller, "because he did not want his advisors to know they were talking," said longtime campaign official Sam Nunberg. And Trump attorney Michael Cohen added, "Stone called Trump all the time." Stone, therefore, was someone who could quietly provide entrée to Trump without the need to deal with the campaign bureaucracy or get caught up in the media frenzy.

Also critical was that Stone greatly supported Israel's harsh occupation of the Palestinians and its war drums when it came to Iran. Following Trump's AIPAC speech, Stone noted approvingly that "Donald Trump is a radical Zionist." He added that the candidate hit all the "hot buttons" in his speech, including vowing to tear up the Iran nuclear deal.

Another Trump aide heavily involved in the conspiracy, according to the FBI documents, was Stone's associate Jerome Corsi, who appears to have been the original contact who connected the Israelis to Stone. An ultraconservative author and journalist with a doctorate in political science from Harvard in 1972 and a shelf of books harshly critical of liberals and Democrats, Corsi became the literary light of the extreme right. He had originally gained fame in 2004 for his attacks on the military record of then presidential candidate John Kerry, a Swift Boat commander during the war in Vietnam. The attacks, which became known as "swiftboating," were eventually discredited.

For the secret agent, key was Corsi's adulation for Israel and support of its warmongering against Iran. He was even invited to speak on the topic by the Israeli Knesset, Israel's parliament, where the two might have met. Among his books: *Atomic Iran: How the Terrorist Regime Bought the Bomb and American Politicians*; *Showdown with Nuclear Iran: Iran's Messianic Mission to Destroy Israel and Cripple the United States*; and *Why Israel Can't Wait: The Coming War Between Israel and Iran*.

Hidden behind his online pseudonym, "jrlc," Corsi was also a virulent Islamophobe. Posting on the conservative online forum FreeRepublic.com, he has called Islam "a virus" and "a worthless, dangerous Satanic religion," and said that "Islam is a peaceful religion as long as the women are beaten, the boys buggered, and the infidels killed."

After first making contact with Corsi, the secret Israeli agent and Stone connected. Then on May 17, he wrote, "Hi Roger, I hope all is well. Our dinner tonight for 7PM is confirmed. I arrive at 4PM. Please suggest a good restaurant that has privacy." The original plan was for Stone and the agent to meet alone, but possibly for security reasons Stone wanted to bring along Corsi as backup. "I am uncomfortable meeting without Jerry," Stone wrote, and thus changed the dinner to Wednesday, May 18.

According to indications picked up by the FBI and as laid out in the sealed 2018 search warrant, the same day Stone communicated with the secret Israeli agent he suddenly began Googling some very strange terms, including "guccifer" and "dcleaks." Strange because it would be nearly a month before those same terms would make headlines around the world. On June 14 the *Washington Post* announced that the Democratic National Committee had been hacked by Russian government agents. And the next day, someone calling himself "Guccifer 2.0" took credit for the attack. Claiming to be an American hacktivist, he was actually a Russian GRU employee. Soon afterward, many other hacked Democratic Party documents would be released by the website "DCLeaks," also a front for the GRU.

Somehow, the Israeli agent passed on to Stone critical details of a Russian cyberattack on the DNC a month before it became known to anyone outside of the Kremlin and GRU. Thus the two critical questions: How did the Israeli know, and why was he revealing the details to a close associate of Trump rather than the Obama administration, Israel's supposed ally?

On May 18, the day following the Google search, Stone, Corsi, and the Israeli agent met for dinner at the posh 21 Club on New York's Fifty-second Street. With its balcony lined with painted iron lawn jockeys, it was a regular Trump hangout. On the top of the agent's agenda was getting Stone to quickly and quietly set up a confidential meeting with the candidate. Wasting little time, the next day the agent pressed Stone in an email: "Did You Talk To Trump This Morning? Any News?" But Stone was coy. "Contact made—interrupted—mood good."

Then at some point in early June, Stone learned from the Israeli agent that Julian Assange, the head of WikiLeaks, was about to release something "big." At the time, Assange was living in the Ecuadorian embassy in London. Stone in turn relayed the details to Rick Gates, Trump's deputy campaign manager, and told him as well that Assange appeared to have Clinton's emails. Yet it wasn't until later, on June 12, that Assange would publicly announce that they "have emails relating to Hillary Clinton which are pending publication."

This was the first of many tips to Stone that appear to have come from his newly befriended Israeli agent. Two days later, the Democratic National Committee announced that they had been hacked by Russia. And the next day, Stone again began Googling both "Guccifer" and "dcleaks" hours before Guccifer 2.0, the online persona that the Russian hackers were hiding behind, publicly claimed responsibility. And days before the DCLeaks website appeared.

On June 21, as Guccifer released more documents, the Israeli agent quietly notified Stone that he was in New York accompanied by another senior official and would like a meeting with Trump. "RS: Secret," said the message. "Cabinet Minister [redacted] in NYC. Available for DJT [Donald J. Trump] meeting." Other parts of the message were also redacted, but in a sidenote the FBI revealed the cabinet minister's official title: "According to publicly-available information, during this time [redacted] was a Minister without portfolio in the cabinet dealing with issues concerning defense and foreign affairs."

At the time, the only minister without portfolio in the Israeli government was Tzachi Hanegbi. And Wikipedia, the likely source of the FBI agent's "publicly-available information," uses nearly identically language to describe Hanegbi. According to the entry, on May 30, 2016, Hanegbi, fifty-nine, was "appointed Minister without portfolio in the Fourth Netanyahu Cabinet, dealing with issues concerning defense and foreign affairs." He was one of Prime Minister Netanyahu's longest and closest confidants. Also, Israeli press reports at the time indicated that Hanegbi was in the United States on that precise date as part of a delegation attending the unveiling of Israel's new F-35 stealth fighter jet.

Married to an American from Florida and fully fluent in English, Hanegbi is tall and nearly bald, with a wraparound fringe of dark hair. Among his previous jobs was minister of intelligence supervising Mossad and Shin Bet, the internal security service. He was born in Jerusalem, the son of members of the Stern Gang, a self-described Jewish terrorist organization that fought against the British occupation government in Palestine in the late 1940s. The question is, why would Netanyahu send a trusted high-level confidant, with an intelligence background and close American links, to attempt a highly secret meeting with Trump, a presidential candidate?

Trump was very busy, hustling from city to city on the campaign trail and

hitting several rallies a day. Taking valuable time to meet a couple of Israeli officials was not a high priority, especially without any idea what the meeting would
be about. So on June 25, Hanegbi returned to Israel. "Roger, Minister left," said
the Israeli agent. "Sends greetings from PM. When am I meeting DJT? Should I
stay or leave Sunday as planned?" The FBI noted, "Based on statements here and
below, I believe 'PM' refers to the 'Prime Minister.'" The next day, Stone replied,
"I would not leave as we hope to schedule the meeting mon or tues."

At the same time Netanyahu was pressing his clandestine agent to meet
secretly with Trump, he was coming under growing pressure from President
Barack Obama on Palestine, which may explain the need for urgency. Both
Obama and Kerry were strongly urging Netanyahu to finally resolve the Palestinian issue. And a key element of that solution was agreeing to negotiate
an equitable division of Jerusalem, since both sides claimed it as their capital.
But if his secret agent could confidentially meet with Trump and get a com-
mitment to, if elected, support the prime minister's position, then Netanyahu
could ignore Obama. A big election win for Trump, therefore, would also be
a big election win for Netanyahu. And Netanyahu was thus incentivized to
secretly do everything possible to help put Trump in the White House. Especially since the candidate was already fully committed to another Netanyahu
key issue: canceling the nuclear deal with Iran.

———

Suddenly there was a change in plans. The agent was ordered by Netanyahu
to postpone the appointment with Trump and instead get on the next plane
for Rome. In a last-minute effort to find a solution to Jerusalem and the Palestinian issue, a meeting in the Italian capital was set up between Netanyahu,
U.S. secretary of state John Kerry, and the European Union's foreign policy
chief, Federica Mogherini. And Netanyahu wanted his aide, the agent, at his
side. At the meeting, the elephant in the room was a forthcoming report by
the Middle East Quartet, negotiators from the United States, the European
Union, the United Nations, and Russia. It was expected by all to be extremely
critical of Israel for its apartheid-like settlement policies and its treatment of
the occupied Palestinians.

The night before the meeting, Netanyahu and Kerry got together for
dinner at Pierluigi, a popular seafood restaurant in Piazza de Ricci, a block
from Rome's Tiber River. "What is your plan for the Palestinians?" Kerry
asked Netanyahu as the prime minister began chain-smoking a batch of
thick Cuban cigars, likely supplied by Arnon Milchan as part of the bribery
scheme. "What do you want to happen now?" Netanyahu simply offered a
vague, unrealistic idea involving a regional initiative, but Kerry wasn't buying.
"You have no path of return to direct talks with the Palestinians, or a channel

to talks with Arab countries," Kerry told the prime minister. "You've hit the glass ceiling. What's your plan?" he asked again. What Kerry didn't know was that Netanyahu *did* have a plan. It was to use his secret agent, possibly sitting with them at the dinner table, to help put Trump in the White House. In that way he wouldn't have to worry about a plan, or the Palestinians.

To make matters even worse, at the same time that the Rome meeting was taking place, California Democratic senator Dianne Feinstein, vice chairman of the Senate Intelligence Committee, sent Netanyahu a letter harshly rebuking his government for demolitions of private Palestinian homes in the occupied West Bank. "I strongly urge your government to halt these demolitions," she wrote. Feinstein added that she had also discussed the issue with Tzachi Hanegbi, the minister without portfolio who had tried to meet secretly with Trump a few days earlier.

With much of the world ganging up on him, including members of Congress, Netanyahu was desperate to get Trump to come to his rescue. Therefore, on June 28, after the meeting finished up in Rome, his aide once again transformed into a secret agent and quickly dashed off another message to Stone. "RETURNING TO DC AFTER URGENT CONSULTATIONS WITH PM IN ROME. MUST MEET WITH YOU WED. EVE AND WITH DJ TRUMP THURSDAY IN NYC."

The meeting with Trump was rescheduled for 1 p.m. on Wednesday, July 6, before the candidate took off for a rally in Sharonville, Ohio. In preparation, the Israeli agent flew into New York City the day before and checked into the St. Regis, the stylish French Beaux-Arts–style hotel on East 55th Street. The next morning, he had planned to meet with Stone in the hotel's lobby for a pre-meeting discussion. "At the St Regis With Lt General. Waiting For You Thank You," he wrote.

But there were major problems involving secrecy. Stone at his home in Florida had come down with a bad cold and was too ill to travel, so he arranged for Corsi to make the introduction. That made the Israeli agent uncomfortable because of the secrecy of the discussion. "I have to meet Trump alone," he said, and they agreed that Corsi would leave after the introduction. There was still another problem, however. Trump also wanted the meeting to be secret, but the agent was accompanied by a lieutenant general. So once again the meeting had to be postponed.

Unlike the United States, where the highest military rank is a four-star general, in Israel it is a three-star lieutenant general, and there is only one, the chief of the General Staff, the commander in chief of the Israel Defense Forces (IDF). It is the equivalent of the chairman of the Joint Chiefs of Staff. And at the time, that was Lieutenant General Gadi Eizenkot. But it was very unlikely that Eizenkot was the person waiting in the lobby of the St. Regis to meet with Trump. He had little to do with the election and actually sided with Obama on the issue of Iran. In January 2016, he said that the nuclear deal "had actually removed the most serious danger to Israel's existence for the foreseeable future, and greatly reduced the threat over the longer term."

Instead, it may have been Eizenkot's predecessor, Benny Gantz, who retired as head of the IDF in February 2015 but still held the rank of lieutenant general in the reserves and was often referred to by his military title. He was in charge of the IDF during Israel's war on Palestinians in Gaza in 2014. It was a war that produced a "vastly disproportionate" number of civilian deaths, fourteen hundred of the nearly twenty-three hundred people killed in the conflict, according to Human Rights Watch. Gantz would later boast that "parts of Gaza were sent back to the Stone Age."

In May 2020, Gantz became the second most powerful person in Israel under Netanyahu, as the alternate prime minister, and in a power sharing agreement he was originally scheduled to take over as prime minister in November 2021.* At the time of the canceled meeting with Trump, however, he was chairman of Fifth Dimension, a very invasive Israeli private intelligence company run by a former deputy head of Mossad, with another former Mossad member as CEO. And Gantz may have had a number of reasons to meet with Trump, including offering his company's private spy services to the campaign, giving him a unique, albeit secret, advantage.

———

Thus Netanyahu and his cronies were determined to get Trump elected at all costs, including with another secretive Israeli spy company with close ties to Israeli intelligence, Psy Group. An Orwellian private Israeli intelligence firm, its motto was "Shape Reality." On behalf of the Ministry of Strategic Affairs, the company had earlier carried out Project Butterfly to clandestinely attack Americans who supported the BDS boycott movement. Then, in April 2016, it offered Trump campaign official Rick Gates another secret operation, "Project Rome." The subtitle of the six-page proposal clearly spelled out its objective to covertly interfere with the U.S. presidential election: "Campaign Intelligence & Influence Services Proposal."

The op plan's secrecy was paramount. "We recommend keeping this activity compartmentalized and on need-to-know basis since secrecy is a key factor in the success of the activity," it said. To further mask the true nature of the work, code names were used. "Due to the sensitivity of some of the

———

* Due to Netanyahu's loss to Naftali Bennett in the recent election, Gantz instead now serves as Israel's minister of defense.

activities and the need for compartmentalization and secrecy, Psy Group will use code names." Trump, therefore, was "Lion," Hillary Clinton was "Forest," and Ted Cruz was "Bear." "This document details the services proposed by Psy Group for the 'Lion' project between now and July 2016," the proposal noted. It therefore focused on the primaries and getting Trump the nomination, and if he won, then a more elaborate scheme would be developed to win the general election.

Much of the secrecy was likely designed to hide any direct connections between Trump, the Israeli government, and its intelligence organizations. Also, the secret Project Rome proposal read like an official Ministry of Strategic Affairs or Mossad operational document. There were numerous spy agency terms and references, including "multisource intelligence collection," "covert sources," "automated collection and analysis," and "intelligence dossier on each target, including actionable intelligence." After the intelligence was collected, it would then be fed to the influence operators. "Once the information has been uncovered or extracted, it is delivered to the Influence platform for use in the campaign as needed," said the proposal.

The "Influence+process" platform then involved targeting American voters through "authentic-looking 3rd party platforms"—that is, fake news sites—and also with the use of "tailored avatars," thousands of phony social media accounts on platforms such as Facebook, and other forms of deception. "The purpose of these platforms is to engage the targets, and actively convince them or sway their opinion towards our goals." The "targets" were the unwitting American voters and the goals, ultimately, were those of Israel, with the operation being carried out by a massive team of Israeli covert operators. "The team will include over 40 intelligence and influence experts," the document said. Then there were the "physical world ops like counter protesters, hecklers, etc." The techniques were nearly identical to those used by the Israeli firm Archimedes Group to secretly throw elections around the world.

The price tag for the operation was $3,210,000, with another $100,000 for media expenses and $400,000 more for "negative opposition." It appears that Gates wisely passed. But the covert high-level approaches to Roger Stone to get directly to Trump continued.

————

"Hi Roger," the agent wrote on July 8. "Have you rescheduled the meeting with DJT? The PM is putting pressure for a quick decision." Stone wrote back that Trump would not be back in New York until after the Republican National Convention, so the meeting would have to be postponed until then. He added, "Sorry about the fiasco last week, however you can't just bring the General without tell[ing] me."

As Trump stormed the Midwest for votes, in Moscow Guccifer 2.0 was making final preparations for another major release of documents. The issue was how best to pass them on to Julian Assange at WikiLeaks. A month earlier Assange had requested the Ecuadorian embassy to increase his internet capacity, possibly to better access the large data transfers.

Then on July 14, Guccifer transferred to WikiLeaks an email with the subject "big archive." A one-gigabyte encrypted attachment was also sent. Guccifer then tweeted an encrypted file and instructions on how to open it. Four days later, on July 18, Assange notified Guccifer that he had received the data and that release of the hacked Democratic National Committee emails was planned for later in the week.

The next day in New York, Donald Trump was in his office venting at the press for its barrage of criticism over his wife Melania's Republican convention address the night before. There were questions about authenticity, plagiarism, and whether she had borrowed passages from First Lady Michelle Obama. In between bouts of anger and frustration over the coverage, and joy at the prospect of officially becoming the Republican nominee that night, he took a phone call from Roger Stone.

"Roger, how are you?" said Trump.

"Good," Stone replied. "Just want to let you know I got off the telephone a moment ago with Julian Assange. And in a couple of days, there's going to be a massive dump of emails that's going to be extremely damaging to the Clinton campaign."

Trump was pleased. "Uh, that's good. Keep me posted," he said into a small black speaker box on his desk. Sitting nearby was Michael Cohen. "Do you believe him? Do you think Roger really spoke to Assange?" Trump asked.

"I don't know," said Cohen. "Roger is Roger, and for all you know, he was looking on his Twitter account. I don't know the answer."

Eventually, both Stone and Assange would admit that neither had ever communicated with the other in any way. Nor was there ever any evidence that Stone communicated with anyone involved with WikiLeaks. And with the exception of exchanging a few nominal messages with Guccifer, later reviewed by the FBI, there was no indication of how Stone could have known what he knew—unless the information had once again been passed to him by Netanyahu's agent. And just as before, he was 100 percent accurate.

Three days later, on July 22, just as Hillary Clinton was preparing to announce her choice of a running mate on the eve of the Democratic National Convention, Wikileaks released its tranche of approximately twenty thousand emails stolen from the DNC. "I guess Roger was right," Trump told Cohen. Paul Manafort, his campaign manager, agreed. Sitting on the tarmac in his plane, about to take off for his next speech, Trump delayed the flight for half an hour to work the messages into the speech.

While there was never any evidence that Stone learned of the releases from either WikiLeaks or the Russians, during that same period both he and Jerome Corsi were instead clandestinely meeting with the Israeli agent, who apparently provided the details during meetings or phone calls. Israel's NSA, Unit 8200, was certainly targeting the Russians, as indicated by their tip-offs to Stone in May. Later they may also have been begun targeting Assange as well. After all, the agency employs some of the most highly trained signals intelligence specialists in the world, is equipped with NSA-level intercept capabilities, and the election was certainly one of Netanyahu's highest intelligence priorities. Even reserve lieutenant general Benny Gantz, with his private Mossad at Fifth Dimension and its connections to the Israeli government, would likely have been able to penetrate WikiLeaks. And passing on the intelligence to Trump would help assure his cooperation on a variety of issues important to Netanyahu, the top of which was the ongoing negotiations with the Obama administration over Palestine.

Trump, meanwhile, was hungry for more and told his campaign manager to keep in touch with Stone about future WikiLeaks releases. And at a news conference he announced, "Russia, if you're listening, I hope you're able to find the 30,000 emails that are missing. I think you will probably be rewarded mightily by our press." Within five hours, Moscow began spear-phishing Clinton's personal office email accounts for the first time.

Stone had tried to contact Assange directly to get access to unreleased emails but was never successful. "Get to Assange," he told Corsi in an email, "and get pending WikiLeaks emails... they deal with [the Clinton] Foundation, allegedly." In turn, an hour later Corsi forwarded Stone's message to Ted Malloch, a fellow conservative author living in London. The two had discussed Assange in the past, but Malloch also never made contact.

Four days later, however, the Israeli agent was back in touch with Stone and Corsi and very anxious to connect with Trump now that the convention was over and he was officially the Republican nominee for president. On Wednesday, July 29, he sent a message to Stone: "HI ROGER," he wrote. "HAVE YOU SET UP A NEW MEETING WITH TRUMP? I PLAN TO BE BACK IN THE US NEXT WEEK. PLEASE ADVISE. THANK YOU." Stone then sent a message to Manafort about finding a time for him and Manafort to communicate, writing that there was "good shit happening." The next day the two spoke on the phone for sixty-eight minutes. The following day, July 31, Stone had two phone calls with Trump that lasted over ten minutes.

Then on Sunday, August 2, despite Corsi's lack of success in connecting with Assange either personally or as a last-ditch effort through Malloch, he was nevertheless able to send a very detailed message to Stone about WikiLeaks' future plans:

> Word is friend in embassy [Assange] plans 2 more dumps. One shortly after I'm back. 2nd in Oct. Impact planned to be very damaging... Time to let more than [Clinton campaign manager John] Podesta to be exposed as in bed w enemy if they are not ready to drop HRC. That appears to be the game hackers are now about. Would not hurt to start suggesting HRC old, memory bad, has stroke—neither he nor she well. I expect that much of next dump focus, setting stage for Foundation debacle.

Corsi later told Stone that there was "[m]ore to come than anyone realizes. Won't really get started until after Labor Day." And he told Malloch that Podesta's hacked emails would be released prior to election day in November and would be helpful to the Trump campaign. After which, he said, "we" are going to be in the driver's seat. The information, Corsi told Malloch, was coming directly from Assange, who was in contact with Stone. But that was untrue since neither Corsi nor Stone ever connected with Assange. The details, including the first indication that Podesta was a target, were coming from somewhere else. And once again, the most likely source was Netanyahu's secret agent. (I met with Assange twice while he was holed up avoiding arrest in London's Ecuadorian embassy, but both times he declined to discuss any details concerning the leaked documents.)

At the time, pressure was building on Netanyahu from Obama and the Europeans to settle with the Palestinians. And his aide, in turn, was becoming desperate to meet with Trump. "Roger-As-per PM we have one last shot before moving on," he wrote to Stone on August 9. "Can you deliver? History will not forgive us. TRUMP IN FREE FALL. OCTOBER SURPRISE COMING !" What the "October Surprise" consisted of was left unexplained but implied a spectacular new release of stolen emails, possibly centering on Podesta.

Three days later Netanyahu's secret agent was even more frantic. He told Stone that his government was prepared to "intervene" in the U.S. presidential election to help Trump win the presidency, and also offered to share critical intelligence to make it happen. It was a treacherous act by Israel. "Roger, hello from Jerusalem," he wrote. "Any progress? He is going to be defeated unless we intervene. We have critical intell. The key is in your hands! Back in the US next week." Stone replied cryptically, seemingly concerned about the potential consequences of acting as an agent of Israel. "Matters complicated. Pondering," he wrote. Then, the following week, on August 20, Corsi suggested getting together with the secret agent to determine "what if anything Israel plans to do in Oct."

From the messages it appears that either Israel had its own "October

Surprise" planned or was referring to Guccifer's planned release of the Podesta emails before the election. It was likely that Israel had advance knowledge of what was taking place in Moscow regarding the Guccifer operation, including the penetration of Podesta's emails and their release as part of an "October Surprise." After all, Russia's cybersecurity was less than ironclad since the operation had originally been penetrated by the Dutch Joint Sigint Cyber Unit, which warned the NSA about the hacking of the DNC a year earlier. And if Israel did have advance knowledge of what was taking place, why didn't they simply notify the Obama administration, the government in power, as would be expected by an ally? Instead, they chose to secretly intervene in the presidential election by passing the "critical intell" clandestinely to Trump.

The day after Corsi suggested getting together with Netanyahu's agent, Stone for the first time publicly indicated that Podesta would soon become a target of WikiLeaks—thereby predicting the event six weeks before it happened. "Trust me, it will soon the [sic] Podesta's time in the barrel. #CrookedHillary," said his tweet. With neither Assange nor Guccifer as the source of either Corsi or Stone, it once again clearly pointed to the Israeli agent who was in communication with both of them about the "October Surprise."

The "October Surprise" and offer of critical intelligence apparently got Trump's attention. The next month he and his Jewish Orthodox son-in-law, Jared Kushner, met privately with Netanyahu in his Trump Tower penthouse. And as Netanyahu hoped, Trump came through. That same day he publicly announced that if he was elected his administration would finally "recognize Jerusalem as the undivided capital of the State of Israel." Since 1947, there has been virtual unanimity within the international community, and among U.S. presidents, that the future of Jerusalem must be the subject of negotiations between Israel and the Palestinians. Now Trump was vowing to trash tradition, along with the Palestinians, and support Netanyahu's agenda.

With little surprise, Minister Without Portfolio Tzachi Hanegbi, who had hoped to meet Trump with the secret agent earlier in the summer, was close by if not at the private meeting itself. Press accounts mentioned him as being in New York City at the same time. And in a radio interview he accused Obama of being "naive and messianic" and no longer "acting like the most powerful man in the world." "Instead," he said, Obama "is behaving like someone working in Hillary Clinton's campaign office."

Around the same time, Stone had a conversation with Manafort, who by then had left the campaign but stayed in communication with Trump's political circles. "John Podesta was going to be in the barrel," he told him, repeating the claim he made by tweet on August 21, and that "there were going to be leaks of John Podesta's emails." A few days later, on September 29, Stone called Trump in his black, bulletproof limo as he was on the way to New York's LaGuardia Airport. After concluding the call, Trump told Rick Gates, who was sitting next to him, that "more releases of damaging information would be coming."

Finally, on October 7, WikiLeaks unleashed 2,050 Podesta emails very damaging to Hillary Clinton and her campaign, as Stone had predicted a month and a half earlier. But soon after, he began getting very paranoid about potential criminal charges. It was unlikely, however, that he was worried about prosecutors discovering close links to Assange or the Russians, since there were none, except for a few nonconspiratorial email exchanges with Guccifer. Instead, it was far more likely that what greatly concerned him were his numerous hidden communications and dealings with the secret Israeli agent. Discovery of his messages discussing clandestine foreign intervention in a presidential election, the "October Surprise," and arrangements for a secret meeting between a foreign agent and Trump were certainly enough to rattle his nerves.

By secretly assisting Netanyahu's agent make contact with a presidential candidate, aware that he intended to interfere in the election on behalf of his country, both Stone and Corsi could have faced very serious charges as agents of a foreign power under Section 951 of the criminal code. It is often referred to as the "espionage lite" section because it makes it a crime to covertly assist a foreign government without registering. The less serious and better-known Foreign Agents Registration Act, by contrast, focuses instead largely on acting on behalf of a foreign "principal" or company without registering.

Even before the actual Podesta email dump in October, Stone and Corsi became very nervous that someone would discover their Israeli back channel. Soon after Stone's Podesta "time in the barrel" tweet in August, he and Corsi tried to find a way to somehow account for that unique insight. On August 30, said Corsi, "I suggested Stone could use me as an excuse, claiming my research on Podesta and Russia was the basis for Stone's prediction that Podesta would soon be in the pickle barrel." He added, "I knew this was a cover-story, in effect not true, since I recalled telling Stone earlier in August that Assange had Podesta emails that he planned to drop as the 'October Surprise.'" The next day, he said, he emailed to Stone "a nine page background memorandum on John Podesta that I had written that day at Stone's request."

Following the October Surprise and the Podesta dump, the cover-up became more drastic. Stone ordered Corsi to delete emails relating to Podesta, and then hid his own communications with Corsi about WikiLeaks. Stone also pointed his finger at Randy Credico, a onetime friend who had a radio program in New York, as his back channel to WikiLeaks. Credico had interviewed Assange on his program, but that was four days *after* Stone's tweet about Podesta's upcoming time in the barrel. Credico denied under oath that he acted as a secret back channel for Stone, and there was never any evidence to show he did.

———

In a predawn raid on January 25, 2019, nearly thirty heavily armed FBI agents stormed Roger Stone's Fort Lauderdale, Florida, home and placed him under arrest. He was charged with seven criminal offenses, including one count of obstruction of an official proceeding, five counts of false statements, and one count of witness tampering. Later that day he was released on a $250,000 signature bond. Defiant, he said he would refuse to "bear false witness" against Trump.

Finally, on November 15, 2019, after a weeklong trial and two days of deliberations, Stone was convicted on all counts and sentenced to forty months in federal prison. But on July 10, 2020, a few days before he was to turn himself in, Trump commuted his sentence, personally calling him with the news.

Throughout the entire chain of events, including the trial, the Mueller Report, and the nearly one-thousand-page Senate Intelligence Committee Report, no hint of the involvement of Israel or the secret Israeli agent ever surfaced. Despite the clear violations of U.S. law and months of clandestine high-level interference in the presidential election, no arrests were made, no details were released, and no congressional hearing or investigations took place. Once again, because Israel was the guilty party, the entire matter would be covered up for political reasons. Nor was there ever a hint in the press. Practicing pack journalism and groupthink, they were solely transfixed on Russia.

But the Israeli interference in the presidential election to put Trump in the White House took place not just from the top down of the Trump campaign, but also from the bottom up.

———

From the rooftop of The Harp of David restaurant on Mount Zion in Jerusalem, the shouting could be heard on the street below. Every time there was a mention of Hillary Clinton, people in Trump T-shirts and red "Make America Great Again" baseball caps booed and cried "Lock her up!" and "Hillary for prison!" On the evening of October 26, 2016, "The Biblical Restaurant," as it calls itself, played host to a noisy crowd of Trump supporters, serving them a cuisine from the Bible that emphasized the "seven spices" of ancient Canaan. Beyond, bright lights lit up the Western Wall and Temple Mount in the Old City. On a large video screen, Donald Trump addressed the crowd. "Together, we will stand up to enemies like Iran bent on destroying Israel and her people," he said. The previous month the Israeli JTA news organization ran the headline "Donald Trump Says Israel Will Be Destroyed Unless He Is Elected." Fearmongering about Iran was at the top of Team Trump's priority list for winning over the several hundred thousand American voters in Israel.

The "Trump in Israel" rally also featured several Trump advisors, among them David Friedman, fifty-eight, who would eventually be named Trump's ambassador to Israel. An Orthodox Jewish bankruptcy lawyer from Long Island and a pro-Israel extremist, he fit in well among the crowd. Friedman was chief fund-raiser for a yeshiva deep in the West Bank settlement of Beit El, one run by a militant rabbi who called on Israeli soldiers to stand their ground and refuse orders to evacuate settlers. He had also accused President Obama of "blatant anti-Semitism," an insult so tired and overused by the pro-Israel crowd to have become virtually meaningless. And he compared J Street, a liberal American Jewish group, to "kapos" who cooperated with the Nazis. "He has made clear that he will appeal to a small minority of Israeli—and American—extremists," noted Daniel C. Kurtzer, ambassador to Israel under President George W. Bush.

With offices on the fifteenth floor of a Jerusalem high-rise above a comedy club on Ben Yehuda Street in Tel Aviv, Republican headquarters in Israel was a busy place as donations from Americans poured in during the months leading up to the election. Some came from Americans visiting the country, some from Americans who were living there. Many Americans had dual citizenship, but as long as they requested absentee ballots, their votes would count. And on the top of the agenda for the Republican organization was close, daily coordination with the Trump campaign as it launched a massive get-out-the-vote campaign in Israel.

Apparently sensing a change in national priorities for the transplanted Americans, the slogan "Make America Great Again" was unceremoniously dumped. Instead, the focus was "Trump: Make Israel Great Again." In July the campaign opened seven offices, including one in the illegal West Bank settlement of Karnei Shomron, the first time such an act had been conducted by a U.S. political party. There a right-wing rabbi agreed to let the campaign use his house, festooned with a Hebrew-language Trump banner, as the local headquarters. In the kitchen, activist settlers in dark blue Trump T-shirts pounded laptop keyboards on a wooden table.

Far from home, the approximately two hundred thousand expat Americans in Israel, about the population of Fort Wayne, Indiana, would nevertheless play an important role in the very narrow 2016 U.S. presidential election. And in the months leading up to the vote, few were more energized than Marc Zell. Silver-haired, with a "Trump 2016" button shining in his lapel, he founded the Republican organization in 1992 even though he felt that fellow Republican James A. Baker, the secretary of state under then President George H. W. Bush was, no surprise, another "anti-Semite." He has also called comedian Sarah Silverman a "self-hating Jew" and said she "needs a muzzle." Today, a dual U.S./Israeli citizen, Zell lives in Tekoa, a West Bank settlement declared illegal under international law, and advocates on behalf of the right-wing settler movement.

Much of the campaign took place behind closed doors with the Republican and Trump organizations in Israel ignoring even the most basic U.S. laws when it came to money and foreign influence. Despite strict legal prohibitions against foreign involvement in U.S. political activities, Trump and the Republicans quickly packed the campaign with far-right pro-settler non-American Israeli citizens. According to *Haaretz*, the Trump campaign issued a statement claiming that their "ultimate goal is to recruit 'tens of thousands' of non-Americans in Israel to campaign...In its statement, the local Trump team said this was the first time a U.S. presidential campaign in Israel had actively enlisted non-Americans in its efforts." This despite the strict laws prohibiting the active participation of foreign nationals in most campaign activities.

In July 2016, after meeting with Republican Party and Trump campaign officials at the national convention in Cleveland, Tzvika Brot, thirty-seven, a non-American Israeli citizen, was put in charge of Trump's campaign in Israel. It was a clear and blatant violation of the law which states, "A foreign national shall not direct, dictate, control, or directly or indirectly participate in the decision-making process...in connection with elections for any Federal, State, or local office or decisions concerning the administration of a political committee." It also makes no difference whether the person works for free or is paid.

Brot was a local Israeli political consultant with close ties to Prime Minister Netanyahu and his far-right Likud Party—so close that Netanyahu once offered him the prestigious job of director of communications in the Prime Minister's Office, but Brot turned it down. Similarly, the Trump campaign spokesperson, Dana Mizrahi, another non-American, was also closely linked to the Netanyahu administration. In addition, she had previously served as spokesperson for a campaign in which human rights activists, writers, and artists were "outed" as "moles" in service to Israel's enemies because of their left-wing views.

As banners and balloons imprinted with Trump's name in Hebrew went up in shopping malls across the country, the Republicans began scrambling for money wherever they could find it—legal or illegal, it didn't matter. Brot, the campaign manager, even admitted on Army Radio in Israel that the Republican organization freely accepted donations from Israelis who were not American citizens, a serious criminal violation of U.S. law. Top Trump officials certainly had knowledge of the group's activities since according to the Israeli news organization Ynetnews, Vice President–elect Mike Pence and Trump's Jewish son-in-law, Jared Kushner, "advised the Israeli team during the campaign."

Zell tried to argue that the Republican organization was immune from

U.S. campaign finance laws because it was "a registered non-profit in Israel." But election experts quickly dismissed that claim as laughable. It is "illegal for any non-U.S. citizen to make a contribution to the Trump campaign or the Republican party," said Larry Nobel, legal counsel to the Washington-based Campaign Legal Center. He previously spent thirteen years as legal counsel for the Federal Election Commission. Nobel added, "It is illegal for any foreign (non-U.S.) individual or entity to solicit contributions for the Trump campaign or the U.S. Republican party and for the campaign or party to accept those contributions." There are no exceptions for American political parties in Israel, or anywhere else.

In fact, the Republicans made it very easy for anyone from anywhere to donate any amount to the party, whether $10 or $100,000. They even announced publicly that they would let Israelis without U.S. citizenship register with the party in Israel for a minimum payment of 33 shekels ($8.60). Nor did the group's website contain a function that blocks Israelis and other non–U.S. citizens from donating. In the United States, however, donors are required to provide their U.S. address, and the software provides no option to type in a non-American address. The Republicans in Israel don't take any address. U.S. law also requires any political action committee (PAC) to register with, and disclose its donors to, the Federal Election Commission. But the Republicans refused.

The result is massive campaign fraud. But U.S. law means little to Israelis like Brot, a foreigner who has no legal right becoming involved with U.S. elections, let alone leading a political campaign for the presidency. "To us, Israel is the 51st state from the elections standpoint," he said, echoing the belief of the Republican Party in Israel. "Israel is a very red state," according to Kory Bardash, the Republican Party co-chair in Israel. But Israel is no more part of the United States than China or Argentina. Nor do Israelis like Brot pay any U.S. taxes, so they have no right to play any role in politics or government.

Throughout the summer and into the fall of 2016, Israel massively and illegally interfered in the U.S. presidential election. A top agent of Netanyahu was secretly offering intelligence and other covert assistance to Trump to get him elected; foreign cash in untold amounts was being pumped into Republican Party coffers, while Israelis, foreigners with no connection to the United States, were heavily involved in a U.S. presidential campaign. All with virtually no oversight or scrutiny by the FBI or the U.S. media, both of which had personnel in Israel at the time. Where were the FBI arrests, the congressional investigations, or the breaking news headlines? "Israeli intervention in US elections vastly overwhelms anything the Russians may have done," said MIT professor emeritus Noam Chomsky. "I mean, even to the point where the prime minister of Israel, Netanyahu, goes directly to Congress, without even informing the president, and speaks to Congress, with overwhelming applause, to try to undermine the president's policies."

By 2020, little had changed. In August, Republicans Overseas Israel chairman Marc Zell launched another campaign for Trump, this time with the slogan "Thank you, President Trump!" And managing the campaign was another non-American, Israeli Ariel Sender, who worked with non-American Israeli Tzvika Brot in the 2016 Trump campaign. They are partners in the same Israeli lobbying firm. And along with Trump, Zell refused to accept Biden's win, blaming it, ironically, on voter fraud. "[Seventy] million Americans are sobbing tonight over the corruption of their most sacred democratic institution," he tweeted on November 7, with the hashtag #LegalVotesOnly.

One person who is likely counting on the FBI again looking the other way in the next presidential election is former vice president Mike Pence. In March 2022, he flew to Israel aboard one of the late Sheldon Adelson's Boeing 747s. Following the multibillionaire's death in January 2021, Miriam, his Israeli-born wife, inherited most of Adelson's wealth as well as much of his political power. And Pence, a far-right evangelical, was on the receiving end of that power during his trip to Israel. Among his excursions was a trip to the illegally occupied West Bank and a tour of Hebron with two of Israel's most notorious extremists, Knesset member Itamar Ben-Gvir and far-right activist Baruch Marzel.

It was a "great honor," Pence said, to meet Ben-Gvir, the ideological successor to the late Rabbi Meir Kahane, a violent racist whose Kach movement (later known as Kahane Chai) was classified as a terrorist organization in the United States; and Boston-born Marzel, a settler living in Hebron and the former leader of Kach. Marzel has been banned from both Twitter and Facebook for hate speech, and in 2019 he was banned from running for the Knesset for inciting racism against Palestinians. Matt Duss, a foreign policy advisor to Senator Bernie Sanders, tweeted that Pence's meeting would be "like a foreign leader coming to the US and hanging out with the Proud Boys." And Benzion Sanders of the Israeli human rights organization Breaking the Silence tweeted that Pence was "empowering Jewish Supremacy the same way he empowers White Supremacy."

During his visit, Pence also dined with Miriam Adelson and met with both Prime Minister Bennett and former prime minister Netanyahu.

Just as the FBI counterspies were AWOL when it came to a high-level foreign mole burrowing deep into the Trump campaign, they were also not to be found when two more foreign moles burrowed high up in the Hillary Clinton campaign.

CHAPTER 28

——— ◆ ———

The Agent

Beneath a fringe of trees on either side of Iredell Lane, a small road near the Hollywood Hills, protesters waited in anticipation in front of elaborately sculpted iron driveway gates and private tennis courts. A few doors away, set back from the road was a three-story villa protected by police with long black batons. Soon, motorcycles and squad cars flashed by in a kaleidoscope of reds and blues. And racing behind them was a conga line of boxy Chevy Suburbans, black as midnight, men with clenched jaws staring from every window.

Suddenly the crowd erupted—taunts and boos, then a shower of green as handfuls of dollar bills were angrily tossed at the cars. Moments later, Hillary Clinton arrived at George Clooney's Studio City home for a $33,400-a-person fund-raiser. "Plutocrat's Ball!" shouted a protester in his late twenties wearing a straw hat and a tan "Bernie for the Future" T-shirt. Unlike Bernie Sanders, with his grassroots donation policies, and an average campaign contribution of $27, Hillary Clinton needed a Brink's armored truck to follow her from rally to rally.

By mid-April 2016, Clinton had made ten visits to Los Angeles, which included twenty-two fund-raisers. Now she was back at her favorite ATM for more cash, this time a high-priced dinner with Clooney, where the $33,400 would get you in the door, another $5,400 would buy you a selfie with Clinton for two, and $353,400 would put you at the same table as George and Hillary. The night before, the Clinton/Clooney road show was in San Francisco for an identical cash-for-contact event.

Inside, crowded around Clooney's bar with its photos of the Rat Pack in *Ocean's Eleven*, the original and the remake staring Clooney, was Hollywood's deep-pocketed elite. Among them were DreamWorks SKG cofounders Jeffrey Katzenberg and Steven Spielberg, and billionaire media mogul Haim Saban, along with their wives. And nearby was Andy Khawaja. Sports club trim with well-developed biceps, he was the creator of a reality television show on the 4KUniverse channel called *Model Turned Superstar*. The idea was to bring together a hundred barely clad models from around the world to compete in exotic locations, such as swimming with sharks in the waters of Bora Bora, for a million-dollar prize and Hollywood stardom. Appropriately, he was married to a striking Lithuanian-born blonde-haired, blue-eyed model, Ana Stoliarova-Khawaja, who goes by Ana Kha.

But Khawaja also had another job. He was a clandestine agent working for a foreign spy. A spy who was also mingling with guests at the party. A spy whose assignment was to become a mole in the Clinton campaign. Once on the inside, he would report back to his foreign government on Clinton's plans and intentions. And after she entered the White House, he would become an agent of influence, secretly steering her to make decisions favorable to his government. To that end, he needed to get as close to Clinton as possible, for as long as possible throughout the campaign, no matter the cost. And as long as the FBI was hunting under every rock for nonexistent Russian foreign agents, a real spy would have free rein.

The spy was George Nader, a paunchy Middle Easterner with a broad, dimpled smile, a facial tic, and a shadowy career connecting discreet handshakes, passing on high-level whispers, and turning influence into a weapon. Unknown to the Clinton campaign, he was a senior advisor to Crown Prince Mohammed bin Zayed. Based in the United Arab Emirates' capital of Abu Dhabi, a city of towering skyscrapers, placid lagoons, and man-made islands, Crown Prince Mohammed became the de facto ruler of the UAE due to the ill health of his half brother, UAE president Sheikh Khalifa bin Zayed. And in 2019, the *New York Times* named him "the most powerful leader in the Arab world."

He was also the wealthiest. "He may be the richest man in the world," noted the *Times*. "He controls sovereign wealth funds worth $1.3 trillion, more than any other country." In the same way the crown prince stayed fit through rigorous exercise, he kept that power and wealth through rigorous gamesmanship. The trick was balancing superpower off superpower, region off region, and powerful leader off powerful leader. And that was where his spy Nader came in, with his ability to find the right player able to push the right button to get the crown prince the right outcome.

Born in 1959 in the ancient northern Lebanese city of Batroun, Nader moved with his family to Cleveland, Ohio, when he was fifteen. Sworn in as a U.S. citizen and eager to become a journalist, in 1980 he started his own magazine, *Middle East Insight*, at first published out of his home, and later turned it into an influential journal. That led to interviews with major players in the region, including former Palestine Liberation Organization chairman Yasser

Arafat and Ayatollah Khomeini, the former head of Iran who led the 1979 revolution. He even played a role in the shuttle diplomacy between Syria and Israel over the Golan Heights in 1998.

Nader also worked secretly with a variety of intelligence organizations over the years, including those in the United States. "George Nader did some very discreet work for us of a humanitarian nature," said James Baker, secretary of state under President George H. W. Bush, "having to do with the then-ongoing crisis over the taking of hostages, American citizens as hostage. And George worked very closely and very discreetly with us on that." Depending on which way the political winds catch a flag, sometimes a country is a friend and sometimes a target.

For Nader, it was a busy time. He was also assisting the crown prince in secret negotiations with a number of Gulf and Middle Eastern leaders on a yacht in the Red Sea. In addition to the UAE's crown prince, among those on board were the then deputy crown prince of Saudi Arabia, Mohammed bin Salman; Abdel Fattah al-Sisi, the president of Egypt; Crown Prince Salman of Bahrain; and King Abdullah of Jordan. The discussions centered on ways to create a new, more proactive and aggressive joint organization to counter the increasing power of Iran and Turkey throughout the region. What they needed was to somehow find a way to secretly influence the new U.S. president to back them and follow their advice. Nader agreed to quietly take on the mission.

His solution would take the form of secretly spending millions of dollars to buy up-close-and-personal influence with Hillary Clinton, the leading candidate for president and the likely next occupant of the White House. Money buys access, and access gets you results. Nader's problem, however, was that he could not do it himself; his name was too closely associated with the UAE and its royal family. His cash would immediately be flagged. He would need a clandestine agent, an American straw man, a wealthy political nobody willing to take a risk and secretly and illegally donate millions of UAE dollars without revealing its foreign source. In other words, millions in dirty cash.

Enter Andy Khawaja, the man at Clooney's bar sipping champagne and nibbling canapés with Hollywood's plutocracy. According to government documents, he was little more than a professional con man. His TV show, *Model Turned Superstar*, was simply a sideline. His fortune actually came from his company, Allied Wallet. Little known, it functioned as a sort of credit card processor for fraudsters, swindlers, and rip-off artists bilking the public out of more than $100 million. It was the go-to company for Ponzi and pyramid scheme operators, phony debt collectors, coaching and education scams, and other fraudulent activities.

Khawaja and Nader had first met months earlier, in the fall of 2015, when Khawaja decided to visit the UAE. Like Nader, a Lebanese American and fluent in Arabic, he requested an audience with Crown Prince Mohammed and at one point was introduced to Nader. Soon the two began discussing a joint business venture, but the topic quickly turned to the election and the offer to become Nader's secret agent. Until 2015, Khawaja had never made a political contribution to anyone. But in November of that year he witnessed what money can buy. For a donation of $2,700 he received an invitation to the home of Hollywood film director Rob Reiner, where he had his picture taken with a smiling, toothy Hillary Clinton, and got to mingle with stars such as actor Ted Danson. And for $27,000 he could have attended an even more exclusive reception.

Now with Nader's bags of cash and secret help, Khawaja was about to be transformed from a political nobody hustling credit card companies to someone who shared champagne toasts and inside gossip with a former president and the likely next president in the living room of his own home—with Nader, as always, by his side. Thus, beginning in March 2016, Nader began secretly pumping millions of illegal dollars into Clinton's insatiable campaign coffers through his obscure American agent, Andy Khawaja.

In no time, Khawaja became one of Hillary Clinton's heaviest donors. On April 7, he paid $33,400 for his ticket to George Clooney's dinner for Clinton. Then, just four days later, he tossed in another $150,000 to the Hillary Victory Fund, assuring an extra-warm welcome at Clooney's home for both him and his spy, George Nader. The next day, Nader reported back to his spymaster—likely the crown prince—in the UAE's capital of Abu Dhabi. "Wonderful meeting with the Big Lady," he wrote. "Can't wait to tell you all about it." Continuing to burrow his way into Clinton's inner circle of donors, in March and April alone Nader, through his agent Khawaja, contributed a total of $275,000.

By May, with more hidden cash flowing, more doors were opening, more favors were arriving, and more intelligence and influence were accruing for Nader's foreign masters. "Had a magnificent session with Big Lady's key people," he boasted. "You will be most amazed by my progress on that side!" Often commuting back and forth between his villa in Abu Dhabi, his chalet in Lebanon, and Clinton events in the United States with Khawaja, on June 2 Nader wrote his spymaster that he was "leaving very early morning to catch up with big Lady over the weekend...Can I come over for 10 minutes...to get your blessings and instruction before I leave please?"

The Big Lady was scheduled to appear at a star-clogged fund-raising concert in Griffith Park on June 6, with ticket prices topping out at $50,000.

Among those taking to the stage in the park's Greek Theatre were Cher, John
Legend, Stevie Wonder, Ricky Martin, Eva Longoria, Jamie Foxx, and Christina Aguilera. Also appearing was Congressman Adam Schiff of the House
Intelligence Committee, who would lead the charge accusing the Trump
campaign of being a patsy for Russian spies and influence peddlers. While
he never uncovered any dirty Russian money going to the Trump campaign,
Schiff's own campaign received more than $8,000 in dirty cash from the
UAE's foreign agent. And with a donation of another $250,000 to Hillary's
campaign and committee, Nader and his agent were guaranteed some quality time at the concert for quality influence with Clinton. The following day,
armed with a new load of intelligence to share, Nader secretly texted his spymaster in Abu Dhabi: "Had a terrific meeting with my Big Sister H You will
be most delighted!"

Now fully burrowed in, the mole and his agent began making arrangements to throw their own fund-raisers for both Hillary and her husband,
former president Bill Clinton, in the agent's home. It was a major move. In
spite of the very suspicious backgrounds of the two, the Clinton campaign
nevertheless agreed—provided they could cough up a million bucks. In a
secret message back to the UAE, Nader referred to the event as a "birthday
party" and Clinton as "my sister." "The birthday party has been set up. &
party have been arranged for my sister and it's going to be huge for her. She
is very excited and happy. All arranged buddy:) as you will see I'm a man of
my word."

Up until now, Khawaja had been fronting all of the money on his own,
including the million dollars for the Bill and Hillary Clinton fund-raiser in
his home, on Nader's promise that it would be fully repaid by his bosses in
Abu Dhabi. In fact, the money Khawaja was passing out was already dirty,
having been ripped off from the innocent victims of his fraud-racked company. But with the fund-raiser scheduled for June 26, Khawaja was beginning
to get nervous and agitated since the check had not yet arrived. As a result,
on June 13, with Bill Clinton due to show up at his door on the twenty-sixth
and Hillary due in a separate fund-raiser two days later, Khawaja sent a secret
message to Nader telling him the "package" had not yet arrived.

"I told them about the upcoming deadline and events and they assure me
that it will be over there in coming days! It will be over there in time for the
26th event! That is all!" Nader wrote back.

"Just make sure you guys don't look bad buddy," Khawaja replied. "I did
[my] part and more. It's all up in your hands now."

"Good!" said Nader. "I am sure you can take care of it till the package
arrive! No way I can press them anymore! You have to understand that will

backfire if I push anymore! It will be there! I have seeing the approval of the first package! I am not worry about it at all I hope you deliver as promised!"

Secrecy was critical. To hide the payments, they discussed using a false invoice, making it look as though it was a legitimate commercial transaction. As a result, on June 15, one of Khawaja's employees sent Nader an email. Attached was a phony invoice from Khawaja's company for 10 million euros for a supposed license of Allied Wallet's software for one of Nader's companies.

But with just a few days to go, there was still nothing and Khawaja complained again. "The issue has been taken care of and is in order! Nothing more can be done about it!" an agitated Nader responded. On Friday, June 24, Nader notified his spymaster, "traveling on Sat morning to catch up with our Big Sister and her husband: I am seeing him on Sunday and her in Tuesday Sir! Would love to see you tomorrow at your convenience…for your guidance, instruction and blessing!"

That Sunday, accompanied by several black SUVs loaded with Secret Service agents, former president Bill Clinton arrived at Khawaja's home, a $15 million Italian-style villa named Grande Belleza (Big Beauty) at 3100 Benedict Canyon Drive in Beverly Hills. With 11,500 square feet of living space, a 1,700-square-foot master bedroom, a dozen indoor and outdoor fireplaces, an infinity pool, water fountains, movie theater, waterfall, wine bar and wine cellar, steam and sauna rooms, an elevator, six bedrooms, and eleven baths, it was certainly up to Clinton fund-raiser standards. It was also all paid for with Khawaja's dirty money.

"Meeting with Bill Clinton was superb!" Nader told his spymaster. Two days later, Hillary Clinton's own entourage of Secret Service SUVs pulled through the gates of Grande Belleza and parked in the large circular motor court. "Meeting with Big Lady went extremely well," noted the mole. But despite the success, Khawaja was still being stiffed by Nader's boss, the crown prince. At one point, Nader wrote to Khawaja, "I have also discussed the company issue [the phony receipt] and will send you a note on the matter as per HH instruction!" HH stood for His Highness, Crown Prince Mohammed.

Nevertheless, having Bill and Hillary Clinton over for cocktail parties in his home, dining with movie stars, and driving around Hollywood in his Ferrari with a mysterious spy seated next to him—as if he was George Smiley or James Bond—was a con man's dream, giving Khawaja enormous credibility with future victims. With no intention of stopping, on July 14 he wrote a check for $550,000 for box seats at the Democratic National Convention in Philadelphia, scheduled for the end of July, and, ever the good agent, invited his spy.

Nader wanted to attend, but his spymaster in Abu Dhabi thought it unwise—there were too many chances of blowing his cover—so he declined. "I have a dilemma," he wrote to an associate in Abu Dhabi; "invited to attend the [Democratic] convention next week with Andy as a VIP guest where I meet all the major principles! On 29/30 July invited to a very small dinner with the Lady: just 5 people altogether!" But, he noted, his spymaster is "cautious and not terribly excited about the big event. He thinks I am better off with the smaller private one but the convention you are too exposed!"

As a result, the intimate high-priced meetings with Hillary Clinton would continue. Among them was a brunch at his agent's house with Hillary, but this time limited to just Khawaja and his wife, Nader, and one other person. It would provide some quality time to impart some quality influence and learn some quality intelligence for his spymasters.

Finally, the same day Khawaja bought his convention tickets, he received his "baklava"—code for cash—from Nader. "Fresh hand made Baklava on the way designed especially for that private event at your house later this month! First tray on the way!" wrote Nader. "You have got to lose some weight for the upcoming tray of Baklava next week. Once you taste it and you like the choices more on the way soon." The "baklava" consisted of 2.5 million euros, about $3 million.

On August 22, the private, intimate brunch in Khawaja's home scheduled for that day had fallen through. Clinton had become greedier and Khawaja hadn't come up with enough cash. She thought her presence was now worth five times more than he was offering. "Too small of birthday gift and the time is worth 5 times more they say," Khawaja wrote to Nader, using "birthday gift" as code for donation. Instead, Khawaja paid to cohost a larger event that same day, with his fellow mole as always by his side. "I just had dinner with my Big Sister and had a very very productive discussion with her," wrote Nader to his spymasters.

Throughout the remainder of the summer and fall, the lunches, dinners, and cocktails with Clinton would continue, the freshly made baklava would keep flowing, the spying would never stop, and the secret influence would go on being peddled. In Las Vegas, Clinton's managers told Khawaja he would have to cough up another million bucks if he wanted to have another dinner party for Hillary, which he did. And as usual, Nader wrote back to his spymaster about his success. "Had a simply Terrific Magnificent brainstorming and discussion with the Big Lady This evening!" he declared. Later he wrote to Khawaja, "I am leaving early morning back to join HH [His Highness Crown Prince Mohammed]. Have already told him about the Wonderful Event with Our Sister and he was thrilled and want to know all about it in person."

For months, Nader had been spying on Hillary Clinton with the help of his agent, Khawaja. He would meet with her and her inner circle, pick up inside details of her plans and future policies, push his influence agenda, then fly back to Abu Dhabi and brief the crown prince, before returning for another expensive dinner with the candidate. But much of what he was learning greatly troubled the prince. Based on Nader's intelligence, Clinton appeared to be fully prepared to continue normalizing relations with Iran, the longtime rival and nemesis of the UAE, Saudi Arabia, and Israel. That included support of the nuclear agreement, which the prince believed was very flawed and dangerous.

Based on Nader's intelligence reports, there were also worries over Clinton's future support for the UAE and Saudi Arabia's joint military actions in Yemen. Largely with U.S.-supplied arms, the two countries had invaded Yemen in March 2015 to expel militants aligned with Iran. But the war had dragged on, creating a humanitarian disaster in the process, and many vocal critics. By the Obama administration arming the UAE with advanced weaponry, noted former State Department official Tamara Cofman, "We have created a little Frankenstein." As a result, Clinton's support seemed to be wavering. Trump, on the other hand, appeared to be willing to continue pouring weapons into the UAE while adopting a largely hands-off policy on the war. Therefore, with his belligerent tough guy talk about Iran, Trump was far more appealing to the crown prince than Clinton. It was time for his mole to begin burrowing into the Trump camp as well.

Ever the Machiavellian, George Nader began secretly playing both sides against the middle. Hedging his bets in case the unexpected happened and Clinton lost, he began making quiet overtures to Team Trump. On July 19, the day Trump was formally nominated at the Republican convention in Cleveland, Nader sent a message to his spymaster in Abu Dhabi saying he was "developing a steady, consistent and constructive relationship with both camps!" He then began dividing his time between Clinton's salmon-and-Sancerre dinners and Trump's barbecue-and-beer rallies.

In November, both Khawaja and Nader attended Clinton's election night party in Manhattan. Upon hearing of Trump's win, Nader must have used every facial muscle to secretly repress a broad grin while feigning severe disappointment after spending millions of dollars to get Clinton elected. As if at a roulette table, all along he had been secretly betting on both black and red, Clinton and Trump, in order to become a White House mole no matter who won. And in the end, he wanted the ball to land on red. It was time to put all his efforts on developing sources in the Trump camp.

Within days of the election, Khawaja donated a million dollars to the

Trump inaugural committee. In return, he received two tickets to the inauguration, one for him and one for Nader. Later, Khawaja even had his picture taken in the Oval Office, standing next to Trump behind his presidential desk. And now in a super-sleazy political pay-to-play move, no doubt as a payoff for Khawaja's millions in donations in dirty money to the Clinton campaign and the Democratic Party, Senate Democratic leader Charles Schumer had a gift for Khawaja. He appointed him to the U.S. Commission on International Religious Freedom, an independent, bipartisan federal body, despite Khawaja's long history of fraud and a client list of porn operators and scam artists.

George Nader's double life began to implode on January 17, 2018, as he stepped off an Emirates Airways jet at Washington's Dulles International Airport. He was traveling from Dubai and was on his way to attend a gala dinner at Mar-a-Lago to celebrate the one-year anniversary of Trump's inauguration. By then, however, the Mueller probe was fully under way and Nader's name had surfaced. As a result, FBI agents questioned him upon arrival. They also seized his three cell phones to check for text messages and emails.

But all they were interested in was Russia, and nothing pointed to any connection with Moscow. They ignored, however, any intelligence connection between the Clinton and Trump campaigns and the UAE government.

By accident, however, they discovered that the phones did contain a dozen sexually explicit videos featuring boys as young as two, including one showing baby goats performing fellatio on a three- or four-year-old boy. Another shows a boy thirteen or fourteen years old penetrating a goat from behind. "The goat reacts and makes noise each time the boy thrusts," said the FBI's complaint. Knowing he was in deep trouble, Nader asked for a limited grant of immunity to tell what he knew about the 2016 election. Granted the immunity, he went into detail before a secret grand jury about his activities. He was then allowed to leave.

It was only then that the FBI finally began discovering what it and the Secret Service should have noticed at the start of the campaign. It is inexplicable that the foreign influence operation was allowed to take place for so long under the noses of both organizations. A simple background check would have turned up the fact that Nader was not only working for a foreign leader but was also a convicted felon and serial pedophile. In 1991 he pled guilty to transporting videotapes, hidden in candy tins, containing child pornography. The check would also have uncovered a May 2003 conviction in the Czech Republic for "sexual abuse and impairing morals" after he abused ten underage boys. Among the cases was one where Nader had requested oral sex from a fourteen-year-old in a room at Prague's Hilton Hotel. Following the boy's refusal, Nader masturbated in front of him and paid the boy the equivalent of $100. He was sentenced to a year in prison, after which he was deported.

And according to U.S. prosecutors, in both 1997 and 2002, Nader brought fourteen-year-old boys into the country. Interviewed by the FBI back then, one boy told the agents he had viewed child pornography with Nader, and the other said he was sexually abused by him. Even earlier, Nader repeatedly had come under scrutiny by law enforcement agencies for similar behavior. In 1985, a federal grand jury in Washington, DC, indicted him on two counts of mailing and importing child pornography. But the charges were dismissed because the government had illegally seized evidence in the case. It was during that period, as he was awaiting trial, that Nader became a U.S. citizen. In addition, twice during 1988, Nader received in the mail sexually explicit material featuring underage boys. Although he was not charged, his home was searched and child pornography was found in his toilet.

Following the investigation, in April 2018 charges finally were brought against Nader. But because by then he was safely out of the country the indictment was placed under seal and kept secret. Unaware of the pending charges, Nader landed at John F. Kennedy International Airport on June 3, 2019, and was arrested and charged with transporting sexually explicit videos. They had been shared with "multiple people," according to a prosecutor, who added that Nader had "hands-on contact with more than a dozen minor boys." On January 13, 2020, Nader pled guilty to bringing a fourteen-year-old boy to the United States for sex and to possessing child pornography. Although the charges carry a maximum penalty of thirty years, prosecutors instead agreed to recommend the mandatory minimum of ten years.

Finally, on November 7, 2019, a secret fifty-three-count indictment was unsealed. Nearly four years after they began their covert influence operation, Nader, Khawaja, and others in his company were charged with conspiring to conceal more than $3.5 million in political donations to Hillary Clinton. By then, Nader was already in custody and later pled guilty. But the FBI, in one final blunder, had managed to allow Khawaja to flee to the Lithuanian capital of Vilnius five months earlier. He was accompanied by his Lithuanian-born model-turned-superstar wife, along with hundreds of millions of dollars in dirty money from his crooked credit card processing company, Allied Wallet.

Although, on behalf of the U.S. Justice Department, Lithuanian authorities arrested Khawaja, he was released on bail after several months, and there is little prospect of his extradition. According to a local newspaper report on the "U.S. billionaire," "The amount paid to the Prosecutor's Office's account is not disclosed. But according to sources, it is the largest in the history of

Lithuania—about one million euros." Then on August 26, 2021, the U.S. Justice Department charged Khawaja in a $150 million payment processing scheme involving Allied Wallet. But as noted in the Justice Department press release, "Khawaja is a fugitive." A very wealthy fugitive with no plans to show up in court. "The Republic of Lithuania is his and his family's permanent residence," his lawyer wrote.

————

There remains, however, the question as to whether Clinton herself should have at least been investigated for possible violation of campaign finance laws. As a former secretary of state, she should have been aware of the odd behaviors of Nader and Khawaja, the constant pumping of millions of dollars into her campaign for face time and questions about the Middle East, and her campaign's demands for more and more millions for more and more dinners and more and more face time. And why over eight months did she never bother checking out the odd pair, one donating millions while nibbling pretzels at the bar, with the other obviously interested in influence?

By election day 2016, Clinton had raised an eye-popping $1.14 billion to Trump's $712 million, with unknown amounts of illegal foreign cash pouring into both campaigns since the FBI wasn't watching. Nor were they watching as moles burrowed deep into both presidential campaigns, thus illegally interfering in the U.S. democratic process. These were critical failures. Even worse, deep in the bureau's own ranks was another mole, one fingering clandestine American spies to Chinese intelligence. Many of whom would be killed.

BOOK SEVEN

THE LIQUIDATORS

◆

CHAPTER 29

The Crash

Cranberry, Pennsylvania, not far from Pittsburgh, was an unlikely meeting ground for spies, especially invisible ones. It is the kind of town where the opening of the Milk Shake Factory made the local TV news. But sitting on a nearby hilltop, like a flying wing too heavy to get off the ground, was a quarter-billion-dollar structure of steel, concrete, and tempered glass in the shape of a wide V. It was Westinghouse Electric's nuclear power engineering headquarters, and filling nearby homes were the company's four thousand engineers and other technical employees. As a world leader in nuclear power plant construction, Westinghouse Electric was also a prime target for foreign spies.

For nearly two years, from 2014 to 2016, the GRU's Ivan Yermakov had been roaming stealthily through the company's computer system from his desk in Moscow's Khamovnichesky Barracks, spying on the company's dealings with Ukraine. But as he was planting malware and taking up residence in the computer hard drives, he might have virtually bumped into another intruder. Also skulking around inside the company's server room and mainframes at the same time was Yermakov's Chinese counterpart, Sun Kailiang, a stiff-backed military officer with an athletic physique and a cautious smile.

Sun Kailiang worked for the Network Support Department (NSD), part of the People's Liberation Army and China's equivalent of the GRU. His organization, Unit 61398, like the GRU's Unit 26165, targeted the United States and was made up largely of cryptomathematicians, cryptologists, and computer scientists. Other members included Wang Dong, a chubby-faced veteran operator with rimless glassed whose moniker was "UglyGorilla," and Gu Chunhui, otherwise known as "KandyGoo," whose neatly parted black hair and high cheekbones lent him a studious appearance.

Unlike Yermakov, breaking into Westinghouse from the courtyard of a Napoleon-era barracks, Sun conducted his break-ins from a white, modern twelve-story tower in Shanghai. It's part of a complex of well-protected buildings in the Pudong District, an architectural playground of spiraling glass and concrete skyscrapers of endless geometric designs, as if from an old children's coloring book of the world of tomorrow.

But as a sign in front of a pale ten-foot concrete wall makes clear, Unit 61398 is definitely off the tourist map. "Restricted Military Zone," it says near a uniformed guard in an archway behind a steel gate. "No Photography Permitted." Above tall narrow windows with curtains drawn tight is a five-pointed red star containing the Chinese characters for August 1, the sign of the People's Liberation Army (PLA). Nearby is Liu's Mutton Soup Restaurant, where a bowl of lamb stew goes for 8 yuan. Externally, the only thing the building has in common with the home of the GRU spies is a rooftop loaded with parabolic satellite dishes, hidden behind a high wall, to receive the stolen data from Westinghouse and a thousand other targets.

Ironically, China's codebreakers and their counterparts in the NSA are descendants of the same father: Herbert Osborn Yardley. A U.S. Army cryptanalyst during World War I, in 1920 he created America's first civilian eavesdropping and codebreaking agency, the Black Chamber, the NSA's earliest predecessor. Then in 1938 the Chinese government secretly hired Yardley to create their own Black Chamber. At the time, the nationalist Chinese Kuomintang led by Chiang Kai-shek and the Chinese Communists headed by Mao Zedong had put aside their civil war and joined forces to fight the invading Japanese. After a few years Yardley, ill and homesick, returned to Washington, but his nascent Chinese Black Chamber would continue to evolve into a codebreaking dynasty, one largely targeted against the descendant of his American Black Chamber.

Although fellow ghosts inside Westinghouse, Yermakov and Sun were after different secrets, like shoppers in the same clothing store, one looking for shoes, the other for hats. Where Yermakov was interested in documents dealing with the transfer of nuclear fuel to Ukraine, Sun was after critical nuclear power plant design information, data that may help China one day be an active competitor of Westinghouse in the field. Eventually, Sun and his colleagues would load their shopping baskets with more than 1.4 gigabytes of data, about 700,000 pages of email and attachments, while Yermakov filled his with gigabytes of emails detailing secret discussions about fuel supplies and plans for Westinghouse to replace the aging Russian reactors in Ukraine with their own.

Early every morning hundreds of Unit 61398's cyber workers stand on platforms and board Shanghai's Metro Line 6, fast modern cars that are painted white with a wide magenta strip and plastic magenta seats. The train heads north, twisting and turning as it parallels the winding curves of the

Huangpu River, and the workers exit at the last stop, Gangcheng Road Station. Nearby is Gaoqiao, an old city from the Southern Song Dynasty with a narrow, stone-paved main street and ancient buildings displaying intricate wooden façades and weathered, unpainted shutters.

But it was not eleventh-century architecture that led to the site selection for Unit 61398; it was instead twenty-first-century geography. Just a dozen miles east, across a narrow channel, sits Chongming Island at the mouth of the Yangtze River, where it meets the East China Sea. Although a spit of land little known to most, the island serves as a sort of meeting place for much of the world. Packed tightly in dense fiber optic cables that transit the island for a millisecond are the voices, documents, and messages of millions of people, businesses, and governments around the globe.

The internet's metaphoric "clouds" are actually cables wrapped in thick layers of copper, aluminum, and polyethylene that sit safely among the bottom dwellers on the seabed. But like seals that become vulnerable to polar bears when they come up for air, the cables lose their protection when they crawl out of the sea onto land, as they do on Chongming Island. Emerging from the black silt of the broad Chongming shoal are eight international optical cables able to support the two-way conversations of twenty million people around the world simultaneously, while speeding their emails and other data along at 5.12 terabytes per second.

Among the cables are SEA-ME-WE3, or South-East Asia–Middle East–Western Europe 3, the longest wire in the world, stretching twenty-four thousand miles and linking nearly thirty-five countries on four continents, from the United Kingdom and much of Europe to the Middle East, Africa, Australia, and Asia. Other cables that interconnect on Chongming Island include the Trans-Pacific Express and New Cross Pacific, both of which carry American communications across the Pacific.

Once on Chongming Island, the cables remain buried underground for four miles before finally surfacing at a small, isolated landing station in a wetlands area near the Dongtan Bird Reserve. Surrounded by tall pampas grass with feathery, silver-gray tussocks that sway in the breeze, it is where phone calls and data destined for China are routinely and automatically extracted and enter the nation's networks. The rest continue to speed toward their international destinations as the cable returns to the ocean's depths. But before that happens, Sun and his colleagues secretly get access to the contents of the worldwide cables.

To accomplish this, the unit maintains a secret facility on Chongming Island across a narrow dirt road from the cable landing station. Housed in a large walled compound, it is made up of a collection of modern four- and five-story off-white buildings along with a round airport-style control tower, on top of which sits a large parabolic dish antenna. As if to confirm ownership of the compound, a sign is posted nearby warning against digging because cables belonging to the national defense are buried below. At the bottom of the sign, in bright red letters, are the words "Military Unit 61398."

Inside the compound's buildings, the data transiting the cables pass through computers containing superfast deep-packet inspection software searching for key words, such as "Westinghouse," and other indicators of intelligence value. That information is then forwarded a dozen miles away to Unit 61398 headquarters as well other locations where thousands of analysts like Sun, "UglyGorilla," and "KandyGoo" analyze it and report it up to headquarters.

In addition to the enormous amount of worldwide data received from the cables crossing Chongming Island, on the other side of Shanghai, in Nanhui, a rapidly developing new area on Hangzhou Bay, still more international optical cables enter the country. Among them is Fiber Optic Link Around the Globe (FLAG), a seventeen-thousand-mile cable that connects all of the United States via New York City to Europe, Africa, the Middle East, and most of Asia. And close to the landing station, about half a mile up an inlet from Luchao Port, is another large Unit 61398 monitoring station with a tower similar to the one on Chongming Island.

At the same time that members of the unit are rifling through the world's undersea cable systems at Nanhui and Chongming Island, others in Shanghai are draining international communications satellites of phone calls and data. A dozen miles to the northwest of the unit's high-rise is the Baoshan section of the city, a port and industrial area where a forest of cranes stack colorful steel containers like children's blocks. Nearby, inside a high-walled compound, more than a dozen egg-white parabolic dishes rise from the ground like toadstools after a heavy rain. Pointing at different azimuths, they target key international communications satellites high over the Pacific.

The problem, however, was that as China was tapping into communications links to spy on the United States, the United States was also tapping into communications links to spy on China. This often required a combination of human and technical capabilities, which meant the NSA and CIA working jointly on projects. Among them was TAREX, the Target Exploitation Program, which was based at the U.S. embassy in Beijing and involved what was known as "close-access operations." They included clandestine activities such as bribing Chinese telecom or government employees to physically place malware in a computer system.

"Over 70 percent of all the signals intelligence that's produced in China is human enabled," a former senior CIA official told me. "We'll send officers in and they'll go, 'Hey, Wei, you work at the Ministry of Post and Telecommunications, right? You make $3,000 a year—how would you like to make $30,000 for a day? Take this Nortel switch and swap it out for the one that's in there now.' And that puts the device in the system so NSA can then collect from it. So we enable NSA, but they don't like us [CIA] to publicize it."

In the cat-and-mouse game of cyber espionage, sometimes China's cyber spies win and NSA's cyber defenders lose. In 2015 it was discovered that China's cyber force had broken into the Office of Personnel Management and stolen over twenty-one million sensitive records. The data contained private details about government employees and civilians, including their Social Security numbers and other personal information. It was among the largest breaches of government data in the country's history.

But in the summer of 2016, in secret meetings throughout Washington, the U.S. intelligence community was trying to come to grips with an even more serious loss—that of human lives. Somehow China was able to discover the identity of many of the CIA's local agents and execute or imprison them. Entire clandestine networks were suddenly jeopardized in the worst penetration in the agency's history, and no one had a clue. Only years later would the full picture of the blunders by the FBI, CIA, and NSA begin to come into focus. A massive combination of technical and human failures that China was able to capitalize on resulted in what was likely the largest loss of critical intelligence in U.S. history.

————

Sunrise was still a half hour away and the temperature was just at the freezing mark when the lineman removed the blocks from the worn tires of the EP-3E ARIES II, a gray-and-white four-engine propjet with a donut-shaped "Big Look" radar attached to its lower belly. It was Sunday, April 1, 2001. "Kilo Romeo 919," said a voice in the tower, "clear to taxi." Moments later the pilot, Navy lieutenant Shane Osborn, released the parking brake and eased the four power levers forward, his knuckles white. As the engines coughed blue-black exhaust fumes like a heavy smoker, the aircraft crawled slowly toward the runway on Okinawa's Kadena Air Base.

One of eleven left in the fleet, the tired 1960s-era spy plane bristled with porcupine-like antennas. It would be a risky mission. Assigned to the NSA's Sensitive Reconnaissance Operations Program (SRO), the crew was scheduled to once again fly along the Chinese coast to update lists of signals, pick up a few conversations, and see if some ships or subs had moved from point A to point B or point C.

It was intelligence overkill. In addition to its vast number of cyber spies at

Fort Meade focused on China, the NSA also had the world's largest and most expensive fleet of spy satellites orbiting over the country every ninety minutes, as well as half a dozen expansive and costly listening posts stretching from northern Japan to South Korea to Okinawa. There, hundreds of agency operators sat with their ears constantly tuned to Chinese frequencies and their eyes scanning Chinese intercepts 24/7. And then just two miles from Kadena was the NSA's Hanza Remote Collection Facility, a massive electronic ear facing China, and scores of additional intercept operators. But within the intelligence bureaucracy, more spies mean more power for those in charge, whether they are needed or not. Hence the daily EP-3E patrols.

At 4:47 a.m., the word came from the tower. "Wind 010 at eight [knots]. Cleared for takeoff." Osborn, a native Nebraskan with a dark receding hairline and heavy caterpillar brows, moved the power levers forward again and placed his feet on the rudder pedals. Loaded with twenty-nine tons of jet fuel, the plane lumbered forward. Then as the airspeed indicators hit 133 knots, Osborn pulled back on the yoke and the aircraft's nose wheel lifted gently from Runway 4 Left.

In addition to Osborn, there were five other members of the flight crew, including two more pilots; the three would take turns resting and flying. Behind them, in the near-windowless tubelike fuselage, eighteen analysts, eavesdroppers, and linguists hunched over racks of gray machines with blinking scopes and black dials that lined the long bulkhead on either side of the cabin. The mission was to monitor China's signals environment, especially their South Sea Fleet's tactical communications, radars, and weapon systems.

Just aft of the door on the left side of the fuselage sat the Science and Technology (S&T) operator. His assignment that day was to collect and process signals associated with China's SA-10 surface-to-air missiles. According to top secret documents, this was done with one of the most highly classified computers on the plane, the SCARAB. Tall and boxy with a handle on top, it contained a unique processor code-named LUNCHBOX that was able to search and identify forty different worldwide weapons-related signals, code-named PROFORMA.

A few seats away, another operator studied the screen of a black Tadpole Ultrabook IIi laptop. On it were some of the NSA's most highly secret programs, including the RASIN (short for Radio Signals Notation) manual, the agency's bible. Listed inside were critical details about every signal in the world that NSA was intercepting. The laptop also contained MARTES, an ultrasensitive codebreaking program that deciphered enciphered Chinese voice communications.

Shortly after takeoff, Osborn left the cockpit and entered the ops area. "It looks like good weather en route to the track orbit and back to Kadena," he told the crew. "Mission time is just over nine hours today." Back on the flight deck, he proceeded southwest, flying at 21,500 feet between Taiwan and the Philippines before following China's coastline on his SRO track past Hong Kong. A short time later he began approaching China's Hainan Island, home to the military's Lingshui Airfield, remaining about sixty miles off the coast.

For almost a year, tensions over the U.S. spy flights, about two hundred a year, had been building on the island, as well as in Beijing. In May 2000, Chinese military officers aired their complaints during a conference with their American counterparts in Honolulu. The annual meetings were established to discuss ways to avoid accidents at sea and in the air, and at the May meeting the Chinese officials made it very clear that the flights had become a growing problem. It was "the most important topic" at the meeting, one Chinese officer told the *Washington Post* at the time. The flights were approaching "too close to the coast, and it might cause trouble," he said, adding, "The atmosphere wasn't good." But the Americans paid little attention.

It was an arrogant and belligerent stance for the United States to take since no American president would ever tolerate near-daily spy flights fifty miles off America's coasts by China, Russia, or any other country. Such flights are often viewed as a preparation for war. But rather than reduce the provocative flights, the NSA instead increased them from about two hundred a year to five days a week, even on Christmas Day. It was therefore less about collecting intelligence and more about flaunting power and flexing muscles.

In response, on about every third mission Chinese fighters would conduct inspection flights, pulling up close and parallel with the American pilots and sometimes gesturing from the cockpit. The United States did basically the same thing on the very infrequent occasions that Russian aircraft flew near the U.S. mainland. As the NSA's spy flights close to China increased, the Chinese fighter pilots became more aggressive, and the situation was becoming more and more dangerous.

Nearly a half century earlier, in 1956, another Navy reconnaissance aircraft was flying off China's coast when it suddenly had a confrontation with Chinese fighters. As a result, the plane crashed into the sea, killing all sixteen crew members on board. The incident shocked President Dwight Eisenhower. "We seem to be conducting something that we cannot control very well," he told Admiral Arthur M. Radford, then chairman of the Joint Chiefs of Staff, in a secret meeting. "If planes were flying 20 to 50 miles from our shores," Eisenhower continued, "we would be very likely to shoot them down if they came in closer, whether through error or not." Close-in airborne eavesdropping was dangerous business.

As Osborn continued his mission off Hainan Island, the plane was on autopilot as it cruised over the South China Sea at 22,500 feet and about 180 knots. Outside the weather was clear, with seven-mile visibility and a broken cloud layer below at 15,000 feet. And in the operational spaces, the eavesdropping activity was light, with the interception of an occasional early warning radar and routine military communications. It was, after all, a Sunday, raising even more questions about the reasons for the costly and hazardous mission.

But the morning quiet would soon be shattered. On Hainan Island at 8:48 a.m., technicians manning the regional air defense network spotted the aircraft and flashed the details to Lingshui Airfield, which sounded an alarm. Standing by in ready status in their dark blue aviator's uniforms, fighter pilots Wang Wei and Zhao Yu raced for their aircraft, single-seat J-8II Finback interceptors armed with Israeli Python air-to-air missiles. At Mach 2.2 and with a ceiling of almost 60,000 feet, they flew fast and high with improved avionics supplied by the United States in the late 1980s.

With the increase in spy flights came an increase in aggressive inspections. Since December there had been forty-four interceptions, with six coming within thirty feet, and two within ten feet. Wang Wei, a thirty-three-year-old PLAN (People's Liberation Army Navy) lieutenant commander from the silk city of Huzhou near Shanghai, had eleven hundred hours of flight time under his belt. He was also a veteran of another EP-3E inspection the previous January.

As the alarm sounded at Lingshui Airfield, followed by the scramble for the jets, Chinese linguists in the EP-3E's ops spaces immediately picked up the activity. Through their earphones they could hear the ground controller, the pilot communication checks, the fighter pre-flight activities, and a takeoff sequence. Across the Pacific, in a World War II–era bombproof bunker beneath a pineapple field in Hawaii, NSA linguists and intercept operators were also listening intently to the activity at Lingshui. Part of an alert system for spy planes, code-named KNICKELBACK, analysts quickly sent out a warning to the reconnaissance plane. The expansive bunker, known as the Kunia Regional Sigint Operations Center, was the NSA's major Pacific listening post.

At 8:51 the EP-3E acknowledged the warning via secure satellite communications, and four minutes later Osborn spotted the jets approaching about a half mile out and climbing rapidly to his altitude. At the time, he was about seventy miles from Hainan Island, and with the mission coming to an end, he was preparing to return to Okinawa. Within minutes, however, the fighters had reached the lumbering spy plane, and while Zhao Yu hung back about a half mile, Wang Wei rapidly closed in. "Hey, he's right off our wing," someone from the back end reported to Osborn. "He's tight, that's the closest I've seen!"

In the ops spaces, Marcia Sonon was in an awkward crouched position. Searching for the Chinese fighters, she was looking out a small round window on the left side over the wing. A Navy lieutenant with bright red hair, she was the plane's COMEVAL, the communications intelligence (COMINT) evaluator. Reporting to her were the six COMINT operators on the right side of the aircraft. They focused on intercepting Chinese voice communications and the PROFORMA weapons-related signals. "He's closing to three o'clock," she told Osborn. "He's definitely armed. I can see missiles on his wing. He's got his oxygen mask on." A moment later her calm tone turned tense and stressed. "He's getting really close! Fifty feet. Now he's about forty feet," she said, her voice rising. "Oh my God, he's coming closer! Right now he's about ten feet off our wing." Wang Wei rendered a salute, but Sonon couldn't make out what he meant. In the cockpit, Osborne looked right in his face. "This isn't good," he said. Then Wang Wei fell back about a hundred feet off the left wing.

A minute later, Wang Wei had returned, this time closing to just five feet before making another gesture and dropping back again. Then a third approach, but this time he had difficulty slowing his fast interceptor to match the propjet's slow speed and suddenly he was directly below the EP-3E's left wing. In severe trouble, he immediately radioed the base, telling them he was unable to maneuver and being sucked in by the spy plane. Seconds later, his jet impacted the plane's left outboard propeller just forward of the J-8II's vertical stabilizer, tearing the tail off the Chinese aircraft and sending its nose crashing into the front of the EP-3E, which was then still on autopilot.

Instantly Osborn felt the bang as a cloud of glittering debris exploded in front of the left wing and he heard what sounded like a monster chainsaw hacking through metal. Then, a fraction of a second later, as the jet hit the front of his plane, the EP-3E's fiberglass nosecone flew over the windscreen and metal fragments punctured the fuselage like machine-gun fire. Immediately there was an explosive decompression as screams filled the cockpit and the cabin. "I was pretty certain we were dead at that point," said Osborn. "We were upside down in a large reconnaissance aircraft. I had lost my nose. I could hear the wind screaming through the plane, and I knew that number one prop was violently shaking. We were pretty much inverted. I was looking up at the ocean, so it was not a good feeling...I thought twenty-four people were going to die in the middle of the ocean, and I wondered if anyone would know why."

At that same moment, twenty-six-year-old Navy lieutenant junior grade John Comerford felt a shock wave rip down his spine. "I was scared," he later said. Tall, with a thick patch of carrot-colored hair, the 1997 Annapolis grad had been nicknamed by Osborn "Johnny Ballgame" because the two would have a good time on the weekends together. As the senior evaluator (SEVAL), he had overall responsibility for the reconnaissance personnel. "Honestly, based on how things felt—I didn't have a whole lot of visual reference—but based on how things felt, and the shaking of the plane, yeah, there was a time there that I really thought to myself, 'Wow, this guy—this guy just killed us.'"

Flying behind the two planes in his J-8II, Zhao Yu witnessed the collision and frantically radioed Wang Wei. "Your plane's vertical tail has been struck off!" he yelled. "Remain stable, remain stable!" "Roger," Wang Wei replied, but about thirty seconds later Zhao Yu saw his partner's jet roll to the right side and plunge toward the South China Sea. Although Wang Wei managed to bail out, his parachute did not open in time and his body would never be found.

By now the spy plane was out of control, gear crashing all around, a disintegrating number one engine hurling shrapnel, and horrified screams in the cockpit and the ops area as it began an inverted dive. Osborn instinctively swung the yoke hard right and jammed his foot on the right rudder pedal to regain control. But the dive angle steepened, and he was looking up at the sky instead of down at the choppy blue-black waves of the sea below. After the plane tumbled for about a mile and a half, Osborn shouted into the PA system, "Prepare to bail out!" In the ops area, the crew scrambled for their parachutes, survival vests, and helmets. But then he managed to bring the aircraft under partial control, and after falling another mile, he was able to regain full control, leveling off at 8,000 feet. Minutes later Osborn changed the order to prepare to ditch.

At 9:13, eight minutes after the collision, copilot Jeff Vignery, a redheaded Kansan, put out an emergency call over the international distress frequency, 243.0 MHz. "Mayday! Mayday!" he shouted. "Kilo Romeo 919! We are going down!" It was then 8:13 p.m. in Washington, but despite all of its eavesdropping assets, the NSA never received the emergency call because even during sensitive reconnaissance missions it never bothered to monitor the international distress frequencies. Nor were the communications in the ops spaces any better. Moments after the collision, the secure communications operator attempted repeatedly to transmit the two-word message "GOING DOWN" on a secure network for reconnaissance operations. Code-named Sensor

Pace, it was a low-data-rate digital satellite network, but the message was never received.

Finally, the navigator began repeatedly transmitting Mayday calls on another secure satellite system, the Pacific Tributary Network, and at least one transmission was eventually received by both the NSA's Kunia bunker in Hawaii and the agency's Special Support Activity at Fort Meade. Part of the agency's National Security Operations Center, the SSA instantly sent out a top secret CRITIC message. Reserved for the highest emergencies, or indications of war, CRITICs (for Critical Intelligence) are designed to immediately alert the president and top government officials to a major event.

Within minutes, the SSA watch commander set up a special high-level conferencing system known as a NOIWON (National Operational Intelligence Watch Officer's Network) bringing together the crisis centers at the White House, CIA, Pentagon, State Department, and NSA. Other discussions were conducted over a watch officers' secure chat room known as ZIRCON chat. In concert with the National Reconnaissance Office, eavesdropping and imaging satellites were steered toward the crisis area.

On board the aircraft, there were only bad and worse choices. No one had ever bailed out of an EP-3E, and because of the damage there was a good possibility of the jumpers smashing into the tail. And even if they made it to the sea beneath their parachutes, the twenty-four crew members would be scattered over a wide distance in shark-infested waters. There was a life raft, but because of the airspeed, it would land far from the survivors. Ditching into the sea, however, was an even worse idea. Because of the lack of control, and the bulbous doughnut-shaped Big Look radar on the bottom, the plane would likely flip nose down and immediately sink.

Finally, Osborn gained partial control of the aircraft, which gave him a third choice: Make for the nearest land. But that was Hainan Island, their eavesdropping target. Thus they would be handing Chinese intelligence an entire NSA spy plane filled bulkhead to bulkhead with top secret coding and crypto equipment, intercept gear, and a library of highly sensitive documents, most classified above top secret. Nevertheless, between losing secrets or lives, Osborn chose in favor of saving the crew and turned toward Hainan's Lingshui Airfield. "Activate the emergency destruction plan," he yelled over the PA, assuming there was such a plan.

In the ops spaces, it was chaos, with no one in charge and no coherent method to the destruction. Despite the fact that NSA spy planes flew almost daily missions along hostile borders, there was no guidance or procedures on what to do in an emergency if it was necessary to divert to the target country. Nor had there ever been training on how to destroy a planeload of NSA secrets in flight. These were just further blunders by NSA director Michael Hayden, who was in charge of the airborne missions under his dual role as chief of the Central Security Service, the military side of NSA. He was about to hand the Chinese an entire flying listening post packed with the nation's highest secrets.

Much of the blame for the chaos, compromise of material, and lack of training also fell on Osborn and the plane's signals intelligence officers, according to a top secret NSA damage assessment. "The aircrew's overall performance in safeguarding classified materials under their charge was poor," it said, citing "a general lack of training, practice in emergency destruction, capabilities, and sound policy."

LTJG John Comerford, the senior evaluator, was in charge of the NSA's signals intelligence personnel in the back end and therefore responsible for overseeing the emergency destruction of the critical documents and equipment. But according to the NSA report, rather than supervise the destruction, he instead "isolated himself from knowledge of actions taking place in the rest of the cabin. As a result, he had no situational awareness of the status and scope of emergency destruction and was unable to effectively monitor and direct the actions of the crew." Wielding a fire ax, he began smashing equipment and dumping material out a hatch, but paid little attention to directing an organized destruction effort.

Also, inexplicably, he never bothered to tell the crew that rather than ditching in the South China Sea they were going to land on Hainan Island. Therefore, many crew members simply stood by the door preparing to exit rather than taking part in the emergency destruction. Others found the task overwhelming due to the lack of direction and the fact that the plane was overstuffed with reams and reams of top secret documents. Many of the documents were useless, unnecessary, and never should have been brought aboard. And while the ax was used to damage some laptop computers, left unharmed were the internal hard drives containing the sensitive data. Similarly, with the racks of highly sensitive intercept equipment along the aircraft's bulkheads, crew members smashed the keyboards and display screens but left such critical system components as tuners and signal processors unscathed.

Among those Comerford failed to inform about the landing in China was Lieutenant Marcia Sonon, the COMINT evaluator in charge of the voice intercept crew. Assuming the plane was going to ditch, instead of destroying or jettisoning all the highly sensitive COMINT materials, the crew simply packed them in locking leather satchels and, along with the highly sensitive MARTES laptop computer, stored them in a cabinet.

It was a short flight to Lingshui, but despite numerous Mayday calls and requests for assistance on an international distress frequency (243.0 MHz), there was no response from the Chinese airfield's controllers. No one, however, bothered to contact the airfield on its own frequency even though members of the crew had that information. Nevertheless, after a pass over the runway, flying low over orange roofs, swaying palm trees, rice fields, and an operations tower blackened with mildew, Osborn touched down. It was 9:34 in the morning, twenty-nine minutes after the collision. As he tapped the brakes with his flight boots to slow the aircraft down, ahead of him on the runway he saw a thin lineman in sandals directing the aircraft to the edge of the runway. Once the plane came to a stop, it was surrounded by about two dozen military personnel, six to eight of them armed with AK-47 assault rifles, though none were pointed at the aircraft.

At 9:41, over secure satellite communications, Comerford reported to the NSA's SSA, the Kunia bunker, and the Pacific Reconnaissance Operations Center in Hawaii. "On deck at Lingshui," he said. He then told Osborn his orders were to stay put as they evaluated the situation. "They want us to hold on a few minutes," Comerford said. Instead, before awaiting instructions or passing on any information about the collision, the status of the classified information, or their situation, Osborn ordered the plane's power turned off, thereby eliminating any chance of further communications with NSA or the outside world.

Moments later, in the ultimate absurdity, the first thing Osborn did was to ask a PLA officer for his cell phone to call NSA headquarters. "Can I use your phone to make a call?" he said, standing in the doorway. "I have to tell my command that we are safe."

"That is not possible," the officer said. "We will take care of that. Do not worry."

Ordered off the plane, Osborn at first resisted and then turned to Comerford. "Hey, Ballgame. It's time to get off."

"Okay, you're right," said Comerford, and he lowered the door's folded ladder.

Once everyone was off the plane, the PLA officer headed for the ladder.

"You are not allowed aboard the aircraft," Osborn said. "It's American property."

"It's okay, we'll guard it for you," said the officer, no doubt laughing to himself.

From the plane, the crew was escorted to a bus where they waited, drinking bottled water and smoking packs of Bao Dao cigarettes, filling the air with thick gray smoke.

"Everything did go alright in the backend, right?" Osborn asked Comerford.

"Everything's good back there," he replied, seemingly oblivious to the inadequate emergency destruction that had taken place. Although the plane had an emergency action plan, neither Comerford nor anyone else ever consulted it. "Notwithstanding the chaotic circumstances on the aircraft following the collision," the top secret NSA damage assessment noted, "we conclude that the crew had sufficient time to jettison all sensitive materials… The incident revealed a systemic complacency regarding policy, planning, and training support to EP-3E SRO missions."

The report also pointed a finger directly at the NSA's leadership, including Director Hayden. "No specific guidance existed regarding Mission Commander or aircrew actions should an SRO aircraft be forced or, through emergency, be required to land in the PRC," it said. It added, "Crew training for emergency destruction was minimal and did not meet squadron requirements; this deficiency was the primary cause of the compromise of classified material."

For the next eleven days, until their release, the crew was treated well, housed first in a military barracks and then in a simple hotel. They were questioned about the cause of the midair collision while Washington and Beijing worked out agreements for their return. But while the crew was eating rice, seaweed, and chicken feet, Chinese signals intelligence specialists were studying the top secret documents and dissecting the equipment on the spy plane as if it were an alien spacecraft. It was an enormous intelligence windfall.

Because Lieutenant Marcia Sonon, the COMINT evaluator, was never informed by Comerford of the plan to land in China, all of the highly secret communications interception computers, equipment, and documents were neatly stowed in cabinets rather than destroyed or thrown into the sea. This gave Chinese intelligence an incredible insight into the NSA capabilities against their country.

Among the undamaged computers were the two most sensitive on the aircraft, according to the NSA's report. "The most potentially damaging compromised items were the carry-on LUNCHBOX PROFORMA processor," it said, "and a laptop computer with MARTES software tools for collecting, analyzing, and processing signals. The aircraft also had an extensive inventory of SIGINT documentation in both hardcopy and electronic media."

What most concerned NSA on the MARTES computer was the RASIN manual, RASIN Working Aid, and associated material. This was the agency's index of every signal they were targeting in China, Russia, and everywhere else in the world. "Together, the RASIN manual and aforementioned files provided a comprehensive overview of how the U.S. Cryptologic System exploits an adversary's signal environment," said the report.

Ultimately, the damage went well beyond China itself to other adversaries. "The aircraft carried significant technical data on target nations such as Russia, North Korea, and Vietnam," the report said. This included "Russian-designed PROFORMA [weapons-related] signals used by North Korea, Russia, Vietnam, and possibly the PRC," as well as "PROFORMA data for nearly 50 nations." It added, "The Electronic Order of Battle (EOB) database carried on the EP-3E provided information on the location, number, and type of radars worldwide."

Still other documents revealed the fact that the NSA was able to spy on the PLA Navy's Submarine Launched Ballistic Missile program, locate its submarines, and eavesdrop on their communications. They could now change their communication methods and develop better ways to successfully hide.

Compromises also included the Intercept Tasking Database and Collection Requirements. It outlined all the key targets in China the agency was interested in, and even details on a new communications system the PLA had yet to deploy. The PLA also got near-complete access to the plane's electronic intelligence systems. "Emergency destruction of the installed ELINT equipment by the crew was largely ineffective," said the report. A further problem for the NSA was the fact that the inventory of classified materials aboard, left by the EP-3E crew in Kadena before they departed "was not accurate, detailed, or verified." Therefore, no one knew just what was on the plane and what might have been compromised.

The aircraft was also loaded down with encryption devices, cryptographic keys, and entire codebooks, some for a month in advance. Much of it, said the report, was "in excess of what was needed for the mission." Sixteen cryptographic keys and codebooks as well as sixteen cryptographic devices were left on board undamaged. Other keying materials were simply torn and left in the plane. "The PRC would probably be able to reconstruct the key tape," it said.

With keys and devices in hand, and the right technical ability, the Chinese had fifteen hours to decipher highly secret communications across the Pacific before the NSA was able to distribute new keys worldwide, an enormous intelligence coup. The compromised materials also "might enable PRC SIGINT units to decrypt limited U.S. Pacific area encrypted transmissions for 31 March and 1 April," said the report. The crypto devices proved unique prizes. "There is strong evidence that the PRC has aggressively sought to obtain these equipments," said the report. One reason might be that they already had a source who could supply them with keying materials on a regular basis.

The ramifications of the EP-3E disaster would be enormous and have a long-range and very detrimental legacy for the United States. In 2019, the Chinese government credited the incident that took Wang Wei's life with being the catalyst to spur the country's military modernization. "His death was an accident, but it set off many changes," said Beijing-based military expert Zhou Chenming. "What happened 18 years ago spurred China to step up the modernization of its military, especially aircraft development for the air force and navy." Beijing-based naval expert Li Jie agreed. "The 2001 crash taught China a lesson—that a strong country cannot rely on a vibrant economy alone but also needs a strong military. That's what they refer to as 'comprehensive national strength.'"

Equally serious, the EP-3E incident provided China with an enormous capability to discover exactly what successes the NSA had been able achieve over the years and decades. Now they knew which codes they had broken and which targets they were intercepting, giving Chinese intelligence the ability to modify the systems and plug the NSA's ears for years or decades to come. Next, they were determined to do the same with the CIA's human spies, to find them and eliminate them with a bullet or a jail cell. And following a secret meeting in Hong Kong a week before the crash, they were off to a very good start.

CHAPTER 30

The Rendezvous

It was a very dangerous time to be a foreign spy. On March 25, 2001, FBI spokesman Paul Bresson suddenly announced that five hundred agents would be forced to undergo lie detector tests. "These are people in positions that place them in contact with highly sensitive material," he said. At the same time, FBI director Louis J. Freeh ordered a review of all "sensitive investigations" to determine which employees had access to information outside their regular duties.

A few weeks before, the FBI had suffered the worst blow in its history. It turned out that the agency charged with uncovering foreign spies had instead employed a top Russian mole for nearly a quarter of a century. Until he was arrested on February 18, 2001, while loading a dead drop, Robert Hanssen had been one of the counterintelligence division's top officials. His espionage was described by the Department of Justice as "possibly the worst intelligence disaster in U.S. history." It would be surpassed just two weeks later with the unintended gift to China of NSA's plane full of secrets.

By then, Chinese intelligence was on a very big roll. On the same day that the FBI announced the start of its mole hunt, strapping hundreds of agents to polygraph machines, a former CIA officer secretly agreed to become a Chinese mole inside the FBI. And like Hanssen, he would go undetected for decades.

In the spring of 2001, four years after the handover from Britain to China, much of Hong Kong remained a world of neon and noise. But now a great many of the tourists haggling over Rolex watches, checking into the Peninsula, and packing Lan Kwai Fong and other nightlife districts had a decidedly Mandarin accent. "Five years ago, everyone looked down on you if you spoke Mandarin," said a Beijing executive living in Hong Kong. "Now, they know we're the big bosses with the money." Despite predictions that the former colony would turn into a gray vista of hunched workers and nameless noodle shops, travelers from mainland China had become the principal source of visitors to Hong Kong. They were even spending more per capita than their American and Japanese counterparts. And March 2001 was an especially busy time. As soon as the Hong Kong Arts Festival ended, the Hong Kong International Film Festival began.

Deep in the shadows, the city had also become a major crossroads for Eastern and Western spies. "Hong Kong is a place where foreign intelligence agencies conduct a lot of activity," admitted Li Gang, the deputy director of Beijing's Liaison Office in the city. As the arts crowd checked out of their rooms and the film fans checked in, two former American spies quietly slipped into another hotel for a discreet rendezvous with their Chinese counterparts. They were brothers who had both worked as clandestine CIA officers in China, and now they were about to switch sides.

Alexander Yuk Ching Ma and his older brother David were both veterans of the CIA's clandestine operations division. David was born in Shanghai in 1935, a time of smoky jazz clubs, bustling casinos, and opium dens. The Pudong District, on the eastern bank of the Huangpu River, became the country's major financial hub, and decades later it would also become its high-tech eavesdropping hub.

In 1961, at the age of twenty-six, David moved to Los Angeles, became a naturalized U.S. citizen, and six years later joined the CIA in an entry-level capacity, possibly as a translator. But in the late 1960s the United States was in the middle of its desperate war with North Vietnam, which was aided by China. As a result, a throng of new recruits were continuously making their way to Camp Perry, known as "The Farm," the CIA's boot camp for spies, near Williamsburg, Virginia. The problem was, nearly all had the physical appearance of cheering fans at a Notre Dame football game. Few would blend into a crowd on a street in Asia. Also, very few spoke Chinese or Vietnamese, especially with any fluency. That was good for David, and in 1971 he was promoted to the officer ranks within the CIA's clandestine service. Entrusted with the identities of many of the agency's human sources in China and elsewhere, as well as its system of covert communications (known as "covcom"), he spent years in the Far East.

In 1983, David resigned after it was determined that he was inappropriately using his government position to assist Chinese nationals in obtaining entry into the United States. But months before, as if taking his place, his thirty-year-old brother Alex had joined up and also became a clandestine officer. He was born in Hong Kong and, like David, lived for a time in Shanghai. Both also graduated from the University of Hawaii at Manoa. Following extensive training at The Farm, he was also provided with the identities of the agency's networks of spies, the various covcom details, and was sent to the Far East. Seven years later he left the agency, and around 1995 he moved to China, there oddly being no restrictions on former spies moving to their target nations. Therefore, little is known about his activities there.

David, however, ran into serious legal and financial trouble. In 1998, while living in Los Angeles, he pled guilty to two counts of defrauding a lending institution. In December he began serving a five-month sentence at Taft Correctional Institution, a low-security federal prison near Bakersfield, California, followed by five years of probation and $145,623 in restitution—money he didn't have. Then in 2000, his brother Alex returned from China, telling Customs and Border Protection officers that he was an "importer and exporter" and was carrying $9,000 in U.S. currency. Not long after, both brothers turned up in Shanghai.

For three days, beginning on March 24, 2001, Alex and David allegedly met secretly in a hotel room with at least five officials from China's Ministry of State Security (MSS) and passed on highly classified information. According to government charges, details included the covers used by CIA officers and CIA activities in China; cryptographic information used in classified and sensitive CIA communications and reports; information concerning CIA officer identities as well as those of CIA human assets in China; the CIA's use of operational tradecraft; and CIA secure communications practices—that is, covcom details. The brothers were then handed $50,000 in cash.

Afterward, as laid out in the indictment, both Alex and David returned to California, but they kept in touch with their handlers. Alex eventually agreed to become a mole for China's intelligence service within the FBI, and on the day after Christmas 2002, he applied for the position of special agent. By then, however, he was about forty-nine years old and was informed that he was over the age limit. But in 2004 he was nevertheless hired as a Chinese translator since he spoke several Chinese dialects. In many ways, this was an even better position for a spy since he would have access to a very broad range of information, including intercepted Chinese conversations. The day before he started his new job, he called a suspected accomplice, possibly David, to give him the good news that he would now be working full-time for "the other side."

By then the FBI was reeling from another extremely damaging, and extremely embarrassing, counterintelligence disaster involving China. In 2003 it was discovered that the bureau's key U.S.-based China asset, Katrina Leung, was, like Alex, a double agent working for China. Worse, she was simultaneously sleeping with two of the FBI's top China agents. Among them was her longtime handler, through whom she had been passing false information for more than a decade, information that often was quickly passed on to the White House.

Assigned to the Honolulu FBI office, Alex and his wife moved into a $600,000 condominium on Hawaii Kai Drive, a short walk to the ocean on the southeastern corner of Oahu. Strongly built, with a broad natural grin, Alex wore squarish glasses above puffy cheeks that seemed to glow when he smiled, which was often. Over at least the next six years and possibly much longer, he took over the role of FBI mole where Robert Hanssen left off, except for a different spymaster. It was as though no lessons had ever been learned by the bureau.

The method was simple. Attracting no suspicion, Ma would gather up piles of highly secret materials and simply walk out the door with them, just as Hanssen had done for decades. Some he photographed with a digital camera, others he downloaded from his computer onto a flash drive, while still others he copied onto CD-ROM discs. Some dealt with guided missiles and weapon systems, and others revealed the identity of confidential sources, putting their lives at risk. In addition, Ma had extensive knowledge of the CIA's highly secret covcom techniques by which CIA officers communicated with their sources. Every few months, once he had accumulated a load of secrets, he would call his handlers. They would then book him a hotel room in Shanghai, pick him up at the airport, and take him into town, where he would hand over his secrets and be debriefed by agents of the Shanghai State Security Bureau (SSSB).

Although just across town from Sun Kailiang and the other eavesdroppers and codebreakers of China's Network Support Division, their professional rivals the SSSB existed in a different universe. Rather than extracting data from muddy undersea cables, they needed to pull it from the brains of foreign spies. Spies that first had to be identified, bribed, and recruited. The SSSB was the regional office of the Ministry of State Security, China's equivalent of both the CIA and FBI. Headquartered in Beijing at Xiyuan (Western Garden), next to the vast ensemble of lakes, gardens, and palaces of the Summer Palace, its logo still displays the hammer and sickle of the Communist Party. At the time, it was run by Minister of State Security Xu Yongyue, a stern-faced senior party official from Zhenping County, the jade capital of China, in the province of Henan. And in charge of the SSSB was Cai Xumin, who received a very significant promotion to vice minister of the MSS in 2004, likely due to his recruitment of Ma.

Following the rendezvous and document drops in Shanghai, Ma would simply fly back to Honolulu. At one point a curious U.S. customs official pulled him aside for a secondary search and discovered he was carrying

$20,000 in cash and a shiny new set of golf clubs. But no questions were raised, no actions were taken, and later that day Ma sent an email to his SSSB handler with an attachment containing additional classified information. Other money paid to him by the MSS was regularly deposited in a bank account in Hong Kong.

David Ma also secretly remained in the loop. Living in Arcadia, a wealthy Los Angeles bedroom community, he established himself as a consultant on immigration rights for the many Asian immigrants in the nearby communities, such as Alhambra and Monterey Park. Familiar with their needs and fluent in various Chinese dialects, including Mandarin, Cantonese, Shanghai, and Chaozhou, he opened several businesses. They included the Chinese American Civil Rights Organization and AsiAmerica Immigration & Consultancy, Inc. Ironically, in 2005 he was quoted in a *Los Angeles Times* article about Chinese espionage. As China's economy continued to boom, he said, he could understand the temptation of some Chinese Americans who wanted to do business there to help the government any way they could. "I'm not saying all of them are spies," he said. "But for some of them it is outright greed because they need to do business with [the Chinese government]. It's just like barter or exchange."

Because of his businesses, David became very well known within the Chinese communities in Los Angeles, which was ideal for the SSSB and MSS. Critical for them was discovering community members who had become confidential informants on China for the CIA and FBI. In February 2006, Alex Ma, China's mole in the FBI, sent David photos he received from his handlers of five suspected human sources. Accompanying the pictures was a photo of five dogs sitting on a park bench, which was a coded way of asking him to supply the identity of the sources. Shortly thereafter, David sent Alex an email identifying two of the informants. And a memory card belonging to Alex had pictures of the five sources along with a list of five names.

A few months later, Alex arranged for his wife, Amy Ma, who was also born in Hong Kong, to fly to Shanghai to meet with his handlers and to deliver an encrypted laptop computer to them. An email message soon came back thanking him for sending his wife and delivering "the present." Over the years, without suspicion, Alex continued to fly back and forth to Shanghai every few months with stashes of secrets. And in June 2008, his handler phoned him to say that his "company" would have a lot of work orders in the coming year.

In May 2010, a few months after another clandestine rendezvous to hand over documents to his handler, Alex received a phone call from an MSS officer apologizing for not seeing him during a recent visit to China and extending an invitation to meet in Shanghai in the future. He also asked Alex to get in touch with David and see if he would be willing to discuss their "business venture." About the same time, the MSS was also bringing on board another veteran CIA clandestine officer, one who had just reapplied to the agency, possibly to become a mole. Known as Zhen Cheng Li in China, he was Jerry Chun Shing Lee to his colleagues at Langley.

Born in Hong Kong like Alex, Lee grew up in Hawaii and became a naturalized U.S. citizen. At seventeen, in 1982, he joined the U.S. Army, serving for four years but remaining in the reserves. A few years later he enrolled at Hawaii Pacific University, graduating in 1992 with a degree in international business management. A year later he earned a master's degree in human resource management and shortly thereafter joined the CIA as a case officer in the clandestine service. Over the following fourteen years, he was dispatched on numerous overseas assignments, including to China, where he, like Alex and David Ma, had access to the agency's clandestine networks, both human and covcom.

By July 2007, Lee had become frustrated by his lack of advancement at the CIA. "He was quite critical about the organization and his time there; the fact that he didn't get credit, he didn't get promoted, he didn't get the assignments he deserved," said one of his associates. As a result, Lee resigned and moved to Hong Kong, taking a job with Japan Tobacco International (JTI). Employing about forty thousand people around the world, the company sells 120 brands of cigarettes, including both Camel and Winston outside the United States.

But a key problem for the company was tobacco smugglers and counterfeiters. Asian crime syndicates were exporting tons of counterfeit cigarettes out of China with the help of corrupt officials. To combat the syndicates, the company had established a Brand Integrity Unit under a veteran CIA officer, David Reynolds, who had worked at the agency from 1988 to 2002. Afterward he was assigned as a U.S. consular officer in Guangzhou for two years. Lee claimed that his last job at the CIA was the agency's official liaison in Beijing to Chinese intelligence, the MSS, and he was hired by Reynolds.

Now, with an office on the forty-second floor of Tower 1 in Times Square, the city's flashy, upscale shopping and restaurant complex at Causeway Bay, Lee could see all of Hong Kong spread out below him. But adjusting to private industry was difficult and he soon ran into problems. Company officials began to suspect that he was alerting corrupt Chinese officials about the firm's investigations and the pending raids and arrests by law enforcement. "Several of the shipments of counterfeits purchased as part of the investigations were seized by the Chinese authorities or simply disappeared, and one of our contract investigators was arrested and imprisoned in China," said a manager. All evidence pointed toward Lee, and as a result, executives at JTI alerted the FBI, but apparently no action was ever taken.

Lee was finally fired in mid-2009, and soon afterward a Chinese official warned the company that he was not only continuing to share information with MSS officers, but was also actively working with them. And once again JTI officials passed the information to the FBI. "I certainly reported it to the appropriate authorities," said a company supervisor. It was good information, but once again it seemed to go nowhere within the bureau. At about the same time, Lee hooked up with a potential business partner, Barry Cheung Kam-lun, a former Hong Kong police officer who, Lee knew, had close ties to the MSS. And on April 26 the two traveled across the Hong Kong border to neighboring Shenzhen for a private dinner with MSS officers.

It was time for the official pitch. After excusing Barry, the intelligence officers and Lee reached an agreement that he would begin passing secrets to them and act as their spy. In exchange, they handed him a briefcase full of cash, $100,000, along with an agreement to take care of him "for life." It would be the first of hundreds of thousands of dollars he would receive, and within a few weeks he began receiving his taskings, key among them apparently becoming a mole in the CIA, as Alex Ma had done in the FBI. That same month, he applied for reemployment with the CIA. But given his less than illustrious career and departure from the agency, it went nowhere.

Instead, possibly as a cover, Lee and Barry Cheung Kam-lun established their own company, FTM International, to enter the "Big Tobacco" wars and conduct their own brand integrity investigations. After investing nearly $400,000, they set up shop in the down-market Wan Chai area, renting space in Dannies House. Unlike JTI's soaring skyscraper in Times Square, Lee's new office was in a tired thirteen-story orange high-rise with battered air-conditioning units stuck out the windows like giant steel bird feeders.

But two years later, fed up with Hong Kong and having run out of secrets to sell, Lee decided to move his family back to Virginia, where he had been offered a potential job by the CIA. It had been secretly created to lure him back to the United States, and in August 2012, during a three-day stopover in Hawaii, agents conducted a black bag job on his hotel room. What they found was damning. Inside a small, clear plastic travel pack was a forty-nine-page datebook and a twenty-one-page address book, both of which contained top secret handwritten operational notes from his CIA days. Most critically, they included the true names of secret human sources as well as the dates and operational locations of the meetings. Another clandestine search was conducted on his hotel room in Fairfax, Virginia, soon after he arrived, and the information remained in his possession.

But inexplicably, rather than Lee being arrested, the decision was made to simply question him repeatedly over the following year. Finally, after the fifth interview in June 2013, with the questions becoming more and more revealing of what the bureau knew, Lee fled with his family back to China-controlled Hong Kong. Once more he was out of reach, and once more the FBI had bungled it. Over the next few years, Lee did security work for the cosmetics company Estée Lauder and the auction house Christie's. Then in January 2018, apparently believing the danger had blown over, he boarded a Cathay Pacific flight to New York's John F. Kennedy International Airport. It was a serious mistake. His name had been flagged on the airline's manifest and he was arrested as soon as he landed. After first vowing to fight the espionage charges, in May 2019 he agreed to plead guilty and was sentenced to nineteen years in prison.

Around the same time, the FBI finally discovered the Chinese mole who had bored his way into the organization sixteen years earlier. In August 2020, an agent posing as an MSS officer approached Alex Ma in Honolulu and snared him in a sting operation. To convince Ma of his bona fides, he showed him a video of the meeting between him, David, and the SSSB agents at the time they signed on as spies in 2001. The pretend MSS officer then offered Ma $2,000 in cash as a "small token" of appreciation for Ma's assistance to China. Ma offered to continue working for the MSS and stated that he wanted "the motherland" to succeed. Shortly afterward he was arrested on charges of espionage and as of the fall of 2022 was awaiting trial. With regard to David, then eighty-five years old, the decision was made not to arrest him due to his advanced stage of Alzheimer's disease.

But many questions were left unanswered, among them how the video of the 2001 meeting came into the FBI's possession. The entire three days of meetings were filmed by someone. If the filming was done by FBI, there is the question of why it took nearly two decades to make the arrests. Birney Bervar, Ma's defense attorney, said government authorities have known about the allegations since 2001. And if it instead was filmed by the MSS or SSSB, how did the FBI get it? From a defecting Chinese intelligence official, using the files and film to get asylum and a good deal of money from the CIA?

And then there is the question of how many years Alex Ma worked for the FBI and sold secrets to China. Oddly, the government makes no mention of when Ma left the bureau, but they admitted that he "obtained decades worth of national defense information." Since that would have included his seven years at the CIA, it's possible he continued as a mole inside the FBI until his arrest in 2020. But if so, the FBI isn't saying.

What is clear is the seriousness of the CIA's and FBI's years of multiple failures. According to government documents, "In the case of the individuals whose identities Ma and his co-conspirator [David] revealed to the MSS, the danger is acute—they could be captured or killed...Ma and his co-conspirator knew the names and covers of CIA officers and assets, the operational tradecraft used by the CIA overseas, including methods of secure communication [covcom], and cryptographic information (i.e., how the CIA disguises the contents or significance of its communications)."

Beginning around 2010, the same time Ma was commuting between the FBI field office in Honolulu and Shanghai with his loads of secrets, recruited CIA assets in China began to quickly, and very unexpectedly, disappear. "You could tell the Chinese weren't guessing," said one former intelligence official, who described the reaction within the CIA's China team as "shellshocked." "The Ministry of State Security were always pulling in the right people. When things started going bad, they went bad fast," he said. According to one report, as a last resort CIA case officers began passing out fat wads of cash to their endangered sub-agents, hoping they could find a way to escape capture. The officials estimated that over several years, upwards of thirty or more sources were executed as a result of the security failures by the FBI, as well as others by the CIA and NSA.

For years, on the north wall of the CIA's original headquarters building, the agency has maintained a memorial to employees who have died in the line of service, beginning in 1947. On May 23, 2022, during a ceremony, two new stars were affixed to the white Alabama marble. "Each year, we gather in this sacred place to mourn and remember," said CIA director William J. Burns. "We look upon this Memorial Wall, etched with sacrifice, and honor those Agency officers who gave their lives in the service of our country." But the stars are limited to official agency employees. There is no wall, however, for the many secret sub-agents who greatly risked, and then lost, their lives in hostile environments like China, many paying with their blood for the incompetence, bungled security, traitorous acts, and other failures by those they trusted in the FBI and U.S. intelligence community.

And the screwups were not limited to China. A former senior CIA clandestine service official told me that due to poor technical security Iran also compromised weaknesses in the agency's covcom system. "The Iranian Intelligence Service, the MOIS [Ministry of Intelligence], grabbed one of our assets inside Tehran," he said. "And he had his covcom device. They were able to reverse engineer it, and they uncovered the whole net by finding out where the signals were going. The problem was, it was multiple nets, but it was the same equipment. So when they figured this one out, they figured out the rest. People got executed and there was a huge investigation at the agency. This was a huge scandal."

While the intelligence and counterintelligence disasters differ greatly in detail, their one common denominator seems to be that there are never any consequences for utter failure in the intelligence community, and it is instead often a career booster. Despite losing half a billion pages of top secrets, and then most of the NSA's deadly cyberweapons, letting them fall into the hands of North Korea and causing a worldwide cyberpandemic, Admiral Mike Rogers suffered no consequences. He was neither fired nor demoted, nor even given a reduction in pay. Nor, apparently, was anyone else at NSA disciplined.

And after General Michael Hayden, the NSA director, lost an entire spy plane to China, largely as a result of incompetent planning and training; totally missed the attacks on 9/11; and got the war in Iraq completely wrong, nevertheless he was promoted to principal deputy director of national intelligence and later director of the CIA.

And then there was General Clapper, who was having dinner with the head of North Korea's intelligence agency at the same time that his counterpart was conducting the largest cyberattack against a U.S. company in history. That followed Clapper's failed cyberwar attack against Kim Jong Un's nuclear facilities, a key factor leading to the cyberpandemic, also on his watch. And then, due to very high-level CIA leaks to the press, the United States lost its most important spy in the Kremlin, a few years before Russia's war in Ukraine (see Chapter 33). With no negative consequences, Clapper simply left and became a high-paid talking head on CNN.

Nor were the directors of the CIA or FBI or any of their senior staff ever fired for the many screwups involving China. Former CIA director George Tenet was in fact awarded the Presidential Medal of Freedom, the highest civilian award in the country, by President George W. Bush for his bad intelligence leading to the disastrous war in Iraq.

Corrective action can therefore start with taking away stars, jobs, and pay for failure and incompetence.

Soon there would not even be consequences when former CIA and FBI agents secretly became involved in a Russian plot to violently overthrow an American ally and assassinate its prime minister.

BOOK EIGHT

THE ASSASSINS

CHAPTER 31

The Aquarium

The runners began to gather near Luzhniki Stadium beneath the morning clouds, thin and gray like slabs of slate. It was the last Sunday in September 2016, Marathon Day in Moscow, and participants did warm-ups in foil-wrapped thermal jackets, drank in long gulps from plastic water bottles, and adjusted belly packs and caps with the marathon logo, two tags forming a heart. The twenty-eight thousand enrolled starters from seventy countries would run 42.2 kilometers from the embankment of the Moscow River, over Krymsky Bridge, down Tverskaya Street, past the Bolshoi, and along the red-brick walls of the Kremlin.

Across town from the athletes in their damp, perspiration-stained T-shirts, and the cheering spectators lining the embankment that morning, Eduard Shirokov was immersed in work at "the Aquarium" despite it being a Sunday. It was the nickname for the modern concrete and glass complex at Khoroshovskoye Shosse in northwest Moscow that was home to the GRU, Russia's military intelligence organization. By 2016, the buildings had become spy central, with helicopters landing urgently on the rooftop helipad, clandestine wars being fought on multiple fronts, and covert agents engaging in risky operations in various parts of the globe.

But Shirokov was part of a special organization within the Aquarium, Unit 29155, tasked with assassinations, destabilizing governments, and other sensitive operations. It is housed separately, behind high concrete walls at the headquarters of the 161st Special Purpose Specialist Training Center, a Spetsnaz facility on the east side of Moscow. Laid out on Shirokov's desk were secret spy satellite photos of Montenegro, a small European country preparing for a new election—an election Shirokov was making sure would never happen. Instead, he was planning the assassination of Prime Minister Milo Đukanović and the violent overthrow of his country. And time was getting short. At 7:17 that evening, after leaving his office, he stopped down the street at Western Union and sent a money wire for $800 for travel expenses to the man who would carry it out. He was flying to Moscow from Belgrade, Serbia, the next day.

Shirokov's real name was Eduard Shishmakov, and at forty-five he was barrel-chested, with a puffy face, rimless glasses, and a thick dark brown mustache that hung just below the edges of his mouth. A spy who had once been blown, he now needed an alias whenever he was engaged in a new operation, and the previous month he had received a new passport and credit cards with his new name.

For decades, Shishmakov had been a rising GRU military intelligence officer. He was born into an army family and spent his high school years on a Soviet military base in Halle, East Germany. Deciding on a naval career, he graduated "with distinction" from the Black Sea Military Navy Institute in Sevastopol and then, selected for intelligence, entered the Military Diplomatic Academy. Nicknamed "the conservatory," it is the GRU's four-year graduate school for spies and attachés where courses cover such topics as organizing deep-cover operations, agent recruitment, and counterintelligence evasion. The complex of sand-colored cement buildings sits behind an iron fence at 50 Ulitsa Narodnogo Opolcheniya in the northwest of Moscow.

Shishmakov learned his lessons well. By 2013, posted as a naval attaché at the Russian embassy in Warsaw, Poland, he managed a number of successful recruitments, including a Polish Army lieutenant colonel working in the Ministry of Defense. For 5,500 euros, the officer turned over data on hundreds of Polish military personnel who had criminal records, and therefore were potential recruits as spies. Shishmakov also convinced a Polish-Russian lawyer to commit economic espionage for the GRU. But when several of his spies were arrested, he was revealed as a Russian agent, and in October 2014 he was expelled from Poland. Now he had a new assignment.

Very early on a Moscow morning, two days after the marathon, Shishmakov stood at a plate-glass window and stared into the inky predawn darkness. He was at an empty gate in Terminal E at Moscow's vast Sheremetyevo Airport. Below, in the harsh radium-blue glow of fluorescent lights, baggage handlers in small steel cabs pulled luggage-filled trailers, and beyond, an occasional jet would land, its tires screeching and its engines screaming. He was watching for the distinctive markings of an Air Serbia jet, a stylized double-headed eagle on the tail. On board was the man who was going to carry out his operation in Montenegro, Sasa Sindjelic, an agent he had recruited as an assassin two years earlier, in 2014.

———

The Dinaric Alps are a steep, jagged chain of limestone mountains that stretch like a black wall along the eastern coast of the Adriatic Sea. Beyond, protected like a fortress, is Montenegro, a diminutive country the size of Connecticut with a population about that of Washington, DC. In 1907 the Anglo-French journalist William Le Queux decided to explore Montenegro and found it "the wildest, most desolate mountain region." "By order of Prince Nicholas," he wrote, "every man must carry his revolver when outdoors."

More than a century later, despite its peaceful declaration of independence from Serbia in 2006, some of that wildness remains, as do the dangers. In 2016 Montenegro was at the center of a shadowy tug-of-war between Russia and the United States, making it a very busy summer and fall for GRU agents. At the same time they were releasing emails to interfere with the November election in the United States, they were also planning to interfere with the October election in Montenegro. But rather than releasing emails, they were planning to release bullets.

At 11 p.m. on election day, October 16, 2016, the plan was to assassinate the prime minister, launch a bloody coup, and take over the country. Like a modern-day *Game of Thrones*, which was filmed just over the border in Dubrovnik, Croatia, House Obama and House Putin were both determined to capture Montenegro in a battle for control of the Mediterranean Sea.

On October 15, 2016, the day before the election, the *Admiral Kuznetsov*, the flagship of the Russian navy, and the country's only aircraft carrier, was due to set sail along with its task group from Severomorsk. Located near Murmansk, the port was the headquarters for Russia's Northern Fleet. Their destination would be the Mediterranean and operations off the coast of Syria. The problem was, the ships might soon have no place to refuel or obtain repairs.

For years, Russia faced major difficulties in conducting operations in the Mediterranean. Once a mission was completed, the only place for repair and refueling was Tartus, a small Russian-leased naval facility on the coast of Syria. But given the uncertainty of the country, its future could not be guaranteed. One possible solution was Montenegro. It controlled the only stretch of coastline available to Russian warships between Gibraltar and eastern Turkey not already in the hands of NATO.

A new country with an old history of Russian friendship, Montenegro had a shared belief in the Orthodox religion and beaches packed with sunburned Russian tourists. In 2016, the country welcomed over three hundred thousand Russian visitors, and the popular tourist destination of Budva has become known colloquially as "Moscow on the Sea." Therefore, beginning in September 2013, negotiations got under way for a possible long-term naval base at the ports of either Bar or Kotor. But with the United States putting pressure on the country's prime minister, Milo Đukanović, not to enter into an agreement, it was a hard sell.

For most of nearly three decades, Đukanović had been either president or prime minister of Montenegro, beginning when he was twenty-nine and the country was a rump republic inside communist Yugoslavia. With an athletic frame beneath a mane of gray hair, Đukanović, nicknamed "Milo the Blade," was a die-hard basketball fan with a closet full of dark Italian suits, and allegations of corruption, money laundering, and tobacco smuggling. A man who enjoyed taking chances, he was now engaged in a very dangerous game, attempting to play one nuclear-armed superpower off another. As the Kremlin whispered in one ear, the White House whispered in the other, hoping to keep the Mediterranean a near-exclusive sea for NATO members only.

The United States was engaged in geopolitical bullying; it was using NATO to generate friction and heighten tensions rather than the opposite, the treaty's original purpose. But by deliberately generating a hostile atmosphere, it was also providing NATO its raison d'être. In reality, there was no way that Montenegro was essential to NATO. Its total armed forces consisted of less than two thousand active personnel; it had no air force, no military academies, and not even a coast guard despite its coastline. And much of the public was against joining NATO, the organization that had bombed the country in the 1990s. A poll in December 2016 found that 39.5 percent of Montenegrins supported NATO membership, while 39.7 percent were against.

What Montenegro did have was plenty of corruption. In 2015, Đukanović was named the world's "Criminal of the Year in Organized Crime" by the investigative journalists' network OCCRP for building "one of the most dedicated kleptocracies and organized crime havens in the world." In March 2019, fed up with decades of official cronyism and unaccountable theft, thousands converged on the capital's main square to protest. They then marched through the center of the city chanting, "Milo thief." "We are not the danger for this country," Marija Backovic, a protesting teacher, told the crowd. "Those that are destroying it for thirty years are the real danger."

In December 2015, after two years of back-and-forth negotiations with both East and West, Đukanović came down on the side of the United States and NATO. Inside the Kremlin, the anger was immeasurable. "The continued eastward expansion of NATO and NATO's military infrastructure cannot but result in retaliatory actions from the east, i.e. from the Russian side," President Vladimir Putin warned through his spokesman, Dmitry Peskov. And the Russian Foreign Ministry spokesperson, Maria Zakharova, would later tweet, "The current Montenegro authorities will bear full responsibility for the consequences of their anti-Russian stance." As Montenegro prime minister Duško Marković noted, "In Russia's official military doctrine, the expansion of NATO is listed as the number one security threat, higher than terrorism."

The anger had been festering for decades, since the very end of the Cold War. In January 1990, West German foreign minister Hans-Dietrich Genscher declared, "What NATO must do is state unequivocally that whatever happens in the Warsaw Pact, there will be no expansion of NATO territory eastwards, that is to say, closer to the borders of the Soviet Union." Later U.S. secretary of state James Baker told Russian leader Mikhail Gorbachev in Moscow that "there would be no extension of NATO's jurisdiction for forces of NATO one inch to the east." Gorbachev then stated that "any extension of the zone of NATO is unacceptable." Baker replied, "I agree." After all, the alliance had been created in 1949 to deter the Soviet Union and its Warsaw Pact from venturing westward into Europe. And by 1991 both were gone.

Boris Yeltsin, Gorbachev's successor, was given similar promises by the Clinton administration according to recently declassified top secret documents. During a meeting with Yeltsin in Moscow in 1993, Secretary of State Warren Christopher told the Russian president that rather than NATO, the idea was to create a Partnership for Peace agreement. Under such an arrangement, Russia would be included along with all European countries. Having long pushed to become part of Europe, Yeltsin was overjoyed. "This really is a great idea, really great," he told Christopher. "Tell Bill that I am thrilled by this brilliant stroke." It was a scam, and Clinton and NATO would soon make their move.

In the spring of 1994, William J. Burns, a senior State Department official who had spent the past eight years in Washington, entered the ornate, mustard-colored U.S. embassy in Moscow as the new minister-counselor for political affairs. Near the entrance of the chancery was an Orthodox church so infused with eavesdropping equipment that embassy personnel referred to it as "Our Lady of Telemetry," or "Our Lady of Immaculate Reception."

Soon after arriving, Burns saw the disconnect between the administration's steamroller push to expand NATO eastward toward the Russian border and Yeltsin's fears of losing face and territory. "Sitting in the embassy in Moscow in the mid-1990s, it seemed to me that NATO expansion was premature at best, and needlessly provocative at worst," he wrote in 2019. "It was wishful thinking," he argued, "to believe that we could open the door to NATO membership without incurring some lasting cost with a Russia coping with its own historic insecurities." As Burns recognized, the Russians had reasons for their anxiety; unlike the United States, they had been invaded multiple times and suffered twenty-seven million deaths in World War II. And he attempted to warn Washington.

Another declassified memo, this one dated March 1995, encapsulates

the Clinton administration's supreme arrogance when it came to U.S. foreign policy toward Russia. It's from Strobe Talbott, the number two official
at the State Department, to his boss, Secretary of State Warren Christopher.
"It's Russia that must move toward us, toward our way of doing things," he
wrote. "For some Americans, not to mention a lot of Russians (and other
non-Americans), this may be an obnoxious confirmation of our doctrine of
'exceptionalism.' Well, tough. That's us; that's the U.S. We are exceptional."

Five months later, NATO launched Operation Deliberate Force, a sustained bombing campaign against the Bosnian Serb Army in the former
Yugoslav republic of Bosnia and Herzegovina. As four hundred NATO aircraft conducted 3,515 sorties, Yeltsin saw into the future. "This is the first
sign of what could happen when NATO comes right up to the Russian
Federation's borders," he said. "The flame of war could burst out across the
whole of Europe." Despite the warnings from Burns and others, in early 1997
invitations to join were extended to Poland, the Czech Republic, and Hungary, thereby going back on previous understandings and moving the West's
military force ever closer to Russia's border.

"We have no idea what we're getting into," complained New York senator Daniel Patrick Moynihan. "We're walking into ethnic historical enmities."
George Kennan, the former U.S. ambassador to Moscow and architect of
America's successful containment of the Soviet Union, also saw only disaster
ahead. "I think it is the beginning of a new Cold War. I think the Russians
will gradually react quite adversely and it will affect their policies. I think it is
a tragic mistake. There was no reason for this whatsoever. No one was threatening anybody else. This expansion would make the founding fathers of this
country turn over in their graves. We have signed up to protect a whole series
of countries, even though we have neither the resources nor the intention to
do so in any serious way."

Finally, in 1999 the three were admitted to the heavily armed pact. And at
almost the same time, without UN approval, NATO launched another massive attack in the Balkans. This time the target was Yugoslavia (today Serbia and Montenegro), to protect Kosovo's Muslim population. A non-NATO
member, the country was an ally of Russia. For seventy-eight days, the bombs
rained on Belgrade, a city of 1.5 million people, as well as on Montenegro.
Among them were deadly cluster munitions, banned by international conventions, which left a grim legacy: thousands of unexploded bomblets. Richard Lloyd, of the U.K. Consulting Group on Landmines, estimated that more
than 250,000 bomblets were ejected by the 1,400 cluster bombs that were
dropped.

And according to a scathing report by Amnesty International, NATO violated international law by targeting locations where civilians were sure to be killed, among them a radio and television headquarters. That bombing, which killed sixteen people, "was a deliberate attack on a civilian object and as such constitutes a war crime," according to the report.

A brutal, illegal war very close to his doorstep had always been Yeltsin's worst nightmare. Now there were two wars in less than half a decade. The following year, Yeltsin's nightmare became Putin's reality upon his election as president. Then just four years later NATO admitted into its military bulwark Latvia, Estonia, and Lithuania. Suddenly the United States and its allies were now standing toe to toe, soldier to soldier, and weapon system to weapon system with Putin on Russia's border. Nearby neighbors Bulgaria, Romania, Slovakia, and Slovenia, much of the former Soviet bloc, also joined.

In 2005, Burns was named U.S. ambassador to Russia. Looking back, he noted the failure of the Clinton administration to comprehend the gravity of NATO's encirclement of Russia. "If you wanted to understand the grievances, mistrust, and smoldering aggressiveness of Putin's Russia, you first had to appreciate the sense of humiliation, wounded pride, and disorder that was often inescapable in Yeltsin's," he said.

It would be as if Russia suddenly placed military forces and weapons not just in Cuba, but in Mexico and much of Central America as well—after launching a two-month bombing campaign in another nearby country. The United States, citing the Monroe Doctrine of 1823, would never stand for it, as the Kennedy administration demonstrated by nearly launching a nuclear war over missiles in Cuba. "Everybody knows if Russia had troops in Mexico or Canada there would be invasions tomorrow," said Harvard's Cornel West. "Here are you, right at the door of Russia, and can't see yourself in the mirror."

Despite the obvious dangers, the United States and NATO continued to speed eastward, ignoring all warning signs and off-ramps. "NATO has put its front-line forces on our borders," Putin complained in 2007, adding that "it represents a serious provocation." Nevertheless, a year later in Bucharest, NATO and the United States issued a cavalier statement indicating that they next intended to go eyeball-to-eyeball with Putin on his southern border as well, with the admittance of Ukraine and Georgia. Viewed through those Russian eyeballs, it was a classic military pincer movement. Suddenly the United States was building an "Iron Ring" around Russia, complained Senator Moynihan, who saw the looming dangers. The comment left Senator Joe Biden, an enthusiastic supporter of NATO enlargement, confused. "I don't quite get it," he said.

Around the same time, Burns, then ambassador to Russia, issued another even more dire warning to Secretary of State Condoleezza Rice. "Ukraine's entry into NATO," he wrote, "is the brightest of all red lines for the Russian elite (not just Putin). In more than two and a half years of conversations with key Russian players, from knuckle-draggers in the dark recesses of the Kremlin to Putin's liberal critics, I have yet to find anyone who views Ukraine in NATO as anything other than a direct challenge to Russian interests." By 2016, with NATO's plans to both encircle western Russia and at the same time largely cut off its critical access to the Mediterranean Sea, Putin had had enough. Montenegro, he believed, was his.

————

Sasa Sindjelic, the man chosen to organize the assassination of Đukanović and the overthrow of his country, was a tough, tall, bull-shaped Serbian nationalist, with close-cropped red hair. A man with a well-deserved reputation for violence, Sindjelic was the leader of an anti-NATO paramilitary biker gang called the Serbian Wolves. In Serbia he had served a seven-year prison sentence for an attack on government officials and possession of explosive devices, and he was currently wanted for murder in nearby Croatia.

A pro-Moscow activist, in 2014 he also spent time assisting injured veterans of the fighting in the Russian-occupied Donbas region of Ukraine. Months earlier, angry protests had broken out in Maidan Square in Ukraine's capital of Kiev over the government's decision to reject an economic agreement with the European Union in favor of one with Russia. It was a protest in which the United States overtly and covertly played a key role, helping to turn it into an anti-Russian coup, what became known as the Maidan uprising. And it was one more item, in bold print, on President Vladimir Putin's long list of grievances against Washington. Viewed through the eyes of those in the Kremlin, it was a bit like Russian agents traveling to Mexico City to ferment an anti-U.S. coup in Mexico. Later, pro-Russian protests broke out in the eastern Donbas region of Ukraine and Russian forces moved in, launching a war of occupation.

As tanks flying Russian flags rolled toward the disputed border on the backs of long green army trucks, Sasa, who spoke Russian as well as Serbian and some English, assisted a group of Cossack fighters at a makeshift refugee camp in Rostov-on-Don. Shishmakov was there on a recruiting mission for the GRU, mingling with a few of the Cossacks in their camouflage vests and high black fur hats known as *papakhas*. They pointed to Sasa as a hard and dedicated pro-Russian worker, and Shishmakov, who was familiar with the Serbian Wolves, went up to greet him. "He introduced himself as Eddie," Sasa said, "and shook my hand." Seating themselves at a table, they chatted about Serbia and their mutual distrust of NATO, and Eddie gave Sasa his phone number and said if he was ever in Moscow to give him a call.

Over the coming months, Eddie would contact Sasa occasionally over Viber, a popular instant messaging service in Russia and Eastern Europe, and ask him about conditions in Serbia. And then in 2015 he invited him to come to Moscow and paid for his ticket. After picking him up at the airport, on the long drive into the city in Eddie's SUV with darkened windows, he told Sasa that he had spoken with his colleagues about him and they were impressed by his views and attitude. But the one thing that would ensure their trust in him would be if he would submit to a polygraph exam.

Sasa was surprised but reluctantly agreed as they pulled up to a tall, interconnected seven-story office building, likely within the 161st Special Purpose Specialist Training Center, and entered a spacious room through a heavy steel door. As they waited for the polygrapher, Sasa was nervous. "If you don't want to do this right now," Eddie said, "just tell me and I'll tell them to leave." Sasa agreed, and a short while later the examiner placed pneumographs around his chest, a blood pressure device on his arm, and electrodes on his fingers.

Then for four to five hours Eddie and the polygrapher took turns pumping Sasa with questions to determine if he might be a double agent. Had he been to any embassies recently? No, he answered. Where did his money come from? He told them he worked on prefabricated homes and sold T-shirts on the side, and for a while did security work for Soko Group in Belgrade. He detailed his criminal record and family ties. When it was over, they went to another room and Eddie lit a cigarette. "Don't worry, it's okay," he said, the smoke corkscrewing between them in the still air, "they would have the results in a day or so." Grabbing the analysis of the polygraph exam, Eddie met with others to discuss Sasa's suitability as a potential assassin.

The next day, Eddie met Sasa at his hotel, and Sasa was relieved when told he had passed the test. To celebrate, they went to lunch at Samarkand, an Uzbek restaurant a short fifteen-minute drive from the GRU offices. With a belly dancer, rice plov, and steamed dumplings known as manty, it was an enjoyable place to hear good news. They chatted about Serbian politics, and then as they headed for the car to drive back to the airport, Eddie asked Sasa what he owed him for expenses. About $300, Sasa estimated, to cover the hotel, dinner, and breakfast. Eddie reached into his pocket and pulled out a wad of bills—about $5,000—and handed it to Sasa. Eddie had a new source and potential assassin.

By January 2016, Putin's covert war had begun. Eight miles southeast of the clandestine agents at the Aquarium were the cyber warriors at Khamovnichesky Barracks. And at the same time Eddie was focused on election day in Montenegro, Ivan Yermakov was focused on election day in the United States. For both, the goal was the same: Get an anti-NATO government installed. In Montenegro that meant knocking out Milo Đukanović and putting the pro-Russian Democratic Front (DF) in power, and in the United States it meant knocking out Hillary Clinton and putting Donald Trump in power. But rather than a bloody coup d'état, Yermakov's goal was to influence the election through stealth, with malware rather than warfare.

Trump made no secret of his opposition to NATO, even suggesting it be killed. "Either they have to pay up for past deficiencies or they have to get out," he said about other member countries not paying their share of dues. "And if it breaks up NATO, it breaks up NATO." He added, "It was really designed for the Soviet Union, which doesn't exist anymore." Unlike with the Soviet Union, however, Putin's Russia had no Warsaw Pact to counter NATO. But he did have the GRU.

With nine months to go before the October parliamentary election, there was little noticeable change in daily life in Podgorica, Montenegro's capital. In the old neighborhood of Stara Varoš, workers in winter coats and colorful scarfs crisscrossed the narrow streets beneath a stone clock tower that during the Ottoman times called Muslims to prayer. And across the cable-stayed Millennium Bridge, visitors clutching oddly folded maps boarded tour buses and snapped selfies in front of the Hotel Podgorica with its façade made of a thousand stones.

But underneath the calm exterior, a violent coup d'état was taking shape. Russia was secretly controlling the opposition DF party, which strongly opposed joining NATO. The FSB, Russia's internal security service, had long had a spy in the organization, Anani Nikic, posing as a translator. And the two leaders of the group, Andrija Mandic and Milan Knežević, who would assume power following the coup, were secretly working with Moscow and making covert trips there.

In charge of the operation was the GRU's "Eddie" Shishmakov. As originally planned, the on-the-ground commander of the coup would hire paid mercenaries in Montenegro and across the border in Serbia. They would purchase automatic weapons, tear gas masks, body armor, handcuffs, coils of barbed wire, and other supplies and hide them in Podgorica. Coordination would be done over encrypted cell phones supplied by Eddie.

At 11 p.m. on election night, after the polls closed, a crowd of DF supporters would gather in front of the Parliament Building and stage a noisy protest. Secretly joining them would be dozens of the armed mercenaries, some dressed as local police officers. Also standing by in the shadows would be about fifty Russian special forces soldiers. Then, as one of the DF officials took the stage, the mercenaries dressed as Montenegrin police would open fire on the crowd. Led by the plainclothed mercenaries, the angry crowd, blaming Đukanović, would then storm the building, take over Parliament, assassinate the prime minister, and install the leaders of the Front as head of the new government.

The key was getting the right person to organize the ground operation, and Eddie and the Front leaders focused on a former Serbian intelligence officer, Slavko Nikie. In early February, Mandic and Knežević traveled to Serbia's capital of Belgrade to brief him on the plot. But on closer examination, Nikie appeared unreliable. As a result, absent a Plan B, that left Eddie scrambling. In March, without revealing the operation, he expressed his frustration to Sasa. "It's enough," he wrote. "It cannot be tolerated anymore. In Montenegro, the authorities should be toppled, Đukanović...that gang." That month the DF leaders again secretly flew to Moscow for a meeting but came back without much encouragement.

By early fall, Eddie's frustration was morphing into panic. As a result, on Sunday, September 25, with less than a month to go before the October 16 election, he once again contacted Sasa. Sasa hesitated; he said he was involved with a construction job and had a wife and small child to take care of. "No, no, no," Eddie told him, "you should go now. I'm covering all the expenses. I'm sending you some money right now, just go, you have to come!"

A little after seven that night, Eddie left his GRU office and went down the street to Western Union to send a money wire to Sasa for $800 to cover the plane fare. The next day, Monday, September 26, Sasa picked up the cash from Western Union and boarded the first plane he could get, a midnight flight to Moscow getting in around 4 a.m. At Terminal E at Moscow's Sheremetyevo Airport, Eddie stared into the blackness watching for the Air Serbia jet with the double-headed eagle on the tail.

A short time later, as the early dawn's ghostly gray shadows were beginning to form on the tarmac, the Air Serbia jet pulled up to the gate. Sasa walked out of the Jetway carrying a briefcase and an overnight bag, and there to greet him was Eddie and an airport security officer. Eddie handed Sasa a plastic badge to hang from his neck and asked him not to say anything as the security officer led them down some freshly polished corridors. But just before arriving at passport control, they took a right through a locked door and entered a maze of off-limits hallways and dimly lit stairwells before emerging into the terminal, thereby avoiding any record of Sasa entering Russia.

Eddie said little as they drove to the building where Sasa had taken his polygraph exam. They entered the same apartment as before through the heavy steel door. After locking away Sasa's cell phone to prevent any eaves-dropping, Eddie suggested that Sasa take a nap in the bedroom, and after he rested, they would have a long talk.

Sasa awoke to the sound of the opening of the steel door, which reminded him of a vault. But now another man had joined Eddie. He was younger, athletic, with the build of a tennis player, and his blond hair was cut short, Caesar-style. Eddie's deputy in the operation, his *nom de inspiciendum*, was Vladimir Popov and his cover job was that of a photographer and journalist employed by *Morskoye Strakhovanie*, a Russian insurance magazine special-izing in the maritime industry.

As a tool of his make-believe trade, he often had a camera with a long white zoom lens hanging from his shoulder. The phony job gave him an excuse to travel extensively in the West, snapping pictures at various ports. Eddie also used the periodical as a cover when necessary. In reality, Popov was Vladimir Moiseev, thirty-six, a lieutenant colonel in the GRU. Born in a small village in Siberia near Chelyabinsk, he had earned an engineering degree from the Tyumen Military Engineering Institute before joining a GRU airborne Spetsnaz unit.

For the next several hours, as Popov remained largely quiet, Eddie described to Sasa the dire situation with the anti-NATO campaign and the difficulties in trying to get positive changes in Montenegro through elections. "There were problems," Eddie explained. "We were backing some people there, the Democratic Front, and have already spent a huge amount of money on them, but they can't win an election. Milo Đukanović is always stealing them."

Then, as he went into detail about the plot on voting night, on a large table he laid out a series of satellite photos of the Parliament Building, a boxy, Soviet-era structure built in 1954 as a bank, when Podgorica was named Titograd and Montenegro was part of Yugoslavia. The photos clearly showed the streets around the building, pedestrian crossings, and the park across the street. The massive scale and complexity of the coup caught Sasa by surprise. "Doing something like that would take a minimum of five to six months of secret preparation," he said, adding that he had a new baby at home and could not spend time in Montenegro.

Eddie said they were in a bind in terms of time, but that they already had people in Montenegro and Sasa's job would be to remain in Serbia and recruit the mob and mercenaries who would go to the rally on election night, and also to find someone to purchase the weapons. He said they would need at least fifty Kalashnikov assault rifles, fifty handguns, as much ammo as he could get, as well as police uniforms, coils of barbed wire, gas masks, and an assortment of other police and military-style equipment. The weapons, he suggested, could be transported to Podgorica in a truck with a false bottom and then stored in a rented house.

Eddie then gave Sasa a Lenovo mobile phone with an encryption program and a speed dial to quickly reach him. Similar encrypted phones, he said, would be given to other members of the coup. To hide their origin, the phones had been purchased online from a website in Bulgaria. It was critical, Eddie said, that only Sasa would be aware of his and Moscow's involvement.

Sasa worried that the small group of armed mercenaries would likely be outnumbered by Montenegro's police and special tactical forces. But Eddie said they wouldn't be a problem. His men would be armed with assault weapons while the local police would have only pistols. Also, a team of Russian commandos was planning to attack the base in the mountains that housed the tactical forces and take them out of action. It was very risky, Sasa told Eddie. But after a lot of back-and-forth he said he would do it because of his ideological convictions against NATO. "I was aware of the risk I was getting into," Sasa would later say. "But I agreed to do it out of respect for Eddie."

Then Eddie told Sasa his people had been constantly following Đukanović for weeks as he pulled out another photo, this one of a two-story white building with pinkish columns. "It's the American embassy," he said. "Đukanović will likely try to flee there and that will not be allowed to happen." From the Parliament Building, where he would be preparing for his victory speech, it was only a short distance across the bridge over the Morača River to the embassy.

But Đukanović would never reach the bridge.

Before driving Sasa back to the airport, and once again escorting him around passport control, Eddie gave him $10,000 in cash and said there would be a lot more coming when they met in a few days in Belgrade where Eddie was planning to oversee the coup. At 8:45 p.m. Sasa boarded an Aeroflot jet for the three-hour flight back home.

By 2016 in Belgrade, the memory of Josip Broz Tito, Yugoslavia's communist founder and leader for decades until his death in 1980, had all but vanished. And for many, the brutal wars that followed were slipping ever more distantly from memory. At the Hotel Majestic that October, crowds packed into BeoGourmet for a weekend of fine wine and epicurean pleasures; across town at the Crowne Plaza, climatologists were listening to lectures at the International Conference on Environmental Science and Technology; on Bokeljska Street an LGBT organization was screening a film in honor of Intersex Awareness Day; and the October Belgrade Jazz Festival, which went dark for fifteen years in 1990, had now become one of the most influential jazz events on the annual European circuit.

But for others, NATO's seventy-eight-day bombing campaign in 1999, launched to end President Slobodan Milosevic's attacks on ethnic Albanians in Kosovo, remained in the forefront of their memory, as did their deep nationalistic desire for a "Greater Serbia," one that again incorporated Montenegro. Theirs was the Belgrade of battered trams and gritty bars with whispering men in long gray coats. And it was in those areas that Sasa was hoping to find his recruits to storm Montenegro's Parliament Building for his Kremlin spies.

Within days of arriving back in Belgrade, Sasa found a source to provide the weapons and act as the on-the-ground commander to lead the armed assault on election night: Mirko "Paja" Velimirovic. A locksmith, tavern owner, and ex-cop with Serbia's Ministry of Internal Affairs in Serb-dominated North Kosovo, Paja had the physique of a bouncer at a cheap bar, a droopy black mustache, and a face veiled behind a mat of salt-and-pepper whiskers. He called himself a "Chetnik duke," a reference to an ultranationalist paramilitary organization that glorified the massacre and expulsion of Bosnian Muslims from lands deemed Serbian.

Paja told Sasa that he had access to a large supply of weapons left over from the war in Kosovo, and that he could smuggle them into Montenegro. He also agreed to take charge of the on-the-ground operation on the night of the election and pose as a member of the Montenegrin special police. It was decided that they would all wear small blue ribbons on their uniforms to distinguish the hired guns from the real police. Sasa would later give Paja $30,000 and three boxes of ammo.

Another person Sasa convinced to become a co-conspirator and masquerade as a Montenegrin special police officer, as well as help out with organizing the attack, was General Bratislav Dikić. At forty-six he was the former commander of an elite Serbian special police unit known as the Gendarmery, but he was now out of work. The previous year he had been fired after reports surfaced of his alleged involvement in organized crime. Sasa agreed to pay him about $20,000 for his services.

On October 2, with just two weeks before the election, Eddie and Popov landed at Belgrade's Nikola Tesla International Airport and took a taxi to Le Petit Piaf, a small boutique-style hotel on steep, cobblestoned Skadarlija Street in the city's bohemian quarter. Once a gathering place for poets and artists a century ago, today the old town street is lined with cafés, art shops, and open-air restaurants. At night, bathed in a moonlike glow, Balkan folk bands perform beneath wrought iron streetlamps, and bakeries stay open until dawn.

After arriving, Eddie sent a message to Sasa for a meet-up to discuss his progress. By now there was great pressure from the Kremlin on the two Russian agents to organize the overthrow of the Montenegro government, install the DF, and scrap the NATO deal. Soon, the aircraft carrier *Admiral Kuznetsov* and its battle group would arrive in the Mediterranean on their way to operations off Syria. And as before, they would likely be denied refueling access at NATO member ports.

The venue for the debriefing was Belgrade Fortress in Kalemegdan Park, a mammoth white battlement surrounded by tall stucco walls that glittered in the sun. It sat on a rocky cliff, overhanging the surging confluence of the Danube and Sava Rivers, and contained elevated lookout points for viewing the city, and dark low recesses for discreet conversations. Over the coming days, it was where they would regularly rendezvous, and where Eddie would give Sasa wads of cash, eventually totaling 200,000 euros in new banknotes, to bribe his contacts and buy the weapons, uniforms, and equipment needed for the operation.

And as Eddie and Sasa talked, Popov would remain out of sight at a distance, watching for watchers from other spy agencies, and snapping pictures with his long zoom lens of anyone suspicious. To protect themselves, Popov would occasionally follow Sasa after the meeting to see where he went and who he met. At one point on the way back to his car, Sasa stopped at Shindra, a small local neighborhood bar with cold Jelen beer and a friendly waitress. The next day Eddie questioned him about why he was there and who he was talking to.

In Podgorica as election day drew near, national flags began to flutter and billboards suddenly sprang up along the roads and highways proclaiming "Eternal be our Montenegro." Long black Audis shuffled high-ranking officials to campaign parties and meetings with diplomatic delegations. But at DF campaign headquarters, leaders Andrija Mandic and Milan Knežević were counting on winning with bullets instead of ballots thanks to Moscow's money and men.

CHAPTER 32

◆

The Exfiltrators

As a security measure, Eddie had set up a firewall between Sasa's team in Belgrade and the Front's team in Podgorica. The DF leaders, therefore, knew their role in the election night plan, but they had no idea of the identity of the others. And likewise, Sasa knew the DF was involved in the operation, but was never given any specific names.

Critical in the lead-up to the coup was finding the right campaign manager, someone who was savvy and tough, and the person they were counting on was Paul Manafort, newly resigned as the top advisor for Donald Trump's presidential campaign. Caught up in a nasty scandal involving previous work in Ukraine, he resigned under a dark cloud in August 2016. Now damaged goods and nearly broke, he was looking for money and a new job. He also had a long history with Montenegro, working for Russian billionaire Oleg Deripaska.

According to the almost entirely redacted section on the coup in the Senate Intelligence Committee report, "By 2016, Deripaska was involved in funding and executing an aggressive Russian-directed campaign to overthrow the Montenegrin government and assassinate the Prime Minister in a violent coup . . . These efforts supported a pro-Russia and anti-NATO Montenegrin opposition party, the Democratic Front (DF)."

At forty-eight, Deripaska was tall with an impish grin, cropped blond hair, and cobalt eyes. The *Guardian* once compared him to Daniel Craig, adding that he "shares the Bond actor's reputation for toughness." He also knew Paul Manafort very well. Long before the political consultant became Donald Trump's campaign manager, he had Deripaska as a client. And to a large degree, that meant having Vladimir Putin as a client, since Deripaska was not only a close associate of the Russian president but often acted as his proxy in a variety of countries around the world, including Montenegro.

In 2005, Deripaska purchased a majority stake in Montenegro's giant aluminum company, KAP, "a deal that was likely done in coordination with the Russian government to extend Russian influence in Montenegro," said the Senate report. He then hired Manafort to further "Russian government efforts to exert influence over the country." That meant finding ways to quietly support the leaders of the DF.

But by 2014, Manafort had jumped ship. Nearly broke after binge-spending sprees, and owing Deripaska upwards of $19 million, he became elusive after the Russian sued him. Then, following his ill-fated turn with Trump, he was back patching things up with his former client, looking for new work. Leaders of the DF saw his fall from grace with Trump and were counting on him becoming their campaign manager. Manafort did talk to several politicians in Montenegro, but in the end he passed.

Instead, the DF turned to another veteran campaign manager, a shadowy Israeli with a long history of working for governments involved in coups, conflicts, and corruption. And someone, Montenegrin prosecutors would charge, who employed a team of former CIA and FBI agents to quickly exfiltrate the plotters following the coup and assassination. Which may be why the section is redacted from the Senate Intelligence Committee report.

With a Nixonian five o'clock shadow and a high forehead surrounding an ever-retreating widow's peak the color of coal dust, Aron Shaviv has the good looks of a TV pitchman. Born in England, he grew up in Canada before moving to Israel as a teenager. For most of his life he has operated in the netherworld of espionage and politics, hype and propaganda. They are likely some of the qualities that attracted the DF and its Russian backers to him as their campaign manager. According to his now deleted bio, Shaviv "honed his leadership and decision-making skills while serving as a captain in the Israeli Defense Forces and a field agent for a civilian intelligence agency," most likely the Mossad. He also worked for the secretive Ministry of Strategic Affairs. "I used to do surveillance, that's my background, that's exactly what I used to do," he told me.

Later Shaviv became a political hired gun for Israeli politicians and anyone else who could pay his high price, often taking on clients in areas with a history of corruption and political coups d'état, like Guinea, Mali, and Sudan. "I've worked in Libya, I still work in Iraq, and I've worked in Mali," Shaviv said, "where I had a whole team kidnapped." He added, "I'm very highly paid. I'm probably the highest-paid person in this field I want to say globally, outside of the U.S." In Thailand in 2014, Shaviv was on the wrong end of a coup when General Prayut Chan-o-cha took over the government from his client, Prime Minister Yingluck Shinawatra, who had been impeached, forced from office, and later convicted of corruption. "I was in the room with Yingluck Shinawatra, the prime minister, when the coup went down."

Close to former prime minister Benjamin Netanyahu, Shaviv served as his chief strategist in his successful 2015 campaign. And he had a long history of working with Russians in elections. Before Netanyahu, he served as a campaign consultant for Avigdor Lieberman. A racist Israeli politician with great admiration for Vladimir Putin, Lieberman was minister of finance in former prime minister Naftali Bennett's right-wing government in Israel. Lieberman's anti-Muslim bigotry was so over-the-top that it even shocked Netanyahu's former ambassador to the United States. "He accused anti-Zionist Arab politicians of treason—'Your place is in prison, not the Knesset'—and demanded loyalty oaths from Israeli Arabs," noted former ambassador Michael Oren. "Such populism, brutish even by Israeli standards, earned Lieberman an international reputation as a racist. The sight of every poster, and every call for loyalty oaths, made me cringe."

Just as the racism of his clients didn't bother Shaviv, nor did their human rights abuses or corruption. Another of his clients was billionaire Israeli Dan Gertler, an Orthodox Jew who drained billions from the impoverished citizens of the Democratic Republic of Congo, one of the poorest countries on the planet, through corrupt deals involving his gold and diamond mines. In 2017, the United States formally sanctioned Gertler for his "extensive public corruption."

Working for Lieberman, who was born in the Soviet Union, Shaviv developed a great many contacts within the Russian community since Russian immigrants heavily supported Lieberman's party. Now Shaviv was on his own as a campaign consultant and his background with Lieberman and the Russians allowed him to specialize in former Soviet Bloc countries. Among his clients were the heads of state in Serbia, Bulgaria, and Romania, and also municipal leaders in Ukraine, thus his name and reputation were well known to the leaders of the DF.

Shaviv's exfiltration team was led by Joseph Assad, a forty-five-year-old former CIA operations officer. A naturalized American, Assad was a child when his Christian family fled from Lebanon to Egypt during the civil war in the mid-1970s. Following high school, Assad moved to the United States to attend Palm Beach Atlantic University, a private conservative Christian college. His future wife, Michele, like Assad a devoted Christian, was also a student there.

In 2002 after receiving their master's degrees they both joined the CIA as operations officers and bounced around embassies in the Middle East, from Yemen to Saudi Arabia to Iraq to the United Arab Emirates. Then in 2012, after a decade in the field and several headquarters assignments, they quit the agency and formed a small security company in Abu Dhabi called Peregrine

Consultants, LLC, that was fronted out of Box 62986 at a local post office. Three years later the couple moved back to Florida and set up Peregrine Group, LLC, in another post office box, this time Box 808 at 137 S. Courtenay Parkway in Merritt Island.

At first Shaviv downplayed the coup attempt, calling it "the world's worst conspiracy theory," but he later acknowledged that the evidence was there. "Certainly, it seems as if there were enough kind of pieces to piece it together," he said. "And if there was, fine, I'm willing to accept it . . . But I certainly wasn't part of it." Shaviv said it was just out of an abundance of caution that he happened to fly in a very expensive six-man CIA-led exfiltration team, complete with gear, to a peaceful city in a peaceful country for a peaceful election with no history of violence.

He said the team was there not to exfiltrate the coup plotters, but just him. "He's there to protect me and me only and that's the be-all and end-all of his assignment," Shaviv told me. I asked him why he would need such a very expensive five-man team flown from the United States, and another electronic surveillance expert flown in from Israel, for a simple parliamentary election in a peaceful micro-country where the major industry is tourism. "As the election came closer and closer we were being harassed by the authorities," he said. "Every single time I would land in Podgorica [the capital], I'd flash my passport, I'd be taken into a room, they'd keep me there for twenty minutes, an hour." There was little, however, a joint CIA/FBI/Israeli exfiltration team could do about that, and he could offer no other examples of harassment or danger.

Shaviv then said that Assad's only job was to simply act as a security advisor. "His task is the risk assessment," he said. "He's worked with me over many years." But it was clear that from the beginning Assad's job, and that of the others, was going to be far more than that of passive risk consultants.

When not exfiltrating Shaviv from elections, Assad worked as a contractor for the Orlando-based Patriot Defense Group. Run by Brian Scott, also a CIA veteran, the firm earned around $50 million selling spy training back to the spies as the intelligence agencies and Pentagon outsourced training contracts to his company. Assad's job was to train students in CIA tradecraft at the company offices in Maitland, Florida.

Hoping to bring along a few other former intelligence officers to help in the exfiltration effort, Assad turned to Scott. According to restricted, internal FBI documents, Assad told Scott that he had been contacted by "an Israeli/Canadian political adviser for a Montenegrin political party, 'DF' . . . The political adviser is well known and may have provided advice to Israeli Prime Minister Netanyahu." What he needed, Assad said, "included

counter-surveillance as well as evacuation and extraction planning sometime after October 6, 2016 [ten days before the Montenegrin election] in/
around the Montenegrin capital, Podgorica." Not the usual election campaign support. Scott told Assad that he was interested but wanted to make a
few checks.

Scott said he then contacted Tiziano Mousu, a company "asset" known as
"Krill" and living in Malta, to see if he wanted to become involved in the plot.
"Krill laid out the then current political climate of Montenegro and advised
he had close contact with the Montenegrin ruling party including the most
senior level of the Montenegrin government," he told the FBI agents. But, he
added, Mousu said he wanted nothing to do with the operation if it involved
the Democratic Front "due to allegations that it was involved with Russian
intelligence."

Later, Scott testified at the trial in Montenegro at the request of the special
prosecutor. In his testimony, he says he told Assad "that protective counter-
security and evacuation planning was difficult without the support of host
nation police services." But Assad told Scott "he would be fine as he had two
former FBI special agents working with him. I expressed my opinion that was
not acceptable overseas given their expertise is inside the domestic U.S." Yet
despite the fact that his company received millions of dollars from the CIA
every year, Scott apparently never bothered to tell the agency or the FBI that
one of his employees, along with several FBI agents, was about to assist a Russian intelligence–backed organization in a friendly ally plan an exfiltration
during a national election.

———

Assad then talked four former FBI agents into joining him in the operation.
Together the agents had collectively spent more than a century with the FBI.
Three were associated with the D&R Agency, a private investigation company
operating out of an office in Fort Lauderdale's Museum of Art Plaza. According to an investigation by Montenegrin prosecutors, the former agents the
prosecutor named as part of his investigation included John J. DiPaolo, president of the firm, who spent much of his career based in Miami and focused
on organized crime and money laundering investigations.

Another was R. Scott Rivas, the CEO of the firm, who was a senior leader
of the Miami SWAT team and supervised several international terrorism
squads. A third former agent was Jorge Miyar, the company's investigative
manager, who also spent time in Miami and was the operations supervisor
in Baghdad in 2004. And the fourth agent was Ladislao "Ladi" Carballosa,
whose assignments included a number of tours at the CIA. He was with a
Washington, DC, private investigation firm, Ahearn Consulting Group. All

were contacted but I only heard back from Assad, who required the payment of a "consulting fee" to hear his side of the story, which I declined.

On October 10, according to Montenegro's special prosecutor, the former CIA ops officer and his fellow FBI agents arrived in Montenegro, six days before the election. They brought with them devices to prevent the tracking of mobile phone signals, a satellite phone, and other equipment. And once in country, they were housed in two private homes in suburban Podgorica, rented several months earlier for about $25,000 by a DF staffer.

In addition to the former FBI agents, Assad also asked an Israeli private investigator who specialized in scanning for surveillance devices to join them. He was Yoram Frig, a hulking surveillance expert with a dark stubble haircut and offices in Tel Aviv and the coastal resort of Agios Tychonas in Cyprus. His usual equipment consisted of an OSC-5000 Omni-Spectral Correlator. Priced at around $21,000, it consists of a hard briefcase packed with antennas, a spectrum analyzer to automatically store all signals encountered in a memory for later review, built-in demodulators for converting signals, triangulation equipment to pinpoint bug locations, and many other technical surveillance devices.

Prosecutors believed that the equipment was to help the conspirators avoid the police as they fled across the border into Albania during their escape. Like Shaviv, Frig had a number of clients in the Balkans and Eastern Europe, among them Tom Doshi, an Albanian politician and owner of the largest pharmaceutical company in the country. In 2018 the U.S. State Department announced that Doshi was barred from entering the United States, along with his immediate family, "due to his involvement in significant corruption."

On Friday, October 14, two days before the election, Milan Knežević, one of the two Front leaders, gave a speech in Podgorica's central square that was a preview of what he had planned. Prime Minister Đukanović, he said, would soon be sent to the capital's Spuž prison. "This dictator will kneel in Spuž while he cleans the floors," he emphatically declared. The party also announced that supporters would hold a large rally outside the Parliament Building as the results were announced on election day.

———

Back in Serbia, as election day was getting close, a key concern for Eddie and the Russians was the possibility that as the attack began, the coup plotters would be overwhelmed by Montenegrin special forces. But the GRU had already infiltrated and prepositioned about fifty of their own well-armed special forces troops into Serbia, and they were hiding out in the mountainous Zlatibor region close to the Montenegrin border. The plan was to cross into Montenegro on the night before the election and, if necessary, neutralize Montenegrin special forces at their nearby camp. Then they would travel to Podgorica to assist the plotters in the planned post-election takeover of the Parliament Building.

Three days before the election, Paja Velimirovic, the man responsible for buying the weapons, met again with Sasa in Belgrade. Paja said he had found a supplier, but he needed more cash, about $20,000. Flush with Moscow's money, Sasa gave it to him, but now both he and Eddie were also beginning to become suspicious. They had good reason. The day before, Paja had walked into the Montenegro police headquarters and told them about the plot. Hoping to catch the conspirators, and at the same time prevent the coup, the police asked Paja to continue playing along.

Leaving Sasa, Paja drove back to Montenegro and secretly met again with the police. They pulled out a pile of military weapons so he could take some pictures and pretend they were the guns he had just purchased. Later that day he returned to Belgrade, and as he and Sasa went shopping for police uniforms, gas masks, razor wire, and other supplies, he showed Sasa the photos. Sasa then instructed Paja to return to Montenegro and rent a safe house to hide the recruited mob in the hours before the coup. But instead, Paja returned again to the police headquarters to report on his meeting with Sasa.

As his suspicions about Paja increased, Sasa decided to replace him as the on-scene commander with General Bratislav Dikić, the former chief of Serbia's special police. But the last-minute switch presented some problems. Sasa had an encrypted Russian cell phone he needed to get to Dikić, then in Podgorica, who would in turn hand it to one of the Front leaders, apparently Knežević, so Knežević and Eddie could coordinate the coup. As a result, despite his suspicions, Sasa met with Paja again, this time in the Serbian city of Požarevac, a farming area about fifty-five miles from Belgrade at the confluence of the Danube, Great Morava, and Mlava Rivers. Sasa gave him the Russian encrypted phone and instructions to hand it to "Nikola," his code name for Dikić, who would then give it to Knežević.

The next day, the day before the election, Paja traveled to Podgorica to meet with the mob of mercenaries and make the handoff of the phone, but Dikić was delayed. Instead, Paja returned to police headquarters and, as the officers listened in, called Sasa. "So listen to me, Sasa, and please don't interrupt me," he said. "People are getting nervous, man! Listen to what I'm telling you...I am still waiting for this guy [Dikić], whoever will come here."

But Sasa sensed he was overreacting to a simple delay, and some restlessness by the hired mob. "Don't behave like a kid!" he chastised Paja. "You must simply wait...It's your problem that they are nervous. Keep them under control." Then he turned sarcastic. "If you are bored, you can go to the Parliament already now." But Paja was not amused. "Hey, listen to me. You know we can't go to Parliament now!" Sasa had heard enough. "Just sit tight. He will call you. Meet him and hand him over the phone," he said and hung up.

Later Paja and Dikić met and Paja handed him the encrypted phone and the address of the safe house where the weapons were supposedly stored. But when Dikić showed up at the location, the Montenegrin police were there waiting and quickly arrested him. Over the next hours mass arrests took place, and on the morning of the election news of the aborted coup and the arrest of twenty people was announced.

The news no doubt sent shock waves through members of the Front. "I stepped out, there are police and law enforcement and army people in Podgorica," said Shaviv. "All over, basically on every street corner." Suddenly, rather than waiting for the election results, both former CIA officer Joseph Assad and Israeli surveillance expert Yoram Frig, and possibly the former FBI agents, quickly fled the country on what was likely the planned escape route. At about 2 p.m., hours before the polls closed, they drove across the land border at Bozaj into Albania, about a dozen miles away. Then from the Albanian capital of Tirana they flew to Istanbul. Shaviv left the next day.

Hearing about the arrests, Sasa, in Serbia, went into hiding and secretly met up with Eddie, who pumped him with questions about the location of the weapons. Sasa said he had no idea and that only Paja knew where they were. "Eddie said that it was Paja's fault, that he ratted us out and that he should be killed," Sasa later said. Eddie then suggested a way to "finally resolve the matter in Montenegro." He asked Sasa to personally assassinate Prime Minister Đukanović. Sasa, however, declined, arguing that because he was now a wanted man in Montenegro he would be arrested the minute he entered the country. Instead, he said, "He asked me to find someone who is skillful in using a sniper rifle and explosives and who is willing to do that, adding that money is not a problem. As far as Đukanović is concerned, he said that they knew where he moved in Podgorica, as he was under surveillance."

With the arrests, the voting took place as normal, and as the Russians anticipated, the Front lost, winning only eighteen out of eighty-one seats in Parliament. Đukanović's DSP party won thirty-six seats and was able to form a majority government with three other minority parties. And eight months later, on June 5, Montenegro officially became NATO's twenty-ninth member. Thus ensuring that, in this modern-day *Game of Thrones*, Americans may one day give their lives and blood for one of the world's most corrupt countries led by one of the world's most corrupt authoritarians.

"He views anyone who doesn't want to plunder the country with him as a traitor," said Draginja Vuksanovic, a respected university professor in Montenegro, about Đukanović. In 2020, Freedom House even degraded the country from a democracy to a "hybrid regime," little more than a kleptocracy, charging years of abuse of power and strongman tactics employed by Đukanović. "Many members of the ruling party are believed to have ties to organized crime, further cementing the DPS's grip on power," said the human rights group. Nevertheless, the ink had barely dried on the membership agreement when NATO agreed to send troops to Montenegro to defend against potential Russian "hybrid warfare."

With the announcement of the arrests, Serbian police and intelligence organizations began assisting officials in Montenegro, and eight days after the election, on October 24, they detained Eddie and Popov. In their possession they discovered counterfeit Montenegro special police uniforms, a cache of over $135,000 in euros, and sophisticated encrypted telecom equipment. According to Russian authorities, the two agents were in Belgrade simply researching an article about the Russian military in the region during the First World War, an excuse British foreign secretary Jeremy Hunt called "absurd." Almost immediately the Kremlin sent to Belgrade one of its most senior officials to try to defuse the situation and retrieve the two Russian spies.

The official was Nikolai Patrushev, a veteran of the KGB who replaced Putin as director of the successor FSB. Since 2008 he has been secretary of the Kremlin's National Security Council, a position somewhat analogous to the White House national security advisor. The fact that such a high-level official, and ex–spy chief, would be flown to Belgrade on a moment's notice reflected the seriousness of the situation. Unwilling to create a damaging diplomatic row with the powerful superpower, Serb officials simply allowed Eddie and Popov to fly back to Russia on Patrushev's government jet.

Just a few days after the Russians departed Belgrade, Serb officials began to wonder if their own country might have been part of a larger Russian conspiracy. On October 29, Serbian police discovered a large cache of weapons close to Prime Minister Aleksandar Vučić's family home in Jajinci, along the route he normally took to work. The arsenal, which included a grenade launcher, four hand grenades, and more than a hundred rounds of 7.62mm ammunition, as well as ammunition for automatic weapons, had been stashed in a car parked in the forest about fifty feet from a road. Later, the police found another car, this time in a garage in Belgrade. Inside was a Heckler & Koch submachine gun, ammunition, TNT, a detonator paired with a mobile phone, and a gun.

With everyone else either arrested or safely out of the country, on November 1, Sasa turned himself in to the Montenegrin police, gave a full statement of his activities, and cooperated in the investigation. "If I had not surrendered myself, I would have been killed," he said. Investigators seized 125,000 euros from his bank account and also discovered in his possession three hundred-dollar bills whose serial numbers indicated that they had been processed in Moscow at Bank of America and later at Sber Bank.

After a long investigation, the multiple trials ended on March 28, 2019, and the following September, Supreme Court judge Susan Mugos issued a 678-page verdict. Nearly all those arrested either pled guilty or were found guilty and received sentences of up to fifteen years in prison. They included the two top leaders of the Front, Andrija Mandic and Milan Knežević, and the two Russians, Eddie and Popov, who were tried in absentia. But the Russian agents no doubt quickly received new identities and spent weeks explaining to GRU officials what went wrong. The special prosecutor said he suspected Russia spent between 15 and 17 million euros on the plot.

Soon after the verdicts were announced, British foreign secretary Jeremy Hunt expressed his relief and concern. "The guilty verdicts announced today against the 2 Russian intelligence officers responsible for plotting this coup were the conclusion of Montenegrin legal proceedings of unprecedented transparency," he said. "The failed coup attempt against Montenegro in 2016 was one of the most outrageous examples of Russia's attempts to undermine European democracy."

Then, on February 5, 2021, Montenegro's Court of Appeals annulled the verdict against those charged due to procedural violations and the case was returned to the high court for retrial.

An arrest warrant was issued for Anani Nikic, the Front Russian translator suspected of being a covert Russian FSB agent, and he was detained in April 2017 in Rostov, an area of Russia near the Russian-occupied territory of Ukraine. But in November the Kremlin granted him political asylum.

With regard to the others, Shaviv and Assad were key targets of the investigation and on August 12, 2018, an Interpol "Red Notice" international arrest warrant was issued for Assad by Montenegro's special prosecutor, Sasa Cadenovic. He faced up to ten years in prison for "creating a criminal organization," according to the charges. The following month he was arrested while visiting the United Arab Emirates, where he had previously been posted with the CIA and later ran a private intelligence agency. A Red Notice was also issued for Shaviv.

Interpol later canceled both of the Red Notices since the organization does not involve itself with internal coups. "INTERPOL's practice has generally been to forbid the use of the Organization's channels for the circulation of requests for police cooperation related to acts committed in the context of an unconstitutional seizure of power," it said. Such actions, "would have significant adverse implications for the neutrality of the Organization." Through his lawyer, Assad claimed his innocence. "This is a deception campaign against a loyal American who had no role in any crimes or coup in Montenegro," he said.

An arrest warrant had also been issued for Yoram Frig, the Israeli electronic surveillance specialist, but he voluntarily surrendered to Montenegrin authorities for questioning. He told the special prosecutor that he "came to Montenegro on the invitation of the ex-CIA agent Joseph Assad and that he was supposed to provide electronic services for a gathering of the Democratic Front," thus further implicating Assad.

––––––––

Then, in January 2019, the special prosecutor issued an order expanding the investigation into the four American FBI agents, naming them as suspects for "creating a criminal organization" and the crime of "attempted terrorism." Six months later, in July, Cadjenovic expanded it again, when he discovered that nearly $2 million had allegedly been transferred to Shaviv and Assad by three individuals with Russian names in the months leading up to the election, from July to October 2016. The money traveled via a complex network of front companies, from the Czech Republic to a Cypriot account of a Seychelles company called "Derker," a company founded by Shaviv and jointly owned by both Shaviv and Assad. From there, money flowed to Shaviv's Strategy and Campaign account in Israel and Assad's Peregrine account in Abu Dhabi.

Shaviv was evasive when I brought up Assad and their secretive company, Derker. "I'm not confirming it, I'm not denying it, that we were partners in that company," he said. "If we were partners then how we divide it between us...I really don't want to get into this, I don't want to get into my business structure." He added, "I don't work with him anymore because of this incident."

Despite the possible involvement of a former CIA officer and four former FBI agents in a planned Russian assassination and coup attempt in what is now a NATO member, there has been surprisingly little interest by the U.S.

Justice Department or the FBI—possibly precisely because of the alleged involvement of CIA and FBI agents in the plot and the embarrassing questions they raise.*

The utter hypocrisy of the American message was not lost on the defendants sitting in prison. After their sentencing, the U.S. embassy in Podgorica issued a Twitter message calling it a "historical day for Montenegro." That prompted former DF leader Milan Knežević to send an open letter to U.S. ambassador Judy Rising Reineke. Referring to the former American agents, he accused her of incriminating her own citizens. "You have in fact supported an indictment in which at least five U.S. citizens were accused of having participated in a coup attempt to prevent Montenegro from joining NATO," he said.

———

Moscow's plot to violently overthrow a European country and assassinate its leader, in order to prevent its NATO membership, should have been a wake-up call for Washington. But instead of raising the alarm, bringing together allies to denounce the action, and issuing harsh sanctions against Russia, both the Obama and Trump administrations did and said virtually nothing. It may have been because of the suspected involvement of the former U.S. intelligence personnel, something that the Russians would have certainly pointed out. After all, it would be difficult to issue sanctions against Russia for a coup attempt in which former members of the CIA and FBI were accused of playing a key role, the exfiltration of the coup plotters. And because of the silence by both the Obama and Trump administrations, President Putin may have assumed there would be similar inaction by President Biden if he decided to launch a takeover of Ukraine. A green light of sorts.

The plot also raises very serious questions about the quality of U.S. intelligence. How could James Clapper, the director of national intelligence, have been unaware that Russia was plotting the violent takeover of a friendly European country—and killing its leader—when even his former employees were allegedly playing a major role? And then there was the tens of billions invested in NSA and CIA capabilities. To be caught by surprise by a Russian coup plot in a soon-to-be NATO member country was certainly a major intelligence failure.

———

* In March 2022, Congress passed a new law banning former spies from hiring themselves out to foreign governments for thirty months after they stop working for the U.S. government. The new law also requires that former intelligence officials report any foreign government work to the U.S. intelligence community and Congress for five years after they leave service.

Around the same time that Nikolai Patrushev, Putin's top national security advisor and former FSB chief, flew to Belgrade to rescue Eddie and Popov, another official flew to Montenegro to try to ease tensions there. He was Oleg Smolenkov, the senior aide to Putin's top foreign policy advisor, Yuri Ushakov.

He was also the CIA's most secret and highest-ranking spy in the Kremlin. And as he was overtly helping Moscow deal with its interference in Montenegro's election, covertly he was passing on to his CIA handlers details of Moscow's interference in the U.S. election, as well as critical intelligence on Ukraine.

He would soon be plotting his own escape.

BOOK NINE

THE
FEARMONGERS

CHAPTER 33

The Agent-in-Place

Around Christmas 2016, Oleg Smolenkov had suddenly become very worried. For years he had been the CIA's top spy in the Kremlin, a very rare agent-in-place, and currently he was reporting on President Putin and his government's involvement with the U.S. election.

But then the messages began arriving, coded messages from his agency handler that his life might be in danger.

The man deep in the shadows was a bland forty-seven-year-old bureaucrat with a receding swatch of thick light brown hair that hung slightly over his collar. He had a hefty frame, a thick neck, and often hid his eyes behind a pair of hip retro sunglasses with small black oval-shaped lenses. As a state advisor, he was a top government official, with a hefty salary and an office near the Kremlin.

Born in Ivanovo, a textile manufacturing region about 160 miles northeast of Moscow, Smolenkov grew up without a father and was raised by his mother, a public health worker. Following college, he began work as an aspiring diplomat with the Ministry of Foreign Affairs, and around 2006 he was assigned as a second secretary to the Russian embassy in Washington. It is likely while there that he was recruited or volunteered as a spy for the CIA.

By the fall of 2016, much of the American media was approaching the point of hysteria in its coverage of the Russiagate investigation, and leak after leak was bringing suspicion ever closer to Smolenkov. Networks were in hot competition with each other for rent-a-spooks, former top-ranking intelligence officials, once sworn to secrecy, now hungry to hype the threat of Russian espionage for six-figure paydays.

CNN hired former director of national intelligence James Clapper and former NSA and CIA director Michael Hayden. MSNBC, meanwhile, signed on John O. Brennan, the former director of the CIA, and Frank Figliuzzi, the former FBI counterintelligence chief. "My hobby, which is increasingly growing, is just talking on television," Figliuzzi said when we met for lunch. "They told me my contract was based on a guesstimate of about a hundred hits a year, a hundred appearances a year. I'm now approaching two hundred, and I've been doing it for nine months. So," he said, exuding a very large grin, "time to renegotiate the contract!" As of August 18, 2019, the terms "Frank Figliuzzi," "Russia," and "MSNBC" turned up 13,200 results on Google.

Along with the dozens of other armchair ex-spies, agents, and counter-spies who pack green rooms like a crowded safe house, they arrive at the studio in limos, have their faces dusted with powder, and then march on set armed with their agency's talking points. "The downside of outsourc-ing national security coverage to the TV spies is obvious," wrote Jack Sha-fer, *Politico*'s senior media writer. "Imagine a TV network covering the auto industry through the eyes of dozens of paid former auto executives and you begin to appreciate the current peculiarities."

Both Clapper and Brennan seemed to jump at the chance to use their past intelligence credentials for partisan propaganda purposes and Russia fearmon-gering, thereby enhancing their second careers as high-paid talking heads. Shortly before the 2020 election, they even signed a letter, along with forty-nine other "intelligence experts," deriding stories in the *New York Post* about a laptop owned by Joe Biden's son Hunter. The stories focused on suspicious emails con-tained on the computer, stories Clapper, Brennan, and the others said had "the classic earmarks of a Russian information operation."

In fact, in March 2022 the stories turned out to be correct and had nothing to do with Russian disinformation. "Spies Who Lie: 51 'Intelligence' Experts Refuse to Apologize for Discrediting True Hunter Biden Story," crowed the headline in the *New York Post*. Many of the phony "disinformation" allega-tions claimed by Clapper and the other former intelligence officials originated within the FBI, whistleblowers told Republican Senator Chuck Grassley, the ranking member of the Senate Judiciary Committee. In July 2022, he sent a letter to FBI director Christopher Wray alleging that "there was a scheme in place among certain FBI officials to undermine derogatory information con-nected to Hunter Biden by falsely suggesting it was disinformation."

In an article titled "Spies Are the New Journalists," *Tablet* magazine's Lee Smith noted, "The media and intelligence officials have forged a relationship in which the two partners look out for the other's professional and political interests. Not least of all, they target shared adversaries and protect mutual friends."

Much of the deliberate fearmongering was being driven by politicians. Channeling the worst of Senator Joe McCarthy, former senator Hillary Clinton charged in 2019 that presidential candidate Tulsi Gabbard, a congresswoman from Hawaii, was being "groomed" by the Russians. And she accused former presidential candidate Jill Stein of being a "Russian asset." "Yes," Clinton said in a television interview, "she's a Russian asset, I mean, totally."

Regarding Russiagate, *Vanity Fair*'s T. A. Frank pointed to "a serious credibility cost to the press." "Many news outlets," he noted, "already struggling with credibility problems going into 2016, redoubled their worst traits in the name of what they thought was a higher truth. Mainstream media has hyped the Russia stories so much that less Resistance-minded readers have started to doubt much of their work altogether."

By far the most serious leak took place on December 14, 2016, when NBC News led its evening broadcast and website with the headline "U.S. Officials: Putin Personally Involved in U.S. Election." The report went on to state, "Two senior officials with direct access to the information say new intelligence shows that Putin personally directed how hacked material from Democrats was leaked and otherwise used. The intelligence came from diplomatic sources and spies working for U.S. allies, the officials said... Ultimately, the CIA has assessed, the Russian government wanted to elect Donald Trump... Now the U.S. has solid information tying Putin to the operation, the intelligence officials say. Their use of the term 'high confidence' implies that the intelligence is nearly incontrovertible."

While largely true, this story and others like it created a real blowback problem. The fact that "spies" were close enough to gather "intelligence" that was "nearly incontrovertible" indicating that "Putin personally directed" the hacking operation could only mean someone close to Putin's inner circle was working for the CIA. Fearing a Russian mole hunt, the agency immediately began planning a highly secret and elaborate exfiltration operation for Smolenkov—and contemplating life without his valuable reports on Ukraine and numerous other critical topics.

This was a huge blow to understanding Putin. Smolenkov was not some corporate executive being asked to transfer to a new sales territory. He was a high-level American spy working at the center of power in his own government. At the time he switched sides in Washington, he was an aide to the Russian ambassador to the United States, Yuri Ushakov, who would eventually serve in that post for a decade. And while there, Smolenkov apparently developed a close working relationship with him. As a result, when Putin became prime minister in 2008, and Ushakov returned to Moscow to become his top foreign affairs advisor, Smolenkov was at his side as his key aide. There, the two worked out of the Presidential Administration Building at 4 Staraya Square.

Similar in function to the Eisenhower Executive Office Building next to the White House, the Presidential Administration Building is a gray neoclassical structure about a dozen blocks from the Kremlin. Formerly it had served as the headquarters of the Central Committee of the Communist Party of the Soviet Union, home of the party apparatus. It was also where, on February 7, 1990, the Soviet Communist Party leaders voted to end their monopoly on power and create a presidential system of government. Now the CIA had a mole there.

Soon Smolenkov was promoted to state advisor of the 3rd Class, the civilian equivalent of an army two-star general. With a salary of about $136,000 a year, he was in the upper bracket of Russia's middle class. Appointed as his assistant was Antonina Agafonova, twenty-five, an attractive and stylish blonde student about to graduate from Moscow Regional Institute of Management and Law with a degree in organization management. Before long, they would have an affair, she would leave her husband and take their son, and she and Smolenkov would get married. They moved into Antonina's modest one-bedroom apartment in a pink-fronted building on Kargopolskaya Street in Moscow's Otradnoye district. A working-class neighborhood, it was nine miles north of the Kremlin. In addition to Ivan, Antonina's son, the couple would have two daughters.

As Ushakov's top aide, Smolenkov would have had access to key details on Putin's plans and decisions involving virtually every part of the world. "Oleg Smolenkov was a member of the inner circle of Yury Ushakov," said Ilya Shumanov, a Russian affairs expert at the Wilson Center. He had access to intelligence information and also to military and defense secrets since his portfolio included involvement with the government's Military-Industrial Commission. One former longtime associate recalled that Smolenkov would sometimes show "excessive curiosity" about certain topics, "which did not look like a simple interest."

While it is doubtful that Smolenkov would have had regular access to the closely held secrets of the GRU, the group conducting the DNC hacking operations and email releases, it is highly likely that details may have been discussed in relation to the effects the operation was having on U.S.-Russia relations. Therefore, while Smolenkov may not have been able to tip off the CIA to the operation beforehand, his intelligence would likely be crucial in providing a view into ongoing decision making. And among the most critical information he passed on was the fact that Putin directly ordered the hacking and release of the DNC and Clinton emails. After all, Putin believed that Clinton, secretary of state at the time of the Maidan uprising in Kiev, was responsible for fomenting much of the anti-Russian movement and coup plotting, even giving a "signal" to Russia's opponents. And then there were his fears regarding NATO and Montenegro.

Because of the information's extraordinary fragility, those reports were handled out of channels, directly between Brennan and President Obama, without a mention even in the President's Daily Brief. Nor was even the NSA allowed key details concerning Smolenkov, an extremely unusual decision. But Brennan would also share much of the Russia-related intelligence with FBI director James Comey at a time when the bureau was drowning in leaks and misconduct.

Now, secretly informed that he and his family needed to immediately and permanently disappear, Smolenkov balked. It is unlikely anyone else in his family suspected he was an American agent. And he was unwilling to suddenly tell them that their lives as they'd known them were now over and they were to quickly pack up, move to a new country, and assume new lives and new identities.

Smolenkov also had a number of serious obligations. His mother, Valentina Nikolaevna Smolenkova, was very unstable. Bedridden, she often let out screams and needed his care. She lived alone in another part of Moscow, in a thirty-eight-square-meter one-room apartment on Zoya and Aleksandr Kosmodemyanskikh Street. If he suddenly left, there would be no one to take care of her. And then there was his wife's mother, who worked for the Foreign Ministry. Revenge by the government against family members left behind was still another concern. Plus, there was the issue of custody of his wife's twelve-year-old son, Ivan, by another marriage. His father had visiting rights and it could be considered kidnapping if they suddenly removed him permanently from the country. This was not a Hollywood movie, it was real life—his and his family's real life.

Despite the warning, Smolenkov decided that, for now, he would keep up the charade and hope for the best. But the partisan leaks would keep on coming and become even more hazardous to his and his family's health. Thus, as the American media exploded in the aftermath of the Clinton email release, there was likely no one who had a greater fear of the potential repercussions than Oleg Smolenkov. His life was literally hanging by a headline, one that might contain just the right pieces of a puzzle to reveal his role as a spy in the Kremlin—puzzle pieces that would put him in a cold Siberian work camp for decades, if he were not shot. And there was no greater generator of hype and hysteria than the Steele dossier.

————

It was midsummer when FBI agent Michael Gaeta stepped off the plane in London, but it felt more like early spring. There was a chill breeze beneath the chalky cauliflower clouds that hung low over the city, and the temperature barely hit the mid-60s. Assigned to the U.S. embassy in Rome, Gaeta was on

his way to Grosvenor Gardens, a row of weary gray neoclassical houses converted to assorted offices near Victoria Station. Behind the unmarked black
pillar-framed door to number 9-11 was Orbis Business Intelligence, Ltd.,
one of the dozens of small private intelligence companies run by ex-spooks
exploiting for profit their days in the field as phony diplomats or as bureaucrats back in London in stuffy closet-sized government offices.

Gaeta's appointment was with Orbis's Christopher Steele, an ex-MI6 officer who had spent a few years under diplomatic cover in Moscow in the early
1990s, and a few more in the 2000s running the agency's Russia desk back in
London. Now Steele was on the outside being paid hundreds of thousands of
dollars by clients who wanted to know what was on the inside. In its first nine
years, his company hauled in approximately $20 million. As a result, unlike
during his civil servant days, Steele now lived in a pricy house in suburban
Surrey on almost an acre of land, had joined a golf club, and drove to and
from work in a classy Land Rover Discovery Sport.

In June 2016, Steele was hired and eventually paid $168,000 to dig up
political dirt in Russia on Donald Trump for Hillary Clinton and the Democratic National Committee. A few months earlier he had done the same
thing for the conservative newspaper the *Washington Free Beacon*. The new
contract came from Fusion GPS, a Washington consulting and opposition
research firm hired by the Clinton team's law firm, Perkins Coie, at a rate of
$50,000 a month. It was run by an ex–*Wall Street Journal* reporter, Glenn
Simpson, and the company would eventually be paid more than $1 million
for its anti-Trump work.

The week before Gaeta flew to London, Steele submitted the first of a mul-
tipart report on Trump and Russia to Simpson. Then, to curry favor with the
FBI, which was one of his profitable clients, and justify the $95,000 they had
thus far paid him as a confidential informant, he quickly telephoned Gaeta
in Rome, his so-called bureau handler. But it was bad timing. "Can it wait a
while?" Gaeta asked. "You know, it's Fourth of July week." But Steele was insistent. "No, you need to see this immediately." The two were acquainted from an
earlier investigation into FIFA, the governing body of the World Cup.

On that chilly July Tuesday in London, the day after America's Independence Day, Gaeta climbed the stairs at Grosvenor Gardens and pressed the
bell for Orbis Business Intelligence, Ltd. In Steele's office, surrounded by the
images of Tolstoy, Gogol, Lermontov, and Pushkin, their faces painted on
Russian dolls, Gaeta studied the dossier that had been prepared for Simpson and the Hillary Clinton campaign. "It was explosive," he would later say,
but he was also very suspicious. "I assumed," he said, that Steele's investigation "was attached to somebody, politically motivated," and that "whoever is

paying for this information is at some point going to somehow broadcast this information."

The problem was, it lacked even the slightest verification. "Do you have any corroboration of this? Is there any independent corroboration?" he asked Steele. "Is there a videotape? Is there an audiotape? Do you have anything else? And the answer was 'no.'"

Gaeta flew back to Rome in the late afternoon and spent a week trying to decide what to do with the strange report that, unverified, consisted of little more than a collection of odd rumors and conspiracy theories. So on July 12 he telephoned the assistant special agent in charge (ASAC) of public corruption in the New York field office and asked him what to do with Steele's dossier. "Hold on to it," the official told Gaeta. Two week later, on July 28, the ASAC told Gaeta to send the Steele reports to FBI attorneys in the New York field office. He did, and by August 1, Gaeta was told by the ASAC, they had reached "a very high level" at FBI headquarters. Soon, for many, the Steele dossier would become the Rosetta Stone for the Russiagate investigation. In reality, it was a Tower of Babble.

Much of the private intelligence business is based on a myth the practitioners like to exploit: once a spy always a spy. But once a spy leaves the field, and even worse, leaves the government, they simply become shoe salesmen without shoes. The result is spying from a distance in both time and miles, an unsustainable option. In Steele's case, it had been seven years since he left the government and nearly a quarter century since he served in Moscow. He had not even traveled to Russia or any of the former Soviet states, his areas of supposed expertise, since 2009. Whatever in-country contacts he might have had, therefore, were likely dead, long gone, or impossible to reach without greatly risking their safety.

It is also completely unethical for ex-spies to attempt to coopt or buy off sources originally recruited while they were with a government intelligence agency. That was never part of the bargain when they were hired. It could be extremely dangerous for the clandestine sources in a hostile country, and it could damage or cripple ongoing intelligence operations. Nevertheless, with large profits to be made, many of them secretly try, with varying levels of success.

For Steele, with no direct, physical access to in-country sources, he, like most ex-spooks, was left to spy from the comfort of his high-backed office chair, relying instead on often questionable and unreliable second- and third-hand sources. That can be very dangerous, as the war in Iraq demonstrated with its overreliance on sources who turned out to be liars, fraudsters, and know-nothings angling for visas, cash, and favors. And with regard to Iraq, the spies hunting for sources were active-duty CIA officers rather than has-been former agents trying to score big bucks and secretly play politics.

Without any sources within the Kremlin, Moscow, or anywhere in Russia, Steele was left to rely on Igor Danchenko, a freelance researcher just across the Potomac River from his client, Simpson. Entrusting such a secret and important mission—digging up dirt in Russia on a presidential candidate—to Danchenko was a sign of Steele's desperate lack of real sources. Later Danchenko would tell the FBI in a secret debriefing that the assignment was to find "compromising materials" not only on Trump but also on Hillary Clinton. It's possible Steele wanted to play both sides of the fence for double the money. The whole idea made Danchenko very uncomfortable. It was a "strange task to have been given," he would later say. And he knew nothing about the subject. As the FBI would note, he was "clueless as to who Paul Manafort was."

Slim, with a boyish face and a receding, spiky brown hairline, Danchenko was far from a highly experienced clandestine operative with an intimate knowledge of the Washington/Moscow political netherworld. Instead, he was a forty-one-year-old academic with a background in Russian oil, gas, and economic analysis. Raised on the edge of Siberia, he had left Russia years before to attend graduate school in Kentucky. He also had a drinking problem, having been arrested several times in the Washington area for drunk and disorderly conduct and thrown in Prince George's County Jail. He was released on the condition he undergo substance abuse and mental health counseling, according to criminal records. He also would later tell the FBI that he and one of his "sources" "drink heavily together."

With his background, it would have been difficult to find someone less qualified for such a sensitive assignment than Danchenko. Now as Steele's "principal source," he was left to find his own "principal source." Never before having had a need for such a person, he simply turned to his "social circle" and pestered his bar mates with questions. They offered little of use beyond a few rumors. Finally, as a shot in the dark he called Olga Galkina, an old friend from high school now living on the island of Cyprus and working for a tech company. The two had been classmates in Perm, a railway junction on the Trans-Siberian Railway in the shadow of the Ural Mountains. Nearly a thousand miles east of Moscow, and a former transit stop for political prisoners on their way to the Siberian gulags, it was called the last stop to nowhere.

After high school, both Galkina and Danchenko studied at Perm State University. Danchenko later moved to the United States to attend graduate school in political science at the University of Louisville. And Galkina, an attractive woman with dark hair cut in a short pixie style, went for advanced study in philology at the Peoples' Friendship University in Moscow. With an ability to speak five languages, she eventually specialized in public relations. Despite the distance, however, she and Danchenko would stay in touch and occasionally exchange emails.

At the time Danchenko contacted Galkina in 2016, she was living with her young son in Limassol, the capital of Cyprus. She worked as a press secretary and belonged to an intellectual Russian expat social club created to discuss poetry. Her boss was Aleksej Gubarev, the owner of XTB Holding SA and its subsidiary, Webzilla. An enterprise data service company, it was housed in a modern three-story cement building in Agios Athanasios, just outside the capital. Previously, Galkina had been based in Moscow working for Gazeta.ru, a popular online news service, and then later as head of the press service for Russia's nuclear watchdog, the Environmental, Technological and Nuclear Supervision Agency.

For Galkina, it was a difficult period. In August 2016 she became involved in a messy dispute with Gubarev, her boss, a Russian-born Cyprus resident, and was fired in November. But around the time of her dismissal, at the end of October, Danchenko started dropping her friendly notes on Facebook and getting back in touch with her. He then began fishing for anything that might be useful to pass on to Steele for his dossier on Trump. But it was just more unsubstantiated rumors and street gossip. Trump's attorney, Michael Cohen, she heard somewhere, had met in Prague with Russian intelligence agents to discuss ways to finance the hackers attacking the DNC and hide their activities. It never happened, but that made little difference—it would nevertheless wind up in Steele's dossier as if from a Moscow insider rather than an unemployed tech worker on the island of Cyprus, who happened to be the high school chum of the source.

Without any insiders within the Kremlin or even Russia, Danchenko was forced to turn to a source much closer to home, a Floridian deep inside the Clinton campaign itself, the organization paying for the Russia investigation. The source was Charles Dolan Jr., a top unpaid advisor to the Hillary Clinton campaign with a long history of Clinton and party involvement. He had previously served as a state chairman for President Bill Clinton's 1992 and 1996 campaigns and spent seven years as head of the Democratic Governors Association.

And instead of the Trump campaign having extensive connections to the Kremlin, it was instead the Clinton campaign. Until 2014, Dolan had spent nearly a decade as a public relations flack for Putin, working with his inner circle to spin unfavorable publicity. He was employed by Ketchum, a New York–based public relations firm. It was a position that also raised questions about the Foreign Agents Registration Act. The Justice Department may look at this, noted Joshua Ian Rosenstein, an expert on FISA, "to see on whose behalf he was actually working."

In June 2016 both Danchenko and Dolan happened to be in Moscow. As Steele's top investigator was desperately going from bar to bar hunting for dirt on Trump, Dolan was there staying at the Ritz-Carlton Hotel and meeting with the manager about a forthcoming conference, a meeting in which the manager gave Dolan a tour of the presidential suite, a gaudy, gold-leaf affair overlooking the Kremlin. What would emerge is the most explosive, and highly publicized, report in the dossier—that in 2013 the Russians secretly videotaped Trump cavorting with a pair of prostitutes in the presidential suite at the Moscow Ritz-Carlton. For entertainment, Trump allegedly asked the two to engage in an act of watersports, peeing on each other on his bed.

Later, Danchenko would give FBI investigators a convoluted explanation of what happened next, an explanation in which he left out any mention of Dolan, one of his secret sources, who may or may not have had any connection to the event. In Danchenko's version, it was he who was meeting with the manager of the Ritz and his assistants, questioning them Columbo-style about the pee tape. "I circled around it, you know, enough for them to say, 'look, yeah, there is a—you know, a funny thing. There might be a tape of Mr. Trump, might be sexual, but, you know, things that happen at Ritz-Carlton stay at Ritz-Carlton,'" he said. At another point he stopped a low-ranking hotel employee who did "not say much," which he "interpreted as corroboration of what the first three told me." Which apparently was nothing, if the unlikely event happened at all. Then he saw some men in the hotel who looked to him like FSB officers, and a few women who looked like prostitutes. That scene, he said, "sort of, to an extent, corroborates the story to me."

Through it all, Danchenko claimed he never bothered to actually take any notes or jot down any names. He would eventually admit to investigators that he had "zero" corroboration for his claims in the dossier. He also had "no idea" where the claims sourced to him came from. And the gossip he passed along, he said, simply came from "word of mouth and hearsay," as well as conversations "with friends over beers" that should be taken with "a grain of salt."

His investigation complete, Danchenko flew off to London to report his results to Steele, who included the dubious, ludicrous, and uncorroborated pee-tape account in his dossier before sending it off to Glenn Simpson, who passed it on to Clinton. The FBI also received their copy and were taking the dubious reports very seriously. They even used the dossier multiple times as one of the elements in a secret wiretap application from the Foreign

Intelligence Surveillance Court. The target was Carter Page, an innocent American businessman.

With the FBI counterspies on board and using the dossier in their Russiagate investigation, the hope was that Trump would be charged with something, thus eliminating him as a presidential candidate. Next, Steele and Simpson began to "broadcast this information," as FBI agent Gaeta had suspected would happen from the very start. To peddle details from the dossier to the press for the benefit of the Clinton campaign, the two set up what amounted to an invitation-only pop-up shop in downtown Washington. Simpson rented a room in the funky, eclectic Tabard Inn, a hangout for journalists, and invited reporters from the *New York Times*, the *Washington Post*, CNN, the *New Yorker*, and other organizations. Steele, a highly paid FBI informant, then provided them with off-the-record anti-Trump briefings derived from his dossier.

"These encounters were surely sanctioned in some way by Fusion's client, the Clinton campaign," wrote the *New Yorker*'s Jane Mayer, who was one of those invited. She added that Steele "provided no documentary evidence" and "neither *The New Yorker* nor any other news organization ran a story about the allegations." But three journalists in particular did completely swallow Steele's fake news conspiracies and largely became his megaphone and media champions. They were Michael Isikoff of Yahoo News, David Corn of *Mother Jones*, and Rachel Maddow of MSNBC's *Rachel Maddow Show*. Maddow gushed about Steele's "deep cover sources inside Russia."

Other gullible journalists included those at CNN, as well as Greg Gordon and Peter Stone of the McClatchy news service. They credited the leaks as coming from "Steele's Kremlin sources, cultivated during 20 years of spying on Russia." Instead, they were the product of a local DC researcher with no intelligence experience. Few news organizations were spared. The *Wall Street Journal*, *Washington Post*, and ABC News also fell headfirst for the bogus Steele reports.

The media hype generated by the deliberately leaked, largely phony, but sensational Steele dossier would add to an increasing paranoia of anything connected to Moscow. It was part of a deliberate red-baiting disinformation campaign by the Clinton team. Soon Washington would be enveloped in Russiagate, along with a Cold War–style fear and suspicion of anything Russian. In the end, following two years of intense investigation, Special Counsel Robert Mueller concluded that the Russians interfered with the election with its hacking and trolling operations, which by then had long been known. But more important, "the investigation did not establish that members of the Trump Campaign conspired or coordinated with the Russian government in its election interference activities." Instead, the Federal Election Commission fined both the Clinton campaign and the DNC for deliberately hiding their funding of $1,024,407.97 for the Steele dossier. And Danchenko was arrested and charged with lying to the FBI.

Days later, in an enormous embarrassment, the *Washington Post* was forced to take the highly unusual step of removing large portions of articles it had published about the Steele dossier. "The Danchenko indictment doubles as a critique of several media outlets that covered Steele's reports in 2016 and after its publication by BuzzFeed in January 2017," wrote the *Post*'s media critic, Erik Wemple. "CNN, MSNBC, *Mother Jones*, the McClatchy newspaper chain and various pundits showered credibility upon the dossier without corroboration—and found other topics to cover when a forceful debunking arrived in December 2019 via a report from Justice Department Inspector General Michael Horowitz."

———

During the spring of 2017, as the Russiagate rumor mill continued to grow, with its constant flow of breathless, politically driven "leaks" warning of Russian spies in our midst, the CIA feared the worst for Oleg Smolenkov. As a result, the CIA's spy in the Kremlin was given one final ultimatum: Let us get you out or let them execute you.

For Smolenkov, whose family likely knew nothing of his secret life, the decision to suddenly flee was no doubt wrenching. Unlike Hollywood's James Bond, Smolenkov's home life was low-key. His wife, Antonina, was also employed by the Department of Presidential Affairs but was on parental leave. And her mother had been working as a dentist within the Ministry of Foreign Affairs for over twenty-five years. Antonina's father was a retired Moscow policeman. Smolenkov's own mother lived alone in the city and required frequent care for her debilitating mental illness. Adding to the concerns, because their son's natural father had visiting rights, an international arrest warrant could also be issued for Antonina charging her with kidnapping.

Most troubling, in preparation for a future article, the *Washington Post* began asking sensitive questions that indicated they knew, and were about to report, that the CIA had a very important source close to Putin. Among the information leaked to the paper were details about a CIA "eyes only" report delivered by courier in early August 2016 to President Obama. Viewed by *Post* reporters as "an intelligence bombshell," it was the product of a source deep inside the Russian government, someone who was able to capture Putin's specific instructions on the election hacking operation's objectives. Key among them: to defeat or at least damage Democratic nominee Hillary Clinton, and help elect her opponent, Donald Trump.

Based on the enormous sensitivity of the information, it was clear that this was no ordinary intelligence report but rather the kind that was likely from a very well-placed human source. Like the previous leak, it was so sensitive that CIA director John O. Brennan had decided to even keep it out of the President's Daily Brief. To further restrict the information, the same protocols were put in place in the White House Situation Room as applied during the planning sessions for the Osama bin Laden raid.

The "bigot list," those witting of the information, was extraordinarily small, including Brennan and Clapper. Both were now highly paid media sources expected to produce such blockbuster scoops for their employers. Brennan, in fact, became a senior national security analyst for NBC News, the network that broadcast a similar highly sensitive report four months earlier. It was a very interesting coincidence, given that he was among the few people on the bigot list for both. That December 2016 report was headlined on its website as "U.S. Officials: Putin Personally Involved in U.S. Election." It noted, "Two senior officials with direct access to the information say new intelligence shows that Putin personally directed how hacked material from Democrats was leaked and otherwise used." It was that report which triggered the CIA's first warning to Smolenkov.

Now, with a new report about to come out, there was no time to wait. Smolenkov's CIA handlers immediately reactivated their escape plan and the agent was told he had no choice. Make up a cover story at work, pack up as quickly as possible, then get on a plane with your family to Montenegro. Once there, await instructions. Or wait instead for the knock on the door.

Smolenkov and his handlers at the CIA had decided that Montenegro was the best place to arrange the exfiltration because he could travel there for work without drawing too much suspicion. He had earlier flown there in an attempt to calm the waters with the local government following Russia's failed coup attempt. Those efforts also involved U.S. embassy officials, and therefore meeting with Americans in Montenegro would likely not draw too much suspicion. At the same time, because the country was a popular Russian vacation destination, it would not be unusual for him to take his family along for some summer beach time.

Nevertheless, the choice of Montenegro for the rendezvous was very risky. It was an extremely tense time. The trials had just started for the coup plotters and the country was only weeks away from becoming the newest member of NATO, with protesters planning on staging a demonstration. As a result, the Russian government was forbidding Russian officials from traveling there. But after several weeks of phone calls, supposedly to set up meetings aimed at continuing his efforts to improve relations, Smolenkov managed to slip through the cracks.

By early June 2017 the arrangements were made. Agafonov, their son Ivan's natural father, was told that the family along with Antonia's mother was going on a vacation to Montenegro, and on June 8 he had a phone call with Ivan. By then, time was getting very short, and on Wednesday, June 14, they boarded an Aeroflot jet and took to the sky. Looking out the window, all except for Oleg likely had no idea they would probably never see their homeland again.

Three and a half hours later they landed at the coastal resort city of Tivat with its glitzy Monaco-style Porto Montenegro. Located on the fjordlike Bay of Kotor, it had become a haven for the superrich with their equally super yachts, glimmering white frigate-size boats with knifelike bows. Among those occasionally bobbing in the turquoise water alongside Jetty 5 was the 590-foot-long *Azzam*. The longest motor yacht ever built, it was commissioned by UAE president Khalifa bin Zayed at a cost of around half a billion dollars.

A week after arriving, on June 21, Ivan visited his page on VKontakte, the Russian equivalent of Facebook. Antonina also visited the page. But there would be no more visits to VK, or any other social network, by Ivan or anyone else in the family. Later that day, they quietly boarded a CIA-chartered yacht for the short trip across the Adriatic to Italy where a government jet flew them to the United States. Left behind, and possibly never informed of her family's secret, was Antonina's mother, who returned to Moscow alone. "I was supposed to return home a week earlier," she later said. "Oleg said he would be delayed on holiday."

Two days later, the *Washington Post* published its story linking Putin to the hacking operation, largely alerting the Kremlin that they had a CIA spy in their inner circle. A spy who had suddenly vanished.

By then the former mole and his family had secretly moved into a CIA-supplied million-dollar mansion at 78 Partridge Lane in Stafford, Virginia. The home had six bedrooms, six bathrooms, a home cinema, a gym, an outdoor Jacuzzi in the courtyard, and was commuting distance to agency headquarters for easy debriefings. Back home their sudden disappearance caused great alarm. In August, Agafonov complained that his son, Ivan, had not been returned as agreed, and the next month he placed a note on his social network page, "Did he die?" Finally, on September 6, 2017, nearly three months after the family disappeared in Montenegro, a formal criminal case was opened under Art. 105 of the Criminal Code of the Russian Federation: murder. And a search was launched by the FSB and the SVR. Then in March

2019 the family disappeared once again as the CIA found a more hidden and secure place for them to live.

In the end, the United States lost its key and irreplaceable Kremlin spy at one of the most dangerous times in history. Just a few years later the United States and Russia would fight a deadly proxy war in Ukraine, a war in which President Putin would hint, multiple times, at possible nuclear retaliation against the United States. Now the United States had no one in the Kremlin to warn if President Putin should ever decide to turn those threats into reality. That critical loss made Putin the ultimate winner in Russiagate.

Yet despite the enormous security breach, there was apparently no investigation, even though among the very few people who knew about Smolenkov's critical role were Brennan and Clapper, who quickly became highly paid media informants after leaving office. In the intelligence community, it seems, it is only the low-level whistleblowers, like Chelsea Manning, who get investigated and prosecuted.

Soon, the same breathless Russophobic media coverage that almost got Smolenkov executed would only grow louder. And the FBI, its starched-shirt reputation trashed by scandals, and unable to uncover any real spies, needed to quickly find a Russian to arrest.

CHAPTER 34

◆

The Mad Hatter

On a steamy Sunday in July 2018, at about half past noon, a caravan of unmarked SUVs exited the FBI's Washington, DC, field office, an eight-story concrete building that exudes all the charm of a supermax prison. The cars moved swiftly across the city; speed was critical. There were indications that the target, a Russian who had canceled the lease on her apartment and packed her belongings, was about to take flight.

Just before one o'clock, the SUVs turned off Wisconsin Avenue and into a parking lot at 3617 38th Street NW, a low redbrick apartment building near American University. Armed agents in bulletproof vests filled a narrow corridor outside apartment 208. Inside, rather than a highly trained spy with a packed suitcase, a dozen passports, and an Aeroflot ticket back to Moscow, a wisp-thin twenty-nine-year-old grad student was watching the Wimbledon men's finals on TV. And instead of bolting to Russia, Maria Butina, in tan capri pants and a black-and-white-striped top, was preparing for a long drive in a boxy U-Haul truck to South Dakota. Having just graduated from American University with a master's degree in international relations, she was about to start working as a consultant in the cryptocurrency industry. With her in the apartment was her close friend of five years, a Republican activist named Paul Erickson, who would be traveling with her to his home in Sioux Falls.

"Everything was boxed up," Erickson told me. "The last thing to do was to pack the electronics, to unplug the TV and the internet. And then pound, pound, pound! I answered the door, and there was a team of six agents in the hallway." As three agents surrounded Erickson, the other three beelined for Butina. "The team went in, dragged her out, spun her around, cuffed her in the hallway, and announced her arrest," Erickson recalled, the image still vivid in his mind. She was charged with being an unregistered agent of the Russian government. "And so I had to stand and watch her being cuffed and frog-marched out of the building into a waiting black SUV. And to this day, I look up, I peek through the window every time before I walk into the parking lot to see if there's three giant black Suburbans, freshly washed."

Seconds after the arrest, Erickson called Butina's attorney, Robert N. Driscoll, who rushed from his Virginia home to the FBI field office. Despite his pleading and protests, the counterintelligence case agent, Michelle Ball, ordered Butina transported to the infamous Central Cell Block. The city's worst hellhole, it was a crumbling, leaking, overcrowded human waste pit resembling a dungeon hidden beneath the district's police station. Among the prisoners released a few days before was Graylan Hagler, a local pastor jailed for protesting at the Supreme Court. "It was a metal shelf for a bed, literally," he said. "Roaches were walking all over that as well as the ceilings and up the walls and on the floors. So you are spending the night killing roaches."

A few months before her arrest, Maria Butina and I met for lunch at Mari Vanna, a Russian-cuisine restaurant and nightclub on Connecticut Avenue near Dupont Circle in downtown Washington. Around the corner is the Washington headquarters for ABC News, and half a block toward the White House is the venerable Mayflower Hotel. Spidery houseplants hang from the ceiling, family photos dot the "shabby chic" walls, and its dacha-inspired interior is cluttered with Soviet-era bric-a-brac, like the colorful tchotchkes and nesting dolls that cram the shelves. On tables near crystal bowls of sushki, a traditional Russian tea bread, were steamed dumplings known as pelmeni, and servings of ruby red borscht packed with beets and carrots. And nearby, I would later learn, was an FBI surveillance team that had followed her there.

We first met a year and a half earlier, in October 2016. I was the national security columnist for *Foreign Policy* magazine, a documentary filmmaker for PBS, and the author of a number of books on intelligence activities, and she had just started graduate school at American University. The venue was a talk in Washington about ways of achieving peace in the Middle East. At the time, I was planning a long train trip from Beijing to Ulan Bator, Mongolia, and from there to Moscow on the Trans-Mongolian and Trans-Siberian Railways. Someone pointed me to Maria Butina and said I should meet her since she was born and grew up in Siberia. I introduced myself and we began a casual friendship as I picked her brain about life in that vast, cold area of Russia.

Over the next year and a half we would occasionally meet for lunch and at lectures and parties. Then, following my trip to Siberia, and another, a monthlong journey aboard a massive container ship, the APL *Columbus*, from California to China, Vietnam, and Sri Lanka to learn a little about the supply chain, we had that lunch at Mari Vanna. At the time, I had little interest in the Trump-Russia controversy. The breathless reporting it generated reminded me of the pack journalism at the start of the war in Iraq, when groupthink dictated that Saddam Hussein possessed weapons of mass destruction. (I ended up writing a book about it called *A Pretext for War*.) Also, on distant trains and aboard ship, with little internet availability, I had not been able to follow the latest developments in the scandal.

During the lunch, however, Maria showed me several online stories that, based on government leaks, implied she was a spy at the center of a complex and convoluted Russia conspiracy. Some FBI allegations accused her of being a secret conduit for tens of millions of dollars from Putin to Trump. Others charged that, with her red hair, she was a real-life "red sparrow" spy-seductress. What was missing, however, was a shred of evidence. Instead, it was simply overhyped innuendo and conjecture, the basis of much of the Russiagate conspiracy. But it was enough to turn her life into a nightmare. Once-friendly students were now keeping their distance, and she had to keep dodging journalists and photographers even on campus. And later would come the arrest and imprisonment in solitary confinement.

"I'm a huge fan of *Alice in Wonderland*," Maria once told me. "I love the story, for some reason it fascinates me. It seems to be simple, but it's so complicated a story." Three years earlier, like Alice, she began tumbling down a deep rabbit hole. And on that hot Sunday in July, in that roach-infested cell, she suddenly hit bottom.

"Who in the world am I?" asked Alice. "Ah, that's the great puzzle."

To a large extent, it all began when Maria met the Mad Hatter, Patrick Byrne.

———

Three weeks before the January 6, 2021, attack on the U.S. Capitol, when insurrectionists violently attempted to change the vote in the presidential election, Patrick Byrne was standing on a darkened Washington street in jeans, a black hoodie, and a neck gaiter. It was 6:15 p.m. on Friday, December 18, 2020, and his goal was to somehow get a face-to-face with President Donald Trump and urge him to activate the military and overturn the outcome of the election. With him was retired lieutenant general Michael Flynn, briefly Trump's national security advisor until arrested for lying to the FBI; Flynn's attorney Sidney Powell; and a former Trump staffer, Emily Newman.

Six feet eight inches tall, with a thick mop of rusty hair and a passing resemblance to a less wrinkled Robert Redford, Byrne was the founder and former CEO of the e-commerce furniture supply company Overstock. In 2021, the company would earn $2.8 billion in revenue. He also had an impressive academic background, with a B.A. from Dartmouth College, his master's degree as a Marshall Scholar from Cambridge University, and his Ph.D. from Stanford.

Convinced that Biden had stolen the election from Trump with the help of China and Venezuela, and having made close to $100 million when he sold his company, Byrne had become the principal moneyman financing much of the effort to put Trump back in office. The "election was hacked," he said, and he had "the data, the electronics, everything" to prove it. Key was getting access to critical ballots, and having cyber experts analyze them for tampering while others searched for bits of bamboo shoots proving China's involvement. And also access to the election software, which, Byrne claimed, "was developed in Venezuela, by Hugo Chavez for him to rig his elections." The problem, however, was the elaborate cover-up involving a "shredding truck" paid to shred "3,000 pounds of ballots," he said.

"A few days after the election I rented a block of rooms in the Trump International Hotel and I brought with me a bunch of people I call 'dolphin speakers,' hackers, and when I say hackers, I don't mean bad guys, I mean white-hat hackers, people who are court certified." Byrne chose Trump's Washington hotel, he said, because he considered it "the safest place in D.C. for a command bunker."

A bunker that would cost Byrne over $800,000 for a number of weeks. And by mid-December, it was time to crash the White House.

"We had a vague plan regarding how we were going to get through all the rings of Police, Secret Service, and Marines without any invitation," he said, "and get to the Oval Office. Beyond that, we'd be playing it by ear." On his cell phone, Byrne contacted a staffer on the National Security Council he had briefly met and asked if he could stop by for a chat. Moments later, the group was invited into the Eisenhower Executive Office Building next to the White House. And after a short discussion, Garrett Ziegler, an aide to Trump advisor Peter Navarro, escorted them into the West Wing. Then, as they stood in the hallway, a surprised Trump heading to his office recognized Flynn. "After a moment he beckoned us in," said Byrne. "Within seconds General Flynn, Sidney Powell, and I were all sitting in the Oval Office with President Donald J. Trump, with the door shut behind us."

It was an extraordinary four-hour-plus meeting, one in which the president was urged to involve the military and spy agencies to overturn the election results. The day before, Flynn, a retired general and the former head of the Defense Intelligence Agency, said that President Trump could deploy the military to redo the 2020 election. "He could order, within the swing states if he wanted to, he could take military capabilities and basically rerun an election in each of those states," he said. "People out there talk about martial law like it's something that we've never done. Martial law has been instituted 64 times."

Seated in a row in front of Trump's heavy wooden Resolute Desk, the group discussed ways in which the president could send in troops and spies to seize voting machines and redo the ballot counting. Byrne, a compulsive conspiracy theorist, long believed that China was behind a massive operation to rig the election results. "China's involved in this," he would later claim. "I think we're living through the assassin's mace." It was a reference to a centuries-old Chinese concept of overcoming an enemy with a surprise weapon, in this case the U.S. presidential election results. "It would be so Chinese to do it this way."

Key to uncovering the conspiracy was issuing a presidential order, or "finding." "Sidney and Mike began walking the president through things from our perspective," said Byrne. "He could 'find' [i.e., issue a finding] that there was adequate evidence of foreign interference with the election." And then, Byrne added, "all he had to do was one small thing: direct a federal force." At that point Flynn and Powell presented Trump with the document for his signature. Created two days earlier, it was titled "Presidential Findings: To Preserve Collect and Analyze National Security Information Regarding the 2020 General Election." Eventually Trump rejected it. But had he signed the order, it would have placed extraordinary powers in the hands of the nation's top military and intelligence officials to overturn the election.

"Effective immediately, the Secretary of Defense shall seize, collect, retain and analyze all machines, equipment, electronically stored information, and material records," the finding said. Then, "Within 7 days of commencement of operations, the initial assessment must be provided to the Office of the Director of National Intelligence. The final assessment must be provided to the Office of the Director of National Intelligence no later than 60 days from commencement of operations. The Director of National Intelligence shall deliver this assessment and appropriate supporting information to the President..."

Another curious document may also have been presented to Trump, one that further elaborated on the proposed involvement of the spy agencies in overturning the election. The memo recommended that President Trump issue an extraordinary order allowing a team to secretly access NSA's highly classified intercepts to search for evidence of foreign involvement in the election. The team would be made up of "trained senior intelligence analysts," it said. Among other things, the document laid out a plan whereby the team "will run targeted inquiries of NSA raw signals that may not have been processed yet to pursue suspected foreign interference of the 2020 election vote count manipulation." Finally, printed on the bottom of the document were the words "DISPOSE OF VIA SHREDDING."

Although there is no indication who actually originated the document, it was dated December 18, the same day that Byrne and the others met with Trump. And Byrne recalled that the group brought numerous papers to the Oval Office with them. "Sidney and her staff printed up some documents," he said. "There may or may not have been a memo dated December 18 from Sidney for the president to sign. I believe I saw that off her printer in her suite in the hotel."

During the Oval Office meeting, Byrne suggested that Trump put Flynn, the former military intelligence chief, in charge as his "field marshal" and appoint Sidney Powell his special counsel. "If you do I put your chances at around 50–75%," he said. "You should see how well [Flynn] has this planned, it would run like clockwork." Later, to the surprise and shock of everyone, Byrne repeated several times an elaborate story of how he was involved in a multimillion-dollar bribery attempt of Hillary Clinton during the presidential campaign. "I know how this works. I bribed Hillary Clinton $18 million on behalf of the FBI for a sting operation," he claimed.

It was an indication of just how deep Byrne's paranoid conspiracy theories ran. For safety, he would also later give up flying in his private jet. "I fly commercial now so as to not get blown up," he said. "Because I assume they're not going to blow up a commercial airliner to get me." "I'm a sucker for conspiracy theories," he admits. Soon the cabal would follow Trump upstairs to the Yellow Oval Room in his private quarters to continue the plotting past midnight over Swedish meatballs. According to one of the participants, Byrne was "nonstop housing meatballs."

The late-night meeting had been exhilarating for Trump. Encouraged and energized by what he had heard from Byrne and the others, he could now see a path to victory. At 1:42 in the morning, a little more than an hour after everyone departed, he decided to take action and began tapping out a tweet to his followers. "Big protest in D.C. on January 6th. Be there, will be wild!" The tweet, according to the congressional January 6th Committee, would be "pivotal." "The tweet led to the planning for what occurred on January 6th," said committee vice chair Liz Cheney, "and the violence on that day."

Even before the meeting with Trump, Byrne began flying what he said were "many dozens" of people to Washington to take part in briefings and rallies. Among them, he said, were "fifteen pro-freedom Latinos from Texas" who were flown to Washington to take part in a large rally on December 12. They included, he was later told, Enrique Tarrio, the national chairman of the Proud Boys, along with several other Proud Boys. In the following weeks, according to a June 2022 indictment, Tarrio and four of his lieutenants would plan and coordinate the movements of as many as three hundred people who stormed the Capitol on January 6. Charged with "seditious conspiracy," their purpose, said the indictment, was "opposing the lawful transfer of presidential power by force." Byrne was also in Washington that day but says he stayed away from the Capitol and only later learned that Tarrio and the other Proud Boys were on the December flight. "The names of very few of those people have reached me," he said.

In the end, Byrne's meeting with Trump helped convince the former president to send the "pivotal" tweet announcing the "wild" protest on January 6. Shortly before, Byrne flew a key planner of the Capitol attack to Washington. A man wallowing in fantasies and conspiracies, with over $100 million in the bank, can be a very big danger to himself, and especially to those around him.

Five years earlier Byrne had first met Maria Butina, an attractive young Russian, as she was preparing to enter graduate school in Washington. And just as he was positive that China and Venezuela had stolen the election from Trump, and that Clinton was involved in a multimillion-dollar "Deep State" bribery scheme, he was convinced that Butina must be an insidious Russian spy. Believing he had been secretly deputized by the U.S. Senate to search the Deep State for evildoers, he now made Butina his target. And from that moment onward, her life would be forever altered.

———

"It's Burning Man for Libertarians," said financial writer Gary Alexander of the Libertarian Party's annual three-day thinkathon in Las Vegas. Known for its wonkish, freedom-themed speeches, the convention bills itself as "the world's largest gathering of free minds." In July 2015, those free minds mingled with the free spenders in Planet Hollywood, a hotel and casino with a hip vibe and an uptempo atmosphere midway up the Strip and across from Bellagio's famous fountains. A key draw was the sixty-one-thousand-square-foot gaming area that occupied a broad pit with a mini-baccarat table, craps tables, roulette wheels, a high-limit card room, and over twelve hundred slot machines. And for a 3 a.m. dinner there was a Gordon Ramsay burger joint.

It was the political season. A few weeks earlier, a short distance away at the Venetian Hotel, Sheldon Adelson had formed his secret task force of millionaires and billionaires to fight the boycott movement on behalf of Benjamin Netanyahu. And at Planet Hollywood, at the last minute, just four days before the Libertarian conference, Donald Trump had asked to speak to the crowd and was granted a time slot. He had just announced his candidacy a few weeks before. Among those in the audience was Maria Butina, who at the time was preparing for graduate school to study international relations and deciding which one to attend. She had been brought there by her close friend Paul Erickson, who had long been involved in politics and was among those invited.

Taking advantage of the unexpected appearance of Trump, Butina stood in line with other attendees in the large Celebrity Ballroom during the question-and-answer session. "I'm from Russia," she said when her turn came, holding a microphone up to her lips. "My question will be about foreign politics. If you will be elected as president, what will be your foreign politics, especially in the relationships with my country? Do you want to continue the policy of sanctions that are damaging both economies? Or do you have any other ideas?" Trump replied, "I know Putin, and I'll tell you what, we'll get along with Putin . . . I would get along very nicely with Putin, I mean, where we have the strength. I don't think you'd need the sanctions. I think we would get along very, very well."

Following the Trump talk, Butina decided to attend another lecture at the conference, one by Overstock CEO Patrick Byrne. She had developed an interest in blockchain and cryptocurrencies like bitcoin, and it would later be one of her principal areas of focus at American University. And Byrne had gained a reputation as an expert in the field, even becoming the first major retailer to begin accepting bitcoin. He also established an offshoot company, tZERO, to further develop crypto ventures.

At fifty-three, Byrne had never been married and often boasted of his short-term sexual conquests. "I am a lifelong bachelor," he declared on his webpage. "I give great tryst. I have no Act III whatsoever, but my Acts I and II are dynamite." He also boasted of his lifestyle: "I'm a pot-smoking, hippy, libertarian, bachelor, Catholic, lapsed Catholic, living in Utah." His father, Jack Byrne, was a prominent financier, insurance executive, and close associate of Warren Buffett. And from an early age, Patrick Byrne looked to Buffett as a mentor.

Following his talk, Butina asked him if he would like to be a speaker to a group interested in blockchain and economics in Russia. Byrne said it sounded interesting but suggested that they discuss it further the next day over lunch in his suite. Butina was surprised by the invitation but agreed. By then, Byrne was swimming in a sea of paranoia. After their very brief encounter he became convinced that Butina, because she was from Russia, was a hired assassin out to kill or drug him.

"The truth is, when she came into the room, I had two makeshift weapons made out of wooden pieces of furniture. I of course wasn't going to hurt her, but I was prepared to defend myself," he told me, looking very serious and concerned. "And to be honest, in Vegas I always have a handgun in my luggage. So, I was prepared if this turned into something strange." A couple of years later,

Byrne would be arrested at Salt Lake City International Airport attempting to carry a loaded .40-caliber Glock 23 handgun onto a passenger plane.

Byrne also arranged the furniture in an attempt to determine if Butina was a Russian seductress, dispatched from Moscow to possibly tap into his secrets about online furniture sales. "I had set it up so we could sit next to each other, or we could sit across the table professionally," he said. "Curious to see how she would sit. Curious to see if she was trying to throw some seduction into this, in which case I would start thinking she was a 'red sparrow.'" But Butina was all business. "She sat across from me professionally, was super professional, brisk, to the point. Could have been a Bain consultant," he said.

As with his uninvited crashing of the Oval Office to suggest a military takeover of the election, Byrne had long suffered from an imagination that could occasionally turn dangerous. Years earlier he had helped the FBI target some crooked Wall Street brokers and hedge fund operators. "It included everything from hiring economists to unscramble trading records and building programs to give them to show them how to spot the illegal trades," Byrne said. He then added, "I also did all kinds of illegal things ... I was dressed as a bum at somebody's brownstone at three in the morning. I was hacking his computer and downloading crap from the Ukraine to hack his firewall and steal his computer data."

Since then, Byrne developed an almost childlike worship of the bureau. It is so extreme that he tries never to even say the initials out loud, as some religious groups refuse to say the word "God." "I don't even like using the initials, the FBI," he said. "I'm just going to call them federal agents or Men in Black."

After assisting in the case, Byrne says that he was given a secret assignment by the Senate Judiciary Committee to find and root out, vigilante-style, evildoers within the Deep State. This authorization came in the form of a mysterious letter he was never allowed to touch. "I had to stand with my hands behind my back so I could read this letter," he told me. "You can't go kill anybody," he says the officials told him. "But this will be sitting in a safe in the Department of Justice and it will make it very unlikely you're going to get prosecuted." Byrne had thereby become a modern-day superhero: Peter Parker by day, Spider-Man by night.

Byrne now believes the letter no longer exists because of a conspiracy by Obama to "sanitize" him. "My belief is the copy of that letter that was over in the Justice Department was probably destroyed at the end of the Obama administration. At least no one from the Department of Justice has confirmed the existence of the letter. And I have other reasons to think that they sanitized me on the way out." Nevertheless, Byrne continued his secret search for evildoers within the Deep State, and after their brief meeting he quickly became convinced he had finally found one. Rather than a simple grad student, Butina was actually a Russian spy out to destroy America. And he would prevent that from happening.

Soon after their lunch, therefore, he quickly notified a federal official of the meeting. "When I heard back from someone," he told me, "communication was reopened with the Men in Black. It had been a long, long time." But the FBI, according to Byrne, seemed uninterested. "I was surprised at the lack of response from the channel I was given to communicate with if anything happened like this," he said. Nevertheless, convinced he had at last found the Deep State evildoer he was commissioned to root out, he would continue his relentless pursuit of Butina until she was finally behind bars.

———

In a sense, Maria Butina grew up under the eyes and ears of U.S. intelligence. On November 6, 1988, a Titan 34D rocket was launched from Vandenberg Air Force Base in California. On board was a highly classified KH-11 imaging satellite placed in an orbit taking it over the Soviet Union several times a day. Four days later Maria was born in the remote Siberian city of Barnaul, then part of the Soviet Union, near the border with Kazakhstan. According to recently declassified CIA documents, Barnaul, home to a secret Soviet space tracking facility and an SS-20 missile base, was a key target of the KH-11 satellite. Other NSA satellites eavesdropped on the area.

In Barnaul, a crossroads between Russia, China, Mongolia, and Kazakhstan, her family lived in a one-room apartment with a shared kitchen. "There were no phones at the time, no email, so we wrote letters," she told me. "We didn't have enough food, we couldn't buy candy." Because of a bad case of pneumonia, she spent a great deal of time recuperating with her grandparents in the small village of Kulunda, about five hours south by train. "I grew up in homeschooling with my grandmother—she's a geography teacher," Butina told me. Her grandfather taught her chess and "was a huge Stalin supporter," she said. "He had a kind of old Soviet car, and on the back window of his car he always had a portrait of Stalin—or sometimes he switched it to Lenin." He had come to Siberia as an electrician during Stalin's reign, and lit some of the very first lightbulbs there.

Shy and tall for her age, by the time Butina started elementary school, in 1994, the Soviet Union had disintegrated, and Russia was struggling. With the introduction of capitalism, her father gave up his job, bought some tables and chairs, and began a small furniture company in Barnaul. "My dad is a person who always accepted risk," said Maria. "He was a university professor, but he abandoned his safe life to become a businessman." Even by 1998 when Butina was ten, her school, closer to Mongolia than Moscow, could not afford to purchase computers. "My first computer classes, believe it or not, the keyboard was drawn by hand by our teacher on a piece of paper... So by the time we got computers, we had already learned how to type on a keyboard." Nevertheless, in 2010 she graduated from nearby Altai State University with honors and twin master's degrees in political science and education. She also became a candidate for a Ph.D., writing a dissertation on the challenges of political organizations as alternatives to traditional political parties.

Following in her father's footsteps, and with his help, Butina started a furniture business with a company called Home Comfort. "I grew up in this period of freedom in the 1990s when everyone believed that the Soviet Union had collapsed and we got freedom, it's going to be great. We all believe that now we're not going to be involved in these Chechen wars, we'll be building good capital in a good way. People will be earning money and we'll be helping the world in a good way. We will be part of Europe again. This is why I created my own business because that was inspiration."

Soon she began thinking large, wanting to finally escape the sameness of Siberia for the exhilaration of the big city. Also, her dream from as far back as she could remember was getting involved in politics and changing things for the better. But that meant leaving Barnaul, so in August 2011 she put a manager in charge of her company and boarded a plane for Moscow. But as she stepped off the plane at the age of twenty-two, the vastness of the city stunned her. "I was frightened by the number of people, especially at rush hour," she noted in her blog at the time. "And the noise is frightening."

Much like in Alaska and northern Canada, guns were commonplace in Siberia, where hunting was taken for granted. And there was also a movement to legalize handguns for personal protection, as crime was rising. As a result, Butina had formed a small gun rights group in Barnaul made up of several dozen locals in the area. Now in Moscow, she found the well-established furniture business difficult to penetrate. As a result, she decided to see if there was an interest in a similar gun rights group there. There was, and she formed a small clublike organization called "The Right to Bear Arms." In Moscow, however, it was a very risky undertaking. Gun ownership in Russia has always been highly restricted. With few exceptions, handguns are illegal, and guns for hunting and sport are difficult to obtain.

Over several years, the group grew, and among the most important members was Alexander P. Torshin. A passionate pro-gun enthusiast, he was deputy chairman of the Federation Council, the upper chamber of Russia's parliament, the Duma. As a senator, he represented the Republic of Mari El, a small, insular region that hugs the Volga River about five hundred miles east of Moscow. With her interest in politics, Butina became fascinated by Torshin, the first real politician she had ever met. And eventually Torshin took her on as an unpaid intern, just as college and graduate students throughout Washington work as paid and unpaid interns for politicians and government officials.

With politics and gun rights in common, Torshin encouraged Butina to connect with the American NRA. It was a group very familiar to Torshin since he had gone to a number of their conventions and even spoken to the group. Butina therefore joined, paid her membership dues, and invited them to send someone over to give a talk at their second annual meeting in Moscow. It was a reciprocal invitation following the NRA's invitation to Torshin.

That meeting took place at the end of October 2013. Stepping off a Delta jet from Washington was David Keene, sixty-seven, whose thick sweep of snow white hair, combed JFK-style, gave him the appearance of a retired judge. Instead, he was the former president of the National Rifle Association. Following the invitation, Keene wanted to go but worried about his health and asked an old friend, Paul Erickson, to come along as his "body man," Erickson told me. "He said we think that this group is probably real, but we don't know, it's worth a trip to meet this woman."

At fifty-two, Erickson was thin, with the physique of a basketball player, and dark curly hair that formed a half circle beneath a balding crown. For years he had maintained long and close ties to America's conservative power centers. If Keene had been the movement's general, Erickson was its veteran guerrilla fighter. Sandwiched between campaign stints for conservative Republicans like Ronald Reagan, Pat Buchanan, Richard Viguerie, and Mitt Romney were far-flung missions in support of anti-Soviet rebel forces.

Erickson also had a very dark and very hidden side. Charming, polite to a fault, at the same time he was denouncing liberals and Democrats for their unsound economic policies, he was secretly defrauding investors out of millions of dollars in dubious financial schemes ranging from nursing homes to oil fields. But on that Halloween eve in Moscow in 2013, it was not a right-wing con man Maria Butina saw emerge from the airport customs area with Keene, but a charming, successful American businessman and a respected political strategist with a broad smile and a warm and ingratiating manner.

By the end of the visit both Keene and Erickson were surprised and also convinced that Butina's group was genuine. "We watched over the course of nine hours that day her run this thing like the Trans-Siberian Railroad, boom, boom, boom," Erickson told me. "And by the time we finished that day, two things were clear to us. The organization was real; it was not a false front. And more to the point, the members were real." But it was not without risk in a country where nearly all guns are outlawed, Putin distrusted activist organizations, and surveillance is pervasive. "We saw her office in Moscow that day," said Erickson. "She kept a 'go' bag by the door at the office and one in her home. When you get arrested and have to go to prison: a toothbrush, a change of underwear."

Eventually, Butina and Erickson grew close and began seeing more of each other as she would come to the United States to attend NRA conventions, accompanying Torshin as his translator. At one point, to make it clear that she was working for him as an intern, or unpaid assistant, rather than a paramour, she had him issue her cards listing her as his assistant. And Erickson would occasionally fly to Moscow. In June 2015, following an NRA convention in Nashville, Butina began looking into graduate schools in the United States for a master's degree in international relations. It was at that point that Erickson invited her to join him at the annual Libertarian Party meeting in Las Vegas, which was when she met Patrick Byrne.

———

Despite the bureau's lack of interest in Butina as a spy, Byrne kept in touch with her after she flew back to Moscow. And the emails grew more and more romantic. Byrne was as attracted to the mysterious Russian as he was suspicious of her. And Butina was charmed by the handsome, larger-than-life businessman. But as in the hotel room, Byrne was also attempting to set a trap for her. And he therefore kept trying to convince his FBI contacts that Butina was a Kremlin spy, based on nothing but his increasingly unhinged "Deep State" paranoia and childlike "Men in Black" fantasies.

"Finally, in September of 2015, I received something that sounded like they wanted me to meet her again," Byrne told me. "But I wanted to make sure there was an unambiguous decision being made, because I didn't want to meet her again and then have them show up in my life and give me a hard time." Tired of the indecision, Byrne told his FBI contacts to make up their mind. "In an effort to make things clear, I sent a binary message along the lines of: Not wanting to get in a hassle with the U.S. government, I am not going to meet Maria again unless I hear the word, 'Greenlight.' They responded: 'Greenlight.'"

With that, Byrne invited Butina to meet him in New York for a romantic weekend, and Butina agreed. They got together at The Bowery, an opulent, high-priced seventeen-story hotel in the former Skid Row part of Manhattan. Byrne obviously enjoyed his role as an "undercovers" agent for the FBI and told Butina he wanted to continue it—of course, without telling her she was sleeping with an unofficial freelance FBI informant who would report their every whisper to federal agents.

"So, at the end of our first three-day tryst, I proposed the following," Byrne said. "Every six weeks or so suits me just fine. Pick a city you want to see while you're in America, like Miami, or San Francisco, I'll just send you a ticket and we'll make a weekend of it." Living in Moscow, Butina was having second thoughts, but said if they did get together again it would have to be someplace closer, such as in Europe. Byrne therefore wasted little time. He booked a cruise on a charter yacht sailing out of Montenegro's lavish Porto Montenegro from September 24 to 28. The company was Camper & Nicholson's International, whose catalog lists charter yachts from the port beginning at about $117,000 a week and running to $584,000 a week for the seventy-three-meter *Titania*. But Butina canceled. As a result, to Byrne's disappointment their rendezvouses devolved into simply friendly and occasional platonic dinners rather than romantic trysts. So much for the "red sparrow."

Nevertheless, Byrne dutifully reported both the September pillow talk and the dinner chatter to the FBI. But there was little to report since Byrne quickly became convinced that he had been mistaken, that Butina was *not* the Deep State spy he had originally suspected but instead just who she said she was. "I was telling them she's not a spy," said Byrne. "From my first ninety-minute discussion with her, I thought she might be the best thing that ever happened to Russia. And even Russian-U.S. relations. Which is what she said she wanted."

From their own investigation of Butina, the agents quickly came to the same conclusion that she was simply an innocent grad student. "The federal agents showed up and started talking to me about this, I'd say, January through March of 2016," Byrne said. "The Men in Black were sort of just brushing all this off...Any interest in the U.S. government went, as far as I could tell, to zero. Absolute zero...I was kind of surprised, there was no appetite, not only no appetite but the FBI was telling me, 'That's ridiculous, that's ridiculous, that's absolutely ridiculous, she's just some grad student.'"

By March 2016, with nothing suspicious about Butina and her activities over the past six months, the bureau decided to pull the plug on the operation. The FBI agents, said Byrne, told him that "the agency [CIA] has spent a couple of weeks studying her and they've decided there's nothing to her and she's not connected to anybody...In fact, we think it's time you break up with her and get her out of your life." Byrne complied. "So I did," he said. "Roughly, by text. Curtly. Simply told her I was tired of being 'the other guy.' What was she going to say to that? It was unlike me not to be kinder. Thus, when I was told to cut her out of my life, I did. Just like that."

Three months later, the *Washington Post* carried the front-page headline "Russian Government Hackers Penetrated DNC, Stole Opposition Research on Trump." Suddenly caught flat-footed, the FBI began scrambling for

Russians to surveil and arrest. The agents therefore contacted Byrne. "Boy, were we wrong," he says they told him. "You were right about Maria and right about the Russians. Get on this, all Maria all the time. All Russia all the time. Gloves are off, Patrick, you get on this." Byrne agreed, and a surprised Butina once again heard from the Mad Hatter. Without her knowing it, she now had an FBI bull's-eye on her back. For the bureau, she was the only game in town.

CHAPTER 35

The Scapegoat

Now, in the toxic atmosphere of Russiagate, nearly every action Butina took would be looked at in retrospect by the FBI counterspies through a conspiratorial lens, as proof she was a spy, even including her simple question to Trump. That same conspiracy-mongering quickly became rampant in much of the press. Calling Butina a "quasi-spy" on National Public Radio, David Corn, Washington bureau chief of *Mother Jones*, said, "She asked him the most important question there for the Kremlin," as if she had been sent on a secret diabolical mission by Putin. As a foreign student about to enter grad school to study international relations it was a logical question to ask about her own country. And she had reservations at the hotel long before Trump's last-minute decision to appear there, making the Moscow spy operation quite an intelligence coup.

Corn also thought it was suspicious that Butina would ask people to friend her on Facebook. "Will you be my Facebook friend? Will you Snapchat with me?" he said, as if it was standard Russian spy tradecraft rather than the actions of a typical college student.

By August 2016, when Maria Butina stepped off a plane from Moscow to begin her two-year grad school course at American University, Russiagate was in full steam. Slim and attractive, with the figure of a dancer and long rose-colored hair that spiraled gently down her back, Butina fit the stereotype of a seductive Russian spy, like Anna Chapman, the redheaded Russian sleeper agent arrested in New York City in 2010; Jennifer Lawrence, who played the redheaded Russian spy-seductress in the film *Red Sparrow*; and Keri Russell, who starred in the popular television show *The Americans* as a dedicated Soviet spy posing as a typical U.S. citizen.

It was a very hazardous time to be Russian in the city. "Washington's young émigré crowd is beginning to feel like they're living in a spy novel. And they're the bad guys," noted *Politico*'s Ben Schreckinger in an article about being young and Russian in Washington during Russiagate. "Now, more so than ever, the capital's young Russiantonians find themselves living in a battlefield of the new Cold War. Their Tinder dates keep asking them if they're spies. Their landlords are interrogating them. Their résumés are getting tossed in the trash, and when they do get the job, their boss might warn them not to mention their nationality to people at the office...And for Russians who do get the job, office life in Washington can be awkward. Dmitry Sivaev, an urban development specialist at the World Bank, recalled his annoyance when a former boss told him not to mention to colleagues that he was Russian."

Nor was Russia fearmongering limited to Washington. On cable television it became rampant. "The most irredeemable outpost of the national media is cable news," wrote media critic Michael Massing in *The Nation*. "In the past, Fox News stood out for the nakedness of its partisanship and the purity of its ideology; now, both MSNBC and CNN are mirror versions of it, tailoring their programming to the demands of their Trump-loathing audiences. With their noxious talking heads, irritating breaking-news flashes, nonstop commercials (20 or more minutes out of every 60 on CNN), performative White House correspondents, paucity of reporting, and constant drumbeat of *Trump, Trump, Trump, Trump*, watching these networks is a demoralizing and soul-sapping experience."

It is little wonder, given the deplorable state of the U.S. media. According to a 2022 study by the Reuters Institute and the University of Oxford, news trust in the United States is the absolute lowest among the forty-six countries polled by the report, at 26 percent. Another study, by the *Columbia Journalism Review* in 2018, points to Twitter helping to transform journalists from independent-minded reporters into robotic packs, all reading and following the same Tweets, many of which are ill informed. "Journalism can get caught up in a kind of pack mentality in which a story is seen as important because other journalists on Twitter are talking about it, rather than because it is newsworthy," said the study. "The researchers argue it can also distort the way a story is reported."

As Russiagate exploded, Butina became an easy target since ethnic profiling was nothing new for the FBI. J. Edgar Hoover targeted Black leaders like Martin Luther King as "communists." Then following the 9/11 attacks more than a thousand Muslims were quickly rounded up, mostly in secret, and deprived of their rights. "The decision of whom to question often appeared to be haphazard, at times prompted by law enforcement agents' random encounters with foreign male Muslims or neighbors' suspicions," said a 2002 Human Rights Watch report. "The Department of Justice has subjected them to arbitrary detention, violated due process in legal proceedings against them, and run roughshod over the presumption of innocence."

The same thing happened when the media focus turned to China and the FBI in turn launched its "China Initiative" in 2018. "Almost every student that comes over to this country is a spy," said President Trump, no stranger to racist fearmongering. "The China initiative engaged in blatant racial profiling," charged Judy Chu, a congresswoman from California. "It reinforces harmful stereotypes that Asian Americans are the perpetual 'others' and it ruined numerous lives in the process." She then pointed to the result. "After over three years of investigations, over 150 defendants, and at least 77 cases, the DOJ's China Initiative has secured one single conviction in a court of law," Chu said.

According to a 2018 analysis by *Time* magazine of Justice Department data, the bureau's loss in credibility was long-term and endemic. The number of convictions in FBI-led investigations declined in each of the five preceding years, dropping nearly 11 percent over that period. At the same time, public support also sank, declining ten points to 61 percent in just a two-month period. "We've seen ups and downs, but I've never seen anything like this," Robert Anderson, a former senior FBI official, told *Time*.

And around the same time the bureau was expending enormous resources engaged in constant surveillance of Butina at American University, it was completely ignoring reports of massive sexual abuse at Michigan State University, eventually totaling upwards of two hundred victims. The women were young Olympic athletes sexually abused by Dr. Larry Nassar, the doctor for the USA Gymnastics national team and Michigan State sports.

According to a highly critical 2021 Justice Department IG report, despite being alerted to the crimes, senior FBI officials failed to respond to the allegations "with the utmost seriousness and urgency that they deserved and required." It was only when a newspaper article appeared more than a year later that they finally took action, and according to the report, they "made numerous and fundamental errors when they did respond." And the FBI special agent in charge, W. Jay Abbott, then led a cover-up and lied repeatedly to the IG's office. Yet, unlike Butina, who never lied to the FBI and was still prosecuted, Abbott was never prosecuted for the cover-up or the lying. Senator Richard Blumenthal called the IG report "absolutely chilling" and a "gut punch to anyone who cares about effective law enforcement." And the *New York Times* called the report "another damaging blow to the F.B.I.'s reputation."

Ethnic hatemongering was also rampant at the FBI and throughout the intelligence community, as Dan Gilmore discovered. At the time he was an administrator with the intelligence community's top secret Intelink, which among other things ran in-house classified blogs for those within the spy world. Soon he became shocked by the level of racism and bias expressed by employees of the FBI, CIA, NSA, and other intelligence agencies. "After a couple years, it became a dumpster fire. Professionalism was thrown out the window, and flame wars became routine," he said. "Hate speech was running rampant on our applications. I'm not being hyperbolic. Racist, homophobic, transphobic, Islamaphobic, and misogynistic speech was being posted in many of our applications."

Gilmore's comments were corroborated by Tara Lemieux, a senior cyber-security assessor who worked for Intelink, which is administered by the NSA, from 2012 to 2020. "This is unconscionable and the [U.S. intelligence community] needs to take immediate and meaningful action, as there is no room for personal bias in matters of national security," she said. "The NSA is likely hoping this goes away."

––––––––

Ironically, the same summer the FBI was focusing on Butina, and supposed Chinese spies, the United States was crawling with *real* spies and foreign agents.

In Malibu making movies and billions was Israel's top-level, longtime U.S. spy Arnon Milchan. And in Las Vegas, Sheldon Adelson had established his clandestine task force of Americans, acting as foreign agents of Israel, to fight the boycott movement. Gilad Erdan's Ministry of Strategic Affairs had launched its secret Israel Cyber Shield covert operations in the United States, as well as its Blue Network of clandestine operatives and money sources, and its hidden nationwide troll farms. And Israel's covert Psy Group was actively spying and intimidating people around the country along with the Canary Mission thugs. All were using intelligence from American spies associated with its Israel on Campus Coalition organization and the Israeli embassy.

And then there was the UAE's spy and his agent at the heart of the Hillary Clinton campaign; an Israeli mole burrowing into the Trump campaign; Hal Martin walking out of NSA with his half billion pages of top secret documents; and the Shadow Brokers auctioning off most of NSA's highly dangerous cyberweapons. By then the FBI's counterintelligence operations were near a collapse. In a new effort to uncover spies, the bureau set up a unit called the National Security Recruitment Program. But because of "sloppy" and "careless activity by FBI employees" and "possible digital compromise," after just two years it was totally scrapped.

One element, code-named Stagehand, involved using contract employees to develop false identities and "legends"—fake backgrounds—for use in counterespionage operations. But it quickly became a major disaster. In 2017, Senator Chuck Grassley learned of the problems from a whistleblower and sent a letter to then FBI director James Comey alerting him that the program had been completely blown. "Every single investigation or criminal prosecution that involved Stagehand between 2008 and 2011 was compromised," Grassley wrote, "and the identities and sensitive information of FBI undercover agents were disclosed to foreign governments."

He added, "The whistleblower further alleged that in January 2012, the FBI's Inspection Division (INSD) launched an inspection of the infiltration of Stagehand, but that the resulting INSD report amounted to a cover-up." Grassley then asked the bureau to send him the report, which they never did, apparently attempting to cover up the cover-up. "In my January 2016 letter I requested information about how the FBI handled this matter, including a copy of the report that resulted from the INSD's inspection. However, the FBI failed to provide a copy of the report to the Committee in the year since it was first requested."

On top of everything else, the Counterintelligence Division was penetrated by Russian and Chinese moles almost continuously for three decades or more, first Hansson and then Ma. Awash in scandals, failures, and lack of results, and desperate to get positive headlines to show their relevance during Russiagate, the counterspies quickly grabbed for the low-hanging fruit: Maria Butina.

With no real Russian spies around, just embassy intelligence officers with diplomatic immunity (as the United States has in Moscow), they were left with an idealistic young Russian grad student who had to borrow money to pay for her tuition. Grasping at straws, they asked their flaky informant, Patrick Byrne, to once again reestablish a connection with Butina. "Given the harshness with which I had ended things with Maria the first time, it took me a while to win back Maria through emails, texts, and phone calls," he said.

In October 2016, he invited Butina to fly out to Utah to celebrate the opening of his new Overstock headquarters outside Salt Lake City in Midvale. Designed with typical Byrne flare, and dubbed The Peace Coliseum, it was a round, three-story, $100 million, 231,000-square-foot office building designed to look like a glass-and-concrete version of the Roman Coliseum from the outside. From the air looking down, four walkways intersect in the circular courtyard to form a peace sign. The courtyard also contains a large fire pit where employees can gather with their laptops and exchange ideas or simply relax.

Butina decided to give Byrne another chance, but in the end it again simply remained platonic. Instead, Byrne, who continuously believed that Butina was innocent, began to turn more and more against the bureau. "I became certain that there was no legitimate law enforcement or national security interest being served," he said. "I thought she was just what she was telling me she was: an idealistic liberal intellectual who is trying to make the world a better place." Nevertheless, the government agents pressed ahead. "The FBI

and the Justice Department needed a scalp in the midst of the frenzy about…
Russiagate," said John Kiriakou, a former CIA officer turned whistleblower
about torture, who was prosecuted and imprisoned for his revelations.

At first, they were convinced that Butina must be acting as a secret conduit for tens of millions of dollars from the Kremlin to Trump via the NRA,
simply because she had attended a few conventions. Therefore, as they often
do to gain favorable publicity, the bureau leaked details of their probe to the
press. "FBI Investigating Whether Russian Money Went to NRA to Help
Trump," blared a headline in the nationwide chain of McClatchy newspapers,
which also heavily promoted the Steele dossier conspiracy theories. Mentioning Butina, the article said the investigation "signals a new dimension in
the 18-month-old FBI probe of Russia's interference."

But as the bureau would eventually discover, there was absolutely no evidence of any kind showing massive amounts of Russian money flowing to the
NRA or Trump, let alone via Maria Butina. And Butina's only contribution to
the NRA was her annual dues. Nor was any money flowing from the Kremlin
to Butina, who had to continuously borrow money to pay for her tuition.
With her family in Siberia unable to help, she was not even able to make the
payments for her final semester. The publicity, however, had a devastating
effect on her. "At American University I was cut out from everything," she
told me. "Classmates didn't sit next to me because they believed that I am this
agent who came here to elect Trump."

Their leak having bombed, the FBI next decided to take a page out of Hollywood and charge that Butina was in fact a real-life "red sparrow" sent by the
Kremlin to seduce her way into the highest levels of government. In charge of
the case was forty-five-year-old Michael Orlando, the assistant special agent
in charge of counterintelligence at the Washington Field Office. Years earlier
he was assigned to the Honolulu FBI office around the same time that alleged
Chinese mole Alex Ma was there stealing every secret he could under the
noses of the counterintelligence agents—and then flying off to Shanghai to
deliver the packages and be debriefed by his handler. It is unclear when Ma
left the bureau, but he was not arrested until 2020.

To gather proof, the bureau assigned two of its crack counterspies, Kevin
Helson, forty-five, a slow-talking former blood and fingerprint analyst from
Tennessee, and Michelle Ball, thirty-three, a perky brunette with a sideswept
bang, large dimples, and a toothy smile. Fresh out of the FBI Academy, she
had spent the previous five years as a local anchor and reporter for a Biloxi,
Mississippi, TV station covering car crashes and advising on where to go for
the weekend. There is no indication she knew anything about Russia or espionage, except what she may have watched on *The Americans*. Nevertheless,

the pair were badge-carrying counterspies on the trail of Maria Butina. "They were interested in sex," according to one of the people interviewed by Ball. She brought up a few names, but again it was a dead end. "They couldn't establish that," he said, "but that's what they wanted to know."

Given the lack of evidence tying Butina to the Kremlin, espionage, influence, or any Russiagate conspiracy, the Mueller team in charge of the Russiagate investigation paid no attention to her. At one point I asked Special Counsel Robert Mueller why he never included Butina in his investigation. "She didn't come under my bailiwick," he told me, indicating that there had never been anything suspicious about her. His "bailiwick" being Russiagate and Russian influence operations. Nevertheless, despite the fact that the Mueller investigation had no interest, a local District of Columbia federal prosecutor with a history of grabbing for headlines decided to go after her. Short and bulky, Gregg A. Maisel had a reputation for pushing weak but spotlight-attracting cases.

Maisel had previously been severely criticized by the court for abusive prosecution in another high-profile case, and also for unnecessarily keeping someone in jail. In an unusual public spanking, in 2012, Maisel was reprimanded in open court by a senior judge for "unbelievably inexcusable behavior" as a result of what amounted to a deliberate wrongful prosecution. That case involved the pirate takeover of a Danish merchant ship. Like Butina's case, it was high-profile but without merit. In such cases, prosecutors seek maximum positive publicity while scaring the defendant into a guilty plea, thereby avoiding a likely loss at trial. "The criminal law does not exist to go to push something to the outer limits," D.C. senior judge Ellen Huvelle admonished Maisel, saying he had "misled" her. "That's not what a criminal case is about. You should not be prosecuting a case that you cannot win. It is an outrage."

In addition to charging that Maisel was wasting "taxpayers' money for a case that won't have the legs to stand on," Judge Huvelle gave him another verbal tongue-lashing for deliberately holding the defendant in jail regardless, something she vowed she would not let happen. "Not if I can stop it," she said, adding, "You brought him here. You bamboozled him here…So you fought tooth and nail to lock him up. You brought him here under false pretenses, now you tell me he can't be free while you take up an extremely novel difficult legal principle?"

And around the same time Maisel was taking on the Butina case, the entire District of Columbia U.S. Attorney's office was being severely criticized for abusive prosecution of more than two hundred protesters arrested and charged with felonies during the Trump inauguration. In the end, the prosecutors were only able to secure a single guilty plea to a felony charge. "It's hard not to feel cynical about the enormous amount of power that prosecutors have to overcharge people," said one defense attorney, Michael A. Webermann, "disrupt their lives, and then drop cases before having to face any consequences in court."

Assigned as the lead prosecutor in Butina's case was Erik Kenerson. Thin, balding, and bearded, he had spent most of his career prosecuting local street crimes and apparently only made the news twice. The first time was when he prosecuted another American University student on charges—later dropped—involving the aiming of a laser pointer at a U.S. Park Police helicopter. The other involved a man arrested after telling Secret Service agents he had been summoned telepathically for a meeting with President Trump and that he was carrying an asteroid in a canvas bag in his trunk. They were hardly résumé builders, but a high-profile case involving the actual arrest of a Russian agent in the United States associated with Russiagate could be a stepping-stone to greater glory.

Maisel and Kenerson were determined to paint Butina as the Kremlin's sexy "red sparrow." It was a charge guaranteed to attract enormous publicity. In a court hearing shortly after her high-profile SWAT-team arrest, Kenerson dramatically declared that they had uncovered evidence that Butina had offered a person sex "in exchange for a position within a special interest organization." However, he adamantly refused to reveal the source of the evidence or the identity of the "special interest organization," even to Butina's lawyers. As a result, the speculation throughout the media was that it was likely a political party, possibly the Democrats or the Republicans. And given the Russiagate hysteria of the times, the results were predictable.

"Who Is Maria Butina? Accused Russian Spy Allegedly Offered Sex for Power," read the headline in *USA Today*. CNN, never known for subtlety or objectivity, carried the breaking news banner "The Russian Accused of Using Sex, Lies, and Guns to Infiltrate U.S. Politics." "Real-Life 'Red Sparrow'? Court Filings Allege Russian Agent Offered Sex for Access," blared an ABC News banner. "Maria Butina Had Ties to Russian Spies and Offered Sex for Access to U.S. Political Circles, Court Documents Claim," screamed a breathless *Newsweek* headline.

It even made headlines on the other side of the planet. The *New Zealand Herald* declared in large bold print, "Accused Red Sparrow-Style Russian Agent Traded Sex for Influence, Prosecutors Say," and the *South China Morning Post* headline read, "Alleged Russian Spy Maria Butina Traded Sex for U.S. Political Access, Prosecutors Say." Within days, a simple Google search using the phrase "Maria Butina" and "sex" produced more than three hundred thousand hits, and she became the butt of jokes on shows like *Full Frontal with Samantha Bee.*

As part of the Russiagate hysteria, a senior Treasury Department official then began illegally leaking Butina's innocent banking records to BuzzFeed News. "Here is the Money Trail from the Russian 'Agent' and her Republican partner," read the headline. And FBI counterintelligence agents continued to illegally leak false information. "FBI counterintelligence officers," read the article, say the "banking activity could provide a road map of back channels to powerful American entities such as the National Rifle Association, and information about the Kremlin's attempt to sway the 2016 U.S. presidential election." It didn't, since there never was a link, and in 2021 the Treasury official, Natalie Mayflower Edwards, was prosecuted and sent to prison.

For Butina, still in her twenties, just out of grad school and hoping to begin her career, the blatantly sexist slander was devastating. "Every major newspaper in the U.S. and abroad called me a whore based on nothing," she told me from jail, fighting back tears. "I am Russian. I will be burned because I'm a witch...It's just a pure sexist story. I'm still considered to be the source of the money, a honeypot, all this crazy stuff...They saw a movie and went looking for a 'red sparrow.' Well, this is not a movie and I'm not a 'red sparrow.'" She was frustrated and disillusioned. "I came here because kids of my generation believed in the U.S., because our laws are based on yours. This is the human rights place. They just smashed my reputation."

Perhaps even worse was Butina's sadness that her family in Siberia had to read and hear all the lies. "It hurts me so much that my parents saw all this sex-scandal speculation on the news. It has been very hard to them to see my name, a person who earned three master's degrees, a justice believer, being smashed in the dirt so much."

It would be months before Butina's attorney, Robert Driscoll, was finally able to force Kenerson and Maisel to reveal the evidence on which they based their charges. In reality it simply turned out to be a three-year-old text from her phone that was a joke to a longtime friend, a Russian public relations employee at her gun rights organization in Moscow. Humorously complaining about taking Butina's car for an annual inspection, he wrote, "I don't know what you owe me for this insurance [but] they put me through the wringer." Facetiously, Butina replied, "Sex. Thank you very much. I have nothing else at all. Not a nickel to my name." She added a humorous smiley face emoji at the end. The friend then wrote back in the same humorous vein that sex with Butina did not interest him, also adding a smiley face emoji. Butina was also a longtime friend of the colleague's wife and child. In months of investigation, after interviewing dozens of witnesses and reviewing years of email and text messages, that was the best the prosecutors could come up with.

Kenerson's deliberately misleading and headline-grabbing "special interest organization" therefore turned out to be not the Democratic or Republican Party, but Butina's own Moscow gun rights club. Thus she was supposedly offering sex to someone "in exchange for a position within" her own organization, which she founded and ran, thereby making no sense at all. The charges were an outrageous abuse of power. Attorney Driscoll, who was representing Butina pro bono because he deeply believed in her innocence, discovered many more. They included, he wrote to the judge, "deleted sentences, misquoting her messages; truncated conversations, taking them out of context; replaced emoticons with brackets, twisting tone; and mistranslated Russian communications, altering their meaning."

Caught in his deception, Kenerson claimed it was just a simple misunderstanding. Judge Tanya Chutkan didn't buy it. "It took approximately five minutes for me to review those emails and tell that they were jokes," she said. Kenerson then made sure that the defense would be muzzled to prevent them from telling the truth, and thereby revealing his deliberate sexist slander. "They eventually got a gag order put in place because I went on TV and said it was untrue," Driscoll told me.

When the true details behind the charges were finally released more than three months after the explosive headlines, they were barely mentioned in the press. As a result, the wild charges will forever dominate people's memories, as well as Google searches for Butina, not the long-delayed truth.

When I asked Frank Figliuzzi, the former head of the FBI's counterintelligence division, about the conduct of Maisel and Kenerson, he was angry. "I am troubled and hope there is a full inquiry," he told me. "This is disturbing. The question is whether this is convenient ineptitude or something far deeper... Further, there is the possibility of a civil suit for slander/libel which could force DOJ to determine whether these prosecutors were within the scope of their employment or whether the assertions were so irresponsible that they were acting 'outside the scope.'"

"They manipulated the evidence," was the opinion of a former assistant U.S. attorney familiar with the Washington, DC, office where Kenerson worked. It was a place he had spent many years prosecuting cases, and therefore he preferred that his name not be mentioned. "The government is basically calling her a whore in a public filing," he told me. "I think it was an attempt to influence media coverage... This seems like somebody panicked, they moved too early, now they're trying to figure out what to do."

A senior CIA official who held one of the highest jobs in the Clandestine Service, and who worked closely with the FBI on many spy cases, offered his professional view of the bureau's counterintelligence work. "They want to generate headlines. They don't care if the information is credible or not," he said, asking to remain anonymous because of his past clandestine work. "They form an opinion and that stays with them until the completion of the case...Bank robbers, kidnappers, fraud, embezzlement, they're very good at it. But when it gets into the espionage realm, they're rank amateurs." He added, "I feel sorry for Butina; she got caught up in this whole vortex. They're just interested in putting another notch in their belt and they don't care who gets hurt in the process."

Driscoll, Butina's attorney, is a former deputy assistant attorney general with the Justice Department's Civil Rights Division. Over the years he has handled numerous political and national security–related cases, but never anything like this. "I would wake up periodically at night and think this case is taking place in some alternative reality," he told me. "A 'spy' who uses no tradecraft and posts her every move on social media."

Lacking evidence of espionage, money laundering, passing cash to the Trump campaign, violating Russian sanctions, being a "red sparrow," or any other crime, prosecutors finally turned to the rarely used Section 951, acting as an unregistered agent of a foreign power. It is exactly the charge they should have instead brought against the scores of Americans acting as agents of Israel operating throughout the country at that very moment. But Israel is off-limits, and Russia makes headlines. Therefore, the prosecution attempted to show that Butina was actually an unpaid agent of her old mentor, Alexander Torshin, and that between them they had cooked up an elaborate plot to influence the election.

Among the supposed key pieces of evidence uncovered by Helson, the lead FBI agent on the case, was a four-year-old email exchange with Erickson, Butina's former close friend, at the time she was considering grad schools. In the old email she fantasized about a possible "diplomacy" project aimed at building constructive relations between Russia and the United States. Such a project, she suggested, would require a budget of $125,000 for her to attend conferences and the Republican National Convention. But what was never mentioned by Helson was that nothing ever happened. It was simply idle chatter, wishful thinking, idealistic dreaming, nothing more.

In his affidavit, Helson also described a search of Butina's computer during which he discovered another four-year-old conversation, this time with Torshin, in which they discussed an article Butina had published in *The National Interest* calling for improved U.S.-Russia relations. "BUTINA asked the RUSSIAN OFFICIAL [Torshin] to look at the article," Helson's FBI affidavit states, "and the RUSSIAN OFFICIAL said it was very good."

In other words, she sent Torshin an article to read. Torshin read it and liked it. Therefore, Butina is a spy.

Such was the quality of the FBI's case.

When Scott Walker announced his presidential candidacy, Torshin asked Butina to "write [him] something brief," which she did. This, too, became another piece of evidence for Helson, the former blood-splatter analyst, and his partner, Ball, the former Biloxi TV anchor. Further proof that Butina was a covert Kremlin operative. Such mundane revelations went on and on for a dozen pages.

From beginning to end, there was not a scintilla of evidence that Butina was ever under the orders, direction, or control of either the Russian government or Torshin. Torshin exhibited no power or authority over her, and she had no obligation to fulfill any order or request. She could not be fired, demoted, or reassigned by him.

"I've never been employed, I've never been paid by the government," Butina told me, and no evidence of it was ever been presented by the FBI or the prosecutors. What started with promised heartstopping scenes of sex, spies, millions, and secrets ended instead with selfies on Facebook with glad-handing politicians and dinners with long-winded academics. And then there were the endless chats about peace between the United States and Russia with Torshin, an old fan of former Russian president Mikhail Gorbachev and his close friendship with the West.

On November 23, 2018, Butina went to sleep on a blue mat atop the gray cement bed in her cell in the Alexandria Detention Center. It was her eighty-first day in solitary confinement. Hours later, in the middle of the night, she was awakened and marched to a new cell, 2E05, this one with a solid steel door like the other, but now with no food slot, preventing even the slightest communication. No reason was given, but her case had reached a critical point and it was apparently decided to apply additional pressure on her. Realizing what little real evidence they had, prosecutors were hoping to get her to plead guilty rather than go to trial. They even agreed to drop the major charge against her: acting as an unregistered foreign agent of Russia.

Born and raised in the wide-open spaces of Siberia, Butina was terrified of solitary confinement. She was also six thousand miles from her family. Fifteen days later, now in solitary for over three straight months and threatened with spending the next decade and a half of her life in prison, she signed the agreement pleading guilty to the lesser charge, one count of conspiracy. She knew she was innocent, but she saw little hope as a Russian, in the midst of the Russiagate hysteria, facing a Washington jury. On April 26, 2019, she was sentenced to eighteen months in prison, and given credit for time already served.

A week earlier, the much-anticipated Mueller Report was released, officially titled "Report on the Investigation into Russian Interference in the 2016 Presidential Election." Nowhere in its 448 pages was Maria Butina's name. And in 2022, an unredacted version of the report was released that revealed the identities of people Mueller considered charging but whose names were redacted in the original report. Again, Maria Butina was not among them. Nevertheless, she ended up becoming the only Russian to take the fall for the entire scandal.

As Butina was transferred from jail in Alexandria to a federal prison in Tallahassee, Florida, to serve out the remainder of her sentence, Patrick Byrne admitted his regret at having set the entire prosecution in motion. "She's the only Russian they had for this whole charade," he told me. "I thought their case was chickenshit." He also accepted much of the blame. "I used her as bait," he said. "She spent a year and a half in jail that she should not have because I used her in my own scheme. I've behaved monstrously toward not just any woman but one of the finest women I've ever met, and the finest Russian I've ever known, and just a really fine woman. I know it was horrible."

Finally, on October 25, 2019, Butina was released from her cell, escorted by U.S. marshals to Miami International Airport, placed on a regularly scheduled Aeroflot jet, and deported back to Moscow. Once airborne, Butina watched through the window as the last of Florida, and the United States, disappeared in the gray haze of a billowing cloud. Alice had at last emerged from the rabbit hole.

Butina had come to the United States five years earlier as an idealistic graduate student, hoping to someday find a way to create better relations between the United States and Russia. It was her childhood dream. She left bitter and forever scarred by a country that politically and publicly abused her. Seduced by an erstwhile FBI informant, fraudulently branded by the Justice Department as a Russian whore, and slandered by the American media as a spy-for-sex, she saw deep into America's soul. In 2021, Butina was elected to Russia's parliament, the Duma. And one day, she may sit in the Kremlin and make critical decisions on relations between Russia and the United States.

ACKNOWLEDGMENTS

Many thanks to Sean Desmond, my editor and publisher at Twelve, for his courage to take on such a controversial topic, his constant personal attention, and his wisdom in turning a pile of words into a beautiful book. And also my gratitude to production manager Bob Castillo, who deciphered my manuscript with the skill of a cryptologist.

Thanks also to Kristine Dahl, my literary agent at ICM, for her hard work during the pandemic to help me think through yet another book, our fourth together. They never get easier, but her advice and encouragement always push me toward the finish line.

ENDNOTES

———◆———

Introduction

ix **fraudulently changing odometers:** See United States Court of Appeals, Sixth Circuit, *United States of America v. J.T. Haun*, June 6, 1996; **watering down orange juice:** See United States Court of Appeals, Sixth Circuit, *United States of America v. Friedrich R. "Fred" Kohlbach, et al*, June 23, 1994.

BOOK ONE: THE SABOTEURS

Chapter 1: The Dinner

3 **Retired general James Clapper:** Unless otherwise indicated, details of General Clapper's North Korea visit are from James R. Clapper with Trey Brown, *Facts and Fears: Hard Truths from a Life in Intelligence* (New York: Penguin, 2018).

3 **Sitting next to him:** General Kim Yong Chol background from North Korean Government Information website (in Korean [Choseonmal]), https://nkinfo.unikorea.go.kr/nkp/theme/viewPeople.do?nkpmno=945.

4 **Iraq:** See Stephen Kinzer, *Overthrow: America's Century of Regime Change from Hawaii to Iraq* (New York: Times Books, 2006).

4 **"the U.S. tried to change":** Lindsey A. O'Rourke, "The U.S. Tried to Change Other Countries' Governments 72 Times During the Cold War," *Washington Post*, December 23, 2018, https://www.washingtonpost.com/news/monkey-cage/wp/2016/12/23/the-cia-says-russia-hacked-the-u-s-election-here-are-6-things-to-learn-from-cold-war-attempts-to-change-regimes/. See also Stephen Kinzer, *Overthrow: America's Century of Regime Change from Hawaii to Iraq* (New York: Times Books, 2006).

4 **direct support to Saudi Arabia:** See Annelle R. Sheline and Bruce Riedel, "Biden's Broken Promise on Yemen," Brookings Institution, September 16, 2021, www.brookings.edu/blog/order-from-chaos/2021/09/16/bidens-broken-promise-on-yemen/.

4 **punishing blockade:** See "Yemen Civilian Deaths Double Since UN Monitors Removed: NGO," Al Jazeera, February 10, 2022, https://www.aljazeera.com/news/2022/2/10/yemen-civilian-deaths-double-since-un-monitors-removed-ngo-says.

4 **hundreds of thousands of deaths:** Joyce Sohyun Lee, Meg Kelly, and Atthar Mirza, "Saudi-Led Airstrikes in Yemen Have Been Called War Crimes. Many relied on U.S. Support," *Washington Post*, June 4, 2022, www.washingtonpost.com/investigations/interactive/2022/saudi-war-crimes-yemen/.

4 **extensive acts of torture:** Carol Rosenberg and Julian E. Barnes, "Gina Haspel Observed Waterboarding at C.I.A. Black Site, Psychologist Testifies," *New York Times*, June 3, 2022, www.nytimes.com/2022/06/03/us/politics/cia-gina-haspel-black-site.html. Haspel was in charge of the "black site" in Thailand at the time. Yet not only was she not prosecuted for violating laws against torture, she was instead promoted to head the CIA. At her confirmation hearing Senator Richard Burr, chairman of the Senate Intelligence Committee, told Haspel, "You are without a doubt the most qualified person the president could choose to lead the CIA and the most prepared nominee in the 70-year history of the agency. You have acted morally, ethically and legally over a distinguished 30-year career." Her confirmation thus told the world that America views torture as a positive, moral, ethical, and legal action that should be promoted. See also National Security Archive, https://nsarchive.gwu.edu/document/16782-document-12-gina-haspel-report-cia.

4 **"made it clear that he will not give up"**: Jung H. Pak, *Becoming Kim Jong Un: A Former CIA Officer's Insights into North Korea's Enigmatic Young Dictator* (New York: Random House, 2020), p. 83.

5 **"that a state without nuclear capability"**: Top Secret/SI/TK, NSA, 12/7/16, "Ambassador Wendy Sherman Speaks on North Korea," Edward Snowden Archive.

5 **"If you had nukes"**: Doug Bandow, "Kim Won't Be Duped Like Qaddafi, *Foreign Policy*, May 30, 2018, https://foreignpolicy.com/2018/05/30/kim-wont-be-duped-like-qaddafi/.

5 **"Gaddafi pleaded for the United States"**: Clapper, *Facts and Fears*, p. 165.

5 **"plagued by deeply flawed intelligence"**: Azmat Khan, "Hidden Pentagon Records Reveal Patterns of Failure in Deadly Airstrikes," *New York Times*, December 18, 2021, www.nytimes.com/interactive/2021/12/18/us/airstrikes-pentagon-records-civilian-deaths.html.

5 **"with special skill sets"**: Clapper, *Facts and Fears*, p. 272.

6 **Lieutenant Kim was an aide:** By 2022, General Kim had become one of the most powerful officials in North Korea. As director of the United Front Department of the Workers' Party of Korea, he was in charge of all relations with South Korea, including espionage, diplomacy, and policy making. The UFD is part of a shadowy group of Central Committee organizations known as the "Third Building." In March 2022, hackers from his former RBG successfully penetrated the email account of a former director at South Korea's National Intelligence Service.

6 **Army major general Pak Chung Kuk:** "In Pueblo's Wake," *Time*, February 2, 1968, http://content.time.com/time/subscriber/article/0,33009,837782-1,00.html.

7 **nearly led to a nuclear war:** Chris McGreal, "Papers Reveal Nixon Plan for North Korea Nuclear Strike," *Guardian*, July 7, 2010, www.theguardian.com/world/2010/jul/07/nixon-north-korea-nuclear-strike.

Chapter 2: The Studio

8 **"defined MGM"**: Scott Eyman, *Lion of Hollywood: The Life and Legend of Louis B. Mayer* (New York, Simon & Schuster, 2005), p. 12.

8 **Mandeville Canyon:** Jane Carlson, "Live Nation CEO Buys 2 Houses for $14.7 Million," *Hollywood Reporter*, February 22, 2013, www.hollywoodreporter.com/lifestyle/style/live-nation-ceo-buys-2-423250/.

9 **earned more than $250,000 a year:** Tatiana Siegel, "New Life for Amy Pascal: From $250K+ Assistant to $250M in Cuts," *Hollywood Reporter*, November 25, 2013, www.hollywoodreporter.com/news/general-news/new-life-amy-pascal-250k-659570/.

9 **"I thought I should have your job"**: Tim Arango, "Sony's Version of Tracy and Hepburn," *New York Times*, October 24, 2009, www.nytimes.com/2009/10/25/business/media/25sony.html.

9 **"Sony Pictures has made incredible progress"**: Sony Pictures, Press Release, "Sony Pictures Announces New Sustainability Targets," April 16, 2013, www.sonypictures.com/corp/press_releases/2013/04_13/041613_sustainability.html.

9 **meetings in New York:** WikiLeaks, Email 26444, Sony to Amy Pascal, "Lynton—Four Square/MRP Meetings—NYC," October 16, 2014, https://wikileaks.org/sony/emails/emailid/26444.

9 **by private helicopter:** WikiLeaks, Email 57713, Sony to Amy Pascal, "Lynton—MPG Meetings NYC," August 22, 2014, https://wikileaks.org/sony/emails/emailid/57713.

10 **"[David] is obsessed"**: WikiLeaks, Email 128221, Michael Lynton to Lili, "Re: Travel questions," February 25, 2014, https://wikileaks.org/sony/emails/emailid/128221. See also Kali Holloway, "9 Obscene Ways the Rich Spend Their Money," *Salon*, June 2, 2015.

10 **"Principal Gifts"**: WikiLeaks, Email 116639, Lili Lynton to Michael Lynton, "Re: Travel questions," February 2, 2014, https://wikileaks.org/sony/emails/emailid/116639.

10 **"This is great news!"**: WikiLeaks, Email 127173, Ronald Margolin to Michael Lynton, "Re: Lynton Info," February 10, 2014, https://wikileaks.org/sony/emails/emailid/127173.

10 **"No one outside the board"**: WikiLeaks, Email 118265, Tom Rothman to Michael Lynton, March 12, 2014, https://wikileaks.org/sony/emails/emailid/118625.

10 **"I have not been a good godfather"**: WikiLeaks, Email 132469, Liza Chapman to Michael Lynton, November 17, 2014, https://wikileaks.org/sony/emails/emailid/132469.

11 **"I do not really know anyone at Brown"**: WikiLeaks, Email 118064, Michael Lynton to Liza Chapman, November 20, 2014, https://wikileaks.org/sony/emails/emailid/118064.

11 **an alumnus of both the college and business school; on the Harvard Board of Overseers:** Meg P. Bernhard and Theodore R. Delwiche, "Overseer Connects Harvard Fundraising Apparatus to West Coast, Sony

Emails Suggest," *Harvard Crimson*, April 27, 2015, www.thecrimson.com/article/2015/4/27/overseer-email -roles/.

11 **donated about $360,000 in rare photographs; donated an additional $550,000:** WikiLeaks, Email 122040, Michael P. Mattis to Michael Lynton, October 30, 2013, https://wikileaks.org/sony/emails/emailid/122040. See also WikiLeaks, Email 130986, Michael Lynton to Michael P. Mattis, October 7, 2014, https://wikileaks.org /sony/emails/emailid/130986.

11 **"this summer's most cartoonishly":** Ann Hornaday, "'White House Down' Movie Review," *Washington Post*, June 27, 2013, www.washingtonpost.com/goingoutguide/movies/white-house-down-movie-review /2013/06/27/55285f92-ddbf-11e2-b197-f248b21f94c4_story.html.

11 **"Is 'After Earth' the worst movie ever made?":** Joe Morgenstern, "Muddle-'Earth,'" *Wall Street Journal*, May 30, 2013, www.wsj.com/articles/SB10001424127887324412604578515000854294308.

12 **"This was a SHOCKER":** WikiLeaks, Email 200591, Stephen Basil-Jones to Steven O'Dell, "Untitled Seth Rogan Xmas Project," February 13, 2014, https://wikileaks.org/sony/emails/emailid/200591#searchresult.

12 **"The unanimous point of view":** WikiLeaks, Email 197252, Peter Taylor to multiple addressees, May 30, 2014, https://wikileaks.org/sony/emails/emailid/197252.

12 **"Above all":** WikiLeaks, Email 193874, Sun Yong Hwang to Steven Odell, "Re: The Interview—DCP Screenings," June 3, 2014, https://wikileaks.org/sony/emails/emailid/193874.

12 **"It never occurred to me":** Michelle Lanz, "How 'The Interview' Screenwriter Dan Sterling Became 'The Guy That Brought Down Sony,'" The Frame, 89.3KPCC, December 15, 2014, https://archive.kpcc.org/programs /the-frame/2014/12/15/40758/how-the-interview-scribe-dan-sterling-became-Sony/.

12 **"In the original version of the script":** Martin Fackler, Brooks Barnes, and David E. Sanger, "Sony's International Incident: Making Kim Jong-un's Head Explode," *New York Times*, December 14, 2014, www.nytimes .com/2014/12/15/world/sonys-international-incident-making-kims-head-explode.html.

13 **Rogen, who would make $8 million on the film:** *Variety* staff, "Sony Hackers Reveal Seth Rogen and James Franco's Pay for 'The Interview,'" *Variety*, December 3, 2014, https://variety.com/2014/film/news/sony -hackers-reveal-seth-rogen-and-james-francos-pay-for-the-interview-1201370629/.

13 **"Maybe the tapes of the movie":** "'The Interview' Trivia," IMDB.com, undated, www.imdb.com/title /tt2788710/trivia/.

13 **"If it does start a war":** Josh Rottenberg, "Seth Rogen and Evan Goldberg Like That Kim Jong Un Doesn't Get the Joke," *Los Angeles Times*, December 3, 2014, www.latimes.com/entertainment/movies/la-ca-rogen -goldberg-20141207-story.html.

13 **"Wikipedia mostly":** Steve Weintraub, "Seth Rogen, Evan Goldberg, and James Franco Talk Real-Life Inspiration, Improvisation, Franco's Instagram, and More on the Set of The Interview," Collider, October 1, 2014, https://collider.com/seth-rogen-james-franco-evan-goldberg-the-interview-set-interview/.

13 **asking his Alexa to fart:** Noah Vega, "Seth Rogan Asks Alexa to Fart," YouTube, March 27, 2020, www.youtube .com/watch?v=U3w8Wg-uSko.

13 **"Red Ink Runs at Sony Again":** CBS News, October 31, 2013, www.cbsnews.com/news/red-ink-runs-at -sony-again-cuts-profit-forecast/.

13 **"No cost is too sacred to cut":** Gideon Spanier, "Sony Moves Away from the Big Screen to Make Quality TV," *Independent*, November 22, 2013, www.independent.co.uk/news/business/news/sony-moves-away-from-the -big-screen-to-make-quality-tv-8957555.html.

13 **Lynton, who made $13 million in 2013:** Ben Fritz, *The Big Picture: The Fight for the Future of Movies* (Boston: Houghton Mifflin Harcourt, 2018), p. 17.

13 **And Pascal, who made $12 million:** Fritz, *The Big Picture*, p. 17.

13 **"Oh please, it's an investor conference":** WikiLeaks, Email 165130, Amy Pascal to Doug Belgrad, July 18, 2014, https://wikileaks.org/sony/emails/emailid/165130.

13 **The article, headlined:** Siegel, "New Life for Amy Pascal."

14 **"So stupid":** WikiLeaks, Email 73265, Amy Pascal to Scott Rudin, November 25, 2013, https://wikileaks.org /sony/emails/emailid/73265.

14 **"I wish I was there so much":** WikiLeaks, Email 144438, Amy Pascal to Andrea Giannetti, November 26, 2013, https://wikileaks.org/sony/emails/emailid/144438.

14 **"Should I ask him if he liked DJANGO?":** WikiLeaks, Email 60731, Amy Pascal to Scott Rudin, "Re: Ridealong. I bet he likes Kevin Hart," November 26, 2013, https://wikileaks.org/sony/emails/emailid/60731.

14 **"12 years"**: WikiLeaks, Email 60731, Scott Rudin to Amy Pascal, November 26, 2013, https://wikileaks.org/sony/emails/emailid/60731.

14 **"The film used every racist image"**: Tim Shorrock, "How Sony, Obama, Seth Rogen and the CIA Secretly Planned to Force Regime Change in North Korea," AlterNet, September 5, 2017, www.alternet.org/2017/09/how-sony-obama-seth-rogen-and-cia-secretly-planned-force-regime-change-north-korea/.

14 **"Now imagine this assassination farce"**: Justin Wm. Moyer, "Why North Korea Has Every Reason to Be Upset About Sony's 'The Interview,'" *Washington Post*, December 16, 2014, www.washingtonpost.com/news/morning-mix/wp/2014/12/16/why-north-korea-has-every-reason-to-be-upset-about-the-interview/.

14 **"Want to go kill Kim Jong Un?"**: Abby Phillip, "North Korea Threatens 'Merciless' Retaliation over James Franco and Seth Rogen Assassination Comedy," *Washington Post*, June 25, 2014, www.washingtonpost.com/news/worldviews/wp/2014/06/25/north-korea-threatens-merciless-retaliation-over-james-franco-and-seth-rogen-assassination-comedy/.

15 **"To allow the production and distribution"**: Asawin Suebsaeng, "What Does North Korea Have to Say About Seth Rogen and James Franco Trying to Kill Kim Jong Un in 'The Interview'?," *Mother Jones*, June 13, 2014, www.motherjones.com/politics/2014/06/north-korea-not-respond-yet-seth-rogen-james-franco-interview-movie-trailer/.

15 **"There was a lot of high-fiving"**: Josh Rottenberg, "Seth Rogen and Evan Goldberg Like That Kim Jong Un Doesn't Get the Joke," *Los Angeles Times*, December 3, 2014, www.latimes.com/entertainment/movies/la-ca-rogen-goldberg-20141207-story.html.

Chapter 3: Pyongyang

17 **one of his top cyber warriors**: Unless otherwise indicated, details regarding Park Jin Hyok can be found in United States of America v. Park Jin Hyok, United States District Court for the Central District of California, Case No. MJ18-1479, June 8, 2018, www.justice.gov/opa/press-release/file/1092091/download. Hereafter cited as Park Criminal Complaint.

17 **"Knowing this email is being hacked"**: WikiLeaks, Email 36716, George Clooney to Amy Pascal, September 6, 2014, https://wikileaks.org/sony/emails/emailid/36761.

18 **In 2019 it ranked eighth**: Martyn Willims, "Kim Chaek University Ranks 8th in International Programing Contest," North Korea Tech, May 4, 2019, www.northkoreatech.org/2019/05/04/kim-chaek-university-icpc-2019/.

19 **four million by 2015**: "North Korea's Ruling Elite Are Not Isolated," Insikt Group, July 25, 2017, https://go.recordedfuture.com/hubfs/north-korea-internet-activity.pdf.

20 **"Visitors to North Korea"**: Jung H. Pak, *Becoming Kim Jong Un: A Former CIA Officer's Insights into North Korea's Enigmatic Young Dictator* (New York: Ballantine, 2020), p. 91.

20 **Austrian roaster Helmut Sachers**: Min Chao Choy, "North Korea's Café Culture is Growing, but Coffee Is Still a Luxury Brew," NK News, May 8, 2022, www.nknews.org/2020/09/north-koreas-cafe-culture-is-growing-but-coffee-is-still-a-luxury-brew/.

20 **1,230-seat *Rainbow***: Julie Makinen, "North Korea Is Building Something Other Than Nukes: Architecture with Some Zing," *Los Angeles Times*, May 20, 2016, www.latimes.com/world/asia/la-fg-north-korea-architecture-20160520-snap-story.html.

20 **"Consumerism has been entrenched"**: Pak, *Becoming Kim Jong Un*, p. 91.

21 **Since 1998, the country has launched five satellites**: Josh Smith, "Explainer: Why North Korea's Satellite Launches Are So Controversial," Reuters, March 7, 2022, www.reuters.com/world/asia-pacific/why-north-koreas-satellite-launches-are-so-controversial-2022-03-07/.

21 **Hwasong-15 rocket**: Hyonhee Shin and Josh Smith, "S.Korea says N.Korea Staged 'Largest ICBM' Fakery to Recover from Failed Test," Reuters, March 30, 2022. www.reuters.com/world/asia-pacific/skorea-says-nkorea-staged-largest-icbm-fakery-recover-failed-test-2022-03-30/.

21 **reconnaissance satellite in orbit**: Smith, "Explainer."

21 **have the capability of reaching U.S. cities**: David E. Sanger and William J. Broad, "U.S. Says North Korea Is Testing a New Intercontinental Missile," *New York Times*, March 10, 2022, www.nytimes.com/2022/03/10/us/politics/north-korea-intercontinental-missile.html.

21 **ordered an Air Force RC-135S Cobra Ball**: U.S., U.S. Indo-Pacific Command, "INDOPACOM Increases ISR, BMD Readiness in Response to Continued DPRK Missile Launches," March 9, 2022, www.pacom.mil/Media/News/News-Article-View/Article/2960710/.

21 **a server hidden at Thammasat University:** Ryan Sherstobitoff, "Analyzing Operation GhostSecret: Attack Seeks to Steal Data Worldwide," McAfee, April 24, 2018, www.mcafee.com/blogs/other-blogs/mcafee-labs /analyzing-operation-ghostsecret-attack-seeks-to-steal-data-worldwide/.

Chapter 4: Tokyo

23 **"Mr. Kaz Hirai, CEO, was very much concerned":** WikiLeaks, Email 191563, Noriaki Sano to Stephen Basil-Jones, June 23, 2014, https://wikileaks.org/sony/emails/emailid/191563.

24 **"Have to keep whole interview thing under wraps":** WikiLeaks, Email 47351, Michael Lynton to Amy Pascal, June 18, 2014, https://wikileaks.org/sony/emails/emailid/47351.

24 **"we need sonys name off this asap everywhere":** WikiLeaks, Email 166167, Michael Lynton to Amy Pascal, June 20, 2014, https://wikileaks.org/sony/emails/emailid/166167.

25 **"start some real thinking":** WikiLeaks, Email 128396, Bruce Bennett to Michael Lynton, June 25, 2014, https://wikileaks.org/sony/emails/emailid/128396.

25 **"Spoke to someone very senior in State":** WikiLeaks, Email 128714, Michael Lynton to Bruce Bennett, June 26, 2014, https://wikileaks.org/sony/emails/emailid/128714.

25 **"We made relationships with certain people":** Dave Itzkoff, "James Franco and Seth Rogen Talk About 'The Interview,'" *New York Times*, December 16, 2014, www.nytimes.com/2014/12/21/movies/james-franco-and -seth-rogen-talk-about-the-interview.html.

25 **"I think probably Hollywood is full of CIA agents":** The Guardian, "Ben Affleck on Argo: 'Probably Holly-wood Is Full of CIA Agents…,'" YouTube, November 8, 2012, www.youtube.com/watch?v=LCq97j4VakQ. In the film *Argo*, about the rescue of American embassy personnel during the Iran hostage crisis, Affleck played Tony Mendez, the CIA's master of disguise.

25 **"I'm the U.S. government official who told Sony":** "Daniel Russel, 'Remarks at USCI's China's Growing Pains Conference,'" USC Annenberg, USC U.S.-China Institute, April 22, 2016, https://china.usc.edu/daniel-russel -%E2%80%9Cremarks-usci%E2%80%99s-china%E2%80%99s-growing-pains-conference%E2%80%9D -april-22-2016.

25 **"We cannot be cute here":** WikiLeaks, Email 27823, Michael Lynton to Amy Pascal, "Re: Seth/Evan," July 9, 2014, https://wikileaks.org/sony/emails/emailid/27823.

25 **"We are gonna get rid of [his] face":** WikiLeaks, Email 27823, Amy Pascal to Michael Lynton, July 9, 2014, https://wikileaks.org/sony/emails/emailid/27823.

25 **"Speaking of making Kaz comfortable":** WikiLeaks, Email 32066, Doug Belgrad to Amy Pascal, August 2, 2014, https://wikileaks.org/sony/emails/emailid/32066.

26 **"Sony Altering Kim Jong Un Assassination Film":** Tatiana Siegel, "Sony Altering Kim Jong Un Assassination Film, 'The Interview' (Exclusive)," *Hollywood Reporter*, August 13, 2014, www.hollywoodreporter.com/news /general-news/sony-altering-kim-jong-assassination-725092/#!.

26 **"A source close to Sony's decision-making":** WikiLeaks, Email 103485, Leah Weil to Aimee Wolfson, "Privi-leged: Clearance Issues," August 13, 2014, https://wikileaks.org/sony/emails/emailid/103485.

26 **"Well, this is pretty much the worst headline imaginable":** WikiLeaks, Email 21914, Seth Rogen to Amy Pascal, August 13, 2014, https://wikileaks.org/sony/emails/emailid/21914.

26 **"As I sit and process this a bit":** WikiLeaks, Email 103485, Leah Weil to Aimee Wolfson, August 13, 2014, https://wikileaks.org/sony/emails/emailid/103485.

27 **"Just woke up":** WikiLeaks, Email 167316, Amy Pascal to Seth Rogen, "Re: Please Call Me ASAP," August 13, 2014, https://wikileaks.org/sony/emails/emailid/167316.

27 **"I don't know what that means":** WikiLeaks, Email 81100, Seth Rogen to Amy Pascal, "Re: Please Call Me ASAP," August 13, 2014, https://wikileaks.org/sony/emails/emailid/81100.

27 **"My conundrum is simple:** WikiLeaks, Email 20615, Seth Rogen to Amy Pascal, August 13, 2014, https:// wikileaks.org/sony/emails/emailid/20615.

27 **"Doug [Belgrad] and I agreed to a strategy":** WikiLeaks, Email 79566, Michael Lynton to Amy Pascal, August 13, 2014, https://wikileaks.org/sony/emails/emailid/79566.

27 **"I'm doing nothing now":** WikiLeaks, Email 161030, Amy Pascal to Michael Lynton, August 13, 2014, https:// wikileaks.org/sony/emails/emailid/161030.

27 **"We have to protect the movie":** WikiLeaks, Email 52366, Amy Pascal to Michael Lynton, August 13, 2014, https://wikileaks.org/sony/emails/emailid/52366.

27 **"That does not fly with me"**: WikiLeaks, Email 47129, Seth Rogen to Amy Pascal, August 13, 2014, https://wikileaks.org/sony/emails/emailid/47129.

27 **"Feels like he will drive you nuts for a while"**: WikiLeaks, Email 38151, Michael Lynton to Amy Pascal, August 15, 2014, https://wikileaks.org/sony/emails/emailid/38151.

27 **"The THR [*Hollywood Reporter*] story has been widely picked up"**: WikiLeaks, Email 27026, Doug Belgrad to Amy Pascal, Michael Lynton, August 13, 2014, https://wikileaks.org/sony/emails/emailid/27026.

28 **"No one is asking you to lie about the process"**: WikiLeaks, Email 151429, Amy Pascal to Seth Rogen, August 15, 2014, https://wikileaks.org/sony/emails/emailid/151429#searchresult.

28 **"The head melting shot described vividly"**: WikiLeaks, Email 21571, Seth Rogen to Amy Pascal, Doug Belgrad, August 15, 2014, https://wikileaks.org/sony/emails/emailid/21571.

28 **"Just arrived in Bali"**: WikiLeaks, Email 38151, Amy Pascal to a friend, August 15, 2014, https://wikileaks.org/sony/emails/emailid/38151.

28 **"Can I be lost in the jungle?"**: WikiLeaks, Email 160351, Amy Pascal to Doug Belgrad, August 15, 2014, https://wikileaks.org/sony/emails/emailid/160351.

28 **"Adding some melting"**: WikiLeaks, Email 54616, Doug Belgrad to Amy Pascal, Michael Lynton, August 15, 2014, https://wikileaks.org/sony/emails/emailid/54616#searchresult.

28 **Dassault Falcon 900:** See N90TH Dassault Falcon 900C leased to Sony, https://rzjets.net/aircraft/?page=4&typeid=85.

28 **operating loss of $181 million:** Daniel Miller, "Sony's Film Division Contributes to Company's Weak Second Quarter," *Los Angeles Times*, October 31, 2013, www.latimes.com/entertainment/envelope/cotown/la-et-ct-sony-film-unit-contributes-to-weak-quarter-20131031-story.html.

28 **"Meeting pretty rough"**: WikiLeaks, Email 61449, Michael Lynton to Amy Pascal, October 10, 2014, https://wikileaks.org/sony/emails/emailid/61449.

28 **"Shana Tova from temple"**: WikiLeaks, Email 148371, Amy Pascal to Seth Rogen, September 25, 2014, https://wikileaks.org/sony/emails/emailid/148371.

29 **"Burning face not as important as watermelon head explosion"**: WikiLeaks, Email 141067, Amy Pascal to Seth Rogen, September 25, 2014, https://wikileaks.org/sony/emails/emailid/141067#searchresult.

29 **"We took out three out of four of the face embers"**: WikiLeaks, Email 41526, Seth Rogen to Amy Pascal, Doug Belgrad, September 26, 2014, https://wikileaks.org/sony/emails/emailid/41526.

29 **"I think this is a substantial improvement"**: WikiLeaks, Email 22168, Amy Pascal to Kaz Hirai, September 27, 2014, https://wikileaks.org/sony/emails/emailid/22168#searchresult.

29 **"I need one night without dreaming about head explosions"**: WikiLeaks, Email 86114, Amy Pascal to Seth Rogen, September 30, 2014, https://wikileaks.org/sony/emails/emailid/86114.

Chapter 5: Sony Down

30 **"I don't care if Aaron is sleeping with the girl or not"**: WikiLeaks, Email 40925, Amy Pascal to Doug Belgrad, November 14, 2014, https://wikileaks.org/sony/emails/emailid/40925.

30 **"despicable"**: WikiLeaks, Email 51275, Amy Pascal to Mark Gordon, September 18, 2014, https://wikileaks.org/sony/emails/emailid/51275.

31 **"Amy, it's closed"**: WikiLeaks, Email 36789, Scott Rudin to Amy Pascal, November 19, 2014, https://wikileaks.org/sony/emails/emailid/36789.

31 **"Pay the damage"**: Park Criminal Complaint.

32 **"We've already warned you"**: Park Criminal Complaint.

32 **"Things have come to a standstill"**: David Robb, "Sony Hack: A Timeline," Deadline, December 22, 2014, https://deadline.com/2014/12/sony-hack-timeline-any-pascal-the-interview-north-korea-1201325501/.

32 **"We are investigating an IT matter"**: Robb, "Sony Hack."

32 **1.2 million downloads:** Andrew Wallenstein and Brent Lang, "Sony's New Movies Leak Online Following Hack Attack," *Variety*, November 29, 2014.

33 **"We Will PUNISH You Completely"**: Park Criminal Complaint.

33 **"This morning, I received a link"**: Kevin Roose, "Hacked Documents Reveal a Hollywood Studio's Stunning Gender and Race Gap," Splinter, December 1, 2014, https://splinternews.com/hacked-documents-reveal-a-hollywood-studios-stunning-ge-1793844312.

33 **"I'm not destroying my career"**: WikiLeaks, Email 82438, Scott Rudin to Amy Pascal, February 28, 2014, https://wikileaks.org/sony/emails/emailid/82438.

33 **"We will clearly show it to you"**: Park Criminal Complaint.

34 **"The lapse in judgment happened"**: Mark Seal, "An Exclusive Look at Sony's Hacking Saga," *Vanity Fair*, March 2015.

34 **"It's not only the great works of European art"**: Scott Foundas, "Film Review: 'The Monuments Men,'" *Variety*, January 29, 2014, https://variety.com/2014/film/reviews/film-review-the-monuments-men-1201075441/.

34 **"So depressed"; "We will protect you"**: WikiLeaks, Email 93447, George Clooney to Amy Pascal, January 30, 2014, https://wikileaks.org/sony/emails/emailid/93447#searchresult.

34 **"Cohn expected sex"**: Erin Blakemore, "This Tinseltown Tyrant Used Sexual Exploitation to Build a Hollywood Empire," History.com, September 1, 2018, www.history.com/news/this-tinseltown-tyrant-used-sexual-exploitation-to-build-a-hollywood-empire.

35 **"Nobody stood up"**: Mike Fleming Jr., "Hollywood Cowardice: George Clooney Explains Why Sony Stood Alone in North Korean Cyberterror Attack," Deadline, December 18, 2014.

35 **"I think they made a mistake"**: CNN, *Anderson Cooper 360°* transcript, December 19, 2014, http://edition.cnn.com/TRANSCRIPTS/1412/19/acd.01.html.

35 **"once the DVD leaks to the North"**: WikiLeaks, Email 128396, Bruce Bennett to Michael Lynton, June 25, 2014, https://wikileaks.org/sony/emails/emailid/128396.

35 **"The president, the press and the public are mistaken"**: CNN, *Anderson Cooper 360°* Degrees transcript, December 19, 2014.

35 **"We will respond proportionally"**: Justin Sink, "President: Sony Made a Mistake," *The Hill*, December 19, 2014, https://thehill.com/homenews/administration/227708-obama-sony-made-a-mistake/.

36 **"the chief culprit"**: "North Korea Berates Obama over The Interview Release," BBC News, December 27, 2014, www.bbc.co.uk/news/world-asia-30608179.

37 **"I launched thousands of copies"**: "Balloon Activist Sends 'Thousands of copies' of The Interview to North Korea," *Guardian*, April 8, 2015, www.theguardian.com/film/2015/apr/08/balloon-activist-sends-thousands-of-copies-of-the-interview-to-north-korea.

37 **"All I did was get fired"**: Jeremy Gerard, "Amy Pascal to Tina Brown: 'All I Did Was Get Fired'—Media," Deadline, February 13, 2015, https://deadline.com/2015/02/amy-pascal-tina-brown-sony-fired-1201372825/.

BOOK TWO: THE EXTORTIONISTS

Chapter 6: The Man in the Mirror

42 **"THIS CONOP CONTAINS"**: United States of America v. Harold T. Martin, III, Government's Response to Defendant's Motion for a Detention Hearing, October 20, 2016, Case 1:16-mj-02254-BPG. Hereafter cited as U.S. v. Martin, Motion.

42 **50 terabytes:** U.S. v. Martin, Motion.

42 **"I have 20 years in the IC"**: Letter from Hal Martin to author, Harford County Detention Center, Bel Air, Maryland, December 6, 2016. Hereafter cited as Martin letter.

42 **earned $3.6 billion:** Matthew Rosenberg, "At Booz Allen, a Vast U.S. Spy Operation, Run for Private Profit," *New York Times*, October 6, 2016, www.nytimes.com/2016/10/07/us/booz-allen-hamilton-nsa.html.

42 **"Are you a hacker?"**: Advertisement for Booz Allen Dark Labs, 2016, www.reddit.com/r/netsec/comments/3zfj6v/rnetsecs_q1_2016_information_security_hiring/cznjgh4/?context=3.

43 **"I spent a little over two and a half years there"**: Martin letter.

43 **"You could read anyone's email in the world"**: NDR.de, German television, "Snowden-Interview: Transcript," January 26, 2014, https://web.archive.org/web/20140128224439/http:/www.ndr.de/ratgeber/netzwelt/snowden277_page-3.html.

43 **"millions of implants"**: Ryan Gallagher and Glenn Greenwald, "How the NSA Plans to Infect 'Millions' of Computers with Malware," *The Intercept*, March 12, 2014, https://theintercept.com/2014/03/12/nsa-plans-infect-millions-computers-malware/.

43 **"TAOist at heart"**: October 23, 2016, HAL999 Google Profile.

43 **From TAO he transferred to S31:** Martin letter.

43 **"I wanted to do CNA"; "heavily involved"; "offensive software"**: Martin letter.

44 **He was a fan:** Details of Martin's likes and imaginings are from his allocution at sentencing, July 19, 2019. Hereafter cited as Martin allocution.

44 **Major Motoko Kusanagi:** See Motoko Kusanagi in Ghost in the Shell Wiki, https://ghostintheshell.fandom .com/wiki/Motoko_Kusanagi.

44 **"a special breed of warrior":** Hal Martin, "Human Dimension," *Cyber Defense Review*, February 12, 2015.

44 **he married his first wife, Marina:** Ian Duncan, "Former NSA Contractor Depicted in Court as a Hoarder Addicted to Stealing Classified Information," *Baltimore Sun*, October 21, 2016, www.baltimoresun.com /maryland/bs-md-harold-martin-nsa-hearing-20161021-story.html.

44 **"Virtual Interfaces for Exploration of Heterogeneous":** Hal Martin and Wayne T. Lutters, "Virtual Inter-faces for Exploration of Heterogeneous & Cloud Computing Architectures," USENIX, Proceedings of the 28th Large Installation System Administration Conference, November 9–14, 2014, www.usenix.org/system/files /conference/lisa14/lisa14-poster-martin.pdf.

44 **"Who is that 'man in the mirror'?";** "Major Pugachev, fighting to be free"; "new Number Six, episode 17"; Harry Palmer: Martin allocution.

45 **"Guccifer 2.0":** Eric Lichblau and Noah Weiland, "Hacker Releases More Democratic Party Documents," *New York Times*, August 12, 2016, www.nytimes.com/2016/08/13/us/politics/democratic-party-documents-hack .html.

45 **Nghia Hoang Pho:** United State of America v. Nghia Hoang Pho, Information, U.S. District Court for the District of Maryland, November 29, 2017, Case 1:17-cr-00631-GLR.

45 **The tip-off came from Israel's equivalent of NSA:** Nicole Perlroth and Scott Shane, "How Israel Caught Russian Hackers Scouring the World for U.S. Secrets, *New York Times*, October 10, 2017, www.nytimes .com/2016/08/13/us/politics/democratic-party-documents-hack.html.

46 **extensive interview with Edward Snowden; "I think that's amazing":** James Bamford, "Edward Snowden: The Most Wanted Man in the World," *Wired*, August, 2014, www.wired.com/2014/08/edward-snowden/.

46 **"political persecution":** James Bamford, "Israel's N.S.A. Scandal," *New York Times*, September 16, 2014, www.nytimes.com/2014/09/17/opinion/israels-nsa-scandal.html?_r=2. In 2015, forty-three veterans of Unit 8200—many still serving in the reserves—revealed that data from intercepts was gathered on Palestinians' sexual orientations, infidelities, money problems, family medical conditions, and other private matters. Such information, they said, could then be used to coerce Palestinians into becoming collaborators or create divi-sions in their society. The informants declared that they had a "moral duty" to no longer "take part in the state's actions against Palestinians."

46 **Pho had installed Kaspersky:** Kaspersky, "Preliminary Results of the Internal Investigation into Alleged Incident Reported by US Media," October 24, 2017, https://usa.kaspersky.com/about/press-releases/2017 _preliminary-results-of-the-internal-investigation-into-alleged-incident-reported-by-us-media. See also Kaspersky Securelist, "Investigation Report for the September 2014 Equation Malware Detection Incident in the U.S.," November 16, 2017, https://securelist.com/investigation-report-for-the-september-2014-equation -malware-detection-incident-in-the-us/83210/.

47 **Red Magic:** Ellen Nakashima, "NSA Employee Who Worked on Hacking Tools at Home Pleads Guilty to Spy Charges," *Washington Post*, December 1, 2017, www.washingtonpost.com/world/national-security /nsa-employee-who-worked-on-hacking-tools-at-home-pleads-guilty-to-spy-charge/2017/12/01/ec4d6738 -d6d9-11e7-b62d-d9345ced896d_story.html.

47 **"one of the most sophisticated cyber-attack groups in the world":** Stephanie Mlot, "Sophisticated Global Spyware Operation Linked to NSA," *PC Magazine*, February 17, 2015, www.pcmag.com/news /sophisticated-global-spyware-operation-linked-to-nsa#:~:text=%22The%20Equation%20group%20is %20probably,have%20seen%2C%22%20Kaspersky%20said.

47 **unmasking TAO in a public report:** "Equation: The Death Star of Malware Galaxy," Kaspersky Securelist, February 16, 2015, https://securelist.com/equation-the-death-star-of-malware-galaxy/68750/.

48 **"Personal security products":** Top Secret Strap2 UK Eyes Only, "Application for Renewal of Warrant GPW/1160 in Respect of Activities Which Involve Modification of Commercial Software," GCHQ, June 13, 2008, https:// s3.documentcloud.org/documents/2106826/gchq-application-for-renewal-of-warrant-gpw-1160.pdf.

48 **According to a top secret NSA document:** Top Secret//Comint//Rel to USA, AUS, CAN, GBR, NZL, "An Easy Win: Using SIGINT to Learn About New Viruses. Project CAMBERDADA," NSA, June 22, 2015, https:// theintercept.com/document/2015/06/22/project-camberdada-nsa/.

49 **"I was terrible at math":** Warren Strobel, "New NSA Director Was Horrified as a Child When He Learned About Illegal Government Spying," Reuters, May 20, 2014, www.businessinsider.com/r-post -snowden-the-nsas-future-rests-on-admiral-rogers-shoulders-2014-19?r=US&IR=T.

49 **"he managed to avoid significant notice"**: Adrianne Jeffries, "Who's the New Guy Running the NSA?," The Verge, July 7, 2014, www.theverge.com/2014/7/7/5876817/nsa-michael-s-rogers.

49 **"My grades were not very good"**: Mike Rogers interview, Auburn Alumni Association, June 5, 2017, https://m .facebook.com/watch/?v=10158657827045005&_rdr.

49 **"I'm not a computer engineer"**: Jeffries, "Who's the New Guy Running the NSA?"

50 **"We're sending a message"**: *Meet the Press*, NBC News, October 14, 2016, www.nbcnews.com/meet-the-press /video/biden-we-re-sending-a-message-to-putin-786263107997.

50 **"It's highly likely that any war"**: Richard Clarke, comments to author, June 5, 2019.

50 **"So…figure out how we talk"**: HAL999999999 Twitter message, www.politico.com/f/?id=00000168-30d2 -d7a7-a1ea-f6f327d70000.

50 **outside in his car**: U.S. v. Martin, Motion.

Chapter 7: Shadowland

51 **"How much you pay for enemies cyberweapons?"**: "Equation Group—Cyber Weapons Auction," Pastebin, August 13, 2016, https://archive.ph/rdYpc#selection-623.1-623.84.

52 **"There are a lot of people in Ft. Meade shitting bricks"**: Patrick Howell O'Neill, "Hackers Claim to Be Selling NSA Cyberweapons in Online Auction," Daily Dot, August 15, 2016, www.dailydot.com/debug /shadow-brokers-nsa-equation-group-hack/.

52 **"Without a doubt, they're the keys to the kingdom"**: Ellen Nakashima, "Powerful NSA Hacking Tools Have Been Revealed Online," *Washington Post*, August 16, 2016, www.washingtonpost.com/world/national -security/powerful-nsa-hacking-tools-have-been-revealed-online/2016/08/16/bce4f974-63c7-11e6-96c0 -37533479f3f5_story.html.

52 **"This is real"**: "EP 53: Shadow Brokers," *Darknet Diaries*, undated, https://darknetdiaries.com/transcript/53/.

52 **suddenly crashed**: Eric Geller, "NSA Website Recovers from Outage Amid Intrigue," *Politico*, August 16, 2016, www.politico.com/story/2016/08/nsa-website-hacking-rumors-227088.

52 **"Still considering it"**: Kim Zetter, "How a Russian Firm Helped Catch Alleged Data Thief," *Politico*, January 9, 2019, www.politico.eu/article/how-a-russian-firm-helped-catch-alleged-data-thief/.

54 **In March 2022, following Russia's invasion of Ukraine**: "List of Equipment and Services Covered by Section 2 of the Secure Networks Act," Federal Communications Commission, www.fcc.gov/supplychain/coveredlist.

55 **"expedited our plan"**: Details of the SWAT arrest from USA v. Harold T. Martin, III, sealed transcript of hearing, November 14, 2018, Document 192.

56 **winner in the World's Toughest Mudder competition**: Blair Ames, "Becoming the Toughest Mudder Is Year-Long Pursuit," *Buffalo News*, February 22, 2014, https://buffalonews.com/lifestyles/health-med-fit/becoming -the-toughest-mudder-is-year-long-pursuit/article_5c96ae04-d870-5b35-be50-ccdae1e5b87c.html.

56 **"unconscionable"**: Ellen Nakashima, "Judge: Government's Treatment of Alleged Leaker Thomas Drake Was 'Unconscionable,'" *Washington Post*, July 29, 2011, www.washingtonpost.com/blogs/checkpoint-washington /post/judge-governments-treatment-of-alleged-leaker-thomas-drake-was-/2011/07/29/gIQAPcVThI_blog .html.

57 **"Would one not then infer"**: Martin Brinkmann, "Computer Online Forensic Evidence Extractor," ghacks .net, updated December 8, 2014, www.ghacks.net/2008/04/29/computer-online-forensic-evidence-extractor/.

57 **"The Defendant's interrogation lasted approximately four hours"**: USA v. Harold T. Martin, III, Memorandum Opinion, December 17, 2018, Document 181.

58 **arrest under wraps for six months**: USA v. Harold T. Martin, III, Government's Response to Defendant's Motion for a Detention Hearing, October 20, 2016, Document 21.

58 **"I thought the third world war had started"**: Nicholas Fandos and Scott Shane, "A 'Sad Case' Suspect, Scared Pale as Police Swarmed His House in N.S.A Case," *New York Times*, October 5, 2016, www.nytimes .com/2016/10/06/us/politics/harold-martin-nsa-contractor.html.

58 **"The Justice department unsealed"**: Jo Becker, Adam Goldman, Michael S. Schmidt, and Matt Apuzzo, "NSA Contractor Arrested in Possible New Theft of Secrets," *New York Times*, October 5, 2016, www.nytimes .com/2016/10/06/us/nsa-leak-booz-allen-hamilton.html.

59 **75 percent of its dangerous and potentially deadly cyberweapons**: Ellen Nakashima, "Prosecutors to Seek Indictment Against Former NSA Contractor as Early as This Week," *Washington Post*, February 6, 2017, www.washingtonpost.com/world/national-security/prosecutors-to-seek-indictment-against-former-nsa -contractor-as-early-as-this-week/2017/02/06/362a22ca-ec83-11e6-9662-6eedf1627882_story.html.

59 **Mike Damm:** https://twitter.com/mikedamm.

59 **announced on Twitter that he was the highest bidder:** Mike Damm, tweet, August 15, 2016, https://twitter .com/mikedamm/status/765218627024891904.

59 **"We say roser not get money back":** "TSB-Message2," https://swithak.github.io/SH20TAATSB18/Archive /Messages/TSB/Message2/.

59 **"This is probably some Russian mind game":** David E. Sanger, "'Shadow Brokers' Leak Raises Alarming Question: Was the N.S.A. Hacked?," *New York Times*, August 16, 2016, www.nytimes.com/2016/08/17/us /shadow-brokers-leak-raises-alarming-question-was-the-nsa-hacked.html.

59 *Mass Effect 2: Lair of the Shadow Broker:* "Shadow Broker (enemy)," Mass Effect Wiki, https://masseffect .fandom.com/wiki/Shadow_Broker_(enemy).

59 **"It is pointless to challenge me":** "Shadow Broker," Villains Wiki, https://villains.fandom.com/wiki /Shadow_Broker.

60 **"If theshadowbrokers be using own voices":** "TSB-Message10," https://swithak.github.io/SH20TAATSB18 /Archive/Messages/TSB/Message10/.

60 **refers to then vice president Joe Biden as "DirtyGrandpa":** "Message#5—Trick or Treat?," October 30, 2016, https://medium.com/@shadowbrokerss/message-5-trick-or-treat-e43f946f93e6.

60 **"Shadow Brokers is not in the habit of outing":** "EP 53: Shadow Brokers," *Darknet Diaries*, undated, https:// darknetdiaries.com/transcript/53/.

60 **"[The Shadow Brokers] had operational insight":** Scott Shane, Nicole Perlroth, and David Sanger, "Security Breach and Spilled Secrets Have Shaken the N.S.A. to Its Core," *New York Times*, November 12, 2017, www .nytimes.com/2017/11/12/us/nsa-shadow-brokers.html.

61 **"CIA is cyber B-Team, yes?":** "Message#5—Trick or Treat?"

61 **"Auction is sounding crazy but is being real":** "TheShadowBrokers Message #3," October 1, 2016, https:// medium.com/@shadowbrokerss/theshadowbrokers-message-3-af1b181b481.

61 **"fostering hatred":** John F. Burns, "Britain Identifies 16 Barred from Entering U.K.," *New York Times*, May 5, 2009, www.nytimes.com/2009/05/06/world/europe/06britain.html.

61 **"Dr. Savage is correct":** "TSB-Message 10."

62 **"Fuck running from these bastards?":** "TSB-Message 10."

62 **Through such server passed:** Michael S. Schmidt, "Second Review Says Classified Information Was in Hillary Clinton's Email," *New York Times*, September 7, 2015, https://www.nytimes.com/2015/09/08/us/politics/second -review-says-classified-information-was-in-hillary-clintons-email.html.

62 **"Secrets between government and governed":** "Grammer Critics: Information vs Knowledge," Steemit, https://steemit.com/shadowbrokers/@theshadowbrokers/grammer-critics-information-vs-knowledge.

62 **"TheShadowBrokers is not being irresponsible criminals":** Joseph Cox, "They're Back: The Shadow Bro-kers Release More Alleged Exploits," Vice, April 8, 2017, www.vice.com/en/article/5387an/theyre-back-the -shadow-brokers-release-more-alleged-exploits.

62 **"When you are ready to make the bleeding stop":** "Message#5—Trick or Treat?"

Chapter 8: Apocalypse

63 **China:** See "The Bvp47—a Top-tier Backdoor of US NSA Equation Group," Pangu Lab, February 23, 2022, www.pangulab.cn/en/post/the_bvp47_a_top-tier_backdoor_of_us_nsa_equation_group/. See also "Chinese Experts Uncover Details of Equation Group's Bvp47 Covert Hacking," The Hacker News, February 23, 2022, https://thehackernews.com/2022/02/chinese-experts-uncover-details-of.html.

64 **"So long, farewell peoples":** "REPOST: TheShadowBrokers Message#8—January 2017," Steemit, https:// steemit.com/shadowbrokers/@theshadowbrokers/repost-theshadowbrokers-message-8-january-2017.

64 **eighty-three buildings:** "Facts About Microsoft," https://news.microsoft.com/facts-about-microsoft/.

64 **over forty thousand employees:** Karen Weise, "Ahead of the Pack, How Microsoft Told Workers to Stay Home," *New York Times*, March 15, 2020, www.nytimes.com/2020/03/15/technology/microsoft-coronavirus -response.html.

65 **"Dear President Trump":** "Don't Forget Your Base," Steemit, https://steemit.com/shadowbrokers /@theshadowbrokers/don-t-forget-your-base.

66 **"Where is being 'free press'?:** "Message#5—Trick or Treat?," October 30, 2016, https://medium.com /@shadowbrokerss/message-5-trick-or-treat-e43f946f93e6.

66   **"Last week theshadowbrokers be trying to help peoples"**: "Lost in Translation," Steemit, https://steemit.com /shadowbrokers/@theshadowbrokers/lost-in-translation.

66   **"Password = Reeeeeeeeeeeeeee"**: "Lost in Translation."

66   **"This isn't a data dump"**: hackerfantastic.crypto, tweet, April 14, 2017, https://twitter.com/hackerfantastic /status/852922058707263489?ref_src=twsrc%5Etfw.

Chapter 9: Yongbyon

67   **Nuclear Scientific Research Center**: The 2022 Annual Threat Assessment, prepared by the U.S. Office of National Intelligence, noted that Pyongyang is "probably" expanding its uranium enrichment program and that the current sanctions regime is likely not enough to convince the leadership to change course. "In January," the report added, "North Korea began laying the groundwork for an increase in tensions that could include ICBM or possibly a nuclear test this year—actions that Pyongyang has not taken since 2017." See "Annual Threat Assessment of the U.S. Intelligence Community," Office of the Director of National Intelligence, February 2022, https://docs.house.gov/meetings/IG/IG00/20220308/114469/HHRG-117-IG00-Wstate -HainesA-20220308.pdf.

69   **Finally, on May 9**: Park Criminal Complaint, p. 106.

Chapter 10: Cyberpandemic

70   **Anthony Brett**: Jamie Bullen, "'They Should Be Hung Drawn and Quartered': Patients' Fury as Operations Are Axed Because of NHS Cyber Attack," *Mirror*, May 12, 2017, www.mirror.co.uk/news/uk-news /they-should-hung-drawn-quartered-10411020.

70   **Patrick Ward**: Jonathan Mitchell, "NHS Cyber Attack: London Hospital Cancels Patient's Heart Surgery After 10-Month Wait," *Evening Standard*, May 13, 2017, www.standard.co.uk/news/health/nhs-cyber-attack-london -hospital-cancels-patient-s-heart-surgery-after-waiting-10-months-fro-operation-a3538411.html.

70   **Richard Harvey**: Kevin Rawlinson, "NHS Left Reeling by Cyber-Attack: 'We Are Literally Unable to Do Any X-Rays,'" *Guardian*, May 13, 2013, www.theguardian.com/society/2017/may/13/nhs-cyber-attack-patients -ransomware.

70   **Ray Neal**: Charlotte Wace, "'It's Life and Death to Us,' Patients Tell Cyber Crooks as One Surgeon Reveals the NHS Attack Led to a Computer Blackout During a Heart Operation," *Daily Mail*, May 13, 2017, www .dailymail.co.uk/news/article-4503420/It-s-life-death-NHS-patients-say-cyber-attack.html.

71   **Martin Hardy**: Dan Bilefsky, "British Patients Reel as Hospitals Race to Revive Computer Systems," *New York Times*, May 13, 2017, www.nytimes.com/2017/05/13/world/europe/uk-hospitals-cyberattack.html?action =click&module=RelatedLinks&pgtype=Article. See also Wace, "'It's Life and Death to Us.'"

71   **Grant Gowers**: Wace, "'It's Life and Death to Us.'"

71   **"The emergency department has no IT facilities"**: Rawlinson, "NHS Left Reeling by Cyber-Attack."

72   **nearly twenty thousand appointments had to be canceled**: Owen Hughes, "WannaCry Impact on NHS Considerably Larger Than Previously Suggested," DigitalHealth, October 27, 2017, www.digitalhealth .net/2017/10/wannacry-impact-on-nhs-considerably-larger-than-previously-suggested/.

72   **"One major hospital group is having a rough time"**: Felix Palazuelos, "How the WannaCry Ransomware Attack Affected Businesses in Spain," *El País*, May 19, 2017, https://english.elpais.com/elpais/2017/05/19 /inenglish/1495181037_555348.html.

72   **"The global reach is unprecedented"**: Robert Hackwill, "Europol Admits Stunned by Scale of Cyberattack," Euronews, May 14, 2017, www.euronews.com/2017/05/14/europol-admits-stunned-by-scale-of-cyberattack.

72   **"Humanity is dealing here with cyberterrorism"**: Andrew E. Kramer, "Russia, This Time the Victim of a Cyberattack, Voices Outrage," *New York Times*, May 14, 2017, www.nytimes.com/2017/05/14/world/europe /russia-cyberattack-wannacry-ransomware.html.

73   **"The spread is immense"**: "ALERT: Massive Ransomware Attack Is the Biggest Ever," SemTech IT Solutions, May 14, 2017, www.semtechit.com/blog/alert-massive-ransomware-attack-is-the-biggest-ever/.

73   **Marcus Hutchins came to the rescue**: Andy Greenberg, "The Confessions of Marcus Hutchins, the Hacker Who Saved the Internet," *Wired*, May 12, 2020, www.wired.com/story/confessions-marcus-hutchins-hacker -who-saved-the-internet/.

73   **$130,634.77 in bitcoin from 327 payments**: "Dissection of WannaCry Ransomware," Quadrant360 Consulting, August 23, 2021, https://quadrant360.com/penetration-test/dissection-of-wannacry-ransomware/.

73   "It's very important everyone understands": Marcus Hutchins, tweet, May 12, 2017, https://twitter.com /MalwareTechBlog/status/863191272969973760.

Chapter 11: Eternal Blowback

76   "A New Ransomware Outbreak": Dan Goodin, "A New Ransomware Outbreak Similar to WCry Is Shutting Down Computers Worldwide," *Ars Technica*, June 27, 2017, https://arstechnica.com/information-technology /2017/06/a-new-ransomware-outbreak-similar-to-wcry-is-shutting-down-computers-worldwide/.

76   servers at Heritage Valley began crashing and dying: Andy Greenberg, "How the Worst Cyberattack in His- tory Hit American Hospitals," *Slate*, November 5, 2019, https://slate.com/technology/2019/11/sandworm -andy-greenberg-excerpt-notpetya-hospitals.html.

76   "We confirm our company's computer network was compromised": Merek, tweet, June 27, 2017, https:// twitter.com/merck/status/879716775021170689?lang=en.

77   "It appears these two global ransomware attacks": Taylor Hatmaker, "In Aftermath of Petya, Con- gressman Asks NSA to Stop the Attack If It Knows How," Techcrunch, June 28, 2017, https://techcrunch .com/2017/06/28/ted-lieu-petya-notpetya-no-kill-switch/.

77   "Many of the versions we see spreading in the wild today": "WannaCry & EternalBlue Remain at Large & Most Prevalent Malware After the Vulnerability Patched," *Cyber Intel*, March 10, 2021, https://cyberintelmag .com/malware-viruses/wannacry-eternalblue-remain-at-large-most-prevalent-malware-after-the-vulnerability -fixed/.

77   "They've been very successful": Andy Greenberg, "North Korean Hackers Stole Nearly $400 Million in Crypto Last Year," *Ars Technica*, January 16, 2022, https://arstechnica.com/information-technology/2022/01 /north-korean-hackers-stole-nearly-400-million-in-crypto-last-year/?comments=1.

78   "world's third biggest hacking powerhouse": Kim Myong-song, "N. Korea 'World's 3rd Biggest Hacking Powerhouse,'" *Chosun Ilbo*, January 24, 2022, https://english.chosun.com/site/data/html_dir/2022/01/24 /2022012401130.html.

78   "decapitation"..."perform this function": Donald Kirk, Daily Beast, August 3, 2022, https://www.thedaily beast.com/us-to-enrage-kim-jong-un-with-assassination-dry-run.

BOOK THREE: THE SPIES

Chapter 12: The Propagandist

81   "Watch how you talk to me!": WikiLeaks, Email 68428, Scott Rudin to Amy Pascal, February 28, 2014, https:// wikileaks.org/sony/emails/emailid/68428.

81   Milchan was number 240: "#240 Arnon Milchan," Forbes.com, https://images.forbes.com/lists/2006/10/6BJX .html.

81   another half billion dollars hidden away: Uri Blau, "Arnon Milchan, Witness in Netanyahu Trial, Held $500m in Tax Haven, Pandora Papers Show," *Haaretz*, October 7, 2021, www.haaretz.com/israel-news/2021-10-07 /ty-article/.premium/witness-in-netanyahu-trial-held-500m-in-tax-haven-pandora-papers-show/0000017f -dc28-d856-a37f-fde8f83b0000.

82   "Those who wear the BDS label": "Full Transcript of Netanyahu's 2014 AIPAC Address," *Times of Israel*, March 4, 2014, www.timesofisrael.com/full-transcript-of-netanyahus-aipac-address/.

82   "This is not the best time to be seen": Itamar Eichner, "From DiCaprio to Eastwood, Netanyahu's Star- Studded LA Dinner," Ynetnews, March 5, 2014, www.ynetnews.com/articles/0,7340,L-4494923,00.html.

82   "I couldn't believe the amount of security": Danielle Berrin, "Bill Maher: The Confident Blasphemist," *Jewish Journal*, April 2, 2014, https://jewishjournal.com/culture/arts/128081/bill-maher-the-confident-blasphemist/.

82   "Posing for pictures is anathema": Elaine Dutka and Alan Citron, "Column One: A Mogul's Bankroll— and Past: Arnon Milchan Has Emerged as One of Hollywood's Most Powerful Producers. His Background Is Unusual: Agribusiness and Munitions," *Los Angeles Times*, February 28, 1992, www.latimes.com/archives /la-xpm-1992-02-28-mn-2957-story.html.

82   "He remains the town's most secretive mogul": Ann Louise Bardach, "The Last Tycoon," *Los Angeles* maga- zine, April 2000, www.lamag.com/longform/the-last-tycoon/.

83   "the most unpopular nation barring one": James Sanders, *South Africa and the International Media, 1972–79* (London: Frank Cass Publishers, 2000).

83 **"Sure, it sounds like fun"**: Bardach, "The Last Tycoon."

83 **"morality flies out the window"**: Anthony Sampson, "South Africa's Scandal Spreads to the West," *Washington Post*, March 25, 1979, www.washingtonpost.com/archive/opinions/1979/03/25/south-africas-scandal-spreads-to-the-west/c2e56978-14db-43db-97dd-85dc2159e48b/.

84 **"a full-scale psychological war"**: James Adams, *The Unnatural Alliance: Israel and South Africa* (London: Quartet Books Limited, 1984), p. 149.

84 **"You should keep your paperwork"**: Joseph Gelman and Meir Doron, "The Player," *Tablet*, July 19, 2011, www.tabletmag.com/sections/israel-middle-east/articles/the-player.

84 **"I have enough men to commit murder"**: Mary Braid, "Obituary: Hendrik van den Bergh," *Independent*, August 21, 1997, www.independent.co.uk/news/people/obituary-hendrik-van-den-bergh-1246509.html.

84 **"probably the most feared man in South Africa"**: Braid, "Obituary: Hendrik van den Bergh."

84 **Milchan became involved**: Gelman and Doron, "The Player." Jane Hunter, *Israeli Foreign Policy: South Africa and Central America* (Boston: South End Press, 1987), p. 18.

84 **"a vitally important co-operation"**: Chris McGreal, "Apartheid-Era Minister Carried 'Nuclear Trigger' in Hand Luggage to South Africa," *Guardian*, June 3, 2010, www.theguardian.com/world/2010/jun/03/south-africa-nuclear-trigger-israel.

84 **"enjoyed every minute there"**: Benjamin Beit-Hallahmi, *The Israeli Connection: Who Israel Arms and Why* (New York: Pantheon, 1987), p. 160.

84 **"'the alliance of pariah states'"**: Beit-Hallahmi, *The Israeli Connection*, p. 161.

85 **"an indefatigable schemer"**: Eric Weiner, "Shimon Peres Wears Hats of Peacemaker, Schemer," NPR, June 13, 2007, www.npr.org/templates/story/story.php?storyId=11020066&t=1621810011890.

85 **"Arnon is a special man"**: "Film Mogul, Power Broker, Ex-Spy, Arnon Milchan Is Central to Netanyahu Graft Probe," *Times of Israel*, January 7, 2017, www.timesofisrael.com/film-mogul-power-broker-ex-spy-arnon-milchan-is-central-to-netanyahu-graft-probe/.

85 **a secret reactor**: Officially known as the Negev Nuclear Research Center, with the acronym KAMAG.

85 **"a desolation that not even imagination can grace"**: "Israeli Idealists Look to the Negev as the Last Frontier," Israel 21c, September 18, 2007, www.israel21c.org/israeli-idealists-look-to-the-negev-as-the-last-frontier/.

86 **Blumberg checked out Milchan**: Meir Doron and Joseph Gelman, *Confidential: The Life of Secret Agent Turned Hollywood Tycoon Arnon Milchan* (Jerusalem: Gefen Publishing House, 2011). Caution should be taken in reading this book, "part of which was written in the first person," says *Haaretz*, since Milchan appears to have been the book's unnamed ghost co-author. Unsurprisingly, it therefore paints Milchan simply as a larger-than-life heroic figure. According to *Haaretz*, in 2011, Milchan "helped write his own biography, 'Confidential: The Life of Secret Agent Turned Hollywood Tycoon,' by Meir Doron and Joseph Gelman," and "the book doesn't stop heaping superlatives on its star." See Eytan Avril, "Nukes, Planes and Champagne: How Israeli Prime Ministers Have Worked for Billionaire Arnon Milchan," *Haaretz*, June 30, 2019, www.haaretz.com/israel-news/.premium.MAGAZINE-how-israeli-prime-ministers-have-worked-for-billionaire-arnon-milchan-1.7420636.

86 **"Eschel Rhoodie expressed his envy"**: Beit-Hallahmi, *The Israeli Connection*, p. 155.

86 **Rhoodie even sold Milchan his condominium**: William E. Burrows and Robert Windrem, *Critical Mass: The Dangerous Race for Superweapons in a Fragmenting World* (New York: Simon & Schuster, 1994), p. 458.

86 **$100 million to spend**: Hunter, *Israeli Foreign Policy*.

87 **"The Whites of South Africa understand"**: "South Africa: The Soweto Uprising: A Soul-Cry of Rage," *Time*, June 28, 1976, https://content.time.com/time/subscriber/article/0,33009,911814,00.html.

87 **"The idea was that we"**: Milchan interview on *Uvda* (Israeli television program, in Hebrew), November 25, 2013.

87 **"They recognized me as someone"**: Milchan interview on *Uvda*.

87 **Nicknamed "Jackboot John"**: Details about Vorster from "Vorster: Man on a Wagon Train," *Time*, June 28, 1976, http://content.time.com/time/subscriber/article/0,33009,911815,00.html.

87 **laid a wreath on a mass grave**: "Vorster and Rabin Meet in Jerusalem," *New York Times*, April 10, 1976, www.nytimes.com/1976/04/10/archives/vorster-and-rabin-meet-in-jerusalem.html?searchResultPosition=1.

87 **"They are both situated"**: Chris McGreal, "Israel and Apartheid: A Marriage of Convenience and Military Might," *Guardian*, May 23, 2010, www.theguardian.com/world/2010/may/23/israel-apartheid-south-africa-nuclear-warheads.

87 **its biggest weapons customer**: Jonathan Broder, "Israel Grows Sensitive over Links to South Africa," *Chicago Tribune*, April 2, 1977.

87   **powerful counterinsurgency weapons:** Phillip W. D. Martin, "Stop Israel's Secret Help in Arming South Africa," *Christian Science Monitor*, December 1, 1989. https://www.csmonitor.com/1989/1201/emart.html.

87   **"We created the South African arms industry":** Chris McGreal, "Brothers in Arms—Israel's Secret Pact with Pretoria," *Guardian*, February 7, 2006, www.theguardian.com/world/2006/feb/07/southafrica.israel.

88   **Uzi submachine guns:** William E. Farrell, "Israeli Arms Industry Has Grown Fivefold Since '73," *New York Times*, January 15, 1977, www.nytimes.com/1977/01/15/archives/israeli-arms-industry-has-grown-fivefold -since-73.html.

88   **"This is much worse than apartheid":** McGreal, "Brother in Arms."

89   **"on the advice of both Prime Minister Vorster":** Sanders, *South Africa and the International Media, 1972–1979*.

89   **1,160 screenings worldwide:** Ron Nixon, *Selling Apartheid: South Africa's Global Propaganda War* (London: Pluto Press, 2016).

90   **"the correct payload":** Chris McGreal, "Revealed: How Israel Offered to Sell South Africa Nuclear Weapons," *Guardian*, May 24, 2010, www.theguardian.com/world/2010/may/23/israel-south-africa-nuclear-weapons.

90   **secret South African court records:** Court of South Africa, Cape Province Division, The State versus Johann Philip Derk Blaauw, case no.270/87, Top Secret, September 9, 1988, p. 24.

90   **Among those serving as escorts:** Gelman and Doron, "The Player."

Chapter 13: The Producer

92   **As part of Operation Hollywood:** William E. Burrows and Robert Windrem, *Critical Mass: The Dangerous Race for Superweapons in a Fragmenting World* (New York: Simon & Schuster, 1994), pp. 458–59.

92   *Ipi Tombi*: "Arnon Milchan Biography," Film Reference, www.filmreference.com/film/68/Arnon-Milchan .html. See also "LEGEND Press Kit Photos," www.figmentfly.com/legend/background3.html.

92   **"the exploitation of blacks by South Africans":** C. Gerald Fraser, "Black Committee Urges Boycott of 'Ipi Tombi,'" *New York Times*, December 28, 1976, www.nytimes.com/1976/12/28/archives/black-committee -urges-boycott-of-ipi-tombi-from-south-africa.html.

92   **"The protesters contended the musical":** Fraser, "Black Committee Urges Boycott of 'Ipi Tombi.'"

93   **"Shut down *Ipi Tombi*":** Hardy Price, "S. African Playwright Team Gets Harsh U.S. Reception from Critics," *Arizona Republic*, June 15, 1980, www.newspapers.com/image/119951727/.

93   **"The closing of 'Ipi Tombe' ":** Fraser, "Black Committee Urges Boycott of 'Ipi Tombi.'"

93   **happened to meet film producer Elliott Kastner:** See Jack Mathews, *The Battle of Brazil* (New York: Crown, 1987), p. 16.

93   **Nicholson ended up suing Kastner:** Don Stradley, "The Missouri Breaks: Looking Back at the One That Got Away," July 2013, https://donstradley.blogspot.com/2013/07/the-missouri-breaks-1976.html.

93   **"Suddenly we are doing business together":** Ann Louise Bardach, "The Last Tycoon," *Los Angeles* magazine, April 2000, www.lamag.com/longform/the-last-tycoon/.

93   *Black Joy*: "Arnon Milchan Biography," Film Reference, *Black Joy* (with Elliott Kastner), Wincast, 1977. See also "LEGEND Press Kit Photos."

93   **"I don't like how the script is turning out":** Details on *Black Joy* from Sally Shaw, "But Where on Earth Is Home?: A Cultural History of Black Britain in the 1970s Film and Television," Volume 1 (doctor of philosophy thesis, 2014, University of Portsmouth), p. 234.

94   **During the May event, Rhoodie:** Meir Doron and Joseph Gelman, *Confidential: The Life of Secret Agent Turned Hollywood Tycoon Arnon Milchan* (Jerusalem: Gefen Publishing House, 2011), p. 123.

94   **Roman Polanski:** "Polanski Pleads Not Guilty in Drug-Rape Case," *Los Angeles Times*, April 16, 1977. "Polanski Flies to Paris as Officials in U.S. Ponder Prosecution Move," *New York Times*, February 3, 1978.

94   **"He's fun":** Bardach, "The Last Tycoon."

94   **"I went with them":** Sara Leibowitz-Dar, "LAKAM Chief Benjamin Blumberg Tells His Story," *Ma'ariv* (in Hebrew), April 7, 2012.

94   **"Kastner had the style of an amiable gorilla":** Sampson quotes and interaction with Milchan from Anthony Sampson, "Arms and the Man," *Guardian Weekend*, May 19, 2001.

95   **"He's as cheap as they come":** Bardach, "The Last Tycoon."

95   *The Last Supper of a Greedy Man*: Doron and Gelman, *Confidential*, p. 159.

96   **"I never saw such luxury":** Leibowitz-Dar, "LAKAM Chief Benjamin Blumberg Tells His Story."

97   **"was my partner":** Allison Kaplan Sommer, "Hollywood Producer Opens Up About Past as Israeli Operative," *Haaretz*, November 23, 2013, www.haaretz.com/.premium-arnon-milchan-secret-agent-1.5294466. See also

Stuart Winer, "Hollywood Producer Arnon Milchan Reveals Past as Secret Agent," *Times of Israel*, November 25, 2013: "Aside from setting up arms deals, Milchan also tried to get other Hollywood figures involved in his clandestine work, notably the late director Sydney Pollack," Winer wrote. "Pollack was allegedly involved in buying arms and military equipment for Israel during the 1970s and, according to Milchan, knew just what he was getting into."

98 **produce a film about Dayan:** Fred Ferretti, "On Location with 'King of Comedy,'" *New York Times*, August 23, 1981, www.nytimes.com/1981/08/23/movies/on-location-with-king-of-comedy.html.

98 **De Niro sat at a dinner table next to a smiling Dayan:** See image of Dayan and De Niro at dinner at https://i.pinimg.com/originals/70/9d/d8/709dd888314ca92ccd03df42f2b9dadf.jpg.

98 **"for the producer to be real partners":** Ferretti, "On Location with 'King of Comedy.'"

99 **"The revelations about Rhoodie":** Sampson, "Arms and the Man."

99 **"My close Israeli friend Dr. Dror Sadeh":** Dr. Alan Berman, "The VELA Incident: A Statement Written by Dr. Alan Berman," Wilson Center, Washington, DC, October 26, 2019, https://digitalarchive.wilsoncenter.org /document/220120. According to Berman, Sadeh's time at Dimona proved deadly. While working there, he said, Sadeh "had been the victim of an accident that led to his receiving excessive dosages of radiation that eventually led to his death from cancer."

Chapter 14: The Bang

101 **nuclear pariah states like Israel:** See Robert E. Harkavy, "Pariah States and Nuclear Proliferation," *International Organization* 35, no. 1 (Winter 1981): 135–63, www.jstor.org/stable/2706559?read-now=1&refreqid =excelsior%3Aa8817c9b661728363f22b22a28bb43ca&seq=29#page_scan_tab_contents.

101 **refused to sign:** "Arms Control and Proliferation Profile: Israel," Arms Control Association, July 2018, www .armscontrol.org/factsheets/israelprofile.

103 **"We've got them in space":** Rick Neale, "Patrick AFB's Secret Lab Watches for Nuclear Explosions Worldwide," *Air Force Times*, April 21, 2019, www.airforcetimes.com/news/your-air-force/2019/04/21 /patrick-afbs-secret-lab-watches-for-nuclear-explosions-worldwide/.

103 **"low-yield atmospheric nuclear detonation":** Details of alert from Secret, "Alert 747," Division 1243, Sandia National Laboratories, May 1, 1980, https://nsarchive2.gwu.edu/NSAEBB/NSAEBB190/08.pdf.

103 **"The initial examination":** Secret, NOFORN, Department of Energy Memorandum, from John Deutch to Henry Owen, November 8, 1979, https://nsarchive.gwu.edu/document/19603-national-security-archive-doc -2-john-deutch.

103 **"the signal from this disturbance":** Secret, "Possible Nuclear Explosion," National Security Council Memorandum, from Science and Technology to Zbigniew Brzezinski (Only), November 9, 1979, https://nsarchive .gwu.edu/document/19604-national-security-archive-doc-3-white-house.

104 **"There is no indigenous population":** Fred Pearce, "US and UK Accused of 'Squeezing Life out of' Ascension Island," *Guardian*, September 11, 2013, www.theguardian.com/uk-news/2013/sep/11/ascension-island -population-cut-uk-government.

104 **In 2006, 109 miles off the coast of New York:** Mark K. Prior, Ross Chapman, and Arthur Newhall, "The Long-Range Detection of an Accidental Underwater Explosion," paper submitted to present at Forum Acusticum 2005, http://acoustics.whoi.edu/multi/videos/Mark_Prior_ECUA_2010_paper2.pdf.

105 **"large impulsive release of energy":** Naval Research Laboratory, Memorandum, Alan Berman, Director of Research, to John M. Marcum, Executive Office of the President, Office of Science and Technology Policy, "Hydroacoustic Evidence on the Vela Incident," December 11, 1980, https://digitalarchive.wilsoncenter.org /document/116758.pdf?v=7d24a38cb7521b316076381e7b127ce1.

105 **Takeshi Morikawa:** Antarctic Geophysical Note No. 44, "Vela Incident was Proved to Be Marine Nuclear Explosions by the Syowa Seismographic Records," National Institute of Polar Research, March 30, 2017, http:// polaris.nipr.ac.jp/~geophys-notes/Note/note44/index.html.

105 **"the Syowa auroral patch":** "Evaluation of Some Geophysical Events on 22 September 1979," Los Alamos Scientific Laboratory, April 1981, https://nsarchive2.gwu.edu/NSAEBB/NSAEBB190/12.pdf.

105 **at the time of the nuclear blast:** White House, "The Daily Diary of President Jimmy Carter," Carter Presidential Library, www.jimmycarterlibrary.gov/assets/documents/diary/1979/d092179t.pdf.

105 **watching 408 films during his single term:** Matt Novak, "Every Single Movie That Jimmy Carter Watched at the White House," Gizmodo, September 15, 2015, https://gizmodo.com/every-single-movie-that-jimmy -carter-watched-at-the-whi-1728538092.

106 **"that according to a JAEIC":** Secret, White House Situation Room, Situation Room Log, "Reflections of South African Nuclear Event," October 25, 1979, https://nsarchive.gwu.edu/document/19602-national-security-archive-doc-1-white-house.

106 **"get my *toucus* to work":** Stephen Green, *Living by the Sword: America and Israel in the Middle East, 1968–87* (Brattleboro, VT: Amana Books, 1988), p. 112.

106 **"strong positive evidence" and "no negative evidence":** Summary of Conclusions of a Mini-Special Coordination Committee Meeting, Washington, September 22, 1979, *Foreign Relations of the United States*, 1977–1980, Volume XVI, p. 1086 (GPO).

106 **conduct a total of twenty-five sorties:** Secret, "History of the Air Force Technical Applications Center, Patrick Air Force Base, Florida, 1 January 1979—31 December 1980, Volume 1," https://nsarchive2.gwu.edu/NSAEBB/NSAEBB190/15.pdf.

107 **"There was indication of a nuclear explosion":** Jimmy Carter, *White House Diary* (New York: Farrar, Straus & Giroux, 2010), p. 357.

107 **pumpkin-carving contest:** Steve Hendrix, "From JFK to Omarosa: The White House Situation Room's History-Making Moments," *Washington Post*, August 13, 2018, www.washingtonpost.com/news/retropolis/wp/2018/08/13/from-jfk-to-omarosa-the-white-house-situation-rooms-history-making-moments/.

107 **A briefing board had been sent over:** Secret, White House Situation Room, Situation Room Log, "Reflections of South African Nuclear Event," October 25, 1979, https://nsarchive.gwu.edu/document/19602-national-security-archive-doc-1-white-house.

107 **"Limited satellite detection information suggests":** Summary of Conclusions of a Mini-Special Coordination Committee Meeting, Washington, September 23, 1979, *Foreign Relations of the United States*, 1977–1980, Volume XVI (GPO).

107 **"The Intelligence Community has high confidence":** Secret/Sensitive Memorandum, from Ambassador Gerard Smith to Dadiv D. Newsom, "South Atlantic Problem," October 23, 1979, https://nsarchive.gwu.edu/document/22325-13-gerard-c-smith-david-newsom-south-atlantic.

107 **The CIA agreed in a separate secret report:** Confidential, Director of the CIA to Ralph Earle, II, Director, U.S. Arms Control and Disarmament Agency, January 21, 1980. Attachment: Secret, "The 22 September 1979 Event," https://nsarchive2.gwu.edu/NSAEBB/NSAEBB190/03.pdf.

107 **"assessed the probability of a nuclear test as 90% plus":** Secret, National Security Council Memorandum, Jerry Oplinger to Henry Owens, "South Atlantic Event," January 25, 1980, https://nsarchive.gwu.edu/document/19606-national-security-archive-doc-5-jerry-oplinger.

107 **"[South Africa] had enough fissile material":** Avner Cohen and William Burr, "Revisiting the 1979 VELA Mystery: A Report on a Critical Oral History Conference," Wilson Center, August 31, 2020, www.wilsoncenter.org/blog-post/revisiting-1979-vela-mystery-report-critical-oral-history-conference.

107 **"A Secret Test by Israel"; "developing the fission trigger":** Norman Dombey, "Double Flash," *London Review of Books*, May 26, 2010, www.lrb.co.uk/blog/2010/may/double-flash.

108 **"Hamilton Jordan was specifically apprehensive":** Kai Bird, *The Outlier: The Unfinished Presidency of Jimmy Carter* (New York: Crown, 2021), pp. 258–60.

109 **Egypt, Syria, and Iraq had made it clear:** David Albright and Corey Gay, "A Flash from the Past," *Bulletin of the Atomic Scientists*, November 1997.

109 **"it is not clear that there has been a nuclear detonation":** Sec State Wash DC to All Diplomatic Posts Worldwide, Subject: Suspected Nuclear Explosion—Secretary Vance Press Conference of October 26 in Gainesville, Florida, November 1, 1979.

109 **"My questioning":** Leonard Weiss, "My Involvement with the 1979 Vela Satellite (6911) Event," November 22, 2019, Wilson Center, Washington, DC, https://digitalarchive.wilsoncenter.org/document/220121.

110 **picked nine scientists:** Secret, "Ad Hoc Panel Report on the September 22 Event," May 23, 1980, https://nsarchive2.gwu.edu/NSAEBB/NSAEBB190/09.pdf.

110 **triggered by a meteoroid:** Secret, White House Science and Technology [Staff] Report to National Security Adviser Zbigniew Brzezinski, "Evening Report," November 9, 1979, https://nsarchive.gwu.edu/document/19604-national-security-archive-doc-3-white-house.

110 **"Israel certainly has more than 100":** Richard Garwin interview, Voices of the Manhattan Project, National Museum of Nuclear Science & History, 2008, www.manhattanprojectvoices.org/oral-histories/richard-garwins-interview.

110 **"Israel remains the most powerful and well-equipped military force"**: Dalia Dassa Kaye and Shira Efron, "Israel's Evolving Iran Policy," International Institute for Strategic Studies, July 23, 2020, www.iiss.org/blogs /survival-blog/2020/07/israels-evolving-iran-policy.

111 **"Israel ranks as the 8th most powerful country"**: Yvette J. Deane, "Israel Ranks as 8th Most Powerful Country—U.S. News Report," *Jerusalem Post*, March 4, 2019, www.jpost.com/israel-news /israel-ranks-as-8th-most-powerful-country-us-news-report-582387.

111 **"It's an open secret"**: Nir Gontarz, "A U.S. President Who Truly 'Loves Israel' Would Cut Aid to It," *Haaretz*, July 18, 2022, https://www.haaretz.com/opinion/2022-07-18/ty-article-opinion/.premium/a-u-s-president -who-truly-loves-israel-would-cut-aid-to-it/00000182-11df-d11c-a1da-5dffc1cb0000.

111 **Even CIA director Stansfield Turner:** "Blast from the Past," *Foreign Policy*, September 22, 2019, https:// foreignpolicy.com/2019/09/22/blast-from-the-past-vela-satellite-israel-nuclear-double-flash-1979-ptbt -south-atlantic-south-africa/.

111 **"there will be continued internal dissent"**: Secret, National Security Council memorandum, Jerry Oplinger to Henry Owen, "South Atlantic Event," January 23, 1980, https://nsarchive.gwu.edu/document /22345-33-jerry-oplinger-henry-owen-south-atlantic.

111 **"main objective [of the new review]"**: Secret, National Security Council memorandum, Jerry Oplinger to Henry Owen, "South Atlantic Event," January 25, 1980. https://nsarchive.gwu.edu/document/19606 -national-security-archive-doc-5-jerry-oplinger.

111 **"We have a growing belief among our scientists"**: Carter, *White House Diary*, p. 405.

111 **the panel completed its report:** Secret, "Ad Hoc Panel Report on the September 22 Event," May 23, 1980, https://nsarchive2.gwu.edu/NSAEBB/NSAEBB190/09.pdf.

112 **"For political reasons"**: Bird, *The Outlier*, p. 457.

Chapter 15: The Triggerman

114 **Seated on a chair on the seventh floor:** "On Location with 'King of Comedy,' " *New York Times*, August 23, 1981, www.nytimes.com/1981/08/23/movies/on-location-with-king-of-comedy.html.

114 **the production closed for good just eight performances:** " 'So Nice to Be Civilized' Closes," *New York Times*, June 10, 1980, https://timesmachine.nytimes.com/timesmachine/1980/06/10/111165002.html?pageNumber=47.

114 **"The show," a *New York Times* reviewer wrote:** Mel Gussow, " 'Nice to Be Civilized,' a Musical Neighborhood," *New York Times*, June 4, 1980, https://timesmachine.nytimes.com/timesmachine/1980/06/04/113944238 .html?pageNumber=74.

115 **annual Kidspalooza festival:** Joyce Hanz, "Kidspalooza Returns to Parks Township This Weekend," Trib Live, May 31, 2022, https://triblive.com/local/valley-news-dispatch/kidspalooza-returns-to-parks-township-this-weekend/.

115 **Homeland Security vehicles arrived:** Scott C. Johnson, "What Lies Beneath," *Foreign Policy*, March 23, 2015, https://foreignpolicy.com/2015/03/23/what-lies-beneath-numec-apollo-zalman-shapiro/.

115 **"devoid of adequate physical safeguards"**: Top Secret, FBI Memorandum, NUMEC, Atomic Energy Act, Obstruction of Justice, November 9, 1979, https://nsarchive.gwu.edu/sites/default/files/documents/3149996 /40-Interview-of-Charles-A-Keller-Assistant.pdf.

116 **Zalman Shapiro:** "Zalman Shapiro, Scientist and Supporter of Israel, Passes Away at 96," *Pittsburgh Jewish Chronicle*, July 28, 2016, https://jewishchronicle.timesofisrael.com/zalman-shapiro-scientist-and-supporter -of-israel-passes-away-at-96/.

116 **"a contingent of Israelis"**: Thomas Bullock, *Diary of a Cold War Patriot*, self-published, 2017, p. 112.

116 **Shapiro entered into an agreement:** "NUMEC to Train Israeli Scientists," *Simpson's Leader-Times* (Kittanning, PA), September 20, 1960.

117 **"The first attempt at oxidizing metal plutonium"**: Bullock, *Diary of a Cold War Patriot*, p. 120.

117 **Following a supposed "picnic" with his family:** John Hadden, *Conversations with a Masked Man: My Father, the CIA, and Me* (New York: Arcade Publishing, 2016), p. 23.

117 **"Given the aforementioned circumstances"**: Top Secret, Letter from CIA Director Richard Helms to The Honorable Ramsey Clark, Attorney General, April 2, 1968.

117 **"He is known to generally travel"**: Secret, FBI Memorandum, Director to SAC Pittsburgh, Subject: Dr. Zalman Mordecai Shapiro IS [Intelligence Service] Israel, Atomic Energy Act, June 13, 1968.

118 **"Source advised that [Shapiro] is closely associated"**: Secret, FBI Pittsburgh Office, Subject: Dr. Zalman Moedecai Shapiro, June 13, 1968.

118 "The clear consensus of CIA": Quoted in a letter from Congressman Morris K. Udall to Secretary of Energy B. James Edwards, March 9, 1982, contained in Department of Energy Budget Request for Fiscal Year 1983, Oversight Hearing before the House Subcommittee on Energy and the Environment of the Committee on Interior and Insular Affairs.

118 "They have this vast network of sympathizers": Interview of Glenn R. Cella by the Association for Diplomatic Studies and Training, Foreign Affairs Oral History Project, July 18, 2006, https://adst.org/OH%20TOCs/Cella .Glenn.pdf.

118 "more active than anyone but the KGB": Charles R. Babcock, "U.S. an Intelligence Target of the Israeli, Officials Say," *Washington Post*, June 5, 1986, www.washingtonpost.com/archive/politics/1986/06/05/us -an-intelligence-target-of-the-israelis-officials-say/80e52393-3b43-4a5a-8d5d-ce4fd2bf0532/.

118 Raymond Wannal: David K. Shipler, "U.S.-Israel Relationship Makes Keeping Secrets Hard," *New York Times*, December 22, 1985, https://timesmachine.nytimes.com/timesmachine/1985/12/22/243812.html ?pageNumber=1.

118 "Foreign Intelligence and Security Services": SECRET, NOFORN, NOCONTRACT, ORCON, "Israel: For- eign Intelligence and Security Services," CIA, March 1979, https://ia601909.us.archive.org/29/items/israel -foreign-intelligence-and-security-services/EBB-PollardDoc1.pdf.

118 "had a handwritten note literally from [the] president": Statement of Jessica Mathews, "Revisiting the 1979 VELA Mystery: A Report on a Critical Oral History Conference," Wilson Center, Washington, DC, www .wilsoncenter.org/blog-post/revisiting-1979-vela-mystery-report-critical-oral-history-conference.

119 "Who shut off the investigations?": Hadden, *Conversations with a Masked Man*, p. 238.

119 "As reported in the paper": Bullock, *Diary of a Cold War Patriot*, p. 163.

119 Among the victims is Patty Ameno; $80 million: John R. Emshwiller, "Waste Land: One Town's Atomic Leg- acy: A $500 Million Cleanup," *Wall Street Journal*, November 22, 2013, www.wsj.com/articles/SB10001424052 7023048684045791942319222830904.

119 about 40 percent of the claimants had died: Michael Yates, "Poisoning People in Apollo," Counterpunch, May 23, 2012, www.counterpunch.org/2012/05/23/poisoning-people-in-apollo/.

119 "a widely held attitude among Israeli officials": Wolf Blitzer, *Territory of Lies: The Exclusive Story of Jonathan Jay Pollard: The American Who Spied on His Country for Israel and How He Was Betrayed* (New York: Harper & Row, 1989), p. 280.

120 previously served as the editor: Wolf Blitzer, Jewish Virtual Library, www.jewishvirtuallibrary.org/wolf -blitzer.

121 "continued to lose money": Unless otherwise indicated, comments from Emilie Smyth are from *Family His- tory of a Successful Aerospace Executive: A Story Related by Jon Schiller, PhD*. The self-published book was written by Emilie about her family life with her husband, Richard Kelly Smyth, using his alias "Jon Schiller."

123 "Arnon Milchan [had] requested": Charles R. Babcock, "Computer Expert Used Firm to Feed Israel Tech- nology," *Washington Post*, October 31, 1986, www.washingtonpost.com/archive/politics/1986/10/31 /computer-expert-used-firm-to-feed-israel-technology/dac7f8f5-560c-4f42-8b8a-c03892ae1140/.

124 "I thought we ought to face up to the fact": Seymour M. Hersh, *Sampson Option: Israel's Nuclear Arsenal and American Foreign Policy* (New York: Random House, 1991), p. 213.

124 "Anything that was seen as even remotely critical": Interview of Glenn R. Cella by the Association for Diplo- matic Studies and Training, Foreign Affairs Oral History Project, July 18, 2006, https://adst.org/OH%20TOCs /Cella.Glenn.pdf.

124 "Do you think there's any chance": Interview of Glenn R. Cella.

Chapter 16: The Pitch

126 "Hope to receive delivery schedule this week": Department of the Treasury, U.S. Customs Service, Report of Investigation, March 21, 1985, "Illegal Export of Munitions Items to Israel." Hereafter cited as Customs Service Investigation Reports. Telex from Ernest P. Smyth to Milchan, re: PINTO (the code name for krytrons), Octo- ber 1, 1979.

126 a truck from Overseas Airfreight: Customs Service Investigation Reports, telex from Ernest P. Smyth to Overseas Airfreight re: "Authorization to ship our package Air Freight Collect to Israel," January 7, 1980.

127 "Anyone who lives in California is a star-fucker": Milchan interview on *Uvda* (Israeli television program, in Hebrew), November 25, 2013.

127 **Biehl worked alongside Edward Teller:** Biography of Ernest O. Lawrence, Lawrence Livermore National Laboratory, www.llnl.gov/ernest-o-lawrence-co-founder. See also Herbert York, *The Advisors: Oppenheimer, Teller and the Superbomb* (San Francisco: W. H. Freeman and Company, 1976), p. 133.

127 **due to his position on the:** See "Hearing Record of the Public Hearing on the Draft Environmental Impact Statement, Livermore Site, Livermore, California," April 12, 1979, www.energy.gov/sites/prod/files/2015/05 /f22/EIS-0028-Record_of_Public_Hearing_on_the_DEIS_April_1979.pdf.

127 **Joint Strategic Target Planning Staff:** "History of the Joint Strategic Target Planning Staff: Background and Preparation of SIOP-62," Top Secret, Headquarters, Strategic Air Command. See also Army War College, "Strategic Target Planning and the JSTPS," March 1988, https://apps.dtic.mil/sti/pdfs/ADA195083.pdf.

128 **Dr. Ivan Getting:** See U.S. Space Force and National Academies biographies: www.afspc.af.mil/Portals/3 /documents/Pioneers/1998_Getting.pdf, https://nap.nationalacademies.org/read/12473/chapter/22.

128 **Robert Mainhardt:** John Spangler, "MBA Gyrojet Mark I Model B Pistols and Carbines: Rocket Science Meets Reality," American Society of Arms Collectors Bulletin, undated.

129 **"He's maybe the third most powerful man in Israel":** William E. Burrows and Robert Windrem, *Critical Mass: The Dangerous Race for Superweapons in a Fragmenting World* (New York: Simon & Schuster, 1994), p. 462.

129 **"That's it for me":** Burrows and Windrem, *Critical Mass*, p. 463.

130 **"I never even saw Sharon":** Sara Leibowitz-Dar, "LAKAM Chief Benjamin Blumberg Tells His Story," *Ma'ariv* (in Hebrew), April 7, 2012.

130 **"For years I worked for the country":** Leibowitz-Dar, "LAKAM Chief Benjamin Blumberg Tells His Story."

BOOK FOUR: THE SMUGGLERS

Chapter 17: Escape

133 **"Richard thought the robbery was espionage":** Unless otherwise indicated, comments from Emilie Smyth are from *Family History of a Successful Aerospace Executive: A Story Related by Jon Schiller, PhD.* The self-published book was written by Emilie about her family life with her husband, Richard Kelly Smyth, using his alias "Jon Schiller."

135 **"There is this movie that I have been working on":** Meir Doron and Joseph Gelman, *Confidential: The Life of Secret Agent Turned Hollywood Tycoon Arnon Milchan* (Jerusalem: Gefen Publishing House, 2011), p. 153.

136 **"People that I talked to said":** Jack Mathews, *The Battle of Brazil* (New York: Crown, 1987), p. 15.

136 **"In Hollywood they don't like working with an arms dealer":** Stuart Winer, "Hollywood Producer Arnon Milchan Reveals Past as Secret Agent," *Times of Israel*, November 25, 2013, www.timesofisrael.com /hollywood-producer-arnon-milchan-reveals-mossad-past/.

137 **"Officially [Rosen] was Israel's ambassador":** Ben Caspit, *The Netanyahu Years* (New York: Thomas Dunne, 2017), pp. 64–65.

137 **"I was stunned and dismayed":** Unless otherwise indicated, comments from Richard Kelly Smyth are from his self-published book, *Irrational Indictment & Imprisonment for Exporting Krytrons to Israel*, 2008, using his alias "Dr. Jon Schiller."

137 **"Richard did not think Fahey had a 'right to know' "; "continued to lose money in spite of all Richard's efforts":** Emily Smyth, *Family History of a Successful Aerospace Executive.*

138 **a secret grand jury was empaneled:** John M. Goshko, "Israel Got U.S.-Made Devices," *Washington Post*, May 14, 1985.

138 **"The first time I heard the word 'krytron' ":** Thomas L. Friedman, "Israelis Deny Knowing of Export Bar for Device Usable in A-Bomb," *New York Times*, May 18, 1985, www.nytimes.com/1985/05/18/world/israelis -deny-knowing-of-export-bar-for-device-usable-in-a-bomb.html.

138 **"I'm asking for your help":** Meir Doron and Joseph Gelman, *Confidential: The Life of Secret Agent Turned Hollywood Tycoon Arnon Milchan* (Jerusalem: Gefen Publishing House, 2011), p. 17.

138 **Milchan would later donate large sums of money:** Gidi Weitz, " 'You Can't Meet with the Netanyahus Empty-Handed. There Is No Such Thing," *Haaretz*, July 5, 2022, www.haaretz.com/israel-news/2022-07-05 /ty-article-magazine/.highlight/you-cant-meet-with-the-netanyahus-empty-handed-there-is-no-such -thing/00000181-ce46-dc67-adab-cfc759600000.

139 **"The U.S. government was prosecuting me":** Richard Kelly Smyth (a.k.a. Schiller), *Irrational Indictment & Imprisonment for Exporting Krytrons to Israel.*

139   **"Israel was not aware of any ban"**: Friedman, "Israelis Deny Knowing of Export Bar."

140   **"I don't know what the fuck this thing is"**: Unless otherwise indicated, details on Gilliam and *Brazil* are from Mathews, *The Battle of Brazil*, p. 36.

143   **"Frankly, we are in a limbo situation"**: Jane Applegate, "Accused Engineer Fails to Appear at Nuclear Device Trial," *Los Angeles Times*, August 21, 1985, www.latimes.com/archives/la-xpm-1985-08-21-me-1095-story .html.

144   **"This is a nightmare"; "Sources close to the case"**: Applegate, "Accused Engineer Fails to Appear at Nuclear Device Trial."

144   **"Tell my mother I'm safe"**: Jane Applegate, "Brief but to the Point: 'Tell Her I'm Safe,'" *Los Angeles Times*, October 21, 1985.

144   **$9.9 million at the box office**: Box Office Mojo, *Brazil*, December 20, 1985, www.boxofficemojo.com/release /rl3360065025/weekend/.

144   **"No one has asserted that Mr. Milchan"**: Mathews, *The Battle of Brazil*, p. 92.

144   **"Arnon has to screw everyone"**: Ann Louise Bardach, "The Last Tycoon," *Los Angeles* magazine, April 2000, www.lamag.com/longform/the-last-tycoon/.

144   **"You just never know"**: Andrew Yule, *Losing the Light: Terry Gilliam and the Munchausen Saga* (New York: Applause Books, 1991), p. 62.

Chapter 18: Deceit

146   **could fill a six-by-ten-foot room**: Top Secret Umbra, United States of America v. Jonathan Jay Pollard, Declaration of the Secretary of Defense Caspar W. Weinberger, January 8, 1987, p. 5.

147   **"no drastic action would be taken against you"**: Top Secret Umbra, Director of Central Intelligence, "The Jonathan Jay Pollard Espionage Case: A Damage Assessment," October 30, 1987.

147   **"Rafi just kept blowing me off"**: Elliot Goldenberg, *The Spy Who Knew Too Much: The Government Plot to Silence Jonathan Pollard* (New York: S.P.I. Books, 1993), p. 101.

147   **Washington Hospital Center**: It is now MedStar Washington Hospital Center.

148   **"As we drove up Wisconsin Avenue"**: Goldenberg, *The Spy Who Knew Too Much*, p. 119.

148   **"A diplomatic vehicle was going into the compound"**: Noltkamper testimony, U.S. v. Anne Henderson Pollard, U.S. District Court for the District of Columbia, November 27, 1985.

148   **"I immediately said, 'Throw him out'"**: "Former Mossad Handler: Pollard Rejected Escape Plan," *Jerusalem Post*, December 2, 2014, www.jpost.com/israel-news/former-mossad-handler-pollard-rejected-escape-plan-383418.

149   **"This is where the knife really went deep"**: "Pollard's Ex-wife: I Still Don't Understand Why He Divorced Me," *Times of Jerusalem*, November 20, 2015, www.timesofisrael.com/pollards-ex-wife-i-dont -understand-why-we-divorced/.

149   **"Any country that could do this to a loyal agent"**: Wolf Blitzer, *Territory of Lies: The Exclusive Story of Jonathan Jay Pollard: The American Who Spied on His Country for Israel and How He Was Betrayed* (New York: Harper & Row, 1989), pp. 213, 218.

150   **In 2020, 116 fugitives were arrested**: "The Costa del Sol, the Hideout of the Fugitives: Why Do Murderers and Drug Traffickers Live There?," Tekdeeps, December 30, 2020, https://tekdeeps.com/the-costa -del-sol-the-hideout-of-the-fugitives-why-do-murderers-and-drug-traffickers-live-there/.

151   **Attending the Deauville American Film Festival**: "El Festival de Cine de Deauville, Francia," *El Nuevo Herald*, September 6, 1987.

152   *Man on Fire* **flamed out at the box office**: Caryn James of the *New York Times* said that the film "always seems about to slip into unconsciousness." James, "Film: Scott Glenn in 'Man on Fire,' Thriller," *New York Times*, October 10, 1987, www.nytimes.com/1987/10/10/movies/film-scott-glenn-in-man-on-fire-thriller.html. And Lloyd Sachs of the *Chicago Sun-Times* wrote, "Unfortunately, when it's required to make sense, 'Man on Fire' doesn't." Sachs, "'Man on Fire' Disintegrates on Film," *Chicago Sun-Times*, October 27, 1987.

152   **$87 million in the United States and $160 million worldwide**: Box Office Mojo, *The War of the Roses*, February 23, 1989, www.boxofficemojo.com/title/tt0098621/.

152   **"This should be the title of the movie"**: Marvin R. Shanken, "An Interview with Arnon Milchan," *Cigar Aficionado*, September/October 2008, www.cigaraficionado.com/article/an-interview-with-arnon-milchan-6231.

152   **grossing $178,406,268**: Box Office Mojo, *Pretty Woman*, October 12, 1990, www.boxofficemojo.com/title /tt0100405/.

153 **Mitzpe Yam Street in Beit Yanai:** Shuki Sadeh, "Yes, It's Public Space, Just Don't Tell the Public About It," *Haaretz*, September 24, 2020, https://mideastenvironment.apps01.yorku.ca/2020/09/yes-its-public-space-just -dont-tell-the-public-about-it-haaretz/.

153 **spent another $3.5 million:** Shuki Sadeh and Hagai Amit, "How Hollywood Mogul Arnon Milchan Uses His Benjamins to Influence Israeli Politics," *Haaretz*, February 13, 2017, www.haaretz.com/israel-news/.premium .MAGAZINE-how-hollywood-mogul-uses-his-benjamins-to-influence-israeli-politics-1.5432261.

153 **Milchan put the woman in touch:** Chaim Levinson, "How Mossad Chief Got Arnon Milchan to Boost Music Career of Oligarch's Daughter," *Haaretz*, February 13, 2019, www.haaretz.com/israel-news/.premium-how-ex -mossad-chief-enlisted-hollywood-mogul-to-help-putin-associate-1.6934148.

153 **a member of Cohen's inner circle:** "Report: Israel Police Investigating Mossad Chief's Ties with Netanya- hu's Billionaire Friend," *Haaretz*, January 18, 2017, www.haaretz.com/israel-news/report-police-probing -mossad-chief-s-ties-with-milchan-1.5487388.

153 **"We did a few operations together":** Gidi Weitz, "How a Drunk, Unstable Billionaire Became Netanyahu and Mossad Chief's Confidant," *Haaretz*, April 29, 2021, www.haaretz.com/israel-news/.premium.HIGHLIGHT .MAGAZINE-unstable-billionaire-james-packer-netanyahu-mossad-chief-s-confidant-1.9759071.

155 **"To: Arnon Milchan, Big Time Movie Producer":** Richard Kelly Smyth (a.k.a. Schiller), *Irrational Indictment & Imprisonment for Exporting Krytrons to Israel*, pp. 78–80.

Chapter 19: The Fix

159 **"young, slim, good-looking":** Andrew Yule, *Losing the Light: Terry Gilliam and the Munchausen Saga* (New York: Applause Books, 1991), p. 38.

159 **Ilana Dayan:** See her appearance on JN1 (Jewish News 1), Tel Aviv, November 26, 2013. See also David Caspi, "Arnon Milchan Admits to Arms Dealing in the '70s: The New Regency chairman and veteran pro- ducer tells the Israeli investigative program 'Uvda' that he and others, including Sydney Pollack, secretly assisted the government," *Hollywood Reporter*, November 21, 2013, www.hollywoodreporter.com/news /general-news/arnon-milchan-admits-arms-dealing-658717/. Allison Kaplan Sommer, "Hollywood Producer Open Up About Past as Israeli Operative," *Haaretz*, November 26, 2013, www.haaretz.com/.premium-arnon -milchan-secret-agent-1.5294466.

162 **"Then began a series of emotional calls":** Nir Hasson, "Milchan Begged Netanyahu for Help, Former Aide Testifies. Within Days, He Got a U.S. Visa," *Haaretz*, July 6, 2022, www.haaretz.com/israel-news/2022-07-06 /ty-article/.highlight/netanyahu-trial-witness-describes-orderly-mechanism-for-gifts-as-testimony -continues/00000181-d355-d974-afbd-ff57433c0000.

162 **"He asked me to reach out to Dan Shapiro":** Jeremy Sharon, "Milchan Aide Testifies Netanyahu Intro- duced Her Boss to Kerry to Help Him Get Visa," *Times of Israel*, July 6, 2022, www.timesofisrael.com /milchan-aide-testifies-netanyahu-introduced-her-boss-to-kerry-to-help-him-get-visa/.

162 **"Why is Arnon so worried?":** Hasson, "Milchan Begged Netanyahu for Help."

162 **"very agitated":** Gidi Weitz, "Netanyahu Graft Affair: Israel Police Wanted to Question Kerry and Ex-U.S. Envoy but Were Blocked by AG," *Haaretz*, February 23, 2017, www.haaretz.com/israel-news/2017-02-23 /ty-article/.premium/israeli-ag-blocked-plan-to-question-kerry-shapiro-in-netanyahu-graft-affair/0000017f -e5f4-df5f-a17f-fffe6ea60000.

163 **"If the Netanyahu couple arrives":** Chen Maanit, "Sara Netanyahu Asked Me to Sign a Friendship Affidavit, Billionaires' Aide Tells Court," *Haaretz*, July 12, 2022, www.haaretz.com/israel-news/2022-07-12/ty-article /.premium/cross-examination-of-hollywood-moguls-assistant-begins/00000181-f11f-db6b-a5a7-f9ffd3270000.

163 **"Am I at the Oscars?":** Alex Ben Block, "Inside the Hollywood Scandal That Looms over Israel's Election," *Los Angeles* magazine, April 9, 2019, www.lamag.com/citythinkblog/netanyahu-israel-election-arnon-milchan/.

163 **Unhelpful was his habit of guzzling bottles of vodka:** Damon Kitney, "Warren Beatty and Me: The Inside Story of James Packer's Breakdown," *The Australian*, October 6, 2018, www.theaustralian.com.au/weekend -australian-magazine/warren-beatty-and-me-the-inside-story-of-james-packers-breakdown/news-story /c837f9323e436a58%E2%80%A6.

163 **"a kind of convenience in moving from house to house":** Gidi Weitz, "How a Drunk, Unstable Bil- lionaire Became Netanyahu and Mossad Chief's Confidant," *Haaretz*, April 29, 2021, www.haaretz.com /israel-news/.premium.HIGHLIGHT.MAGAZINE-unstable-billionaire-james-packer-netanyahu-mossad -chief-s-confidant-1.9759071.

164 **"I was a political cadaver"**: Gidi Weitz, "'Mr. Prime Minister, Do You Believe What You're Saying? It's Embarrassing': The Netanyahu Interrogation Transcripts," *Haaretz*, September 26, 2020, www.haaretz.com /israel-news/.premium.HIGHLIGHT.MAGAZINE-do-you-believe-what-you-re-saying-the-netanyahu -interrogation-transcripts-1.9184340.

164 **"Bibi personally tells me everything"**: Michael Bachner, "Netanyahu Allegedly Leaked Info on Iran to Hollywood Mogul Arnon Milchan," *Times of Israel*, November 10, 2020, www.timesofisrael.com/netanyahu -allegedly-leaked-info-on-iran-to-hollywood-mogul-arnon-milchan/.

164 **appointing Milchan as honorary consul in Los Angeles**: "Netanyahu Said to Have Offered to Nominate Billionaire Milchan for President," *Times of Israel*, May 22, 2022, www.timesofisrael.com/netanyahu -said-to-have-offered-to-nominate-billionaire-milchan-for-president/.

164 **"The prime minister wants to speak with Secretary Kerry urgently"**: Barak Ravid, "Netanyahu, Agitated and Aggressive, Asked Ex-U.S. Envoy to Help Milchan Get Visa," *Haaretz*, February 17, 2017, www .haaretz.com/israel-news/2017-02-17/ty-article/.premium/agitated-netanyahu-asked-ex-u-s-envoy-to-help -milchan-get-visa/0000017f-ea31-ddba-a37f-ea7f7b130000.

165 **"One day I got a phone call from abroad"**: Sharon, "Milchan Aide Testifies Netanyahu Introduced Her Boss to Kerry to Help Him Get a Visa."

165 **"He doesn't pay any taxes in the United States"**: Eytan Avriel, "This Israeli Hollywood Mogul Didn't Pay Taxes for a Decade. Here's How," *Haaretz*, July 18, 2022, https://www.haaretz.com/israel-news/2022-07-18 /ty-article-magazine/.premium/u-s-israeli-mogul-arnon-milchan-didnt-pay-taxes-anywhere-for-a-decade -heres-how/00000182-1046-d1ad-a1b7-1fe60f960000.

165 **"According to an accumulation of evidence in recent years"**: Avriel, "This Israeli Hollywood Mogul."

165 **"on at least 31 days during the current year"**: See IRS, "Substantial Presence Test," https://www.irs.gov /individuals/international-taxpayers/substantial-presence-test.

165 **"created a global tax haven"**: Efrat Neuman, "'Arnon Milchan Law' Turned Israel Into Tax Haven for Billionaires. They Left When It Expired," *Haaretz*, December 4, 2019. https://www.haaretz.com/israel-news /business/2019-12-04/ty-article/.premium/tax-exemption-lured-billionaires-to-israel-they-left-when-it -expired/0000017f-e2d7-d9aa-afff-fbdf7d780000.

166 **"U.S. intelligence officials trooped up to Capitol Hill"**: Jeff Stein, "Spy vs. Spy: Espionage and the U.S.-Israel Rift," *Newsweek*, March 25, 2015, www.newsweek.com/israel-spying-iran-nuclear-talks-barack-obama -benjamin-netanyahu-white-house-316623.

166 **"No other country close to the United States"**: Jeff Stein, "Israel Won't Stop Spying on the U.S.," *Newsweek*, May 6, 2014. https://www.newsweek.com/israel-wont-stop-spying-us-249757

167 **"There is a small community of ex-CIA"**: Jeff Stein, "Israel's Aggressive Spying in the U.S. Mostly Hushed Up," *Newsweek*, May 24, 2014, www.newsweek.com/israels-aggressive-spying-us-mostly-hushed-250278.

167 **"Former counterintelligence officials describe"**: Scott Shane, "Leak Offers Lot at Efforts by U.S. to Spy on Israel," *New York Times*, September 5, 2011, www.nytimes.com/2011/09/06/us/06leak.html.

167 **"U.S. officials said Israel has long topped the list"**: Adam Entous, "Israel Spied on Iran Nuclear Talks with U.S.," *Wall Street Journal*, March 23, 2015, www.wsj.com/articles/israel-spied-on-iran-talks-1427164201.

167 **"Israel should be assumed"**: Julian Pecquet, "Leaked Documents Reveal US Sees Israel as a Spying Threat," *The Hill*, August 29, 2013, http://thehill.com/blogs/global-affairs/middle-east-north-africa/319513-leaked -documents-reveal-us-sees-israel-as-a-major-spying-threat.

167 **"Dealing with the Israelis was"**: Stein, "Israel Won't Stop Spying on the U.S."

167 **"You catch them red-handed"**: Stein, "Israeli Aggressive Spying in the U.S. Mostly Hushed Up."

167 **Frank Figliuzzi Jr.**: Interview with Frank Figliuzzi Jr., August 2, 2018.

168 **"I haven't observed many other countries"**: Tom Perkins, "Pro-Israel Donors Spent Over $22 Million on Lobbying and Contributions in 2018," *Guardian*, February 15, 2019, www.theguardian.com/us-news/2019 /feb/15/pro-israel-donors-spent-over-22m-on-lobbying-and-contributions-in-2018.

168 **"Our prime minister and his wife are hedonistic"**: Weitz, "'Mr. Prime Minister, Do You Believe What You're Saying?'"

168 **expenditures as little as 20 shekels**: Gidi Weitz, "Netanyahu Trial Witness Didn't Say 'Bribery,' but Painted a Very Clear Picture," *Haaretz*, July 6, 2022, www.haaretz.com/israel-news/2022-07-06/ty-article/.premium /netanyahu-trial-witness-didnt-say-bribery-but-painted-a-very-clear-picture/00000181-d2af-d98d-a5db -deef19850000.

168 **"Milchan never gave anybody anything without a reason"**: Gidi Weitz, "You Can't Meet with the Netanyahus Empty-Handed. There Is No Such Thing,'" *Haaretz*, July 5, 2022, www.haaretz.com/israel-news/2022-07-05 /ty-article-magazine/.highlight/you-cant-meet-with-the-netanyahus-empty-handed-there-is-no-such -thing/00000181-ce46-dc67-adab-cfc759600000.

168 **"He has deep pockets and short arms"**: Weitz, "'You Can't Meet with the Netanyahus Empty-Handed.'"

169 **"Sara would ask for boxes of six or 12 bottles"**: "Milchan's Assistant Claims Netanyahu Personally Requested Gifts," Ynetnews, November 13, 2017, www.ynetnews.com/articles/0,7340,L-5042510,00.html.

169 **Hinnawi Wine Store:** See Eli Senyou, "Report: Sara Netanyahu Told Investigators Champagne Received as Friends," Ynetnews, January 13, 2017, www.ynetnews.com/articles/0,7340,L-4907044,00.html.

169 **"We received crates of champagne"**: Shuki Sadeh and Hagai Amit, "How Hollywood Mogul Arnon Milchan Uses His Benjamins to Influence Israeli Politics," *Haaretz*, February 13, 2017, www.haaretz.com/israel -news/.premium.MAGAZINE-how-hollywood-mogul-uses-his-benjamins-to-influence-israeli-politics -1.5432261.

169 **"Sara was afraid of being recorded"**: "Milchan's Aide: Sara Netanyahu Asked Gifts Be Inconspicuous," Ynetnews, February 1, 2018, www.ynetnews.com/articles/0,7340,L-5079626,00.html.

169 **"She's scared to death"; "I don't work for your wife"**: Sharon, "Milchan Aide Testifies Netanyahu Introduced Her Boss to Kerry to Help Him Get Visa."

169 **included a bracelet:** MAKOTV, "Revealing 'Fact': This is the Prestigious Bracelet that Sarah Netanyahu Received from James Packer—and the receipt for a total of more that $40,000," MAKOTV, Israel (in Hebrew), November 15, 2021, www.mako.co.il/news-law/2021_q4/Article-c19fca8d1b42d71026.htm?sCh =31750a2610f26110&pId=173113802. See also "New Evidence Alleges Netanyahu Illicitly Got Luxury Jewelry, Clothes for His Wife," *Times of Israel*, November 15, 2021, www.timesofisrael.com/new-evidence-in -netanyahu-trial-alleges-ex-pm-illicitly-got-luxury-jewelry-clothes/.

169 **the glitzy Caprice:** "Prosecutors Ask Court to Add New Witnesses in Netanyahu's Case 1000," *Times of Israel*, April 12, 2022, www.timesofisrael.com/prosecutors-ask-court-to-add-new-witnesses-in-netanyahus-case -1000/.

169 **"He said there's no choice"**: Sharon, "Milchan Aide Testifies Netanyahu Introduced Her Boss to Kerry to Help Him Get Visa."

169 **"He would phone and say"**: Sue Surkes, "Mogul Tells Police He Felt 'Disgusted' by Netanyahus' Gift Requests—Report," *Times of Israel*, June 7, 2019, www.timesofisrael.com/mogul-tells-police-he -felt-disgusted-by-netanyahus-gift-requests-report/.

170 **$85,000 worth of "leaves"**: Rahel Jaskow, "Full Text: The Criminal Allegations Against Netanyahu, as Set Out by Israel's AG," *Times of Israel*, May 18, 2019, www.timesofisrael.com/full-text-the-criminal-allegations -against-netanyahu-as-set-out-by-israels-ag/.

170 **dip his cigars in a glass of Cointreau:** Chen Maanit, "Hollywood Mogul's Aide Testifies She Bought the Netanyahus Cigars, Coats, Jewelry at Their Demand," *Haaretz*, July 5, 2022, www.haaretz.com /israel-news/2022-07-05/ty-article/.highlight/netanyahu-trial-key-witness-to-open-evidence-stage-of-gifts -for-favors-case/00000181-ca6a-d83b-a3d3-da6b8e8d0000.

170 **"We would buy iPads every two days because of his fears"**: "Key Witness in Trial Denies Netanyahu Got Luxury Gifts out of Genuine Friendship," *Times of Israel*, July 12, 2022, www.timesofisrael.com /key-witness-in-trial-denies-netanyahus-got-luxury-gifts-out-of-genuine-friendship/.

170 **Milchan showed up at the Israeli police office:** Gidi Weitz, "This Time, Netanyahu Can't Hide from the Allegations Against Him," *Haaretz*, February 15, 2018, www.haaretz.com/israel-news/.premium-this-time -netanyahu-can-t-hide-from-the-allegations-against-him-1.5821233.

170 **"Gifts that I don't bring voluntarily"**: Gidi Weitz, "Netanyahu Worries That Star Witness Milchan Will Drop Bombshell," *Haaretz*, February 12, 2021, www.haaretz.com/israel-news/.premium-netanyahu -worries-that-star-witness-will-drop-bombshell-1.9533081.

170 **"feel sick"**: Gidi Weitz, "Netanyahu Asked for Pricey Gift; Milchan: It Made Me 'Sick,'" *Haaretz*, February 8, 2017, www.haaretz.com/israel-news/.premium-netanyahu-asked-for-pricey-gift-milchan-it-made-me-sick -1.5495767.000.

171 **quarter of a million dollars:** Judy Maltz, "The Israeli James Bond? Arnon Milchan and His Ties to the Secret Services," *Haaretz*, February 15, 2018, www.haaretz.com/israel-news/.premium-the-israeli-james -bond-milchan-and-his-ties-to-the-secret-services-1.5822493.

171 **"Arnon was shocked"**: Chen Maanit, "Sara Netanyahu Asked Me to Sign a Friendship Affidavit, Billionaires' Aide Tells Court," *Haaretz*, July 12, 2022, www.haaretz.com/israel-news/2022-07-12/ty-article/.premium /cross-examination-of-hollywood-moguls-assistant-begins/00000181-f11f-db6b-a5a7-f9ffd3270000.

171 **Later, according to Klein, Sara would attempt to pressure her:** Yonah Jeremy Bob, "Sara Netanyahu Crossed Lines and Tried to Get Me to Withdraw Testimony—Witness," *Jerusalem Post*, July 5, 2022, https://www.jpost .com/israel-news/article-711222.

Chapter 20: The Trial

172 **flew to London:** Gidi Weitz, "Hollywood Producer Arnon Milchan Interrogated over Suspicion That He Bribed Netanyahu," *Haaretz*, September 6, 2017, www.haaretz.com/israel-news/arnon-milchan-interrogated -over-suspicion-he-bribed-netanyahu-1.5448532.

172 **pursued him to his home in Malibu:** Weitz, "Netanyahu Worries That Star Witness Milchan Will Drop Bomb- shell," *Haaretz*, February 12, 2021, www.haaretz.com/israel-news/.premium-netanyahu-worries-that-star -witness-will-drop-bombshell-1.9533081.

172 **"This man destroyed my life":** Weitz, "Netanyahu Worries That Star Witness Milchan Will Drop Bombshell."

172 **"Don't throw me under the bus because of him":** Gidi Weitz, " 'You Can't Meet with the Netanyahus Empty-Handed. There Is No Such Thing,' " *Haaretz*, July 5, 2022, www.haaretz.com/israel-news/2022-07-05 /ty-article-magazine/.highlight/you-cant-meet-with-the-netanyahus-empty-handed-there-is-no-such -thing/00000181-ce46-dc67-adab-cfc759600000.

172 **"Do you want me to fall on the ground laughing?":** Sue Surkes, "Mogul Tells Police He Felt 'Disgusted' by Netanyahus' Gift Requests—Report," *Times of Israel*, June 7, 2019, www.timesofisrael.com/mogul -tells-police-he-felt-disgusted-by-netanyahu-gift-requests-report/.

173 **"I'm sad":** Amy Spiro, "Arnon Milchan Will Not Face Corruption Charges in Israel," *Variety*, May 1, 2019, https://variety.com/2019/film/news/arnon-milchan-producer-not-face-corruption-charges-israel-benjamin -netanyahu-1203152821/.

173 **"Among other results of Milchan's utter failures":** Gene Maddaus, " 'Rules Don't Apply' Investors Accuse Arnon Milchan of Fraud," *Variety*, March 23, 2018, https://variety.com/2018/biz/news/rules-dont -apply-arnon-milchan-fraud-1202735008/.

174 *Did you see the quantities of champagne bottles?:* Weitz, " 'Mr. Prime Minister, Do You Believe What You're Saying? It's Embarrassing': The Netanyahu Interrogation Transcripts," *Haaretz*, September 26, 2020, www.haaretz.com/israel-news/.premium.HIGHLIGHT.MAGAZINE-do-you-believe-what-you-re-saying -the-netanyahu-interrogation-transcripts-1.9184340.

175 **They would lead, according to close associates:** Yosi Verter, "Could the Probe into Sara Net- anyahu Bring Down King Bibi?," *Haaretz*, January 2, 2016, www.haaretz.com/israel-news/.premium -could-probe-into-sara-netanyahu-bring-down-bibi-1.5384443.

175 **with $215,000 worth of lavish "gifts":** Weitz, "Netanyahu Worries That Star Witness Milchan Will Drop Bombshell."

175 **with bribing Netanyahu to change the "Milchan" law:** David Caspi, "Israeli Police Recommend Charging Producer Arnon Milchan with Bribery," *Hollywood Reporter*, February 13, 2018, www.hollywoodreporter. com/business/business-news/israeli-police-recommend-charging-producer-arnon-milchan-prime-minister -bribery-1084390/.

176 **"It was not my job to help Milchan"; "Despite all the pressure":** Sue Surkes, "Lapid on His Testimony Against PM: I Acted 'Like Any Law-Abiding Citizen,' " *Times of Israel*, February 14, 2018, www.timesofisrael.com/lapid -on-testimony-against-pm-i-acted-like-any-law-abiding-citizen/.

176 **But after yearlong negotiations:** Spiro, "Arnon Milchan Will Not Face Corruption Charges in Israel."

176 **"He won't attack me":** Weitz, "Netanyahu Worries That Star Witness Milchan Will Drop Bombshell."

176 **President Donald Trump denied the request:** Gidi Weitz, "Revealed: U.S. Refused Israeli Request to Ques- tion Kerry, Shapiro in Netanyahu Corruption Case," *Haaretz*, January 2, 2019, https://www.haaretz.com/israel -news/2019-01-02/ty-article/.premium/u-s-refused-israeli-request-to-question-kerry-shapiro-in-netanyahu -corruption-case/0000017f-e31d-d804-ad7f-f3ff93900000.

176 **"living at the expense of others":** "Netanyahu Asked Kerry 3 Times to Help His Benefactor Arnon Milchan with US Visa," *Times of Israel*, January 7, 2017, www.timesofisrael.com/netanyahu-asked-kerry-3-times -to-help-his-benefactor-arnon-milchan-with-us-visa/.

177 **"It was a war zone"**: Moran Sharif, "Like a Regular Guy, Netanyahu Sat Around and Waited for His Judges for 20 Minutes," *Haaretz*, February 11, 2021, www.haaretz.com/israel-news/2021-02-11/ty-article-magazine /.premium/like-a-regular-guy-netanyahu-waited-for-his-judges-for-20-minutes/0000017f-e5c4-dc7e-adff -f5ed32d50001.

177 **"a drugged cockroach in a bottle"**: Yossi Verter, "Netanyahu Is 'On His Knees' Seeking a Plea Deal. As Usual, Way Too Late," *Haaretz*, January 21, 2022.

177 **"When he realized that I didn't intend to let him"**: Yossi Verter, "Settler Violence, Netanyahu's Trial and COVID: Haaretz Interview with Prime Minister Bennett," *Haaretz*, January 28, 2022, www.haaretz .com/israel-news/.premium.HIGHLIGHT.MAGAZINE-settler-violence-netanyahu-s-trial-and -covid-haaretz-interview-with-bennett-1.10572407.

178 **"I would not like to see Netanyahu in jail"**: "Israel's PM Bennett: 'Netanyahu Threatened Me,'" i24, January 27, 2022, www.i24news.tv/en/news/israel/politics/1643316822-israel-s-pm-bennett-netanyahu-threatened-me.

178 **a massive shredding operation**: Michael Hauser Tov, "Netanyahu Ordered Illegal Shredding of Docs at His Office Before Bennett Took Over, Sources Say," *Haaretz*, June 17, 2021, www.haaretz.com/israel -news/.premium-netanyahu-ordered-illegal-shredding-of-docs-before-bennett-took-over-sources-say-1 .9916551.

178 **"Before I left, I took documents"**: Gil Hoffman, "Netanyahu's Cabinet Secretary Admits to Shredding Files on Tape—Report," *Jerusalem Post*, December 30, 2021, www.jpost.com/breaking-news/article-690121?_ga =2.264166020.989822878.1640773506-1229034299.1617710680&utm_source=ActiveCampaign&utm _me%E2%80%A6.

178 **"We decided to come with our truck"**: "Netanyahu's Moving Out, but Not Soon Enough for Critics," Repub-licWorld, June 21, 2021, www.republicworld.com/world-news/middle-east/netanyahus-moving-out-but-not -soon-enough-for-critics.html.

178 **"The defendant and his family fled"**: Amrit Burman, "Israel's Ex-PM Benjamin Netanyahu Vacates Official Residence After 12 Years," RepublicWorld, July 11, 2021, www.republicworld.com/world-news/rest-of-the -world-news/israels-ex-pm-benjamin-netanyahu-vacates-official-residence-after-12-years.html.

178 **"There will never be a peace plan with the Palestinians"**: Nir Hasson, "'Great Joy but Even Worse Anxiety': One Last Night with the Anti-Netanyahu Protesters," *Haaretz*, June 13, 2021, www.haaretz.com/israel-news /elections/.premium.MAGAZINE-great-joy-but-even-worse-anxiety-one-last-night-with-anti-netanyahu -protesters-1.9900650.

178 **"Until Sunday I'll fight"**: Hasson, "'Great Joy but Even Worse Anxiety.'"

178 **"unacceptable"; "outrage"; "betrayal"**: Allison Kaplan Sommer, "'We're Outraged': Liberal U.S. Jews Feel Betrayed by New Israeli Government," *Haaretz*, February 3, 2022, www.haaretz.com/us-news/.premium .HIGHLIGHT-we-re-outraged-liberal-u-s-jews-feel-betrayed-by-new-israeli-government-1.10589115.

179 **"The time has come for the country to move"**: "Netanyahu Should Take the Plea Deal—Editorial," *Jerusalem Post*, January 18, 2022, www.jpost.com/opinion/article-693900.

179 **"A bribery conviction, should there be one"**: Verter, "Netanyahu Is 'On His Knees' Seeking a Plea Deal."

179 **"It's about time Israel had a prime minister"**: "Netanyahu Asked Kerry 3 Times to Help His Benefactor Arnon Milchan with US Visa."

179 **"They were insufferable"**: Orly Halpern, "A Silver Lining of Israel's Political Trumoil: Naftali Ben-nett's Neighbors Can Finally Get Their Driveways Back," *Forward*, June 29, 2022, https://forward.com /fast-forward/508357/a-silver-lining-of-israel-political-turmoil-naftali-bennett-neighbors-can-finally-get -their-driveways-back/?utm_source=Iterable&utm_medium=email&utm_campaign=campaign_4572802.

179 **"never agree to allow"**: Noa Shpigel, "'Antisemitic': Netanyahu Blasts Likud Lawmaker for Suggesting Cooperation with Arab Party," *Haaretz*, June 26, 2022, www.haaretz.com/israel-news/elections/2022-06-26 /ty-article/.premium/antisemitic-netanyahu-blasts-likud-mk-for-suggesting-cooperation-with-arab -party/00000181-9efd-db6b-afbf-fffff6b40000.

179 **"One benefit of a victory"**: Anshel Pfeffer, "'Binyamin Netanyahu on Steroids' Limbers Up for an Israeli Elections Comeback," *Times* (London), June 23, 2022, www.thetimes.co.uk/article/binyamin-netanyahu-on -steroids-limbers-up-for-an-israeli-elections-comeback-rb6vqkrp2?utm_source=Sailthru&utm_medium =email&utm_campaign=Best%20of%20Times%20June%2024&utm_term=audience_BEST_OF_TIMES.

180 **"smearing Israel abroad"**: Anshel Pfeffer, "Yar Lapid's Journey: From Late-night Host to Israel's Prime Min-ister," *Haaretz*, June 29, 2022, www.haaretz.com/israel-news/elections/2022-06-29/ty-article-magazine

/.highlight/yair-lapids-journey-the-late-night-host-about-to-be-israels-next-prime-minister/00000181
-ae27-d941-a5bd-aea7f6700000.

180 **chose to move into Villa Hanna Salameh:** Nir Hasson, "New Israeli PM Lapid to Move into Jerusalem Home
That Arabs Fled in 1948," *Haaretz*, July 1, 2022, www.haaretz.com/israel-news/elections/2022-07-01/ty-article
/.highlight/lapid-to-move-into-a-jerusalem-home-from-which-arabs-fled-in-1948/00000181-b875-d415
-a78b-bc7f94390000.

180 **ethnic cleansing:** Hussein Ibish, "A 'Catastrophe' That Defines Palestinian Identity: For the People of Palestine, the Trauma of 70 Years Ago Never Ended," *Atlantic*, May 14, 2018, www.theatlantic.com/international
/archive/2018/05/the-meaning-of-nakba-israel-palestine-1948-gaza/560294/. See also Ilan Pappe, *The Ethnic
Cleansing of Palestine* (New York: Simon & Schuster, 2007).

180 **"incomparably broad and draconian":** Editorial, "Israel Must Repeal Its Discriminatory Absentee Property Law,"
Haaretz, November 2, 2021, www.haaretz.com/opinion/editorial/2021-11-02/ty-article-opinion/.premium
/israel-must-repeal-its-discriminatory-absentee-property-law/0000017f-db94-df62-a9ff-dfd75e030000.

180 **"I remember [Milchan] and me sitting with George Clooney":** This and subsequent testimony by Lapid
comes from Gidi Weitz, "When Lapid Warned Hollywood Mogul Milchan About Netanyahu," *Haaretz*, July 1,
2022, www.haaretz.com/israel-news/2022-06-30/ty-article/.premium/when-lapid-warned-hollywood-mogul
-milchan-about-netanyahu/00000181-b5df-d21b-a1eb-f7df95e50000.

180 **"I interviewed the Dalai Lama":** Weitz, "When Lapid Warned Hollywood Mogul Milchan About Netanyahu."

180 **"Lapid's 22 months as finance minister were a disaster":** Pfeffer, "Yar Lapid's Journey."

181 **five long years; "It's difficult to guess":** Weitz, " 'You Can't Meet with the Netanyahus Empty-Handed.' "

181 **"All those who are clucking their tongues at the Netanyahus' ":** Gideon Levy, "Bibi Haters Have a New Her-
oine," *Haaretz*, July 13, 2022, www.haaretz.com/opinion/2022-07-13/ty-article/.premium/lets-hear-it-for
-hadas-klein/00000181-f88f-d16e-af91-fcafe6e60000.

181 **commercials for Warburtons bagels and Kia automobiles:** Kevin Maher, "From Mean Streets to Bread
Ads," *Times* (London), April 20, 2021, www.thetimes.co.uk/article/robert-de-niro-from-mean-streets-to
-bread-ads-q9qm5sl2d.

181 **"Fees for De Niro":** Amy Kaufman and Meg James, "The Man Who Played Hollywood: Inside Randall
Emmett's Crumbling Empire," *Los Angeles Times*, June 30, 2022, www.latimes.com/entertainment-arts
/business/story/2022-06-30/randall-emmett-bruce-willis-pacino-lala-kent.

181 **the actor was millions of dollars behind on his taxes:** Emily Kirkpatrick, "Robert De Niro's Lawyer Claims
He's Being 'Forced to Work' to Support His Estranged Wife's 'Thirst for Stella McCartney,' " *Vanity Fair*,
April 19, 2021, www.vanityfair.com/style/2021/04/robert-de-niro-divorce-grace-hightower-forced-to-work
-support-lifestyle-stella-mccartney.

182 **"gratuitous unwanted physical contact"; "You fucking don't answer my calls":** Ruth Weissmann, Emily
Saul, and Lia Eustachewich, "Robert De Niro Subjected to Female Employee to Creepy and Abusive Behavior: Lawsuit," Page Six, October 3, 2019, https://pagesix.com/2019/10/03/robert-de-niro-subjected-female
-assistant-to-creepy-and-abusive-behavior-lawsuit/.

182 **totaling over $4,228,000:** OpenSecrets, "Money to Congress," www.opensecrets.org/industries/summary
.php?ind=Q05&cycle=All&recipdetail=M&sortorder=U.

182 **had accumulated sixteen hundred tons of nuclear waste:** Rebecca Tuhus-Dubrow, "What Should America Do
with Its Nuclear Waste?," *Washington Post*, April 17, 2022, www.washingtonpost.com/magazine/2022/04/11
/america-nuclear-waste-san-onofre/.

183 **"the Israeli government is doing":** Jon Gambrell, "Secretive Israeli Nuclear Facility Undergoes
Major Project," AP News, February 25, 2021, https://apnews.com/article/secret-israel-nuclear-construction
-ecd8b6f3ffb329aa1fc566b9f9336038.

183 **"significant new construction":** "Satellite Images Show Significant New Construction at Israel's Dimona
Reactor Site," *Nuclear Engineering International*, February 2021, www.neimagazine.com/news/newssatellite
-images-show-significant-new-construction-at-israels-dimona-reactor-site-8542583.

184 **"With limited geological options for disposal":** "Planning for Nuclear Power Plant Site Visits," WM2020
Conference, March 2020, Phoenix, AZ, www.pnnl.gov/sites/default/files/media/file/PlanningForNuclear
PowerPlantSiteVisits.pdf.

184 **the distressing headline:** "Israel Among World's Least Popular Nations," *Haaretz*, May 25, 2013, www.haaretz
.com/bbc-poll-israel-among-world-s-least-popular-nations-1.5269605.

BOOK FIVE: THE INFILTRATORS

Chapter 21: Adelson's Army

189 **"shall remain strictly confidential"**: Nathan Guttman, "Will Sheldon Adelson's Push to Fund Anti-BDS Campaign Backfire on Campus?," *Forward*, June 4, 2015, https://forward.com/news/309413/sheldon-adelson -bds-campaign-campus-vegas/.

189 **eighth richest human**: Ben Jacobs, "Republican Contenders Visit Vegas to Woo Growing Jewish Donor Base," *Guardian*, April 27, 2015, www.theguardian.com/us-news/2015/apr/27/republican-jewish-coalition -ted-cruz-jeb-bush-barack-obama-foreign-policy.

190 **$40 billion**: "Sheldon Adelson Net Worth," Celebrity Net Worth, 2021, www.celebritynetworth.com /richest-businessmen/richest-billionaires/sheldon-adelson-net-worth/.

190 **"the Sheldon Adelson suck-up fest"**: Molly Ball, "The Sheldon Adelson Suck-Up Fest," *Atlantic*, April 2, 2014, www.theatlantic.com/politics/archive/2014/04/the-sheldon-adelson-suck-up-fest/360028/.

190 **Afikim Caddy**: Kia Makarechi, "Sheldon Adelson's Weekend Retreat Tests Candidates, Mocks Democracy," *Vanity Fair*, March 31, 2014, www.vanityfair.com/news/politics/2014/03/sheldon-adelson-s-weekend -retreat-tests-candidates-mocks-democracy.

190 **In 2012 he spent over $150 million**: Theodoric Meyer, "Buying Your Vote: How Much Did Sheldon Adelson Really Spend on Campaign 2012?," ProPublica, December 20, 2012, www.propublica.org/article/how-much -did-sheldon-adelson-really-spend-on-campaign-2012. See also Peter Stone, "Sheldon Adelson Spent Far More on Campaign Than Previously Known," *Huffington Post*, December 3, 2012, www.huffpost.com/entry /sheldon-adelson-2012-election_n_2223589.

190 **"It's not complicated"**: Jacobs, "Republican Contenders Visit Vegas."

190 **"His priority is Israel"**: Kenneth P. Vogel, "Sheldon Adelson: Wild Card," *Politico*, March 31, 2014, www .politico.com/story/2014/03/sheldon-adelson-las-vegas-2016-elections-republicans-105192.

190 **"I had this crazy Jewish billionaire"**: Connie Bruck, "The Brass Ring: A Multibillionaire's Relentless Quest for Global Influence," *New Yorker*, June 23, 2008, www.newyorker.com/magazine/2008/06/30/the-brass-ring.

190 **"The uniform that I wore in the military"**: Truth Seeker, "Sheldon Adelson 2010 Speech Israel Media Media Watch," YouTube, November 26, 2010, www.youtube.com/watch?v=jHQLg7C3zD8.

191 **"Greetings from Jerusalem"**: "PM Netanyahu's Greetings to Participants at the Anti-BDS Summit in Las Vegas," Government of Israel, June 6, 2015, www.gov.il/en/departments/news/spokevegas060615.

191 **"an anti-Semitic tsunami"; "little to no sign"; upwards of $50 million**: Nathan Guttman, "Secret Sheldon Adelson Summit Raises up to $50M for Strident Anti-BDS Push," *Forward*, June 9, 2015, https://forward.com /israel/309676/secret-sheldon-adelson-summit-raises-up-to-50m-for-strident-anti-bds-push/.

191 **At the same time the summit was taking place; $30 million; $900 million**: Itamar Eichner, "Israel to Allocate NIS 100 Million for BDS Battle; In Letter, Netanyahu Tells Attendees at Emergency BDS Summit in Las Vegas, 'You Are on the Front Lines of Fight Against BDS, and Israel Must Stand with You," Ynetnews, June 6, 2015, www.ynetnews.com/articles/0,7340,L-4665676,00.html.

191 **donate $6.4 million to Hillary Clinton's campaign**: Open Secrets, "Saban, Haim & Cheryl: Donor Detail," www.opensecrets.org/outsidespending/donor_detail.php?cycle=2016&id=U0000000380&type=I&super =N&name=Saban%2C+Haim+%26+Cheryl. See also Sharon Waxman, "Haim Saban Wants You to Know How Many Millions He's Given Hillary Clinton," The Wrap, February 7, 2016, www.thewrap.com/haim-saban-hillary -clinton-millions-donated-campaign/.

192 **"I am seeking your thoughts"**: Letter, Hillary Rodham Clinton to Haim Saban, July 2, 2015, www .documentcloud.org/documents/2158218-hillary-clintons-letter-to-haim-saban-against-bds.html.

192 **"The driver cannot have failed to see her"**: Harriet Sherwood, "Rachel Corrie Death: Struggle for Justice Culminates in Israeli Court," *Guardian*, August 27, 2012, www.theguardian.com/world/2012/aug/27 /rachel-corrie-death-israel-verdict.

192 **"On the night of Corrie's death"**: Sandra Jordan, "Making of a Martyr," *Observer*, March 23, 2003, www .theguardian.com/world/2003/mar/23/internationaleducationnews.students.

192 **"gross violation of human rights"**: Michael Paulson, "Tutu Urges Jews to Challenge Oppression of Palestinians," *Boston Globe*, October 28, 2007, http://archive.boston.com/news/local/articles/2007/10/28 /tutu_urges_jews_to_challenge_oppression_of_palestinians/.

192 **"We know too well that our freedom is incomplete"**: Speeches of Nelson Mandela, Republic of South Africa, www.mandela.gov.za/mandela_speeches/1997/971204_palestinian.htm. In 2021, Mandela's grandson, Mandla

Mandela, urged countries to boycott the Miss Universe event that was due to be held in Israel that December, citing the occupation of Palestine, which he compared with that of South Africa. "We must not support or legitimize the victimization of our Palestinian brothers and sisters," he said. Nadda Osman, "Mandla Mandela Calls for Boycott of Miss Universe Competition in Israel," Middle East Eye, October 22, 2021, www.middleeasteye.net/news/israel-south-africa-mandela-grandson-calls-boycott-miss-universe-competition-apartheid.

192 **"The Palestinian narrative":** "South African Official Calls for Israel to Be Declared an 'Apartheid State,'" *Jerusalem Post*, July 26, 2022, https://www.jpost.com/bds-threat/article-713140.

193 **Between 2006 and 2012, violent settlers' attacks:** "Settler Violence: An Armed Wing of Settlement Expansion in the Occupied Palestinian Territory; Case Studies from the Northern West Bank," Première Urgence Internationale (PUI) and Médecins Du Monde—France (MDM), May 2016, https://mdm-me.org/wp-content/uploads/2016/05/RAPPORT-PALESTINE-ENGLISH-V3.pdf.

193 **settlers from the Mitzpeh Yair outpost:** Gideon Levy, Alex Levac, "Israeli Settlers Beat a 78-year-old Palestinian Farmer with Clubs. Then They Came Back to Attack His Family," *Haaretz*, January 8, 2021, www.haaretz.com/.premium.MAGAZINE-settlers-beat-a-palestinian-with-clubs-then-they-returned-to-attack-his-family-1.9431849?utm_source=mailchimp&%E2%80%A6.

193 **"Violence by settlers":** "Settler Violence = State Violence," B'Tselem, November 25, 2021, www.btselem.org/settler_violence.

193 **about six million Israelis live on 85 percent of the area that was Palestine:** Chris McGreal, "Brothers in Arms—Israel's Secret Pact with Pretoria," *Guardian*, February 7, 2006, www.theguardian.com/world/2006/feb/07/southafrica.israel.

193 **"clear similarities to the racist apartheid regime":** "Forbidden Roads: The Discriminatory West Bank Road Regime," B'Tselem, 2004, www.btselem.org/publications/summaries/200408_forbidden_roads.

193 **"Apartheid was about keeping the best parts":** McGreal, "Brothers in Arms—Israel's Secret Pact with Pretoria."

193 **Israel also now allows its draft-age youth:** Hagar Shezaf, "Instead of Army Service, Israel Allows People to Volunteer at Illegal West Bank Outposts," *Haaretz*, March 17, 2022, www.haaretz.com/israel-news/.premium-the-israeli-state-allows-for-national-service-at-illegal-west-bank-outposts-1.10679893?utm_source=mailchimp&utm%E2%80%A6.

193 **Israeli forces killed over five hundred children:** Josh Nathan-Kazis, "A New Wave of Hardline Anti-BDS Tactics Are Targeting Students, and No One Knows Who's Behind It," *Forward*, August 2, 2018, https://forward.com/news/407127/a-new-wave-of-hardline-anti-bds-tactics-are-targeting-students-and-no-one/.

194 **"The authorities detained thousands":** "2015/16—The State of the World's Human Rights—Israel and Occupied Palestinian Territories," Amnesty International, February 24, 2016, www.ecoi.net/en/document/1036995.html.

194 **On July 22, 2019:** Jeff Halper, "The Meaning of Israel's Massive Housing Demolitions in East Jerusalem," *The Nation*, August 6, 2019, www.thenation.com/article/archive/israel-occupation-palestine-housing-east-jerusalem/.

195 **"to Judaize Palestine":** "End Home Demolitions—An Introduction," ICAHD, March 15, 2020, https://icahd.org/2020/03/15/end-home-demolitions-an-introduction/.

195 **"The bulldozer is coming":** Steve Hendrix and Shira Rubin, "Ahead of Biden Visit, Israel Launches Biggest Eviction of Palestinians in Decades," *Washington Post*, May 22, 2022, www.washingtonpost.com/world/2022/05/22/israel-palestinian-masafer-yatta-biden/.

195 **house demolitions had eclipsed a thousand:** Austin Ahlman, "Israel Surpasses 1,000 Demolitions in the Occupied West Bank Since Joe Biden Took Office," *The Intercept*, February 25, 2022, https://theintercept.com/2022/02/25/israel-palestine-west-bank-demolitions/.

195 **home of a ninety-five-year-old physically disabled woman:** Nati Yefet, "Israel to Demolish Home of 95-Year-Old Physically Disabled Bedouin," *Haaretz*, February 23, 2022, www.haaretz.com/israel-news/.premium-israel-to-demolish-home-of-95-year-old-physically-disabled-bedouin-1.10628398.

195 **"Gangs of settlers carry out raids":** Michael Sfard, "Violent Israeli Settlers Are Starting to Resemble the KKK," *Haaretz*, February 10, 2022, www.haaretz.com/israel-news/.premium.HIGHLIGHT.MAGAZINE-violent-israeli-settlers-are-starting-to-resemble-the-kkk-1.10605081.

195 **"We, members of the Jewish people":** "Israeli Minister Slammed for Rebuking 'Subhuman' Settlers After Vandalism of Palestinian Graves," *Haaretz*, January 6, 2022, www.haaretz.com/israel-news/.premium-minister-slammed-for-calling-settlers-subhuman-after-vandalism-of-palestinian-grav-1.10519470.

196 **"In boardrooms and campuses"; considered the country's expulsion:** Dan Perry, "Analysis: Fair to Boycott Israel? Global Momentum Grows," Associated Press, June 6, 2015, https://apnews.com/article /f5eae76ab13a477983bbc3b5991e39a7.

196 **the National Union of Students in the UK:** Jodi Rudoren and Sewell Chan, "E.U. Move to Label Israeli Set- tlement Goods Strains Ties," *New York Times*, November 11, 2015, www.nytimes.com/2015/11/12/world /middleeast/eu-labels-israeli-settlements.html.

196 **Norway, although not a member:** "Conrad Myrland, "Norway's New Labeling Policy Is a Double Standard Against Jews—Opinion," *Jerusalem Post*, June 22, 2022, www.jpost.com/opinion/article-710087.

196 **a critical Human Rights Watch report:** "Occupation, Inc.: How Settlement Business Contribute to Israel's Violations of Palestinian Rights," Human Rights Watch, January 19, 2016, www.hrw.org/news/2016/01/19 /occupation-inc-how-settlement-businesses-contribute-israels-violations-palestinian.

196 **"encourage affiliates, employers and pension funds":** Cnaan Liphshiz, "British Trade Unions Reaf- firm Support for Boycotting Israel," *Jerusalem Post*, September 14, 2019, www.jpost.com/diaspora/british -trade-unions-reaffirm-support-for-boycotting-israel-601638.

197 **"For too long the international community has stood idly by":** Congress Motions, [2020] Motion 66, "Soli- darity with Palestine and Resisting Annexation," Trades Union Congress.

197 **the British Labor Party Conference voted:** "UK Labour Party Votes for Motion Calling Israel an Apart- heid State," Middle East Monitor, September 27, 2021, www.middleeastmonitor.com/20210927-uk -labour-party-votes-for-motion-calling-israel-an-apartheid-state/.

197 **"Hotovely is a proud supporter":** "Cambridge: 'Anti-Apartheid' Protest Greets Israeli Ambassador at Uni- versity," Middle East Monitor, February 9, 2022, www.middleeastmonitor.com/20220209-cambridge -anti-apartheid-protest-greets-israeli-ambassador-at-university/.

197 **"Israel has blatantly codified a racist governing principle":** Resolution, United Methodist Church, 2022 New England Annual Conference, June 9–11, 2022, https://neumc-email.brtapp.com/files/fileshare/ac+2022 /pre+con+materials+5-2-22.pdf.

197 **"Israel's laws, policies and practice":** Michael Starr, "US Presbyterian Church: Israel Is Apartheid State, Creates Nakba Remembrance Day," *Jerusalem Post*, June 29, 2022, www.jpost.com/christianworld/article -710725.

198 **"discrimination against Palestinians":** "WCC Central Committee Statement on Threats to a Just Peace in Israel and Palestine," World Council of Churches, June 18, 2022, www.oikoumene.org/resources/documents /wcc-central-committee-statement-on-threats-to-a-just-peace-in-israel-and-palestine-and-to-the-christian -presence-in-the-holy-land.

198 **"commission of the crimes of apartheid and persecution":** Michael Starr, "N. Carolina Dems Want Nakba Day, Accuse Israel of Apartheid, Killing Abu Akleh," *Jerusalem Post*, June 28, 2022, www.jpost.com/diaspora /article-710623.

198 **"As a Jewish Educator":** Michael Arria, "Seattle Teachers Union Endorses BDS, Demands End to Police Part- nership with Israel," Mondoweiss, June 18, 2021, https://mondoweiss.net/2021/06/seattle-teachers-union -endorses-bds-demands-end-to-police-partnership-with-israel/.

198 **"Over 1,500 Palestinians":** "Resolution in Solidarity with the Palestinian People," May 19, 2021, https://docs .google.com/file/d/1dqNbz8SteV4ZY6u6jM4xfOG-etXXmpxg/edit?filetype=msword.

198 **"a very big deal":** Chemi Shalev, "Portman's V for Vendetta Against Netanyahu Touches Raw Nerve for Israel," *Haaretz*, April 22, 2018, www.haaretz.com/israel-news/.premium-portman-s-v-for-vendetta-against -netanyahu-touches-raw-israel-nerve-1.6013647.

198 **"The mistreatment of those suffering":** Amir Tibon, " 'It's Not BDS, It's Netanyahu': Portman Explains Why She Nixed Prize Ceremony in Israel," *Haaretz*, April 21, 2018, www.haaretz.com/us-news/2018-04-21 /ty-article/.premium/natalie-portman-responds-to-genesis-prize-boycott-backlash/0000017f-f27e-d487 -abff-f3fe93280000.

198 **"I find his racist comments horrific":** "Genesis Prize Cancels Ceremony After 2018 Winner Natalie Port- man Says Won't Visit Israel," *Haaretz*, April 21, 2018, www.haaretz.com/israel-news/natalie-portman -forces-genesis-prize-to-cancel-israel-ceremony-1.6012937.

199 **an organization so secret:** "Bill Calling to Keep Strategic Affairs Ministry's Efforts to Combat Delegitimiza- tion Secret Passes First Reading," Israeli Government, Knesset News, July18, 2017, https://main.knesset.gov.il /EN/News/PressReleases/Pages/Pr13526_pg.aspx.

199 **even its location was long hidden:** Uri Blau, "Inside the Clandestine World of Israel's 'BDS-Busting' Ministry," *Haaretz*, March 26, 2017, www.haaretz.com/israel-news/MAGAZINE-inside-the-clandestine-world -of-israels-bds-busting-ministry-1.5453212.

199 **"see themselves as the heads of a commando unit":** Blau, "Inside the Clandestine World of Israel's 'BDS-Busting' Ministry."

199 **the European Union financed an investigation:** "Kept in the Dark: Treatment of Palestinian Detainees in the Petah Tikva Interroration Facility of the Israel Security Agency," B'Tselem, October 2010, www.btselem.org /download/201010_kept_in_the_dark_eng.pdf.

199 **An earlier report by Human Rights Watch:** "Torture and Ill-Treatment: Israel's Interrogation of Palestinians from the Occupied Territories," Human Rights Watch, June 1994, www.hrw.org/reports/pdfs/i/israel /israel946.pdf.

200 **"Investigators left me tied to a chair":** Nir Hasson, "Tortured into Confession: Two Palestinians Recount Hellish Interrogation," *Haaretz*, May 23, 2022, www.haaretz.com/israel-news/2022-05-23/ty-article/.premium /tortured-into-confession-two-palestinians-recount-hellish-interrogation/00000180-f6c5-d469-a5b4 -f6fdd5cc0000.

200 **"not interested and unable to stop the use of torture against Palestinians":** Lubna Masarwa, "Israeli Anti-Torgure Body Refers Israel to International Court," Middle East Eye, June 10, 2022, www.middleeasteye.net /news/israel-anti-torture-body-refers-international-criminal-court.

200 **"We just had a historical conference in Las Vegas":** Israel National News—Arutz Sheva, "Adam Milstein Speaks About the Campus Maccabees Summit," YouTube, June 8, 2015, www.youtube.com/watch?v =wm40qg0RYAw.

201 **According to the law:** 18 U.S. Code § 951—Agents of Foreign Governments. See www.law.cornell.edu/uscode /text/18/951.

201 **"I believe this goes on beyond living memory":** Amy Klein, "The Spinka Money Trail—And the Informant Who Brought Them Down," *Jewish Journal*, January 11, 2008, https://jewishjournal.com/news/united-states /15956/.

202 **"People are very shell-shocked":** Rebecca Spence, "Case of Informant Reverberates Through L.A. Orthodox Community," *Forward*, January 23, 2008, https://forward.com/news/12542/case-of-informant-reverberates -through-la-s-orth-01183/.

202 **Milstein's bond:** For his involvement in the Spinka ring, see United States District Court for the Central District of California, United States of American v. Tuvia Milsztein, aka Adam Milstein, September 19, 2008, Case 2:08-cr-01122-JFW, https://ecf.cacd.uscourts.gov/doc1/03116646000

202 **"There is an obvious concern":** Amended Government's Position Re: Sentencing of Tuvia Milsztein, April 15, 2009.

202 **"This was simply a case about greed":** U.S. Department of Justice, "New York Rabbi Sentenced to Two Years in Federal Prison in Scheme to Defraud Federal Tax Authorities," press release, December 21, 2009, www.justice .gov/archive/usao/cac/Pressroom/pr2009/148.html.

202 **"meet with Israel's Prime Minister":** Attachment, United States District Court, Central District of California, Stipulation Permitting Travel by Defendant, September 25, 2009.

Chapter 22: The Blue Network

203 **$202 billion in "ill-gotten funds":** "Congressional-Executive Commission on China, 2013 Annual Report," www.cecc.gov/publications/annual-reports/2013-annual-report.

204 **"Much of Mr. Adelson's casino profits":** Josh Rogin, "McCain: Adelson Funding Romney Super PAC with 'Foreign Money,'" *Foreign Policy*, June 15, 2012, https://foreignpolicy.com/2012/06/15/mccain-adelson -funding-romney-super-pac-with-foreign-money/.

204 **nearly two hundred thousand Israelis and ex-Israelis:** Amir Tibon, "This Powerful Adelson-Funded Israel Lobby Could Soon Rival AIPAC's Influence in Washington," *Haaretz*, October 31, 2017, www .haaretz.com/us-news/.premium-the-adelson-funded-group-that-could-rival-aipacs-influence-in-d-c -1.5461209.

204 **Netanyahu sent over members of his war cabinet:** "The IAC 2015 National Israeli-American Conference," www.israeliamerican.org/national-washington-dc/videos/iac-2015-national-israeli-american-conference.

204 **"move from defense to offense"**: Chemi Shalev, "Justice Minister Shaked: U.S. Criticism 'Unacceptable' and 'Distorts Reality,'" *Haaretz*, October 18, 2015, www.haaretz.com/.premium-minister-shaked-u-s-criticism -unacceptable-1.5410264.

204 **"Attila the Hun"**: Truth Seeker, "Sheldon Adelson 2010 Speech Israel Media Media Watch," YouTube, November 26, 2010, www.youtube.com/watch?v=jHQLg7C3zD8.

205 **"I don't think the Bible says anything about democracy"**: Zehava Galon, "Those Loyal to Democracy in Israel Must Wake Up," *Haaretz*, February 27, 2022, www.haaretz.com/opinion/.premium-those-loyal-to -democracy-in-israel-must-wake-up-1.10639797.

205 **"Democracy is overrated"**: Chemi Shalev, "Adelson's IAC: American-Israeli Expat Society, AIPAC For or Both?," *Haaretz*, October 20, 2015, www.haaretz.com/israel-news/.premium-adelsons-iac-american-israeli -expat-society-aipac-foil-or-both-1.5411124.

205 **"The State of Israel was created for the Jewish people"**: Peter Beinart, "The New American Jewish Struggle over Israel: Hawks Versus Ultra-Hawks," *Haaretz*, November 12, 2014, www.haaretz.com/opinion/.premium -the-new-u-s-jewish-struggle-over-israel-1.5327746.

205 **"There are enough democratic countries"**: Galon, "Those Loyal to Democracy in Israel Must Wake Up."

205 **"If you don't calm down"**: Jonathan Ofir, "Israeli Lawmaker Warns Palestinians of Another 'Nakba' If They Fly Palestinian Flag," Mondoweiss, May 24, 2022, https://mondoweiss.net/2022/05/israeli-lawmaker -warns-palestinians-of-another-nakba-if-they-fly-palestinian-flag/.

205 **"We feel that we have the natural knowledge"**: "IAC Goes to Washington... And Plans to Stay," *Jewish Journal*, March 4, 2015, https://jewishjournal.com/news/united-states/164072/.

205 **"He challenged them to establish"**: Adam Milstein, blog, "Why We Set Up the Israeli-American Council," *Times of Israel*, November 7, 2013, https://blogs.timesofisrael.com/why-we-created-the-israeli-american-council/.

205 **changed its name to the Israeli-American Council**: "Israeli Leadership Council Changes Name," *Jewish Journal*, March 13, 2013, https://jewishjournal.com/mobile_20111212/113955/.

205 **"Would you be willing to recognize"; "Which raises the question"**: Chemi Shalev, "Adelson's IAC: American-Israeli Expat Society, AIPAC Foil or Both?," *Haaretz*, October 20, 2015, www.haaretz.com/israel-news /.premium-adelsons-iac-american-israeli-expat-society-aipac-foil-or-both-1.5411124.

206 **sex-segregated department stores**: Caroline Hawley, "Israeli Shop Opens Only to Women," BBC News, April 20, 2006, http://news.bbc.co.uk/2/hi/middle_east/4923618.stm

206 **laws forbidding women**: "Haredi Teacher Said Fired for Getting Her Driver's License," *Times of Israel*," August 30, 2016, www.timesofisrael.com/ultra-orthodox-teacher-said-fired-for-getting-her-drivers-license/. See also Ran Bar-Zik, "A 'Bug' That Leaves the Data of Ultra-Orthodox People Exposed Has Devastating Results," *Haaretz*, April 4, 2022.

206 **female bus passengers**: Lawrence Bush, "Back of the Bus," *Jewish Currents*, January 6, 2013, https:// jewishcurrents.org/january-6-the-back-of-the-bus.

207 **"narrative in the world won't be"**: Uri Blau, "Inside the Clandestine World of Israel's 'BDS-Busting' Ministry," *Haaretz*, March 26, 2017, www.haaretz.com/israel-news/MAGAZINE-inside-the-clandestine-world-of -israels-bds-busting-ministry-1.5453212.

207 **"In order to win"**: Itamar Eichner, "Israel vs. Boycott Movement: From Defense to Offense," Ynetnews Magazine, December 7, 2017, www.ynetnews.com/articles/0,7340,L-4987758,00.html.

207 **"We are a different government"**: Quoted in *The Lobby—USA*, Parts 1, 2, 3, and 4, at "Watch the Film the Israeli Lobby Didn't Want You to See," The Electronic Intifada, November 2, 2018, https://electronicintifada .net/content/watch-film-israel-lobby-didnt-want-you-see/25876.

207 **"Blue Network"**: Yossi Lempkowicz, "Ties Between BDS Organizations and Terror Groups," European Jewish Press, June 27, 2018, https://ejpress.org/ties-between-bds-organisations-and-terror-groups/.

207 **"One of the principles for success"**: "Bill Calling to Keep Strategic Affairs Ministry's Efforts to Combat Delegitimization Secret Passes First Reading," Israeli Government, Knesset News, July18, 2017, https://main .knesset.gov.il/EN/News/PressReleases/Pages/Pr13526_pg.aspx.

208 **"take down" members of Parliament**: Ewen MacAskill and Ian Cobain, "Israeli Diplomat Who Plotted Against MPs Also Set Up Political Groups," *Guardian*, January 8, 2017, www.theguardian.com/world/2017 /jan/08/israeli-diplomat-shai-masot-plotted-against-mps-set-up-political-groups-labour.

208 **"more than £1 million"**: Simon Walters, "Israel Plot to 'Take Down' Tory Minister: Astonishing Undercover Video Captures Diplomat Conspiring with Rival MP's Aide to Smear Deputy Foreign Secretary," *Daily Mail*,

January 7, 2017, www.dailymail.co.uk/news/article-4098082/Astonishing-undercover-video-captures-diplomat
-conspiring-rival-MP-s-aide-smear-Deputy-Foreign-Secretary.html.

208 **"The diplomat in question"**: Patrick Wintour, "Boris Johnson Rejects Calls to Discipline Israel over Diplomat's Plot, *Guardian*, January 10, 2017, www.theguardian.com/politics/2017/jan/10/boris-johnson-rejects
-calls-discipline-israel-diplomats-take-down-mps-plot.

208 **"disgusting interference in our public life"**: Alan Duncan, *In the Thick of It: The Private Diaries of a Minister*
(London: HarperCollins, 2022), p. 62.

208 **found no validity to the charges**: Graham Ruddick, "Ofcom Clears Al-Jazeera of Antisemitism in
Exposé of Israeli Official," *Guardian*, October 9, 2017, www.theguardian.com/media/2017/oct/09/ofcom
-clears-al-jazeera-ntisemitism-expose-israeli-embassy-official.

208 **"a serious investigative documentary"**: "Ofcom Broadcast and On Demand Bulletin," Ofcom, October 9,
2017, www.ofcom.org.uk/__data/assets/pdf_file/0033/106989/issue-338-broadcast-on-demand-bulletin.pdf.

209 **"Ambiguity is part of our guidelines"**: *The Lobby—USA*.

210 **funded by $36 million from the ministry**: Uri Blau, "Spying on Linda Sarsour: Israeli Firm Compiled BDS Dos-
sier for Adelson-Funded U.S. Group Battling Her Campus Appearances," *Haaretz*, May 25, 2018, www.haaretz
.com/us-news/.premium-spying-on-sarsour-israeli-firm-compiles-bds-dossier-on-activist-1.6115514.

210 **Sagi Balasha**: LinkedIn account. In it, he lists himself as "Co-Founder & CEO of Concert in Tel Aviv from
January 2016 to October 2018." He describes Concert as: "Concert mission is to counter and undermine
the global Israel deligitimization movement by providing the information, coordination and tools to enable
the pro-Israel community to combat the demonization and hatred towards the State of Israel and improve
dramatically the country's positive perception and standing in world public opinion." He also lists himself
as CEO of the Israeli-American Council from September 2011 to December 2015, www.linkedin.com/in
/sagi-balasha-24b09721/?originalSubdomain=il.

210 **Concert directors**: Noa Landau, "Israel Sets Up Secret Firm with Top Ex-generals, Envoys for Online 'Mss
Awareness' Campaign 'To Fight Delegitimization,' " *Haaretz*, January 9, 2018, www.haaretz.com/israel-news
/.premium-ex-diplomats-generals-in-state-funded-firm-to-clear-israels-name-1.5729945.

210 **turned the ministry down**: Josh Nathan-Kazis, "Jewish Groups Reject Israel Funding for Fear of Being
Branded Foreign Agents," *Forward*, May 29, 2018, https://forward.com/news/401876/israeli-ministrys
-repeated-efforts-to-fund-american-jewish-groups-rejected/.

210 **"anxious and frustrated"; "anxious to figure out a way to spend the money"**: Nathan-Kazis, "Jewish Groups
Reject Israel Funding."

210 **"surveillance and espionage"**: Itamar Benzaquen, "New Petition Challenging Israel's Secret Information Warfare Campaign," The Seventh Eye, March 5, 2018, www.the7eye.org.il/288393.

211 **"The ICC pools resources"**: *The Lobby—USA*.

211 **"We built up this massive national political campaign"**: *The Lobby—USA*.

212 **heavily funded by Milstein**: Alex Kane, "Right-Wing Donor Adam Milstein Has Spent Millions of Dollars to Stifle the BDS Movement and Attack Critics of Israeli Policy," *The Intercept*, March 25, 2019, https://
theintercept.com/2019/03/25/adam-milstein-israel-bds/.

212 **paid over $1 million**: Josh Nathan-Kazis, "When Jewish Leaders Decide to Harass College Kids—To 'Sup-
port' Israel," *Forward*, December 31, 2018, https://forward.com/news/416569/why-did-jewish-leaders-think
-they-should-target-college-kids-to-help/.

212 **likening students protesting Israel's occupation**: Nathan-Kazis, "When Jewish Leaders Decide to Harass College Kids."

212 **"We have a lot of communications capabilities"**: *The Lobby—USA*.

212 **"Obviously I'm an AIPAC-trained activist"**: *The Lobby—USA*.

Chapter 23: The Eavesdroppers

215 **"Every 'juicy' telegram"**: Yossi Melman, "U.S. Spied on Israel's Washington Embassy, Claims Ex-envoy,"
Haaretz, November 29, 2010, www.haaretz.com/1.5146151.

215 **"It was pretty clear that the Israelis were responsible"**: Daniel Lippman, "Israel Accused of Planting Mysterious Spy Devices Near the White House," *Politico*, September 12, 2019, www.politico.com/story/2019/09/12
/israel-white-house-spying-devices-149135.

215 **"As a young soldier serving in the Israeli army"**: Shamai K. Leibowitz, "In Defense of Divestment," *Against the
Current*, January/February 2005, https://againstthecurrent.org/atc114/p339/.

216 **"Twenty-five years ago I stared":** Tom Hayden, "I Was Israel's Dupe," Counterpunch, July 20, 2006, www .counterpunch.org/2006/07/20/i-was-israel-s-dupe/.

216 **"Even before I was a Democrat":** Nathan Guttman, "New Foreign Affairs Committee Chairman Draws Praise from All Sides," *Forward*, April 24, 2008, https://forward.com/news/13244/new-foreign-affairs -committee-chairman-draws-prais-01741/.

217 **"a flagrant violation of international law":** United Nations, "Israel's Settlements Have No Legal Validity, Constitute Flagrant Violation of International Law, Security Council Reaffirms," United Nations Security Council, December 23, 2016, www.un.org/press/en/2016/sc12657.doc.htm.

217 **"I would urge the Administration to make every effort":** Cnaan Liphshiz, "Sen. Chuck Schumer, World Jewish Congress Urge Veto of UN Anti-Settlement Resolution," *Forward*, December 23, 2016, https://forward.com/news /breaking-news/358205/sen-chuck-schumer-world-jewish-congress-urge-veto-of-un-anti-settlement-res/.

218 **"You don't think Israel's a sensitive topic?":** Interview with a former head of the FBI's Counterintelligence Division.

218 **she was lobbying hard:** Harold Meyerson, "Harman's Two-Front War," *LA Weekly*, May 24, 2006, www .laweekly.com/harmans-two-front-war/.

218 **he promised that Haim Saban would threaten:** Neil A. Lewis and Mark Mazzetti, "Lawmaker Is Said to Have Agreed to Aid Lobbyists," *New York Times*, April 20, 2009, www.nytimes.com/2009/04/21/us/politics /21harman.html.

218 **a recipient of more than half a million dollars:** Open Secrets, "Money to Congress," Nancy Pelosi, www .opensecrets.org/industries/summary.php?ind=Q05&cycle=All&recipdetail=H&mem

219 **going directly to someone at the White House; "This conversation doesn't exist":** Lewis and Mazzetti, "Lawmaker Is Said to Have Agreed to Aid Lobbyists."

219 **"I'm a one-issue guy, and my issue is Israel":** Connie Bruck, "The Influencer," *New Yorker*, May 3, 2010, www .newyorker.com/magazine/2010/05/10/the-influencer.

219 **"completed crime"; "deemed the matter particularly urgent":** Jeff Stein, *Congressional Quarterly*, April 20, 2009.

219 **"I'm proud of my friendships"; never realized she had been recorded:** Ron Kampeas, "What's Behind Harman Allegations?," Jewish Telegraphic Agency, April 22, 2009, https://www.jta.org/2009/04/22/politics /whats-behind-harman-allegations

219 **agent finally leaked on April 20, 2009:** Stein, *Congressional Quarterly*. Lewis and Mazzetti, "Lawmaker Is Said to Have Agreed to Aid Lobbyists."

220 **"Thanks to a confidential source":** Richard Silverstein, "Israeli Intelligence Operations Target U.S. Congressional Leaders," *Tikun Olam: Make the World a Better Place* (blog), April 28, 2009.

220 **"I've been informed by a confidential source":** Richard Silverstein, "Jewish Leader Colludes with Israeli Embassy in Monitoring House Member 'Hostile' to Israel," *Tikun Olam: Make the World a Better Place* (blog), April 28, 2009.

220 **"saw things which I considered were violation of the law":** United States District Court for the District of Maryland, Southern Division, United States of America v. Shamai Kedem Leibowitz, May 24, 2010, p. 8. Case 8:09-cr-00632-AW, Document 27, Transcript of Sentencing.

220 **Six years later it was discovered:** Adam Entous, "Israel Spied on Iran Nuclear Talks with U.S.," *Wall Street Journal*, March 23, 2015, www.wsj.com/articles/israel-spied-on-iran-talks-1427164201.

220 **"It is one thing for the U.S. and Israel to spy on each other":** Julian Borger, Mairav Zonszein, and Sabrina Siddiqui, "US Accuses Israel of Spying on Nuclear Talks with Iran," *Guardian*, March 24, 2015, www.theguardian .com/world/2015/mar/24/israel-spied-on-us-over-iran-nuclear-talks.

221 **quietly approached by officials:** Josh Nathan-Kazis, "Israeli Spy Firm That Approached Trump First Proposed Dirty Tricks Against BDS," *Forward*, October 11, 2018, https://forward.com/news/411798/israeli-spy -firm-that-approached-trump-first-proposed-dirty-tricks-against/.

221 **Psy Group:** Simona Weinglass, "Israel Ducks Blame for Firm with Ex-Intel Officers That Bid to 'Shape' US Vote," *Times of Israel*, August 25, 2020, www.timesofisrael.com/israel-ducks-blame-for-firm-with-ex-intel -officers-that-bid-to-meddle-in-us-vote/.

222 **a strategic partnership with Cambridge Analytica LLC:** Byron Tau and Rebecca Ballhaus, "Israeli Intelligence Company Formed Venture with Trump Campaign Firm Cambridge Analytica," *Wall Street Journal*, May 23, 2018, www.wsj.com/articles/israeli-intelligence-company-formed-venture-with-trump-campaign-firm -cambridge-analytica-1527030765.

222 **data of up to eighty-seven million Facebook users:** Cecilia Kang and Sheera Frenkel, "Facebook Says Cambridge Analytica Harvested Data of Up to 87 Million Users," *New York Times*, April 4, 2018, www.nytimes .com/2018/04/04/technology/mark-zuckerberg-testify-congress.html.

222 **Project Butterfly:** Psy Group Project Butterfly Plan, May 2017, www.forensicxs.com/wp-content /uploads/2021/05/Entous-Butterfly.pdf.

222 **All links to the donors would be hidden:** Nathan-Kazis, "Israeli Spy Firm That Approached Trump First Proposed Dirty Tricks Against BDS."

222 **"you don't kill them but you do have to deal with them":** Adam Entous and Ronan Farrow, "Private Mossad for Hire," *New Yorker*, February 11, 2019, www.newyorker.com/magazine/2019/02/18/private-mossad-for-hire.

222 **Psy Group approached the donors through:** Nathan-Kazis, "Israeli Spy Firm That Approached Trump First Proposed Dirty Tricks Against BDS."

222 **Misha Galperin:** "Mourning and Memory," Wexner Foundation, July 22, 2015, www.wexnerfoundation.org /mourning-and-memory/. Daphna Berman, "Natan Sharanski: Act III, Scene 1," *Moment* magazine, July–August 2012, https://momentmag.com/natan-sharansky-act-iii-scene-i-2/.

223 **"The Butterfly initiative uses":** Psy Group Project Butterfly Plan, May 2017, www.forensicxs.com/wp-content /uploads/2021/05/Entous-Butterfly.pdf.

223 **One of those targeted was Hatem Bazian:** Adam Entous, "How a Private Israeli Intelligence Firm Spied on Pro-Palestinian Activists in the U.S.," *New Yorker*, February 28, 2019, www.newyorker.com/news/news-desk /how-a-private-israeli-intelligence-firm-spied-on-pro-palestinian-activists-in-the-us.

Chapter 24: The Thugs

225 **The largest private owner of apartments; controlled over thirteen thousand:** Prometheus LinkedIn page, www.linkedin.com/company/prometheus-real-estate-group/.

225 **contributing over a quarter million dollars:** "Jaclyn Safier, Federal Election Campaign Contributions," Little-Sis, https://littlesis.org/person/103927-Jaclyn_Safier.

225 **the board of directors of Presidio Trust:** "Digest of Other White House Announcements," December 31, 2018, www.govinfo.gov/content/pkg/DCPD-2018DIGEST/pdf/DCPD-2018DIGEST.pdf.

225 **"The level of greed on display":** Business Wire, "Housing Rights Advocates Take On Prometheus Real Estate Group CEO in Socially Distant Car Protest in S.F.," www.businesswire.com/news/home/20200513005206 /en/Housing-Rights-Advocates-Take-on-Prometheus-Real-Estate-Group-CEO-in-Socially-Distant-Car -Protest-in-S.F.

226 **he came under investigation:** Matthew Mosk and John Santucci, "Billionaire Behind Pardon Effort Pledged Massive Donation to Trump: Sources," ABC News, December 10, 2020, https://abcnews.go.com/Politics -/billionaire-pardon-effort-pledged-massive-donation-trump-sources/story?id=74656249.

226 **"record of anti-Muslim, anti-immigrant and anti-black bigotry":** Allison Kaplan Sommer, "From Project Veritas to the Tea Party, San Francisco Jewish Federation also Funding Far-Right Fringe Groups, Not Just Canary Mission," *Haaretz*, October 10, 2018, www.haaretz.com/us-news/.premium-sf-jewish-federation -funded-far-right-groups-as-well-as-canary-mission-1.6547447.

226 **"You know what's going on over there":** Joe Eskenazi, "Diller Family's $5 Million Will Boost Jewish Studies: Grant to Level Playing Field for Israel at Cal," *J. The Jewish News of Northern California*, October 4, 2002, https://jweekly.com/2002/10/04/diller-family-s-5-million-will-boost-jewish-studies-grant-to-level-playing/.

227 **Project Censored named Canary Mission:** "Canary Mission Blacklists Pro-Palestinian Activists, Chilling Free Speech Rights," Project Censored, www.projectcensored.org/6-canary-mission-blacklists-pro-palestinian -activists-chilling-free-speech-rights/.

227 **"anti-Semitic and anti-American radicals":** David Greenberg et al., "The Blacklist in the Coal Mine," *Tablet*, October 26, 2016, www.tabletmag.com/sections/news/articles/the-blacklist-in-the-coal-mine -canary-missions-fear-mongering-agenda-college-campuses.

227 **It's "classic McCarthyism":** Aviva Stahl, "A Shadowy Website Targets Student Protesters With 'Classic McCarthyism,'" *Village Voice*, October 28, 2016, www.villagevoice.com/2016/10/28/a-shadowy-website -targets-student-protesters-with-classic-mccarthyism/.

227 **quickly grew to more than two thousand names:** Josh Nathan-Kazis, "Canary Mission's Threat Grows, from U.S. Campuses to the Israeli Border," *Forward*, August 3, 2018, https://forward.com/news/407279 /canary-missions-threat-grows-from-us-campuses-to-the-israeli-border/.

228   **"It's essentially a spying operation"**: Aaron Liss, "Canary Mission Releases Personal Information of UC Davis Students, Faculty Who Criticize Israel," *California Aggie*, October 12, 2018, https://theaggie.org/2018/10/12 /canary-mission-releases-personal-information-of-uc-davis-students-faculty-who-criticize-israel/.

228   **"It was scary"**: Eric Berger, "JCRC Criticizes Blacklisting of St. Louis College Student," *STL Jewish Light*, February 21, 2019, https://stljewishlight.org/news/news-local/jcrc-criticizes-blacklisting-of-st-louis-college -student/. See also Aisha Sultan, "Sultan: Burroughs Grad Blacklisted by Pro-Israel Site. She's Jewish," *St. Louis Post-Dispatch*, February 15, 2019, www.stltoday.com/lifestyles/parenting/aisha-sultan/sultan-burroughs -grad-blacklisted-by-pro-israel-site-she-s/article_e3a91102-1fdc-5f7b-8400-3ccb66b1e0e2.html.

228   **"demonizing Israel at a Jewish event"**: Nathan-Kazis, "Canary Mission's Threat Grows."

228   **"My first quarter at UCLA"**: Alex Kane, " 'It's Killing the Student Movement': Canary Mission's Blacklist of Pro-Palestine Activists Is Taking a Toll," *The Intercept*, November 22, 2018, https://theintercept.com/2018/11/22 /israel-boycott-canary-mission-blacklist/.

228   **"THERE ARE NO SECRETS"; "pretty unbelievably terrifying"**: Josh Nathan-Kazis, "A New Wave of Hardline Anti-BDS Tactics are Targeting Students, and No One Knows Who's Behind It," *Forward*, August 2, 2018, https:// forward.com/news/407127/a-new-wave-of-hardline-anti-bds-tactics-are-targeting-students-and-no-one/.

229   **Her 2020 novel**: Laleh Khadivi, "A Beautiful, Urgent Novel of the Palestinian Struggle," *New York Times*, August 26, 2020, www.nytimes.com/2020/08/26/books/review/against-the-loveless-world-susan-abulhawa.html.

229   **fired from her job**: Maddie Hanna, "Former Athletic Trainer Says Agnes Irwin School Illegally Fired Her for Social Media Posts Critical of Israel," *Philadelphia Inquirer*, March 17, 2022, www.inquirer.com/news/agnes -irwin-school-natalie-abulhawa-fired-israel-palestine-20220317.html.

229   **"Employment discrimination against Palestinian Americans"**: "Apologize and Remedy the Harm Done to Natalie; Remove Anti-Palestinian Bias from Agnes Irwin School," CAIR Philadelphia, March 16, 2022, https:// pa.cair.com/civil-rights/abulhawa/.

229   **Canary Mission acts as a key intelligence asset**: Noa Landau, "Official Documents Prove: Israel Bans Young Americans Based on Canary Mission Website," *Haaretz*, October 4, 2018, www.haaretz.com/israel -news/.premium-official-documents-prove-israel-bans-young-americans-based-on-canary-mission -site-1.6530903.

230   **"show clearly that the [Canary Mission] site"**: Noa Landau/Haaretz, "Israel Uses Canary Mission Black-list Info to Bar Activists," *Forward*, October 4, 2018, https://forward.com/news/411453/israel-uses-canary -mission-blacklist-info-to-bar-activists/.

230   **"We have a steadfast policy"**: Caleb Melby, "Prometheus Billionaire Emerges with San Francisco Rentals," Bloomberg, September 18, 2014, www.bloomberg.com/news/articles/2014-09-18/prometheus-billionaire -emerges-with-san-francisco-rentals.

230   **Diller Foundation donated $100,000**: Josh Nathan-Kazis, "REVEALED: Canary Mission Blacklist Is Secretly Bankrolled by Major Jewish Federation," *Forward*, October 3, 2018, https://forward.com/news/411355 /revealed-canary-mission-blacklist-is-secretly-bankrolled-by-major-jewish/.

230   **donated another quarter of a million dollars**: Josh Nathan-Kazis, "Second Major Jewish Charity Admits Funding Group Tied to Canary Mission Blacklist," *Forward*, October 11, 2018, https://forward.com /news/411895/second-major-jewish-charity-admits-funding-canary-mission-blacklist/.

230   **manages assets of more than $1.3 billion**: Erin Ben-Moche, "Jewish Community Foundation Awards $3 Mil-lion in COVID-19 Relief to 19 L.A. Groups," *Jewish Journal*, December 24, 2020, https://jewishjournal.com /news/326511/jewish-community-foundation-awards-3-million-in-covid-19-relief-to-19-l-a-groups/.

231   **"I'd never heard of this happening before"**: Ben Sales, "With the Rise of Federation-Managed 'Donor-Advised Funds,' Politics Can Complicate Jewish Giving," Jewish Telegraph Agency, March 28, 2017, www.jta .org/2017/03/28/united-states/when-politics-gets-in-the-way-of-jewish-giving.

231   **the Central Fund of Israel**: Central Fund of Israel, 2016 IRS 990 Form, www.citizenaudit.org/2017_07 _EO/13-2992985_990_201701.pdf/.

231   **2016 and 2017 the fund made grants**: Nathan-Kazis, "Second Major Jewish Charity Admits Funding Group Tied to Canary Mission Blacklist."

231   **three hundred or so other "charities"**: Jill Jacobs, "Your Tax Dollars Are Propping Up the Intellectual Heirs to an Israeli Terrorist," *Washington Post*, January 11, 2019, www.washingtonpost.com/outlook/your-tax -dollars-are-propping-up-the-intellectual-heirs-to-an-israeli-terrorist/2019/01/10/3683c6e0-0efa-11e9 -8938-5898adc28fa2_story.html.

231 **Central Fund's revenues were $25 million; "For years the federations"**: Uri Blau, "From Textiles to the West Bank: Unraveling the Story of One of the Main U.S. Donors to the Settlements," *Haaretz*, December 15, 2015, www .haaretz.com/.premium-unraveling-the-story-of-one-the-main-u-s-donors-to-the-settlements-1.5377041.

231 **980 Sixth Avenue**: Central Fund of Israel, 2016 IRS 990 Form, www.citizenaudit.org/2017_07_EO/13 -2992985_990_201701.pdf/.

231 **back room of J.Mark Interiors**: See donation solicitation site to pro-settler organization, Women in Green, https://womeningreen.org/how-to-help/.

231 **The family business is run by Jay Marcus**: Uri Blau, "Haaretz Investigation: U.S. Donors Gave Settlements More Than $220 Million in Tax-Exempt Funds over Five Years," *Haaretz*, December 7, 2015, www.haaretz .com/haaretz-investigates-u-s-donors-to-israeli-settlements-1.5429739.

231 **second home in Efrat**: Central Fund of Israel, 2016 IRS 990 Form.

232 **Jonathan Jack Ian Bash**: Nathan-Kazis, "Canary Mission's Threat Grows."

232 **annual budget of about $40 million**: Gary Rosenblatt, "Is Aish International Intentionally Misleading High-Profile Donors?," Jewish Telegraph Agency, June 7, 2017, www.jta.org/2017/06/07/ny/in-heavens -name-the-battle-for-reb-noachs-legacy.

232 **"failing score"**: "Aish Hatorah," Charity Navigator, www.charitynavigator.org/ein/943094990.

233 **"a politicized form of Judaism"**: Michael Schulson, "Radical Mission: What Is Aish HaTorah Trying to Teach Young Jews?," Religion & Politics, October 22, 2013, https://religionandpolitics.org/2013/10/22/radical -mission-what-is-aish-hatorah-trying-to-teach-young-jews/.

233 **"It's him, it's him"**: *The Lobby—USA*, Parts 1, 2, 3, and 4, at "Watch the Film the Israeli Lobby Didn't Want You to See," The Electronic Intifada, November 2, 2018, https://electronicintifada.net/content/watch-film -israel-lobby-didnt-want-you-see/25876.

233 **"First of all, investigate who they are"**: *The Lobby—USA*.

233 **A 2019 opinion piece he wrote**: Adam Milstein, "The Nazi-Like Boycott of Jews Is a Global Menace: Why BDS Is All About Eradicating the State of Israel," CBN News, August 30, 2019, www1.cbn.com/cbnnews /israel/2019/august/the-nazi-like-boycott-of-jews-is-a-global-menace-why-bds-is-all-about-eradicating-the -state-of-israel.

233 **Another in his newsletter**: Adam Milstein, "The BDS Movement: Proudly Following in Hitler's Footsteps," Adam Milstein Newsletter, July 23, 2019, www.adammilstein.org/the-nazi-like-boycott-of-jews-is-a-global-menace/.

234 **"alarmingly resembles the Nazi movement"**: "July 2019 Milstein Family Foundation Newsletter," https://myemail.constantcontact.com/Antisemitism-is-in-the-mainstream.html?soid=1125321731257 &aid=EcU2AbpFYnQ.

234 **In a carefully worded statement**: "Pro-Israel Donor Adam Milstein Denies Report That He Funds Canary Mission," *Forward*, August 28, 2018, https://forward.com/fast-forward/409081/pro-israel-donor-adam -milstein-denies-report-that-he-funds-canary-mission/.

234 **Honest Reporting**: See Project Nemesis, https://projectnemesis.net/honest-reporting/.

234 **OpenDor Media**: See OpenDor Media, 2020 Annual Report, https://opendormedia.org/wp-content/uploads /2021/01/opendor-media-annual-report-2020-web.pdf.

234 **Aish HaTorah's Dov Heller**: See Rabbi Gavriel Horan, "Reaching Israelis in America," Aish, May 24, 2012, https://aish.com/reaching_israelis_in_america/.

Chapter 25: The Trolls

235 **"If you boycott against Israel"**: Andrew Cuomo, "Gov. Andrew Cuomo: If You Boycott Israel, New York State Will Boycott You," *Washington Post*, June 10, 2016, www.washingtonpost.com/opinions/gov-andrew -cuomo-if-you-boycott-israel-new-york-state-will-boycott-you/2016/06/10/1d6d3acc-2e62-11e6-9b37 -42985f6a265c_story.html?tid=a_inl.

235 **"has had no truer friend"**: Conor Skelding, "Cuomo Quietly Releases Israel-Boycott Opposition List, Perplexing Targeted Companies," *Politico*, December 9, 2016, www.politico.com/states/new-york/albany/story /2016/12/muted-release-of-and-mixed-reaction-to-cuomos-bds-blacklist-107815.

235 **"Shame on Governor Cuomo"**: "Groups Respond to Cuomo's Unconstitutional Executive Action on BDS," Center for Constitutional Rights, June 6, 2016, https://ccrjustice.org/home/press-center/press-releases /groups-respond-cuomos-unconstitutional-executive-action-bds.

235 **a key target of Erdan's spies and Canary Mission thugs**: Rebecca Vilkomerson's Canary Mission dossier page, https://canarymission.org/individual/Rebecca_Vilkomerson.

236 **secretly unleashing his latest weapon:** "Israel Launches 'Iron Dome of Truth' Website at Celebrate Israel Parade," *Times of Israel*, June 5, 2017, www.timesofisrael.com/israel-launches-iron-dome-of-truth -app-at-celebrate-israel-parade/.

236 **"Israel is an apartheid state":** Eric Cortellessa, "In Platform, Movement for Black Lives Accuses Israel of 'Genocide,' Backs BDS," *Times of Israel*, August 3, 2016, www.timesofisrael.com/in-platform-black-lives -matter-accuses-israel-of-genocide-backs-bds/.

236 **"Thought Police"; "With frightening speed":** "Minister Erdan's Thought Police," editorial, *Haaretz*, March 22, 2017, www.haaretz.com/opinion/editorial/minister-erdan-s-thought-police-1.5451861.

237 **"We started to establish a project":** Quoted in *The Lobby—USA*, Parts 1, 2, 3, and 4, November 3, 2018, https://electronicintifada.net/content/watch-film-israel-lobby-didnt-want-you-see/25876.

237 **"Innovation in AI-powered surveillance":** Sophia Goodfriend, "How the Occupation Fuels Tel Aviv's Boom-ing AI Sector: Israel Hones Invasive Surveillance Technology on Palestinians Before It Is Exported Abroad," *Foreign Policy*, February 21, 2022, https://foreignpolicy.com/2022/02/21/palestine-israel-ai-surveillance-tech -hebron-occupation-privacy/.

237 **Eran Vasker:** Uri Blau, "Spying on Linda Sarsour: Israeli Firm Compiled BDS Dossier for Adelson-Funded U.S. Group Battling Her Campus Appearances," *Haaretz*, May 25, 2018, www.haaretz.com/us-news /.premium-spying-on-sarsour-israeli-firm-compiles-bds-dossier-on-activist-1.6115514.

237 **previously worked for Israeli police:** Eran Vasker's webpage at RocketReach, https://rocketreach.co/adv -eran-vasker-email_5864407.

238 **budgeted $570,000 to create:** Itamar Benzaquen, "The Israeli Government Is Paying for Anti-BDS Journal-ism," The Seventh Eye and *+972 Magazine*, December 20, 2017, www.972mag.com/the-israeli-government-is -paying-for-anti-bds-journalism/.

238 **"Call it a human 'botnet'":** Josh Nathan-Kazis, "Shadowy Israeli App Turns American Jews into Foot Sol-diers in Online War," *Forward*, November 30, 2017, https://forward.com/news/388259/shadowy-israeli-app -turns-american-jews-into-foot-soldiers-in-online-war/.

238 **twenty thousand online potential trolls:** See Israeli American Council, "IAC National Summit," bio of Yarden Ben Yosef, founder and executive director of Act.il, www.israeliamerican.org/iac-national-conference /team-member/yarden-ben-yosef-0.

239 **"a world expert in cognitive influence operations"; "an elite intelligence unit":** IAC, bio of Yarden Ben Yosef.

239 **"We work with the Ministry of Foreign Affairs":** Ben-Yosef quoted in "30 Under 30," *Israel Forbes*, 2018, https://forbes.co.il/lists/2018under30/.

239 **"We talk with each other":** Nathan-Kazis, "Shadowy Israeli App Turns American Jews into Foot Soldiers in Online War."

239 **"In the months before the app's launch"; "We're working with the IDF and the Shin Bet":** Ruben Weiss, "A Lesson in Hasbara," Ynetnews, June 27, 2017, www.ynetnews.com/articles/0,7340,L-4981081,00.html.

239 **Erdan Gilad personally visited:** Weiss, "A Lesson in Hasbara."

239 **the Zionist Organization of America:** Lidar Grave-Lazi, "Training Activists in the Social Media War Against BDS," *Jerusalem Post*, July 3, 2016, www.jpost.com/Israel-News/Training-activists-in-the-social -media-war-against-BDS-459329.

239 **"[Congresswoman] Omar":** Abe Silberstein, "It's Time for the Conference of Presidents to Kick Out Mort Klein," *Forward*, June 8, 2020, https://forward.com/opinion/448321/its-time-for-the-conference-of -presidents-to-kick-out-mort-klein/.

239 **"Nicolet... was visibly excited":** Weiss, "A Lesson in Hasbara."

239 **"This is a new kind of war":** Grave-Lazi, "Training Activists in the Social Media War Against BDS."

240 **"Spearheaded by the Ministry of Strategic Affairs":** Allison Kaplan Sommer, "Sexy Women, 'Missions' and Bad Satire: Israeli Government App Recruits Online Soldiers in Anti-BDS Fight," *Haaretz*, June 13, 2017, www.haaretz.com/israel-news/.premium-how-israel-recruits-online-foot-soldiers-to-fight-bds-1.5483038.

240 **1,580 missions a week; "Every 5.4 minutes"; as young as thirteen years old:** Asa Winstanley, "Inside Isra-el's Million Dollar Troll Army," The Electronic Intifada, June 12, 2019, https://electronicintifada.net/content /inside-israels-million-dollar-troll-army/27566.

240 **"receive points":** Sommer, "Sexy Women, 'Missions' and Bad Satire."

240 **letter of congratulations:** Nathan-Kazis, "Shadowy Israeli App Turns American Jews into Foot Soldiers in Online War."

240 **manipulate Google's algorithm:** Allison Kaplan Sommer, "Israeli-Sponsored App Tries to Manipulate Google in Fight Against BDS," *Haaretz*, January 9, 2018, www.haaretz.com/israel-news/.premium-israeli -sponsored-app-tries-to-manipulate-google-in-fight-against-bds-1.5729933.

240 **as young as thirteen years old:** Winstanley, "Inside Israel's Million Dollar Troll Army."

240 **"[We have] five situation rooms":** Yarden Ben Yosef, "The Digital Battle over the Narrative of the Gaza Protests," The Arena, May 29, 2018, www.eng.arenajournal.org.il/single-post/yarden-ben-yosef-digital -battleground-eng.

240 **"mimic those used by the Israel Defense Forces":** "Student Startup Gives Pro-Israel Advocates a Unified Voice," *Times of Israel*, July 27, 2017, www.timesofisrael.com/this-student-startup-gives-pro-israel -advocates-a-unified-voice/.

241 **Combined Jewish Philanthropies of Greater Boston:** Nathan-Kazis, "Shadowy Israeli App Turns American Jews into Foot Soldiers in Online War."

241 **They were instructed to push a new Facebook page:** Ishmael N. Daro, "How an App Funded by Sheldon Adelson Is Covertly Influencing the Online Conversation About Israel," BuzzFeed News, September 20, 2018, www.buzzfeednews.com/article/ishmaeldaro/act-il-social-media-astroturfing-israel-palestine.

241 **exposed the names and pictures:** Behind Israel's Troll Army, tweet, April 26. 2018, https://twitter.com /AntiBDSApp/status/989529791282982912.

241 **"in excess of 500 students":** "Video Activism," Root Funding, https://rootfunding.com/causes/839141.

242 **sat on its board of directors:** Milstein LinkedIn page, www.linkedin.com/in/adammilstein/details/experience/.

242 **an organ of the Ministry of Strategic Affairs; In 2016, for example:** Aiden Pink, "U.S. Pro-Israel Groups Failed to Disclose Grants from Israeli Government," *Forward*, August 31, 2020, https://forward.com/israel /453286/us-pro-israel-groups-failed-to-disclose-grants-from-israeli-government/.

242 **"Is Linda Sarsour Really a Feminist?":** "Is Linda Sarsour Really a Feminist? Learn About What She Really Believes in This Video Produced by Video Activism Participant Emily Biffinger," October 10, 2017, https://m .facebook.com/story.php?story_fbid=1265958676846757&id=667743300001634&_rdr.

242 **passed to Hasbara through its cover organization:** Pink, "U.S. Pro-Israel Groups Failed to Disclose Grants from Israeli Government."

242 **"We are the elite":** Video Activism Facebook page, July 28, 2017, www.facebook.com/videoactivism/posts /check-out-this-awesome-video-emily-biffinger-made-to-sum-up-her-experiences-on-t/1265241746918450/.

242 **"slandering and delegitimizing Israel":** Jonathan Greenblatt, tweet, April 6, 2022, https://twitter.com /jgreenblattadl/status/1511889120955535363.

242 **"shocked me—and broke my heart":** Michael Arria, "GEICO Cancels Event with Linda Sarsour After Backlash from Pro-Israel Groups," Mondoweiss, https://mondoweiss.net/2022/04/geico-cancels-event-with-linda -sarsour-after-backlash-from-pro-israel-groups/.

242 **"This is disgraceful":** Yousef Munayyer, tweet, April 7, 2022, https://twitter.com/yousefmunayyer/status /1512225992223432704.

242 **paying tens of thousands of dollars:** Itamar Benzaquen and The Seventh Eye, "*Jerusalem Post* Took Government Money to Publish Anti-BDS Special," *+972 Magazine*, October 4, 2020, www.972mag.com/israeli -propaganda-bds-jerusalem-post/.

242 **special supplement:** "Unmasking BDS," *Jerusalem Post*, June 2019, https://cdn.the7eye.org.il/uploads/2020/09 /jerusalem-post-msa-june2019.pdf.

243 **"narrative in the world":** Uri Blau, "Inside the Clandestine World of Israel's 'BDS-Busting' Ministry," *Haaretz*, March 26, 2017, www.haaretz.com/israel-news/MAGAZINE-inside-the-clandestine-world-of-israels-bds -busting-ministry-1.5453212.

243 **In a major report:** "A Regime of Jewish Supremacy from the Jordan River to the Mediterranean Sea: This Is Apartheid," B'Tselem, January 12, 2021, www.btselem.org/publications/fulltext/202101_this_is_apartheid.

243 **"What acts like apartheid":** Yossi Sarid, "Yes, It Is Apartheid," *Haaretz*, April 25, 2008, www.haaretz.com/1.4973854.

243 **human rights groups are labeled terrorist organizations:** "Report of the Special Rapporteur on the Situation of Human Rights in the Palestinian Territories Occupied Since 1967," United Nations Human Rights Council, March 22, 2022, https://reliefweb.int/report/occupied-palestinian-territory /report-special-rapporteur-situation-human-rights-20.

244 **"extreme measure"; "It's simple, we were given evidence":** Hagar Shezaf, "European Diplomats: Israel Failed to Submit Sufficient Evidence Against Outlawed Palestinian NGOs," *Haaretz*, June 8, 2022, www.haaretz.com

/israel-news/2022-06-08/ty-article/.highlight/israel-failed-to-submit-sufficient-evidence-against-outlawed
-palestinian-ngos-sources-say/00000181-4222-df72-a5cb-c2ff61970000.

244 **"People here were told":** Shany Littman, "Labeled a Traitor, She Fled Israel. Now She Wants to Decon-
struct Zionism," *Haaretz*, January 28, 2022, www.haaretz.com/israel-news/.premium.HIGHLIGHT
.MAGAZINE-labeled-a-traitor-she-fled-israel-now-she-wants-to-deconstruct-zionism-1.10572707.

244 **"It's heart-rending":** Craig Timberg, "Pegasus Hack Reported on iPhones of Human Rights Watch Official," *Washington Post*, January 26, 2022, www.washingtonpost.com/technology/2022/01/26/pegasus
-hack-reported-iphones-human-rights-watch-official/.

244 **its own lengthy report:** "A Threshold Crossed: Israeli Authorities and the Crimes of Apartheid and Persecution," Human Rights Watch, April 27, 2021, www.hrw.org/report/2021/04/27/threshold-crossed/israeli
-authorities-and-crimes-apartheid-and-persecution.

245 **"We think that in the coming year":** Lazar Berman, "Lapid: 2022 Will See Intense Effort to Paint
Israel as Apartheid State," *Times of Israel*, January 3, 2022, www.timesofisrael.com/lapid-2022-will-see
-intense-effort-to-paint-israel-as-apartheid-state/.

Chapter 26: The Reckoning

246 **in February 2022, the esteemed human rights organization:** "Israel's Apartheid Against Palestinians: A Look
into Decades of Oppression and Domination," Amnesty International, February 2022, www.amnesty.org/en
/latest/campaigns/2022/02/israels-system-of-apartheid/.

246 **"the denial of nationality and citizenship to Palestinians":** In March 2022, Israel's Knesset passed the
so-called Citizenship Law, which bars the naturalization of Palestinians from the occupied territories
who are married to Israeli citizens, thereby forcing thousands of Palestinian families to either emigrate or
live apart. Such a law has existed for decades but was now made permanent. It was heavily criticized in the
Human Rights Watch report on apartheid. See Henriette Chacar, "Israel's Knesset Passes Law Barring Palestinian Spouses," Reuters, March 10, 2022, www.reuters.com/world/middle-east/israels-knesset-passes
-law-barring-palestinian-spouses-2022-03-10/.

246 **"COMMENT on this tweet":** Behind Israel's Troll Army, "Israel's app isn't happy about @amnesty's report
on Israeli apartheid. Below are some of the many 'missions' the app has launched on social media seeking to
discredit and slander Amnesty, with the hashtag #AmnestyLies," tweet, February 1, 2022, https://twitter.com
/AntiBDSApp/status/1488568955782549513. In 2022, Israel finally threw in the towel on its troll army and
deactivated Act.il. Michael Bueckert saw it coming. The vice president of Canadians for Justice and Peace in
the Middle East, he followed the app since it began five years earlier. "It was destined to fail," he said, "because
the problem facing Israel today is not the result of misinformation or lies, but of a growing awareness of the
realities of Israeli apartheid itself—and this is something that an app is incapable of solving."

247 **2021 survey by the Jewish Electoral Institute:** "National Jewish Survey," Jewish Electoral Institute, June 28–
July 1, 2021, www.jewishelectorateinstitute.org/wp-content/uploads/2021/07/JEI-National-Jewish-Survey
-Topline-Results-July-2021.pdf.

247 **"The results were shocking to many":** Arno Rosenfeld, "What If a Quarter of Jews Really Do Think
Israel Is a Genocidal, Apartheid State?," *Forward*, July 15, 2021, https://forward.com/news/473044/what
-if-a-quarter-of-jews-really-do-think-israel-is-a-genocidal-apartheid/. In February 2022, Harvard Law
School's International Human Rights Clinic released a formal study which found that Israel's treatment of
Palestinians in the West Bank amounted to the crime of apartheid. Entitled "Apartheid in the Occupied
West Bank: A Legal Analysis of Israel's Actions," it did not escape the wrath of Ambassador Gilad Erdan,
who branded its authors "anti-Semites." "Those who wrote the report on behalf of Harvard," he said, "decided
to delegitimize the Jewish state because of their antisemitic views." See "Apartheid in the Occupied West
Bank: A Legal Analysis of Israel's Actions," Harvard International Human Rights Clinic, February 28, 2002,
http://hrp.law.harvard.edu/wp-content/uploads/2022/03/IHRC-Addameer-Submission-to-HRC-COI
-Apartheid-in-WB.pdf. Re: Erdan, see Steve France, "Harvard Law School 'Apartheid' Report Leaves Israel's
Defenders Speechless," Mondoweiss, April 5, 2022, https://mondoweiss.net/2022/04/harvard-law-school
-apartheid-report-leaves-israels-defenders-speechless/?utm_source=mailpoet&utm_medium=email&utm
_campaign=daily-email-hgs-mailpoet.

247 **Pew poll was released in 2022:** "Modest Warming in U.S. Views on Israel and Palestinians; Young Americans' Attitudes Are as Favorable Toward the Palestinian People and Government as Toward Israel," Pew

Research Center, May 26, 2022, www.pewresearch.org/religion/2022/05/26/modest-warming-in-u-s-views -on-israel-and-palestinians/.

247 **"We are anti-Zionist"; "a HUGE step toward Judaism":** Allison Kaplan Sommer, " 'Anti-Zionist' Congregation Stirs Emotion in Chicago's Jewish Community," *Haaretz*, April 6, 2022, www.haaretz.com/us-news/.premium .HIGHLIGHT-anti-zionist-congregation-stirs-emotion-in-chicago-s-jewish-community-1.10723970?utm _source=mailchimp&utm_medium=content&utm_campaign=daily-brief&utm_content=d2efca2a5d.

247 **one of at least half a dozen congregations:** Arno Rosenfeld, "Chicago Synagogue Officially Designates Itself 'Anti-Zionist,' " *Forward*, March 31, 2022, https://forward.com/news/484838/in-likely-first-chicago -synagogue-officially-designates-itself-anti/.

247 **"The American Jewish rabbinate is turning pro-Palestinian":** "The American Left and Israel" [Professor Eric Alterman, in conversation with Dr. Yael Sternhell, Tel Aviv University, May 24, 2022], YouTube, https://youtu.be /yRGhaQ4ybqg.

248 **"The vast majority of ammunition used":** Daniel Boguslaw, "Israel Used U.S. Weapons to Destroy U.S. Assets and Aid Projects in Gaza," *The Intercept*, May 19, 2022, https://theintercept.com/2022/05/19/israel -gaza-us-weapons-aid-projects/?utm_medium=email&utm_source=The%20Intercept%20Newsletter.

248 **forty-two civilians were killed:** "Israeli Air Strike Survivor at HRC: Hold Perpetrators Accountable for 'Wiping Out My Family,' " Euromedmonitor, March 25, 2022, https://euromedmonitor.org/en/article/5000 /Israeli-air-strike-survivor-at-HRC:-Hold-perpetrators-accountable-for-%27wiping-out-my-family%27.

248 **"I remember that my mom":** Daniel Estrin, "22 Members of One Family Killed in Gaza," NPR, May 23, 2021, www.npr.org/2021/05/23/999563043/gaza-residents-access-damage-amid-ceasefire.

249 **"unprecedented":** "UN Moves Forward with Unprecedented Open-Ended Probe Against Israel," *Times of Israel*, December 25, 2021, www.timesofisrael.com/un-moves-forward-with-unprecedented-open -ended-probe-against-israel/#:~:text=The%20resolution%20called%20for%20the,with%20an%20 %E2%80%9Congoing%E2%80%9D%20mandate.

249 **established a special permanent "Commission of Inquiry":** "Human Rights Council Establishes International Commission of Inquiry to Investigate Violations in the Occupied Palestinian Territory, Including East Jerusalem, and in Israel," United Nations Human Rights Council, Office of the High Commissioner, May 27, 2021, www.ohchr.org/en/press-releases/2021/05/human-rights-council-establishes-international -commission-inquiry?LangID=E&NewsID=27119.

249 **The commission was approved overwhelmingly:** *Times of Israel*, "UN Moves Forward with Unprecedented Open-Ended Probe Against Israel."

249 **similar commission of inquiry:** "Report of the Commission of Inquiry on Human Rights in the Democratic People's Republic of Korea," United Nations Human Rights Council, February 17, 2014, www.ohchr.org/en /hr-bodies/hrc/co-idprk/reportofthe-commissionof-inquiry-dprk.

249 **"I conclude that the Israeli settlements":** "Israeli Settlements Amount to War Crime, UN Rights Official Says," *Haaretz*, July 9, 2021, www.haaretz.com/israel-news/israeli-settlements-amount-to-war-crime -un-rights-official-says-1.9985923.

249 **"I know my loss is too great":** Euromedmonitor, "Israeli Air Strike Survivor at HRC."

249 **Israel announced it would not cooperate:** Erin Brady, "Israel Again Rejects an International Call for Possible War Crimes Inquiry," *Newsweek*, February 17, 2022, www.newsweek.com/israel-again-rejects-international -call-possible-war-crimes-inquiry-1680371. See also Jonathan Lis, "Israel Won't Cooperate with UN War Crimes Probe, Accuses Chair of 'Anti-Israel Agenda,' " *Haaretz*, February 17, 2022, www.haaretz .com/israel-news/.premium-israel-won-t-cooperate-with-un-inquiry-into-alleged-war-crimes-in-may -gaza-war-1.10619238?utm_source=mailchimp&utm_medium=content&utm_campaign=daily-brief&utm _content=ba2948eeb3.

250 **"I am so sorry":** "Israel Rejects Palestinian Accusations of 'Apartheid' at UN Meeting," *Haaretz*, February 24, 2022, www.haaretz.com/israel-news/israel-rejects-palestinian-accusations-of-apartheid-at-un-meeting-1 .10631744?utm_source=mailchimp&utm_medium=content%E2%80%A6.

250 **In August 2022 he ordered the Israeli military:** Hagar Shezaf, Jack Khoury, "Israel Raids Outlawed Palestinian Rights Groups' Offices in West Bank," Associated Press, August 18, 2022, https://www.haaretz.com /israel-news/2022-08-18/ty-article/.highlight/israel-raids-outlawed-palestinian-rights-groups-offices-in -west-bank/00000182-af5a-d1f9-a59e-ff7a07050000.

250 **"All the questions were about my journalism"; imprisoned at least twenty-six Palestinian journalists:** Yuval Abraham, "Israel Charges Palestinian Journalists with Incitement—For Doing Their Jobs," *The Intercept*, April 5,

2022, https://theintercept.com/2022/04/05/israel-palestine-journalists-incitement/?utm_medium=email&utm_source=The%20Intercept%20Newsletter.

250 **"most likely"**: Ellen Francis, "Al Jazeera to Refer Killing of American Journalist to War Crimes Court," *Washington Post*, May 27, 2022, www.washingtonpost.com/world/2022/05/27/aljazeera-journalist-killing-israel-shireen-abu-akleh-icc/.

251 **"They were shooting directly at the journalists"**: Zeena Saifi et al., "'They Were Shooting Directly at the Journalists': New Evidence Suggests Shireen Abu Akieh was Killed in Targeted Attack by Israeli Forces," CNN, May 24, 2022, www.cnn.com/2022/05/24/middleeast/shireen-abu-akleh-jenin-killing-investigation-cmd-intl/index.html.

251 **"examined more than five dozen videos"**: Sarah Cahlan, Meg Kelly, and Steve Hendrix, "How Shireen Abu Aleh was Killed," *Washington Post*, June 12, 2022, www.washingtonpost.com/investigations/interactive/2022/shireen-abu-akleh-death/.

251 **signed a letter:** Congress of the United States to Secretary of State Antony Blinken and Director of the FBI Christopher Wray, May 19, 2022, https://static1.squarespace.com/static/5faecb8fb23a85370058aed8/t/6287a9e9065a8f5aecd18b8e/1653058025476/FINAL+LETTER+Shireen+Abu+Abkleh.pdf.

251 **"gunfire from IDF positions was likely responsible"**: Press release, "On the Killing of Shireen Abu Akleh," U.S. Department of State, July 4, 2022, www.state.gov/on-the-killing-of-shireen-abu-akleh/.

251 **"I've raised more money"**: "In the Heart of Motor City, Vice President Biden Addresses Yeshiva Beth Yehuda, November 13th, 2011," The White House, November 18, 2011, https://obamawhitehouse.archives.gov/blog/2011/11/18/heart-motor-city-vice-president-biden-addresses-yeshiva-beth-yehuda.

252 **"As recently as last year"**: "Remarks by the Vice President to the AIPAC Policy Conference," The White House, March 4, 2013, https://obamawhitehouse.archives.gov/the-press-office/2013/03/04/remarks-vice-president-aipac-policy-conference.

252 **described Biden to the Israeli press as a "Zionist"**: "'Joe Biden Loves Israel': Listen to U.S. Ambassador Thomas Nides," *Haaretz*, July 4, 2022, www.haaretz.com/israel-news/podcasts/2022-07-04/ty-article-podcast/joe-biden-loves-israel-listen-to-u-s-ambassador-thomas-nides/00000181-c998-d11e-a1e9-df9bfb810000.

252 **Israel's biggest eviction of Palestinians in decades:** Steve Hendrix and Shira Rubin, "Ahead of Biden visit, Israel Launches Biggest Eviction of Palestinians in Decades," Washington Post, May 22, 2022, https://www.washingtonpost.com/world/2022/05/22/israel-palestinian-masafer-yatta-biden/.

252 **And in August 2022:** "Israel Approves Construction of 1,400 Settlement Units in East Jerusalem," Middle East Monitor, August 5, 2022, https://www.middleeastmonitor.com/20220805-israel-approves-construction-of-1400-settlement-units-in-east-jerusalem/.

252 **"No one is ever held responsible"**: Gideon Levy, "Ripping Up the Evidence: How Israel Maintains Global Impunity," Middle East Eye, June 20, 2022, www.middleeasteye.net/opinion/israel-global-impunity-maintained-how.

252 **"The political system of entrenched rule"**: "Report of the Special Rapporteur on the Situation of Human Rights in the Palestinian Territories Occupied Since 1967," United Nations Human Rights Council, 28 February–1 April 2022, https://reliefweb.int/sites/reliefweb.int/files/resources/EN_78.pdf.

253 **"In recent months Israel has intensified"**: "Israel/OPT: Israel Is Committing Apartheid, Says UN Special Rapporteur," Amnesty International, March 23, 2022, www.amnesty.org/en/latest/news/2022/03/israel-opt-israel-is-committing-apartheid-says-un-special-rapporteur/. In the spring of 2022, Italian human rights lawyer Francesca Albanese was elected to a six-year term to replace Michael Lynk, whose term expired. Albanese is an expert on the Palestinian refugee crisis, the longest and most protracted refugee situation since World War II, and has published several books on the topic. She also spent ten years with the UN, including the UN's Relief Works Agency in Palestine. "I was horrified by what I saw," she said. "It was much more than my body could handle. At that time, I clearly saw and felt the apartheid policy. But at that time, I didn't have the tools to deal with [it] … The Israeli government and its supporters' repeated claim of exceptionalism have been overused, and it has led to abuses and double standard. It is about time for the international community to question and act upon it." See Daoud Kuttab, "Israel's Occupation Has Crossed the 'Red Line of Legality,' Says New UN Rapporteur," Al-Monitor, April 7, 2022, www.al-monitor.com/originals/2022/04/israels-occupation-has-crossed-red-line-legality-says-new-un-rapporteur.

253 **"I am a Jew. I am an Israeli citizen"**: Rafael Silver, "I Know Israel Practices Apartheid Because I Helped Enforce It," Mondoweiss, March 28, 2022, https://mondoweiss.net/2022/03/i-know-israel-practices-apartheid

-because-i-helped-enforce-it/?utm_source=mailpoet&utm_medium=email&utm_campaign=daily-email
-hgs-mailpoet.

253 **"We're a values-led company"**: "Ben & Jerry's Will End Sales of Our Ice Cream in the Occupied Palestinian
Territory," Ben & Jerry's press release, July 19, 2021, www.benjerry.com/about-us/media-center/opt-statement.

253 **"It is a rejection of Israeli policy"**: Bennett Cohen and Gerry Greenfield, "We're Ben and Jerry. Men of Ice
Cream, Men of Principle," *New York Times*, July 28, 2021, www.nytimes.com/2021/07/28/opinion/ben-and
-jerry-israel.html.

253 **"I'm against some of [Israel's] actions"**: Ben Samuels, "Ben & Jerry's vs. Ben & Jerry's: Israeli Licensee Sues
Ice Cream Giant," *Haaretz*, March 3, 2022, www.haaretz.com/israel-news/.premium-ben-jerry-s-vs-ben
-jerry-s-israeli-licensee-sues-ice-cream-giant-1.10650106?utm_source=mailchimp&utm_medium
=content&utm_campaign=haaretz-news&utm_content=e342d86e1b.

254 **"The boycott of Israel is a new sort of terrorism"**: Ravit Hecht, "Ben & Jerry's and 'Terrorism'? Lapid
and Herzog Are Embarrassing Israel," *Haaretz*, July 23, 2021, www.haaretz.com/opinion/.premium
-ben-jerry-s-and-terrorism-lapid-and-herzog-are-embarrassing-israel-1.10023414?utm_source=mailchimp
&utm_medium%E2%80%A6.

254 **"severe consequences"**: Dan Williams and Siddharth Cavale, "Israel PM Warns Unilever Boss over Ben &
Jerry's Boycott," Reuters, July 20, 2021, www.reuters.com/world/middle-east/israel-pm-warns-unilever-severe
-consequences-ben-jerrys-decision-2021-07-20/.

254 **"the dehumanization of the Jewish people"**: David Rosenberg, "Ben & Jerry's Could Be the First in a
Wave of BDS Victories," *Haaretz*, July 21, 2021, www.haaretz.com/israel-news/.premium-ben-jerry-s-the
-first-real-bds-success-1.10016419?utm_source=mailchimp&utm_medium=content&utm_campaign
=%25E2%2580%25A6.

254 **"Unilever's war on the Jewish state"**: Jacob Baime, "The Story of Unilever's War on the Jewish State," *Jerusalem
Post*, April 17, 2022, www.jpost.com/opinion/article-704422.

254 **"Following Erdan's call"**: Samuels, "Ben & Jerry's vs. Ben & Jerry's."

254 **"Over 30 states in the United States"**: Ben Samuels, "Israel Wants U.S. to Enforce Anti-BDS Laws Against Ben
& Jerry's. Will It Work?," *Haaretz*, July 20, 2021, www.haaretz.com/us-news/.premium.HIGHLIGHT-israel
-wants-u-s-to-enforce-anti-bds-laws-against-ben-jerry-s-will-it-work-1.10014760.

254 **"immediately block the sale"**: Ishaan Tharoor, "Israel's Spat with Ben & Jerry's Overshadows Its Spyware Scandal," *Washington Post*, July 26, 2021, www.washingtonpost.com/world/2021/07/26/israel-ben-jerrys-spyware/.

254 **a group of congressmen and senators**: Samuels, "Ben & Jerry's vs. Ben & Jerry's."

255 **"We find the IIPB's [Illinois Investment Policy Board] punitive actions"**: "Illinois Rabbis for Free Speech
on BDS," Mondoweiss, March 11, 2022, https://mondoweiss.net/2022/03/we-rabbis-and-cantors-object-to
-illinois-divesting-from-unilever-to-punish-ben-jerrys-settlement-boycott/?utm_source=mailpoet&utm
_medium=email&utm_campaign=daily-email-mailpoet.

255 **"The anti-Semites will not defeat us"**: Yair Lapid, tweet, June 29, 2022, https://twitter.com/yairlapid
/status/1542130728166690816.

255 **"We do not agree with it"**: " 'Inconsistent with Our Values': Ben & Jerry's Opposes Ice Cream's Return to
Israeli Settlements," *Haaretz*, June 30, 2022, www.haaretz.com/israel-news/2022-06-30/ty-article/.premium
/inconsistent-with-our-values-ben-jerrys-opposes-ice-creams-return-to-west-bank/00000181-b3fd-da42
-abdd-b7ffdd260000.

255 **on July 5, 2022, Ben & Jerry's took action**: Jonathan Stempel and Jessica DiNapoli, "Ben & Jerry's Sues
Parent Unilever to Block Sale of Israeli Business," Reuters, July 6, 2022, www.reuters.com/legal/litigation
/ben-jerrys-sues-parent-unilever-block-sale-israeli-business-2022-07-05/.

255 **General Mills**: AFSC, tweet, May 31, 2022, https://twitter.com/afsc_org/status/1531805362701189120.

255 **"Why We Must Boycott Pillsbury"**: Charlie Pillsbury, "Why We Must Boycott Pillsbury," *Minneapolis Star
Tribune*, April 28, 2021, www.startribune.com/why-we-must-boycott-pillsbury/600051334/.

255 **KLP, the enormous Norwegian pension fund**: David Rosenberg, "In the BDS Fight, 'D' is the Letter
Israel Should Really Worry About," *Haaretz*, October 31, 2021, www.haaretz.com/israel-news/.premium
.HIGHLIGHT-in-the-bds-fight-d-is-the-letter-israel-should-really-worry-about-1.10340922.

255 **New Zealand's $33 billion national pension fund**: Ali Abunimah, "New Zealand State Pension Fund Divests
from Israeli Banks," The Electronic Intifada, March 3, 2021, https://electronicintifada.net/blogs/ali-abunimah
/new-zealand-state-pension-fund-divests-israeli-banks.

256 **"As a board, we are proud"**: Crimson Editorial Board, "In Support of Boycott, Divest, Sanctions and a Free Palestine, Harvard University, April 29, 2022, www.thecrimson.com/article/2022/4/29/editorial-bds/.

256 **"I must admit I saw this coming"**: Dany Bahar, "I Attended Harvard and Have Researched BDS. The Crimson Editorial Is Not Just Noise," *Forward*, May 2, 2022, https://forward.com/opinion/501283/harvard-crimson-bds-editorial-is-not-just-noise/.

256 **"proudly and unapologetically"**: Student Government resolution, https://docs.google.com/document/d/1dm4Sv9QsbzgdyrOhpVABkEZuLskrkcWp9MgjiQRDsG4/edit

256 **"in the ongoing apartheid, genocide, and war crimes"**: "US: CUNY's Law Faculty Becomes Latest University Department to Endorse BDS," Middle East Eye, May 19, 2022, https://www.middleeasteye.net/news/us-universitys-law-faculty-endorse-bds-movement.

257 **successfully prevented $30,000 in student funding**: Samantha Sinutko and Samuel Yoo, "University Prohibits GradGov from Subsidizing Israel Trip," [Georgetown] *Hoya*, February 25, 2022, https://thehoya.com/university-prohibits-gradgov-from-subsidizing-israel-trip/.

257 **"apartheid colonial state"; "ethnic cleansing of more than 350+ Palestinian villages and towns"**: Ash Obel, "Australian Student Union Calls for Boycott of 'Apartheid Colonial State' Israel," *Times of Israel*, August 15, 2022, https://www.timesofisrael.com/australian-student-union-calls-for-boycott-of-apartheid-colonial-state-israel/.

257 **"solidarity with the Palestinian people"**: Lucy Knight, "Sally Rooney Turns Down an Israeli Translation on Political Grounds," *Guardian*, October 12, 2021, www.theguardian.com/books/2021/oct/12/sally-rooney-beautiful-world-where-are-you-israeli-publisher-hebrew.

257 **Earlier she signed**: "A Letter Against Apartheid," www.againstapartheid.com/.

257 **"de facto annexation"**: Ben Samuels, "Sally Rooney Explains Her Israel Boycott: 'BDS Is Anti-racist,'" *Haaretz*, October 12, 2021, www.haaretz.com/israel-news/sally-rooney-explains-her-israel-boycott-bds-is-anti-racist-1.10287709.

258 **"supports the Palestinian people"**: Hillel Italie, "Sally Rooney Holds Off on Hebrew Translation of New Novel," Associated Press, October 12, 2021, https://apnews.com/article/entertainment-business-israel-race-and-ethnicity-racial-injustice-7ff0e9604fa3b2215e2aa80b16babae4.

258 **seventy notable writers and publishers**: Asaf Shalev, "Sally Rooney's Boycott of Israeli Publishers Gets Backing of 70 Writers," *Haaretz*, November 23, 2001, www.haaretz.com/israel-news/sally-rooney-s-boycott-of-israeli-publishers-gets-backing-of-70-writers-1.10408509?utm_source=mailchimp&utm_medium=c%E2%80%A6.

258 **"This is hateful behavior at its finest"**: Behind Israel's Troll Army, "Israel's anti-BDS app is directing users to post comments on social media accusing novelist Sally Rooney of antisemitism for boycotting an Israeli publisher," tweet, October 12, 2021, https://twitter.com/AntiBDSApp/status/1447930898675081218.

258 **"Those who seek to protest"**: Manar Waheed and Brian Hauss, "The Latest Attack on Free Speech in the Israel-Palestine Debate," ACLU, June 5, 2018, www.aclu.org/blog/free-speech/rights-protesters/latest-attack-free-speech-israel-palestine-debate.

258 **"The AIPAC PAC is now the largest"**: Ron Kampeas, "AIPAC's New PAC Is Now the Country's Biggest Pro-Israel PAC, and Endorses 3/4 of Republicans Who Embraced Election Falsehoods," Jewish Telegraphic Agency, April 21, 2022, www.jta.org/2022/04/21/politics/aipacs-new-pac-is-now-the-countrys-biggest-pro-israel-pac-and-endorses-3-4-of-republicans-who-embraced-election-falsehoods.

258 **$1 million; another $8.5 million**: Ben Samuels, "Israeli-U.S. Billionaire Saban Donates $1 Million to AIPAC's Super PAC," *Haaretz*, April 13, 2022, www.haaretz.com/us-news/2022-04-13/ty-article/.highlight/israeli-u-s-billionaire-saban-donates-1-million-to-aipacs-super-pac/00000180-5bb2-d718-afd9-dfbea3a70000.

259 **took in nearly $16 million**: Eric Alterman, "Altercation: AIPAC Goes Full Trump," *American Prospect*, April 29, 2022, https://prospect.org/politics/altercation-aipac-goes-full-trump/.

259 **109 of the 147 Republicans**: Kampeas, "AIPAC's New PAC Is Now the Country's Biggest Pro-Israel PAC."

259 **"invoked the Nazis"**: Jacob Kornblun, "4 GOP Candidates in Key House Races Invokes the Holocaust Against Mask and Vaccine Mandates," *Forward*, October 1, 2021, https://forward.com/fast-forward/476208/several-gop-candidates-in-key-house-races-equate-covid-19-measures-vaccine/.

259 **In June 2022 he said he no longer supports AIPAC**: Jacob Henry, "De Blasio Says He No Longer Supports AIPAC and Wouldn't Accept Its Endorsement If Offered," *Forward*, June 27, 2022, https://forward.com/fast-forward/507800/de-blasio-says-he-no-longer-supports-aipac-and-wouldnt-accept-its-endorsement-if-offered/?utm_source=Iterable&utm_medium=email&utm_campaign=campaign_4548084.

259 "At the end of the day": Refaella Goichman, "This Anti-BDS Initiative Failed. So Israel Throws Another $30 Million at It," *Haaretz*, January 26, 2022, www.haaretz.com/israel-news/.premium.MAGAZINE-this-anti -bds-initiative-failed-so-israel-throws-another-100-million-nis-at-it-1.10565661?utm_source=%E2%80%A6.

BOOK SIX: THE MOLES

Chapter 27: The Asset

263 "Roger, hello from Jerusalem": See United States District Court for the District of Columbia, "In the Matter of the Search of Information Associated with the Google Account of [redacted]." Search and Seizure Warrant. Case 1:18-sc-01518, Assigned to Beryl A. Howell, May 4, 2018.

263 "References to some sort of Israeli involvement": Chemi Shalev, "No Stone Unturned in Trump-Netanyahu Mutual Intervention Alliance," *Haaretz*, April 30, 2020, www.haaretz.com/israel-news/2020-04-30/ty-article/.premium /no-stone-unturned-in-trump-netanyahu-mutual-intervention-alliance/0000017f-dfa8-d3a5-af7f-ffae23eb0000.

263 "change reality according to our client's wishes": Simona Weinglass, "Who Is Behind Israel's Archimedes Group, Banned by Facebook for Election Fakery?," *Times of Israel*, May 19, 2019, www.timesofisrael.com /who-is-behind-israels-archimedes-group-banned-by-facebook-for-election-fakery/.

264 In Nigeria in 2018: Isabel Debre, "Israeli Company Targeted Nigerian Election in Facebook Disinforma-tion Campaign," *Times of Israel*, May 18, 2019, www.timesofisrael.com/israeli-company-targeted-nigerian -election-in-facebook-disinformation-campaign/.

264 "Make Nigeria Worse Again": "Inauthentic Israeli Facebook Assets Target the World," DFR Lab, May 17, 2019, https://medium.com/dfrlab/inauthentic-israeli-facebook-assets-target-the-world-281ad7254264.

264 world in at least thirteen countries: "Inauthentic Israeli Facebook Assets Target the World."

264 three million people following their phony Facebook: "Removing Coordinated Inauthentic Behavior from Israel," Meta, May 16, 2019, https://about.fb.com/news/2019/05/removing-coordinated-inauthentic -behavior-from-israel/.

264 "The tactics employed by Archimedes Group": "Inauthentic Israeli Facebook Assets Target the World."

264 Elinadav Heymann: Sarah E. Needleman, "Facebook Bans Israeli Firm over Fake Political Activity," *Wall Street Journal*, May 16, 2019, www.wsj.com/articles/facebook-bans-israeli-firm-over-fake-political-activity -11558030115.

264 director of the NGO European Friends of Israel: Omer Kabir, "These Are the People Behind a Coordinated Fake News Campaign Targeting African Countries," Tech Calcalist, May 20, 2019, www.calcalistech.com /ctech/articles/0,7340,L-3762506,00.html.

264 including anti-boycott legislation: Elinadav Heymann, "EU Tantrums Hurt Palestinians More Than Israel," *Jerusalem Post*, November 1, 2014, www.jpost.com/opinion/eu-tantrums-hurt-palestinians-more -than-israel-380494.

264 "the closest thing this side of the Atlantic": Powerbase, "European Friends of Israel," https://powerbase.info /index.php/European_Friends_of_Israel#cite_note-4.

264 But in May 2019 Facebook caught on: "Removing Coordinated Inauthentic Behavior from Israel."

264 "is a drop in the bucket": Simona Weinglass, "Archimedes Group, Outed by Facebook for Election Fakery, Works from Holon Office," *Times of Israel*, May 23, 2019, www.timesofisrael.com/archimedes-group-outed -by-facebook-for-election-fakery-works-from-holon-office/.

264 "IDF intelligence likes to use avatars": Weinglass, "Archimedes Group, Outed by Facebook for Election Fakery."

265 "Her anti-semitic acts don't have a place in the congress: See https://twitter.com/AntiBDSApp/status /1095848960521093121?s=20; https://twitter.com/AntiBDSApp/status/1095853062672056320/photo/1; https:// twitter.com/AntiBDSApp/status/1095848960521093121/photo/1.

266 "There has probably never been a person": Raviv Drucker, "What About Netanyahu's Other Lawyer?," *Haaretz*, November 29, 2016, https://www.haaretz.com/opinion/2016-11-29/ty-article/.premium/what -about-netanyahus-other-lawyer/0000017f-e9d6-dc91-a17f-fddf12290000.

266 "The Mossad gritted its teeth": Amir Oren, "Did Milchan and Packer Push Netanyahu to Pick Their Buddy to Head the Mossad?," *Haaretz*, January 20, 2017, https://www.haaretz.com/israel-news/2017-01-20/ty -article-magazine/.premium/did-milchan-packer-push-pm-to-pick-their-buddy-as-mossad-chief/0000017f -e989-da9b-a1ff-edefcea30000.

266 a "discreet man": Judy Maltz, "A Discreet Man for Sensitive Missions: Meet Issac Milho, Netanyahu's Confidant Detained by Israeli Police," *Haaretz*, November 7, 2017, https://www.haaretz.com/israel-news/2017-11-07/ty-article/.premium/meet-isaac-molho-netanyahus-confidant-detained-by-israeli-police/0000017f-dc78-db5a-a57f-dc7a5b5d0000.

266 a heavily redacted 2018 FBI search warrant: Unless otherwise indicated, quotes and details are derived from United States District Court for the District of Columbia, "In the Matter of the Search of Information Associated with the Google Account of [redacted]." Search and Seizure Warrant. Case 1:18-sc-01518. Assigned to Beryl A. Howell, May 4, 2018.

267 "because he did not want his advisors to know they were talking"; "Stone called Trump all the time": U.S. Senate, "Report of the Select Committee on Intelligence on Russian Active Measures Campaigns and Interference in the 2016 U.S. Election, Volume 5: Counterintelligence Threats and Vulnerabilities," www.intelligence.senate.gov/sites/default/files/documents/report_volume5.pdf, pp. 230, 227. Hereafter cited as Senate Intelligence Committee Report.

267 "Donald Trump is a radical Zionist": Greg Richter, "Roger Stone on AIPAC Speech: 'This Is the New Trump,'" *Newsmax*, March 21, 2016, www.newsmax.com/newsmax-tv/roger-stone-new-trump-aipac-israel/2016/03/21/id/720207/.

268 "a virus"; "a worthless, dangerous Satanic religion"; "Islam is a peaceful religion as long as": Duncan Black, "MMFA Investigates: Who Is Jerome Corsi, Co-author of Swift Boat Vets Attack Book," Media Matters, August 8, 2004, www.mediamatters.org/jerome-corsi/mmfa-investigates-who-jerome-corsi-co-author-swift-boat-vets-attack-book.

268 Googling some very strange terms: *Ibid.*, Documents 29-11, 29-18.

268 "Hi Roger, I hope all is well" "Did You Talk To Trump This Morning?": United States District Court for the District of Columbia, Affidavit in Support of an Application for a Search Warrant, Case 1:19-mc-00029-CRC Document 29-7.

269 "have emails relating to Hillary Clinton": *Report on the Investigation into Russian Interference in the 2016 Presidential Election*, Special Counsel Robert S. Mueller, III, March 2019, Volume 1, p. 52, www.justice.gov/archives/sco/file/1373816/download.

269 Tzachi Hanegbi: His Wikipedia page: https://en.wikipedia.org/wiki/Tzachi_Hanegbi.

269 Married to an American from Florida: Gil Stern Hoffman, "Knesset Expected to Approve Hanegbi Appointment as Deputy Foreign Minister," *Jerusalem Post*, May 27, 2014, www.jpost.com/diplomacy-and-politics/knesset-expected-to-approve-hanegbi-appointment-as-deputy-foreign-minister-354558.

269 minister of intelligence supervising Mossad and Shin Bet: Government of Israel, The Knesset, Members of the 24th Knesset, Knesset Member Tzachi Hanegbi, https://main.knesset.gov.il/en/MK/APPS/mk/mk-personal-details/45.

270 dinner at Pierluigi..."What is your plan for the Palestinians?": Barak Ravid, "Netanyahu Offered Opposition Leader to Push Together for Regional Peace Initiative–and Then Backtracked," *Haaretz*, March 5, 2017, https://www.haaretz.com/israel-news/2017-03-05/ty-article-magazine/.premium/netanyahus-peace-plan-which-he-abandoned-for-political-survival/0000017f-dc83-db5a-a57f-dceb34da0000.

271 "I strongly urge your government to halt these demolitions": Letter, Senator Dianne Feinstein to Prime Minister Netanyahu, June 28, 2016, www.feinstein.senate.gov/public/_cache/files/f/0/f03cf404-73a6-4d55-96d5-9dd8c99f88db/DFA2B0BBF2FEDDD8CB0444481A7AF27D.2016-06-28-feinstein-letter.pdf.

272 "had actually removed the most serious danger": "Trump Says He Told Netanyahu the Iran Deal Is 'Horrible for Israel,'" Jewish Insider, October 7, 2016, https://jewishinsider.com/2016/10/trump-says-he-told-netanyahu-the-iran-deal-is-horrible-for-israel/.

272 "vastly disproportionate": Omar Shakir, "Jerusalem to Gaza, Israeli Authorities Reassert Domination," Human Rights Watch, April 30, 2021, www.hrw.org/news/2021/05/11/jerusalem-gaza-israeli-authorities-reassert-domination.

272 chairman of Fifth Dimension: Shuki Sadeh and Refaella Goichman, "How Putin's Blacklisted Oligarch Friend Is Linked to Key Israeli Political Players," *Haaretz*, January 3, 2019, www.haaretz.com/israel-news/.premium-how-putin-s-blacklisted-oligarch-friend-is-linked-to-key-israeli-political-players-1.6803271.

272 "Project Rome": "Psy Group, Project 'Rome': Campaign Intelligence & Influence Services Proposal," https://int.nyt.com/data/documenthelper/360-trump-project-rome/574d679d1ff58a30836c/optimized/full.pdf.

274 "Roger, how are you?": Senate Intelligence Committee Report, pp. 229–31.

275 "Russia, if you're listening": Morgan Winsor, Michael Edison Hayden, Candace Smith, and John Santucci, "Trump Says He Hopes Russian Hackers Find Clinton's Deleted Emails," ABC News, July 27, 2016, https://abcnews.go.com/Politics/donald-trump-spoken-vladimir-putin-urges-russian-president/story?id=40922483.

275 "Get to Assange": District Court for the District of Columbia, United States of America v. Roger Jason Stone, Jr., Indictment, p. 4, www.documentcloud.org/documents/5694704-Stone-Indictment-012419.html. Hereafter cited as Stone Indictment.

275 "good shit happening": Senate Intelligence Committee Report, p. 236.

276 "Word is friend in embassy": Stone Indictment, p. 4.

276 "[m]ore to come than anyone realizes": Senate Intelligence Committee Report, p. 239.

277 "Trust me, it will soon the [sic] Podesta's time in the barrel": Senate Intelligence Committee Report, p. 241.

277 Jared Kushner, met privately with Netanyahu: Barak Ravid, "Trump Tells Netanyahu: If Elected, U.S. Would Recognize Undivided Jerusalem as Israel's Capital," *Haaretz*, September 25, 2016, www.haaretz.com /israel-news/trump-to-pm-i-d-recognize-undivided-jerusalem-as-israeli-capital-1.5442362.

277 "recognize Jerusalem as the undivided capital of the State of Israel": Ravid, "Trump Tells Netanyahu."

277 Press accounts mentioned him: "Hanegbi Highlights Israeli Development Projects at Palestinian Donor Conference [in New York City]," BICOM, Britain Israel Communications and Research Center, September 21, 2016, www.bicom.org.uk/news/hanegbi-highlights-israeli-development-projects-palestinian-donor-conference/.

277 "naive and messianic": Raoul Wootliff, "Israeli Minister Slams 'Naïve and Messianic' Obama," *Times of Israel*, September 22, 2016, www.timesofisrael.com/israeli-minister-slams-naive-and-messianic-obama/.

277 "John Podesta was going to be in the barrel": Senate Intelligence Committee Report, p. 244.

278 "more releases of damaging information": Senate Intelligence Committee Report, p. 244.

278 "I suggested Stone could use me as an excuse": Jerome R. Corsi, *Silent No More: How I Became a Political Prisoner of Mueller's "Witch Hunt"* (Franklin, TN: Post Hill Press, 2019), p. 78.

278 "a nine page background memorandum on John Podesta": Corsi, *Silent No More*.

279 "Together, we will stand up to enemies like Iran": "Video: Trump Touts Link to Jewish Values in Video Shown at Rally in Jerusalem," *J. The Jewish News of Northern California*, October 28, 2016, https://jweekly .com/2016/10/28/video-trump-touts-link-to-jewish-values-in-video-shown-at-rally-in-jerusale/.

279 "The Biblical Restaurant": Website of The Harp of David restaurant, http://www.harpofdavid.co.il/.

279 "Donald Trump Says Israel Will Be Destroyed": "Donald Trump Says Israel Will Be Destroyed Unless He Is Elected," Jewish Telegraph Agency, September 6, 2016, www.jta.org/2016/09/06/politics/donald-trump -says-israel-will-be-destroyed-unless-he-is-elected.

279 the "seven spices" of ancient Canaan: GoJerusalem.com, www.gojerusalem.com/items/709/Davids-Harp -Restaurant/.

280 Friedman was chief fund-raiser for a yeshiva: Isabel Kershner and Sheryl Gay Stolberg, "David Friedman, Choice for Envoy to Israel, Is Hostile to Two-State Efforts," *New York Times*, December 16, 2016, www.nytimes .com/2016/12/16/world/middleeast/david-friedman-us-ambassador-israel.html.

280 accused President Obama of "blatant anti-Semitism"; "kapos": Marsha B. Cohen, "New Senior Adviser to US Ambassador to Israel: Ideology Trumps Experience," Lobe Log, August 28, 2017, https://lobelog.com /new-senior-adviser-to-us-ambassador-to-us-israel-ideology-trumps-experience/.

280 "He has made clear that he will appeal": Kershner and Stolberg, "David Friedman, Choice for Envoy to Israel, Is Hostile to Two-State Efforts."

280 daily coordination with the Trump campaign: Andrew Tobin, "Trump Backers Launch Campaign in the West Bank," *J The Jewish News of Northern California*, September 9, 2016, https://jweekly.com/2016/09/09 /trump-backers-launch-campaign-in-the-west-bank/.

280 massive get-out-the-vote campaign: Andrew Tobin, "Donald Trump Supporters Launch Push for American 'Swing State' Votes in Israel," Jewish Telegraph Agency, August 5, 2016, www.jta.org/2016/08/05/politics /donald-trump-supporters-launch-push-for-american-swing-state-votes-in-israel.

280 "Trump: Make Israel Great Again": Jonathan Marcus, "Trump and the Middle East: An Impossible Disengagement," BBC News, December 30, 2016, www.bbc.com/news/world-us-canada-38407226.

280 illegal West Bank settlement of Karnei Shomron: Andrew Tobin, "Trump Backers Launch Campaign in the West Bank," *J. The Jewish News of Northern California*, September 9, 2016, https://jweekly.com/2016/09/09 /trump-backers-launch-campaign-in-the-west-bank/.

280 James A. Baker: Raphael Ahern, "How Israel's Leading Republic Learned to Love The Donald," *Times of Israel*, August 11, 2016, www.timesofisrael.com/how-israels-leading-republican-learned-to-love-the-donald/.

280 Sarah Silverman: "Head of GOP in Israel Says 'Self-Hating Jew' Sarah Silverman 'Needs a Muzzle,'" *Jewish Journal*, March 26, 2017, https://jewishjournal.com/culture/arts/hollywood/217137/head-gop-israel-says-self -hating-jew-sarah-silverman-needs-muzzle/.

281 **"ultimate goal is to recruit"**: Judy Maltz, "Trump Campaign in Israel Enlists 'Thousands' of Right-Wingers to Get Out the Vote," *Haaretz*, September 19, 2016, www.haaretz.com/israel-news/2016-09-19/ty-article/.premium /trump-campaign-in-israel-enlists-right-wingers-to-win-votes/0000017f-e87c-da9b-a1ff-ec7f60120000.

281 **Tzvika Brot:** "Trump Launches Campaign in Israel: 'Israelis Can Win Elections,'" Walla News (in Hebrew), August 3, 2016, https://news.walla.co.il/item/2984929.

281 **"A foreign national shall not direct"**: See 11 CFR § 110.20—Prohibition on contributions, donations, expenditures, independent expenditures, and disbursements by foreign nationals (52 U.S.C. 30121, 36 U.S.C. 510). See also "'Things of Value' and the Foreign Contribution Ban, Congressional Research Service, October 28, 2019, https://sgp.fas.org/crs/misc/LSB10358.pdf.

281 **with close ties to Prime Minister Netanyahu:** Judy Maltz, "The Political Ties of the Trump Campaign Team in Israel," *Haaretz*, August 29, 2016, www.haaretz.com/world-news/.premium-the-political-ties-of-the -trump-campaign-team-in-israel-1.5430494.

281 **Netanyahu once offered him the prestigious job:** Maltz, "The Political Ties of the Trump Campaign Team in Israel."

281 **she had previously served as spokesperson:** Maltz, "The Political Ties of the Trump Campaign Team in Israel."

281 **even admitted on Army Radio in Israel:** Chaim Levinson, "Israeli GOP Group Accepts Donations from Non-Americans; Experts Question Legality," *Haaretz*, October 27, 2016, www.haaretz.com/world-news /experts-question-legality-of-non-u-s-donations-to-israeli-gop-group-1.5454085.

281 **"advised the Israeli team during the campaign"**: Nechama Duek, "The Israelis Who Helped Elect Trump," Ynetnews, November 13, 2016, www.ynetnews.com/articles/0,7340,L-4878263,00.html.

282 **It is "illegal for any non-U.S. citizen to make a contribution"**: Levinson, "Israeli GOP Group Accepts Donations from Non-Americans."

282 **They even announced publicly:** Levinson, "Israeli GOP Group Accepts Donations from Non-Americans."

282 **Nor did the group's website contain:** Levinson, "Israeli GOP Group Accepts Donations from Non-Americans."

282 **In the United States, however, donors are required:** Levinson, "Israeli GOP Group Accepts Donations from Non-Americans."

282 **"To us, Israel is the 51st state"**: Levinson, "Israeli GOP Group Accepts Donations from Non-Americans."

282 **"Israel is a very red state"**: Raphael Ahren, "Is the Fifty-First State Red or Blue?," *Haaretz*, July 25, 2008, https:// web.archive.org/web/20160513170847/http:/www.haaretz.com/is-the-fifty-first-state-red-or-blue-1.250377.

282 **"Israeli intervention in US elections vastly overwhelms"**: Andrew Buncombe, "Israeli Intervention in US Elections 'Vastly Overwhelms' Anything Russia Has Done," *Independent*, July 30, 2018, www.independent.co .uk/news/world/americas/us-politics/israel-us-elections-intervention-russia-noam-chomsky-donald-trump -a8470481.html.

283 **"[Seventy] million Americans are sobbing tonight"**: Marc Zell, tweet, November 7, 2020, https://twitter.com /GOPIsrael/status/1325238174587752451?ref_src=twsrc%5Etfw

283 **In March 2022, he flew to Israel:** Allison Kaplan Sommer, "Israel's Far Right, Shunned by AIPAC, Is Embraced by Mike Pence," *Haaretz*, March 10, 2022, www.haaretz.com/israel-news/.premium-israel-s-far -right-shunned-by-aipac-is-embraced-by-mike-pence-1.10666569.

283 **Kach movement:** U.S. Department of State, "Country Reports on Terrorism 2004," April 2005, https://2009 -2017.state.gov/documents/organization/45313.pdf. In May 2022, President Biden dropped Kahane Chai (formerly Kach) from its list of "foreign terrorist organizations," calling the group inactive and the move routine. But William Lafi Youmans, an associate professor at George Washington University, saw it instead as the United States "continuing its light approach towards right-wing violence against Palestinians." "Kach and Kahane Chai splintered into various groups and political parties that continue to espouse, inspire and carry out acts of violence against Palestinian civilians." See "US Removes Ultranationalist Israeli Group from 'Terror' List," Al Jazeera, May 20, 2022, www.aljazeera.com/news/2022/5/20/us-removes -ultranationalist-israeli-group-from-terror-list.

283 **was banned from running for the Knesset:** Marcy Oster, "Israel's Supreme Court Bars 2 Far-Right Candidates from Running for Knesset," Jewish Telegraph Agency, August 26, 2019, www.jta.org/quick-reads /israels-supreme-court-bars-2-far-right-candidates-from-running-for-knesset.

283 **"like a foreign leader coming to the US"**: Matt Duss, tweet, March 9, 2022,https://twitter.com /mattduss/status/1501549447867768834?ref_src=twsrc%5Etfw%7Ctwcamp%5Etweetembed%7Ctwterm %5E1501549447867768834%7Ctwgr%5E%7Ctwcon%5Es1_&ref_url=https%3A%2F%2Fwww.newsweek .com%2Fpence-accused-pushing-jewish-supremacy-over-palestinians-israel-trip-1686578.

283 **"empowering Jewish Supremacy"**: Benzion Sanders, tweet, March 9, 2022, https://twitter.com/BenzionSanders /status/1501538018074763272?ref_src=twsrc%5Etfw%7Ctwcamp%5Etweetembed%7Ctwterm%5E1501538 018074763272%7Ctwgr%5E%7Ctwcon%5Es1_&ref_url=https%3A%2F%2Fwww.newsweek.com%2Fpence -accused-pushing-jewish-supremacy-over-palestinians-israel-trip-1686578.

Chapter 28: The Agent

284 **$33,400-a-person fund-raiser**: Melissa Chan, "George Clooney Admits Money He Raised for Hillary Clinton Is 'Obscene,' " *Time*, April 17, 2016, https://time.com/4297055/george-clooney-obscene-hillary-clinton/.

284 **Jeffrey Katzenberg and Steven Spielberg; Haim Saban**: Annie Karni and Kenneth P. Vogel, "Clinton Asks for $353K to Sit with the Clooneys," *Politico*, March 24, 2016, www.politico.com/story/2016/03 /hillary-clinton-george-clooney-fundraiser-221207.

285 *Model Turned Superstar*: Dave McNary, "Mance Media Launching 'Model Turned Superstar' on 4KUniverse Channel," Yahoo News, April 27, 2016, https://uk.news.yahoo.com/celebrity/mance-media-launching-model -turned-superstar-4kuniverse-channel-151324798.html.

285 **a clandestine agent working for a foreign spy**: United States District Court for the District of Columbia, United States of America v. Ahmad "Andy" Khawaja, George Nader, et al., Indictment, May 7, 2019, Case 1:19-cr-374, https://cdn.cnn.com/cnn/2019/images/12/04/khawaja.et.al_indictment_unsealed.12.3.19.pdf.

285 **The spy was George Nader**: United States of America v. Ahmad "Andy" Khawaja, George Nader, et al.

285 **"the most powerful leader in the Arab world"**: David D. Kirkpatrick, "The Most Powerful Arab Ruler Isn't M.B.S. It's M.B.Z.," *New York Times*, June 2, 2019, www.nytimes.com/2019/06/02/world/middleeast/crown -prince-mohammed-bin-zayed.html.

285 **"He may be the richest man in the world"**: Kirkpatrick, "The Most Powerful Arab Ruler Isn't M.B.S. It's M.B.Z."

285 **Born in 1959 in the ancient**: Sania Akkad and Ian Cobain, "George Nader: How a Convicted Pedophile Became Key to an Emirati Hook-up with Trump," Middle East Eye, July 5, 2019, www.middleeasteye.net /big-story/george-nader-how-convicted-paedophile-became-key-emirati-hook-trump.

286 **"George Nader did some very discreet work"**: Rosalind S. Helderman, Rachel Weiner, and Devlin Barrett, "Complex Portrait of Special Counsel Cooperator Emerges in Newly Unsealed Child Pornography Case," *Washington Post*, March 16, 2018, www.washingtonpost.com/politics/complex-portrait-of-special-counsel -cooperator-emerges-in-newly-unsealed-child-pornography-case/2018/03/16/d91541b0-2939-11e8-874b -d517e912f125_story.html.

286 **He was also assisting the crown prince**: David Hearst, "Exclusive: The Secret Yacht Summit That Realigned the Middle East," Middle East Eye, December 27, 2018, www.middleeasteye.net/news/exclusive -secret-yacht-summit-realigned-middle-east.

286 **credit card processor for fraudsters**: "Allied Wallet Settles with FTC over Fraudulent Payment Allegations," PYMNTS.com, May 21, 2019, www.pymnts.com/legal/2019/allied-wallet-settlement-ftc-fraud-allegations/.

287 **home of Hollywood film director Rob Reiner**: Ted Johnson, "Rob Reiner Hosts Hillary Clinton at Los Ange-les Fundraiser," *Variety*, November 5, 2015, https://variety.com/2015/biz/news/hillary-clinton-rob-reiner -fundraiser-1201634455/.

287 **had his picture taken with a smiling, toothy Hillary Clinton**: "CEO of Allied Wallet, Andy Khawaja, Meets with Hillary Clinton," Alliedwallet.com, undated, www.alliedwallet.com/blog/press-releases/ceo-allied-wallet -andy-khawaja-meets-hillary-clinton/.

287 **Nader began secretly pumping millions of illegal dollars**: Unless otherwise indicated, details of Khawaja and Nader's espionage/influence operation are contained in United States District Court for the District of Colum-bia, United States of America v. Ahmad "Andy" Khawaja, George Nader, et al., Indictment, May 7, 2019, Case 1:19-cr-374, https://cdn.cnn.com/cnn/2019/images/12/04/khawaja.et.al_indictment_unsealed.12.3.19.pdf.

288 **more than $8,000 in dirty cash**: Open Secrets, "Donor Lookup," donations of Ahmad Khawaja, Allied Wallet, www.opensecrets.org/donor-lookup/results?name=ahmad+Khawaja&page=1.

289 **Grande Belleza (Big Beauty)**: "15 Million Beverly Hills Mansion Boasting Endless Views Hits the Market," Cision, May 14, 2022, www.prweb.com/releases/15_million_beverly_hills_mansion_boasting_endless_views _hits_the_market/prweb16559282.htm. See video at: https://vimeo.com/356789219.

289 **It was also all paid for with Khawaja's dirty money**: See United States District Court for the Central Dis-trict of California, Federal Trade Commission vs. Allied Wallet, Inc, et al., Case 2:19-cv-04355, www.ftc.gov /system/files/documents/cases/alliedwallet_proposed_stip_final_ord_aw_and_khawaja_5-21-19.pdf.

291 **"We have created a little Frankenstein"**: Kirkpatrick, "The Most Powerful Arab Ruler Isn't M.B.S. It's M.B.Z."

292 **He appointed him to the U.S. Commission on International Religious Freedom:** "Andy Khawaja Appointed to USCIRF," United States Commission on International Religious Freedom, June 25, 2018, www.uscirf.gov /news-room/releases-statements/andy-khawaja-appointed-uscirf.

292 **sexually explicit videos featuring boys as young as two:** See United States District Court for the Eastern District of Virginia, United States of America v. George Aref Nader, Criminal Complaint, Under Seal, January 17, 2018, Case 1:18-mj-196, www.courthousenews.com/wp-content/uploads/2019/06/Nader-Complaint.pdf.

292 **"sexual abuse and impairing morals"; Among the cases:** See United States District Court for the Eastern District of Virginia, United States of America v. George Aref Nader, Transcript of Detention Hearing, June 7, 2019, https://ecf.vaed.uscourts.gov/doc1/18919771941.

293 **And according to U.S. prosecutors:** Details of sexual charges are contained in the above court documents.

293 **Finally, on November 7, 2019:** See United States District Court for the District of Columbia, United States of America v. Ahmad "Andy" Khawaja, George Nader, et al., Indictment, May 7, 2019, Case 1:19-cr-374, https:// cdn.cnn.com/cnn/2019/images/12/04/khawaja.et.al_indictment_unsealed.12.3.19.pdf.

293 **"The amount paid to the Prosecutor's Office's account is not disclosed":** Dainius Sinkevičius, "Prosecutors Release US Billionaire Detained in Lithuania for Record Bail," Delfi, October 20, 2020 (in Lithuanian), www.delfi.lt/news/daily/lithuania/uz-rekordinio-dydzio-uzstata-prokurorai-i-laisve-isleido-lietuvoje -sulaikyta-jav-milijardieriu.d?id=85619127.

294 **a $150 million payment processing scheme:** "Four Charged in Alleged $150 Million Payment Process- ing Scheme," U.S. Department of Justice, August 26, 2021, www.justice.gov/opa/pr/four-charged-alleged -150-million-payment-processing-scheme.

294 **$1.14 billion to Trump's $712 million:** "Election 2016, Money Raised as of December 31," *Washington Post*, October 24, 2016, www.washingtonpost.com/politics/how-mega-donors-helped-raise-1-billion-for-hillary -clinton/2016/10/22/a92a0ee2-9603-11e6-bb29-bf2701dbe0a3_story.html.

BOOK SEVEN: THE LIQUIDATORS

Chapter 29: The Crash

297 **Sun Kailiang:** "Sun Kailiang," FBI Most Wanted List, www.fbi.gov/wanted/cyber/sun-kailiang.

297 **Wang Dong; Gu Chunhui:** Unless otherwise indicated, details of cyber activities of Unit 61398 are con- tained in United States District Court for the Western District of Pennsylvania, United States of American v. Wang Dong, Sun Kailiang, Wen Xinyu, Huang Zhenyu, Gu Chunhui, Indictment, May 1, 2014, Criminal Case No. 14-118, www.justice.gov/iso/opa/resources/5122014519132358461949.pdf. See also "U.S. Charges Five Chinese Military Hackers for Cyber Espionage Against U.S. Corporations and a Labor Organization for Commercial Advantage," Department of Justice, May 19, 2014.

298 **Chinese Black Chamber:** Herbert O. Yardley, *The Chinese Black Chamber: An Adventure in Espionage* (Bos- ton: Houghton Mifflin, 1983).

299 **Among the cables are SEA-ME-WE3:** See "Submarine Cable Map, Chongming, China," TeleGeography, www .submarinecablemap.com/landing-point/chongming-china. See also "Chongming Cable Landing Station," Submarine Cable Networks, www.transitchina.com/en/stations/asia/china/chongming.

299 **a secret facility on Chongming Island:** James T. Areddy, "Birds Above, Data Below: Where the U.S. Internet Meets China's," *Wall Street Journal*, July 7, 2014, www.wsj.com/articles/BL-CJB-23018.

300 **other side of Shanghai, in Nanhui:** "Nanhui Cable Landing Station (FLAG)," Submarine Cable Networks, www.transitchina.com/en/stations/asia/china/nanhui-flag.

300 **TAREX, the Target Exploitation Program:** Secret/SI/NOFORN, "Classification Guide for the NSA/CSS Tar- get Exploitation (TAREX) Program," National Security Agency, February 6, 2012, www.aclu.org/sites/default /files/field_document/Target%20Exploitation%20Classification%20Guide.pdf.

301 **stolen over twenty-one million sensitive records:** Kim Zetter, "The Massive OPM Hack Actually Hit 21 Mil- lion People," *Wired*, July 9, 2015, www.wired.com/2015/07/massive-opm-hack-actually-affected-25-million/.

301 **"Kilo Romeo 919":** Shane Osborn with Malcolm McConnell, *Born to Fly: The Untold Story of the Downed American Reconnaissance Plane* (New York: Broadway Books, 2001), p. 15.

302 **"Wind 010 at eight [knots]":** Osborn and McConnell, *Born to Fly*, p. 16.

303 "It looks like good weather en route": Osborn and McConnell, *Born to Fly*, p. 8.

303 "the most important topic": Thomas E. Ricks, "Anger over Flights Grew in Past Year," *Washington Post*, April 7, 2001, www.washingtonpost.com/archive/politics/2001/04/07/anger-over-flights-grew-in-past-year /016178cc-aa44-4017-8d01-c8a8a7a91d70/.

303 "We seem to be conducting something": James Bamford, "The Dangers of Spy Planes," *New York Times*, April 5, 2001, www.nytimes.com/2001/04/05/opinion/the-dangers-of-spy-planes.html.

304 Since December there had been forty-four interceptions: Edward Walsh and William Claiborne, "U.S. Faults China on Crash Account," *Washington Post*, April 14, 2001, www.washingtonpost.com/archive/politics /2001/04/14/us-faults-china-on-crash-account/1bcd6ec5-c29d-4758-9993-b0110e47539a/.

305 "Hey, he's right off our wing": "Dangerous Straits," *Frontline*, PBS, Autumn 2001, www.pbs.org/wgbh/pages /frontline/shows/china/interviews/osborn.html.

305 "He's getting really close!": Osborne and McConnell, *Born to Fly*, p. 109–10.

305 "This isn't good": "Dangerous Straits," *Frontline*.

305 "I was pretty certain we were dead at that point": "Dangerous Straits," *Frontline*.

306 "I was scared": Transcript, *Larry King Weekend*, CNN, April 14, 2001. http://edition.cnn.com /TRANSCRIPTS/0104/14/lklw.00.html.

306 As the senior evaluator (SEVAL): Osborne and McConnell, *Born to Fly*, p. 6.

306 "Your plane's vertical tail has been struck off!": Bill Gertz, "The Last Flight of Wang Wei," *Air Force Magazine*, July 1, 2001, www.airforcemag.com/article/0701china/.

306 "Prepare to bail out!"; "Mayday! Mayday!": Osborne and McConnell, *Born to Fly*, p. 116.

306 "GOING DOWN": Top Secret/COMINT/NOFORN/X1, "Cryptologic Damage Assessment and Incident Review, Final Report," National Security Agency, July 2001, https://s3.documentcloud.org/documents /3546567/10th-Anniversary-Edition-EP-3-Damage-Assessment.pdf. Hereafter cited as NSA Damage Assessment.

307 ZIRCON chat: NSA Damage Assessment.

307 "Activate the emergency destruction plan": Osborne and McConnell, *Born to Fly*, p. 120.

308 "The aircrew's overall performance": NSA Damage Assessment.

308 "isolated himself from knowledge of actions taking place": NSA Damage Assessment.

309 "On deck at Lingshui": NSA Damage Assessment.

309 "They want us to hold on a few minutes": Osborne and McConnell, *Born to Fly*, p. 137.

309 "Can I use your phone to make a call?": Osborne and McConnell, *Born to Fly*, p. 139.

310 "Everything's good back there": Osborne and McConnell, *Born to Fly*, p. 141.

310 "Notwithstanding the chaotic circumstances": NSA Damage Assessment.

310 "No specific guidance existed": NSA Damage Assessment.

310 "The most potentially damaging compromised items": NSA Damage Assessment.

312 "His death was an accident"; "The 2001 crash taught China a lesson": Minnie Chan, "How a Mid-air Collision Near Hainan 18 Years Ago Spurred China's Military Modernisation," *South China Morning Post*, April 2, 2019, www.scmp.com/news/china/diplomacy/article/3004383/how-mid-air-collision-near-hainan-18-years -ago-spurred-chinas?module=inline&pgtype=article.

Chapter 30: The Rendezvous

313 "These are people in positions that place them in contact": Eric Schmitt, "Security Move Means 500 at FBI Face Lie Detector," *New York Times*, March 25, 2001, www.nytimes.com/2001/03/25/us/security-move -means-500-at-fbi-face-lie-detector.html.

313 "possibly the worst intelligence disaster in U.S. history": "A Review of the FBI's Performance in Deterring, Detecting, and Investigating the Espionage Activities of Robert Philip Hanssen," Department of Justice, Office of the Inspector General, August 14, 2003, https://irp.fas.org/agency/doj/oig/hanssen.html.

313 "Five years ago, everyone looked down on you": Ron Gluckman, "New Adventure Capitalists," Gluckman .com, www.gluckman.com/HKHandover02.htm.

314 "Hong Kong is a place": Gary Cheung and Klaudia Lee, "HK a Hotbed of Espionage, Says Mainland Official," *South China Morning Post*, December 20, 2003, www.scmp.com/article/438796/hk-hotbed -espionage-says-mainland-official.

314 Alexander Yuk Ching Ma and his older brother David: Unless otherwise indicated, details about Alexander and David Ma are from United States District Court for the District of Hawaii, United States of America v.

Alexander Yuk Ching Ma, Criminal Complaint; and the Affidavit of FBI Special Agent Chris Jensen, August 13, 2020, Case 20-001016 DKW-RT.

316 **Minister of State Security Xu Yongyue:** China Vitae, www.chinavitae.com/biography/311.

317 **"I'm not saying all of them are spies":** Jia-Rui Chong, "New Spy Case Prompts Skepticism," *Los Angeles Times*, November 17, 2005, www.latimes.com/archives/la-xpm-2005-nov-17-me-chinese17-story.html.

318 **Lee had become frustrated:** Scott Shane, "Arrested Former C.I.A. Officer Had Ties to Chinese Spies, Ex-colleague Says," *New York Times*, January 18, 2018, www.nytimes.com/2018/01/18/world/asia/jerry-lee-cia-china-informant-network-ministry-of-state-security.html.

318 **"He was quite critical about the organization":** Josh Meyer, "Mystery of Suspected China-CIA Spy Draws Lawmaker Scrutiny," *Politico*, February 5, 2018, www.politico.com/story/2018/02/05/china-cia-spy-congress-387133.

318 **Japan Tobacco International:** See www.jti.com/asia/hong-kong.

318 **under a veteran CIA officer, David Reynolds:** Raquel Carvalho, "Arrested Ex-CIA Agent Went from Spy Agency to Investigating Counterfeit Cigarettes in Hong Kong, Sources Say," *South China Morning Post*, January 18, 2018, www.scmp.com/news/hong-kong/law-crime/article/2129582/arrested-ex-cia-agent-quit-spy-agency-investigate.

318 **"Several of the shipments of counterfeits":** Raquel Carvalho, "Exclusive: Arrested Ex-CIA Agent Was Fired from Tobacco Firm After Suspicions He Was Spying for China," *South China Morning Post*, January 19, 2018, www.scmp.com/news/hong-kong/law-crime/article/2129593/smoke-and-mirrors-details-revealed-arrested-ex-cia-spys.

319 **a Chinese official warned the company:** Shane, "Arrested Former C.I.A. Officer Had Ties to Chinese Spies."

319 **"I certainly reported it to the appropriate authorities":** Meyer, "Mystery of Suspected China-CIA Spy Draws Lawmaker Scrutiny."

319 **FTM International:** See Hong Kong Company Enquiry Network for FTM International, Limited, www-hongkongcompanylookup-com.

319 **After investing nearly $400,000:** Carvalho, "Arrested Ex-CIA Agent Went from Spy Agency to Investigating Counterfeit Cigarettes in Hong Kong, Sources Say."

320 **he was arrested as soon as he landed:** Adam Goldman, "Ex-C.I.A. Officer Suspected of Compromising Chinese Informants Is Arrested," *New York Times*, January 16, 2018, www.nytimes.com/2018/01/16/us/politics/cia-china-mole-arrest-jerry-chun-shing-lee.html.

320 **$2,000; "small token"; "the motherland":** U.S. v. Alexander Yuk Ching Ma, Affidavit of FBI Special Agent Chris Jensen, August 13, 2020.

320 **"In the case of the individuals":** U.S. v. Alexander Yuk Ching Ma, Government's Memorandum of Law in Support of Motion to Detain Defendant Without Bail, August 19, 2020.

321 **"You could tell the Chinese weren't guessing"; "shellshocked"; fat wads of cash:** Zach Dorfman, "Botched CIA Communications System Helped Blow Cover of Chinese Agents," *Foreign Policy*, August 15, 2018, https://foreignpolicy.com/2018/08/15/botched-cia-communications-system-helped-blow-cover-chinese-agents-intelligence/.

321 **"Each year, we gather in this sacred place":** CIA, "CIA Honors Fallen Officers in Annual Memorial," May 23, 2022.

BOOK EIGHT: THE ASSASSINS

Chapter 31: The Aquarium

325 **Unit 29155:** It is somewhat similar to the assassination squads assigned to the CIA's Special Activities Center. Set up under the Trump administration, the center deploys small teams of commandos—dubbed "paramilitary operations officers" and "specialized skills officers"—to kill people on various target lists. "They are getting people on targeting lists," said one knowledgeable source. "Small teams are locating and killing bad guys. That's what we're doing." It supplements the agency's worldwide drone assassination program. The SAC was previously known as the Special Activities Division, which engaged in torture, kidnapping, secret detention, and the destabilization of foreign governments, including that of Yugoslavia when Montenegro was one of its republics. For details on the SAC, see Aram Roston, "Trump's CIA Has Set Up Teams to Kill Terrorists," BuzzFeed News, March 16, 2018, www.buzzfeednews.com/article/aramroston/cia-trump-kill-teams-terrorists. On Unit 29155 see also Michael Schwirtz, "Top Secret Russian Unit Seeks to Destabilize Europe, Security Officials Say," *New York Times*, October 8, 2019, www.nytimes.com/2019/10/08/world/europe/unit-29155-russia-gru.html.

325 **he was planning the assassination:** Unless otherwise indicated, details regarding the coup and assassination plot come from the court and police testimony of Sasa Sindjelic, the hired assassin and principal member of the conspiracy, as well as other witnesses.

326 **a naval attaché at the Russian embassy in Warsaw:** Dusica Tomovic and Natalia Zaba, "Montenegro Coup Suspect 'Was Russian Spy in Poland,'" BalkanInsight, February 21, 2017, https://balkaninsight.com/2017/02/21/montenegro-coup-suspect-was-russian-spy-in-poland-02-21-2017/.

327 **"the wildest, most desolate":** William Le Queux, *An Observer in the Near East* (London: T. Fisher Unwin, 1907).

327 **the *Admiral Kuznetsov*:** "Carrier Group of Ships of the Northern Fleet Began a Campaign in the Mediterranean Sea," RIA Novosti, October 15, 2016 (in Russian), https://ria.ru/20161015/1479305461.html.

327 **In 2016, the country welcomed; Budva has become known:** Andrew Wrobel, "Has the US Sold Montenegro Out?," *Emerging Europe*, Autumn 2018, https://issuu.com/emerging-europe/docs/ee_autumn_2018/28.

328 **A poll in December 2016:** Dusica Tomovic, "Anti-NATO Groups Demand Referendum in Montenegro," BalkanInsight, February 10, 2017, https://balkaninsight.com/2017/02/10/opposition-activists-demand-nato-referendum-in-montenegro-02-09-2017/.

328 **In 2015, Đukanović was named:** "Djukanovic Named 'Criminal of the Year' in Poll," BalkanInsight, December 31, 2015, https://balkaninsight.com/2015/12/31/djukanovic-beats-gruevski-as-organized-crime-person-of-the-year-12-31-2015/.

328 **"We are not the danger for this country":** Stevo Vasiljevic, "Thousands in Montenegro Rally Against President Djukanovic," Reuters, March 2, 2019, www.reuters.com/article/cnews-us-montenegro-protests-idCAKCN1QJ0LC-OCATP.

328 **"The continued eastward expansion of NATO":** "NATO Invitation to Montenegro Prompts Russia Warning," BBC News, December 2, 2015, www.bbc.co.uk/news/world-europe-34981973.

328 **"The current Montenegro authorities will bear full responsibility":** MFA [Ministry of Foreign Affairs] Russia, tweet, July 14, 2016, https://twitter.com/mfa_russia/status/753582967356854272.

328 **"In Russia's official military doctrine":** "Q&A: Duško Marković, the Prime Minister Stuck Between Putin and Trump in the Balkans," *Time*, February 16, 2017, https://time.com/4673038/dusko-markovic-montenegro-russia-nato/.

329 **"What NATO must do"; "there would be no extension"; "any extension of the zone of NATO"; "I agree":** James M. Goldgeier, *Not Whether but When: The U.S. Decision to Enlarge NATO* (Washington, DC: Brookings Institution Press, 1999), p. 15.

329 **"This really is a great idea":** Warren Christopher, *In the Stream of History: Shaping Foreign Policy for a New Era* (Stanford, CA: Stanford University Press, 1988), pp. 93–94.

329 **"Our Lady of Telemetry"; "Our Lady of Immaculate Reception"; "Sitting in the embassy in Moscow":** William J. Burns, *The Back Channel: A Memoir of American Diplomacy and the Case for Its Renewal* (New York: Random House, 2019), pp. 85, 110.

330 **"It's Russia that must move toward us":** Letter, Strobe Talbott to Warren Christopher, March 24, 1995, cited in M. E. Sarotte, "How to Enlarge NATO: The Debate Inside the Clinton Administration, 1993–1995," *International Security* 44, issue 1 (Summer 2019), 7–41, https://direct.mit.edu/isec/article/44/1/7/12232/How-to-Enlarge-NATO-The-Debate-inside-the-Clinton.

330 **3,515 sorties:** John A. Tirpak, "Deliberate Force," *Air Force* magazine, October 1, 1997, www.airforcemag.com/article/1097deliberate/.

330 **"This is the first sign of what could happen":** John J. Mearsheimer, "Why the Ukraine Crisis Is the West's Fault: The Liberal Delusions That Provoked Putin," *Foreign Affairs*, September/October 2014, www.foreignaffairs.com/articles/russia-fsu/2014-08-18/why-ukraine-crisis-west-s-fault.

330 **"We have no idea what we're getting into":** Eric Schmitt, "'Iron Ring' Around Russia? Comment Provokes Outburst," *New York Times*, March 20, 1998, www.nytimes.com/1998/03/20/world/iron-ring-around-russia-comment-provokes-outburst.html.

330 **"I think it is the beginning of a new Cold War":** Thomas L. Friedman, "Foreign Affairs; Now a Word from X," *New York Times*, May 2, 1998, www.nytimes.com/1998/05/02/opinion/foreign-affairs-now-a-word-from-x.html.

330 **Richard Lloyd . . . estimated:** "NATO's 'Collateral Damage' Still Takes Toll in Kosovo," CNN, April 3, 2000, https://edition.cnn.com/2000/WORLD/europe/04/03/kosovo.damage/.

331 **"was a deliberate attack on a civilian object":** Steven Erlanger, "Rights Group Says NATO Bombing in Yugoslavia Violated Law," *New York Times*, June 8, 2000, www.nytimes.com/2000/06/08/world/rights-group-says-nato-bombing-in-yugoslavia-violated-law.html.

331 **illegal war:** See Katharina P. Coleman, *International Organizations and Peace Enforcement* (Cambridge: Cambridge University Press, 2007), www.cambridge.org/core/books/international-organisations-and-peace-enforcement/A4ADDFD296E68842BF49E3C713D08084.

331 **"If you wanted to understand the grievances":** Burns, *The Back Channel*, pp. 83–84.

331 **"Everybody knows if Russia had troops in Mexico":** Vinson Cunningham, "Cornel West Sees a Spiritual Decay in the Culture," *New Yorker*, March 9, 2022, www.newyorker.com/culture/the-new-yorker-interview /cornel-west-sees-a-spiritual-decay-in-the-culture.

331 **"NATO has put its front-line forces":** Putin speech at the annual Munich security conference in 2007, https:// is.muni.cz/th/xlghl/DP_Fillinger_Speeches.pdf.

331 **"Iron Ring"; "I don't quite get it":** Schmitt, "'Iron Ring' Around Russia?"

331 **"Ukraine's entry into NATO":** Tariq Ali, "Before the War," *London Review of Books*, March 24, 2022, www.lrb .co.uk/the-paper/v44/n06/tariq-ali/before-the-war.

334 **"Either they have to pay up":** Ashley Parker, "Donald Trump Says NATO Is 'Obsolete,' UN Is 'Political Game,'" *New York Times*, April 2, 2018, www.nytimes.com/politics/first-draft/2016/04/02/donald-trump-tells-crowd -hed-be-fine-if-nato-broke-up/.

Chapter 32: The Exfiltrators

340 **the person they were counting on was Paul Manafort:** Simon Shuster, "Russian Ex-Spy Pressured Manafort over Debts to Oligarch," *Time*, December 29, 2018, https://time.com/5490169/paul-manafort -victor-boyarkin-debts/.

340 **"By 2016, Deripaska was involved in funding":** U.S. Senate, "Report of the Select Committee on Intelligence on Russian Active Measures Campaigns and Interference in the 2016 U.S. Elections, Volume 5: Counterintelligence Threats and Vulnerabilities," www.intelligence.senate.gov/sites/default/files/documents/report _volume5.pdf, p. 147.

340 **"shares the Bond actor's reputation":** Luke Harding, "How Metals and a Ruthless Streak Put Russian Patriot at Top of the Rich List," *Guardian*, February 24, 2007, www.theguardian.com/world/2007/feb/24/business .russia.

341 **Manafort did talk to several politicians in Montenegro:** Shuster, "Russian Ex-Spy Pressured Manafort over Debts to Oligarch."

341 **someone, prosecutors would charge:** Samir Kajosevic, "Montenegro Prosecution Suspects Israeli Consultant of Coup Role," BalkanInsight, July 31, 2019, https://balkaninsight.com/2019/07/31/montenegro-prosecution -suspects-israeli-consultant-of-coup-role/. See also Julian E. Barnes, "Ex-C.I.A. Officer's Brief Detention Deepens Mystery in Montenegro," *New York Times*, November 23, 2018, www.nytimes.com/2018/11/23/us /politics/cia-montenegro-russia-coup-joseph-assad.html.

341 **"honed his leadership and decision-making skills":** Shaviv deleted bio.

341 **"I used to do surveillance":** Unless otherwise indicated, all quotes from Aron Shaviv are from an interview on July 8, 2022.

342 **served as his chief strategist:** Kim Sengupta, "Israel Election: Secrets of the Netanyahu Campaign— How He Turned the Election on Its Head," *Independent*, March 17, 2015, www.independent.co.uk /news/world/middle-east/israel-election-the-secrets-of-the-netanyahu-campaign-and-how-he-could-win -even-if-he-loses-10114862.html. See also Gil Stern Hoffman, "Netanyahu Hires New Campaign Consultant for Likud," *Jerusalem Post*, December 4, 2014, www.jpost.com/Israel-Elections/Netanyahu-hires-new -campaign-consultant-for-Likud-383599.

342 **"He accused anti-Zionist Arab politicians of treason":** Michael Oren, "Israel's Prince of Paradoxes," *Atlantic*, August 30, 2019, www.theatlantic.com/ideas/archive/2019/08/avigdor-lieberman-israels-paradox/597010/.

342 **Serbia, Bulgaria, and Romania; Ukraine:** Shaviv deleted bio.

342 **Joseph Assad:** Background from Suzanne Hirt, "Central Florida Couple Uses CIA Training to Rescue 149 Iraqis from ISIS," *Daily Commercial*, May 14, 2016.

342 **Abu Dhabi…Box 62986:** FBI Brian Scott interview.

343 **Florida…Box 808:** Florida Division of Corporations, Filing Information.

343 **the firm earned around $50 million:** Adam C. Smith, "Meet Sniper, CIA Officer, Green Beret, Millionaire Todd Wilcox, a Candidate for U.S. Senate," *Miami Herald*, April 22, 2016, www.miamiherald.com/news /politics-government/article73379327.html.

343 **"an Israeli/Canadian political adviser":** FBI Brian Scott interview.

344 **Later, Scott testified:** Shaviv Strategy and Campaigns, "06 06 2018," YouTube, July 23, 2018, www.youtube .com/watch?v=JqcFl1h_eI4.

344 **talked four former FBI agents into joining him in the operation:** Commission for the Control of INTERPOL's Files, Decision of the Commission, Request Concerning Joseph George Assad, July 2, 2020. See also "New Names Under Investigation in 'Coup,'" Radio Free Europe (in Serbian), January 15, 2019, www-slobodnaevropa-org.translate .goog/a/imena-istraga-drzavni-udar/29711407.html?_x_tr_sl=sr&_x_tr_tl=en&_x_tr_hl=en&_x_tr_pto=sc.

345 **Assad also asked an Israeli private investigator:** Samir Kajosevic, "Montenegro Cancels 'Coup Plot' Warrant for Israeli's Arrest," BalkanInsight, January 21, 2020, https://balkaninsight.com/2020/01/21/montenegro -cancels-coup-plot-warrant-for-israelis-arrest/.

345 **avoid the police as they fled across the border:** Barnes, "Ex-C.I.A. Officer's Brief Detention Deepens Mystery in Montenegro."

345 **"due to his involvement in significant corruption":** Gjergj Erebara, "US Bans Albanian MP for Alleged Corruption," BalkanInsight, April 17, 2018, https://balkaninsight.com/2018/04/17/us-bans-albania-mp-for -significant-corruption-04-17-2018/.

345 **"This dictator will kneel in Spuž while he cleans the floors":** Valerie Hopkins, "Indictment Tells Murky Montenegrin Coup Tail," *Politico*, May 23, 2017, www.politico.eu/article/montenegro-nato-milo -dukanovicmurky-coup-plot/.

347 **At about 2 p.m.:** Commission for the Control of INTERPOL's Files, Decision of the Commission, Request Concerning Joseph George Assad, July 2, 2020.

348 **"He views anyone":** "Montenegro's Milo Djukanovic: The Eternal President," Deutsche Welle, April 14, 2018, www.dw.com/en/montenegros-milo-djukanovic-the-eternal-president/a-43380806.

348 **"Many members of the ruling party":** Montenegro Country Report, Freedom House, 2020, https:// freedomhouse.org/country/montenegro/freedom-world/2020.

348 **NATO agreed to send troops to Montenegro:** Slobodan Lekic, "First NATO Counter-Hybrid Warfare Team to Deploy to Montenegro," *Stars and Stripes*, November 8, 2019, www.stripes.com/news/first-nato -counter-hybrid-warfare-team-to-deploy-to-montenegro-1.606562.

348 **"absurd":** U.K. Foreign & Commonwealth Office, Press Release, May 9, 2019, www.gov.uk/government/news /foreign-secretary-statement-on-the-attempted-coup-in-montenegro-in-2016.

349 **"The guilty verdicts announced":** U.K. Foreign & Commonwealth Office, Press Release, May 9, 2019.

349 **Court of Appeals annulled the verdict:** Svetlana Ðokić, "Verdict for 'coup d'etat' Revoked: Significant Violations of the Provisions of Criminal Procedure Were Committed," Vijesti.me, May 2, 2021 (in Serbian), www .vijesti.me/vijesti/crna-hronika/509713/ukinuta-presuda-za-drzavni-udar.

349 **an Interpol "Red Notice" international arrest warrant:** Julian Borger and Shaun Walker, "Ex-CIA Officer Faces Arrest over alleged Montenegro Coup Plot," *Guardian*, August 12, 2018, www.theguardian.com /world/2018/aug/12/ex-cia-officer-faces-arrest-over-alleged-montenegro-coup-plot.

349 **"creating a criminal organization":** Jankovic, "New Names Under Investigation in 'Coup.'" See also "Montenegro: Extended Investigation into Terrorism Attempts," Radio Free Europe, January 14, 2019, www -slobodnaevropa-org.translate.goog/a/29709366.html?_x_tr_sl=sr&_x_tr_tl=en&_x_tr_hl=en&_x_tr _pto=sc also Borger and Walker, "Ex-CIA Officer Faces Arrest over alleged Montenegro Coup Plot."

350 **"INTERPOL's practice has generally been":** Commission for the Control of INTERPOL's Files, Decision of the Commission, Request Concerning Joseph George Assad, July 2, 2020.

350 **"came to Montenegro on the invitation":** Samir Kajosevic, "Montenegro Cancels 'Coup Plot' Warrant for Israeli's Arrest," Balkan Insight, January 21, 2020, https://balkaninsight.com/2020/01/21/montenegro -cancels-coup-plot-warrant-for-israelis-arrest/.

350 **the special prosecutor issued an order:** Samir Kajosevic, "Montenegro Prosecution Suspects Israeli Consultant of Coup Role," BalkanInsight, July 31, 2019, https://balkaninsight.com/2019/07/31/montenegro -prosecution-suspects-israeli-consultant-of-coup-role/. See also Srdan Jankovic, "New Names Under Investigation in 'Coup,'" Radio Free Europe, January 15, 2019, www-slobodnaevropa-org.translate.goog/a/imena -istraga-drzavni-udar/29711407.html?_x_tr_sl=sr&_x_tr_tl=en&_x_tr_hl=en&_x_tr_pto=sc.

350 **nearly $2 million had allegedly been transferred:** Ivan Cadjenovic, "The Court Ordered the Issue of an International Arrest Warrant; Shaviv and Assad from the Seychelles, with Russian Money, Financed the 'Coup'?," Vijesti, August 8, 2019, www-slobodnaevropa-org.translate.goog/a/imena-istraga-drzavni-udar/29711407 .html?_x_tr_sl=sr&_x_tr_tl=en&_x_tr_hl=en&_x_tr_pto=sc. See also, Ivan Eckhardt, "A Maze of Shells," Dow Jones, June 30, 2020, www.dowjones.com/professional/risk/resources/risk-blog/maze-of-shells.

351 **"You have in fact supported an indictment"**: Samir Kajosevic, "Serbs Convicted in Montenegro Return Home Awaiting Appeals," BalkanInsight, May 13, 2019, https://balkaninsight.com/2019/05/13/serbs-convicted -in-montenegro-return-home-awaiting-appeals/.

BOOK NINE: THE FEARMONGERS

Chapter 33: The Agent-in-Place

355 **"My hobby, which is increasingly growing"**: Interview with Frank Figliuzzi, August 2, 2018.

356 **"The downside of outsourcing"**: Jack Shafer, "The Spies Who Came In to the TV Studio," *Politico*, February 6, 2018, www.politico.com/magazine/story/2018/02/06/john-brennan-james-claper-michael-hayden-former -cia-media-216943/.

356 **signed a letter**: "Public Statement on the Hunter Biden Emails," October 19, 2020, www.politico.com /f/?id=00000175-4393-d7aa-af77-579f9b330000.

356 **"Spies Who Lie"**: "Spies Who Lie: 51 'Intelligence' Experts Refuse to Apologize for Disrediting True Hunter Biden Story," *New York Post*, March 18, 2022, https://nypost.com/2022/03/18/intelligence -experts-refuse-to-apologize-for-smearing-hunter-biden-story/.

356 **"there was a scheme in place"**: Letter, Senator Grassley to Honorable Merrick Garland, Honorable Christopher Wray, July 25, 2022.

356 **"Spies Are the New Journalists"**: Lee Smith, "Spies Are the New Journalists," *Tablet*, June 4, 2019, www .tabletmag.com/sections/news/articles/spies-are-the-new-journalists.

357 **"groomed"**: Meg Cunningham, Beatrice Peterson, "Hillary Clinton Says Republican 'Grooming' a 2020 Candidate for Third-Party Run," ABC News, October 24, 2019, https://abcnews.go.com/Politics /hillary-clinton-russians-grooming-2020-candidate-party-run/story?id=66371944.

357 **"she's a Russian asset"**: Dan Merica, "Hillary Clinton Suggests Russians Are 'Grooming' Tulsi Gabbard for Third-Party Run," October 21, 2019, https://edition.cnn.com/2019/10/18/politics/hillary-clinton-tulsi -gabbard/index.html.

357 **"a serious credibility cost to the press"**: T. A. Frank, "The Hard Truths and High Cost of the Russiagate Scandal," *Vanity Fair*, March 25, 2019, www.vanityfair.com/news/2019/03/the-hard-truths-and-high -cost-of-the-russiagate-scandal.

357 **NBC News led its evening broadcast**: William M. Arkin, Ken Dilanian, and Cynthia McFadden, "U.S. Officials: Putin Personally Involved in U.S. Election Hack: New Intelligence Shows That Putin Became Personally Involved in the Computer Breach, Two Senior U.S. Officials Say," NBC News, December 14, 2016, www .nbcnews.com/news/us-news/u-s-officials-putin-personally-involved-u-s-election-hack-n696146.

357 **an aide to the Russian ambassador to the United States**: "Diplomatic List," U.S. Department of State, http:// search.globescope.com/indexp~2.htm.

357 **Smolenkov was at his side as his key aide**: "What Is Known About Oleg Smolenkov and His Wife," *Kommersant*, September 10, 2019 (in Russian), www.kommersant.ru/doc/4088182?from=doc_vrez.

358 **promoted to state advisor**: "Decree of the President of the Russian Federation of February 4, 2010, No. 143" (in Russian), http://kremlin.ru/acts/bank/30585.

358 **graduate from Moscow Regional Institute**: "What Is Known About Oleg Smolenkov and His Wife."

358 **Kargopolskaya Street**: Marc Bennetts, Julian Borger, and Luke Harding, "Russia Investigated Disappearance of Suspected US Spy as Possible Murder," *Guardian*, September 10, 2019, www.theguardian.com/world/2019 /sep/10/us-spy-russia-kremlin-putin-administration-trump.

358 **"Oleg Smolenkov was a member of the inner circle"**: Ilya Shumanov, telegram message, September 9, 2019 (in Russian), https://t.me/CorruptionTV/1518.

358 **Ilya Shumanov**: "Ilya Shumanov," Wilson Center, www.wilsoncenter.org/person/ilya-shumanov.

358 **"excessive curiosity"**: Ivan Safronov and Svetlana Bocharova, "The Alleged American Spy Has Worked in the Kremlin for at Least Five Years," *Vedomosti*, September 11, 2019 (in Russian), www.vedomosti.ru/politics /articles/2019/09/11/810958-shpion.

359 **His mother, Valentina Nikolaevna Smolenkova**: "Oleg Smolenkov, Manager of the President's Affairs, Is Still Considered Missing," *St. Petersburg*, September 11, 2019 (in Russian), www.piterburger.ru/269170.html.

360 **approximately $20 million**: Jane Mayer, "Christopher Steele, the Man Behind the Tump Dossier," *New Yorker*, March 5, 2018, www.newyorker.com/magazine/2018/03/12/christopher-steele-the-man-behind-the-trump-dossier.

360 **paid $168,000:** Mark Hosenball, "Ex-British Spy Paid $168,000 for Trump Dossier, U.S. Firm Discloses," Reuters, November 1, 2017, www.reuters.com/article/us-usa-trump-russia-dossier-idUSKBN1D15XH.

360 **Perkins Coie, at a rate of $50,000:** Committee Sensitive, Executive Session Permanent Select Committee on Intelligence, U.S. House of Representatives, Interview of Glenn Simpson, November 14, 2017, p. 22, https://docs.house.gov/meetings/IG/IG00/20180118/106796/HMTG-115-IG00-20180118-SD002.pdf.

360 **$95,000 they had thus far paid him:** "Review of Four FISA Applications and Other Aspects of the FBI's Crossfire Hurricane Investigation," Office of the Inspector General, U.S. Department of Justice, December 2019, p. 88, note 205, www.justice.gov/storage/120919-examination.pdf.

360 **"Can it wait a while?":** Secret, Executive Session Permanent Select Committee on Intelligence, U.S. House of Representatives, Interview of Michael Gaeta, December 20, 2017, p. 19, www.dni.gov/files/HPSCI_Transcripts/2020-05-04-FBI_Special_Agent-MTR_Redacted.pdf.

360 **"It was explosive":** Interview of Michael Gaeta, p. 24.

362 **"compromising materials":** Secret, FBI, Interview with Igor Danchenko, February 9, 2017, www.judiciary.senate.gov/imo/media/doc/February%209,%202017%20Electronic%20Communication.pdf.

362 **thrown in Prince George's County Jail:** Danchenko, Igor Yurievich, Inmate 2013-013223, Prince George's County Jail, Upper Marlboro, MD.

362 **"drink heavily together":** FBI, Interview with Igor Danchenko.

362 **called Olga Galkina:** Fridman, et al. v. Bean, LLC, et al., District of Columbia District Court, Exhibit H, Testimony of Olga Galinka, Case 1:17-cv-02041-RJL, https://storage.courtlistener.com/recap/gov.uscourts.dcd.189930/gov.uscourts.dcd.189930.153.8.pdf.

363 **Galkina had been based in Moscow:** Olga Galkina page, Career.Habr, https://career.habr.com/galkinaolga.

363 **working for Gazeta.ru:** www.gazeta.ru/.

363 **Environmental, Technological and Nuclear Supervision Agency:** http://government.ru/en/department/212/events/.

363 **involved in a messy dispute with Gubarev:** Alan Collinson and David Gauthier-Villars, "Russian in Cyprus Was Behind Key Parts of Discredited Dossier on Trump," *Wall Street Journal*, October 28, 2020, www.wsj.com/articles/russian-in-cyprus-was-behind-key-parts-of-discredited-dossier-on-trump-11603901989.

363 **The source was Charles Dolan Jr.:** See United States District Court for the Eastern District of Virginia, United States of America, v. Igor Y. Danchenko, Indictment, Case 1:21-cr-00245-AJT, https://context-cdn.washingtonpost.com/notes/prod/default/documents/fb956512-980f-4f13-8b8f-c26eebb76772/note/5de565a8-06b8-40e8-8572-23d9765d81d2.#page=1.

363 **working with his inner circle; "to see on whose behalf he was actually working":** Isaac Stanley-Becker, "A Spin Doctor with Ties to Russia Allegedly Fed the Steele Dossier Before Fighting to Discredit It," *Washington Post*, November 6, 2021, www.washingtonpost.com/politics/2021/11/06/charles-dolan-steele-dossier-igor-danchenko-indictment/.

364 **"I circled around to it, you know":** FBI, Interview with Igor Danchenko.

365 **The target was Carter Page:** United States Foreign Intelligence Surveillance Court, "In Re Accuracy Concerns Regarding FBI Matters Submitted to the FISC," December 17, 2019, https://int.nyt.com/data/documenthelper/6600-fisa-court-demands-answers-fro/87f1132ddc399b0c99b1/optimized/full.pdf#page=1.

365 **"These encounters were surely sanctioned":** Mayer, "Christopher Steele, the Man Behind the Trump Dossier."

365 **"deep cover sources inside Russia":** Erik Wemple, "Indictment of Steele Dossier Source Is More Bad News for Multiple Media Outlets," *Washington Post*, November 8, 2021, www.washingtonpost.com/opinions/2021/11/08/steele-dossier-msnbc-cnn-danchenko-durham/?utm_source=dlvr.it&utm_medium=twitter.

365 **"the investigation did not establish":** *Report on the Investigation into Russian Interference in the 2016 Presidential Election*, Special Counsel Robert S. Mueller, III, March 2019, Volume 1, p. 2, www.justice.gov/archives/sco/file/1373816/download.

366 **fined both the Clinton campaign and the DNC:** Jonathan Turley, "FEC Fines the Clinton Campaign and DNC for Conduct Related to Steele Dossier," JonathanTurley.org, March 31, 2022, https://jonathanturley.org/2022/03/31/fec-fines-the-clinton-campaign-and-dnc-for-the-steele-dossier/.

366 **charged with lying to the FBI:** United States of America, v. Igor Y. Danchenko, Indictment.

366 **removing large portions of articles:** Paul Farhi, "The Washington Post Corrects, Removes Parts of Two Stories Regarding the Steele Dossier," *Washington Post*, November 12, 2021. www.washingtonpost.com/lifestyle/style/media-washington-post-steele-dossier/2021/11/12/f7c9b770-43d5-11ec-a88e-2aa4632af69b_story.html.

366 **"The Danchenko indictment doubles as a critique"**: Wemple, "Indictment of Steele Dossier Source Is More Bad News for Multiple Media Outlets."

366 **was on parental leave**: Sergel Sinegov, "An Employee of the Presidential Administration Disappeared Without a Trace with His Wife and Three Children," Daily Storm, September 12, 2017 (in Russian), https://dailystorm .ru/news/sotrudnik-upravdelami-prezidenta-bessledno-ischez-s-suprugoy-i-tremya-detmi.

366 **"an intelligence bombshell"**: Greg Miller, Ellen Nakashima and Adam Entous, "Obama's Secret Struggle to Punish Russia for Putin's Election Assault," *Washington Post*, June 23, 2017, www.washingtonpost.com /graphics/2017/world/national-security/obama-putin-election-hacking/.

367 **That December 2016 report**: Arkin, Dilanian, and McFadden, "U.S. Officials: Putin Personally Involved in U.S. Election Hack."

367 **forbidding Russian officials from traveling there**: Shaun Walker, Julian Borger, and Marc Bennetts, "Oleg Smolenkov: Alleged US Spy Who Gave Russia the Slip," *Guardian*, September 14, 2019, www.theguardian .com/world/2019/sep/14/oleg-smolenkov-alleged-us-spy-gave-russia-the-slip.

368 **slip through the cracks**: Stafronov and Bocharova, "The Alleged American Spy Has Worked in the Kremlin for at Least Five Years."

368 **on Wednesday, June 14, they boarded an Aeroflot jet**: Sinegov, "An Employee of the Presidential Administration Disappeared Without a Trace with His Wife and Three Children."

368 **coastal resort city of Tivat**: Walker, Borger, and Bennetts, "Oleg Smolenkov: Alleged US Spy Who Gave Russia the Slip."

368 **Ivan visited his page on VKontakte**: Sinegov, "An Employee of the Presidential Administration Disappeared Without a Trace with His Wife and Three Children."

368 **Antonina also visited the page**: Антонина Дьяконова-Смоленкова page, Facebook.

368 **"I was supposed to return home a week earlier"**: Tom Parfitt, "Kremlin Shaken by Oleg Smolenkov, Superspy Who Sailed to Safety," *Times* (London), September 14, 2019, www.thetimes.co.uk/article/kremlin-shaken -by-oleg-smolenkov-superspy-who-sailed-to-safety-9cfw7h3vt.

368 **Two days later, the *Washington Post* published its story**: Greg Miller, Ellen Nakashima, and Adam Entous, "Obama's Secret Struggle to Punish Russia for Putin's Election Assault," *Washington Post*, June 23, 2017, www .washingtonpost.com/graphics/2017/world/national-security/obama-putin-election-hacking/.

368 **CIA-supplied million-dollar mansion**: Stafford, Virginia, Assessor, http://va-stafford-assessor.publicaccessnow .com/PropertySearch/PropertyDetails.aspx?p=27H%20%20%20%20%20%20%2028&a=16819.

368 **"Did he die?"**: En.crimerussia.com, "Kremlin Spy from Ivanovo: Will Oleg Smolenkov's Escape Be a Lesson to Russian Elite?," September 18, 2019.

368 **criminal case was opened**: "Kremlin Spy from Ivanovo."

Chapter 34: The Mad Hatter

370 **Just before one o'clock**: See James Bamford, "The Russian Spy Who Wasn't," *New Republic*, February 11, 2019, https://newrepublic.com/article/153036/maria-butina-profile-wasnt-russian-spy.

370 **"Everything was boxed up"**: Interview with Paul Erickson, August 7, 2018. Unless otherwise indicated, Erickson's comments are from this interview and several others in Washington.

371 **"It was a metal shelf for a bed"**: Matt Ackland, "'You're Spending the Night Killing Roaches': Pastors Detail Poor Conditions at DC Central Cell Block," Fox5, June 14, 2018, www.fox5dc.com/news /youre-spending-the-night-killing-roaches-pastors-detail-poor-conditions-at-dc-central-cell-block.

372 **"I'm a huge fan of *Alice in Wonderland*"**: Interview with Maria Butina, July 2, 2018.

373 **searched for bits of bamboo shoots**: Chris Anderson, "Cyber Ninjas's Connection to Big Lie Runs Far, Deep and Dangerous," *Sarasota Herald-Tribune*, January 25, 2022, https://news.yahoo.com/opinion-cyber-ninjas -connection-big-210313500.html?guccounter=1&guce_referrer=aHR0cHM6Ly93d3cuZ29vZ2xlLmNvbS8S &guce_refer%E2%80%A6.

373 **"election was hacked"; "was developed in Venezuela"; "shredding truck"**: United States District Court for the District of Columbia, US Dominion, Inc, et al. v. Patrick Byrne, April 20, 2022, Case 1:21-cv-02131-CJN.

373 **"A few days after the election"**: "Press Conference: Patrick Byrne on Stating the Facts on Meetings Between November 4 2020–January 8 2021," Rumble, February 7, 2022, https://rumble.com/vuan99-press-conference -1pm-est.html.

373 **"the safest place in D.C."**: Robert Draper, "Michael Flynn Is Still at War," *New York Times*, February 4, 2022, www.nytimes.com/2022/02/04/magazine/michael-flynn-2020-election.html?referringSource=articleShare.

373 **"We had a vague plan"**: Lee Davidson, "Former Overstock CEO Patrick Byrne Describes Bluffing His Way into Trump's White House," *Salt Lake Tribune*, February 2, 2021, www.sltrib.com/news/politics/2021/02/02/former-overstock-ceo/.

373 **"He could order, within the swing states"**: Jordan Williams, "Michael Flynn: Trump Could Deploy Military to 'Rerun' Election," *The Hill*, December 18, 2020, https://thehill.com/homenews/news/530795-michael-flynn-trump-should-deploy-military-to-rerun-election/?rl=1.

374 **"China's involved in this"**: "Patrick Byrne on Stating the Facts on Meetings Between November 4 2020–January 8 2021."

374 **"Sidney and Mike began walking the president through"**: Patrick Bryne, *The Deep Rig: How Election Fraud Cost Donald J. Trump the White House* (self-published at Deep Rig, LLC, 2001), p. 104.

374 **"Presidential Findings: To Preserve Collect"**: Alan Feuer, Maggie Haberman, Michael S. Schmidt, amd Luke Broadwater, "Trump Had Role in Weighing Proposals to Seize Voting Machines," *New York Times*, January 31, 2022, www.nytimes.com/2022/01/31/us/politics/donald-trump-election-results-fraud-voting-machines.html?referringSource=articleShare.

374 **"Effective immediately, the Secretary of Defense"**: "Presidential Findings to Preserve and Analyze National Security Information Regarding the 2020 General Election," December 16, 2020, www.documentcloud.org/documents/21183521-jan-6-draft.

374 **"will run targeted inquiries of NSA"**: "Counter-Election Fraud NSPM-13 Request," December 18, 2020, https://context-cdn.washingtonpost.com/notes/prod/default/documents/77b709cd-2b04-4249-8200-93b695dbec76/note/b5dca3f1-bcf0-4c08-a16e-ff85e8ed40b5.#page=1.

375 **"Sidney and her staff printed up some documents"**: "Patrick Byrne on Stating the Facts on Meetings Between November 4 2020–January 8 2021."

375 **"If you do I put your chances at around 50-75%"**: Byrne, *The Deep Rig*, p. 106.

375 **"I know how this works"**: Jonathan Swan and Zachary Basu, "Inside the Craziest Meeting of the Trump Presidency," *Axios*, February 2, 2021, www.axios.com/2021/02/02/trump-oval-office-meeting-sidney-powell.

375 **"I fly commercial now so as to not get blown up"**: Patrick Byrne, "A Tasty Morsel: Zeroing In on Some Information I Promised You," patrickbyrne.locals.com, https://patrickbyrne.locals.com/upost/1825346/a-tasty-morsel. Byrne, Flynn, Flynn's brother Joe, and Roger Stone would later form the America Project, which would push a variety of election conspiracy theories. According to its website, the project would "lead a new American renaissance by arming citizens with the tools to fight for their freedoms, building like minded pro-freedom networks and uniting pro-America organizations who want to fight together in support of our nation."

375 **"nonstop housing meatballs"**: Eugene Scott, "Who Is Patrick Byrne, Former Overstock CEO and Election Denier?," *Washington Post*, July 13, 2022, www.washingtonpost.com/national-security/2022/07/13/trump-jan-6-byrne-overstock/.

375 **"Big protest in D.C. on January 6th"**: Transcript, Hearings, United States Congress, January 6th Committee, June 9, 2022.

375 **"many dozens"; "fifteen pro-freedom Latinos from Texas"; Enrique Tarrio**: Jordan Green, "How Rudy Giuliani Turned to a Far-Right Network for Bogus Evidence to Frame 'Antifa' for January 6," Raw Story and Alternet, June 30, 2022, www.alternet.org/2022/06/rudy-giuliani-bogus-evidence-antifa/.

376 **June 2022 indictment**: United States District Court for the District of Columbia, United States of American v. Enrique Tarrio, et al., June 6, 2022, Criminal Case: 21-cr-175(TJK).

376 **"It's Burning Man for Libertarians"**: Gary Alexander, quoted in FreedomFest.com, https://2019.freedomfest.com/testimonials/gary-alexander/.

376 **"the world's largest gathering of free minds"**: Quoted in advertisement for FreedomFest 2021, https://essentialnaples.com/freedomfest-2021-the-worlds-largest-gathering-of-free-minds/.

376 **at the last minute, just four days before**: "Showdown on the Las Vegas Strip: Donald Trump vs. Marco Rubio at Planet Hollywood," Breitbart, July 9, 2015, www.breitbart.com/politics/2015/07/09/showdown-on-the-las-vegas-strip-donald-trump-vs-marco-rubio-at-planet-hollywood/.

376 **He had just announced his candidacy a few weeks before**: "Here's Donald Trump's Presidential Announcement Speech," *Time*, June 16, 2015, https://time.com/3923128/donald-trump-announcement-speech/.

377 **"My question will be about foreign politics"**: Matthew Rozsa, "Who Is Maria Butina?" NRA-linked Gun Activist Charged with Operating as a Russian Agent," *Salon*, July 16, 2018, www.salon.com/2018/07/16/who-is-maria-butina-gun-activist-with-ties-to-the-nra-charged-with-operating-as-a-russian-agent/.

377 **"I give great tryst"**: "Patrick Byrne: Maria Butina and I, Part Deux: Romancing Maria," DeepCapture, August 27, 2019, www.deepcapture.com/2019/08/maria-butina-and-i-part-deux-romancing-maria/.

377 **"The truth is, when she came into the room"**: Interview with Patrick Byrne, Berkeley Faculty Club, Berkeley, CA, February 6, 2020. Unless otherwise indicated, Byrne's comments are from the interview, and also from a private videotape he made discussing his involvement with both the FBI and Maria Butina.

379 **On November 6, 1988, a Titan 34D rocket**: "Titan 34D," Astronautix.com. www.astronautix.com/t/titan34d.html.

379 **A couple of years later, Byrne would be arrested**: "Overstock.com CEO Arrested for Gun," Daily Beast, April 21, 2017, https://www.thedailybeast.com/cheats/2013/01/18/overstock-com-ceo-arrested-for-gun.

379 **recently declassified CIA documents**: Top Secret, CIA, NPIC: "Activity at Selected Soviet Space Tracking Facilities," March 1, 1982.

379 **"There were no phones at the time"**: Interview with Maria Butina, Washington, March 7, 2018. Unless otherwise indicated, Butina's comments are from this interview and several others, including while she was incarcerated in Washington, DC; Alexandria, Virginia; and Tallahassee, Florida.

383 **Three months later, the *Washington Post***: Ellen Nakashima, "Russian Government Hackers Penetrated DNC, Stole Opposition Research on Trump," *Washington Post*, June 14, 2016, www.washingtonpost.com /world/national-security/russian-government-hackers-penetrated-dnc-stole-opposition-research-on-trump /2016/06/14/cf006cb4-316e-11e6-8ff7-7b6c1998b7a0_story.html.

Chapter 35: The Scapegoat

385 **"She asked him the most important question"**: David Corn interviewed on "Piecing Together the Story of Russian Maria Butina," NPR, July 19, 2018, www.npr.org/2018/07/19/630589351/piecing-together-the -story-of-russian-maria-butina.

385 **"Washington's young émigré crowd"**: Ben Schreckinger, "Tinder Woes and Snarky Bosses: Young and Russian in DC," *Politico*, September 10, 2018, www.politico.eu/article/russian-in-dc-spying-security-tinder -woes/.

386 **"The most irredeemable outpost"**: Michael Massing, "Journalism in the Age of Trump," *Le Monde Diplomatique*, August 2, 2018, https://mondediplo.com/openpage/journalism-age-trump.

386 **2022 study by the Reuters Institute and the University of Oxford**: Reuters Institute Digital News Report 2022, https://reutersinstitute.politics.ox.ac.uk/sites/default/files/2022-06/Digital_News-Report_2022.pdf.

386 **"Journalism can get caught up"**: "Do Journalists Pay Too Much Attention to Twitter?," *Columbia Journalism Review*, October 10, 2018, www.cjr.org/the_media_today/journalists-on-twitter-study.php.

386 **"The decision of whom to question"**: "Presumption of Guilt: Human Rights Abuses of Post–September 11 Detainees," Human Rights Watch, August 2002, www.hrw.org/reports/2002/us911/USA0802.pdf.

387 **"Almost every student that comes over"**: Gideon Lewis-Kraus, "Have Chinese Spies Infiltrated American Campuses?," *New Yorker*, March 14, 2022, www.newyorker.com/magazine/2022/03/21/have-chinese-spies -infiltrated-american-campuses.

387 **"The China initiative engaged in blatant racial profiling"**: Phelim Kine, "DOJ's 'China Initiative' Is Dead but Radical Profiling Fears Are Still Very Much Alive," *Politico*, February 24, 2022, www.politico .com/newsletters/politico-china-watcher/2022/02/24/dojs-china-initiative-is-dead-but-racial-profiling -fears-are-still-very-much-alive-00011182.

387 **According to a 2018 analysis**: Eric Lichtblau, "The FBI Is in Crisis. It's Worse Than You Think," *Time*, May 3, 2018, https://time.com/5264153/the-fbi-is-in-crisis-and-america-is-paying-the-price/.

387 **highly critical 2021 Justice Department IG report**: "Investigation and Review of the Federal Bureau of Investigation's Handling of Allegations of Sexual Abuse by Former USA Gymnastics Physician Lawrence Gerard Nassar," Department of Justice, Office of the Inspector General, July 14, 2021, https://oig.justice.gov/reports /investigation-and-review-federal-bureau-investigations-handling-allegations-sexual-abuse.

387 **led a cover-up and lied repeatedly**: Katie Benner, "Justice Dept. to Weigh Prosecuting F.B.I. Agents in Nassar Case," *New York Times*, October 5, 2021, www.nytimes.com/2021/10/05/us/politics/fbi-larry-nassar -gymnastics.html.

387 **"absolutely chilling"**: Juliet Macur and Michael Levenson, "Inspector General Says F.B.I. Botched Nassar Abuse Investigation," *New York Times*, July 14, 2021, www.nytimes.com/2021/07/14/sports/olympics/fbi-nassar-report .html.

388 **"After a couple years, it became a dumpster fire"**: Dan Gilmore, "Why I Left the Intelligence Community," dangilmore.com, March 10, 2022, https://dangilmore.com/2022/03/10/why-i-left-the-intelligence-community/.

388 **"This is unconscionable"**: Jeff Stein and Howard Altman, "Spy Agency Chat Room Hate Speech Draws Hill Scrutiny," SpyTalk, March 28, 2022, www.spytalk.co/p/spy-agency-chat-room-hate-speech?r=2hta&s =w&utm_campaign=post&utm_medium=web&utm_source=direct.

388 **"sloppy" and "careless activity"**: Jenna McLaughlin and Zach Dorfman, " 'Shattered': Inside the Secret Battle to Save America's Undercover Spies in the Digital Age," Yahoo News, December 30, 2019, https://news.yahoo .com/shattered-inside-the-secret-battle-to-save-americas-undercover-spies-in-the-digital-age-100029026 .html.

389 **"Every single investigation"**: Letter, Senator Charles E. Grassley, Chairman, Senate Committee on the Judiciary to FBI Director James B. Comey, Jr., January 9, 2017, www.judiciary.senate.gov/imo/media /doc/2017-01-09%20CEG%20to%20FBI%20(Stagehand).pdf.

389 **"The whistleblower further alleged"**: Letter, Grassley to Comey.

389 **"The FBI and the Justice Department needed a scalp"**: John Kiriakou, "In Search of a Russiagate Scalp: The Entrapment of Maria Butina," Consortium News, May 17, 2022, https://consortiumnews.com/2019/08/28 /john-kiriakou-in-search-of-a-russiagate-scalp-the-entrapment-of-maria-butina/.

390 **the bureau leaked details:** Peter Stone and Greg Gordon, "FBI Investigating Whether Russian Money Went to NRA to Help Trump," McClatchy, May 16, 2018, www.mcclatchydc.com/news/nation-world/national /article195231139.html.

390 **assigned to the Honolulu FBI office:** National Counterintelligence and Security Center, "Senior Official Per-forming the Duties of the Director, National Counterintelligence and Security Center," undated, https://www .dni.gov/index.php/ncsc-who-we-are/ncsc-leadership.

391 **"They were interested in sex"**: Interview with a person who was interviewed by Michelle Ball re: Butina case.

391 **"She didn't come under my bailiwick"**: Conversation with Special Counsel Robert Mueller, June 8, 2019.

391 **"unbelievably inexcusable behavior"**: Martha Neil, "Federal Judge Blasts US Prosecutors for 'Unbelievably Inexcusable Behavior' in Somali Piracy Case," *American Bar Association Journal*, July 23, 2012, www.abajournal .com/news/article/federal_judge_blasts_prosecution_in_somali_piracy_case_for_unbelievably_ine.

392 **"It's hard not to feel cynical"**: Ryan J. Reilly, "DOJ Drops All Charges Against Remaining Trump Inaugu-ration Defendants," *Huffington Post*, June 7, 2018, www.huffingtonpost.co.uk/entry/j20-trump-inauguration -protesters_n_5b3fc53ee4b05127ccf1ee6a.

392 **aiming of a laser pointer:** Spencer S. Hsu, "U.S. Prosecutors to Drop Inauguration Day Laser-Pointing Charge Against A.U. Student," *Washington Post*, March 15, 2017, www.washingtonpost.com/local/public-safety /prosecutors-may-drop-laser-pointing-charge-against-american-university-student/2017/03/15/4a51513e -05b9-11e7-b1e9-a05d3c21f7cf_story.html.

392 **he was carrying an asteroid:** Spenser S. Hsu, "Man Held for Mental Exam After Arrest for False Bomb Threat Near White House," *Washington Post*, March 20, 2017, www.washingtonpost.com/local/public-safety/man -held-for-mental-exam-after-arrest-for-false-bomb-threat-near-white-house/2017/03/20/80e61a58-0da3 -11e7-ab07-07d9f521f6b5_story.html.

392 **"in exchange for a position"**: United States District Court for the District of Columbia, United States of America v. Maria Butina, Government's Memorandum in Support of Pre-trial Detention, July 18, 2018, Case 1:18-cr-00218-TSC.

393 **"Here is the Money Trail"**: Jason Leopold and Anthony Cormier, "Here Is the Money Trail from the Rus-sian 'Agent' and Her Republican Partner," BuzzFeed News, July 31, 2018, www.buzzfeednews.com/article /jasonleopold/maria-butina-paul-erickson-suspicious-bank-money-russia.

393 **Natalie Mayflower Edwards, was prosecuted and sent to prison:** United States of America v. Natalie May-flower Sours Edwards, Complaint, Case 1:19-cr-00064-GHW, https://s3.documentcloud.org/documents /20694930/complaint.pdf.

393 **"Sex. Thank you very much"**: USA v. Butina, Memorandum in Support of Defendant Maria Butina's Motion for Bond Review, August 24, 2018.

394 **"deleted sentences, misquoting her messages"**: USA v. Butina, Memorandum in Support of Defendant Maria Butina's Motion for Bond Review.

394 **"It took approximately five minutes"**: USA v. Butina, Transcript of Status Conference, September 10, 2018.

394 **"They eventually got a gag order"**: Interview with Robert Driscoll.

394 **"I am troubled and hope there is a full inquiry"**: Email message from Frank Figliuzzi, September 9, 2018.

394 **"They manipulated the evidence"**: Interview with a former assistant U.S. attorney.

395 **"They want to generate headlines":** Interview with a former very senior CIA clandestine service officer.

395 **"I would wake up periodically at night":** Interview with Robert Driscoll.

395 **"BUTINA asked the RUSSIAN OFFICIAL":** USA v. Butina, Affidavit in Support of an Application for a Criminal Complaint.

397 **in 2022, an unredacted version of the report was released:** *Report on the Investigation into Russian Interference in the 2016 Presidential Election*, Special Counsel Robert S. Mueller, III, March 2019, www.justice.gov /storage/report_volume1.pdf.

INDEX

———◆———